THE ROUTLEDGE RESEARCH COMPANION TO GEOGRAPHIES OF SEX AND SEXUALITIES

This immensely useful collection of essays rigorously and insightfully addresses urgent questions about sexuality, space and place in an impressive variety of contexts. It will be of benefit not only to geographers, but also to anyone interested in a rich, nuanced analysis of the production and control of sex, sexuality, and sexual and gender identities and subcultures.

Dean Spade, Seattle University School of Law, USA

This volume definitively demonstrates that the study of sexuality is not a sub-field of Geography but rather a crucial and integral component that, taken up seriously, inherently redefines the field. Comprehensive, well-organized, and all-encompassing, it is a must for any syllabus not solely on sexuality studies, but more trenchantly, on human geography. The encapsulation of many decades of work on sexuality and its implications for the study and field of geography is breathtaking.

Jasbir K. Puar, Rutgers University, USA and author of
Terrorist Assemblages: Homonationalism in Queer Times

Comprehensive and authoritative, this state-of-the-art review both charts and develops the rich sub-discipline geographies of sexualities, exploring sex-gender, sexuality and sexual practices. Emerging from the desire to examine differences and exclusions as a key aspect of human geographies, these geographies have engaged with heterosexual and queer, lesbian, gay, bi and trans lives. Developing thinking in this area, geographers and other social scientists have illustrated the centrality of place, space and other spatial relationships in reconstituting sexual practices, representations, desires, as well as sexed bodies and lives. This book reviews the current state of the field and offers new insights from authors located on five continents. In doing so, the book seeks to draw on and influence core debates in this field, as well as disrupt the Anglo-American hegemony in studies of sexualities, sexes and geographies. This volume is the definitive collection in the area, bringing together many international leaders in the field, alongside scholars that are well-established outside the Anglophone academy, and many emerging talents who will lead the field in the decades to come.

Gavin Brown is Senior Lecturer in Human Geography at the University of Leicester, UK.

Kath Browne is Professor in Human Geography at the University of Brighton, UK.

The Routledge Research Companion to Geographies of Sex and Sexualities

Edited by

GAVIN BROWN

University of Leicester, UK

KATH BROWNE

University of Brighton, UK

With Section Editors:

Andrew Gorman-Murray, Robert Kulpa, Maarten Loopmans,

Tiffany Muller Myrdahl, Catherine J. Nash, Joseli Maria Silva,

Andrew Tucker, Paulo Jorge Vieira

Routledge
Taylor & Francis Group

LONDON AND NEW YORK

First published 2016 by Routledge

2 Park Square, Milton Park, Abingdon, Oxfordshire OX14 4RN
52 Vanderbilt Avenue, New York, NY 10017

Routledge is an imprint of the Taylor & Francis Group, an informa business

First issued in paperback 2020

British Library Cataloguing in Publication Data
A catalogue record for this book is available from the British Library

Library of Congress Cataloging in Publication Data
A catalogue record for this book is available from the Library of Congress

ISBN: 978-1-4724-5548-2 (hbk)
ISBN: 978-0-367-66009-3 (pbk)

Typeset in Palatino Linotype
by Apex CoVantage, LLC

Contents

SECTION IV   MOBILE SEXUALITIES
Andrew Gorman-Murray and Catherine J. Nash (editors)

SECTION V   SEXUAL HEALTH
Andrew Tucker (editor)

List of Figures

List of Tables

Notes on Contributors

Kath Albury is an Associate Professor at UNSW Australia, in the School of Arts and Media. Her research focuses on mediated sexual self-representation, sexual subcultures, and the role of user-generated media (including social networking platforms) in young people's formal and informal sexual learning.

Leela Bakshi took part in the 'Count Me In Too' project, which researches LGBT, initially as a participant and subsequently as part of the research team. This has led to a role as an 'activist researcher', working on the 'Making Lives Liveable' project and with university researchers in academic fora that offer opportunities for LGBT activism. A resident of Brighton and Hove, Leela is co-author, with Professor Kath Browne, of *Ordinary in Brighton: LGBT, Activisms and the City* (Ashgate, 2013).

Niharika Banerjea is Associate Professor in the School of Liberal Studies at Ambedkar University, Delhi. Her interests lie in the areas of gender and sexuality, gender and development, space and sexualities, globalization, and qualitative methods and ethnography. She has published in journals such as *Gender Place and Culture*, *Contemporary South Asia* and the *Global Studies Journal*. She is currently co-editing an anthology on friendship and social activism. She is also working on a manuscript about community and queer activism with Sappho for Equality, the activist forum for lesbian, bisexual women and transmen rights in eastern India.

Camila Bassi is a human geography academic. Her doctoral research on Birmingham (UK) and recent research on Shanghai concern the intersection of 'race' and sexuality within and through political economy. Camila's ongoing project within critical geography is to indicate the benefits of a return to, and reinvigoration of, Marx and Marxism. Accordingly, her work offers an original exploration of key ideas from Marx and Gramsci in order to think through more subtle accounts of capitalism – specifically, instances from within that escape its oppressive conditions. Camila makes a case for a return to Marxism as an alternative to the seeming necessity to reconfigure Marxianisms via poststructuralism. She builds on this return to Marxism by critiquing the revolutionary left vanguard of England's anti-war movement through what she argues to be the spirit of Marxism – that is, the task of building a third camp of independent, internationalist, working-class politics. Finally, an excavation of early Marxist work on the Jewish question guides Camila's current writing on the Palestinian–Israeli conflict.

Marianne Blidon is Associate Professor at Paris 1-Panthéon Sorbonne University and associate researcher at INED (National institute of Demographic Studies). She is a feminist geographer, working on gender and sexualities. She was the first French geographer to achieve a PhD on geography of sexualities ('Distance and Meeting: Elements for a Queer Geography'). She has organized several seminars and symposia on gender and queer geographies, helping to legitimize these topics in France. She founded, with other social researchers, a free open-access journal *Genre, sexualité & société* that she led for eight years. She is an editorial board member of the journal *Gender, Place and Culture*. She collaborates with the European Network on Geographies of Sexualities and has published several issues in French journals such as *L'Espace Politique* and *Echogéo*.

Rachele Borghi aka **Zarra Bonheur** describes herself as a queerlesbianfeminist pornoactivademic geographer and is currently at the University of Paris Sorbonne. Her work focuses on post-porn and the transgression of normative space, including reflection on the academic practices and researcher's positionality. She has created the persona of Zarra Bonheur, in order to find a 'teotetic' (theoretical and pragmatic) way out of conceptual cages, to experiment with the embodied research, and to convey subjects, objectives and concepts through her body. Through navigating experimental epistemic pathways, she felt that the new could still spring from the source-rich bibliographic research. She has therefore explored a way – shared by other individuals – that took shape through libraries, self-managed squats, universities, associations' headquarters, and the streets of Italian, French and Spanish cities. For her, sharing practices and reflections with old and new comrades is at the heart of her understanding of militancy, as it is the research and discovery of sensations that puts her body at the centre and makes it, on the one hand, an instrument of pleasure and, on the other, a potential site for subversion. Zarra Bonheur is not the other side, the alter ego of Rachele Borghi or the stage name of the academician. Rather, it is a game. It is an attempt to build a collective creation and experimentation project, a palimpsest of roles and places, travesting Rachele's body and flowing, contaminating, creating and nourishing exchanges of practices, networks and relationships.

Marie-Hélène/Sam Bourcier is a queer activist and theorist. He is an Associate Professor of Cultural Studies, Feminist Studies and Queer Studies at the University of Lille III. He founded Le ZOO, the first queer group in France in 1996. He translated Teresa de Lauretis and Monique Wittig into French and writes extensively on queer epistemology, gender and sexual politics, pornography and post-pornography, queer subcultures and politics. He is the author of the trilogy *Queer Zones 1, Politique des identités sexuelles et des savoirs* (2001), *Queer Zones 2, Sexpolitiques* (2005), *Queer Zones 3, Identités, Cultures, Politics* (2011). He is currently writing a book on sex, neoliberalism and discrimination at university. All his books and papers are available at https://univ-lille3.academia.edu/marieheleneBourcier.

Gavin Brown is a Senior Lecturer in Human Geography at the University of Leicester. He was a founding officer of the Space, Sexualities and Queer Research Group of the Royal Geographical Society (with the Institute of British Geographers). He co-edited *Geographies of Sexualities: Theory, practices and politics* (Ashgate, 2007) with Kath Browne and Jason Lim. He has published widely on the geographies of gay men's lives, radical queer activism and rethinking debates about 'homonormativity'. In recent years, his research has focused as much on the historical geographies of British anti-apartheid solidarity activism, as it has on the geographies of sexualities, and he has a book forthcoming with Routledge on that theme. Follow him on Twitter: @lestageog.

Kath Browne is Professor in Human Geography at the University of Brighton with research interests in sexualities, genders and spatialities. Her current research includes 'Making Lives Liveable: Rethinking Social Exclusion' and explorations of transnational resistances to LGBT equalities. She has worked on LGBT equalities, lesbian geographies, gender transgressions and women's spaces. Kath was a founding member of the Space, Sexualities and Queer Research Group of the Royal Geographical Society (with the Institute of British Geographers). She has authored a number of journal publications, co-wrote with Leela Bakshi *Ordinary in Brighton: LGBT, Activisms and the City* (Ashgate, 2013), and *Queer Spiritual Spaces* (with Sally Munt and Andrew Yip, Ashgate, 2010), and co-edited *Queer Methods and Methodologies* (with Catherine Nash Ashgate, 2010) and *Geographies of Sexualities: Theory, Practices and Politics* (with Gavin Brown and Jason Lim, Ashgate, 2007). Her most recent book, *Lesbian Geographies*, co-edited with Eduarda Ferreira, is forthcoming with Ashgate. Follow her on Twitter: @kathbrowne.

Julie Cupples is Reader in Human Geography and Co-Director of the Global Development Academy at the University of Edinburgh. Her research interests span cultural geography, development studies and media and cultural studies. She is currently engaged in a collaborative research project exploring the geographic dimensions of media convergence, funded by the Marsden Fund of the Royal Society of New Zealand. This project is exploring the democratizing and decolonizing dimensions of the new media environment, with a focus on mainstream entertainment media as well as community and indigenous media operations. She is the author of *Latin American Development* (Routledge, 2013), co-editor of *Mediated Geographies and Geographies of Media* (forthcoming with Springer) and co-author of *Media/Communications/Geographies: Interdisciplinary Perspectives* (forthcoming with Routledge).

Cesare Di Feliciantonio is currently enrolled in a PhD programme in Geography between KU Leuven (Belgium) and Sapienza – University of Rome (Italy). His research interests include a wide range of issues from social and urban geography to critical political economy. Beyond academia, he is a militant in the queer leftist scene in Rome, where he has belonged to various collectives/groups. Currently, he is part of the Roman node of Communia, a national network involving different forms of squatting and grassroots initiatives (communianet.org).

Petra Doan is Professor in the Department of Urban and Regional Planning at Florida State University. In addition to her research on planning in the developing world, she conducts research on planning issues surrounding the LGBTQ community. Most notably she has edited two books, *Queerying Planning: Challenging Heteronormative Assumptions and Reframing Planning Practice* (Ashgate, 2011) and *Planning and LGBTQ Communities: The Need for Inclusive Queer Space* (Routledge, 2015). As an openly trans woman she has also published a number of articles on trans and LGB perspectives on cities in *Gender, Place, and Culture*, *Environment and Planning A*, the *Journal of Planning Education and Research* and *Progressive Planning*.

Gary Downing is a postgraduate research student at the University of Reading, UK. His research interests include sexual and gender identities, the interconnections between young people's online and offline lives, and sociocultural geographies. His recent work has been published in *Children's Geographies*. He is also about to submit his PhD, which explores disabled young people's everyday corporeal realities, their sociosexual and support networks, and their use of the internet and assistive technologies.

Alexandra Fanghanel is a Lecturer in Criminology at the University of Greenwich. She is interested in the production of knowledge, sexuality and subjectification in public spaces. Her research examines questions of fear of crime, securitization, risk and citizenship in public spaces. Alex has also published work on the anthropology of households and families. Some of Alex's work is published in *Geoforum*, *Theoretical Criminology*, the *European Journal of Population* and *Cultural Geographies*.

Emma A. Foster is a Lecturer in International Politics and Gender in the Department of Political Science and International Studies at the University of Birmingham. Her research interests include gender and sexuality, environmental politics and Foucault. She is currently researching issues related to queer ecology and queer(ing) development. Emma has published in a variety of journals including *Gender, Place and Culture*, the *British Journal of Politics and International Relations* and *Globalizations*.

Subhagata Ghosh is a founder member of Sappho for Equality, the activist forum for lesbian, bisexual women and transmen rights in eastern India. Holding a PhD in Bioinformatics, she is professionally involved in the government research and development sector. Science provides her living and sexuality activism bestows her life.

Jen Jack Gieseking (@jgieseking), Assistant Professor of Public Humanities in American Studies at Trinity College, is engaged in research on co-productions of space and identity in digital and material environments, with a focus on sexual and gender identities. Jack's work pays special attention to how such productions support or inhibit social, spatial and economic justice. S/he is presently writing her second book, *Queer New York: Geographies of Lesbians, Dykes, and Queer Women, 1983-2008*. Jack's first book is *The People, Place, and Space Reader*, co-edited with William Mangold, Cindi Katz, Setha Low and Susan Saegert, and recently out with Routledge. S/he has published work on the topic of lesbian and queer spaces in *Area, Radical History Review* and the *Journal of Interactive Technology and Pedagogy*, and has published on related topics in *Qualitative Inquiry* and the *Journal of Urban Affairs*. S/he also blogs and creates data visualizations about urban queer history on her website, jgieseking.org.

Andrew Gorman-Murray is a Senior Lecturer in Geography and Urban Studies at the University of Western Sydney, Australia. He is a social and cultural geographer whose research has focused on geographies of gender and sexuality and the politics of belonging. He has examined LGBTQ experiences and place-making activities across urban and regional Australia, at the scales of the nation, state, city, neighbourhood and home. He has published several edited collections: *Material Geographies of Household Sustainability* (Ashgate, 2011, with Dr Ruth Lane), *Sexuality, Rurality, and Geography* (Lexington, 2013, with Barbara Pini and Lia Bryant), and *Masculinities and Place* (Ashgate, 2014, with Peter Hopkins).

Phil Hubbard has written extensively on the relations of sexuality and the city, and has particular expertise in the regulation of sex work through planning, licensing and environmental controls. This has included international comparative projects funded by the ESRC, Joseph Rowntree and the British Academy: he has given expert testimony to the British All-Party Parliamentary Group on prostitution, and his work has also been cited in Australian and New Zealand parliamentary reviews. His publications include *Sex and the City: Geographies of Prostitution in the Urban West* (1999) and *Cities and Sexualities* (2012).

Jan Simon Hutta is Lecturer at the University of Bayreuth in Germany, working in the Cultural Geography Research Group. He has conducted research in Brazil and Germany on sexual and transgender politics, urban governmentality and relations of affect, subjectivity and space. He received his PhD from The Open University in Milton Keynes, UK. Between 2010 and 2012, he worked for the Transgender Europe's international research project 'Transrespect versus Transphobia Worldwide'. He is a committee member of the Space, Sexualities and Queer Research Group (SSQRG) of the Royal Geographic Society and founding editor of the German-language open-access journal on critical urban research, *sub\urban – Zeitschrift für kritische Stadtforschung*.

Lynda Johnston is a Professor in Geography at the University of Waikato. Her research interests include gender, sexuality, embodiment, tourism and leisure, subjectivities, methodologies, constructions of geographical knowledge and cultures of nature. Lynda is interested in the relationship between bodies and ('real' and discursive) spaces. She concentrates on the formation of subjectivities – gender, sexuality, ethnicity and class – and the ways in which these are performed in different spaces (for example, home, weddings, activist spaces, gay pride parades, beaches, internet). Her publications include *Space, Place and Sex: Geographies of Sexualities* (2010) co-authored with Robyn Longhurst, *Queering Tourism: Paradoxical Performances of Gay Pride Parades* (2005) and *Subjectivities, Knowledges and Feminist Geographies: The Subjects and Ethics of Social Research* (2002), a multi-authored work. *Lynda is currently working on a sole-authored manuscript, Gender Variant Geographies, for Ashgate.*

Gerry Kearns is a Professor of Human Geography at Maynooth University, Ireland. He works at the intersection of historical, political and medical geography. His *Geopolitics and Empire: The Legacy of Halford Mackinder* (Oxford University Press, 2009) was awarded the Murchison Prize from the Royal Geographical Society in 2010. With colleagues, David Meredith and John Morrissey, he has edited a collection of essays on the geography of austerity in Ireland, *Spatial Justice and the Irish Crisis* (Royal Irish Academy, 2014). His work in historical geography includes editing *Irish Historical Geographies: Colonial Contexts and Postcolonial Legacies*, which appeared as two special issues of the journal, *Historical Geography* (2013, 2014). He is currently the Distinguished Historical Geographer for the Historical Geography Specialty Group of the Association of American Geographers and also serves on the Geographical and Geosciences Committee of the Royal Irish Academy. He is currently working on an Irish Research Council-funded project, *The Geographical Turn*, a study of the geographical research and explorations undertaken by Irish artists, and on a book about the cultural politics of AIDS, *Making Space for AIDS*.

Robert Kulpa is interested in critical epistemologies within/of gender and sexuality studies, pertaining to the modes of knowledge production and hegemonic geotemporal 'knowledge situations'. His doctoral research (Birkbeck College, University of London) explored discourses of nationhood and homosexuality in the context of 'post-communist transformations' in Poland. He has also engaged in the study of geographies and temporalities of transnational sexual politics, nationhood and non-normative identities as interlocked with discourses of the 'Occident'/'West' and 'the Rest', 'development', 'human rights' and 'EUropeanization'. Previous publications include *De-Centring Western Sexualities: Central and Eastern Perspectives* (2011), a special issue of *Lambda Nordica* journal, 'Central-Eastern European Sexualities "in Transition"' (2012, both co-edited with J. Mizielinska), and articles in *Sexualities* (2014), *Gender, Place and Culture* (2014) and *Southeastern Europe* (2013). For more information, visit http://independent.academia.edu/robertkulpa.

Nathaniel M. Lewis is a Lecturer in Human Geography at the University of Southampton, UK, and formerly a Canadian Institutes of Health Research (CIHR) Postdoctoral Fellow in the School of Health and Human Performance at Dalhousie University in Halifax, Nova Scotia, Canada. His research focuses on relationships between migration, health and the urban environment among gay-identified men in North America. He serves on the editorial board of *Gender, Place and Culture: A Journal of Feminist Geography*, and his work can be found in a variety of journals such as *Health & Place*, *Geoforum*, *Social & Cultural Geography* and *Annals of the Association of American Geographers*. He has also contributed to recent volumes such as *Planning and LGBTQ Communities: The Need for Inclusive Queer Spaces* (edited by Petra

Doan, Routledge, 2015) and *Masculinities and Place* (edited by Andrew Gorman-Murray and Peter Hopkins, Ashgate, 2014).

Jason Lim a Lecturer in Human Geography at the University of Brighton, UK. His research concerns the interactions between the affective, the material, the practical and the embodied. He has explored how the embodiment of sexuality, gender, race, ethnicity and class can be understood in terms of 'affect'. His work has also addressed how political problems are framed within feminist activism using assumptions about certain proper modes of gendered desire, embodiment, subjectivity and agency. He has worked with Kath Browne (University of Brighton, UK) to examine inequalities and marginalization faced by LGBT groups in the city of Brighton and Hove in the UK. Jason is co-editor of *Geographies of Sexualities: Theories, Practices and Politics* and one of the founding members of the Space, Sexualities and Queer Research Group of the Royal Geographical Society (with the Institute of British Geographers). He has published papers in *Gender, Place and Culture, Geoforum, Environment and Planning A, Sociological Research Online* and the *Journal of Social Policy*.

Robyn Longhurst is Pro Vice-Chancellor Academic and Professor at the University of Waikato. For many years she has taught feminist geography and is committed to providing innovative teaching, learning and postgraduate supervision. Robyn has been awarded both a University of Waikato Teaching Excellence Award and a University of Waikato Research Postgraduate Supervision Excellence Award. She has been Editor-in-Chief of *Gender, Place and Culture: A Journal of Feminist Geography* and Chair of the International Geographical Union Commission on Gender and Geography. Robyn has published on issues relating to pregnancy, mothering, sexuality, 'visceral geographies', masculinities, and body size and shape. Her articles have appeared in journals including *Environment and Planning D: Society and Space, Antipode: A Radical Journal of Geography, Progress in Human Geography, Geoforum, Social & Cultural Geography* and the *Feminist Review*. She is author of *Bodies: Exploring Fluid Boundaries* (2001), *Maternities: Gender, Bodies and Spaces* (2008) and co-author of *Pleasure Zones: Bodies, Cities, Spaces* (2001) and *Space, Place, and Sex: Geographies of Sexualities* (2010). Currently, she is working on a sole-authored manuscript titled *Skype: Bodies, Screens Space* for Ashgate.

Maarten Loopmans is currently an Associate Professor of Geography at the University of Leuven, Belgium. He has a broad range of research interests that span urban geography and planning, political ecology and the geographies of sexualities. These topics are studied in many countries across the globe, both in the Global North and the Global South. His research on sexuality examines the dialectic relationship between norms surrounding sexuality and the production of space. He has written extensively about the spatiality of sex work and sex-work policies in Belgian cities and is currently researching non-heteronormative heterosexualities. His English-language publications include work published in *Environment and Planning A, Social and Cultural Geography* and *Urban Studies*.

Chen Misgav is a Research Coordinator and Research Fellow in the Minerva Humanities Center, Tel Aviv University, and teaches in the Urban Design programme in Bezalel and in the Department of Geography and Human Environment in Tel Aviv University. He is engaged in, and writes about, activism, queer and feminism. He recently completed his PhD titled 'Spatial Activism: Perspectives of Body, Identity and Memory' in the PECLAB (Planning with Communities for the Environment) in the Department of Geography and Human environment at Tel Aviv University, Israel. Chen graduated with an MSc in Town and Regional Planning at the Technion and wrote his thesis on queer perspectives of Tel Aviv. Chen has published journal papers and book chapters in Hebrew, Italian and English.

Sharif Mowlabocus is a Senior Lecturer in Digital Media at the University of Sussex, UK. His research focuses on the intersections between sex and technology, with a particular emphasis on the role that digital technologies are playing in the construction, maintenance and discussion of sexual identities, practices and politics. He has worked with HIV/AIDS organizations on digital community outreach initiatives and has published widely on themes ranging from pornography to dating applications to cinema and queer representation.

Tiffany Muller Myrdahl is the Ruth Wynn Woodward Junior Chair (2012–15) in the Department of Gender, Sexuality & Women's Studies at Simon Fraser University (Burnaby, BC, Canada). She completed her PhD in Geography with a certificate in Feminist Studies at the University of Minnesota in 2008. Her publications appear in *ACME: An International E-Journal for Critical Geographies*, *Social & Cultural Geography*, *Leisure Studies* and the *Journal of Lesbian Studies*, among others, and she serves on the editorial board of *Gender, Place and Culture: A Journal of Feminist Geography*. Her current manuscript, 'Here is Queer: Sexual Difference and Urban Change in a Small Canadian City', is under contract with University of British Columbia Press.

Catherine J. Nash is a Professor of Geography at Brock University in Canada. She is a social and cultural geographer with research expertise at the intersections of feminist geographies and the geographies of sexualities. Her recent research (with Kath Browne), funded by the Social Sciences and Humanities Research Council of Canada, investigates resistances to LGBT equalities in the UK and Canada. She also has a developing research interest in cyberspace, virtual geographies and mobilities. She is co-editor (with Kath Browne) of *Queer Methods and Methodologies* (Ashgate, 2010). Her work has been published in a wide range of journals including *Antipode*, *Area* and *The Canadian Geographer*.

Marcio Jose Ornat is a Professor of Geography in the graduate programme at the State University of Ponta Grossa and Vice-coordinator of the Group of Territorial Studies at the same university. He is one of the founders of the Ibero-Latin American Network for the Study of Geography, Gender and Sexualities. His research focuses on the relationships between space, gender, sexualities and culture, with special attention on transsexualities, homophobia and transphobia. He is a member of the *Renascer* (Reborn) NGO, which works in support of citizenship and the human rights of LGBT groups. He has edited several books, including *Geografias malditas: corpos, sexualidades e espaços* (*Cursed Geographies: Bodies, Sexualities and Spaces*), *Espaço, gênero e masculinidades plurais* (*Space, Gender and Plural Masculinities*) and *Espaço, gênero e feminilidades ibero-americanas* (*Space, Gender and Ibero-American Femininities*).

Natalie Oswin is Associate Professor of Geography at McGill University, Montreal, Canada and has a research interest in sexual citizenship, with a specific emphasis on how sexual politics intertwine with processes of globalization and urbanization. Her publications include articles on South Africa's post-apartheid gay and lesbian movement, the cultural politics of heteronormativity in Singapore and conceptual pieces on queer geographies. She is one of the editors of the interdisciplinary journal *Environment and Planning D: Society and Space*.

Julie A. Podmore is a College Professor in Geosciences at John Abbott College and an Affiliate Associate Professor in Geography, Planning and Environment at Concordia University in Montreal. The intersections between gender and sexuality in urban space have been her sustained research focus – a perspective that is reflected in her publications on Montreal's lesbian geographies. A member of the Sexuality and Gender Diversity research team at the Université du Québec à Montréal, she is currently developing research projects on the intersections between LGBTQ populations, generations and geographies.

Cha Prieur is a PhD student (ABD) and an Assistant Professor in Geography at the Paris-Sorbonne University. Their thesis concerns queer places, communities and sexualities in Paris and Montreal, with a focus on the concepts of 'safe spaces' and 'brave spaces'. Cha is interested in methodological, epistemological and ethical questions of a researcher's place in relation to their subject, fieldwork and people encountered during the fieldwork, and identifies more generally with the fields of gender geography and geographies of sexualities. Cha's perspectives for further research concern the ways in which researchers deal with their emotions in relation to their researches and also interviewees' emotions in the fieldwork, as well as the possibilities of linking together geography and psychotherapy to help researchers in their fieldwork.

Senthorun Raj is a researcher and advocate with a passion for popular culture, social justice and politics. He is currently completing his PhD titled 'Feeling Law: Intimacy, Violence, and Queer Subjects' and is a sessional teacher at the Sydney Law School. He is a contributing writer for the *Guardian* and has published a number of academic papers. He has written on a range of topics including refugee law, queer intimacies, marriage equality, homophobic violence and popular culture. He is also an advisory board member of the sexuality, gender and diversity studies journal *Writing from Below*. In a governance capacity, he serves on the boards of Amnesty International Australia and ACON Health. Sen is a former Churchill Fellow and has worked as the Senior Policy Advisor for the NSW Gay and Lesbian Rights Lobby.

Maria Rodó-de-Zárate is a postdoctoral researcher (PNPD-CAPES) at the State University of Ponta Grossa, Brazil, and a feminist activist. Her main research fields are feminist geographies and geographies of sexualities and youth, with a special focus on intersectionality theory and the development of new visual methodologies such as Relief Maps. She is a member of the Geography and Gender Research Group (Universitat Autònoma de Barcelona) and has spent visiting research periods at CUNY (New York, USA), UEPG (Ponta Grossa, Brazil) and UCD (Dublin, Ireland).

Magaly Rodríguez García is a Lecturer at the History Department of the University of Leuven (KU Leuven). Her research focuses on the League of Nations and its campaigns against traffic in women, prostitution and slavery, as well as on sex work and coerced labour in the global perspective. Her publications include 'The League of Nations and the Moral Recruitment of Women' (2012), 'Prostitution in World Cities (1600s–2000s)' (2014) and 'Child Slavery, Sex Trafficking or Domestic Work? The League of Nations and its Analysis of the *Mui Tsai* System' (2015).

Farhang Rouhani, Professor of Geography at the University of Mary Washington, received his doctoral degree from the University of Arizona in 2001. He is a cultural and political geographer who researches and writes about globalization, state formation and new media politics in Iran, diasporic Iranian and Muslim queer political geographies, and anarchist–geographic theories and practices.

Joseli Maria Silva is a Professor of Geography in the postgraduate programme at the State University of Ponta Grossa. She is a coordinator of the Group of Territorial Studies at the same university and chief editor of the *Revista Latino-americana de Geografia e Gênero*

(*Latin American Journal of Geography and Gender*). She is one of the founders of the Ibero-Latin American Network for the Study of Geography, Gender and Sexualities. Her research focuses on the relationship between space, gender and sexualities, with special attention on transsexualities. She is a member of the *Renascer* (Reborn) NGO, which works in support of citizenship and the human rights of LGBT groups. She has edited several books, including *Geografias subversivas: discursos sobre espaço, gênero e sexualidades* (*Subversive Geographies: Discourses on Space, Gender and Sexuality*), *Geografias malditas: corpos, sexualidades e espaços* (*Cursed Geographies: Bodies, Sexualities and Spaces*) and *Espaço, gênero e poder: conectando fronteiras* (*Space, Gender and Power: Connecting Borders*).

Marlene Spanger is an Assistant Professor at Aalborg University, Denmark. She is a researcher and teacher in the fields of transnational migration, intimacies, gender and sexuality and has a special interest in transactional and intimate relations, sex work and human trafficking, focusing on how multiple subject positions of female migrants intertwine. Other fields of interest are global care chains and transnational family, addressing gendered and racial formations as well as intimate and care relations. Spanger is engaged with poststructuralist feminist theory and discourse analysis theory. Her other relevant publications are: 'Doing Marriage and Love in the Borderland of Transnational Sex Work: Female Thai Migrants in Denmark' in *NORA – Nordic Journal of Feminist and Gender Research* (2013); '"You See How Good-looking Lee Ann is!" Establishing Field Relations through Gendered and Racialised Bodily Practices' in *Qualitative Studies* (2012), 'Human Trafficking a Lever for Feminist Voices? Transformations of the Danish Policy Field of Prostitution' in *Critical Social Policy* (2011) and 'Disturbance and Celebration of Josephine Baker in Copenhagen 1928: Emotional Constructions of Whiteness', in Andreassen and Vitus (eds), *Affectivity and Race: Studies from a Nordic Context* (Ashgate, 2015).

Stephen Taylor is Lecturer in Human Geography at Queen Mary University of London. His research focuses on the geographies of biomedical research in sub-Saharan Africa, with a particular emphasis on emergent urban clinical trial economies in South Africa. He is currently completing a book manuscript based on his ethnographic fieldwork in Cape Town, Durban and Johannesburg that explores the production of scientific facts in South Africa, with special attention to the promises, perils and practical labours of experimentation. He was formerly a postdoctoral fellow at the Department of Geography, University of Cambridge and Queens' College, Cambridge. During this time he conducted research for the World Health Organization on the securitization of polio eradication efforts in Pakistan and Nigeria, and conducted collaborative research at the Rockefeller and Bill & Melinda Gates Foundations on the catalytic role of philanthropy in driving global food security discourses.

Cherie Todd is a Senior Tutor for Student Learning at the University of Waikato, Aotearoa, New Zealand and she has recently completed her PhD titled 'Sex and Gender in World of Warcraft: Identities, Love, and Power' in the Geography, Tourism & Environmental Planning Programme at the University of Waikato. Her PhD examines further the diverse complexities of gaming culture and the relationships between gamers, as well as online/offline identities. Cherie's MA thesis titled 'Gaming and Gender: Home as a Place of (Non) conformity for Women Gamers' examines the experiences of women who game at home and how they negotiate stereotypical and conflicting identities (woman at home/woman gamer). Her research interests focus on social/cultural and feminist geography, and critical social theory.

Andrew Tucker is an MSM Research Specialist at the Anova Health Institute in South Africa. Anova, through its Health4Men initiative, is creating access to MSM-focused competent health services through a variety of training and mentoring programmes in partnership with the South African Department of Health and implementing best-practice prevention, treatment and community engagement models. Dr Tucker was previously a lecturer at the Department of Geography at the University of Cambridge and the Deputy Director of the University of Cambridge Centre for Gender Studies. He has published widely on sexuality and health in sub-Saharan Africa in both geographical and medical journals. His monograph *Queer Visibilities: Space, Identity and Interaction in Cape Town* was published by Wiley-Blackwell in 2009. Dr Tucker is also an Honorary Research Fellow at the Department of Environmental and Geographical Sciences at the University of Cape Town.

Paulo Jorge Vieira is a researcher at the Center for Geographical Studies of the Institute of Geography and Spatial Planning, University of Lisbon and at GETE – Group of Territorial Studies at the State University of Ponta Grossa, Paraná, Brazil. He attended the Masters and Doctorate programme 'Post-Colonialism and Global Citizenship' at the Center for Social Studies and the Faculty of Economics, University of Coimbra (2005-2006). He is currently studying for an MA in Geography – Population, Society and Territory in the Institute of Geography and Spatial Planning, University of Lisbon. Paulo is a member of the editorial team of the *Revista Latino Americana de Geografia e Género* and a committee member of the Space, Sexualities and Queer Research Group of the Royal Geographical Society. His research interests focus on three main areas: social and cultural geography, equality and diversity; gender studies (masculinity) and lesbian, gay and queer studies; and social theory and history and theory of geography (qualitative methodologies and epistemology).

Natasha Vine is a New Zealand queer activist, political scientist and graduate student at Victoria University of Wellington. She has worked with queer and women's rights organizations across New Zealand including UniQ, VUWSA Women's Group and the Young Labour Rainbow Branch.

Gustav Visser, an urban geographer by training, is currently Professor of Geography at Stellenbosch University. His main research interest lies in identity-based consumption and urban morphological change, which is best expressed in his work on sexuality and space in urban South Africa. He also has a strong interest in the tourism and development nexus. His most recent research focuses on Western theorizations of the relationship between gay sexualities and knowledge production, and its links to specific forms of urban space, such as gay ghettos and neighbourhoods.

Audrey Yue is Associate Professor in Cultural Studies at The University of Melbourne. Her recent publications include *Sinophone Cinemas* (Palgrave, 2014), *Transnational Australian Cinema: Ethics in the Asian Diasporas* (Lexington, 2013) and *Queer Singapore: Illiberal Citizenship and Mediated Cultures* (Hong Kong University Press, 2012). She is currently Chief Investigator in the Australian Research Council-funded project on multicultural arts governance and is completing a book project on queer Asian Australian migration.

Acknowledgements

We would like to thank all of the section editors and authors who made this volume possible. Their work and dedication has resulted in a rich and outstanding collection of work that offers both breadth and depth in ways that include but move beyond the Global North.

We want to acknowledge all of those who created this area of investigation, and those who continue to develop this area. Some are included in this collection, but there are many others.

Thanks go to Clara Rivas Alonso for all of her hard work in getting the manuscript to the point of submission.

We would also like to thank Catherine Nash, Cesare di Feliciantonio and Eduarda Ferreira for their (speedy and) insightful comments on an earlier draft of the main introduction. They helped edit the editors and ensured that we remembered to see the world from perspectives other than our own.

Kath would like to thank Donna for her unfailing support and putting up with her loud typing at all times of the day and night!

Gavin would like to thank Seosaimh for his love and encouragement, as well as the insightful words of critique that so often accompanied that support. Thanks also for reminding me to stop and rest.

Chapter 11 uses similar empirical material to an article published in *Gender, Place & Culture*: 'What's Radical about Reality TV? An Unexpected Tale of a Chinese Antihero' (Bassi, **date**)

Figure 11.1 this chapter is reproduced with the permission of AP Archive.

Chapter 15 is an abridged version of Natalie Oswin (2010) 'Sexual Tensions in Modernizing Singapore: The Postcolonial and the Intimate' *Environment and Planning D: Society and Space*, vol. 28, pp. 128–141. It is reproduced with the permission of Pion Ltd, London.

The epigraph at the beginning of Chapter 17 is from *Difference and Repetition*, translated by Paul Patton. Bloomsbury Academic, an imprint of Bloomsbury Publishing Plc. © Gilles Deleuze and also © 1968 Columbia University Press. It is reprinted with the permission of the publishers.

Chapter 1

An Introduction to the Geographies of Sex and Sexualities

Kath Browne and Gavin Brown

Introduction

Sexuality has been present, but obliquely addressed, in human geography for a long time. Whenever geographers discussed demographic transition models, population dynamics or fertility rates, for example, they were, at least implicitly, discussing human sexuality. Such approaches tend to assume, prioritize and only attend to aspects of heterosexual coupledom, parenthood and family arrangements. As in most of the topics we study, as geographers we have learned to be wary of assuming that these normative forms of family and coupledom are universal and do not vary between places or across spatial scales. By contrast, geographies of sexualities scholarship considers the different ways in which human sexualities vary geographically.

Geographies of sexualities scholarship is now in its fourth decade. This approach emerged from the desire to examine geographical differences in sexualities and their spatial specificities as a key aspect of human geographies. This geographical work has engaged with a multiplicity of sexual identities and practices, including lesbian, gay, bisexual, trans, queer and heterosexual/straight as well as myriad other practices and experiences. This rich body of work illustrates the centrality of place, space and other spatial relationships in shaping sexual desires, practices and identities, as well as how they are represented, policed and treated in law and everyday life. Similarly, geographers argue that place and space are central to the production of sexed bodies (Duncan, 1996; Longhurst, 2001).

Often starting from the idea that there is nothing innate or natural to either space/place/ environment or sex and sexualities, these geographies have shown how sex and sexualities are created in, through and by space, place and environment. Moreover, how space and place are organized and used is directly related to sex and sexualities. Space/place are usually understood as heterosexual and meant to be used by two people who are unambiguously sexed (man or woman), exhibit proper gendered behaviours (femininity and masculinity) that are mapped on to that unambiguous physical body and sexual interests that are directed towards the clearly differentiated 'opposite sex'. Heteronormativity refers to the ways in which sexuality, sex and gender are intertwined in ways that are presumed to be natural. It is usually based on particular class, race and able-bodied ideals.

Uncomplicated presentations of heterosexuality are what are expected to be visible in spaces, making heteronormativity the marker of heterosexual space. Heterosexual couples holding hands, for example, are unremarked upon and seen as 'normal' in most public spaces in the Global North (Bell, 1994). In contrast, those who contravene these norms are detected and repudiated, often with verbal and physical violence. For example, those who are not 'properly' gendered – that is, easily read as male/female – can be subject to prejudice, abuse and violence in spaces such as toilets (Browne, 2004). Similarly, couples who are read as both being of the same sex, or those who are seen as beyond the 'correct' boundaries of heterosexual monogamy can also be policed through shouting, comments and physical attack (Valentine, 1996). Yet the sexuality of space tends only to be noticed, and named as such, when it is not heterosexual/straight. Gay spaces are marked as different and named as 'gay', but this is not the case for straight spaces. What this means is that sexualities remake everyday spaces, often as 'normal' (where normal means straight and adhering to gender norms). People using these spaces can conform to the norms of the spaces. As a result, they are not subject to violence, looks or comments. Their 'normality' remains unremarked and invisible. In this way places also remake people's lives, identities and bodies.

Initially, geographies of sexualities focused on the activities and experiences of gay men, before then considering the lives of lesbians, and then bi/bisexual and trans people. Including trans people under the label 'sexualities' is problematic, because trans is not a sexual identity; it is related to gender/sex. For this reason, this book explores sex, as it is related to categorizations of man/woman, male/female, as well as the practices of gender that make sexed bodies. Because geographies of sexualities are often presumed to be about other sexualities, 'normative heterosexuality' or the places that Phil Hubbard (2008) calls 'unsexy spaces' often get overlooked. Sexualities are key to the social relations which produce these 'unsexy spaces' (such as supermarkets, homes and nights out with friends), but because these social relations often go unnoticed and are not considered to be 'sexual', such spaces are often overlooked even by geographers of sexualities (see, however, Meth, 2009; Morrison, 2012a, 2012b; Thomas, 2004; Waitt, Jessop and Gorman-Murray, 2011). The predominance of studies of lesbian and gay spaces by geographers of sexualities also means that there continues to be a lack of geographical work on asexuality, polyamory, kink and BDSM (see Binnie, 1994; Herman, 2007; Klesse, 2007, 2014a, 2014b; Wilkinson, 2009a, 2011).

The term 'queer' has emerged as a dominant conceptual force in Global North considerations of sexualities and sexes, as well as other normative forms of social relations. Queer has diverse definitions. For our purposes, we understand that some people use queer as an identity to move beyond lesbian, gay, bisexual and/or trans (G. Brown, 2007a), whilst others see queer as a mode of thinking that questions how social norms are formed and created (see Giffney, 2004; Browne, 2006; Browne and Nash, 2010; Oswin, 2008; Podmore, 2013a). Queer has questioned the normalization of certain genders (male/female) and also sexualities, including some forms of lesbian and gay sexualities (what can be termed homonormativities – see below).

Whilst there have been many important insights into how bodies and identities question the rigid binaries of gender and sexualities, queer theory's emergence through textual analysis has at times overlooked the lived experience of marginalization, exclusion and self-determination – that is, what it feels like to be other/different and punished in everyday spaces for this. Nonetheless, queer allows us to question the ways in which desire, categories, identities and practices are created, rather than presuming that there is a necessary link between your gender identity, the gender that you are attracted to and what your sexual practices are. Queer, then, allows us to see sexuality and lived experiences as dynamic.

Despite its predominance and analytical potential, there are limits to tying geographical work on sex and sexualities to only queer theory. Doing so encourages us to go about addressing questions in particular ways, when other ways might also be productive (see, for example, Green et al., 2010 for work that does not primarily use queer methodologies). It can also negate the importance of examining sexualities through the identities that continue to matter in people's lives. Given that such identities can mean that people become the target of discrimination and that these identities are important for the creation of community and belonging, they can be a resource for mobilizing collective activism. For example, mapping LGBT places and histories illustrates the ways in which geographies and politics are inherently intertwined, both critiquing and using identities as a mode of analysis (see Brown and Knopp, 2006).

Moreover, queer modes of analyses are not predominant everywhere, and indeed can be seen as reproducing Anglo-American hegemonies in ways that would be at odds with how queer seeks to question all norms. One of the difficulties is the way in which queer travels to different places, as well as the presumption that queer ideas and concepts can be used in identical fashion everywhere (Browne and Nash, 2010). Queer thinking has emerged through Anglo-American linguistic contexts, and the word 'queer' itself and the ideas behind it do not translate easily (see, for example, Pustianaz, 2010).

Thus, for this collection, although many of the chapters might be described as being 'queer geographies', we have chosen not to name the book in this way. Instead, we focus the book on geographies of sexualities and sex, recognizing both the importance and limitations of queer, and seeking a diversity of geographies that investigate sexual lives, desires, identities, bodies and practices.

What follows is a short introduction to some key areas of geographies of sex and sexualities, public/private, urban/rural, Global North/Global South. Such an Introduction, and indeed even the section introductions, cannot cover everything written in geographies of sex and sexualities over the last 40 years. This chapter is designed to give a reader unfamiliar with the area a chance to understand some of the core building blocks of the subdiscipline. It uses three binaries to introduce some of the key ideas in geographies of sexualities. Each of these is developed in further depth in the section introductions and then the chapters that follow.

Public/Private

The public/private divide is a key way through which geography scholars have explored sexual politics, including visibilities and exclusions (Brown, 2000; Tucker, 2009a). Here, we take two paths through this literature, first exploring the role of the state in promoting heteronormative (and, in some cases, homonormative) values and then examining the ways in which everyday spaces are negotiated in relation to the public/private binary. Indeed, some scholarship questions the solidity of the binary itself as the private can become public and what is public is becoming increasingly private. As is the case for many geographers, we are interested in how this and other binaries were used from the nineteenth century onwards to regulate the lives of whole populations through 'public health' and 'birth control' campaigns, and later to encourage people to regulate their own sexual lives (in private). The politics of regulating life in this way is known as 'biopolitics' (see Chapters 29 and 30 for further discussion of this).

Regulating the (real and imagined) relationship between disease and certain forms of sex has been a key form of biopolitics over the last century. Associations between sex and disease are also key areas of research for geographers interested in sexualities. In this context the medicalization and associated demonization of certain sexual acts (see Kearns, Chapter 30 in this volume) is related to shame, and this can encourage the privatization of certain sexual behaviours (as well as associated identities, such as prostitute or gay man). However, public health agendas often intersect with supposedly private sexual lives, as has been the case with diseases such as syphilis, HIV and AIDS when they became key public health concerns (see Brown, 1997a; Legg, 2009, 2012, 2014; Phillips, 2002). However, as Taylor (Chapter 31 in this volume) attests, it is not only public health, but also corporations that have an interest in 'private' sexual lives and the regulation of sexual behaviours. The regulation of sex and sexualities has implications for the individual and collective lives of those who fail to conform to the 'normal' and that includes mental health and suicide (Lewis, 2014b). In this and many other ways, the intersections of health and sexualities extend far beyond sexual health.

Across the globe, nation-states monitor and seek to control sexualities in various ways, including: the governance of reproductive rights; access to marriage; tax and welfare benefits for married couples; and the (unequal) legal regulation of certain sexual acts and identities. Currently, state engagement with sexualities can be classified in terms of heteronormativity and homonormativity, although this distinction soon breaks down. It can be tempting to simply think about heteronormativity in relation to repressive legislation that seeks to condemn and punish 'homosexuality'. Where such legislation has been enacted, it has often driven sexual minorities 'underground' so that they only feel safe expressing their sexualities in private spaces. This, in turn, strengthens a spatial binary between public and private space, whereby all expressions of sexuality become associated with private space. At the same time, this sociospatial division tends to promote some expressions of heterosexuality as not only normal in everyday spaces, but as also key to the development and protection of the state itself. By, for example, outlawing 'unnatural' sexual acts (often sodomy and oral sex) and 'deviant' identities, preventing service in state institutions such as the military and confining the recognition of relationship forms only to men and women, the state itself is sexualized as heterosexual. It is not only by outlawing particular acts that this occurs; the state is also heterosexualized by the ways in which it offers recognition and preferential treatment to some heterosexual relationship forms (Bell, 1994, 1995a; Bell and Binnie, 2000; Richardson, 1996a).

Since the 1990s increasing numbers of countries, such as South Africa, the UK, Brazil and Canada have instigated equalities and human rights legislation that creates protections and rights for some gay men and lesbians. These changes include same-sex marriage, equal employment rights and the right to serve in the military. Seeing state-led sexual politics only in terms of heteronormativity is now problematic (Oswin, 2007a). Yet, to frame all sexual politics in terms of a desire for 'equality' can be problematic as well, and the assertion that all sexual minorities only want equality is inaccurate. Indeed, a group called Against Equality (http://www.againstequality.org) critique mainstream gay and lesbian politics for overlooking the forms of classed and racialized inequalities within lesbian and gay communities that are overlooked by standard equality claims. Rubin (1984) suggests that society prioritizes some expressions of sexuality over others. This is a dynamic process: as new groups are welcomed into the 'charmed circle' of social approved sexualities, so others are pushed out of the circle. The public recognition and hierarchization of some sexual identities, relationships and forms over others continues. The instigation of these rights has seen some queers 'left out in the cold' (Sears, 2005), whilst others, mainly white, monogamous, coupled, middle-class gay men (and, to an extent, lesbians) benefit from these changes. The term 'homonormativity', coined by Duggan (2002) has been used to describe how some people who were once considered 'sexual deviants' have become normalized through these legislative and cultural shifts, whilst others, including queer migrants, queers of colour, disabled queers, those who are poor, non-monogamous or single continue to be demonized and excluded (Isoke, 2014; Nast, 2002; D. Richardson, 2004, 2005; Platero, 2012; Taylor, 2007a; Taylor, Hines and Casey, 2011; Wilkinson, 2013). An engagement with the ways in which normalizations are formed not only by gender/sex, but also by other intersecting identities, including class, race, ethnicities and disabilities, is key to understanding sexual lives, practices, identities and power relations.

Nonetheless, there has been a push-back against the necessary association of white, middle-class gay men with privilege (Elder, 2002; Sothern, 2004). The assumptions that there can be a pure separation of (self-identified) queer lives and politics from the state has also been queried, where scholars have argued that such ideological divisions cannot be realized and that such an argument overlooks the productive possibilities of an LGBT politics that engages overtly with state equalities processes (see Andrucki and Elder, 2007; Brown, 2009; Browne and Bakshi, 2013a; Oswin, 2004). In this way, the desires for equality and freedom are both problematic and have limitations. It is important, then, to look critically at how sexual 'liberation' is understood and attained, given the political and social choices being pursued.

State interventions that seek to eliminate certain sexual acts, practices and relationship forms from public life, can instead privatize them within domestic (private) spaces. The home has been a significant site of geographical research for decades. Initially, humanities research celebrated the positive sense of place associated with home spaces. However, geographers interested in gender and sexualities have queried these assertions (Blunt and Dowling, 2006; Gregson and Lowe, 1995), and architects have explored how housing design presumes certain relationship forms and gendered divisions of labour (Matrix, 1984; Colomina, 1992; Betsky, 1997). The home can also be a place of oppression, where lesbians and gay men experience alienation and discrimination from their families of origin, and other household residents. Moreover, even where same–sex couples live together, they may develop strategies to hide their relationships when certain people come to visit (such as pretending to use two bedrooms) (Johnston and Valentine, 1995). In contrast, when heterosexual family pictures are displayed and shared, there is a celebration of ideal family forms (Rose, 2010). Research on domestic violence has also noted how the associations of privacy and safety with the home can deflect attention from the need to investigate violence and the home (Brickell, 2012; Meth, 2014; Warrington, 2001). Scholars have also noted how homes can be spaces of empowerment and self–expression, including for LGBTQ people (Gorman-Murray, 2007, 2008; Kentlyn, 2008). Paying attention to the mundane practices of making a home together (such as cooking or DIY) can reveal much about the role of homes in the intimate lives of people of all sexualities (Gabb et al., 2013; Meah, 2014, Morrison, 2012a, 2012b).

In contrast to the privacy of the home, as the 'best place for families and reproduction', public spaces for the expression of alternative sexualities and sex itself can be extensively regulated (Browne and Nash, 2014a; Nash and Browne, 2015). Sex itself is policed in relation to 'public decency' that reiterates a public/private divide. In addition to street based sex work, that challenges the public/private divide, numerous studies have documented gay men's/men who have sex with men's use of (semi–) public spaces (including beaches, cemeteries, parks, toilets and bathhouses/saunas) to engage in sex with casual partners (see Brown, 2008; Gandy, 2012; Ingram et al., 1997; Kramer, 1995; McGlotten, 2013). Less well understood are women's use of public space for sex, although there has been some work on queer women's bathhouses (Bain and Nash, 2007; Nash and Bain, 2007). Nonetheless, in public space 'a kiss is not just a kiss' when two women kiss in public spaces, and LGBT people continue to feel unsafe and fear discrimination when displaying affection in public space (Blidon, 2008a; Cattan and Clerval, 2011; Ferreira, 2011; Ferreira and Salvador, 2015).

Digital technologies are increasingly altering the ways in which sexual encounters are mediated, sex work is undertaken, blurring established divisions between public and private space. Applications ('apps') such as Grindr and Tinder, enable individuals to find sexual partners in 'cyberspace' without needing to use public or semi–public spaces. It is worth remembering that these applications rely on their geolocative and other functions. This is explored in Section 7 along with the many other ways that digital worlds are recreating spatial–sexual relations (see Ferreira and Salvador, 2015 and chapters by Albury, Mowlabocus, and Nash and Gorman-Murray).

Urban/Rural

The shift from rural communities to large urban conurbations during industrialization in the Global North contributed to the emergence of the sexual subcultures and identities that we recognize today. Placing people into closer proximity and loosening the ties of community and family was key to creating new social and sexual forms (Hubbard, 2011). Geographies of sexualities began by looking at gay ghettos and other urban areas where gay men claimed territories in the form of shops, bars, clubs and places to live (Lauria and Knopp, 1985; Knopp, 1987, 1990, 1992). These studies showed the importance of proximity and territory in establishing collective identities and also in claiming political power. For example, in San Francisco these areas were able to elect gay politicians, such as Harvey Milk, because of the clustering of gay men around the Castro area (Castells, 1983; Armstrong, 2002; Forest, 1995).

This preliminary scholarship focused primarily on the visible experiences of a particular group of white gay men who were often understood to have disproportionate amounts of disposable income (even if their apparent 'affluence' has continues to be contested). Challenging this Gill Valentine (1993a, 1993b, 1993c, 1995), Linda Peake (1993), Julie Podmore (2001, 2006) and Catherine Nash (2006), amongst others noted the ways in which lesbian geographies queried and contested the territorial assumptions in the literature focused on gay men. Time–space compartmentalization was used to explore how lesbians express their sexual identities differently at different times, and in different spaces, (Valentine, 1993b). We would suggest that just as lesbians *do* cluster, gay and bi men also use time – space compartmentalism as a way of managing different aspects of their lives and identities. This literature has questioned the idea the sexual identities were necessarily territorially based, nor that they needed to be. Indeed Julie Podmore (2001) explored how lesbians found each other in public (heterosexual spaces) through particular dress codes, hair styles, walks and other actions (see Browne and Ferreira, forthcoming).

The focus on gay men is also contested in research examining prostitution and sex work which notes how red light districts in urban areas are facilitated and policed (Hubbard, 1997, 1998, 2001; Hubbard and Whowell, 2008; Laing, Smith and Pilcher, 2015). Seeing sex work as inherently spatial, brings a discussion of heterosexuality to the fore when examining marginalized sexual spaces. Work in this field looks beyond (potentially) marginalized 'red light districts' to consider how new forms of 'adult entertainment' are increasingly central to the economies of many cities (Hubbard, 2011).

Explorations of Bi and Trans lives also question some of the findings in early literatures about sexualities and urban space (Hemmings, 2002; Klesse, 2007). Hemmings (2002) noted that bisexuals have always been present in (and involved in the creation of) both gay and straight spaces despite the fact their presence has largely been visible or unacknowledged. Authors such as Petra Doan (2007, 2009, 2011) and Nash (2011) have noted how supposedly inclusive lesbian, gay, bisexual and trans scenes and urban spaces can be highly marginalizing and spaces of discrimination for trans people. This is similar to findings regarding how lesbians experience LGBT spaces, which are often seen as more friendly to gay men, reproducing a need for lesbian specific space (Chetcuti, 2010; Corlouer, 2013; Ferreira, 2011).

It was not only differing identities that lent complexity to early engagements with urban spaces. Recently, the continuing existence of 'gay ghettos' has been called into question as recent research questions whether major cities in the Global North are witnessing the end of the fixity of gay ghettos (Ruting, 2008) and 'gaybourhoods' as certain gay (and lesbian) identities move into the mainstream (Brown, 2014; Kanai and Kenttamaa-Squires, 2015; Nash and Gorman-Murray, 2014; forthcoming). Ghaziani (2014, pp. 245–59) has argued that 'gaybourhoods' are dynamic and that different clusters of gay businesses and residences come and go over time. In recent years, a combination of more tolerant social attitudes in Europe and North America (along with the growth of online dating apps) has seemingly reduced the need for gay/LGBT people to congregate in particular neighbourhoods for safety and companionship. Many more LGBT people are now choosing to live in the suburbs and smaller cities (Brown-Saracino, 2011; Kirkey and Forsyth, 2001). As more lesbian and gay people have children and other out or semi-visible LGBT populations are ageing, they now look for other services and atmospheres in the places where they choose to live. Even so, traditional gay neighbourhoods continue to be material and symbolic places of safety and freedom for LGBT youth, trans and gender-variant people, as well as others who may find it harder to create a safe space for themselves elsewhere (Gorman-Murray and Nash, 2014; Leroy, 2009). As part of this diversification of residential and leisure options for LGBT people, some researchers have noted the emergence of new 'queer' neighbourhoods which seek to distinguish themselves from older 'gay villages' aesthetically and in terms of the types of consumption opportunities they offer and the 'diversity' of people they claim to include (see Andersson, 2009, 2011; Compton and Baumle, 2012; Nash, 2013a, 2013b; Nash and Gorman-Murray, 2014; Nash and Gorman-Murray, Chapter 22 in this volume). Whether these spaces are more inclusive than older gay neighbourhoods or whether they produce alternative configurations of exclusion will require further research over the coming years. However, it is important not to forget that increasing rent prices and gentrification also means that some LGBT people may not have a 'choice' of living in these neighbourhoods at all, as was contended from the outset of investigations into these areas (Castells, 1983; Collins, 2004a).

Gaybourhoods are not only being questioned in the Global North. Elsewhere they have been critiqued as an Anglo-American spatial formation that resulted from the confluence of various factors, including specific forms of planning cultures. In other contexts, this urban form has never appeared or has assumed completely different forms. This can vary from city to city, as well as internationally (Peixoto Caldas, 2010; Martinez and Dodge, 2010). In other words, geographers should be wary of assuming that these models are universally applicable (Visser, 2013). Concerns over the decline of 'the gaybourhood' and claims that these are no longer necessary are based on specific Anglo-American assumptions (Lewis, 2013a).

Central to discussions of geographies of sexualities from the 1990s has been the urban/rural divide. Research on migration initially focused on urban to rural migrations. Speaking to those who had moved away from rural areas, urban areas were seen as the only place that it was possible to come out, engage with same-sex sexual partners and actively create community (Weston, 1995). When examining heterosexualities in rural areas, the normalization of certain forms of heterosexuality has often been read through associations linking nature and romance, as well as 'wholesome' family life (Little, 2003, 2007). This has meant that others (including racial and urban others) are excluded and marginalized from rural space. Indeed, some authors equate the urban with sexual diversity and promise because of the proximity of people to each other. Rural researchers, however, contest the presumption that gay and lesbian sexualities are confined to urban areas (Phillips et al., 2002). Kramer (1995), for example, demonstrated how gay and bisexual men in rural Dakota developed specific sites and forms of mobility in order to meet men like themselves. Valentine (1997a) showed how US lesbian separatist women used rural areas to challenge man-made urbanities and create alternative communities (see also Browne, 2011). Smith and Holt (2005) showed that a small town in a rural area in the North of England had also developed into a lesbian haven. Finally rural spaces are used in subversive heterosexual ways, including practices of dogging (Bell, 2006).

The urban/rural divide continues to pervade not only geographical literatures, but also popular consciousness about where sexual identities can be performed. Yet there have been some challenges to this. Research demonstrates how migration patterns are not linear and final, even where the initial move is from the rural to the urban (Waitt and Gorman-Murray, 2011a). People move into and out of different areas, they return to places where they grew up and move again (Knopp and Brown, 2003; Lewis, 2014a, 2014b). Many different spaces can be used to find safety and freedom to express gender and sexual identities (see Doan, Chapter 27 in this volume). Of course, these mobilities are not available to all, and the assumption that all sexual and gender minorities can move to urban areas to escape repression in their home towns, has been contested (Gorman-Murray, 2009a; Gray, 2009). Moreover, these studies were often based in the USA, and often focused on coastal cities in that country (Murphy et al., 2010, with notable exceptions including Gorman-Murray, 2013 and Lewis, 2014a). Not only does this fail to account for the diversity of urban spaces in the USA, but it also cannot account for the different experiences of migration that lesbians, gay men, bi and trans people have across the world, including experiences of international diasporas and refugee status (see Blidon, Yue, Raj, Rouhani, Chapters 23, 24, 25 and 26 in this volume). The section on mobilities in this volume explores movements including, but not limited to, migration.

Global North/Global South

In the introduction, the example of same sex-couples holding hands was used to discuss how space is heterosexualized. Whilst this might be out of place in the Global North, in many places in the Global South, it would be men and women holding hands in public that would be seen as disrupting the norms of the sexualities of space. Indeed in some places, men holding hands is an acceptable sign of male friendships. As geographies of sexualities has grown and diversified from its initial beginnings in the study of US cities, the unexamined applicability of concepts developed in these cities about sex and sexualities to other locations has been contested.[1] Three will be introduced here and others can be found in Section III. The three addressed here are: 1) that sexual identity categories and the man/woman binary are universally applicable in all places, at all times; 2) how studies originating in the Global North tend to assume patterns of progress and development that emerge from particular world cities will be replicated in other places; and 3) the geographies of knowledge about sex and sexualities itself.

Gay and LGBT identities are largely associated with specific values located in the Global North, including ideals associated with coupled family forms that differ from other forms of extended kinship. These are not always easily applied to other contexts (Adam et al., 1992; Plummer, 1992; Drucker, 2000; Grewal and Kaplan, 2001; Platero Mendez, 2009; G. Brown et al., 2010; Moussawi, 2013; Cattan and Vanolo, 2014). This means that the assumptions of unidirectional and the unproblematic acceptance of Western gay and lesbian identities in the

---

1   This is not to suggest that writing on the Global South is not a feature of geographies of sexualities (see, for example, Oswin, 2005, 2007a, 2013; Legg, 2009, 2012, 2014; Tucker, 2009a); instead, it is to note how this subdiscipline has been hegemonically constituted through Global North understandings of sex and sexualities, as well as particular practices of scholarship.

Global South have also been critically analysed (see, for example, Povinelli and Chauncey, 1999; Cruz-Malavé and Manalansan, 2002, Kulpa and Mizielińska, 2011).

The presumption of universal models of gender that see it only through man/woman or male/female binaries has long been disrupted by the existence of 'third sexes' in various parts of the world. Examples of third sexes include Hijras in India, Samoan Fa'afafine and Two-Spirited Indigenous Americans (Hutchings and Aspin, 2007). These 'third sexes' and gendered roles associated with them challenge the binaries of Western thought in relation to sex and gender. Moreover, understandings of trans/transgender/transsexual that are articulated in relation to particular models of transitioning and 'gender reassignment' can also be queried beyond the Global North. For example, as Silva and Ornat (Chapter 37 in this volume) demonstrate, *travesti* does not equate to transgender and transgender can be rejected as an identity by *travestis* themselves.

Alongside the ways in which some cultures beyond the Global North can be classified as being 'more progressive' with regard to gendered lives beyond male/female binaries, the presumption that the Global North leads the way in sexual equality agendas is also questionable. These assertions often focus on the 'progress' made in specific cities and the acceptance of some gay men (and lesbians). However, discussions of world cities and ordinary cities (see Kanai, 2014; Oswin, 2015; and the chapters by Muller-Myrdahl, Johnston and Longhurst, and Visser in this volume), show that as geographers we are critical of models that see some cities as 'world leaders' and others as followers. Instead, each city and the lives within them need to be explored on their own terms, recognizing the potentials and limitations of each (see also Robinson, 2006).

However, it is not just the object of examination – that is, 'gay', 'LGBT' or 'heterosexual' men/women – that has been brought into question by critically reflecting on Anglophone and Eurocentric assumptions within the geographies of sexualities. As the editors and authors note in Section III of this book (see the chapters by Hutta, Zarate, and Silva and Ornat), the very way in which knowledge about geographies of sex and sexualities has been created is related to the Global North positioning/identities of scholars. Creating knowledges that move beyond Anglo-American hegemonies not only diversifies the objects of study beyond Global North categories of sexualities and sexed difference; it also can be used to question the premises on which this work is built.

About this Book

The *Companion* is structured around seven themed sections that profile the distinctive contributions geographers make to the study of sexualities: urban sexualities (which also addresses small towns and the urban/rural divide); sexual politics; decolonizing sexualities; mobile sexualities; sexual health; commercial sexualities; and, digital sexualities. Each section brings different ways of thinking that considerably widen the geography of analysis, and conversely push the thinking in sexualities/LGBTQ studies. Each section begins with an introductory chapter authored by the section editor(s), reviewing the core concepts and debates in that specific field of geographic inquiry. Many of these introductions also identify gaps or problems in the field and suggest how scholarship might develop over the years to come. Sections I and II deal with urban sexualities and sexual politics as a frame for how geographical work about sexuality initially developed. We then disrupt this order by explicitly contesting the Anglo-American hegemony within geographies of sexualities through Section III, 'Decolonising Sexualities'. We then move to consider other ways of engaging with sexual geographies through mobilities, sex work and sexual health (an area that has dominated work on sexualities beyond geographies). We conclude by exploring digital sexualities. This is an emerging area that reworks considerations of spatialities in part through the technological reworking of the physical embodiment of gay territories in urban areas.

In this way the *Companion* seeks to provide scholars and graduate students with a comprehensive overview of the current research in geographies of sexual and gender/sex difference. This breadth suggests multiple and diverse, even divergent, paths for future inquiry and developments in the area and beyond into geographies, sexualities, gender identities and queer thinking.

SECTION I
Urban Sexualities

Gavin Brown, Tiffany Muller Myrdahl
and Paulo Jorge Vieira (editors)

Chapter 2

Urban Sexualities: Section Introduction

Gavin Brown, Tiffany Muller Myrdahl, Paulo Jorge Vieira

From the beginning, geographical work on sexuality (and particularly sexual minority lives) has been completely entangled with the study of urban space (Hubbard, 2011). Because sexual identities, as we currently understand them, have been so significantly shaped by urban life, we start the *Companion* with a set of chapters that examine urban sexualities. We review some well-established themes, but also start to look differently at urban sexualities. This introduction reviews the linked trajectories of the geography of sexualities and urban geography. In doing so, it acknowledges more recent work on rural and suburban sexualities – recognizing that such work (and the spaces it studies) usually exists in a relationship to urban space and urban-based scholarship.

There are two key slippages in the geographical literature on urban sexualities that this section identifies and addresses. First, for nearly two decades there has been a frequent elision between the study of urban sexualities and the study of gay space within the city. Geographers have been so busy researching and debating the changing experiences of gay men (and, less frequently, lesbians and bisexuals) in the city that many have overlooked the ways in which other people's sexualities shape their experience of urban life (and shape the city itself). This leads to the second slippage, which is that the study of urban gay space remains focused on those 'homonormative' gay male identities that are lived through the commercial gay centres of major cities in Europe, North America and a handful of other national settings. This work has become caught in a trap of concentrating on the production of gay identities and spaces within small areas of a relatively small set of 'global' cities, such as New York, San Francisco and London against which all other spaces are implicitly assessed. Whilst this section does not ignore (lesbian and) gay lives in metropolitan urban centres in the Global North, it broadens its perspective to include other sexualities, in other types of cities (and work written in languages other than English).

Origins in the Gay 'Ghetto'

Many writers have associated the development of modern homosexualities with the expansion of urban populations over the last two centuries (Abraham, 2009; Bech, 1997). Throughout the 1970s clusters of gay businesses and residential gay populations became more visible in some major cities in Australia, Europe and North America. The earliest geographical work on homosexualities (and, by extension, sexual minorities) attempted to map and examined the growth of these 'gay ghettos', arguing that lesbians and gay men congregated in specific neighbourhoods of US cities for safety, mutual support and to avoid attack (Lyod and Rowntree, 1978).

Much of this work used directories of lesbian and gay bars to locate and map 'gay communities' (Weightman, 1980, 1981). These studies have subsequently been critiqued for their 'patronising, moralistic and "straight" approach to lesbian and gay social and sexual relations' (Bell and Valentine, 1995a, p. 5). It was not until the 1990s that geographers began to publish more sympathetic and 'sex–positive' studies of lesbian and gay venues, drawing on interviews with their clients and extended participant observation within them (Binnie, 1995; Bell, 2001; Rothenberg, 1995). As a result, this work was more nuanced – for example, Brown (2000) argued that the presence of gay bars in the urban landscape was not simply liberating, but could also serve as a 'closet space' that concealed and regulated homosexuality. In many cities, clusters of gay bars initially developed in semi-derelict, industrial or post-industrial districts that were relatively deserted at night, so that gay men could visit the bars discreetly and without embarrassment (Bell, 2001; Ingram et al., 1997).

Geographers examined how gay neighbourhoods were influencing urban politics and reshaping the fabric of US cities (Castells, 1983; Knopp, 1987, 1990; Lauria and Knopp, 1985). In San Francisco, Castells and Murphy (1982) identified an area of 'gay territory' which was simultaneously a residential space, the centre of social and political life, and a focus for business activity. Controversially, in subsequent work, Castells dismissed the prospects for 'lesbian territory' (1983, p. 140). Due to the gendered inequality between men's and women's incomes, he argued, lesbians had more restricted choices in the housing markets (compared to gay men) and this limited the possibilities for lesbian residential enclaves to develop. Despite Castells's predictions, geographers have found evidence of lesbian residential clusters in a number of cities (Adler and Brenner, 1992; Rothenberg, 1995; Doan and Higgins, 2011).

The debate over the existence of 'lesbian territory' raises more fundamental questions about how sexual minority spaces are studied. Podmore (2001) and others (Peace, 2001; Ferreira and Salvador, 2015) argue that the problem lies in the ways in which gay urban geography has tended to focus on territoriality and gay men's attempts at visibility within the urban landscape. Precisely because lesbians (as women) have traditionally had more restricted housing choices, this results in more dispersed residential patterns and social networks that are stretched across space rather than clustered together (Valentine, 1995). Domestic spaces, rather than bar scenes, can be crucial to the articulation of lesbian social networks (Podmore, 2001; however, compare Kennedy and Davis, 1994).

Larry Knopp (1990, 1992, 1995) developed the first major theorization of the relationship between capitalism, sexuality and the production of urban space. This work built on his earlier studies of gay men's involvement in gentrifying urban neighbourhoods (Knopp, 1987, 1990; Lauria and Knopp, 1985). He placed the development of contemporary gay identities within the context of class recomposition and new international divisions of labour after the Second World War. The entry of more women into the workforce in the post-Second World War period reconfigured gender relations in society and began to undermine the ideological significance of 'the family' in policing sexual minorities. In particular, Lauria and Knopp (1985) linked changing gender relations and social attitudes to sexuality to the growth of city-centre service-sector employment which was less tied to 'traditional' masculinities than the manufacturing sector and other heavy industries.

Alongside the growing study of gay leisure districts in a wide range of different cities (Andersson, 2011; Collins, 2006; Giraud 2014; Tucker, 2009a) geographical work on sexualities quickly expanded to include the study of prostitution, red-light districts and the geographical spread of adult entertainment services in urban space (Hubbard, 1998, 2000, 2001; Hubbard and Sanders, 2003; Ribeiro and Oliveira, 2011; Ryder, 2006). This new attention to the moral geographies of sex work expanded the range of sexualities and sexual encounters studied by geographers but consolidated a tendency to focus on once marginal areas of inner cities.

Beyond the (Inner) City

In recent years many commentators have noted a decline in the vitality of those inner city 'gaybourboods' where (lesbians and) gay men have tended to cluster for residential and leisure purposes (Ghaziani, 2014; Nash and Gorman-Murray, 2014). Several factors have been identified as contributing to the decline of these neighbourhoods; but chief amongst these is the acknowledgement that, with increasing social acceptance of sexual minorities and growing legal equality, lesbians and gay men no longer need to cluster together for safety and protection (Nash, 2006, 2013a). Increasingly, the presence of lesbians and gay men has been normalized (Visser, 2008a) in a range of social settings and leisure venues. At the same time, developments in digital and locative technologies (see Section VII in this volume) have meant that sexual minorities no longer have to rely on attending specific bars in order to meet each other (Mowlabocus, 2010a; Nash and Gorman-Murray, 2014).

A key critique of this narrative asks for whom these neighbourhoods are or were ever accessible. By examining who has been excluded from the 'gaybourhood' and how exclusion occurs in practice, this work illustrates the ways in which bisexuals (Hemmings, 2002; Munoz-Laboy, 2004), trans and gender non-conforming people (Nash, 2010), queer people of colour (Catungal, 2013) and women (Gieseking, 2015) are marginalized within gay spaces or those that are marked as LGBTQ-friendly. A second critique attends to the ways in which gaybourhoods have become 'sanitized' as they have been adopted by municipalities for their fiscal and cultural contributions to the city. That gaybourhoods are embraced by many city officials is a sign to some that gaybourhoods reflect a larger trend towards homonormativity that has prioritized domesticity, coupledom and privatized consumption over the public sexual cultures of earlier decades.

The spatialities of homonormativity – where and how it is manifested in and across cities, suburbs and regions – is thus of interest to geographers of sexualities (G. Brown, 2012). Here, homonormativity gets more complicated. For while the 'pink dollar' is sought after (Rushbrook, 2002) and the state is the biggest winner in the push to legalize gay marriage (Brandzel, 2005), attending to the myriad sites within urban space shows that gay and lesbian interest in consumption and domesticity is not a recent phenomenon. Sexual and gender minorities have always lived (and, to some extent, been visible) in the suburbs and smaller cities, as much as the inner cities of major metropolitan centres. Various oral history projects (Kennedy and Davis, 1994; Murphy et al., 2010) illustrate suburban domesticity at work from (before) the 1960s. Of course, it is not just domestic life that is found beyond the city centre – adult entertainment venues, prostitution and public sex environments can be found in (sub)urban territories across cities around the world (da Silva, 2011; Maginn and Steinmetz, 2014).

If homosexuality and other minority sexualities have been strongly associated with urban life, some US-based queer theorists have critiqued the 'metronormativity' (Halberstam, 2005) that informs both popular understandings of gay identities, and the ways in which they have been theorized (Herring, 2010). In the contemporary USA, Herring (2010) suggests that there are now two important strands of 'anti-urbanism' in sexual politics. First, there is a 'deghettoizing' trend which seeks the integration of lesbians and gay men into the suburbs and small-town America (Herring, 2010, p. 11). The second expression of 'queer anti–urbanism' seeks to challenge and critique the ways in which lesbian and gay presence in rural areas is erased by the metronormative associations between major cities and the development of gay identities. This queer anti-urbanism celebrates the lives of those sexual minorities who have stayed put in rural areas (Kramer, 1995; Phillips et al., 2000), rather than leaving for the bright lights of a big city (Weston, 1995).

Many studies have charted rural–urban migrations by lesbians and gay men in a variety of national contexts (Di Feliciantonio, 2014a). However, work from Canada (Lewis, 2014a), the USA (Knopp and Brown, 2003) and Australia (Gorman-Murray, 2007, 2009a) has questioned the assumption that these migrations flow in only one direction. They suggest that lesbians and gay men who grew up in rural areas often move back and forth between rural spaces, small towns and larger cities across their lives as their circumstances change. There are a wide variety of ways in which sexual minorities make viable lives for themselves in rural areas. Mostly they create spaces that look and feel very different to urban-based sexual cultures. These include regular rural festivals (Browne, 2011; Gorman-Murray, Waitt and Gibson, 2012) or experimental land-based communes and intentional communities (Morgensen, 2009; Valentine, 1997a). However, these tend to be more spectacular examples and overlook the ways in which some small rural towns develop reputations as 'gay–friendly' places to live (Smith and Holt, 2005) or visit on holiday (Gorman-Murray, Waitt and Gibson, 2012). Despite their rural locations, some rural and coastal resorts develop many of the features of urban gay life (at least during the holiday season).

Sexualities in a World of Cities

In recent years scholars (G. Brown, 2008, 2012; Browne and Bakshi, 2013a; Muller Myrdahl, 2013) have noted that the same small group of cities – almost all of them major metropolitan centres in the Global North – remain the focus for a significant amount of geographical work on sexualities. Time and again, London (Andersson, 2011; Houlbrook, 2005), New York (Abraham, 2009; Delany, 1999) and San Francisco (Beemyn, 1997; Castells, 1983) have been the subject of urban scholars' studies about the lives of sexual minorities. Just as there has been a call within urban geography to study a wider range of cities, and to study them on their own terms rather than always in comparison to the 'global cities' that are understood as the 'command and control centres' of the global economy (Robinson, 2006), geographers have also been encouraged to study the spatialities of a wider range of sexual cultures, in a wider range of cities, both large and small.

There is a growing body of work about sexual life in cities outside Europe, North America and Australasia, which has been written by 'geographers of sexualities'. However, in looking for geographical work about sexuality and sexual identity in the Global South, it is important to look beyond this specialist subdiscipline (G. Brown et al., 2010). Here, we describe some very different studies of sexual cultures in various cities across the Global South to highlight the range of work that is currently being produced. We consider a variety of work from Brazil and a comparative study of the intimate lives of (mostly) young heterosexual women in Mumbai, Phnom Penh and Taipei (Wills et al., under review).

Work on sexualities in Brazil has developed out of key geographical concepts and debates about the nature of urban space and territory that have been of fundamental importance within the Lusophone geographical tradition (Silva et al., 2013; Silva and Vieira, 2014). The dominant focus within Brazilian geographical research on sexuality in urban space has been the study of prostitution, analysed through a Marxist framework. The issue of prostitution was privileged in these studies due to its connection with the exploitation of the social and economic vulnerability of groups of women and *travestis*.

With the expansion of cultural geography in Brazil in the early 2000s new studies began to interpret urban space from the perspective of how it shaped the identities and experiences of sexual minority groups, particularly gay men and *travestis*. These studies were also concerned with understanding how, in exercising their sexualities, gay men and *travestis* appropriated sections of the city, turning such spaces into their territories, and turning these territories into a focus for these groups' resistance to their exclusion from heteronormative society. For example, the geographer Benhur Pinós da Costa (2010a, 2010b, 2010c, 2012a, 2012b, 2012c) studied the relationship between male homoeroticism and urban space, especially in small towns, introducing the concept of 'micro–territorialization' to describe the appropriation of parts of the city by homoerotic practice. In this work, da Costa makes effective use of phenomenology (a philosophical approach that describes things as people experience them) and symbolic interactionism (an approach, originally from sociology, which studies how people interact with things based on the symbolic meaning those things hold for them). These approaches are frequently overlooked by geographers of sexualities working in Anglophone contexts. His research on male homoeroticism in small cities across Brazil suggests that the appropriation of urban territory to enable forms of disclosure by sexual minorities (more than the presence of gay bars) is significant as a form of resistance to heteronormative constructions of urban space.

Wills et al. (under review) offer a comparison of the spaces of love in Cambodian, Indian and Taiwanese cities. Their study complicates linear narratives of social, cultural and economic progress in Asian countries. They challenge assumptions that 'modernization' leads to a move away from arranged marriages in favour of greater sexual, emotional and spatial freedoms that might further undo rigid social hierarchies. By studying how and where love is experienced and performed in Mumbai, Phnom Penh and Taipei, they outline a politics of love that regulates and governs the spaces through which relations of love are tended. In particular, they examine how public displays of affection by young heterosexual couples continue to be treated with disapproval in each of the cities. However, they acknowledge that in each city public displays of affection are more acceptable (or tolerated) in some places than others. In this way, some public spaces can offer young lovers more privacy to be intimate with each other than they might find in densely packed settlements and overcrowded accommodation. Wills et al. remind geographers to look beyond 'Western' understandings of love when they examine the spatialities of affection, intimacy and love in other contexts. Although they reveal how love is regulated in public spaces, they assert that, through this regulation, love remains a public concern that is seldom reserved only for private, domestic spaces. If, in the past, geographical work on sexualities has sometimes been overconcerned with homoerotic cruising and public homosex, Wills and her colleagues offer a reminder to also pay attention to the full spectrum of intimacies and affection (beyond the sexual), including those that are conducted coyly and through the exercise of personal restraint.

Section Overview

These chapters in the Urban Sexualities section reflect on the ways in which geographers of sexualities have engaged with urban spaces and urban life. As well as identifying what geographers have done well in this regard, they also suggest potential shortcomings, lacunae and challenging new directions for future research.

In her contribution to this section, Julie Podmore unpacks the spatialities of metronormativity: she argues that this critique, however well intentioned in its efforts to wrest attention away from the gaybourhoods of major metropolitan centres, obfuscates and oversimplifies the diversity of queer (and particularly lesbian) urban practices. She highlights the incomplete record of lesbian urbanisms and demonstrates that these gaps are exacerbated by a proscriptive metronormative narrative. Podmore thus refuses to abandon attention to LGBTQ urbanism and indicates that there is much to be gained from a reappraisal of the particular spatialities that have captured geographers' attention for so long. Doing so would bring to the fore the lesbian, queer and other spatialities that geographers have neglected in their efforts to document queer sexualities and include them in the geographic rendering of the city.

In addition to the more familiar urban spaces of North America, which geographers of sexualities have frequently written about (and which are the focus of the chapters by Podmore and Gieseking), the chapters that follow examine sexuality and urban life in Aotearoa/New Zealand (see Johnston and Longhurst), and South(ern) Africa (see Visser). In particular, Visser's chapter considers how some of the central assumptions about sexuality and urban space developed over the last four decades may need to be retheorized in the light of the (re) enactment of anti-gay legislation in India, Russia and Uganda (as well as other countries). Two chapters (Johnston and Longhurst; Muller Myrdahl) address sexual minority lives in small(er), provincial towns. These considerations of small-town life are important for the way in which they decentre on the experience of living in major metropolitan urban centres, which have been the focus of so much geographies of sexualities research over the last four decades. In contrast to a more traditional conception of 'the rural' as isolated, predominantly agricultural and 'natural', small towns contain characteristics of both urban and rural space. They thus enable a consideration of 'urban sexualities' in a wider range of settings than just 'gaybourhoods' in global cities.

The study of urban sexualities needs to expand the range of sexual identities, urban spaces and, indeed, cities, to which it turns its attention. While the chapters in this section predominantly address homosexualities, several chapters focus on the (still under-researched) lives of lesbians and other queer women (see Gieseking; Muller Myrdahl; Podmore), and the chapter by Johnston and Longhurst examines the lives of two older trans women living in Hamilton, Aotearoa/New Zealand. This focus not only addresses sexualities that are 'otherwise', but also looks at the materiality of urban space for the homeless. The chapters in this section deliberately look beyond the major metropolitan centres of the Global North to theorize the various ways in which cities of all kinds shape sexualities and sexualities shape cities.

Conclusions

All the chapters presented here elicit the scope of work that remains for geographers of urban sexualities. Certainly, as Podmore suggests, there is still considerable work to be done in studying the complexity of 'gaybourhoods' in major cities of the Global North. Geographers still have much to offer in terms of historical geographical studies of these areas' development. As these areas shift in location, function and symbolic significance in response to changing sexual politics, there is much for geographers to study, particularly if we stay attuned to the differential impact of these changes on those social groups whose presence in these areas has often been marginalized, overlooked or erased. As gender and sexual minority lives come to be understood as increasingly viable (even desirable) in suburban settings and in smaller towns and cities there are new challenges for geographers of sexualities. Perhaps a key challenge, in some contexts, will be to find new ways of studying urban sexualities that are not automatically shaped by the fault line of a homo/ heterosexual binary. In this way, we might not only begin to see new spaces, but also make room for the study of emerging sexual and gender identities and practices in urban space – such as asexuality and polyamory. At the same time, Visser reminds us that the geography of sexualities literature remains limited in how it can understand the dynamics of sexual lives in cities in the Global South, if we continue to measure and examine Southern cities and sexualities through the ontological categories of Euro-American urban sexual politics (see Section III of this volume).

Chapter 3

Disaggregating Sexual Metronormativities: Looking Back at 'Lesbian' Urbanisms

Julie A. Podmore

Introduction

In 1995 Kath Weston published 'Get Thee to the Big City', in which she critically examined the construction of the 'great lesbian and gay migration' to big cities and its role in shaping narratives of gay and lesbian liberation in North America. While this publication drew attention to the metronormativity of gay and lesbian studies, it was Halberstam's (2005) queer critique that coined and critically advanced the term. At that point, geographers had been empirically critical of the lack of attention to sexualities beyond the metropolis for some time (Bell and Valentine, 1995b; Binnie and Valentine, 1999; Phillips, Watt and Shuttleton, 2000). Since then, many have taken up the project of studying LGBTQ lives beyond metropolitan centres by focusing on rural areas (Gorman-Murray, Pini and Bryant, 2013; Gorman-Murray, Waitt and Gibson, 2008; Smith and Holt, 2005) and, more recently, smaller or 'ordinary' cities (G. Brown, 2008; Browne, 2008; Muller Myrdahl, 2013). In tandem, metronormativity has become a central queer critique of lesbian and gay studies, exemplified by works such as Herring's (2010) examination of the history of American queer anti-urban movements or Tongson's (2011) relocations of queer life to the landscapes of new suburbia, both of which demonstrate the limitations and erasures involved in constructing the urban as the authentic space of LGBTQ lives and liberations.

While the metronormativity critique has drawn our attention to the power relations involved in where we look for geographies of sexualities, the spatial binary it draws between the normative urban and the non-normative elsewhere requires some disaggregation and contextualization. This chapter, therefore, is an attempt to reconsider where and how lesbian (including dyke and queer-identified 'women') urbanisms in the West have been implicated in this dualism. Viewing this debate from the perspective of lesbian geographies, I argue that some metronormativities might be less straightforward than others. Moreover, I suggest that the metronormativity critique relies on the reduction of the queer metropolitan in ways that may reinforce the very homonormativities that they seek to undermine. The chapter begins by asking where lesbians are (epistemologically, spatially and temporally) in relation to the metronormativities critique. Concluding that lesbian metronormativity is at best incomplete, I then turn to the geography of sexualities literature to disaggregate lesbian urbanisms from metronormativity. Finding conceptual ambivalence and under-theorization here, I review the geographical literature on urbanism, considering its potential as a framework for disaggregating metronormativity through the example of lesbian urbanism.

I hope that such a project can be useful for thinking through the spatialities and experiences of other LGBTQ populations.

Lesbian Metronormativities?

Is it possible for lesbian urban spatialities, usually described as ephemeral and invisible, to be associated with the metronormative? Metronormativity is a neologism proposed by Halberstam (2005) to describe the historically specific spatial and temporal narrative that equates gay and lesbian liberation with rural to urban migration. Prevalent in US gay and lesbian histories, this trajectory is intertwined with the culturally specific ideal of 'coming out' and the joining of 'visible' urban communities as a means by which to constitute sexual subjectivity. As Halberstam (2005, p. 37) argues:

> The metronormative narrative maps a story of migration onto the coming-out narrative. While the story of the coming-out narrative tends to function as a temporal trajectory within which a period of disclosure follows a long period of repression, the metronormative story of migration from 'country' to 'town' is a spatial narrative within which the subject moves to a place of tolerance after enduring life in a place of suspicion, persecution, and secrecy. Since each narrative bears the same structure, it is easy to equate the physical journey from small town to big city with the psychological journey from the closet case to the out and proud.

For Halberstam (2005), the concept is useful as it demonstrates the 'devaluation' of the rural in US spatial discourses about sexual subjectivities and can be extrapolated to the global scale to understand the neocolonial dynamic surrounding the construction of non-metropolitan sexualities beyond the urban West. However, like all dualisms, it is an argument that requires some unpacking, especially with regard to what it suggests for the urban. As the hegemonic centre in this asymmetrical relationship, the metropolitan West, with its long history of queer place-making and diversity of queer experiences, is reduced to nothing more than a metaphorical space that represents a hegemonic cultural ideal.

The reduction of the urban in the metronormativities critique is especially apparent when it is contextualized and disaggregated by considering where lesbian urbanisms, both historic and contemporary, might be situated. We might consider the epistemological and temporal underpinnings of the metronormativity critique. It is specifically a post-millennial queer cultural studies critique of US gay and lesbian studies in 1980s and 1990s that seeks to call into question the assumptions of works like D'Emilio's (1983) *Sexual Politics, Sexual Communities*, texts that equate the creation of a gay and lesbian rights movement with the formation of urban gay communities. Certainly, the arguments in many works of this period did somewhat uncritically depend on classic ecological ideas about urbanism for their arguments: cities offered sexual liberation from the family economy, the 'critical mass' needed to form subcultures and political movements, and the anonymity necessary for the appropriation of public and semi-public spaces (Wirth, 1938). However, such works were primarily concerned with understanding post-Stonewall gay community formation, and, by association, the development of the American gay and lesbian rights movement. Lesbian experiences, patterns of community formation and liberation movements were not necessarily structurally central to the 'one-way' linear spatial narratives that such studies constructed. As Taylor and Whittier (1992) have shown, the American lesbian liberation movement in the 1970s and 1980s circulated through a set of submerged communications networks that were not necessarily linked to large urban centres. At least one part of the US lesbian community formation and liberation story revolved around the creation of rural lesbian lands and the rejection of 'the patriarchal city' (Browne, 2011; Valentine, 1997b). Beyond the collective experience, iconic lesbian texts of the temporal journey towards the sexual self from this period did not necessarily involve a spatial movement towards the big city. For example, Audre Lorde's *Zami* (1982) tells a reverse story: growing up in New York City, the main character dreams of queer freedom anywhere in Mexico, migrates to smaller cities in search of herself, stops briefly in the West Village lesbian community, but ultimately leaves the city to settle in Connecticut. Whilst this is not a story of a return to the rural, it suggests that inter-urban mobility, dropping down in the urban hierarchy and even exile from the metropolis have been at least part of the story of finding the lesbian self. Indeed, the historical record is full of queer sexual liberation stories that contradict the metronormative narrative.

Beyond these epistemological and temporal implications, the spatial components of the metronormativity critique are more clearly gendered in ways that obscure lesbian spatialities. Herring's (2010) discussion of metronormativities is instructive here. He begins by presenting the reader with a phallic image of the Empire State Building that was published on a 1982 cover of the New York City gay magazine *Honcho*. He argues that this image suggests a shift towards metronormativity in that it represents the urban as the end-point in a sexual liberation trajectory, the terminus in a one-way movement towards the metropolis: 'Alongside countless other queer productions, it codifies the metropolitan as the terminus of queer world making as many have come to know it' (Herring, 2010, p. 4). A crude critique of this choice to represent lesbian and gay metronormativity via the desires of metropolitan gay men would clearly highlight the gendered aspect of this equation. But the arguments about the narrative terminus and its cultural production are just as compelling. First, Herring is elaborating on the ways in which the metropolitan serves as an end-point in the narrative of sexual liberation. Suggesting that the metronormative narrative ends in visible gay enclaves, he clearly links this trajectory to actual spaces inside New York City with a discussion of the Chelsea addresses listed on the cover of *Honcho*. In other words, the trajectory from rural private domestic obscurity to the metropolitan ends in the gay village, a place of ambivalence and exclusion for lesbians. Second, Herring argues that the metronormative is reproduced through six axes, one of which is the queer aestheticization of the metropolitan. Noting that gay men have long been considered sophisticates of taste in the urban scene, he argues that post-Stonewall queer worlding has revolved around the construction of a stylized cosmopolitan urban norm. Moreover, the cultural production of this version of urbanism, he argues, 'facilitates the ongoing commodification, corporatization, and depoliticization of US-based queer cultures in many locales' (Herring, 2010, p. 16). While positioning lesbians completely outside this version of urbanism and its production would be reductionist, it is certainly possible to question how central lesbian aesthetics have been to such broad world-making processes.

Herring's (2010) own work on queer anti-urbanisms disrupts the metronormativity narrative by providing an array of examples of stylistic and spatial resistances including lesbian anti-urbanisms. Tongson's (2011) *Relocations*, however, takes this critique in directions that are especially useful for disaggregating lesbian urbanisms from metronormativities. The spatial emphasis in *Relocations* is not on making alternative places but on mobility (see the chapters in Section IV of this volume). Focusing on suburban dyke and queer of colour cultural productions and imaginings, this work disrupts metronormativity by speaking from the margins of the metropolis itself, disrupting the territorial and visible with other metropolitan stylings and imaginings. In so doing, Tongson positions dyke urban geographies alongside a host of alternative and peripheral locations in relation to metronormativity. To make this point, she specifically draws on Gates and Ost's (2004) *The Gay and Lesbian Atlas*, a collection that mapped partnered gay and lesbian households in the 2000 US Census. Although sceptical of such evidence, Tongson highlights the locational differences between these households as a means by which to detach a diversity of queer subjectivities from the more metronormative queer worldings of bourgeois white gay men. By pointing to the finding that lesbian urban households are more decentred and are often more strongly concentrated in outer boroughs, Tongson opens the door to resituating lesbians in relation to metronormativities. She argues that such findings confirm '[w]hat has been common lore about the spatial circumstances of gays and lesbians – that gays live in hip neighborhoods in world cities, while lesbians generally have to traverse some bridge, tunnel, or undesirable stretch of freeway to participate in urban life …' (Tongson, 2011, p. 52).

Ambivalent Geographies of Lesbian Urbanism

Geographers of sexualities can certainly be accused of reinforcing a metronormative narrative in terms of the 'object' of our research. While our projects have rarely examined rural-to-urban migrations (see Waitt and Gorman-Murray, 2011a), we have devoted an exceptional amount of attention to the terminus of the metronormative trajectory, the gay village in the urban West (see G. Brown, 2008, 2012; M. Brown, 2013; Visser, 2013). Even as we currently debate the possible de-gaying of such spaces (G. Brown, 2006; Ghaziani, 2014), investigate the development of other 'queer-friendly' urban neighbourhoods (G. Brown, 2006; Gorman-Murray and Waitt, 2009; Nash, 2013b) or examine the place-making practices of LGBTQ populations in smaller cities (G. Brown, 2008; Muller Myrdahl, 2013; Lewis, 2013a), the gay village remains relationally central as a point of reference for the analysis of queer place-making elsewhere. Moreover, attention to homonormativities has refocused our analysis on gay villages as sites of exclusions for young people, people of colour, lesbians and trans people (see, for example, Casey, 2004, Doan, 2007; Nash, 2011; Tucker, 2009b; Valentine and Skelton, 2003), reinforcing the centrality of this most 'visible' form of LGBTQ urbanism. As a result, the more recent research into lesbian urbanisms has been located here, focusing on their exclusions from gay villages and scene spaces (Binnie and Skeggs, 2004; Podmore, 2006, 2013b; Pritchard, Morgan and Sedgley, 2002; Ray, 2004), and, in some cases, how gendered exclusions intersect with normative whiteness and classism (Held, 2015; Kawale, 2004; Taylor, 2007a, 2008).

But the study of lesbian urbanisms has a much longer history within the discipline. Explorations of lesbian community formation and territorial neighbourhood patterns in the urban West began primarily in response to arguments made by Castells (1983) in his study of gay neighbourhood territoriality and urban social movements in San Francisco (Valentine, 2000). Contrasting the territorial organization of gay men in the Castro District with the more dispersed and network-based community formation process of lesbians, Castells argued that gender was a central factor in shaping these differences. Key studies then sought to test these claims: critical of the gendered assumptions of Castells's argument, Adler and Brenner (1992) specifically sought to study lesbian urban and political patterns by replicating his methods and sources; Valentine (1995) used this argument as a starting-point for her investigation of the distinct ways in which lesbians create neighbourhoods and institutional spaces; Peake (1993) responded with a more explicitly feminist and intersectional analysis of urban change; and Rothenberg (1995) examined the factors shaping lesbian neighbourhood choices and community formation. Later works built on these findings, further comparing lesbian and gay neighbourhood formation (Anacker and Morrow-Jones,

2005; Bouthillette, 1997; Cattan and Clerval, 2011; Compton and Baumle, 2012; Kenney, 2001; Lo and Healy, 2000), examining how lesbians negotiate and make use of urban public spaces (Ferreira and Salvador, 2015; Gieseking, 2013, 2015; Podmore, 2001; Rodó-de-Zárate, 2015; Valentine, 1997b) and providing historical studies of lesbian neighbourhood formation processes over time (Podmore, 2006; Geiseking, 2013). Some of this research even suggested that dense lesbian networks may develop in specific small urban centres (Brown-Saracino, 2011; Forsyth, 1997a, 1997b) and that, in these contexts, lesbian communities may be more organized and visible than those of gay men (Nash, 2001).

These findings suggest that lesbian urbanisms might be considered metronormativity's urban other, an ontology that has been reinforced by research frameworks that also construct lesbian spatialities as 'not necessarily' or ambivalently urban in a number of key ways. First, although there are some exceptions, until more recently, most case studies of lesbian urban patterns did not focus on metropolitan centres such as San Francisco, New York, London or Paris. Instead, they primarily represent an incidental collection of medium and small cities and boroughs in the USA, Canada and the UK. Second, in the early years, researchers often had to sacrifice urban context in the interest of the safety of their participants: as Lockard (1986) had done for her study of a large south-western city, Adler and Brenner (1992) were required to withhold the name of the US city they studied to avoid directing readers to the lesbian ghetto; Valentine (1995) adopted the pseudonym 'Melchester' for similar reasons; and Nash (2001) describes how ardent her subjects were about withholding the name of their location to ensure their anonymity. As Adler and Brenner (1992) pointed out, hiding the city meant that they had to sacrifice urban context and comparability. Third, the widespread exploration of the Castells hypothesis served to reinforce the idea that the urban was somewhat incidental to lesbian patterns of congregation and place-making. Most studies refuted the essentialism of Castells's claims by demonstrating that lesbians engaged with the city by congregating in particular neighbourhoods and circulating through their private and semi-private spaces. However, the analysis was still informed by a gender dualism that reinforced the idea that gay men were engaged with public urban processes whereas lesbians could create their networked and more private form of communality wherever that they congregated. Finally, and perhaps as a result, beyond comparison to gay men, this body of literature rarely engages with urban theory. This contrasts significantly with urban studies of gay men and of LGBTQ populations more broadly. For example, the earliest works on gay men situate their community formation processes within the gentrification of the inner city (Knopp, 1990; Lauria and Knopp, 1985). Lesbian geographies, on the other hand – from Valentine's (1993a, 1993b, 1993c, 1995) early case studies to the more contemporary discussions of lesbian exclusions from queer scene spaces – have been more social than urban, with little to say about the dynamics surrounding urban context in which they are set.

Looking for Lesbian Urbanisms

The 'cultural turn' in human geography in the early 1990s is said to have opened the discipline to the expansion of geographies of sexualities and eventually to queer geographies (Oswin, 2013). It also brought a reworking of the conceptualization of urbanism. The traditional ecological interpretation urbanism, described by Louis Wirth (1938) as 'a way of life', was critically reassessed by researchers interested in examining urban diversity and difference (Jacobs and Fincher, 1998). This 'cosmopolitan' interpretation came from a number of different strains, but especially from feminist geographers who were interested in the intersections of difference in shaping the experience of cities. They were also contextualizing the power relations surrounding cities in light of feminist scholarship that suggested that the social breakdown embodied by urbanism had created greater possibilities for women's autonomy than rural life ever had (Wilson, 1991). Another related reworking came from poststructural reinterpretations of neo-Marxist arguments. In *Social Justice and the City* (1973) Harvey had used 'urbanism' to advance his arguments about the production of urban space. Here, urbanism was both a vantage-point from which to view capitalist processes at work in shaping spatial relations and a part of the mode of production – a process that favoured the concentration of capital accumulation in urban centres. Such a concentration made the city the ultimate terrain of class struggle, a place where its contradictions would fuel new social movements (Castells, 1977; Lefebvre, 1968). With renewed interest in Lefebvre's (1991) arguments about the production of space, urbanism was now explored in discursive terms, understood as a set of competing and overlapping representations. Cosmopolitan urbanism, for example, was interpreted as the productive ideal of neoliberal urban governance (Binnie et al., 2006). 'Revanchist urbanism' was used by Neil Smith (1998) to refer to a new set of productive representations by middle-class normative interests seeking revenge on other social groups by taking the city back after leaving it behind.

Such arguments perhaps offer important potential for disaggregating lesbian urbanism from the metronormative narrative, but the study of lesbian urbanism has rarely been attempted within these frameworks (see Chisholm, 2005) for a number of reasons. While poststructuralist feminist reinterpretations did offer new directions by reconsidering the possibilities of urbanism for sexual subjects – with Munt (1998) even exploring the possibility of the lesbian *flâneur* – more material attempts to investigate urbanism interpret it in ways that make lesbian urbanisms difficult to see. When examining competing representations of urbanism, poststructuralists focused on hegemonic structural processes to which lesbians, activists and subcultures would rarely have access. For example, as the only works in this vein to consider the sexualities involved in the production of urbanism, investigations into cosmopolitan urbanism have primarily examined the ways in which homonormativity has been reproduced via the promotion of gay village spaces (Binnie and Skeggs, 2004). Smith's (1998) revanchist urbanism briefly mentions queer sexualities, but largely in terms of their displacement by neoliberal urban policies. As he argued, revanchist urbanism was grounded in 'a vendetta against the most oppressed –workers and "welfare mothers", immigrants and gays, people of color and homeless people, squatters, anyone who demonstrates in public' (N. Smith, 1998, p. 1). Whilst cosmopolitan urbanism seems to involve the integration of 'gays' into the processes of neoliberal governance, revanchist urbanism is responsible for their displacement with no mention of lesbian subjectivities.

As the review of lesbian geographies has suggested, lesbian urbanism has been considered primarily within the more ecological framework of forming gendered subcultures initiated via the Castells hypothesis with little consideration of how lesbian subcultures have been implicated in the production of urbanism. However, around the same time that Castells was conducting research on gay men in San Francisco, Elizabeth M. Ettorre (1978) published the results of her research on a residential lesbian community that formed in the London Borough of Lambeth in the 1970s. She described how a group of politicized lesbian feminists created an alternative community by squatting in a vacating row of council flats that would soon undergo demolition. However, the objective of the article was to situate 'the women's movement' of the period within urban sociological theory, illustrating these arguments through a case study of the 'lesbian ghetto'. Critiquing both the urban ecology and the neo-Marxist interpretations of urbanism (specifically Castells's arguments regarding social formations), Ettorre called for greater attention to women's issues, politics and social organization as part of urban processes by recognizing that patriarchy – in addition to capitalism – is a structural force that results in struggle. Specifically, she frames the women's movement as an urban social movement that needs to be understood in this context. The lesbian–separatist movement is then presented as one faction that refused the spatial separation of women and their assignment to the private sphere. The case study is then used to illustrate how the ideals of lesbian separatism informed the feminist urban practice of creating the collective lesbian ghetto in Lambeth.

In retelling this story, I am not suggesting a return to the study of lesbian-feminist urbanism or refocusing on lesbians as a social movement. Rather, I want to suggest that our focus on Castells's gendered gay and lesbian urbanisms to the neglect of Ettorre's arguments about urban processes and movements could use some reassessment. First, one of the most important aspects of this work is that it focuses on how a lesbian community formed within an urban framework (see also Peake, 1993). According to Ettorre's interpretation, this is not incidental: this group sought to disrupt the patriarchal ordering of urban space by living the city otherwise. This engagement with the city presents an important contrast with the more accepted gender dualism advanced by Castells and explored by others. It is a political act that seeks to disrupt the power relations through the performance of *inhabitance* (Lefebvre, 1974). Second, rather than focusing on their exclusions, Ettorre seeks to reposition both ecological and neo-Marxist interpretations of urbanism in ways that make seeing lesbians as agents of the city possible. The focus is not on normativity and hegemony of a capitalist, patriarchal or heterosexist urbanism that erases and excludes them, but rather on an alternate representation of urbanism that a group of lesbians sought to live. Finally, the urban context in which this alternative community was formed is an important component of the story itself. The community was temporary, created out of government disinvestment in a neighbourhood about to undergo redevelopment, part of the process of industrial restructuring. Whilst the creation of a lesbian commune through squatting in the 1970s is perhaps an atypical lesbian urbanism, this story should draw our attention to the important role of urban processes in shaping how and where lesbians situate themselves within the city.

Conclusion

The objective of this chapter has been to disaggregate lesbian urbanisms from the reductionist rural/urban dualism proposed by the metronormativity critique. Uncomfortable with queer critiques that depict gay and lesbians as normatively anti-rural and ideally cosmopolitan, I have sought to turn this argument on its head by carefully considering the engagement between lesbians and urbanism in the urban West. I began by demonstrating that, spatially speaking, the narrative that metronormativity constructs is quite misplaced and incomplete when considering lesbian urban geographies, especially in terms of their relationship to the queer worlding taking place in this narrative's terminus, the commodified and cosmopolitan gay village, a place that has not necessarily been representative of lesbian subjectivities and subcultures. Given the incomplete character of lesbian metronormativities and the lack of attention to their urbanisms, I turned to the geography and urban studies literature only to find that, among the many case studies of lesbian community and neighbourhood formation patterns, our understandings of lesbian urbanism have been limited by an advancing ambivalence about the urban context in which they are set. While the invisibility of lesbian neighbourhood patterns and the exclusions of lesbians from gay villages detailed in this literature do offer important rebuttals for those who would depict their geographies as metronormative, the discipline's vision of lesbian urbanism is limited by a lack of theorization of the urban – a requirement for situating lesbians within the metronormativities debate. Viewing this literature as incomplete, I turned to poststructural interpretations of urbanism in the geography literature in order to consider their potential for the interpretation of lesbian urbanisms. Here, I have argued that an ecological focus on the gendered comparison between lesbian and gay subcultural neighbourhood formation patterns has been at the expense of an earlier and more critical understanding of lesbian urbanism that involved the politics of living, interpreting, and contesting the urban in context, a disruption of metronormativity itself that requires greater investigation.

Given the multiplicity of lesbian and queer women's identities and the contestation of gender as part of contemporary queer worldings, I hope that my attempt to disaggregate lesbians from a broader LGBTQ framework will not appear anachronistic or essentialist. I would contend that gender, no matter how it is defined or experienced, continues to play an important role in shaping urban geographies and that this needs to be considered when describing LGBTQ spatial narratives as metronormative. I make this argument for many reasons, but most importantly in response to the sense of erasure involved in the reduction of the queer urban to a normative experience in relation to a more unexplored rural. Since few queers find themselves represented by the fiction of the normative, I suspect that many have similarly responded to the metronormativity critique by viewing it as proscriptively premature. Whilst we have been studying LGBTQ urbanism for decades, the emphasis on the particular spatialities that represent this urbanism to the neglect of so very many others should not close the city to our continued investigation.

Chapter 4

Dyked New York: The Space between Geographical Imagination and Materialization of Lesbian–Queer Bars and Neighbourhoods

Jen Jack Gieseking

It's funny – I almost never go to Park Slope [in Brooklyn]. I feel like it's not a lesbian neighbourhood … my girlfriend's aunt lived there in the 1970s and when we moved there in 1989 she was like, 'Oh! It's not a lesbian neighbourhood anymore! All of the Columbus Avenue [implying wealthy, predominantly white elite] people have moved in' … all of the – I don't know like institutions, like, The Rising [Café and Bar], they've disappeared. [Pauses.] But, I guess it doesn't really matter I suppose because if people feel like something's a lesbian neighbourhood then by dint of their believing it, it is. (Sarah 1985 (came out in 1985))

Activist and environmental psychologist Maxine Wolfe wrote, 'That more lesbians go to bars than to women's centres, and that the women who use them are more diverse in terms of age, race, and economics emphasizes the major role they still play in lesbian lives' (1997, p. 315). In a similar vein, my research participant Sarah asserts in her quote that most roads to lesbian–queer spaces lead back to the lesbian neighbourhood and the dyke bar. For decades, the geographies of sexuality literature and lesbian, gay, bisexual, trans and queer (LGBTQ) activists alike have often highlighted these key spaces as essential in the work towards LGBTQ liberation. Even alongside the sea change in LGBTQ acceptance and/ or tolerance, LGBTQ spaces are also marked as untenable and/or unwelcoming for women often because they work differently for lesbians and queer women (see Valentine 1993b, 1993c; Podmore 2001, 2006; Bain and Nash, 2007). What are we to make of the production of lesbian–queer spaces, specifically bars and neighbourhoods, which play such a key role in general LGBTQ life?

As Sarah asserts in her quote, New York's only lesbian neighbourhood seems to be slipping out of the hands of each subsequent generation of women. Gentrification's effects of skyrocketing rental prices increasingly limit the possibility of making a home there for most women, especially people of colour, the poor and young people. Given the emphasis on the roles of bars and parties in lesbian–queer lives before the 1990s per Wolfe, it is revealing that there were over 60 bars for men on a 2008 Pride map of lower Manhattan, and only two bars for women (*Next Magazine*, 2008). There are a myriad other types of places important to lesbians and queer women, but bars retain a prominence in LGBTQ life across generations that requires close examination. The mobility of lesbian bodies within the city and within these spaces especially extends Gill Valentine's (1993b) classic idea that lesbians must enact specific different ways of being and dress in specific spaces at specific times throughout their day. Whilst lesbians and queer women in my study tended to adopt specific avoidance behaviours in specific time-spaces, a closer examination of these spaces reveals that these practices are tied as much to the geographical imagination as the materiality of these spaces.

The setting of the urban is also important to consider. Whilst the city affords women freedom in their financial independence and anonymity, it is equally portrayed as a space of fear and danger for women both in the past and present (Pain and Smith, 2008). Building from these spaces and their social contradictions, my research of lesbian–queer life in New York City asks who and what can be learned from the experiences of lesbian–queer life over time? These quotes and facts reflect similar sentiments to New York lesbians and queer women whose description and, then, experiences of these spaces pointed to a disconnect between their material and imagined qualities.

I address my participants' ideas and experiences of lesbian–queer neighbourhoods and bars in order to reveal the overlaps and distinctions in the ways in which these women imagine and then experience these spaces. This chapter uses a feminist–queer approach alongside the theoretical concept of the geographical imagination to rethink how the experience of contemporary lesbians and queer women in New York City from 1983 to 2008 may differ from more dominant narratives of generalized LGBTQ spaces. I suggest that the historical geographic study of lesbian–queer New Yorkers reveals how the geographical imagination of these women's spaces is as important as their material production. Although the landscape of the city changed drastically during the contemporary period, the way in which these women negotiate their bodies' relationships between the bar and neighbourhood remained consistent. Reading a dyked New York over time sheds light on how gender helps to produce and limit urban geographies of sexuality, both real and imagined. Broadening our understandings of the interplay between the geographical imagination and material manifestations of these spaces offers insights into how lesbians and queer women continue to produce spaces in the face of even more limited economic, social and political power.

Site, Method and Theoretical Framing

While LGBTQ studies of sexuality are increasingly expanding to examine rural and suburban spaces, much of urban queer life remains underexplored. Beyond being a global epicentre of financial, political and cultural capital, New York City remains a worldwide hub of LGBTQ activisms, arts and culture. The city was the location of the 1969 Stonewall riot, which has been attributed with inspiring the modern LGBTQ movement in the USA. In the 1970s and 1980s the city's crime rates allowed LGBTQ people to formalize a gay ghetto in the historically beatnik and always more homosexually-welcoming West Village, as well as other territories throughout New York City and other US, Canadian and European metropoles. New York City eventually became more sanitized, neoliberalized, financialized and, eventually, militarized after 9/11, further limiting the ability to get by for women, people of colour, the working and middle classes, and youth (Delany, 1999). Throughout my period of study (1983–2008), the landscape of the city changed drastically, although I will show that the relationship between the bar and the neighbourhood remained consistently interdependent. With only one history of gay New York written to date (Chauncey, 1994) and no historical studies of lesbians or contemporary LGBTQ history in New York City, this metropolis is an advantageous site for the study of LGBTQ life.

This chapter draws from a larger historical geography of contemporary lesbian and queer society, culture and economies in New York City from 1983 to 2008. My research works across the disparate moments of this period, which range from the beginning of the AIDS epidemic to the rise of internationally syndicated television drama *The L Word*. The project included multi-generation group interviews with 47 self-identified lesbians and queer women. Participants came out (understood broadly and in self-defined ways) between 1983 and 2008, and spent the majority of that time in New York City, which afforded cross-generational dialogue. I simultaneously examined archival records from this period at the Lesbian Herstory Archives in Brooklyn, New York, the largest collection of materials by, for and about lesbians in the world. In this chapter, I foremost draw on themes I developed from group interview conversations.

This study does not use age as a primary marker of generation but rather the year in which participants 'came out'. A participant's coming-out year is denoted after each participant's name. A total of 10 women were black, Latina or mixed race, and the remainder were white or white Jewish; almost all participants identified as middle class or working–middle class, and had attended some college or received further education. I use 'lesbians and queer women' to reference my participants' own naming of their identities and 'lesbian–queer' to describe the experiences of these women as a group while also recognizing that such identity formations may be much more varied (see Browne and Nash, 2009).

I turn to the *geographical imagination* as the analytic tool to address this gap between the material and imagined spaces of everyday lesbian–queer life. David Harvey (1973, 2005) originally theorized the geographical imagination to spatialize and politicize C. Wright Mills's (1961) 'sociological imagination', which is the examination of personal biographies in dynamic relation to the social history in which they are situated. The concept of the geographical imagination has broadened into a tool to describe and analyse both the literal and metaphorical ways people imagine and render space (see Gregory, 1994; Said, 2000). With regard to how the imaginary plays out in LGBTQ communities, scholars have often drawn upon Benedict Anderson's (1983) concept of 'imagined communities', which describes how communities form in image rather than comprehensive knowledge. For example, Anderson highlights nationalism which presupposes a sense of long-distance communion with other citizens who one may or can never know (see Rothenberg, 1995; Valentine, 1995; Weston 1995). Geographer Larry Knopp (2007) has called for a queering of the geographical imagination to afford more multiple LGTBQ spatial ontologies and political actions that promote difference. I take a feminist and queer approach in using the more spatialized geographical imagination, which I deploy as a tool to register how these participants negotiate the fissures between material and imagined spaces with their bodies.

Who are the People in your Neighbourhood, Really?

Whilst LGBTQ people have always existed in urban areas (Aldrich, 2004), LGBTQ spaces were most clearly articulated in neighbourhoods (Chauncey, 1995; Weston, 1995). Even today, prominent 'gaybourhoods' such as Greenwich Village, the East Village, Lower East Side, Chelsea and Park Slope are key spaces in US and global LGBTQ geographic imaginaries. Of these neighbourhoods, Greenwich Village is the most well known. The area also hosts or has hosted many LGBTQ bars, as well as businesses, restaurants, non-profit agencies, cruising grounds and the New York City LGBT Center. Participants in my study felt a great sense of attachment to the Village as a shared destination of all LGBTQ people across racial, class and cultural backgrounds.

Scholars of lesbian and queer spaces have sought to respond to this fixation on neighbourhoods by identifying 'spatial concentrations' of lesbians in various US cities, whether residential, commercial or a combination thereof (Wolf, 1979; Adler and Brenner, 1992; Kennedy and Davis, 1994; Kenney, 1998). Rather than creating long-term, property-owned, residential neighbourhoods, these women do not visibly occupy and control these areas (Gieseking, 2013, 2015). The continuing debate over lesbian neighbourhoods' existence is most often attributed to women having less access to capital (Adler and Brenner, 1992; Rothenberg, 1995). It is unsurprising, then, that, throughout the literature on lesbian and queer spaces, lesbians and queer women are marked and understood as 'invisible'. Reading examples of the Village over time offers insights into how the LGBTQ neighbourhood for all – across races and classes, gender and sexual identities – was always both an idea of an ideal space and an actual experience.

White, working-class and butch-identified Clancy 1986 moved to the Village in the 1980s, desperate to find a safe haven for her butch body. She also sought a community of visibly different others. However, as soon as she began to feel settled in a community, the depths of the AIDS crisis uprooted that comforting sense of place as her newly found community died:

> *In the 80s when all the gay men died who lived in the Village, there was a huge influx of breeders [heterosexuals] because the apartments came on the market, and that's when the West Village changed. By the end of the 80s, early 90s, the West Village was barely even a gay space anymore ... my flower guy and my dry cleaner and the mom and pop stores went out, everyone you used to wave to at night on your way out of work, gone. So it was the end of that neighbourhood-y feeling ... for a while there, it didn't even feel safe in the West Village to hold hands. I think we've bounced that back a bit now, but uh, yeah, that, that was a bit of a shock.*

Clancy reveals how the imagined ideal of the neighbourhood afforded her and other LGBTQ people a space to navigate through and against the multiple ways in which homophobia, heteronormativity, sexism, racism and classism permeate. At the same time, the material reality was actually a perilous and tragic environment that made obvious the homophobia and the LGBTQ lack of power and capital in this period. Clancy later relayed that in the decades she had lived in the Village, the ever-increasing waves of gentrification, mostly via 'breeders', had produced a space that she felt was mostly inhospitable to LGBTQ people and especially to her working-class, butch body.

In the early 1990s geographer Valentine (1993b, 1993c) wrote that spaces in which lesbians could feel safe, let alone comfortable, were severely limited. She paid special attention to the home in terms of the family of origin, workplace and mixed LGBTQ bars in smaller towns often dominated by gay men. Some of my participants found that these experiences had not changed by 2008 (see also Hanhardt, 2013). White, working-class and femme-identified Maral 2002 still lived at home and had not yet come out to her Orthodox Jewish parents. She explained the stress of being out in public, even in a LGBTQ neighbourhood like the West Village. A group of women of various races and classes expressed shock at her position in this territory:

> *Maral: I still don't feel safe, even in New York City. I remember when I was first coming out I didn't even safe walking down Gay Street [in the Village] holding my girlfriend's hand ... my dad is a cab driver so every time a cab would pass by, I'd be like, 'Fuck! Is that my Dad?! Is that my Dad?!'*

> *Tre 2002, Magdalene 2004 and Quinn 1995: Whoa. That is so stressful! God.*

Although the gay neighbourhood is often portrayed as the space of a safe elsewhere, each passing bright yellow cab produces a panopticon effect. Maral's body senses that it is always under surveillance while she needs to continually monitor her actions and self as well. The material affordances of the supposed international gaybourhood of the Village are lost on Maral and, instead, she has merely the idea of Gay Street in which to act as herself. The other women in this interview were older or younger, wealthier or less moneyed, and black or white, yet they *all* connected to her experience with shock, indicating how these women also imagine the Village to be a welcoming place. Still, in many women's stories of their experiences in the Village, other versions of the not-so-safe and much less welcoming neighbourhood leaked out: hate crimes, being followed, being screamed at and harassed, and so on. Even while the Village offers an increased sense of safety to many, the reality of the space is also punctured by limitations, whether specific to one person's family situation or to larger structural inequalities.

'I Could Hardly Wait to Get Back to That Bar' Except 'It's Closed Now'

Conversations with participants often began with participants naming bars and parties as the epitome of a lesbian–queer place. Valarie 1985's quote attests to the 'cool' of such 'gay places':

> That was it: Garbo's! That was the first [lesbian] bar I ever went to. Me and a friend went there. And we just walked in and we like, 'Oh my God, oh my God! We're in a gay place. Oh my God, oh my God. Okay. Be cool, be cool!'

While a wide variety of places remains important to lesbians and queer women (see Nash, 2005), bars have a historical import to lesbians and queer women that changes over time from being a hub of all social activity – imagined or real – to a space that is constantly lost.

In their ground-breaking history of mid-twentieth-century lesbian life in Buffalo, New York, Kennedy and Davis (1994) describe how the bar – lesbian-only or mixed lesbian and gay men – was the only public space available for working-class lesbian socializing from the 1930s to the 1960s; their first full chapter is entitled 'I Could Hardly Wait to Get Back to That Bar'. This sentiment of the bar as the ideal gathering space is reaffirmed by lesbian–queer writers and activists, as noted in the Wolfe quote in the introduction (see also D'Emilio, 1983; Nestle, 1997). However, participants in my project dwell more on the loss and absences of such places, marking their closures as important as anything else in the phrase 'it's closed now'. The sense of nostalgia was pervasive in that there were always so few dedicated lesbian bars and similarly only handfuls of lesbian–queer parties, as the numbers of lesbian and gay male bars in the introduction highlights. The closing of any of these places is therefore considered a deep loss, and these spaces are remembered with significant emotion. At the same time, the limited, shared geographical imagination and materiality of lesbian bars links these women across races, classes and generations.

With a greater number of venues for white women, particularly those that are well advertised and in central locations, lesbians and queer women of colour relayed an even more profound sense of loss when the last lesbian bar for that group closed in the early 2000s. Mixed race, working/middle-class Bailey 1995 spoke out about how she saw this phenomenon affecting lesbians and queer women across races:

> *Well, I was 21. I was working there [at Crazy Nannie's Bar] and everyone there was in their 30s, 40s, 50s. So it wasn't my age group but it was a bar that was primarily African-American lesbian ... a lot of Latin women, working–class white women ... And downstairs it just had that pool table/Megatouch [video game] bar feeling ... upstairs it was a big dance club and bar. It was like Cheers for me ... I remember sitting in there writing a paper on Lil' Kim. [All: Laugh.] Because when I was in there I was like ... home. You know what I mean? [All: Nod.] So when it closed ... now people don't know where to go.*

Rather than realizing the multitude of places and the meanings they can support or how the meaning and function of bars could change over time, participants harkened back to that idealized space of the bar, its closing and their reading of the closure as rendering lesbian–queers invisible. In their stories there was no place to physically locate their body that echoed the difference and attraction of the bars they had once known. The bars most included were: the Duchess and Cubbyhole in the 1980s; Meow Mix, Henrietta Hudson's, Crazy Nannie's, Rubyfruit's and Cubbyhole in the 1990s; and Cattyshack, Ginger's and Cubbyhole in the 2000s. All but three of these bars are closed now. This loss reiterates the fixation on such places as *the* places for galvanizing and enacting LGTBQ liberation.

Generational changes in NYC lesbian bars also express the political and social shifts of the times. Those who came out in the 1980s said they were likely to all wind up in the same places with gay men and trans people because there were fewer bars or parties. Particularly for that generation, political work around the hardest-hitting issues like the AIDS epidemic brought all LGTBQ people together. The number of lesbian–queer bars and parties expanded in the 1990s, as white, working-class Sudie 1999 recalled:

> *Monday night was Doc Holliday's, Tuesday night was Lux, Wednesday night was ... eventually Metropolitan, and then Thursday night sometimes was Meow Mix and then it eventually became something else, Friday night was a party, Saturday night we had off. Maybe something happened on Sunday nights, too. [Laughs.] We all went out five nights a week. I scheduled my classes around it – that's especially when I was young, you know? We were all broke. It was a lot cheaper to just party at someone's house though ... I was like 18.*

By the 2000s all of this changed again. White, working/middle-class Kathy 2005 shared that her recent connection to activisms in the late 2000s recreated the bars as political spaces: 'It's been really great for me ... to know more people, and actually ... hang out with queers! And really angry queers. Instead of just getting drunk and picking the flavor of the evening [at a bar]'. In the end, then, my research suggests that lesbian bars continue to afford the possibility for always slightly more diverse socializing across race, age and class than other social venues, particularly during young adulthood and most especially when coming out. In a landscape of changing attitudes and values toward LGBTQ people, participants noted that bars fall increasingly short of their almost mythical mandate to 'validate the reality of their [lesbian] worlds and their lives as social and sexual beings' (Wolfe, 1997, p. 315). Regardless, operationalizing their geographical imaginations reveals the qualities of the ideal place that generations of urban lesbian and queer bodies, of different races and classes, believe they require at least in some measure in order to sustain their everyday lives and resist injustice.

Discussion and Conclusion: Dyked New York

LGBTQ individuals and groups have historically formed, and have been formed, in urban areas, so much so that Julie Abraham has argued that homosexuals have become 'models of the city itself' (2009, p. xix). For LGBTQ people, the types of urban spaces and places most often represented in the literature range from the scale of the place, namely bars, to the neighbourhood to the city itself. At the same time, women's explicit erasure from the city, in narratives of this group's fear of city spaces, and weaker economic and political power contradict the neighbourhood/bar typology of LGBTQ spaces as being equally safe, useful and/or liberating for all genders, as well as races and classes. Yet, the examination of urban lesbians' and queer women's experiences in this chapter reveals that the intimate scales of LGBTQ bars and neighbourhoods are complicated by gender; this gendered queering of the city is dyked New York.

Beyond the sheer materiality of these spaces and the imagined community socially sustaining lesbian–queer spaces long theorized, these women also imagine the geographical qualities of these material spaces. The meanings and uses of these spaces are also imbricated, where the site of the bar serves as a presumably welcoming space for lesbian–queer bodies, while the neighbourhood is the location for these hangouts and community spaces. Limited in social, economic and political power, these women overcome the limits to produce physical space by a shared geographical imagination of how these spaces should operate. While LGBTQ neighbourhoods operate as a beacon of safety and welcome in the geographical imagination for all of my participants, their materiality is limited through difference and is specific to women's genders, races and classes. With a small number of bars and a limited ability to keep them open, these women express a deep sense of nostalgia for that ideal socially inclusive, politically astute and economically accessible space that always seems to be lost.

The spaces of the bars and neighbourhoods mutually form one another as these women's bodies wind their way between and through these spaces, often finding the bars they seek out are lost to LGBTQ neighbourhoods. Sarah mentions in her opening quote about the Park Slope neighbourhood seeming like it is 'not a lesbian neighbourhood anymore' because 'institutions, like, The Rising [Café and Bar], they've disappeared'. This sentiment shows how much of a role bars play in evidencing and sustaining LGBTQ neighbourhoods for these women. Ignored in their imagined portrayals of these spaces but essential to their actual experiences, it is these women's bodies that help to produce and sustain spaces of both resilience and resistance. This finding elaborates on Valentine's (1993b) idea that lesbians adopt specific avoidance behaviours in specific time-spaces by revealing that these practices are tied both to the materiality and the geographical imagination of these spaces. Further, these women's abilities to navigate the city on the basis of their race, gender and class shape their social lives and spaces, as Bailey's stories of the much more limited spaces available to black women illustrate. An idea of dyked New York, then, reveals the queer flux of these spaces and the multiple affordances to lesbians and queer women, imagined and physical, and specific to identities and experiences.

As my research with lesbians and queer women who came out between 1983 and 2008 in New York City demonstrates, the aspect of change over time reveals changes and consistencies of the urban that need to be addressed more broadly within the literature. My findings reveal that a dyked New York is not constant but always in process and becoming, and thereby part of 'the landscape of contemporary gay life' that incorporates both hegemony and difference (G. Brown, 2009, p. 3). The hegemony of dyked New York is the totalizing social imaginary of the LGBTQ bar and neighbourhood. At the same time, the gap between the imagined and material experiences of LGBTQ neighbourhoods like

Greenwich Village reveals this state of becoming. Equally essential is the shifting import and affordances of lesbian–queer bar culture in the city. Such a queering to hold the tension in dialectic rather than succumb to one side of the binary is the way in which practices of LGBTQ resilience and resistance more fully account for difference. The experiences of my lesbian–queer participants demonstrate how a dyked New York affords a way of reading urban sexualities to account for the imagined and material qualities and contradictions of these spaces.

Acknowledgements

My gratitude to Gavin Brown, Paolo Vieira and Tiffany Muller Myrdahl for their comments and support. This research was supported by the following fellowships and awards for which I remain deeply grateful: Woodrow Wilson Dissertation Fellowship in Women's Studies; Center for Place, Culture, and Politics; Joan Heller–Diane Bernard Fellowship from the Center for Lesbian and Gay Studies; and the CUNY Graduate Center Proshansky Dissertation Award.

Chapter 5

Visibility on Their Own Terms?
LGBTQ Lives in Small Canadian Cities

Tiffany Muller Myrdahl

In March 2013 two anti-gay incidents were reported in the province of Manitoba, Canada. The first made both the mainstream and the gay news circuit: a gay-owned restaurant was being run out of the town of Morris, about 60 kilometres south of Winnipeg. The restaurant owners were targeted by homophobic verbal attacks, the content of which came through loudly in the *Winnipeg Press*: some residents were quoted as saying, 'they should get the hell out of here' and 'a lot of people don't like it. You don't know what they're doing in the kitchen' (McIntyre, 2013). The second incident was less widely reported: the house of an openly gay Winnipeg man was defaced with homophobic slurs.

The responses featured in the media, whether by journalists or reader comments, followed a conventional logic about locating LGBTQ lives: that is, the by-ways of the gay metropolis —whether rural towns or mid-size cities – are uninhabitable for LGBTQ people. One clear example of this discourse was apparent in an article that linked the two incidents, written for the feminist–queer website, autostraddle.com. Here, the author responds to a reader's comment: 'We're lucky that we have cities where people can let their freak flag fly, but saying there are a dozen safe cities for LGBT people to run to isn't a win' (Kristen, 2013). The writer's return to 'safe-city' rhetoric is a striking assumption: despite reporting on hate speech in both Winnipeg and Morris, Manitoba, she clings to an expectation that LGBTQ people can find refuge in the 'right' cities.

But which 'dozen safe cities' in Canada does this author refer to, exactly? In the most recent national statistics (Dowden and Brennan, 2012), a 100 per cent increase in anti-gay hate crimes was documented between 2007–08; this report highlighted Vancouver as having the highest proportion of hate crimes motivated by sexual orientation (26 per cent). While statistics such as these require a substantive unpacking that is beyond the scope of this chapter (for example, the politics of reporting and the boundaries that determine population distribution; compare McDonald and Hogue, 2007), the report suggests that the 'dozen safe cities' notion at work in the writer's account is flawed, as is the lingering perception that the metropolitan centres known for (a certain type of) gay or lesbian culture are the only places in Canada that facilitate spaces of queer belonging (G. Brown, 2008; Gray, 2009; Herring, 2010; Muller Myrdahl, 2013).

Reading rural or urban Manitoba as especially homophobic, or conceptualizing LGBTQ lives as safe in a few select cities that conform to a particular urban aesthetic, is reductive and simplistic. Homophobic sentiment and actions shape LGBTQ and heterosexual lives in cities and towns of all sizes. Moreover, while migration to cities with a large(r) queer population and more institutional support continues to be an attractive (if not necessarily accessible) option for some, the 'Get Thee to a Big City' model of queer migration is no longer as seamless as it once seemed to be (Weston, 1995; Gorman-Murray, 2007; Lewis, 2014a, p. 232). A more productive line of inquiry must examine the geographically-specific negotiations LGBTQ people make as they navigate daily experiences of acceptance and intolerance.

This chapter pursues this line of inquiry, responding as well to an appeal for scholarship on urban sexualities to pay attention to a greater range of cities and to a broader range of spaces within cities. It first offers a cursory review of geographic scholarship on LGBTQ lives in under-studied Canadian cities. Then I present findings from my research conducted in Lethbridge, Alberta,[1] to explore the idea that, for many LGBTQ people living in small cities, urban life is shaped by dual demands: not upsetting the dominant norms-in-place on the one hand, and, on the other hand, using multiple time–space strategies (Valentine, 1993b; Gieseking, 2012) in sites across the city to cultivate a sense of, and space for, queer belonging. As the stories below illustrate, I use queer as a (not essentialist) shorthand for people and practices whose sexualities and/or gender performances and/or identities diverge from and (at least partially) disrupt the hetero-norm. But, significantly, the hetero-norm is a place-specific construct, even as it exists in relation to multi-scalar laws, policies and other sociocultural forces. Thus, I aim to show that appreciating a full(er) range of queer place-specific strategies requires a reconsideration of negotiations that appear to be homonormative or apolitical (Podmore, 2013b).

LGBTQ Lives in Small Canadian Cities

By and large, geographers' attention to sexuality in Canadian cities has focused on Toronto (for example, Nash, 2005, 2006, 2013a, 2013b) and Montreal (for example, Podmore, 2001, 2006, 2013a), with some notice going to Vancouver (for example, Miller, 2005) and Ottawa (for example, Lewis, 2013b; see Nash and Catungal, 2013, for a thorough overview).[2] The disregard for both sizeable cities, like Calgary and Winnipeg, and small regional centres (of which Canada has many) reflects a long-term trend of metrocentric sexualities research and, arguably, the lack of emphasis on feminist geography and geographies of sexualities within many Canadian university departments.

Important exceptions exist, however; this work tells two important stories about queer life in small Canadian cities.[3] First, this scholarship adds a layer of complexity to the urban/ rural binary by highlighting how the rural is inflected through the urban. Typically, the flaws in this binary have been identified through a focus on mobility and the movement between metropolitan centres and rural places by LGBTQ people (Knopp and Brown, 2003; Gorman-Murray, 2007; Annes and Redlin, 2012a; Lewis, 2014a). This sentiment is echoed in Torrie's 2007 work on rural lesbians in British Columbia: she argues that her narrators 'demonstrate that the division between urban and rural is nebulous, that circulation is a

---

1   Entitled 'The Lives of (Sexual) Others: Social Difference and Urban Change in Lethbridge, Alberta', this research is funded by the Social Science and Humanities Research Council of Canada (Project No. 430-2011-0294) and the University of Lethbridge.

2   My focus is strictly on geography literature here, but the same trend holds true for historical scholarship on same-sex sexuality in Canada (see Korinek, 2012, fn. 14).

3   In Canada, the definition of city is determined by the provincial government: for instance, in British Columbia, a city must have a population *greater than* 5,000; in Saskatchewan, a city's population must be *at least* 5,000; and in Ontario, size and history determine whether a municipality is called a city, town, township or village. The municipalities that I reference here range in population from 35,000 (Moose Jaw, SK) to more than 600,000 (Winnipeg, MB). Beyond an indicator of physical size or population base, the use of 'small' here stands in as a way of conceptualizing these cities in relation to the Canadian imaginary of the queer-friendly metropolis.

useful way of understanding how lesbians negotiated geography, and that lesbians' reasons for relocating – or staying where they were – could have little to do with their sexuality' (Torrie, 2007, p. 25).

In other work on queer life in small Canadian cities, the urban/rural binary loses its meaning even further as the rural is understood as a characteristic of small-city life. Sullivan's examination of queer women's lives in Thunder Bay, Ontario is a case in point: although the city had a population of more than 109,000 at the time of her research, she found that 'many of the women interviewed often described the city as rural because of its isolated location, its privileging of masculinity and seemingly conservative disposition. These features mark the city as rural despite many of the urban amenities' (Sullivan, 2009a, p. 81). The 'rural' small city has been documented in other studies of LGBTQ lives, from a population centre of under 35,000 like Moose Jaw, Saskatchewan (Wickenhauser, 2012, p. 35) to a large suburban municipality of 468,000 like Surrey, BC (LoBosco and Badesha, 2014). Even sizeable urban centres are characterized as rural or 'small-town' when LGBTQ interviewees perceive their cities to reflect or promote values that are at odds with what they understand to be a progressive urban aesthetic (see also MacMillan, 2013, p. 147; Muller Myrdahl, under contract).

Second, this work illustrates LGBTQ manoeuvres that are undertaken to negotiate the daily ins and outs of acceptance and intolerance, which are intimately tied to the role of queer visibility and the prevalence of supportive infrastructure such as queer-friendly spaces. Visibility remains a touchstone for LGBTQ organizing (see Hanhardt, 2013). According to Gorman-Murray et al. (2013, pp. 6–7), '[t]he key social and political question in contemporary times is about the political visibility of GLQ folks and how sexual minorities live day-to-day in the tension between belonging and alienation, enacted in both "on-the-street" encounters and in legislation, policy, and planning about social inclusion'.

For LGBTQ people in small Canadian cities, feelings of belonging and alienation are produced in and through sociospatial strategies. For instance, queer-friendly spaces are often also spaces that aim to be welcoming across a broader set of differences. In Thunder Bay, creating a welcoming space for the broader queer community at the LGBTTIQ centre (Pride Central) on the local university campus was one way for queer women to 'bend, push and resist the dominant discourses' of masculinity, whiteness and class privilege to make the rural city more inclusive to marginalized people (Sullivan, 2009a, p. 82; Sullivan, 2009b). Despite these efforts, feelings of isolation persisted for some, who read this space as exclusive and inaccessible to those not affiliated with the university.

Intersecting identities, including class, race or Aboriginal status, informs how the tension around accessibility is navigated. For example, indigenous Two-Spirit and LGBTQ respondents in Winnipeg have recommended the presence or increase of 'visible and accepting services in cities and in First Nations and Métis communities' that are geared towards the particular needs of these communities (Ristock et al., 2010, p. 38). By contrast, whiteness and settler family lineage facilitated community acceptance and municipal leadership in small-town Nova Scotia (McAdam, 2010, p. 30).

In small Canadian cities the visibility of (perceived) racial sameness or difference can take on a unique prominence where the smaller overall population is combined with the legacies and current iterations of colonialism. For instance, in prairie cities, histories of pronounced racism mean that identifying as Native *and* Two-Spirit or LGBTQ can be a challenge for those seeking services and safe spaces (Ristock et al., 2010; compare Holmes, 2012, pp. 195–249). A similar analysis is relevant for racialized newcomers (immigrants and refugees). According to O'Neill and Kia (2012, p. 41), newcomers reported feeling particularly isolated in small urban centres in British Columbia. They noted that regardless of newcomers' legal residency status in Canada, respondents felt unsafe disclosing same-sex sexuality when accessing settlement services. At the same time, these respondents perceived LGBTQ resources to be off-limits because accessing those services seemed to require 'LGB self-identification or self-labelling' (O'Neill and Kia, 2012, p. 41). Queer visibility thus needs to be read with an intersectional lens that attends to the specific historical and contemporary geographies that constitute the small urban context (compare Visser, 2013, p. 272).

Ultimately, the kinds of challenges reported by LGBTQ people in small Canadian cities share much in common with those identified by queers in cities that are presumed to be 'safe'. While the presence of supportive infrastructure – LGBTQ services, queer-friendly spaces, gay-straight alliances, co-optable spaces, and the like – tends to reflect the size of the city, the struggle to make this infrastructure accessible and inclusive is not unique to small cities (compare Catungal, 2013). Moreover, while place-specific permutations of negotiating visibility are evident among queers in small cities, the routes are not unlike those elsewhere, even in so-called gay metropolises. Resiliency in New York City's lesbian–queer culture, writes Gieseking (2012, p. 311), 'depends not only on the acts of visibility but also on acts of concealment and invisibility'. One feature that distinguishes queer life in small cities, then, is how LGBTQ people foster a sense of queer belonging while also contending with a narrower formulation of acceptable norms.

Negotiating Queer Visibility in Lethbridge

With a current population 90,417 (City of Lethbridge, 2013), Lethbridge is a rapidly growing regional centre in southern Alberta. A two-hour drive from Calgary, the province's most populous metropolitan area, Lethbridge is an isolated prairie city: beyond its borders there is little but uninterrupted agricultural and ranch landscape in every direction. Although political conservatism has been consistently challenged by support for centre-left candidates in provincial elections, Lethbridge is known for religious and social conservatism. In the Canadian imaginary of queer-friendly places, it is definitely not among the 'dozen safe cities' that autostraddle.com author Kristen envisaged in the story that began this chapter. Instead, Lethbridge lends itself to well-worn depictions of the scary rural. Narrator J,[4] a 20-something transplant from a small town in British Columbia, captures this sentiment while also denoting its limits:

> When we talk to queer people from different towns, it's like, 'You're out in Lethbridge? That must be scary!' I mean, there's really no queer community in Lethbridge compared to bigger towns, but I think we're doing pretty good for where we are in the Bible Belt, you know? … Lethbridge has a Pride celebration, and now it's a week long and everything … And [we're] being more out and just trying to integrate ourselves into the general community.

---

4   In this research, narrators decide whether to be identifiable: many have chosen to allow their oral history to be public and others have opted to make their oral history transcript available with the use of a pseudonym. In all cases, the oral history interview is transcribed, reviewed, edited and returned to the narrator for their approval. The approved copy is then annotated and indexed in preparation for its submission to the Sir Alexander Galt Museum & Archives in Lethbridge, which will take place in 2015. Because narrators are at different stages of the transcript-approval process, I use limited identifiers in order to maintain a consistent format for the quotes. Narrators are identified by the initial of their first or last name and the age bracket they were in at the time of their interview. Pseudonyms are noted when used.

J's comments underscore one of the emergent themes in the Lethbridge research: many narrators are keenly aware of how their queer lives are supposed to be limited by the small-city context, and while some do feel constrained by the size of the city, others carve out a sense of queer belonging regardless of whether or how day-to-day life may be shaded by contours of social conservatism. This outlook is not unique to Lethbridge, of course, and I return to this point below. It is worth noting that J's perspective should not be read as particular to her youth: in this research, any expectation of generational cohorts – for instance, that younger people would necessarily be less closeted or that older people would inevitably be more interested in exercising discretion in public – did not bear out. The sense of agency that comes through in J's quote is neither shared by all younger narrators, nor is it limited to that subset of participants.

The role that queer sexuality plays in this small city can be gleaned in part by taking note of how queer sociality thrives in the midst of, and plays a role in, re-shaping a conservative social climate. Examples of this abound in the oral history narratives, from the mundane to the exceptional: participants highlight how they make way for sexual difference in all aspects of urban life, from individual workplaces to the city's Business Revitalization Zone to faith communities. The outcome is a small city whose landscape showcases queer life, especially for those who know where to look.

One example is Cabinet of Queeriosities, an exhibition that one narrator curated for the community arts centre in 2011 and 2012. According to its call for submissions, the purpose was to exhibit 'small format works celebrating GLBT (gay, lesbian, bisexual, transgender) history and pride through a diverse range of subject matters and approaches. This call is open to everyone but submissions should in some way address GLBT history and/or pride' (Casa, 16 January 2011). Displayed for five weeks in the community arts centre's main hall, the Cabinet of Queeriosities employed the *wunderkammer* concept to generate conversation across the Lethbridge community. The narrator, L, in her 40s, describes how the exhibit exemplified what she appreciates about making queer life visible in a small city with a vibrant arts scene:

> *I've always been really compelled by the idea that when you bring together a collection of objects, you can create so many different levels of meaning just from juxtaposing different objects together. All sorts of things can happen when you do that ... Nobody even questioned whether they should be in [the show] because they were gay or whatever. It was like, if you were straight and you wanted to make a piece, go ahead. And a lot of straight people did make pieces for it. It was just another community art exhibit, which is another thing that I like about Lethbridge, because that can happen. Everybody can contribute and it makes for a more meaningful and interesting show, because you're getting truly these various forms of dialogues going on within it ... So, it just seemed [to be] about people being able to embrace the things that others don't necessarily understand about them, and bringing them all together in one spot.*

L's comments are suggestive of the breadth of queer life in Lethbridge: there are events that exceed expectations for a southern Alberta city, and some, like Cabinet of Queeriosities, illustrate that small-city activism may not conform to a straightforward version of identity politics.

Some more widespread activities have also found a positive reception in the city: the occasional queer film fest, an annual Trans Day of Remembrance event, and the raising of the Pride flag at City Hall during Pride week all signal LGBTQ people cultivating a small-city landscape in which they feel safe. The flag-raising has emerged alongside social policy changes at City Hall in which the municipal government has committed to making

Lethbridge a 'welcoming and inclusive community' (CMARD Team Lethbridge, 2011). Narrator V (pseudonym), in her 60s, highlights this point, while also implying that these changes are not without struggle:

> *I was a little worried the first year of Pride Fest three years ago [2009] when we raised the flag at City Hall, that there might be protests, that there might be weird things happening with that. But people were driving by and honking and, you know, there didn't seem to be an issue … We are up to three years now. And lots more people from City Hall came out and the police were out and a lot of people from the Aboriginal community are coming out to those events. I think that in City [government], there's an [effort towards] 'Let's make this a more friendly, safer community, and that means accepting everybody'. Even if it chokes people to say the words, to say 'lesbian' out loud. (V (pseudonym), 60s)*

V's quote illustrates the changing social climate of the city and its municipal leadership. Yet her comments are clearly couched within an understanding of the city in which LGBTQ visibility has been circumscribed by feelings of insecurity. For many narrators, queer visibility – from public displays of affection to being 'out' at work – comes with too high a price or, more significantly, does not fit within their perception of the norms of place. Whereas some narrators identified their efforts to deliberately trouble heteronormativity, many others rejected the idea that making their sexuality visible in public is relevant to their lives. Compare the two stories from narrators M (pseudonym) and D, both in their 50s:

> *I'm very polite, so troubling [the norm is] if somebody says, 'oh my husband and I de-duh de-duh', and I go, 'Yeah, that's true; [partner's name] and I find that too'. You know? So I will insert parallel examples. Whatever heteronormativity is happening in terms of description of 'what I did last night', or 'where I am going tomorrow', or the family, or trouble with kids, or whatever, I insert – deliberately, consciously – I insert my life to make it visible. Because I didn't for forty years. I just was silent. I passed … Sometimes I probably still pass. (M (pseudonym), 50s)*

> *I remember I had a guy that I worked with. His son came out. And there was myself and there were another couple of ladies that were gay [at work]. And one day, this particular gentleman, he and I were talking and he was struggling with the fact that his son is gay. And he made the comment to me, he says, 'You're so normal.' And I went, 'Thanks, [name of co-worker].' [Laughs] That's the way I want to be. And that was one of the things that he struggled with, because … the two ladies that worked at the time, they had the tendency to get in people's faces. So I go back to what I said earlier, that's part of the reason why I was accepted as being gay. Yeah, but I'm not in your face about the fact that I'm gay, and I'm not in your face, even with my family. I'm not in their face. A little bit more at times, when I'll put my arm around my girlfriend or I'll say, 'Come on babe, let's go'. But for the most part, that's the extent of it. So it was interesting when he made that particular comment, 'You're so normal', because that's who I've always tried to be. (D, 50s)*

For many narrators, the unspoken tenet of LGBTQ life in Lethbridge is that evidence of sexual or gender difference is not welcome in public and disrupting these dominant norms risks running foul of everything that facilitates the narrators' sense of belonging. The upshot is that the *invisibility* of queer difference shapes the construction of what becomes understood as 'normal' and moulds the community's sense of what is possible (cf. Berlant,

1998). Arguably, then, there is value in queer visibility in Lethbridge, whether in the shape of unique art exhibits like Cabinet of Queeriosities or in the form of more recognizable events like city-sponsored flag-raisings. Visibility should be valued not as an end goal, but as a marker that informs how spaces of belonging are created across social difference.

Yet, to acknowledge the value of LGBTQ visibility and read this visibility as *queer* in its challenge to the dominant norms of place requires rethinking how queerness and (homo)normativity are conceptualized. As Tongson (2011) has shown, queer studies have unwittingly employed certain 'spatial fantasies about sexuality' (ibid., p. 213), including the troublesome premise that normativity is or ever was 'a stable category found in fixed spatial environments' (ibid., p. 10). In other words, queer studies tend to assume that normativity (and queer) looks the same everywhere (G. Brown, 2009). But we need to look only as far as Lethbridge to see the flaws in this theorization. Using Narrator M as an example, her deliberate, conscious action – inserting her life, her same-sex partner, into heteronormativity – may be identified as homonormative in its unwillingness to interrogate liberal rights and privileges, but in Lethbridge, at this particular moment, it also counts as queer activism that disrupts the work of banal heteronormativity.

Normativity and queer visibility, then, are meaningful categories of analysis only when theorized in relation to the specific geographies and temporalities of place. In small cities in particular, strategies to facilitate a sense of queer belonging must be considered with a critical eye to what may, in another context, be read as homonormative or apolitical.

Conclusion

Central to theorizing LGBTQ lives in small cities is accounting for what is distinct and what is not exceptional. One of the elements that sets smaller Canadian cities apart is less access to the kind of LGBTQ-themed resources that large urban centres often have: typically, these cities have fewer institutional resources and few, if any, explicitly gay venues. Yet care should be taken when generalizing. Resources and venues are not just a function of size, but are also related to the relationship between the municipality and the region. That Surrey, BC (population 468,000) has no overtly gay venue, for example, says less about the size of the city and more about the municipality's regional function in relation – and close proximity to – Vancouver's gay scene. Moreover, as historical studies of sexuality in Canadian cities suggest, the landscape can change quickly and, even when resources and venues do exist, some find such sites and spaces inaccessible (see, for example, Korinek, 2012; Millward, 2012).

Another distinct facet of smaller cities is the typically narrower range of acceptable norms and, as a result, the place-specific tactics that LGBTQ communities use to negotiate 'normalcy' and foster a sense of queer belonging. The Lethbridge case suggests that although investments in 'normalcy' are evident from narrators across the lifespan, LGBTQ people insert themselves into the city in myriad ways, using creative events like art exhibits and well-worn methods such as a City Hall flag-raising for Pride week. These forms of queer visibility help to reshape the boundaries of what counts as 'normal' in Lethbridge. Still, for the city to foster a 'welcoming and inclusive community' requires more than enhancing queer visibility or creating a broader definition of 'normal'. What is essential instead is a commitment to cross-cutting anti-oppression education and policy initiatives that recognize how 'normalcy' is always inflected by other forms of (perceived) social difference.

Of course, the need for such a commitment is not unique to small cities; it is echoed in the efforts of several Canadian cities that are working to develop policies and training strategies to ensure that equity is understood through an intersectional lens (CAWI-IVTF, 2014). Likewise, the types of challenges that LGBTQ people face in small Canadian cities are not exceptional. They are similar to the struggles confronted in cities that are purportedly safe for queer self-expression. Regardless of city size or the presence of historically significant gaybourhoods, heteronormativity informs both public and private modes of being and belonging (Berlant, 1998; Berlant and Warner, 1998). Yet the strategies used to navigate the countless ways in which heteronormativity shapes our daily lives are geographically and temporally contingent. Attention to small-city queers and the approaches they take to cultivate a sense of queer belonging offers the important lesson that normativity needs to be theorized in place-specific ways, lest we risk misreading nuanced responses to dominant norms as necessarily homonormative or apolitical.

Chapter 6

Trans(itional) Geographies: Bodies, Binaries, Places and Spaces

Lynda Johnston and Robyn Longhurst

Introduction

In a joint interview Cindy, aged 73, and Sarah, aged 54, talked about their experiences of transitioning from male to female and explained that it is now possible to be designated X instead of male or female in New Zealand passports. Cindy said: '... it means your sex is undetermined.., While this move to using X can be viewed as a positive step towards recognizing that sex and gender are fluid, Cindy explained: '[but] it's not ideal because a lot of computers will not recognize it.' Sarah added: 'It's not totally international.' This meant that when Cindy returned from Sydney to New Zealand she faced a problem: 'The computer wouldn't compute the X and it wouldn't issue a boarding pass.' The issue of the boarding pass was resolved by calling a supervisor, however, and Cindy has since changed her passport to F for female. We begin this chapter with Cindy and Sarah's story about passports because it speaks to some of the challenges, and resistances posed by gender diversity for trans people (also see Doan, 2010, p. 637 on passports).

Browne, Nash and Hines (2010, p. 573) in a themed issue titled 'Towards Trans Geographies' argue that '[g]ender geographies have focused on normatively gendered men and women, neglecting the ways in which gender binaries can be contested and troubled'. We agree and in this chapter on 'trans(tional) geographies' argue that there is plenty of scope to engage not just with the various theoretical fields that surround gendered and sexed 'bodies binaries, spaces and places', but also with the lived experiences of trans people.

We begin by pointing briefly to some of the contributions already made in geography that aim to challenge binary thinking. Second, we outline the methodological process used to collect information from two research participants, Cindy and Sarah, who live in Hamilton, New Zealand. In the third section Cindy and Sarah each offer rich reflections on their journeys in the everyday spaces of work, shopping, 'working men's clubs', bars and toilets. We think it is important to offer culturally and historically specific accounts of trans lives. Browne, Nash and Hines (2010, p. 574) note: 'As trans researchers make clear, trans voices need to be heard and new knowledges created from the specific understanding gained through lived experiences.' We agree and therefore aim in this chapter to contribute to this collection something about the experiences of two people who live in the small city of Hamilton, New Zealand.

Thinking through Trans Bodies, Binaries, Places and Spaces

Over the past two decades geographers and other social scientists have argued that binary thinking, as a strategy adopted by both individuals and collectives in many Western contexts, oversimplifies complex issues (Cloke and Johnston, 2005). It involves dividing a continuous spectrum into separate self-contained elements which exist in opposition to each other – for example, us/them, self/Other, private/public, local/global, black/white and structure/agency – and does not allow for two different types of 'things' to be understood as mutually constituted (Grosz, 1994). Theorists have argued that it is important, therefore, to deconstruct binary pairs. This can help prompt conversations in which a new language is employed in order to open up space for new ways of becoming. One way of thinking about new ways of becoming is provided by Homi Bhabha's (1990a, 1994) notion of 'Third Space'. Bhabha explains that 'by exploring this Third Space, we may elude the politics of polarity and emerge as the others of our selves' (Bhabha, 1994, p. 39; also see Pile, 1994; Soja, 1996). In a similar vein Gillian Rose (1993) argues for the notion of 'paradoxical space', a space in which it is possible to occupy both the centre and the margin (masculine and feminine).

In fact, feminist philosophers (Bordo, 1986; Kirby, 1997; Lloyd, 1993; Grosz, 1993, 1994), feminist geographers (such as Rose, 1993, also see Bondi, 1992; Johnston, 2005; Longhurst, 1995, 1997) and trans scholars (Doan 2007, 2010; Namaste 2000; Stryker 2006) have made important contributions to debates on binary thinking and the need to deconstruct it. In particular, they have paid attention to binary pairs such man/woman, male/female, masculine/feminine, mind/body, rational/irrational, sex/gender, heterosexual/homosexual and culture/nature. For example, Vicki Kirby (1997) discusses the binary pairs mind/body, culture/nature and signification/flesh. The body, Kirby argues, is both written and writes: that is, bodies are more than just texts written upon by representational fields; instead, flesh is articulated by language. Cultural contexts do not simply surround sexed and gendered bodies but also come to inhabit them.

Rather than reiterate further these already well-rehearsed arguments about binaries that have taken place both within and beyond the discipline of geography we now want to concentrate on trans theories (see Hines 2007, 2010 and Nash, 2010 on how trans scholarship intersects with queer geographies). The notion of 'trans' is useful for stressing that gender is fluid and at times unknowable. It unsettles the dominant framing mentioned above of man/woman, male/female, masculinity/femininity and sex/gender. The notion of 'trans' also challenges geographers to think again about these binaries – the way in which they are reasserted and troubled – and how there is no easy separation possible (for example, see Butler, 1990 and 1993 on gender performativity). Browne and Lim (2010, p. 616) describe trans studies as 'a growing field of enquiry that seeks to redress both the absence of trans lives in queer theory (despite the conceptual deployment of trans subjectivities across this field)'. Sally Hines (2010, p. 609) uses the term 'trans' to include a diversity of gender identifications. As one of us has acknowledged elsewhere it is not always possible to 'easily and unproblematically step out of binaries such as man/woman' (Johnston, 2005, p. 120), but the notion of trans can function productively to unsettle these terms, prompting a questioning of their supposed 'naturalness'. Sally Munt (1995) illustrates in her research on the lesbian *flâneur* that subject positions are never completely fixed. This fluidity greatly affects how people experience different spaces at different times (see Doan, 2007, 2010). It is important therefore to understand more about trans people's lives, their experiences of health, recreation, work, politics, travel and occupying a range of spaces and places.[1] Before

---

1   See Hines (2010) who is concerned with mapping some of the specificities of lived trans experiences in the UK; see also Rooke (2010) on trans virtual spaces).

moving on to discuss some of these issues through the lives of Sarah and Cindy, however, we explain a little about the research from which Sarah's and Cindy's stories were drawn.

Sarah and Cindy: Sharing stories

In 2009 Lynda embarked on a research project titled 'Hamilton Pride: Spaces of Sameness and Difference' which was conducted with and through the Hamilton Pride Incorporated Society).[2] As researchers, we are each positioned differently in this project. Lynda has been part of the Hamilton Pride community group since it was founded in 2007 and is, in many ways, an 'insider'. Robyn is not a member of Hamilton Pride, although she sometimes takes part in social and political activities organised by the group. Hamilton Pride's aim is to stand 'together, celebrating and supporting the diversity of Hamilton's rainbow community' (Hamilton Pride Incorporated Society, n.d.) The aim of the research project conducted by Lynda was to understand further the relationship between sexual identity, place, feelings and power for people in Hamilton's gay, lesbian, bisexual and trans communities. It involved participatory methodologies (producing and promoting events such as annual pride festivals, World AIDS Days, International Transgender Day of Remembrance) as well as 13 individual interviews and one joint interview. The joint interview with Sarah and Cindy which we draw on in this chapter was conducted on 31 July 2009 and it lasted for one hour and 40 minutes and was transcribed in full. We focus solely on it in this chapter because Cindy and Sarah occupy a unique place in Hamilton's and Aotearoa New Zealand's trans communities. They were active leaders in the nationally based group Agender New Zealand – a group that supports transgender people and their families throughout New Zealand (see Agender NZ, n.d.) – and the locally-based group Hamilton Pride Incorporated. Furthermore, their interviews are exceptionally rich. Both were able to convey effectively many of the complexities – that is, the prejudices faced and the joys experienced, – of transitioning from male to female. Cindy and Sarah both identify as Pākehā/European. Cindy is aged 73, retired, and describes herself as a post-op transsexual. Sarah is aged 54, works as a motel manager and defines her sexuality as lesbian. Both define their sex/gender as female and both are on very modest incomes.

Neither of us, as the researchers, have experienced first-hand neither a sense of disjuncture between how our bodies 'appear' and how we feel 'in them' in relation to sex and gender nor a desire to change that. We have, however, each experienced marginalization and exclusion on account of other bodily differences, such sexuality, gender, and body size.

In the city where we live, and where Sarah and Cindy live, Hamilton, Aotearoa New Zealand, there is not always much space for 'difference', although some people are warmly accepting. Hamilton is a small city by international standards, with just over 140,000 inhabitants. Within the context of New Zealand, however, it is the fourth largest city. The first settlement of the region in which Hamilton is located was by Māori. The iwi (tribe) Tainui called an area on the west bank of the Waikato River Kirikiriroa which means 'long stretch of gravel'. European colonizers renamed Kirikiriroa 'Hamilton' after Captain John Charles Fane Hamilton, who was killed in a battle in 1864. Māori lived and cultivated gardens along the Waikato River for about 700–800 years, but in the 1860s over 1 million hectares of land was confiscated in the Waikato region, and part of this land provided the basis for Pākehā/European settlement (Hamilton City Council, 2011).

---

2   For information about this group, see Hamilton Pride Incorporated Society (n.d.).

Currently, Hamilton has a population that is higher than the national average in relation to Māori, young people and migrants (Statistics New Zealand, 2013). Despite this, it tends to be relatively conservative given its historical roots as a 'settler town' which grew largely to service the needs of colonial farming families in the district. In fact at the north end of the city is a statue of a Pākehā/European 'farming family' which consists of a husband, wife, and two children, as well as a dog, cow and sheep. Hamilton still has a 'country town' feel about it as it sits in the southern shadow of Auckland which is located one and a half hours' drive north. Although Hamilton tends to be considered as relatively small and conservative, both Sarah and Cindy have lived at various times in even smaller and arguably more conservative places.

Early Days: From Small Towns to Larger Cities

Sarah began the interview, explaining:

> I knew from age seven that I had a thing for wearing female clothes and it just grew from there. I got married at 28 and when I got married I thought 'oh that will cure it'. I hadn't had any sexual experiences till then. It subsided for the first two years, after that it came back. I didn't know why and my wife had three children so I immediately had three children.

Eventually, however, the marriage ended. Sarah says:

> She found out [about the cross-dressing], she found some of my clothes 12 years before we separated. I have to take my hat off to her [read: respect]. She stayed with me for 12 years, hoping that she would help me cure it and yeah we tried but I guess we all know now, there's no cure. The year we separated she just couldn't handle it anymore. I can understand that, so then after that I stayed in Whakatane for about a year and then I came here [Hamilton].

In Whakatane, a small town in the Eastern Bay of Plenty with a population of 18,700, Sarah still cross-dressed but only in private. She comments that, in small towns, if you cross dress:

> [you] are often the only person in that small town that is like that so you stick out like anything and people will pick on you … they run you out of town … although I know one or two people in small towns that have survived … I think it depends a lot on the attitude of the person who has transitioned. I think if you have the right attitude … you are probably going to survive.

It was not until after Sarah moved from Whakatane to Hamilton, and another three and a half years had elapsed, that she made the decision to 'come out full time and live as a female'. What she discovered was a world full of people like herself:

> There's a whole new world out there and I'm still going through the process of discovering that. It's been such an incredible, I mean it's only been a year, it's been an incredible journey to take part in and I'm still learning new stuff every day. I've met literally hundreds of people that I would not have met, if I hadn't, you're obviously

one of them [referring to Cindy] if I hadn't transgender transitioned. I wouldn't have it any other way and I'm incredibly happy and I think I am a more confident and a better person.

But Sarah's gender transitioning was not always easy. She had no contact with her family for five years, and progress with some family members, such as her eldest daughter in Dunedin, continues to be 'slow'. Sarah's daughter wrote to her saying: 'I don't know Sarah, I only know Bob. I don't know how Bob felt keeping this huge secret for so many years from the people that he loved and loved him.' Sarah finds it challenging working through these issues with her daughter.

Cindy also lived for a period, when she was aged 13 to 16, in a small town with a population of approximately 12,000. Then in late 1949–early 1950s her family moved to Hamilton. Cindy's world did not really open up, however, until she discovered the internet which enabled her to connect with others in Auckland Aotearoa, New Zealand's largest city with a population of approximately 1.5 million.

> *I had a cousin that gave me some money and I brought a PC computer and the whole world opened up to me when I typed in 'cross-dressing' ... it just blew me away. The number of people on there and the number of sites for cross-dressers and from then on I joined up with a group called the 'Auckland Cross Dressers' I think it was and I put a note there: 'anyone from Hamilton wishing to have a get together?' And I got this reply from Doreen, and Doreen and I became great friends ... we used to go all over the place together.*

Although she wanted to meet other cross-dressers in Hamilton there were few people in the small city willing to reveal themselves, so Cindy regularly visited Auckland which offered more opportunities and support. Together with newly made friends, Cindy would visit Karangahape Road (commonly referred to as K' Road and known for its shops, cafes and red-light activities) Starbucks coffee shop and a hamburger bar before returning to Hamilton the next day.

While it cannot be assumed that larger city spaces necessarily afford more freedom than smaller towns to trans people, for our participants, Sarah and Cindy, this appeared to be the case. The small rural settlements where each of them spent some time as a young person did not feel accommodating. Auckland, however, provided more opportunities for cross-dressing. Hamilton as a mid-sized city by Aotearoa New Zealand standards appeared to offer both challenges and affirmations in various forms at various times.

'Coming out' in Hamilton: Discrimination and Support

Sarah explains that, when she did 'come out' in Hamilton, everywhere she went in public space

> *... was like climbing a hill, like the supermarket, the dairy, Chartwell Square [shopping centre], the bank, everywhere! I used to spend my time early on looking at people's eyes to see if they were looking at me and most of them weren't. I still do occasionally ... It was really really hard, I mean, I was scared, frightened but excited ... I didn't know what Hamilton would be like, I had no idea.*

Sarah was supported in her engagements in public space dressed as a woman by Cindy who she met prior to 'coming out'. Sarah manages a motel (or 'motor hotel'). She did this for three and a half years as Bob and then for the past year as Sarah. She explains:

> *Eventually I had to go out and spend a whole day out in every motel in our group [franchise] and tell them personally that I was coming out. I think that was a good thing for me, [it] gave me a bit more confidence and also I think it gave me more credibility in their eyes as well rather than just writing and saying what I was doing. So I think that was really good.*

Similarly, Sarah felt the need to talk with friends and acquaintances in the leisure spaces where she spends time. She says:

> *I told the guy at my club, the Cubby Hole, he said 'that's fine, you are still the same person' and I still go there with absolute safety and comfort. I think he actually protects me, in fact I know he does … When he sees me with someone new he checks to see if I'm okay. I'm really lucky.*

Sarah especially likes to go to the karaoke evenings and to 'Ladies Night' on Thursdays which she describes as 'wonderful' because she likes 'being among all these gorgeous chicks and they didn't know I'm a lesbian'. Things were not always as 'wonderful' in some of the other bars and clubs, though, including one in a small town where Sarah no longer goes. She explains:

> *When I was Bob I used to go there [Nottingham Castle, Morrinsville]. It's a very old fashioned … and I would not go there even with company because it's an alien environment for any female, for me, I would be walking into a hornets' nest I think. That's the only place I know of in my life that I've been to that I wouldn't go back to.*

Sarah and Cindy have long enjoyed socializing at charter or working men's clubs which tend to have an older clientele. Cindy says: 'I go down to the Cossie [Cosmopolitan] Club, the RSA [Returned Services Association] but my main club is the Workingmen's Club.' Cindy recalls the first time that she went to this club dressed as a woman:

> *I had a friend who was a lesbian … we had a party one night and she grabbed me and said 'you are coming down all dressed up' and I said 'Okay' so I went down all dressed up … It was like walking into Antarctica. (Lynda: Was it frosty?) It was very cold in there! [laughs]. But hey, I have been a member for 10 years and here I am walking in as a female for the first time and a lot of the guys knew us and of course, oh god! [laughs].*

Eventually, both Cindy and Sarah were accepted by most people at their clubs although their use of the women's toilets prompted some disquiet. Sarah explains that at the 'Workingmen's Club, at the RSA, even at the Cossie Club, there was a lot of resistance to us using the ladies toilets' (see Browne 2004 regarding genderism and the 'bathroom problem'). The women were told that they had to 'use the handicap toilet'. Sarah responded that she is not 'handicapped' and therefore objected to using that toilet. She told the manager:

> *I'm a female, I'm legally a female. I expect to have the right to use a ladies toilet. We have now educated these people to the extent where we are able to comfortably use the*

ladies toilets, but when I first started to go in them, I used to go in there and hope that there was nobody in there or wait until everybody was gone before I would come out again, not anymore.

Cindy's experience was similar. She recounts a story of a manager of one of the other clubs saying to her: 'I don't know how to put this but we have had a complaint from someone about you using the female toilet.' Cindy responded: 'I don't know why, I am a female, you can't discriminate because I am legally a female.' She then showed the manager her birth certificate which read 'Karen Cindy Lewis born Takapuna, female'. The manager then laughed and said: 'Oh we'll have to change the database.' He added, however, that he would still prefer Cindy to use the toilet down the back in order to 'save any hassle'. Cindy explained: 'I went down the back. I don't now. I use the main female toilet, too bad!'

Some of Cindy's and Sarah's stories about their clubs relay difficult situations, but others relay more positive experiences. This mix of narratives illustrates a complex array of negotiations around bodies, spaces and places. Eventually, Cindy stopped wearing pants to the clubs and began wearing dresses and skirts which she says some people, such as the 'barmaid', now prefer. Cindy explains: '[A]s Sarah knows darrn well, I have made more friends in there now since being female than I ever had before and I have had my old workmates come up to me and slap me on the back and say "good on ya, I'll shout you a beer" and I have had a couple do that.' Sarah replies that the atmosphere has changed a lot in the clubs and they enjoy the company of the bar staff but also of the 'ex-railway guys ... even the older ones' who appear to recognize that it is not the pants or skirt that matter but 'what's inside'. Sarah comments:

I have been going there for maybe six or seven months and like I said huge change, when I used to walk in there at first, people would give me some terrible looks aye and walk away, now they will give me a smile, or speak but at least give me a smile, so it's turned around.

Cindy adds that there are still some people who won't talk to them but at least they have 'a lot of supporters that turn around and say "leave them alone"'. Cindy says:

They stand up for us and say 'there's nothing wrong, they are just who they are and they are living their life, just leave them, they live their lives, you live yours, they are doing alright!' Yeah, we have a lot of supporters in there'.

She continues:

I got more blimmin support from the bar staff, well, when I was transitioning of course I had my ears pierced and of course that caused a bit of fun and games. They said 'why did you get your ears pierced?' I said 'I got drunk one night and someone dared me to get them pierced.' So that's how I got over that one but then I started to wear female watches and I got asked 'why do you have a female watch on?' and I said 'well I am going that way' and 'oh ok'. Then they would start to see the breasts starting to grow 'what the heck is happening there?' and I said 'well yup I'm changing.'

It seems that it was not just Cindy and Sarah who were involved in a period of transition but also the people they interacted with in the spaces and places of their everyday lives. Not everyone, however, has been able to make this transition. Cindy notes: '[W]e have a couple of our girls that won't even talk to us while we are in the Workingmen's Club.'

Sarah adds, '[T]here are guys that won't come anywhere near us', to which Cindy replies. 'One especially.' The conversation continues:

Sarah: Because they think if they talk to us people will think … they are part of us. That's crap!

Cindy: One is paranoid, one especially paranoid, the other is not too bad. He will come and talk, like I have had him come up to me but this other one, he said 'no don't you ever talk to me, don't even say hello in the Workingmen's Club.'

Sarah: It's blatant discrimination, that's how I see it.

Cindy: But nah as I say the transition in Hamilton has been great.

Lynda: That's amazing.

Cindy: I used to walk down with a wig on. Of course it never looked right, till my own hair started to grow. When I went to Phuket [Thailand] after I had my operation I went and had extensions put in and I had nice long hair down to about here [gestures to just below her shoulders], and it was permanent, and of course when I went into the Workingmen's Club I always had it tied back and I used to go in and see the hairdresser over here of course, eventually they fell out and the hairdresser just couldn't get over it. She had been doing my hair for quite a while now. She couldn't get over how much my hair has grown. I had a bald patch up here, quite a big one and it's disappeared, almost, still a bit there, but it's disappearing, and she couldn't get over how, even the hair had got thicker and I can't understand it, here I am getting on 73 and my hair is growing [laughs].

Shopping for clothes provides yet another space of both potential tension and acceptance for Cindy and Sarah. Cindy explains that it has been, and continues to be, challenging, especially buying underwear, even though she has not been treated badly in shops. Sarah says that before she came out she would by bras and other undergarments from 'Trade Me' (a well-known New Zealand online buying and selling internet site). Now, however, Sarah goes into shops to buy underwear, although she is still not completely comfortable with this: 'I still feel self-conscious when I go in there and that's because I used to spend so many years of my life going in there and waiting till the shop was empty, hiding behind the display stands [laughs] … and hoping I know the right size.'

Health clinics have tended to be a more accepting space for Sarah. When she felt she needed some assistance she phoned the sexual health clinic at the local hospital and was put in touch with a counsellor who Sarah describes as 'a brilliant lady'. Sarah visited her for approximately a year, and the counsellor put Sarah in touch with a doctor who prescribed her hormone replacement therapy (HRT). Sarah took this for nearly six months before coming out. Also, and very importantly, visiting the clinic opened doors for Sarah to meet others and to share experiences. She says:

I've been lucky, I've met [friend's name] and I've met Cindy and at least I knew a couple of other people that were like me and that really helped a hell of a lot. That gave me a lot more confidence. I don't know how I would have coped, although once I started to tell my friends, I felt confident because they were all supportive.

Conclusion: Farming Family and Riff Raff

Susan Stryker (2006) points out that 'trans' is not just about gender issues. It is also about sex and sexuality. It is about how gendered, sexed and sexual bodies trouble and transgress binaries, spaces and places. In this chapter we have relied on Cindy's and Sarah's stories to convey something of the complexity of trans lives and experiences. We do not claim to represent the many voices of a diverse range of trans but, instead, have attempted to 'dig deep' into the lives of just two people who have been willing to tell their stories about moving from living as a man to being recognized as a woman with clarity, conviction, intelligence and good humour. Cindy and Sarah, while having separate stories, also share in common the fact that they experience both discrimination and empowerment.

Kath Browne and Jason Lim (2010) focusing on Brighton, the 'gay capital of the UK', argue that places, and the ways in which we imagine them, make a difference to trans lives. Interestingly, in this research, Hamilton, as a small city in Aotearoa New Zealand, seems large enough that neither Cindy nor Sarah feel singled out on account of their difference, but small enough that they still feel part of various communities such as the Hamilton Pride organization and their communities at the various charter clubs where they relax. Hamilton as a space does not determine Cindy's and Sarah's various encounters but it does influence them. It is worth noting that not only does Hamilton have a statue of a colonial farming family representing 'family values' (as previously mentioned), but also of Riff Raff, a cross-dressing character – the butler – from the cult film and musical *The Rocky Horror Picture Show*.[3] The film was written by Richard O'Brien, who grew up in Hamilton and plays Riff Raff (see Johnston and Longhurst, 2010, pp. 2–3). This statue, which arguably functions to queer the landscape of Hamilton, has been the site of many events such as Richard O'Brien's 60th birthday celebration (O'Brien cut a cake presented by the mayor), an art project that involved wrapping the statue in rainbow-coloured woollen scarves as part of Hamilton Pride Week celebrations and the International Transgender Day of Remembrance on 20 November 2008 which Cindy and Sarah both attended and described as 'brilliant' and 'humbling because of the turnout'. The statue has become part of the city's identity.

Like Cindy and Sarah, Hamilton itself has undergone something of a trans(itional) geography. The decision 'to support a statue of Riff Raff was bold and contested, yet support prevailed, and the state was erected in 2004' (Johnston and Longhurst, 2010, p. 3). This is extraordinary for a small city which is, at times, overshadowed by conservative farming values. Spaces and bodies are intimately connected. Sarah's and Cindy's experiences cannot be extracted from daily places they inhabit or the people that share these spaces. Hamilton, we think, has also transitioned, and this is in part due to the community leadership of Cindy and Sarah, as well as the placing of Riff Raff in the centre of the city.[4] Gender, sex and sexuality, as well as other markers of subjectivity, are constantly changing and being mapped and remapped across an array of social and cultural landscapes, and it is time that this mapping moved beyond binary divisions. As Petra Doan (2010, p. 64) so eloquently puts it, 'The tyranny of gender dichotomy is an artefact of the patriarchal structuring of gendered space and it is time to lay it aside, not just for trans people, but for all of us'.

---

3   See the statue via a webcam at Riff Raff Statue.Org (n.d.).
4   See G. Brown et al. (2012) for discussion about transition, the nature of change and relations to the past, present and future.

Chapter 7

Sexualities and Urban Life

Gustav Visser

Introduction

An extensive discourse has developed over the past four decades, which suggests a relationship between different sexualities and urban space/places (M. Brown, 2012, 2014; Browne, 2013; Nash and Gorman-Murray, 2014). It is claimed that urban places (particularly larger cities) shape sexualities and that these sexualities shape those places, particularly where gay sexual identities are concerned (M. Brown, 2012; Hubbard, 2011). This chapter briefly reviews one of the debates focusing on the study of urban gay space of gay male identities that are lived through the commercial gay centres of major cities in parts of Europe, North America and a handful of other national settings (Browne, 2013; Nash and Gorman-Murray, 2014). Recent reflections on gay scholarship argue that many views on gay life in urban areas have become entangled in a trap of concentrating on the production of gay identities and urban spaces. It is the contention that this view of gay life in the urban has been conceptualized by drawing on the realities of small areas in a limited number of cities, in specific countries, against which all other gay spaces are implicitly assessed. This chapter argues that, in the process, conceptual understandings of gay sexualities' relationships to urban spaces are incompletely theorized. I contend that a vastly expanded empirical project is required that is informed by a range of other gay lives – lived outside gay ghettos or villages in a handful of Northern metropolitan regions. Drawing on experiences outside the currently mainstream, I argue that differently constructed gay identities are differently spatialized and ultimately incongruent with Northern theoretical constructions of the relationship between gay identity and urban space. The investigation supports the growing scholarship that suggests Northern theorization of necessary links between gay sexual identity and urban space is not universally applicable (Binnie, 2014; M. Brown, 2012, 2014). In addition, a number of future avenues of research are outlined.

Sexualities and Urban Life

Intersections of space and sexuality are key research foci in the field of human geography (Hubbard, 2011). This research focus developed with reference to gay men in urban space as a response to the notion that 'normal' urban spaces were inherently heterosexual, and that the expression of sexualities other than heterosexual was out of place, particularly in public spaces (Bell and Valentine, 1995a). Central to this argument has been the notion that public space is always sexed, mainly as straight, and only occasionally as gay or lesbian, and very seldom as queer sexualities beyond the binary 'markers' of gay/straight (Nash and Gorman-

Murray, 2014). Thinking through the idea of sexualized spaces has been dominated by a focus on gay males in urban space for most of the past four decades.

Most of the early work on gay enclaves in urban areas was on the emergence of areas in urban residential neighbourhoods in the 1960s and 1970s (Podmore, 2013a). This research was predominantly descriptive and focused on the locational choices of increasingly gay and lesbian populations, most often in the urban core of American cities (Nash and Gorman-Murray, 2014, p. 3). Since at least the 1970s a range of scholars have argued that the density, variety and multiple experiences that those contemporary urban landscapes could offer to their inhabitants frequently led to claims that urban and sexual freedoms go hand in hand (Hanhardt, 2013; Harry, 1974; Levine, 1979; Weightman, 1981; Weinberg and Williams, 1975). These claims received further support from Castells's (1983) (see also Castells and Murphy, 1982) investigations of the Castro district in San Francisco (Visser, 2008a, 2013). The overarching theme was that during the 1970s and the early 1980s a number of social scientists began to observe that gay men and lesbian women were creating in a number of Western cities (Valentine, 1995) distinct social, political and cultural landscapes, styled by Levine (1979) as 'gay ghettos', which were later, perhaps more benignly, renamed gay villages. Drawing on these observations, Castells (1983, p. 143) argued that the gay movement 'realized that between liberation and politics it first had to establish a community in a series of [public and private] spatial settings'. Although these earlier investigations have been critiqued on a number of fronts – class, gender and race bias being among them (Giwa and Greensmith, 2012) – they nevertheless reflected the growing significance of commercially concentrated gay areas in major US and UK cities, representing mainly gay male identities and lifestyles, and making them increasingly visible (Casey, 2004, p. 447; Levine, 1979; Valentine, 1995).[1]

As reflected in the earlier work of Knopp (1990), Lauria and Knopp (1985), as well as Weightman (1981), gay urban neighbourhood formation subsequently emerged as a central theme for the geographies of gay sexualities literature (M. Brown, 2012). The 'gay village' was increasingly being analysed, the most important object of investigation being the sexuality and urban places nexus. The most succinct recent summaries of the idea of the sexualities of gay male life in urban places are provided by Michael Brown (2012, 2014), Julie Podmore (2013a), along with Catherine Nash and Andrew Gorman-Murray (2014). In their reflections on gay space development and the change in the form of gay villages in large cities, they refer to investigators who have examined the politics of its development, citing the work of Collins (2004a) and Nash (2005, 2006), as well as Ruting (2008). Drawing on the work of others, such as Rushbrook (2002), Tucker (2009a) and Doan and Higgins (2011), they show that there has been considerable interest in the notion that gay villages, districts or neighbourhoods have been interpreted as complicit in urban regeneration schemes, the exclusions they generate – most often in terms of class and race – and more recently the idea of de-gaying (Casey, 2004; Ghaziani, 2011). Finally, they make the observation that 'these sites also remain conceptually central to the research developing on LGBT-friendly neighbourhoods beyond the gay village' (Podmore, 2013a, p. 264). The city centre or districts known outside gay spatial references as gay are, however, not necessarily to be found in central districts of large cities but have also emerged in suburban contexts – parts of cities that for most of the past century have been understood as spaces of heterosexual socialization and reproduction (Gorman-Murray, 2006a; Nash and Gorman-Murray, 2014). There are increasing examples of gay and lesbian migration away from Central Business Districts CBDs to suburban areas in cities such as Sydney, Australia (Gorman-Murray and Waitt, 2009) and Johannesburg in South Africa since the early 2000s. In the latter city, even the annual gay pride march has been rerouted

---

1   For earlier multidisciplinary research with an explicit focus on the relationship between sexuality and space, see Visser (2013).

to criss-cross a suburban neighbourhood to the north of the CBD. This also gestures towards the issue of gay identity and a necessary urban realm of identity expression. 'Being gay' is no longer confined to 'big cities'. 'The urban' or 'large cities' are not necessarily the spaces that gay identities seek out and where their gay socialization and sexual identity is shaped and developed. There are diverse examples of lived gay lives/communities in places such as Alice Springs, Australia (Johnston and Longhurst, 2010), the North American Great Plains (Annes and Redlin, 2013) and Southern states in the USA (Eaves, 2013), as well as Hastings, Rother and East Sussex in the UK (Browne and McGlynn, 2013), along with rural places in south-western France (Annes and Redlin, 2012b), supporting this view. In addition, rural areas are also part of those spaces that are sexualized as queer, as improbable as it might appear at first (Gorman-Murray, Pini and Bryant, 2013).

The gay/urban nexus has also been expanded towards cities and towns in countries beyond the developed Global North. Initially, this type of research aimed to align those experiences seen in the developed North with those of their case study areas in the South (Visser, 2003a, 2003b). In most cases there appears to be a growing challenge to the notion that gay sexuality is necessarily expressed in urban space through leisure facilities and support services and very seldom leads to the development of consolidated spaces in the forms of gay villages or neighbourhoods (Luongo, 2007; Tamale, 2011). It has been suggested that the link between gay sexuality and urban space could be traced to the idea of safety in numbers. Given the extreme intolerance to sexuality difference in a range of regions outside the developed North this line of reasoning might have suggested numerous gay districts or neighbourhoods in the Global South. Yet, this is simply not the case. The opposite suggestion is that the greater the level of freedom allowed in constitutional or legislative protection, the more likely the change of gay leisure and related services clustering becomes. Once again, drawing on experiences in places with liberal constitutions, this is clearly not the case either. The argument has been made for a post-gay world: one in which the identity marker 'gay' or 'lesbian' is conceptually redundant (Doan and Higgins, 2011; Ghaziani, 2011; Nash, 2013b). The binary between gay and heterosexual spaces is not stable or required: it was a particular Northern moment that was never universally true. The contradictions are seen in the large-scale expansion of consolidated gay space in many large Northern cities, such as Amsterdam, London and Sydney, together with, for example, civil liberties, as compared to mainly an absence of such developments in most other parts of the world. The general tenor in the debates of some Northern researchers is that the binary of included and excluded sexualities in urban space has also not acknowledged the changing nature of the heterosexual world towards different sexualities (Visser, 2013). It is not as if all societies exclude gay people, at least certainly not from a legislative point of view (Visser, 2003a, 2003b), but economically and socially, too. Much of Europe, in addition to countries such as Argentina, Canada and South Africa, and some states in the USA, for example, has equalized the rights of gay and lesbian citizens in all manner of societal spheres. This state of affairs has at least partly been brought about by changes in how heterosexual communities view gay identities and their place in society. This is not to claim that gay identities can be expressed always overtly in the public domain, but at least there are no legal sanctions against them. Then again, such a claim requires considerable qualification as prejudices still exist and gay performativity is edited, or homonormalized, to suit heterosexual expectations of acceptable behaviour (Johnston and Longhurst, 2010; Tucker, 2009a). The general point is that heterosexuals, like homosexuals, are not a uniform, monolithic 'cohort' of people and ideas or a sexuality majority against which gay theorists should solely pit their theoretical claims and activism. As 'being gay' has myriad expressions and has changed over time so, too, has the heterosexual world against which gay theoretical critiques are pitched. The very fact that full citizenship has been extended legislatively to a minority 'cohort', such as homosexuals, demonstrates that, at least in some places, such as Belgium, France, Iceland, Portugal, Spain, Sweden and the Netherlands, to name a few, the manner in which heterosexuals view gay people has moved considerably over time.

The key point is that, at least in law, the position of gay people in many societies has improved dramatically over the past decades. There are, however, dangers in this line of reasoning. Its claims can lead to the suggestion that there is a somewhat linear mode of 'progression', from total exclusion of gay lives to one of acceptance, at play (Podmore, 2013a). It could be argued that this sometimes seems to be a teleological view that gay persons will initially form compacts, then communities, which will lead to mobilization which will find some sort of political traction and spatial consolidation, and lead to inclusion into the heterosexual world at the end of this evolutionary tract. This is not necessarily the case, and it ignores the historical fact that all forms of exclusion and inclusion are fluid and historically, as well as spatially, contingent. Current developments in places such as Russia and a slew of African countries demonstrate how supposed gains in the rights of gay men have and can be lost, with draconian legislation recently introduced, ranging from imprisonment through to execution. Then again, many gay men, despite their context, do create lived gay lives (Tamale, 2011).

This leads to another issue, particularly related to regions beyond the Northern realm of understanding – namely, the debate surrounding gay men and their relationship to urban place and space. The first is the act of naming men who have sex with men as 'gay', and particularly 'gay' in the Northern understanding or interpretation thereof. Although a number of critiques on naming men who engage sex in with men have been presented, there remains a latent idea that 'we know what gay is' (Ghaziani, 2011; Luongo, 2007; Tamale, 2011). A particularly strong debate has been generated in regions where the act of same-sex contact does not equate to a gay identity – for example, many places in Africa and the Middle East. El Feki (2013), Epprecht (2010), Luongo (2007) and Tamale (2011) note how such identities are expressed in complex ways in urban space. Then there is also the example that in some societies femme trans individuals are part of the cultural and social fabric of particular countries as is the case with Brazilian *travesti*, Indian *Hijra*, and Thai 'ladyboys' (Kulick, 1997).

The view can be expressed that the notion of consolidated gay space is not conceptually universally attainable or viable in contemporary lived gay lives, nor should they be (Browne and Bakshi, 2013b; Gorman-Murray and Waitt, 2009; Nash, 2013; Visser, 2008a, 2013). Perhaps the gay village or neighbourhood of the past is, for now, just that: something that happened at a time, in specific places, for locational and temporal-specific reasons, but is not necessarily required or possible in many places. It has been argued that the normalization of gay lives in the developed North has undermined the need for dedicated gay space in the form of designated neighbourhoods (Nash and Gorman-Murray, 2014; Oswin, 2008). There are ample gay places in terms of leisure activities, but even that seems to have become very specific in terms of leisure, with many support services having closed shop (Hubbard, 2011; Nash and Gorman-Murray, 2014). Yet, perhaps such voices are clouded by more progressive developments in some parts of the world. As seen in a range of Southern contexts, this is not the case, and the likelihood of such spaces developing soon is low. The general question appears to be: is there space for gay space in cities, North or South?

Looking Beyond Consolidated Gay Space

While at some level the gay village or consolidated gay space seems to be waning somewhat in importance in parts of the world (Nash, 2013; Nash and Gorman-Murray, 2014), some gay leisure places have become tailored to the needs of gay men seeking very specific forms of sexual expression. Then again, it has to be acknowledged that this occurrence is not new but perhaps simply resurfacing in a more mainstream manner of which a broader public has become aware (see Holleran, 1978; Kramer, 1978; Rotello, 1997). These places are often hidden from the public gaze – clandestine places of sexual discovery and self-actualization, not dependent on a gay village. These sexual desires are expressed mostly in places removed from the consolidated mainstream gay spaces with 'slamming parties' (drug-fuelled sex parties, usually involving injecting crystal meth) or 'bareback gatherings' (deliberately engaging in unsafe sexual intercourse usually in a group-sex or sometimes one-on-one context – Dean, 2009) organized through social networking sites like Grindr, Manhunt and internet portals such as Bareback Real Time that can take place in myriad spatial locations (Bolding et al., 2005; Daly, 2013). In these cases, gay villages, whether in the Global North or the Global South, are abandoned for 'sexual communions' that straddle diverse urban and even rural places. These types of sexual expressions and gatherings are not subject to either the spatial or temporal constraints of consolidated urban space in terms of business hours or local authority planning schemes and permissions, or judgement. These events and places serve the short-term goal of sexual gratification but do not necessarily create or contribute towards a larger gay identity or community – an observation that is relevant to gay men in both the Global North and Global South.

As a consequence, the notion of gay space as a social gel that keeps together and nurtures a 'broader gay identity/ies' appears increasingly questionable. For many gay men in the developed urban North the spatial realm in which gay socialization and physical action takes place appears to have moved into virtual spaces of engagement and identity consolidation that are articulated in potentially any given real or virtual space, and most of the time actualized in what might be seen as heterosexual spaces, with the participants laying no claim to creating or consolidating a differently sexualized identity or space. In addition, given recent events in some regions of the developing South, this strategy might become among the few recourses gay men or men who have sex with men have. The key observation is that understanding links between physical urban spaces and gay sexuality needs to be increasingly read through the impact of virtual and transient sexual communities.

Conceptually, it could be argued that the notion of urban gay life as community and the gay village as an expression thereof requires rethinking across the globe. The manner in which we seek to understand the relationship between lived gay sexuality and urban spaces needs to take a great deal more account of the expanding notion of the gay individual who seeks out fluid and often changing groupings of people – gay or otherwise – in urban life, which greatly complicates the idea of consolidated gay spaces. This issue is currently demonstrated in two very different contemporary trends. The first is the idea that acceptance in many Northern contexts has seemingly diluted the imperative for gay space and place – much of which has been flagged already. The second is its antithesis as observed in a range of regions beyond the Global North, where gay individuals are facing ever harsher sanctions. In this respect, it also means that the focus of any work on gay sexualities needs to revisit an activist past that many of the new generation of gay-focused scholars have perhaps left behind for more intellectual pursuits when the battle for equal human rights appears again to be in question (Cameron, 2014). Perhaps a different route to theorizing the relationship between gay sexuality and space would be scalar and far more place-specific. Politically and/ or socially recent discourse will impact on our ability to theorize the relationship between gay sexuality and urban space. Current legislation in countries as diverse as Nigeria, Russia, Uganda and much of the Muslim world, brings into question the idea that visible consolidated gay spaces in the form of gay villages will and can develop in these countries in the same way in which they did in the Global North. In fact, even the development of mere gay bars or clubs and focused service providers becomes problematic in these places. Yet, there are gay places and spaces in many countries that, in general, would be seen as homophobic. It is against such a backdrop that I would argue for scalar-calibrated analyses. There needs to be sensitivity to the fact that gay lives are accepted at a national scale, but at a micro-level they are not. One can think of legislative meta-narratives such as South Africa or France, where gay life is constitutionally or legally protected, but the actualization of those gay lives is compromised by local resistance to expressions of such identity. On the other hand, a national context can be homophobic yet still present ample social spaces for expression of sexuality difference in places such as Beirut (Moussawi, 2013) or many of the rural plain states in the USA.

Methodologically, these observations present many challenges. If the aim is to regain representative territory in academic discourses, gay studies need to engage larger sample sizes in very diverse spatial contexts. Introspection in the Global North has to be balanced with broader representation from the South. As is increasingly suggested, the notion of developing theory around a handful of investigations in very specific places will not suffice (Nash and Gorman-Murray, 2014). Consequently, larger, intercontinental investigations are required, working from similarly agreed research questions and objectives.

Internal to those debates seeking to understand gay sexualities and urban space intersections in the Global South, but of equal relevance to the Global North, there is a need to open up broader investigatory territory. Gay theory and its desire to link gay men to urban spaces, concentrated or not, will also require different informants – importantly, those who are not gay. This is an issue for scholars investigating both Global Northern and Global Southern gay realities. Investigative studies dealing with gay men in urban spaces seldom include the views of heterosexual participants. The first point of departure would be that current debates have mainly been concerned with how gay people experience heterosexual urban spaces around them, while the converse is not explored. Given the increasing intolerance towards gay people in a number of regions, the question arises as to what way greater acceptance of gay minorities is contingent on understanding gay people in ostensibly straight spaces, and what that means strategically.

SECTION II
Sexual Politics

Kath Browne and Gavin Brown (editors)

Chapter 8

Sexual Politics: Section Introduction

Gavin Brown and Kath Browne

Gay politics, in the form of campaigning for Harvey Milk's historic candidature for the San Francisco Board of Deputies, was a key variable in Castells's (1983) classic study of the formation of gay neighbourhoods. Lesbian and gay social movements and activism – and more recent variations of lesbian, gay, bi and trans (LGBT) and/or queer politics – have been a central theme within the geography of sexualities literature since the 1980s. Geographers have both theorized claims to sexual citizenship and queerer forms of politics that are suspicious of incorporation into state-centred political structures. More recently, geographers have fiercely debated 'homonormativity', 'homonationalism' and the changing sexual politics of neoliberal times. This work has tended to focus on the political demands and organizational methods of sexual and gender minority social movements in the Global North. In contrast, this section thinks more expansively about the geographies of sexual politics and the political geographies of sexuality. While we do not disregard 'traditional' LGBTQ spatial politics that have frequently sought to claim (urban) territory as a springboard for demanding social inclusions and civil rights, this introduction and the section as a whole is also interested in queerer politics, and sexual and gender activisms that spread beyond the LGBTQ umbrella.

Creating a section on sexual politics in a book about sex and sexualities might be read as confining politics to this section. However, writing on sex and sexualities in geographies remains a political act, so every chapter in this book can be considered political. To delimit sexual politics for the purposes of this section, we address specific political forms, recognizing that there are other lines that might be drawn around sexual and sexed politics and that these are equally valid. This introduction will first address equalities and sexual citizenship, exploring changes in sexual citizenships and the place of hetero/homonormativities in geographical scholarships. Following this, we move to explore different forms of activism, outlining those that are related to the state, Pride, AIDS and queer politics. Moving to geopolitics, the introduction recognizes that sexual politics are increasingly globalized as they contest uneven geographies of repressive legislations, 'gay friendly' territories, neo-colonial power relations and expressions of homonationalism.

Equalities and Sexual Citizenships

Sexual citizenship (Bell, 1995a, 1995b; Bell and Binnie, 2000; Evans, 1993) is a term used to describe the interconnections between sexual and political rights and obligations in a specific context, especially as they shape the lives of sexual and gender minorities. It describes the ways in which political geography impacts most directly on the sexual lives of individuals in a given national context. There have been a series of significant shifts in sexual citizenship since geographers first began to think spatially about sexual difference in the 1980s. Over the last 50 years, as the sociologist Jeffrey Weeks (2007) has articulated, there have been a series of 'unfinished revolutions' in relation to sexual politics around the world. Gender relations are now more equal than they were in the mid-twentieth century but they are not yet fully equalized, and there remains significant intransigence around differential gender roles. Women, at least in the Global North, have more control over their bodies, including how, when and if they will have children. Although heterosexuality is still institutionally privileged in most countries, it is now more possible to lead openly gay lives in many places. This has resulted in changing geographies of 'closet space' and new forms of queer visibility – neither of which are globally uniform (M. Brown, 2000; Tucker, 2009a). It is not just homosexuality that has 'come out'; people are now more aware of bisexuality, trans issues and, increasingly, asexual and intersex people (see the chapter by Vine and Cupples in this volume). Sex is everywhere, often openly discussed and no longer as taboo as it was in even the recent past. However, these trends are not unproblematic and have not gone unchallenged. In a number of countries where increasing freedoms are afforded to some adults there are concerns about the sexualization of childhood and the growing commodification of the erotic. Similarly, sexual abuse and domestic violence continue to be significant problems, even as their dynamics are changing and they, too, are becoming less taboo than they were before (Pain, 2014a).

These new equalities are not universal; they challenge religious fundamentalisms and extreme expressions of nationalism of various kinds. There are still many countries in which homosexuality is subject to legal sanctions (Itaborahy and Zhu, 2014), but members of sexual and gender minorities are more visible in certain national and international contexts (including in the UN and at events such as the Olympics) than they were a few decades ago, and cultural attitudes to homosexuality and gender variance continue to shift, albeit not in a simple, linear progression. These social changes mean that sexual citizenship has been discussed in very different terms by geographers writing at different times and in different place-specific historical contexts. For example, Knopp (1998) suggested that gay politics had developed distinct trajectories in the UK, the USA and Australia (over the preceding few decades) because of the different forms that local and national government took in those countries. He suggested that in the USA, far more than in Britain or Australia, minorities needed to cluster together in specific territories in order to maximize their influence, as a voting bloc, in city politics (Knopp, 1998). In cities like London, he suggested, instead of consolidating gay political power in a specific territorial location, gay men in the 1990s were more likely to appropriate and contest everyday public spaces through 'their actions and their self-representations' (Knopp, 1998, p. 162). Whereas American gay men had been attempting from the 1970s to build economic and political influence within the formal institutions of the local and national state, in the UK, he suggested, gay men implemented a 'cultural politics of resistance', challenging dominant social norms outside of formal institutions.

For much of the 1990s, as geographers were establishing the validity of studying sexuality within the discipline, researchers focused much of their attention on the ways in which 'heteronormativity' functions and is reproduced. Heteronormativity is the term used to describe the various ways in which heterosexuality is privileged over forms of desire and, key to this is normative gender presentation, identities and sexed embodiments within the binary of man/woman, male/female. By extension, romantic (heterosexual) coupledom is privileged over other ways of organizing intimate relations.

A whole field of social relations becomes intelligible as heterosexuality, and this privatized sexual culture bestows on its sexual practices a tacit sense of rightness and

64

normalcy. The sense of rightness – embedded in things and not just in sex – is what we call heteronormativity. Heteronormativity is more than ideology or prejudice, or phobia against gays and lesbians, it is produced in almost every aspect of the forms and arrangements of social life: nationality, the state, and the law; commerce; medicine; education; plus the conventions and affects of narrativity, romance and other protected spaces of culture. (Berlant and Warner, 2002, p. 194)

Thus, heterosexuality shapes many of the institutions and spaces that people encounter as they go about their daily lives. Examining how heteronormativity operated spatially was central to much of the early British work by geographers of sexuality (Bell et al., 1994; Valentine, 1993c). Heteronormativity does not only serve to discipline the lives of sexual minorities; it also polices the boundaries of acceptable forms of heterosexuality, marginalizing those who are made to feel as if they do not live up to these normative expectations (Hubbard, 2007).

Since the early 2000s the concept of 'homonormativity' has also gained currency (Duggan, 2002; Bell and Binnie, 2004; D. Richardson, 2004, 2005; G. Brown, 2009). Visser (2008a) acknowledged that this process of 'normalization' involved changes and adaptations in the functioning of 'straight' spaces, as well as adaptations in the behaviour and spatial practices of LGBT people. In the context of the new legal equalities achieved by lesbians and gay men in many countries, and more liberal social attitudes towards sexual difference, homonormativity has been described as 'a [sexual] politics that does not contest dominant heteronormative assumptions and institutions but upholds them and sustains them' (Duggan, 2002, p. 179). In other words, those lesbians and gay men who settle down in long-term relationships are no longer seen to threaten or transgress mainstream heteronormative assumptions about the centrality of the family in social life. Homonormativity has also been used to note the alignment with, and dissent from, hegemonic sexual and gendered forms, including through intersectional engagements with class, race, genders, disabilities and other creations of hegemonic and marginal social differences (Haritaworn et al., 2013; Bailey and Shabazz, 2014; Konrad, 2014; Oswin, this volume). Since the concept of homonormativity began to be commonly used by geographers, the concepts of sexual citizenship have been discussed less frequently. However, as should be clear, these concepts are linked and the social acceptance afforded to lesbians and gay men living 'homonormative' lives is a result of the specific advances in 'sexual citizenship' that have been achieved in the last two decades.

Geographers have been conscious of the aspatiality of much theorizing regarding homonormativities and the ways in which queer people can be complicit in the reproduction of privilege and inequality (G. Brown, 2012; Oswin, 2004). We would caution against focusing only on the study of homonormativity (critically or otherwise) at the expense of continuing to explore the potential of other forms of sexual citizenship. In her ethnography of the 'pansexual BDSM scene' in the San Francisco Bay area, Weiss (2011) demonstrates that 'homonormativity' is not the only expression of the sexual politics of neoliberalism. When exploring the contestation of LGBT equalities in Canada and the UK there is evidence that, rather than subsiding, opposition to sexual and gender rights agendas is growing and needs to be attended to alongside other power relationships (see Browne and Nash, 2014b; Nash and Browne, 2015).

From the inception of the term, studies of homonormativity have tended to focus on how lesbians and gay men have accommodated to heteronormative values. However, if we acknowledge that heteronormativity and homonormativity are linked (and are, essentially, two expressions of the same set of social relations), then it is important also to consider how the redefinition of 'the family' to incorporate certain types of same-sex couples is also being used to regulate and exclude other types of (potentially heterosexual) relationships and households. For example, Gavin Brown (forthcoming) argues that the approval of same-sex marriage in the UK in 2013 needs to be read against the introduction, that same year, of the 'bedroom tax' which penalized households receiving government housing benefit towards the cost of renting a home that was deemed to have more bedrooms than they needed. Just as some (cohabiting) same-sex couples acquired state recognition for their relationships, some single people and others who organized their relationships and families in less conventional ways were delegitimized by the logic of targeted cuts in state welfare spending (Wilkinson, 2013). To link this to a concept that has been overlooked in geography in recent years, the 'charmed circle' of socially acceptable expressions of sexuality has been redrawn (Rubin, 1984) and the fault lines of sexual politics no longer necessarily divide along the hetero/homosexual binary.

Activisms

Activism has been a recurring theme and focus for research in the geographies of sexualities literature over the last three decades. In large part, this is because activism by sex and gender social movements have originated in, and helped to shape, the urban spaces that the geographers of sexualities have tended to study. Alongside Castells's (1983) study of gay politics in San Francisco, Knopp (1987) examined how successes by lesbian and gay social movements in Minneapolis in the mid-1980s began to reshape the city's urban geography. In a British context, Manchester City Council was probably the first local authority to attempt to harness its political links with local lesbian and gay activists to develop the city's gay village as part of a broader urban regeneration and place marketing strategy (Quilley, 1997). In Brighton, the promotion of the city as the 'gay capital of the UK' helped activists to argue for better services and provisions for LGBT people when these failed to be achieved (Browne and Bakshi, 2013a).

Gay liberation politics (in the USA, the UK and other countries) emerged out of those urban neighbourhoods where lesbians and gay men congregated in the late 1960s and early 1970s. As those neighbourhoods became larger and more visible throughout the 1970s, the tensions within those social movements became more apparent. Activist groups frequently split along gender lines, with many lesbians seeing that they had more common interest with other women in the feminist movement than with gay men (Ettorre, 1978). Similarly, tensions often re-emerged between those counter-cultural gay activists who wanted to see sexuality 'liberated' for everyone (dissolving differences between gay and straight), and those more reformist activists who sought human rights for lesbians and gay men, as well as some form of equality with heterosexuals (Collins, 2004a; Sycamore, 2004). This binary continues to be contested in relation to debates about the role of capitalism in the commercialization of lesbian and gay identities (Bassi, 2006; see also Bassi, this volume; di Feliciantonio, this volume), state involvement in LGBTQ organizations and activism (Andrucki and Elder, 2007; Browne and Bakshi, 2013a; Chen, this volume) and, conceptually, in relation to queer thinking and queer complicities (Oswin, 2004).

One of the key tactics of the gay liberation movement, which persists today in various forms, was the appropriation of public space for 'gay pride' events (Brickell, 2000). By taking to the streets, and making themselves visible to wider publics, lesbian and gay activists sought to challenge prejudice and social stigma, demonstrating that they had 'pride' in their sexuality (and were not embarrassed by it). It is a measure of how sexual politics has changed over the last four decades that these are now more commonly referred to as LGBT Pride events, attempting to encompass a broader range of sexual and gender minorities. While even the early pride marches harnessed camp humour alongside anger, many pride events are now more carnivalesque celebrations of local LGBT businesses and communities. Pride festivals have now become major tourist attractions in many locations (Johnston, 2009). Although some radical activists have criticized pride parades for becoming consumption opportunities devoid of politics (G. Brown, 2007a), for other critics they remain more paradoxical 'parties with politics' (Browne, 2007a), exceeding critiques of their homonormative tendencies (di Feliciantionio, this volume). At the same time, in many parts of the world, the constraints on LGBT people making themselves visible in public space mean that pride events, when they occur, are still contested and highly political.

The gay neighbourhoods of North America (as well as Europe and Australia) became laboratories for new forms of politics in the early 1980s as they were forced to find ways of responding to the devastating impacts of the AIDS crisis. While the sex-positive cultures of the 'gay ghettos' facilitated the spread of HIV (before the retrovirus was identified), these close-knit communities also came together to develop 'safer sex' practices, to care for the sick and dying (a task in which lesbians also played a significant role) and to fight for access to appropriate medical treatment (M. Brown, 1995a; Geltmaker, 1997). Although some responses to the early impact of AIDS were the 'implicit activism' (Horton and Kraftl, 2009) of caring for the sick, the AIDS crisis of the mid-1980s in North America also inspired angrier activist responses. ACT UP (the AIDS Coalition to Unleash Power) was formed in New York City in 1987 as 'a diverse, non-partisan group united in anger and committed to direct action to end the AIDS crisis' (Crimp and Rolston, 1990, p. 13). It inspired similar groups to form in major cities across North America and Europe. ACT UP challenged discrimination against people with HIV as well as pressing for them to gain access to clinical trials of experimental drug treatments. Members of ACT UP engaged in direct action and civil disobedience to advance their cause (Shepard and Hayduk, 2002; Wolfe and Sommella, 1997).

For the last 25 years queer activism has presented itself as a radical (and more inclusive) alternative to mainstream lesbian and gay activism. Queer politics initially grew out of AIDS activism, when some activists from ACT UP realized that they had been prioritizing gay men's health issues over broader challenges to the structures and discourses through which heterosexuality reproduced its own privilege. Queer activism developed in tandem with queer theory, with many early queer theorists playing a role in street based polemics in the early 1990s. Groups like Queer Nation (in New York City) sought to transform urban space so that all sexual and gender minorities might feel safe, not just in 'gay' neighbourhoods but in all the spaces that they used in their everyday lives (Berlant and Freeman, 1993). Queer celebrated difference from the norms of heterosexual society and resisted the idea that lesbian, gay and trans people should modify their behaviour or their appearance in order to fit in. Over time, queer activism frequently came to critique the actions of 'homonormative' lesbian and gay politicians and businesses more than it addressed the perpetuation of heteronormativity (G. Brown, 2007a). However, alongside the commonplace use of 'LGBT' as an umbrella term, symbolically (albeit not unproblematically) linking the experiences and interests of lesbians, gay men, bisexuals and trans people, queer politics has opened up a space for new forms of sex and gender politics to emerge.

Geopolitics

The preceding two sections primarily address sexual politics on a national and a subnational scale. In contrast, we now turn to examine how sexual politics shapes international relations and contemporary geopolitics. Sexual politics informs the relationships between nation-states and their respective populations in various ways. In the colonial era, Europeans frequently represented the sexual lives of colonized people in problematically exoticized ways (G. Brown et al., 2010; Epprecht, 2008). In the contemporary world, sexual politics has a material impact on the regulation of immigration, shaping whose relationships are recognized and whose are treated with suspicion or disregard at the border (Luibheid and Cantu, 2005; Marmo and Smith, 2012). With the extension of marriage equality to same-sex couples in some polities at the same time that new laws restricting the rights of sexual minorities have been enacted (or threatened) elsewhere, the politics of sexuality, intimacy and gender have acquired new significance in global geopolitics.

In recent years attacks on the human rights of LGBT people in countries such as India, Russia and Uganda have elicited international condemnation, grassroots campaigns and diplomatic interventions from the USA, Canada and several European countries. Until recently the geopolitics of sexuality was largely implicit in the ways in which diplomacy and international relations contributed to the promotion of different expressions of heteronormative 'family values' (Cowen, 2003; Massaro and Williams, 2013; Oswin, 2007a, 2007b; Sharp, 2001; see also Foster, this volume). In the last two decades the global promotion of lesbian and gay (but, far less frequently, trans) equalities and human rights by a variety of state and non-state actors has made sexuality highly visible in international relations. The EU has positioned itself as a defender of LGBT rights, and sexual politics have been a matter of tense debate within several Central and East European countries before (and after) their accession to membership of the EU (Binnie and Klesse, 2012; Kulpa and Mizielinska, 2011). Indeed, it appears likely that the geopolitical imperative for Russia to distinguish itself from the EU partly contributed to the socially conservative ban on the distribution of 'propaganda' promoting 'non-traditional sexual relationships' in Russia.

There is a common perception that those countries at the forefront of promoting 'progressive' sexual politics (including LGBT equalities) globally are nations like Canada, the Netherlands, the Scandinavian countries and the UK. Several of these countries certainly engage in high-profile acts of popular geopolitics (Dodds, 2014), presenting themselves as promoters of LGBT equality – for example, by sending senior diplomats to support LGBT Pride events in countries where these events are at risk. Yet, when the United Nations Human Rights Commission reiterated its opposition to discrimination and violence on the basis of sexual orientation and gender identity in September 2014, the motion gained significant support from countries outside Europe and North America. The resolution was sponsored by Brazil, Chile, Colombia and Uruguay and 42 other countries acting as co-sponsors. While global attention has been focused on those African and post-Soviet countries with poor human rights records against LGBT people, many commentators appear to have overlooked the development of Latin America as a 'tolerant', 'pro-gay' geopolitical bloc in world politics. Similarly, when examining the promotion of hard-line heteronormativity internationally, and the instigation of legislation that criminalizes homosexuality, it is clear that Christian Right organizations from the USA have significant influence in places such as Uganda (Buss and Herman, 2003; Valentine et al., 2013).

There have been three main critiques of the trend for certain countries (and NGOs based in the Global North) to promote gender and sexual equality through their international relations. The first critique acknowledges that there is a danger that such interventions perpetuate neocolonial relations which recentre the sexual identities, lifestyles and politics of certain metropolitan areas in the Global North (G. Brown et al., 2010; Rushbrook, 2002; Grewal and Kaplan, 2001; Cruz-Malavé and Manalansan, 2002; Puar et al., 2003). Without often intending to do so, privileged activists and commentators from Europe and North America can present themselves as the 'saviours' of people living elsewhere in the world. A second critique is that these politics are 'homonationalist' in that they simultaneously incorporate lesbian and gay rights into the orientation of those countries to the world, as well as other expressions of their nationalisms, but that they also encourage the alignment of some gay constituencies with the interests of the nation (Puar, 2007). In a recent reflection on homonationalism, Puar (2013) acknowledged that this is not simply a practice undertaken by the national state. Instead, Puar (2013, p. 337) argues that homonationalism represents 'the historical convergence of state practices, transnational circuits of queer commodity culture and human rights paradigms, and broader global phenomena such as the increasing entrenchment of Islamophobia. These are just some of the circumstances through which nation-states are now vested with the status of "gay-friendly" versus "homophobic."'

As Puar (2007) and other scholars (El-Tayeb, 2012; Tauquir et al., 2011) have argued, at the very time that some lesbians and gay men have become more incorporated into mainstream society in the Global North (and, arguably, less 'queer' in the process), their rights have been used to justify ideological attacks on Islam and military attacks on Muslim countries, such that the bodies of Muslim people have come to be seen as suspiciously queer. The final critique of the new geopolitics of sexuality is that some countries, most notably Israel, have used their support for lesbian and gay rights domestically and internationally as a means of 'pink-washing' and that this distracts from the human rights violations that they perpetuate against other people (Ritchie, 2014). In recent years Israel has invested heavily in promoting the country as 'the only gay-friendly state' in the region and has promoted Tel Aviv as a desirable gay tourist destination. These popular geopolitical interventions are used to distract attention from the occupation of Palestinian lands and disproportionate military assaults on Gaza (Baum, 2006; Ziv, 2010; see also Misgav in this volume). There is, of course, an element of truth to some aspects of the Israeli propaganda – Israel does offer far greater legal recognition of (and protection for) some sexual minorities than many of its neighbours (Kuntsman, 2009). However, it is important to acknowledge that the political uprisings and unrest across North Africa and the Eastern Mediterranean since 2011 has opened up new, fragile and contradictory spaces for the contestation of conservative sexual politics in the region (Amar, 2013; El Feki, 2013).

The Contributors

The contributions to Section II consider not only different forms of grassroots politics around sexuality, but also the uneven sexual politics of contemporary globalization and geopolitics. The section starts with politics that addresses violence at the bodily scale and extends outwards to consider the ways in which particular forms of sexual politics are reproduced through policies to address environmental concerns affecting the whole planet.

The section begins with Jason Lim and Alex Fanghagel's examination of sexual politics in relation to different expressions of heterosexuality. They explore recent popular challenges to gender-based violence and question what these reveal about contemporary heterosexuality and gender relations. They argue that 'safekeeping – as much as gender-based violence itself – has produced gendered spatial exclusion and entrapment'. This chapter demonstrates how political concerns about unequal gender relations can also serve to reinforce the boundaries of sexual identities.

Emma Foster draws on queer eco-feminism to pose vital questions about the sexual politics of environmental policies. In particular, she examines the heteronormative reproductive futurity of demands for more 'sustainable' living. She argues that sustainability discourses are created by and reproduce ethnocentric forms of heteronormativity that can only conceive of the reproduction of future generations in the context of biological parenthood within heterosexual families. She suggests that queer ecologies can work to re-envision 'nature in creative and (potentially) environmentally-friendly ways', offering exciting new potentials at the intersection of sexual and environmental politics. These are debates which have seldom been explicitly addressed from the perspective of geographies of sexualities, and we are excited to present them here.

Cesare di Feliciantionio considers how, in the context of Southern European austerity, Pride demonstrations in Italy might articulate a sexual politics that exceeds 'homonormative' citizenship claims. He challenges the ubiquitous critiques of Pride marches as 'merely mainstream and commercial', contending that there is a need to account for 'the territorial, social, cultural and political embeddedness of Pride marches' and the politics that they can and do create. Chen Misgav's chapter similarly considers how radical queer groups can both operate within state support *and* disrupt homonormative power relations through an exploration of the 'Trans in the Centre' group and its creation of queer autonomous spaces. In considering radical queer activism in Tel Aviv, Chen questions the homonationalist 'pink-washing' of the Israeli state (from within).

Camila Bassi's exploration of Shanghai's Super Girl competition in 2004-2005, which gave rise to a 'lesbian heyday' in the city, challenges the apparent need to reconfigure Marxism through poststructuralism. Instead, in similar way to how di Feliciantonio problematizes common critiques of Pride parades, Bassi argues that 'commodification of human culture is not crudely or merely capitalist exploitation and social alienation, because there is always human agency'. Popular culture is also at the core of Natasha Vine and Julia Cupples's chapter. They explore the presence of trans women of colour on television and in other mediated spaces to begin a discussion of intersectional geopolitics. Arguing that domestic and foreign policy are underpinned by dominant conceptualizations of race, gender and sexuality, they contend that mediated spaces, as they overlap with 'queer lived experience', can offer new political possibilities that expand state-based geopolitical agendas.

In her chapter, Natalie Oswin discusses how Singapore has promoted specific forms of heteronormativity as part of its citizenship and nation-building strategies. She shows how a postcolonial politics of intimacy in Singapore centralizes particular forms of family, kinship and domesticity. These forms of citizenship queer not only gays and lesbians, but also the 'single, the uneducated, the unskilled migrant workers and many others who have been deemed incapable of creating and sustaining a "quality" population'. This discussion of postcolonialism then leads neatly to Section III, 'Decolonializing Sexualities'.

Conclusion

Sexual politics is a key aspect of geographical work on sexualities. Understanding how sexual politics is spatialized is central to engaging with manifestations of sex and gender social movements, local- and national-level policies, and geopolitical relations between states. Political engagements with sex and sexualities are not static. As some approaches emerge and others decline, the ways in which they develop and travel locally, nationally and transnationally are crucial to the form they take, their relative 'successes' and the critiques that arise in relation to them. The chapters that follow engage with diverse political traditions. They ask critical questions about how we imagine sexual politics in the contemporary world, as well as considering how these politics might develop in the near future.

Chapter 9

Temptresses and Predators: Gender-based Violence, Safekeeping and the Production of Proper Subjects

Jason Lim and Alexandra Fanghanel

Introduction

If violence is crucial for producing and maintaining social order, then gender-based violence can be understood as crucial for the production and maintenance of gender. While the United Nations Committee on the Elimination of Discrimination against Women (1992) defined gender-based violence as any kind of 'violence that is directed against a woman because she is a woman or that affects women disproportionately' – including, but not limited to, sexual violence, domestic violence and intimate-partner violence – other understandings of gender-based violence consider it to be constitutive of regimes of gender. Gender-based violence effectively polices what are considered to be appropriate modes of femininity and masculinity, which means that such policing affects not only women, but everybody. In particular, trans people – those whose gender or sex identity or expression differs from normative expectations regarding assigned sex identity – face gender-based violence whose purpose is to ensure that everybody conforms to normative expectations about the distinctions between genders (see Doan, 2009, 2010; Merry, 2009).

There is a significant literature that considers the spatialities of gender-based violence and a host of related social and political phenomena. Women's fear of crime is a constructed fear of gender-based violence – in particular, sexual violence – that has a very specific set of geographies. In this chapter we will focus on how women's fear of crime in the city has increasingly come to be understood as a mode of producing appropriate femininity through 'safekeeping' – the discourses and techniques by which women are made to regulate and control their own behaviour in order to keep themselves safe from violent crime. In addition to the production of appropriate femininity, safekeeping also produces proper masculine subjects, as well as raced, classed and sexualized subjects. We consider how safekeeping can be understood in terms of a broader process of securitization, and we will discuss a particular example of safekeeping from London, UK, in which women are advised about the risks of travelling in 'minicabs' (taxis that have to be ordered by phone). To conclude this chapter, we will consider some responses to the deleterious effects of both gender-based violence and safekeeping.

A crucial element of our argument is that gender-based violence, in a broad sense, and sexual violence, more specifically, are implicated in the production of not only gendered subject positions, but also sexual subject positions. For example, sexual violence and harassment in urban public space – as well as the discourses thereof – normalize heterosexuality through producing a particular kind of masculine sexual entitlement and a particular imagination of feminine sexual objectification. Safekeeping may seem like the other side of the coin, but it also normalizes particular modes of heterosexuality by producing appropriate forms of femininity through regulated performances of female sexuality. Our focus in this chapter is on cities in the Global North, but it should be noted that there is also a growing geographical literature on gender-based violence and security in various parts of the Global South (see, for example, Brickell, 2008; Fluri, 2011; McIlwaine, 2013).

Women's Fear of Crime: Questioning the Paradoxes

Much research has been conducted on women's fear of crime (see, for example, Fanghanel, 2014; Koskela, 1997, 1999; Pain, 1991, 1997, 2000; Stanko, 1990, 1995, 1997; Whitzman, 2007) and how it is organized around a public/private structuring of space (Pain, 1997; Staeheli, 1996). Harassment and other forms of sexual violence targeted primarily at women operate to police women's presence in public space (Pain, 2000; Valentine, 1993c). Women's fear of these forms of gender-based violence reinforces this gendered exclusion from public space (Koskela, 1999) and spatial entrapment in the home (Pain, 2014a, p. 538). Alongside such spatial concepts as exclusion and entrapment, we might also use concepts related to mobilities to understand how the threat of violence in public space acts to constrain women's mobility (Sheller, 2008, p. 27). Sheller (2008, p. 28) observes that women are often counselled not to go out at night by themselves. She suggests that such advice needs to be understood not only in terms of an individualized constraint on women's potential for independent mobility, but also in terms of how particular spaces – especially in the night-time city – are produced as constraining of women's mobility (ibid., p. 32). That such advice is so frequently proffered speaks of the way in which fear of crime is actively cultivated through a range of discourses and state apparatuses.

Recognizing that women's fear of crime is something that is cultivated and encouraged is important for understanding the paradoxes that surround such fear: that women fear violent crime in public spaces far more than men do, despite men being much more likely to be subject to such violence (Koskela, 1997); that women's fear of experiencing violent crime in public space is much more pervasive than might be warranted by the actual risks of experiencing such crime (Stanko, 1997). Yet, there have been several ways in which the focus on these paradoxes of women's fear of violent crime in public spaces has been challenged. First, fearfulness is just one reading of women's accounts of their experiences of being in the city. Alternative interpretations emphasize how women describe being courageous in situations that safety discourses might suggest should be fearful and being active producers of the city, rather than just potential victims (Koskela, 1997; Wilson, 1991). Second, Stanko (1997, p. 487) has argued that rather than attempting to understand why women's fear of crime is 'wider' than the actual risk of crime, it is necessary to reconceptualize risk. She suggests that the risk women face from men's violence cannot be understood only in terms of findings from crime surveys; rather, such risk is a constitutive part of women's subjectivities. Risk is a construct within discourses of 'safety' and 'security' – discourses that operate through and alongside techniques of subjectivity. In a practical sense, it is part of many women's everyday experience to negotiate, respond to, evaluate and manipulate the 'risk' of male violence and the social control that such 'risk' potentially enacts (Pain, 1997). That to negotiate, respond to, evaluate and manipulate risk are techniques of subjectivity is clear from the costs of getting these techniques wrong: the cost of experiencing sexual violence from a man is a sullied self (Stanko, 1997, p. 488), but the fear is not only of violence, but of being judged by others as performing femininity badly by not being sufficiently prudent about one's safety (ibid., p. 489).

Yet, the feminine subject imagined to be fearful within discourses of safety is white, middle-class and privileged (Stanko, 1997, p. 483). Third, then, the focus on women's fear of crime has been questioned on the basis that fear, risk and safety are not only gendered, but also characterized by other dimensions of power. Even women's fear of gender-based violence perpetrated by men against women cannot be reduced to being a product of patriarchal power relations. Male sexual harassment of women expresses a sense of entitlement to women's bodies that is so powerful because of how masculine sexual agency is normalized and romanticized within heterosexuality (Gardner, 1995). Moreover, male harassment of, and violence towards, lesbians in public spaces often work to regulate public expressions of both sexuality and gender, effecting a normalization of heterosexuality as part of appropriate femininity (Corteen, 2002; Valentine, 1993c). As well as being gendered and heterosexualized, the structuring of oppression in – and exclusion from – public space is also racialized and ethnicized (Cobbina et al., 2008; Ruddick, 1996). Fanghanel's (2014) study of young women's safekeeping practices in the south-east of England shows how such safekeeping practices are techniques of subjectivity in which gender, race and class status are at stake. The young women in Fanghanel's study distanced themselves from racial and classed Others, not only physically, but also through the imaginative erasure of these Others and the spaces associated with them. Whitzman (2007, pp. 2716–17) points to evidence from a number of surveys from the UK, USA and Australia, which suggest that socioeconomic disadvantage – such as social exclusion on the basis of race, low income, being a single parent and living in urban areas characterized by physical deterioration – is the biggest determinant of fear of crime in public space (see also Cobbina et al., 2008). Although women predominate in many of the groups that experience the highest levels of fear of crime in public space, it is clear that gender is not the only dimension of power, privilege and disadvantage that matters.

Fourth (and finally), a focus on the paradoxes of women's fear of violent crime in public spaces has been questioned on the basis that this literature tends to reproduce the public/private dichotomy, with the unintended consequence that attention is diverted away from investigating fear of violence in private space and how it shapes overall fear of violence (Whitzman, 2007). Given that most gender-based violence is perpetrated by abusers already known to their victims and that most of this violence takes place in private space, the need for analyses that address violence in private as well as public spaces is glaring. Warrington's (2001) landmark study on domestic violence not only problematizes the construction of home as a site of safety, but also details the spatial constraints – borne of fear that their abusers will track them down – that women who break free from domestic violence face in refuges and new homes. Pain's (2014a) discussion of domestic violence is situated within a theoretical framework that works against the assumption that the public is characterized by political forms of violence whereas violence in private space is typically apolitical. In examining domestic violence, she draws upon Pain and Smith's (2008) understanding of fear of violence as an 'assemblage' – something that works through the connected activity of a combination of discourses, technologies, institutions, practices, signs, emotions and so on across different spaces and scales – characterized by the intertwined strands of the geopolitical and the everyday.

Gender-based Violence, Security and Governmentality

Pain's (2014a) situation of domestic violence within a theorization of geopolitics is very interesting for our purposes because it places the concept of 'security' centre stage. We would argue that conceptualizations of security – especially those influenced by Foucault (2007) – are particularly useful for understanding the relationship between fear of gender-based violence, safekeeping and the production of gendered subject positions. Security, according to Foucault (2007), can be understood as a *dispositif* – that is, as an assemblage that produces particular kinds of knowledge and articulates this knowledge with institutional, physical, technological and administrative mechanisms – that has developed since the nineteenth century and has become an increasingly important mode of power since the latter half of the twentieth century. Foucault argues that modern states take on the 'biopolitical' role of managing the health and welfare of national populations and that security is one of the most important means of doing this. The *dispositif* of security is characterized by a number of interconnected technologies: the surveillance of the population at both an collective and individual level, the analysis and management of collective and individual behaviour using the knowledge generated by surveillance, the analysis of threats to welfare in terms of calculable risks and probabilities, the production of a fear of the Other whose threat is understood in terms of risk, and a mode of 'governmentality' in which the aims of securing the welfare of the population is achieved through getting individuals to take on the responsibility for assessing risks and probabilities regarding their (and their friends' and loved ones') health, welfare, safety and so on.

Many of these characteristics are evident in the relationship between fear of gender-based violence and safekeeping. Pain (2014a) argues that domestic violence needs to be understood in a context in which the security state produces fear at various scales, from the global to the everyday, in order to get individuals to regulate their own behaviour in relation to the putative threat of violence. Fearful Others are elicited in the collective imagination – whether the figure of the 'Islamist' terrorist or the dangerous male 'predator' lurking on a dark city street. Within a neoliberal context in which rights come with responsibilities, it becomes individuals' responsibility to assess risks and anticipate future dangers (Pain, 2014a, p. 537). If this can be understood as a mode of governmentality, then it is also important to understand the how this governmentality involves a spatiality in which (potential) victims are kept separate from (potential) perpetrators (Merry, 2001). At a collective level, this spatial governmentality of separation works not only through instruments such as restraining orders (Merry, 2001), but also through the very material and political–economic processes of commodifying the neoliberal city (see, for example, Kern's (2010) paper on the selling of condominiums by appealing to women's constructed fear of crime).

In relation to women's fear of gender-based violence in public space –-and as we shall see in the next section – such a spatial governmentality also operates through technologies that promote 'safekeeping' as a mode of individual responsibility. Such safekeeping includes practices of risk minimization through spatial separation – staying at home at night, keeping to well-lit main roads if one has to go out, avoiding certain neighbourhoods – that work to exclude women from public space (Cobbina et al., 2008; Koskela, 1999; Pain, 2014a). Safekeeping also encourages women to behave and dress in public in a manner that is deemed to reduce their risk of being attacked. Women whose behaviour does not conform to the archetype of the Good Woman – middle-class, law-abiding, hides jewellery in public, does not dress in a short skirt or high heels – find themselves subject to censure or, should they actually be attacked in public, unable to access justice because they are constructed as undeserving of protection (see Stanko, 1997, p. 486). The pressure to conform to such standards of judgement is precisely what Stanko (1997) meant when she suggested that techniques of safety are constitutive of femininity. In the context of a *dispositif* of security, we might conceptualize safekeeping as a mode of governmentality in which individuals are normalized – here, within norms of appropriate heterosexual and classed femininity – in order to make populations more easily governable.

Delegating the problem of crimes involving gender-based violence on to would-be victims (O'Malley, 1992, cited in Stanko, 1997, p. 486) marks the abandonment of alternative modes of tackling gender-based violence. The movement away from crime prevention that targets potential perpetrators and the movement towards 'community safety' approaches (Pain, 2000, p. 382) can be understood as part of a *dispositif* of security within the development of the neoliberal state. In a US context, for example, Bumiller (2008) argues that feminist messages about gender-based violence – in particular, sexual violence – have been appropriated by the state. Sexual violence has become constructed as a 'social problem' to be addressed by social workers, therapists, medical professionals and a host of community-sector organizations. The rhetoric of 'providing services' to the marginalized and disadvantaged who are thought to be most at risk of sexual violence – and of working with and in communities – is accompanied, however, by increasing criminalization of black communities (especially young men), surveillance, control and governmentality. Pain (2014a, p. 542) echoes this by noting how security apparatuses in the UK work with communities to elicit watchfulness from their members, while simultaneously demonizing those communities as a danger.

Bumiller (2008) situates the increasing management and control of individual behaviour within the context of a neoliberal vitiation of welfare policies and other state-led means of tackling the structural conditions of poverty, unemployment and marginalization. Rather than addressing the marginalization and poverty that makes individuals more vulnerable to sexual violence – or empowering individuals and communities to be able to address their marginalization – the state simply finds ways to manage sexual violence through managing individual and family behaviour. In the USA this has led to a polarization of gender-based and race-based interests (Bumiller, 2008, pp. 18, 30) as black men become imagined as the primary source of sexual violence. As Garland (1996, p. 461) suggests, criminal justice systems deploy certain imagined figures – such as 'yobs', 'predators' and 'sex beasts' – and it is the classed, gendered and raced individuals who can be imagined using these stereotypes that predominate among those who are incarcerated (despite sexual violence being prevalent among all sections of the population) and that serve as the figures of fear in safekeeping messages. Once again, security and safekeeping involve the production of particular normative subjectivities – variously virtuous, fallen and dangerous.

Sexual Violence and Safekeeping in the City

'Woman is present in cities as temptress, as whore, as fallen women, as lesbian, but also as virtuous woman in danger, as heroic womanhood who triumphs over temptation and tribulation' (Wilson, 1991, p. 6). Woman is a problem in public space. Wilson may have been discussing nineteenth-century constructions of femininity, but it is striking how pertinent these figurations remain today. As a technique within a neoliberal governmentality of self-policing, safekeeping simultaneously promotes a fear of sexual violence and constructs public spaces as menacing to women. Indeed, Judith Butler (1992) also illustrates how this problem plays out in the criminal justice arena. Describing the accusation levelled by the defending attorney to the victim in the New Bedford gang-rape case – 'if you are living with a man, what are you doing running around on the streets getting raped?' (cited in Butler, 1992, p. 52) – Butler identifies, like Wilson, how being outside the home – running around

75

on the streets – renders the victim 'open season' (Butler, 1992, p. 53); outside of the home, when she should be inside the home with her 'man', the victim is in the improper place – the fearful and sexualized city (England and Simon, 2010; Hubbard and Colosi, 2015) – and, thus, could not expect anything else but to be raped.

These individualizing agendas of blame and responsibility have the insidious effect of rendering victims of sexual assault responsible for their own safety. The Manichean virgin/ whore dichotomy that Wilson gestures at becomes crystallized within criminal justice systems, influencing decisions by police not to pursue investigations or by prosecutors not to take a case to trial because they deem the victim to blame for being assaulted by not conforming to the norm of appropriate – that is, virtuous and careful – femininity. Safety awareness campaigns also reproduce this distinction between proper and improper subjects in relation to the menace of rape. Such campaigns are common in various (quasi-)public spaces such as pub and bar toilets, on public transport and on street signage. Targeting a specific subsection of the population (young women using public spaces, usually at night), such safety awareness campaigns reinforce the construction of public spaces as inherently dangerous, fearsome and menacing to women (Brooks, 2011). Such campaigns act in a disciplining capacity to situate proper and improper subjectivities.

Fanghanel (2013), for instance, investigated the CabWise safety awareness campaign run since 2006 by Transport for London, the body responsible for running and regulating public transport in London, UK. Fanghanel (2013) observed that the campaign included posters (and images for the campaign's website and app store) alerting people to the dangers of going home after a night out in an unlicensed minicab. Whilst the campaign might ostensibly be aimed at both men and women, this campaign predominantly preys on women's fear of rape and sexual assault. One of the images used for the campaign's online app store during 2012 shows part of the face of a racially ambiguous man as he looks into a rear-view mirror of his unlicensed minicab. The text accompanying the image states: 'If your minicab's not booked, it's just a stranger's car.' We – the viewers of this poster – are invited to interpret the gaze as menacing, or at least purposeful and intense. We are also invited to make the link between the man's stare, the fact that he is a 'stranger' and the threat of rape. It is significant that the man's appearance suggests that he might be black, Asian or another non-white ethnicity, given that the deployment of images of male bodies of colour is often taken to connote danger (see Day, 2006). The association between 'blackness', ambiguity, signifiers of danger and fear of crime is a common one (Pain, 2000). When safekeeping advice and campaigns like this use these racist stereotypes of who an offender (and who a victim) might be, we can see how safekeeping discourses reproduce imaginations of proper offenders and proper victims, and what the implications of such campaigns might be for the socially marginalized.

Another of the CabWise images that Fanghanel (2013) analysed depicts the face of a young white woman who is crying and screaming as she faces out of the rear passenger seat window of – we are asked to accept – an illegal minicab. The main text accompanying the image reads: 'Stop, no. Stop, please. No, please. Please stop taking unbooked minicabs.' The first part of this text is intended to evoke the language and tone that a rape victim might use to implore her attacker – unseen in this image – to stop sexually assaulting her. That the aggressor is unseen leaves the viewer of the poster to draw on common imaginations of masculine 'stranger danger' (Day, 2001). The female victim, however, appears white, and her affects are similarly unambiguous: she is the 'proper' sort of victim in the 'proper' place to be raped and the 'improper' place to be safe. What is particularly grotesque about these images is that they are part of a campaign intended to promote safe travel, but that simultaneously construct the cost of not so travelling as sexual violence. Many crimes could occur in these illegal minicabs, perpetrated upon men or women. Sexual violence also happens in licensed minicabs and taxis. The so-called 'Black Cab Rapist', who was convicted in 2009, is believed by police to have drugged and sexually assaulted over 100 women during his 13 years as a London taxi driver (note that the 'Black' in 'Black Cab' refers to the most common colour of licensed taxis in London, not to the perpetrator's ethnic identity). The safety advice in the CabWise images not only plays on the fear of sexual violence and perpetuates an individualized responsibility for safety; it also lends succour to those who would blame victims rather than assailants for sexual violence, as well as reproducing 'proper' and 'improper' femininities and masculinities. In doing so, it helps enable sexual violence to occur with impunity because cases are not brought to trial unless victims can be made to fit with imaginations of 'proper' femininity and assailants can be imagined in terms of an 'improper' masculinity (Jordan, 2004; Torrey, 1990).

Conclusions: Contesting Security

Gender-based violence and, moreover, the *dispositifs* of fear and security that surround it are characterized by a variety of spatialities. Attention in the literature has been given to how safekeeping – as much as gender-based violence itself – has produced gendered spatial exclusion and entrapment. Mobilities approaches have contextualized constraints on the freedom of movement of the body within the production of spaces that enable or constrain mobility (Sheller, 2008). Theorizations that use a Foucauldian understanding of security have focused on techniques of governmentality that produce a spatial separation of potential perpetrators and potential victims (Merry, 2001) through mechanisms that make women regulate their own behaviour, especially in public. More generally, *dispositifs* of security generalize techniques that enable individuals and institutions to calculate the risks of violence associated with particular time-spaces. Thus equipped, women are encouraged through safety awareness campaigns and the like to regulate their spatial behaviour and also to regulate the appearance and performances of their own bodies. Critiques of the emphasis given to the public/private dichotomy in analyses of gender-based violence (Whitzman, 2007) have been followed by more complex theorizations of the spatialities of violence, fear and security. Pain (2014a) and Pain and Smith (2008), in particular, have conceptualized the complex assemblages that link all kinds of violence that enact a relation of power through producing fear – and the fearful security responses to such violence. Such assemblages, they argue, intertwine the geopolitical and the everyday, the global and the local, the public and the private, and the body and its encounters, gestures, movements and affects.

If this rethinking of the scales of security challenges the assumption that private violence, such as domestic violence, is apolitical, then assumptions about the sites of contestation of gender-based violence and security *dispositifs* may also need rethinking (Koopman, 2011). Indeed, Pain (2014b, p. 143, citing Abrahams, 1992, pp. 329–30) advocates that activism be thought of as a kind of action through which people attempt to enact political change rather than being understood in terms of its taking place in a formal and public political sphere. In doing so, Pain (2014b) attempts to open up the possibility for thinking about how individuals can – alone, in private and through small acts – resist abusers' attempts to exert power through domestic violence. Koopman (2011, p. 277) also attempts to stake out what she calls an 'alter-geopolitics' that challenges hegemonic policies of (in)security at a variety of interlinked scales and nurtures alternative kinds of non-violent security in connection. Koopman emphasizes the *activity* of building these alternative securities through the mobilization and connection of bodies in a variety of spaces – homes, the jungle, online – as well as through more traditional means, such as taking to the streets in protest. One of the examples that Koopman (2011, p. 277) offers is that of 'Take Back the Night' marches, while Lim and Fanghanel (2013) have written about the 'SlutWalk' marches that took place in a number of cities around the world in 2011 and 2012. What these marches have in common is the coming together of thousands of women (and, more latterly, men) to challenge not only gender-based violence, but also safekeeping advice – and its implicit victim blaming.

Take Back the Night marches started in San Francisco in 1973 and have taken place annually in numerous North American and some European and Australian cities since the mid-1970s. They have given rise to offshoots such as the UK-based 'Reclaim the Night' marches that started in Leeds, UK in 1977 in response to the police's advice to women to stay at home at night while the 'Yorkshire Ripper' murderer was still at large (Hubbard and Colosi, 2015, pp. 593–4; Take Back the Night, 2014). Hubbard and Colosi (2015) situate the Take Back the Night marches within a broader feminist contestation of adult entertainment and pornography in the city, which the protestors argued normalized constructions of women's bodies as sexual objects for male consumption and which thus encouraged sexual violence. Hubbard and Colosi (2015, p. 594) raise the question of whether such an understanding reproduces a view that women cannot negotiate the city by themselves without protection from the law and through planning, and counterpoise this suggestion with Wilson's (1991) argument that the city offers women the possibility of new and varied pleasures, new modes of sociality that do not necessarily privilege male, heteronormative values.

Hubbard and Colosi's argument raises the question of the relation between feminist attempts to challenge violence and safekeeping, female autonomy in the city, the role of capital and the role of the state. Making the city safer for women is a project that is often tied to attempts to increase the amount and profitability of economic activity in the city (see Thomas and Bromley, 2000). While individualized survival or resistance to gender-based violence has its limits, and while the costs of individualized safekeeping need to be challenged, an emphasis on collective social contestation and recognition (Pain, 2014a, pp. 540–41) needs to be accompanied by a wariness of how feminist messages and knowledge become appropriated by capital and by the state (Bumiller, 2008; Pain, 2014a, p. 542; Stanko, 1997, p. 492). Feminist activists and scholars have produced knowledges about alternative securities that are situated in – and that link together – bodies, homes, sexual relationships, state resources, streets, locales, construction of gender, online spaces and representations, and global geopolitics (Koopman, 2011; Stanko, 1997, p. 488). The complex spatialities of these knowledges and activism are necessary in contesting both gender-based violence and the apparatuses of security and fear that are enshrined around such violence.

Chapter 10

Eco-sexual Normativity and Queer(ing) Ecologies

Emma A. Foster

Introduction

To many mainstream environmentalists and environmental policy-makers the link between sexuality and the environment may not be immediately obvious. However, by just scratching the surface of mainstream environmental theory and policy, the importance of sexuality is illuminated, albeit often framed through a Malthusian anxiety about overpopulation and limited resources. This chapter, from a queer perspective, demonstrates the ways in which (hetero)sexuality and environmental policy are problematically interconnected. Ultimately, through a queer eco-critique, this chapter argues that the heteronormative underpinnings of contemporary international environmental policy discourses work counter to combating environmental degradation through their reliance on Western heterosexualized idea(l)s of coupling and family life. Alternatively, I argue, a queer ecological approach offers a new way to conceptualize human-nature dynamics in service of improved inter-human and inter-species relations.

To that end, this chapter, after detailing some background to international sustainable development policy-making, begins by exploring the discourses that inform and are perpetuated in international sustainable development policy, particularly in relation to the United Nations (UN). In so doing, the chapter first discusses the relationship between heteronormativity and international sustainable development policy discourses. Here, I outline the heterosexualized gendered assumptions relating to, for instance, women as victims and saviours of the natural world as underpinning sustainable development policy. Following on from this, the chapter turns to discuss the ways in which sustainable development discourses prescribe environmentally 'healthy' sexual behaviours – a kind of eco-sexual normativity – by encouraging management of sexuality/reproduction/family size to mitigate environmental harm. In this section the chapter looks at the importance of the (nuclear) family and (hetero)sex as a site of (managed) reproduction in sustainable development policy narratives. Moreover, this section highlights the lack of attention afforded to diverse and non-procreative sexual behaviours. At this juncture, I argue that the heteronormative assumptions underpinning sustainable development policy are flawed as a response to environmental degradation. Finally, the chapter proposes new ways of understanding the relationship between humans and the natural world through the lens of queer theory. This section highlights that interpersonal ethics of care that transcend heteronormative family or kinship ties open up possibilities for a more expansive concern for all living or life-supporting entities. This, in turn, highlights how queer approaches to the environment and 'nature', unlike responses to environmental degradation wrapped up in the discourses of sustainable development, can work 'toward radical ecological ends' (Mortimer-Sandilands, 2010, p. 39).

International Responses to Environmental Concerns: Sustainable Development

It is generally accepted that in 1972 the international community, represented by multilateral agreements through organizations such as the UN, recognized the natural environment to be in danger – a danger caused by human activities such as population growth (reproduction) and economic development (consumption and production). In 1972, informed by various reports such as the *Limits to Growth* report (Meadows et al., 1972), the first UN conference to focus on the environment was held in Stockholm, Sweden (known as the UN Conference on the Human Environment). Most notably, this conference led to the creation of the United Nations Environment Program (UNEP) in order to coordinate international efforts to combat environmental problems. Further, this conference, on the international stage, drew attention to the difficulty in reconciling international and national goals of economic development with environmental sustainability.

By 1992 the international consensus on how to ameliorate the tension between economic development and environmental sustainability – namely, the concept of sustainable development – was accepted as the 'way forward'. Sustainable development was a term coined by the Brundtland Commission (also known as the World Commission on Environment and Development) in the 1980s. Although the term is nebulous and can be interpreted by different organizations and individuals in different ways, the general objective of sustainable development is to balance economic development, through the use of tools like technological innovation and economic incentives, with environmental sustainability. In other words, sustainable development seeks to 'manage' economic development in a way that will not compromise the natural habitat to the disadvantage of present and future generations (Brundtland, 1987). In addition, sustainable development became the buzzword for the UN Conference on Environment and Development (UNCED) held in Rio de Janeiro, in 1992 (more affectionately known as the Rio Earth Summit). UNCED produced a number of policy-informing documents such as the *Rio Declaration* and, more comprehensively, *Agenda 21*, which offered guidelines as to how to achieve sustainable development.

It is the concept of sustainable development outlined at UNCED and immortalized on paper through the *Rio Declaration* and *Agenda 21*, with which this chapter concerns itself. Indeed, although sustainable development has been revised and revisioned in many ways, most recently in *The Future We Want* (2012) document launched at the 20-year review of UNCED and the hope afforded to strategies like the 'Green Economy' (Clémençon, 2012), it has remained the concept that has mobilized (inter)national and local policy-making on environmental matters since its international acceptance in 1992.

The (Re)production of Heterosexualized Gender Norms in International Environmental Policy

Agenda 21 (1992) sought to lay the foundations from which sustainable development could be achieved. The rhetoric used in *Agenda 21* promoted a social, political, economic and environmental focus on development planning and practice. This interrelationship between the social, political, economic and environmental elements to development allowed the document to spend some time considering women's place within the sustainable development agenda. In addition to the more holistic understandings of development endorsed by the language used in *Agenda 21*, the fairly easy acceptance of ecological feminist (ecofeminist) understandings of women's special relationship with the natural world (discussed in more detail later in the chapter) to some extent encouraged and legitimized the special attention afforded to women in this document. Indeed, in the preparatory run up to, and during, UNCED there was a strong ecofeminist lobby holding parallel events such as Planeta Femea (Braidotti et al., 1994). Subsequently, one complete chapter in *Agenda 21* is dedicated to 'Women' whereas, perhaps unsurprisingly, the relationship between men and nature is not considered in any sustained way.

Since 1992 many feminists have problematized the nexus constructed between women and nature at UNCED and through its related documents. For example, Rosi Braidotti, who attended Planeta Femea, said of the event:

> ... *there was a masked tendency to emphasize commonalities between women, resulting in an implicitly essentialist position – women as closer to nature than men – as the basis for a collective decision. Some women did see themselves as better environmental managers than men, and as privileged knowers about the environment, but this position was not propagated in a naive way, rather there was a more or less tacit assumption that women see themselves as nurturers of the planet, as people who 'care'. (Braidotti et al., 1994, p. 104)*

Here, Braidotti is commenting on the essentialism implicit in the notion that women are both closer to nature and driven by a higher propensity to care and nurture, which underpins many ecofeminist approaches and which was, to some extent, perpetuated through *Agenda 21*. This idea is problematic in that it conflates women's bodies to their reproductive capacity (as carers and nurturers, as mothers) while simultaneously reproducing the idea that women and nature, and, by 'his' absence, men and culture, are intimately connected. The latter point has historically led to women's subordination within society as 'she' was considered too close to animalism and too distant from reason to engage in that mythic space called the public sphere where voting, decision-making and legitimate wage labour, amongst other processes, occur.

Similarly, Charlotte Bretherton (1998) highlighted how UNCED and *Agenda 21* worked to construct notions of women as problems, saviours and victims of the environment. First, Bretherton highlights how women have been constructed as problems for the environment, as women's bodies reside at the intersection of (hetero)sexuality, procreation and (over) population. Second, and conversely, women, according to Bretherton, are constructed as environmental saviours. This construction is based on notions of women being closer to nature and therefore better environmental decision-makers because they understand the natural world from a more privileged perspective. Finally, Bretherton suggests that international environmental politics recognizes women to be particular victims of the environment as women are considered more likely to suffer the ill-effects produced by environmental degradation. This is because women are more often primary carers for their families and therefore less able to migrate from environmentally devastated habitats and more likely to encounter the difficulties associated with scarcities of food, fuel and water.

Braidotti and Bretherton, as well as other feminist writers such as Melissa Leach (2007), highlight the essentialist and universalizing ways in which women have been constructed in much ecofeminist work as well as in international environmental politics and policy-making. However, it is crucial to note the role of heteronormativity within these gendered constructions (Foster, 2011). Indeed, the conceptualization of women as victims works to reinforce notions of men as protectors (of women) and/or aggressors. This binary in itself reinforces heterosexualized gender dynamics whereby women are considered passive and men active. Also, the privileged position lent to women in this one policy arena, the environment, works to re-establish gender norms which place women as closer to nature and therefore closer to the body than their male counterparts, again reinforcing clichéd notions of femininity which work in the service of the heterosexual imperative (Butler, 1990). However and perhaps most crucially in relation to this chapter, I argue that recognizing women's bodies as actual, and potential, reproductive vessels is crucial to contemporary sustainable development rhetoric. The potential capacity to care and nurture (in line with heteronormative idea(l)s of motherhood) relates to women being special guardians of the environment while their actual reproductive behaviours, when left unmanaged, are pathologized within sustainable development discourses.

Eco-sexual Normativity: Environmental Policies Naturalizing Heterosexuality

As indicated above there is an assumed heterosexuality which underpins the discourses of sustainable development, and this assumed heterosexuality is never clearer than when policy-informing documents like *Agenda 21* and its 2012 revamp *The Future We Want* focus on issues of gender and population. Indeed, this assumed heterosexuality makes apparent a contradiction in environmental policy and mainstream environmental thought. Namely, environmental policy (and, to some extent, the bulk of the theory) whilst recognizing a need to 'manage' population growth also adheres to fantasies of the natural world whereby heterosexuality, and more so procreation, represent the pinnacle of what is natural (read good) behaviour (Little, 2007; Ensor, 2012; Bell, 1995a). The result of this contradiction is that the population is managed through a pro-procreation lens, leading to policies that call for constraint in reproduction within heterosexual family units. In other words, it calls for a post-industrial Western model of heterosexuality across the globe. This point I shall return to later, but first I would like to briefly outline the constructed relationship between natural and procreative heterosexual sex.

Greta Gaard, in a seminal article entitled 'Toward a Queer Feminism' (1997, p. 141) notes that those who 'explore the natural/unnatural dichotomy find that the "natural" is invariably associated with "procreative"'. Moreover, exemplifying this link constructed between nature and heterosexuality/procreation, work done on investigating sexualities as they map on to rural/urban geographies notes that urban 'unnatural' spaces are considered a place for sexual 'deviance', such as sex work and homosexuality (Mortimer-Sandilands, 2005; Bell, 1995a), whereas rural 'natural' environments are considered to be a place where natural heterosex and romantic family life occurs. For example, Jo Little (2007) in her study looking at the construction and lived experience of heterosexuality in the UK countryside, notes how relationships in rural areas are considered to be biologically superior to those in urban areas because couples are able to spend more time together and produce more offspring. Through her analysis of the UK magazine *Country Living* she notes:

> [A] division was drawn between the countryside and the city, with the comment that 'London couples' are so busy that 'fertility clinics have to find them windows of opportunity to make love' … By contrast, 'country people' were seen to be more in tune with the rhythms of nature, requiring no artificial 'help' with fertility. (Little, 2007, p. 862)

This construction of the rural as the environment conducive to hegemonic ideals of heterosexuality is demonstrative of the link drawn between the natural and procreation. Indeed, there has been some scholarship (Mortimer-Sandilands, 2010; Bell, 2000; Gorman-Murray, 2009b; Valentine, 1995; also see Tiffany Muller Myerdahl's chapter in this volume) that notes expressions of non-normative sexualities within 'natural' spaces, but these non-normative expressions ultimately fail to 'challenge the primacy and stability of ... heteronormativity' (Little, 2007, p. 863).

Given strong links constructed between heterosexuality and nature/the natural it is perhaps unsurprising that sustainable development policy discourses, whilst promoting a managed fertility, also rely on notions of procreation to justify the conservation of environmental goods and services for future generations. To clarify this point it is important to consider the definition of sustainable development adhered to by international policy-makers. This definition, taken from the Brundtland Commission (discussed above) reads as follows:

> *Sustainable development is development that meets the needs of the present without compromising the ability of* future generations *to meet their own needs. It contains within it two key concepts: the concept of 'needs', in particular the essential needs of the world's poor, to which overriding priority should be given; and the idea of limitations impose by the state of technology and social organization on the* environment's *ability to meet present and future needs. (Brundtland, 1987, p. 43, emphasis in the original)*

As this definition demonstrates, the notion of intergenerational justice between current and future generations is paramount to securing support for sustainable development. The forthcoming existence of future generations is constructed within dominant understandings of sexuality as reliant on (heterosex and) procreation. In other words, the focus on future generations is very much bound to heterosexual kinship ties. Often in relation to sustainable development discourses one hears rhetoric like 'we should save the planet for our children and our children's children'. This link to biological inheritance presupposes a family unit that is organized around heterosexual kinship ties and has led some commentators, such as Lee Edelman (2004) and Sarah Ensor (2012, p. 409), to problematize and question the 'status of futurity' which is 'predicated on matters of inheritance and procreation' as a precondition for environmental sustainability. Indeed, Edelman in his oft-cited work *No Future*, discussing politics more broadly, notes how the image of the child is invoked to justify nearly every political action within the context of a consensus whereby 'all politics confirms the absolute value of reproductive futurism' (2004, p. 3).[1] Indeed, the environment, as a political problem, and sustainable development, as a potential solution, mobilizes this child imagery along with a promise to future generations all too readily.

Simultaneously, heterosexuality and procreation are paramount whereas fertility and overpopulation are problematized. So, given the primacy of heterosexuality and procreation in sustainable development discourses alongside the simultaneous tension over population growth, what is the 'model' for a sustainable family? There are two crucial discourses within and outside sustainable development policy: one is marked by its absence and the other by its presence. With regard to the former, sustainable development discourses make no mention of non-normative sexualities, even though non-normative sexualities are likely to be less procreative and, as such, arguably have a lower impact on environmental resources. Indeed, we find non-normative sexualities in UN discourses not where population management and

---

1   Also, for a discussion of debates on futurity relating to HIV/AIDS, see Sothern (2007b).

sustainable development are discussed but, rather, in the arena of governance associated with sexual health, particularly HIV/AIDS (see also the chapters by Tucker and Taylor in this volume) and the dangers of sex work (Murray, 1996; Hubbard, 2002; Correa and Parker, 2004). As such, non-normative sexualities are more frequently linked to danger and risk. As a result, the positive contributions that could be made through a discussion of non-normative sexuality in relation to environmental policy is silenced in sustainable development discourses which, after all, rely on the provision of a biologically forged future generation(s).

Second, and as indicated above, the presence of children within sustainable development discourses is necessary to justify this particular form of environmental management. However, the production of these children, according to sustainable development policy, has to be moderated through managed sexuality. In other words, sustainable development policy operates through discourses that encourage the production of some children (so reproductive futurity, as Ensor (2012) puts it, can be anticipated) but not too many children (so the Earth's resources do not deplete). The family model that arises from this tension is formed around heterosexual couples practising 'good' reproductive management and is one that is typical to (or at least presented as ideal for) post-industrial economies – and, as such, is ethnocentric with legacies rooted in particular forms of capitalism, Protestantism, neoliberalism and so on (Foster, 2013). The model is constituted by two heterosexual parents who reside in the same household with an 'appropriate' amount of biologically related children (one minimum, three maximum) spaced (time-wise) 'appropriately' apart (Mortimer-Sandilands, 1999). This model is demonstrative of a discourse that works to pathologize other forms of family life, like extended families, polygamous families, queer families and so on, which may well echo other(ed) geographically, culturally and historically specific trends and traditions. Overall, the nuclear family model is hailed as the correct way of 'doing things' for reproductive management and sustainable development, yet this nuclear family model privileges Western, heterosexual, white, androcentric family organization. Moreover, the privileging of this family model within the context of saving the environment is arguably somewhat paradoxical given that the Western, heterosexual, white, androcentric family is actually a locus of (over)consumption whose environmentally-friendly behaviour is typified through further consumption practices. In other words, this type of family is more likely to increase the strain on environmental goods and services through its consumption practices, and the activities this family may engage with in order to mitigate environmental damage amount to consuming alternative goods like electric cars and free-range eggs (Mortimer-Sandilands, 1993).

The Promise of Ecofeminism and Queer(ing) Ecologies

Ecofeminism is a position which argues that feminist and environmentalist goals are synonymous. As noted earlier in this chapter, ecofeminists contend that women have the capacity to relate to the natural world better than their male counterparts (as they have a greater capacity to care and nurture, as demonstrable through their roles as mothers) and that the oppression of nature is intimately entangled with the oppression of women. Indeed, these themes reverberate through ecofeminist work such as that of Maria Mies and Vandana Shiva (1993), and it is the former proposition, that women have a special bond to nature, which, as previously noted, was co-opted into the rhetoric of UNCED in 1992. As such, ecofeminism has largely been criticized by contemporary feminists for essentializing gender roles and universalizing the experiences of women – as though all women have a particular environmental ethic of care. Indeed, this reading of ecofeminism is certainly problematic to gender theorists of the poststructuralist persuasion and queer theorists alike. However, that is not to say that ecofeminism has nothing to offer. As Greta Gaard (1997) argues, drawing on the notion that the oppression of nature is intimately entangled with the oppression of women, there is scope to 'Queer Ecofeminism'. As Chaia Heller (cited in Gaard, 1997, p. 137) notes, '[l]ove of nature is a process of becoming aware of and unlearning ideologies of racism, sexism, heterosexism, and ableism so that we may cease to reduce our ideas of nature to a dark, heterosexual, beautiful mother'.

So whilst ecofeminists argue that the asymmetry of gendered dynamics reinforces the exploitation of the natural world through reliance on various stratified dichotomies – most notably that nature (and women and the body) is inferior to culture (and men and the mind) – Gaard argues that the asymmetry between the heterosexual (natural) and queer (unnatural) also problematically shapes our understanding of the natural world. This exposes a further contradiction in how nature is imagined, as ecofeminists point to the devaluation of nature (and women) whereas queer theorists point to the devaluation of what is considered unnatural (and queer). As Gaard (1997, p. 141) notes:

> On the one hand, from a Queer perspective, we learn that the dominant culture charges Queers with transgressing the natural order, which in turn implies that nature is valued and must be obeyed. On the other hand, from an ecofeminist perspective, we learn that Western Culture has constructed nature as a force that must be dominated if culture is to prevail. Bringing these perspectives together indicates that, in effect, the 'nature' queers are urged to comply with is none other than the dominant paradigm of heterosexuality ...

In other words, the contradictions that arise when we consider nature, the natural, sexuality, gender, culture and so on only serve to demonstrate the ways in which 'nature' is imagined in ways that sustain and perpetuate the gendered heteronormative order.

Feminism and subsequently queer theory as an intervention into environmental debates, as I hope this chapter has demonstrated, works as a point of departure for eco-criticism. However, from this point of departure, queer theory also allows us to imagine a human–nature relationship that is not predicated on notions of natural heterosexuality (and the gender roles that work in service of this naturalized heterosexuality). For example, undermining the notion of (at least biologically related) future generations as a reason for preserving and conserving the environment opens up a variety of creative paths through which we can reimagine nature. As the well-regarded ecofeminists Andree Collard and Joyce Contrucci imagined in their work, *The Rape of the Wild*, no longer bound to heterosexual family ties, we could develop 'relationship[s] of kinship between human beings and all of creation – vegetation, animals, the elements, and other planets' (Collard and Contrucci, 1988, p. 7). Indeed, love tied directly to heterosexualized relationships (mother, father, husband, wife, son, daughter and so on) specifies that the environment should be protected in an instrumental way for the purposes and use of our direct human relations. However, queer ecology[2] would suggest that love could be constructed as more expansive so that one cares for that which is not just outside our biological kinship, but also outside our species kinship. Our ethic of care could transcend the normative family and instead include trees, non-human animals, rocks, mountains, rivers and so on. Furthermore, and perhaps contrary to traditional environmentalism which offers a static and clichéd understanding of natural

---

2   For a wider discussion of queer ecology, see Mortimer-Sandilands and Erickson (2010); and the 2012 Special Issue of the *European Journal of Ecopsychology* on *Queering Ecopsychology*.

space, a queer ecological perspective also breaks down binaries of urban and rural (Gorman-Murray, 2009b), allowing for a greater potential to appreciate urban spaces and the diversity of identities and relationships that centre on urban ecologies (for example, see Gandy's 2012 discussion of the Abney Park cemetery in London). An expansive and queer ethic of care, whereby family and species boundaries are rendered inconsequential, would encourage a less instrumental valuation of that which is considered in our current paradigm as natural. Indeed, queer ecology poses an environmental ethic that has more in common with the deepest of the deep ecological thinkers (see Naess, 1973, for example) than sustainable development proponents and policy-makers. More simply, it could be argued that queer green is greener than sustainable development green.

Certainly since the mid- to late 1990s there has been a body of literature that has highlighted how seeing the environment through a queer or non-normative lens allows 'for a unique standpoint on resisting destructive relations' (Mortimer-Sandilands, 2005, p. 5) between that which is culturally intelligible as nature and those who are culturally intelligible as humans. For example, Catriona Mortimer-Sandilands, in her article 'Unnatural Passions? Notes Towards a Queer Ecology' (2005), begins by detailing how AIDS amongst non-heterosexual communities in San Francisco offered a new way of understanding life, death, the body and nature. Indeed, here Mortimer-Sandilands notes how caring for those with AIDS was often undertaken by other members of the queer community rather than by biological kin (due to the stigma associated with the disease), thus informing a more expansive ethic of care which could be applied broadly to the natural world. This community could also be described as a 'queer commons' whereby '[t]he sharing and gifting of skills, knowledge, and affection' within these communities works as an alternative to the consumerist individualism of hetero/homonormative spaces (G. Brown, 2009). Similarly, Mortimer-Sandilands has demonstrated how lesbian communities (2002) and, more recently through a reading of the film *Brokeback Mountain*, gay men (2010) can potentially experience the natural environment in profoundly different and erotic ways. Similarly, Scott Herring (2010) in his work *Another Country*, through a dismantling of the relationship often constructed between LGBTQ communities and the urban (as an emancipatory space) discusses the ways in which the rural is negotiated and queered by non-heterosexuals. These experiences and negotiations work to undermine the 'unnaturalness' of non-heterosexual behaviours as well as present new ways of imagining the natural world as valuable – beyond the proposition that we should save the environment for our children and children's children. In a similar vein, Sarah Ensor (2012), through a reading of the never-married conservationist Rachel Carson (who is frequently cited as a founder of contemporary environmentalism), argues that 'Spinster Ecology', through abandoning an investment in future generations, works to produce an environmental ethic which is about 'tending the future without contributing to it' (Ensor, 2012, p. 409) and challenges assumptions on how we best 'move forward' (Ibid., p. 410). Overall, queer(ing) ecologies diversifies how nature can be understood in order to overcome a variety of 'isms' (from racism to speciesism) leading to a human-nature relationship that is more reflexive, more fluid and less exploitative.

Conclusions

The first part of this chapter formed a queer eco-critique of sustainable development, demonstrating the heteronormative assumptions that fundamentally shape contemporary mainstream and policy-relevant understandings of the environment. These understandings of the environment, which work to define the environment as a problem, as well as the policy solution needed to resolve that problem, namely sustainable development, are uncritically premised on, and work to reproduce, ethnocentric gender norms within the framework of heteronormativity. Moreover, the heterosexualized assumptions that underpin mainstream environmental politics and policy-making are problematic to both the natural world and to those marginalized through the said dominant paradigms. For example, the concept of intergenerational justice presented through sustainable development discourses offers an instrumental valuation of nature, in that nature is only valuable in as far as it can maintain the well-being of the human species (in the present and in the future). However, it is well rehearsed within environmental philosophy that an instrumental valuation of nature results in that which is constructed as natural but which offers no apparent utility to humans being neglected and depleted (Naess, 1973). Similarly, an environmental politics reliant on a notion of future generations privileges reproductive (hetero)sexuality and biological inheritance as it is *our* (biological) children who are the target of protection within the discourses of sustainable development. As such, the rhetoric of sustainable development marginalizes non-normative sexual identities and relationships, rendering them invisible within the landscape of environmental protectionism and conservation (Foster, 2013).

This chapter ended through a discussion of queer(ing) ecologies, offering a snapshot of the current work in this field. Indeed, this body of work offers a diverse reading of human-nature relations. By breaking down and reinterpreting understandings of what is meant by 'human' and by 'nature' – by urban and rural, by natural and unnatural – the relations(hips) and power dynamics which stem from these categories are revisioned as fluid and contestable. Moreover, as argued here, by undermining the primacy of 'blood' kinship and by blurring the divisions between species, between the human and non-human, a greater capacity to care (for human and non-human life and non-life) may emerge. To this end, this chapter argued that queer(ing) ecologies works to promote a reimagining of nature in creative and (potentially) environmentally-friendly ways.

Chapter 11

Tunnels of Social Growth within the Leviathan: A Story of China's *Super Girl*

Camila Bassi

Gay Political Economy, Intersectionality and (Intersectional) Marxism

Advancing a Marxist theorization of the contradictory relationship of sexuality and capitalist political economy, this chapter presents a story of China's reality TV show *Super Girl* which gave birth to a unique lesbian heyday in Shanghai during the early millennium.[1] This Marxist approach, as indicated in this introduction, moves beyond an Althusserian notion of containment by political economy – which frames the marketization of culture as an ideological structure of control in line with the prevailing hegemony – and reveals how a turn to intersectionality within sexuality studies is infused with this Althusserian legacy by perceiving intersecting cultural and economic realms as intersecting, ideological structures of control. A leading strand of Marxist geography observes that '[p]recisely because capitalism is expansionary and imperialistic, cultural life in more and more areas gets brought within the grasp of the cash nexus and the logic of capital circulation' (Harvey, 1989, p. 344). Thus, culture becomes locked into an operation of exploitation because 'it sells' (Mitchell, 1995, p. 110). In a poststructuralist queer critique of 'a liberal framework' of work within geographies of sexuality (which depicts homosexual space as opposing and transgressing heterosexual space) an intersectional analysis that is attentive to 'constellations of power across the heterosexual/homosexual divide' is proposed (Oswin, 2008, pp. 89–90). However, in such an intersectional approach, there is slippage into another dichotomy – for example, between the 'colonizing impulses' of a 'queer white patriarch' of the capitalist gay market and the 'anti-colonial efforts' of queer ethnic minorities (Nast, 2002, p. 899). The danger, I caution, of an Althusserian current in Marxist geography and poststructuralist

---

1   This chapter is based on my research in Shanghai on gay political economy, which was conducted between 2008 and 2013, and consisted of interviews, participant observations and secondary documentation. At intervals between January 2008 and April 2009, 21 individuals participated in recorded in-depth interviews (two of whom were interviewed twice and three times respectively). Of these, six were gay male business owners, nine were gay male and lesbian NGO workers, three were lesbian organizers of LGB support groups and three were gay male consumers of the gay scene. That said, all considered themselves consumers of the gay scene and so were also interviewed on this basis. At intervals between March 2007 and April 2013 I visited and recorded participant observations of Shanghai's key commercial gay scene venues, joined a sexual health outreach volunteer to hand out condoms and talk to men at gay cruising grounds, collected an archive of online gay scene resources and web-based local histories, conducted further interviews with five gay men, two lesbian women and one bisexual woman, and compiled an archive of international media coverage of the reality TV show *Super Girl*.

theory lies in bypassing the potential of human agency to consume and construct culture produced by the capitalist market for themselves. The Marxism applied in this chapter challenges the simplistic premise that oppositional culture is limited by its expression in the commodified form, and attunes to both universal *and* specific material realities and capitalist closures *and* openings.

The study of gay political economy has long grappled with the contrary connection of gay identity and existence to capitalism (Binnie, 1995; Butler, 1997a; D'Emilio, 1993; Escoffier, 1997; Fraser, 1995, 1997; Knopp, 1992, 1995, 1998). In the city, capitalism has given birth to conditions for an affluent stratum of gay men to possess a gay life through the market and for market relations to possess gay life – at worst, engendering a depoliticized, individual-centred, pleasure-seeking commercial culture of consumerist alienation (Chasin, 2000; Cornwall, 1997; Evans, 1993; Matthaei, 1997; Mort, 1996; Skeggs, 1999). As Binnie (1995, p. 190) remarks, for many young gay men, political demands 'are not allowed to detract from the freedom which really counts, namely the freedom to consume music, dance, spectacle and sex. This freedom to consume is after all one right which the dominant political ideology has only encouraged …' Class, patriarchal and institutionally racist divisions remain generally unchallenged in gay political economy. Nevertheless, struggles of the 'social periphery against the center' confront a gay hegemony of white, male, middle-class, Eurocentric experience (Seidman, 1993, p. 118). An intersectionality turn in sexuality research examines these material conditions of capitalism by merging cultural and economic aspects of sexuality and class, alongside other markers of oppression (see Adkins, 2002; Binnie, 2004; Binnie and Skeggs, 2004; Heaphy, 2011; McDermott, 2011; Taylor, 2007b; 2011; Skeggs, 1997). With regard to the commercial gay scene, for instance, it is understood as a space 'experienced unequally' through 'intersectionalities including race, age, class, bodily ideals, gender identities and sexual identities' (Browne and Bakshi, 2013b, p. 70; see also Binnie and Skeggs, 2004; Casey, 2007; Holt and Griffin, 2003; Nash, 2011; Taylor, 2007a).

An intersectionality approach has been made theoretically possible, I argue, through an anti-dialectical, Althusserian comprehension of the material, which abets a conceptual collapse and impasse when thinking through the nature of oppression and exploitation, and the means of resistance (Bassi, 2010). Hall (1985, p. 92) acknowledges Althusser as enabling him 'to live in and with *difference*':

> *Althusser's break with a monistic conception of marxism demanded the theorization of difference – the recognition that there are different social contradictions with different origins; that the contradictions which drive the historical process forward do not always appear in the same place, and will not always have the same historical effects.*

But as Miles (1989, p. 65) points out in connection with Hall's notion of historically-specific racisms, Hall fails to 'specify what the many different racisms have in common *qua* racism'. Butler (1997a, p. 275), in her debate with Fraser (1995, 1997) on the relationship of sexuality to political economy, progresses 'Althusser's ground-breaking argument that "an ideology always exists in an apparatus, and its practice, or practices. This existence is material".' Consequently, Butler (1997a, p. 273) insists that the 'operations of homophobia are central to the functioning of political economy', reasoning:

> *Is there any way to analyze how normative heterosexuality and its 'genders' are produced within the sphere of reproduction without noting the compulsory ways in which homosexuality and bisexuality, as well as transgender, are produced as the sexually 'abject', and extending the mode of production to account for precisely this social mechanism of regulation? (Butler, 1997a, p. 274)*

I concur with Fraser (1997, pp. 285–6) who states that what Butler revives here is 'one of the worst aspects of 1970s Marxism and socialist feminism: the overtotalized view of capitalist society as a monolithic "system" of interlocking structures of oppression that seamlessly reinforce one another'. Where, then, are the openings or tunnels within the leviathan?

Michael Brown (2012) expresses a series of anxieties concerning an intersectionality inequity in the investigation of geographies of sexuality: are particular identities believed to be more foundational than others, and certain intersections more politically significant than others? In one way, such questions are resolved in this chapter by a dialectical materialist methodology to the relationship of universality and specificity vis-à-vis sexuality, capitalism and the state (see also Bassi, 2006, 2012). For Althusser, ideology has a material, as opposed to a spiritual, existence that is manifest in an individual's performance and interaction with others and society; it is a 'material existence of "ideas" or other "representations"' (Althusser, 1971, p. 112). For Marx (1846, p. 14), consideration of the material means that we do not start with what humans 'say, imagine, conceive, nor from [humans] as narrated, thought of, imagined, conceived' to arrive at humans 'in the flesh'; one's starting-point is 'real, active' humans and 'their real life-process'. This is not to be mistaken as class-reductionist or economically determinist. Marx warns against a crude materialism, in which humans are the result of circumstances and therefore change as a result of changed circumstances, because what this critically 'forgets' is that humans *change* circumstances (Marx, 1845, p. 156). Furthermore, as Engels (1890, pp. 71–2) spells out:

> We make history ourselves, but first of all, under very definite assumptions and conditions ... history is made in such a way that the final result always arises from conflicts between individual wills, of which each in turn has been made what it is by a variety of particular conditions of life. Thus, there are innumerable crisscrossing forces, an infinite series of parallelograms of forces ...

The (intersectional) Marxism of the next section recognizes that capital seeks to universalize across time and space, and that dialectical change in material reality is also shaped by specific historical and geographical forces and conditions of life. Exploring the evolution of the political economy of television in China, and, through this, the emergence, navigation and consumption of the reality TV show *Super Girl*, the following tells the story of a remarkable lesbian opening.

China's Political Economy of Television and Shanghai's Extraordinary Lesbian Moment

China's first sole, state-owned broadcaster, Beijing Television, later renamed Chinese Central Television (CCTV), began in 1958 as 'the "throat and tongue" of the Chinese Communist Party' (CCP) (Joffe-Walt, 2005; Sun, 2007, p. 188). The post-1979 period of 'opening and reform', which led to the entry of global capital into the country for the first time under CCP rule, has delivered 'a golden age of market expansion' in China's media (Jian and Liu, 2009, p. 527) – a process which the state attempts to control in order to safeguard its reign. There are now approximately 3,000 television stations broadcasting in the country, with a majority of households (both urban and rural) owning at least one television set and receiving a minimum of 35 stations. With around 20 million people entering adolescence annually, China's political economy of television is an expanding youth market (Joffe-Walt, 2005). It is also part and parcel of a cultural struggle. CCP rhetoric stresses economic and moral performance, promising individual riches and global hegemony (Hays Gries and Rosen, 2004; Rosen, 2004). At the same time, a crisis of culture is widely perceived, which is a concern articulated by a majority of my research participants, including the following:

Some people say, 'before the door's closed and now there's no door, the door's already flown away, so it's never gonna close again', so no-one really cares about the culture anymore, and government anymore. (Kimber, Chinese bisexual woman)

Sometimes I wonder if the opening up and reform is really a good thing because people have become so money crazy, they worship money, they think the more you earn the happier you become, but I think otherwise, sometimes you know, money does not bring happiness. (Yutian, Chinese gay man, sexual health outreach worker)

These comments chime with Wang's observation (in Rosen, 2004) of the emergence of an apolitical, material-seeking 'post-communist personality' that rejects life under Mao and reflects the state's drive for wealth. The state response is to propel a popular nationalism, embedded with anti-American and anti-Japanese sentiment (Lam, 2000; Mitter, 2005) and a neoconservative nostalgia for the past (Dutton, 2007). Whilst Confucianism was rejected under Mao, the state now pursues a spiritual moralization and harmonization programme known as 'new Confucianism', in which Confucius has been spun, 'through an extraordinary sleight of hand, into an advocate of profit and economic growth' (Dutton, 2007; Mitter, 2005, p. 295) and a means to acquiescent national culture.

CCTV, originally created to mobilize the masses in its project of socialist modernity, has become a 'remarkably complex, diverse and plural' media organization (Sun, 2007, p. 188). CCTV dominates the market share in news broadcasting, so rather than compete in this genre, the country's provincial television stations incline to the production of entertainment programmes (Jian and Liu, 2009), commonly reproducing versions of successful foreign programmes (Joffe-Walt, 2005). In 2003 the Hunan Broadcasting System (HBS) was the market leader of the provincial stations in the ratings of the national television market (Jian and Liu, 2009) and by 2011 it held the second biggest share of television advertising revenue after CCTV (Hille, 2011). Originating from the agricultural province of Hunan, HBS has 'strongly identified itself as entertainment television for "the common people"', which, in one sense, is a 'coup' that effectively distinguishes the station from CCTV and the political capital of Beijing (Jian and Liu, 2009, p. 528). *Mongolian Cow Sour Yogurt Super Girl Contest*, or *Super Girl*, was a Chinese version of *American Idol* produced by HBS from 2004 to 2011. *Super Girl's* first season in 2004–5 was an exceptional success: its final was viewed by over 400 million people to make 'it the largest television audience in Chinese history and inevitably the largest domestic TV audience in the world' (Joffe-Walt, 2005). *Super Girl's* ratings ranked first in the peak broadcasting time slot in 2005, with an overall profit value that year of RMB 766 million (Jian and Liu, 2009).

I heard about the story of *Super Girl* through my research on Shanghai's gay political economy. Some of my research participants introduced the idea of a heyday in the city's lesbian scene during the years 2004 and 2005:

I have been in the lesbian circle for ten years, I have seen the rises and the downs, and in 2004 and 5, a group of lesbians, before that there were very few lesbians, but during 2004–2005 lots of lesbians came out, and I felt that it was a very, very good period, we did have good time, even though we did not have so many places to go. (Chris, Chinese lesbian, sexual health outreach worker)

Although Chris did not identify a reason for the boom period of 2004–5, Charlene refers to a noticeable lesbian moment at this time in conjunction with the show *Super Girl*:

> *When I'd just arrived in Shanghai in 2005, er ... when I first started work, all these girls, female colleagues were like 'oh!', were you know giving me the eye, and I was like 'what's going on?' you know, 'I don't want to be out at work!', and then they said, 'oh you know there's this* Super Girl *contest and two of the girls', I think it was the runner up and the winner, 'they look so cool, their hairstyle's just like yours, they dress like you, oh wow!' I think it gave them a sense of liberation, so I was very surprised, and at that time I started seeing girls holding hands out on the street, the Ps and Ts [femmes and butches] hanging out on the street. (Charlene, Singaporean lesbian, co-organizer of a Shanghai LGB support group)*

One of the two runners-up, Zhou Bichang, and the winner, Li Yuchun, of the 2004–5 *Super Girl* final (see Figure 11.1) were speculated to be lesbians (Yang and Bao, 2012). The *Super Girl* phenomenon primarily centred on Li Yuchun – namely, on her distinct androgynous look (most notably, her hairstyle) in combination with what people perceived as her defiant attitude (Jakes, 2005). It is also worth noting that Li Yuchun referred to herself by the anglicized name of 'Chris'.

Figure 11.1   *Super Girl* **2004–5 final with Zhou Bichang (left), Li Yuchun (centre) and Zhang Liangying (right)**
Source: Associated Press, 2005.

Hannah's reminiscence explicitly identifies *Super Girl* as a lesbian phenomenon:

> *There's just one more story, one of my favourite moments in my life in China ... they have this competition called* Super Girl *... the girl that won* Super Girl *the first year it was on was a big dyke, like she wasn't out but everyone knew she was a lesbian, all of her fans were lesbians, and she was huge, she became a celebrity, she became a spokeswoman, she was on advertisements, she had that stereotypical Chinese woman dyke style, the short spiky hair, the puffy clothes, kind of boyish looking ... and it became this huge subculture of teenage lesbians ... I started seeing more lesbians on the street feeling free to dress the way they want, you'd see girls on the subway holding hands ... The first winner was Li Yuchun ... it was just this massive thing, the first one was '04 or '05 ... we would go to these fan rallies, my [Chinese] girlfriend even got to go to one of these performances and went up on stage and when she came down the girls were like fainting and touching her, and they were all gay! There were millions of girls watching this stuff! (Hannah, American lesbian, co-organizer of a Shanghai LGB support group)*

Marx (1857–61) clarifies in *Grundrisse: Foundations of the Critique of Political Economy* that the appropriation of human culture in the commodified form is not simply capitalist exploitation and alienation to the detriment of our social being and development. Capital depends on a constant innovation of productive forces that entails not just the division of labour, but also a qualitative 'differentiation of labour in an ever richer form' that produces a differentiation in the items and modes of consumption (ibid., p. 414). Alternatively put, capital drives forth a universalizing and expanding production of specificities that makes social growth possible. Marx (1857–61, p. 470) draws an analogy between capitalism and a leviathan or *'animated monster'*, who is able to lead labour 'by an alien will and an alien intelligence', to describe the transformation of 'the social connection between persons ... into a social relation between things' (ibid., p. 157). Exchange-value and money are the mutual ties of an alienated group of individuals, who carry their 'social power', as well as their 'bond with society', in their 'pocket' (ibid., p. 157). But, crucially, Marx does not stop here. He argues that this social bond is not an innate feature of human nature but is, rather, our product:

> *The alien and independent character in which it presently exists vis-à-vis individuals proves only that the latter are still engaged in the creation of the conditions of their social life, and that they have not yet begun, on the basis of these conditions, to live it ... The degree and the universality of the development of wealth where this individuality becomes possible supposes production on the basis of exchange values as a prior condition, whose universality produces not only the alienation of the individual from himself [sic] and from others, but also the universality and the comprehensiveness of his [sic] relations and capacities. (Marx, 1857–61, p. 162)*

Marx (1857–61, p. 409) refers to 'the great civilizing influence of capital' as the social evolution of individuals through the tunnels of cultural complexity penetrating the capitalist leviathan. As such, in retort to Romantic reactionaries, he states that it is 'as ridiculous to yearn for a return to that original fullness as it is to believe that with this complete emptiness history has come to a standstill' (ibid., p. 162). Whilst the universal relation of capital to labour-power is alienating and exploitative, there are openings through an increasingly differentiated production and consumption process, and an ever-expanding series of specific use-values (the capacities of produced commodities to satisfy human wants or needs) for individuals to experience a new kind of wealth: social wealth. The story of *Super Girl* can in part be understood as one born from capitalist political economy as Marx narrates it in *Grundrisse*. In China's opening and reform period there has been a radical transformation in the political economy of television, which has produced a quantitative and qualitative differentiation of consumption. *Super Girl* was an appropriation of human culture in the commodified form – specifically, a Chinese version of the hit foreign reality TV show *American Idol*. This commodity, at the same time as it bound individuals through its exchange-value and money, was unrestrained in the creation of ever-new use-values. Individual consumption was 'neither bound to particular objects, nor to a particular manner of satisfaction', since the sphere of consumption is 'not qualitatively restricted, only quantitatively', as 'it falls outside the economic relation' (Marx, 1857–61, p. 283). Channels within the leviathan opened up a space for original gratifications and a self-emergent, newly confidant lesbian identity and culture in Shanghai.

To complete the story of *Super Girl*, I turn now to the question of the state. A significant aspect of the popularity of Li Yuchun and some of the other contestants (in the first and later seasons) was the visible representation of an alternative gender and sexual identity and performance to the feminine norm, which disrupted the state hegemony and provoked a state response. The last ever winner of the show, for example, went by the anglicized name of 'Jeremy'.

China's opening and reform era has led to less state control over individuals' private lives, along with a state-fuelled moral panic over the cultural consequences of 'the market', which justifies a continued role for the state as protector. There is a contemporary state 'anti-vulgarity' campaign to clamp down on populist entertainment programmes, which echoes the 1983 'Anti-Spiritual Pollution Campaign' led by the architect of opening and reform, former CCP leader Deng Xiaoping, with its rhetoric of cultural invasion and suspicion of market forces, its concern to uphold spiritual health, preserve national culture and socialist morality, and its accusations of the market corrupting youth (Martinsen, 2006). Soon, in its journey of existence, *Super Girl* was scrutinized by the state regulatory body, the State Administration of Radio, Film and Television (SARFT). SARFT commanded rules for the show in 2006, most notably that contestants need to contribute to the construction of 'a harmonious socialist society' (cited in Jakes, 2006) in line with the state promotion of new Confucianism. In an interview in *China Times* in 2006 (cited in Martinsen, 2006), CCP official Liu Zhongde presented his concerns about *Super Girl*:

> *My views on* Super Girls *are not some blind spouting off; I have a theoretical basis. Cultural products are special commodities. The majority of cultural products possess a commercial side, they are well suited to enter the market and are subject to the influence of the market's rules that regulate production of artworks. But cultural products have another side, distinct from material goods. So the market cannot completely decide the success and failure of cultural products ...* Super Girls *is certainly the choice of the market, but we can't have working people revelling all day in low culture ... Behind the* Super Girls *entertainment lies poison for the youth. Take a look at the youth who are following the* Super Girls *now. See what state of mind they are in, what direction they are headed. Take a look at how the audiences are watching this program, and you'll find that amid unthinking laughter people have been corrupted ... In the case of government departments that oversee culture and art, they should not permit something like* Super Girls *to exist ... Entertainment programs present a problem of guidance to the future of our nationality and country. Look at the youth all over the country who have been hurt. Those participating in* Super Girls *have been hurt, those watching the program have been hurt.*

SARFT makes reference to the vulgarity of *Super Girl* in a public statement in 2007: 'Currently, some television talent shows have vulgar problems ... The performing style, language, hair and clothing of the contestants must be in line with the taste of the masses' (cited in Spencer, 2007). State pressure led to *Super Girl* being off air in 2007, 2008 and 2010, and its axing after its last season aired in 2011. A statement by HBS announcing the end of the show added: 'Instead, the channel will air programmes that promote moral ethics and public safety, and provide practical information for housework' (cited in Branigan, 2011). In contrast, and in what seems like an act of disobedience by the station, on 20 September 2011, a few days after the show had ended, HBS's home webpage featured two female celebrities in a staged kiss (Minter, 2011).

Conclusion

Li Yuchun has become one of the most famous women in China, with a prevalent array of commodities adorning her androgynous look and daring attitude. The story of *Super Girl* reveals a dynamic, contradictory relationship of lesbian identity and existence to China's capitalist political economy. Penetrating the leviathan were satisfactions of new and multifaceted pleasures from the consumption of *Super Girl*, which insecurely co-existed within the rubric of a reconfiguring and reinvigorating nationalist, communist state. At its best, the political economy of television and the production of *Super Girl* generated the material conditions for human agency to create a unique lesbian heyday, and perhaps something more. With hindsight, one of my research participants (a Chinese gay man called Steven) captures the *Super Girl* moment as one of dissent against the CCP itself: 'We want an anti-hero like Li Yuchun!'

The (intersectional) Marxism of this chapter demonstrates a progressive alternative to the ostensible need to reconfigure Marxianisms via poststructuralism. There is a tendency within an intersectionality approach for politics to fall into an Althusserian deadlock capitalism of intersecting structures of oppression, with a consequent impasse on the question of resistance. Although commercial gay culture shores up 'politically and economically conservative processes of profit-accumulation' (Nast, 2002, p. 878), this chapter reveals that the commodification of human culture is not crudely or merely capitalist exploitation and social alienation, because there is always human agency.

Chapter 12

In Italy It's Different: Pride as a Space of Political Contention

Cesare Di Feliciantonio

Introduction: The Mainstreaming (and Boycott) of Pride Parades: A Hegemonic Account

In 2010 Judith Butler declined the Civil Courage Award (*Zivil Preis*) assigned by the organizers of the 2010 Christopher Street Day parade in Berlin, denouncing the commodified character of the initiative and the connivance of the organizers with homonationalist, racist and islamophobic instances (Petzen, 2012). This event appeared to strength the criticisms about the incorporation of LGBT politics – including Pride parades – under the neoliberal agenda celebrating the market values of 'freedom', 'privacy' and 'personal responsibility' (Chasin, 2000; Vaid, 1995). In theoretical terms, Lisa Duggan (2002) has conceptualized these trends as 'new homonormativity' or 'the sexual politics of neoliberalism', associated by other scholars to the exclusion of racial Others under a homonationalist agenda of citizenship (see Nast, 2002; Puar, 2006).

This political shift towards a neoliberal, nationalist agenda found its full evidence in Pride parades that have increasingly adopted business models and foregrounded hegemonic, patriotic symbols, prioritizing normative masculinities and femininities (see, for example, Adam, 2009; Puar, 2006). Accounts of the mainstreaming and commodification of Pride parades have rapidly become dominant across Western/Global North countries, often leading to the boycott of Pride parades by critical queer groups and theorists (see, for example, G. Brown, 2007a).

However this narrative of mainstreaming and 'complicity' with neoliberal and nationalist projects fails to describe the experience of various countries in the Global South or in the 'peripheries' of the Global North where Pride parades are still contentious and even violent (see Renkin, 2014, about the case of Budapest). Although assimilationist groups and claims are present also within these contexts, Pride remains an open space of contention involving leftist and radical groups addressing several (social and economic) claims, far beyond access to conservative institutions like marriage or the army. Based on the Italian case, this chapter is aimed at decentring the hegemonic and monolithic perspective on the mainstreaming and depoliticization of Pride marches across the Global North, highlighting how, in the Italian context, Pride parades still bring political contention. This occurs mainly through the actions of the 'unwanted queers' (for example, trans migrants) and various leftist groups (for example, collectives, social centres, parties) engaged in a wide struggle for social and economic justice.

Following the geographies of social movements literature (for example, Nicholls, 2007, 2009), the chapter stresses the need to consider the territorial, social, cultural and political embeddedness of Pride marches because they are political demonstrations. A monolithic account of the politics of Pride as everywhere depoliticized, commodified and mainstreamed across the West/Global North is at the very least reductive, erasing the role of place and space in shaping politics and activism. Indeed, as stated by Browne and Bakshi (2013a, p. 192) in their study on LGBT ordinary lives (including activism and Pride) in Brighton, 'there is a need to be territorially sensitive in considering social, economic and political contexts of pursuing sexual and gender liberation agendas'; thus, 'the focus can be turned to activisms in each specific context and their possibilities and problems' (ibid., p. 193). This chapter shares this same ontology of non-fixity and diversity as already introduced in the geographical debate on sexual politics, challenging those paths pre-assumed to feature the 'forward' and 'modern' countries of the West/Global North (see, for example, Binnie, 2004; G. Brown, 2009, 2012; Knopp and Brown, 2003; Oswin, 2006). Indeed 'static notions of space and spatiality support the presumption that queer innovations originate in large urban areas and flow unidirectionally to peripheral or nonurban areas for adoption' (Oswin, 2006, p. 778). Opposing this reductionism, Knopp and Brown (2003, p. 422) have invited us to think about 'queer diffusions', highlighting how places shape each other 'in a complex, multilateral, and diffuse process of mutual constitution'.

When emphasizing the contentious and political character of Pride marches in Italy, I do not underestimate their internal conflicts: indeed, a plurality of subjects take part in Pride marches, addressing different claims and experiencing different practices. For instance, much attention has been paid to how lesbians relate to, and appropriate, Pride marches differently (for example, Browne, 2007a; Johnston, 2007). As in other social movements (Della Porta and Diani, 2006), different political horizons co-exist, generating tensions and clashes around some important issues, like the institutionalization of the LGBT movement or the presence of well-known politicians at the marches (Ross, 2009). The ambivalent and contradictory nature of Pride marches, along with my rejection of any presumption of objectivity or comprehensiveness, requires me to clarify my position on the topic: this chapter is primarily based on my experience as a fag/queer,[1] leftist, student militant who has been inside the LGBT and queer scene in Rome since 2006, so a sort of 'Rome-centrism' can result from the analytical perspective.

The remainder of the chapter is divided into three sections. In the next section I give a brief account of the politics of Pride in Italy as it has been from the 1990s, reporting the main instances highlighted by the literature. Through examples taken from recent Pride marches (the 2010 Pride march in Naples and the 2011 EuroPride in Rome), I then discuss the still contentious character of Pride marches in Italy as queer, leftist, critical coalitions have moved towards a radicalization of the contents and the keywords of the demonstrations. Finally, in the conclusions I emphasize the need to avoid monolithic and reductionist accounts, stressing the importance of place and space in framing the politics of Pride.

The Politics of Pride in Italy

A demonstration against the conference organized by a Catholic association on 'Deviant Behaviours of Human Sexuality' in Sanremo in 1972 is usually taken as the first form of public activism on the part of the Italian homosexual community, marking the shift from a

---

1   I prefer not to define myself just as a queer since, in Italian, the word *frocio/a* (literally, 'fag') has historically had a strong political connotation, resembling the political use of the English term 'queer' (for further clarification, see Di Feliciantonio, 2014b).

'homophile' to a 'gay' movement Consoli, 2000).[2] At the same time, a radically leftist collective had been created in Turin in 1971, the United Italian Homosexual Revolutionary Front (Fronte Unitario Omosessuale Rivoluzionario Italiano, FUORI)[3]. Inspired by the widespread social conflict characterizing the country in those years, lesbians, gay men and trans[4] people took to the streets several times between the 1970s and the 1980s, the most emblematic moments being the occupation of Porta Saragozza in Bologne in 1982 and the occupation of a building in the St Paul neighbourhood in Rome (Rossi Barilli, 1999). Nevertheless, it was only in the 1990s that a politics of Pride, as it takes place in many other countries in the West, was established. Following the 1994 Rome Pride – attended by around 20,000 participants – a series of Pride marches has been taking place yearly between the months of June and July (honouring the Stonewall riots) in many different Italian cities. Indeed, since the early 2000s a different city has been selected annually by national assemblies hegemonized by Arcigay[5] to host a 'nationally relevant' Pride march, while the rest of the cities have hosted 'local' marches. This process has created a long series of tensions and disputes, with the Pride of Rome being perceived, in any case, as the 'nationally relevant' one both by the media and the public.[6] Rome has also hosted two internationally relevant Pride marches: the 2000 World Pride and the 2011 EuroPride, both registering an extremely high participation.

Despite the success in terms of participation, Pride marches appear not to have generated a successful change among formal political institutions. Indeed, at the national level there has been no recognition in terms of rights (for example, civil unions or marriage); indeed, a law introducing homophobia as an aggravating circumstance in the Penal Code was rejected by the Parliament in 2009 (Hofer and Ragazzi, 2008; Ross, 2008). As shown by Charlotte Ross (2009), the years of Berlusconi governments were characterized by a pervasive homophobic discourse as a strategy to attract the favour of both Catholic voters and institutions. Nevertheless, the Berlusconi government did not represent an anomaly concerning LGBT issues, as 'the experiences of the LGBT population under Berlusconi fall into a "legislative continuum" since their rights remained unprotected before, during and after this period' (Ross, 2008, p. 204).

The effects of Pride marches appear to have been more relevant in social and cultural terms, with increased visibility and feeling of legitimation/acceptance perceived by LGBT people, especially in metropolitan areas (Bertone et al., 2003; Ross, 2008, 2013; Trappolin, 2004). This can be seen as an extraordinary improvement, given the widespread homophobia in Italian society (see, for example, Gasparini et al., 2012), and the hegemonic power of the Vatican and Catholic institutions in every aspect of social, economic and political life. Indeed, the Vatican has played a key role in stopping the approval of a law on civil

---

2   According to Consoli (2000), the homophile movement, active until the end of the 1960s, was featured by a (silent) claim within the norms and institutions of (heteropatriarchal) society, while the gay movement that emerged in the 1970s aimed at disrupting hegemonic sexual and gender relations.

3   *Fuori* means 'out' in Italian.

4   When the homosexual movement emerged in Italy in the 1970s, homosexual men and trans people were the most active. Demands for the recognition of bisexuality and bisexual rights continued to be ignored at least until the end of the 1980s.

5   Arcigay is the largest Italian gay association. It was created in the 1980s and was based on an ambivalent relation between leisure/commercial business activities and political circles.

6   Despite the success of 'nationally relevant' Pride marches in other cities (for example, Naples 2010, Palermo, 2013), the Pride march in Rome had the highest rates of participation (500,000–700,000 people in 2000, 700,000–1,000,000 people both in 2007 and 2011). The mechanism of the 'nationally relevant' and 'local' Pride marches worked until 2013; from 2014 onwards; apart from the Pride march in Rome, all the other Prides in various cities would take place on the same day, with none of the marches officially designated as 'nationally relevant'.

unions during the period 2006–08 when there was a left-leaning government (Hofer and Ragazzi, 2008; Ross, 2008, 2009). It has also publicly opposed the holding of Pride marches on several occasions, notably in 2000 when the World Pride was organized in Rome as a response to the Christian Jubilee in the same year (McNeill, 2003). Indeed, every 25 years Rome hosts the Christian Jubilee, attracting millions of visitors to the city; given the strongly homophobic character of Catholic institutions, the 2000 Pride aimed at attracting attention to the lack of LGBT rights within the country. The result was a strong institutional and political tension among: 1) LGBT groups and associations; 2) Catholic institutions; 3) right-wing and neofascist political parties, which see themselves as defending the 'Christianity' of the nation; 4) local institutions which, although hesitant, had to guarantee LGBT people the right to demonstrate.

This process of tense negotiations also occurred in many cases other than the 2000 World Pride in Rome (well documented by McNeill, 2003). For instance, Luca Trappolin (2004, 2009) has studied the public (political and media) debate around the 2002 'nationally relevant' Pride march in Padua, showing how deep tensions involving different institutional, social and political levels shaped the march. Whilst the LGBT groups organizing the march were fragmented (Trappolin (2004) traces a main dividing line between the *liberal* and the *radical* groups), some right-wing and neofascist groups opposing the Pride march responded by organizing a protest for the same day. This generated a response from the social centres[7] that organized a counter, anti-fascist demonstration. At the same time, the Church pushed for cancelling the event as 'inappropriate' because of the anniversary of St Anthony, patron of the city, while reluctant local institutions (for example, the municipality and prefecture) were pressed by the Ministry of the Interior to guarantee the demonstration taking place as a fundamental, constitutional right. According to Trappolin (2004), the result of these contrasting tensions was a 'bounded' march as LGBT people were allowed to demonstrate as a discriminated minority that could not cross the (symbolic and physical) borders of the 'holy', Catholic, culturally homogeneous city. The same tensions have been noted by Firrincielli (2005, p. 130) in his video-ethnographic study of the Pride march in Rome in 2005, when all around the route there were posters put up by a neofascist Catholic party, insulting the 'perverts' taking part to the parade.

When highlighting the political and institutional tensions shaping Pride marches *inside* and *outside* the LGBT movement itself, these analyses stress the fundamental politics of visibility that Pride marches entail (Firrincielli, 2005; Ross, 2008, 2013; Trappolin, 2004, 2009). For instance, when studying the 'nationally relevant' Pride march in Turin in 2006, Ross has shown how:

> LGBTQ individuals and groups, in this particular context, have worked to destabilize spaces perceived as heteronormative by publicly insisting on the recognition and validation of their presence within them. This disruption can be understood as a process of 'queering' space, of freeing up multiple (non-normative) modalities of use and existence which it may enable or host. (Ross, 2013, p. 131)

---

7   Social centres (*centri sociali*) represent a specific form of leftist/autonomous political practices mainly in the form of abandoned buildings that are squatted in order to organize counter-cultural events, promote direct political participation and create alternative forms of non-commodified sociability (Chatterton, 2010). In Italy they have had a strong political tradition since the 1980s (see, for example, Mudu, 2004), and have been traditionally associated with the most radical and insurrectional forms of leftist politics. However, since the 2000s Italy has also registered the first cases of neofascist squatted social centres, the most well-known case being Casa Pound in Rome (Castelli Gattinara and Froio, 2014).

On the contrary, some activists/commentators, usually linked to the leftist scene of the LGBT movement, have noted the complicity of Pride marches with hegemonic institutions, denouncing their mainstreaming and commodification (see, for example, Azione gay e lesbica, 2004). More recently, homonationalist tendencies have been recognized as shaping the claims, the language and the campaigns related to the EuroPride march in 2011 (De Vivo and Dufour, 2012; Ferrante, 2014). Through a semiotic analysis of the main advertising material, these authors stress the assimilationist character of the claims addressed, emphasizing how the promoters of the campaign support a racist, nationalist imagery based on a sense of 'nostalgic authenticity' for the country's colonial past. For instance, they stress how the use of the Colloseum and (white, muscled) gladiators within these campaigns recalls the imagery of ancient Rome and its violent colonial expansion in the Mediterranean. However their critical positions fail to recognize the tensions and discrepancies within the LGBT movement, building a unitary and monolithic account of the politics of Pride. This hidden contradiction becomes even more relevant since some of them, notably De Vivo and Dufour, were actively engaged in the organization of the 2011 EuroPride within the leftist, queer and critical network Orgogliosamente LGBT (see next section). These positions appear to raise the same criticisms raised by Gavin Brown (2009, 2012) towards the literature on homonormativity where it gives a reductionist, monolithic account, erasing the diversity of political positions and practices. Following this ontology of diversity, the next section explores the contentious and oppositional character of Pride marches as they challenge the mainstream politics of equality and normalization.

Coalitions and Blocks Bringing Contention

When considering the changes within the politics of Pride in Italy, it is worth noting how Pride marches have increased in number – in terms of both attendance and cities hosting Pride marches – in the same years that there has been a growth and proliferation of the movement for global justice, usually referred in Italy as the 'no global' movement (Rucht, 2005). Indeed, if we look at the self-narratives of Italian queer, critical leftists militants, they make reference to the importance of the 2001 anti-G8 demonstrations in Genoa or the European Social Forum held in Florence in 2002 (see, for example, Azione gay e lesbica, 2004; Busarello, 2011). LGBT groups actively took part in these initiatives both in Genoa and Florence and years later in the mass movement against the Iraq War. In the same period, leftist groups, parties and associations (for example, Rifondazione Comunista[8], Verdi,[9], social centres) were not just supporters of Pride marches when they were permitted to take place, but were also active participants, expanding the political perspective of Pride through their own claims. Here, I will discuss two examples – the Naples Pride of 2010 and the Rome EuroPride of 2011 – to show how coalitions and blocks constituted by queer and leftist groups within Pride marches have been able to make Pride a radical space of contention. This has been made possible by addressing broader social and economic claims beyond 'purely' lesbian and gay ones (for example, marriage or adoption for same-sex couples)

---

8   Rifondazione Comunista was the most influent (post)communist party to emerge after the dissolution of the former Italian Communist Party (Partito Comunista Italiano, PCI). Moreover, the first elected transgender in the Parliament (Vladimir Luxuria in 2006) represented Rifondazione Comunista.

9   The Italian Green Party.

and experiencing new practices. In this sense, these critical blocks and coalitions have been directly engaged in organizing the marches, reshaping them through new contents.

In the case of the 'nationally relevant' Naples Pride of 2010, a LGBTQ/feminist/anti-sexist/anti-racist/anti-fascist coalition was organized following a public call from four queer/feminist collectives from the city (Tiresi@, DeGeneri, Pachamama and Sora Rossa)[10] that were linked to social centres or to the students' movement. The response to their call was massive, with dozens of LGBTQ, feminist and leftist groups (mainly social centres) from all around the country taking part in the block at the demonstration Sharing the concerns of other associations and groups about equal citizenship for LGBT people, the groups composing the coalition added anti-fascism as a leitmotif for the demonstration. Indeed, some months before the Pride demonstration the neo-fascist organization Casa Pound had squatted a building in a lower-/middle-class neighbourhood (Materdei), provoking a strong – and violent – response from all the city's leftist groups. In addition to its concern with anti-fascism, the document produced by the coalition denounced the increasing situation of precarization and loss of social rights in ordinary life, as well as contesting social inclusion as being entirely mediated by the market through the commodification of bodies and desires.

In this way, the coalition emphasized a multiplicity of issues raised by the Pride march, as it involved not just LGBT people but women, migrants, sex workers and all those subjects resisting racism, neofascism and the Vatican's increasing influence on politics and institutions (Tiresi@, 2010). However, these groups did not confine themselves to organizing a critical bloc; they also worked to influence and shape the key discourses of the entire march. For instance, they took part in the general assemblies and meetings of the committee organizing the demonstration, notably the ones aimed at discussing and producing the official political document. When considering the official document of the demonstration these efforts become evident: it included a direct reference to anti-fascism, anti-racism and anti-sexism as main values of the march. Moreover, the claims addressed concern a multiplicity of social and economic issues far beyond same-sex marriage or adoption: for example, the document addresses the right to public health and education, denounces discrimination against non-Christian, non-white – notably Roma – and disabled people and asked for the withdrawal of the 2009 law that had introduced clandestine immigration within the Penal Code (queerblog, 2010). The contentious character of the coalition and the Pride was also expressed in terms of practices. For instance, the militants protested against the presence of Anna Paola Concia, a lesbian member of the Parliament that had proclaimed the need to establish a dialogue on civil unions with neofascist organizations and had participated in a meeting organized by Casa Pound in one of its squats in Rome. When there was a discussion among the organizers about the possibility of inviting Concia to give a speech on the main stage after the demonstration, the groups that made up the coalition strongly opposed this idea, stating that they would promote a boycott campaign against the demonstration if Concia was given the opportunity to speak.

The following year, a coalition was similarly constructed for the EuroPride in Rome, when a network of LGBTQ, feminist and leftist groups (both social centres and Rifondazione Comunista) was created to bring a contentious and leftist perspective into the Pride: Orgogliosamente LGBT. Given the European relevance of the demonstration in times of austerity politics, Orgogliosamente LGBT aimed at challenging the idea of an austere Europe through calling for a European 'social' welfare system. This call found a concrete realization

---

10 All these collectives were linked to the leftist, non-institutional scene of the city. Tiresi@ was a queer collective created during the wide students' protests of 2008 (usually referred as *Onda*). DeGeneri was a feminist/queer collective based at the university. Pachamama and Sora Rossa were feminist collectives linked to the autonomous scene of urban social centres.

on the day of the march. Indeed, the march took place the day before a national referendum on reclaiming the public management of the water system. The 'yes' referendum campaign was constructed by a wide range of locally-based groups all around the country – including most of the social centres. Through this campaign (and its successful result), the defence of the commons has become a leitmotif of the Italian left, following what had already happened in many other national contexts in response to the 'dispossessing' character of capitalism and neoliberalism (see, for example, Harvey, 2004; Spronk and Webber, 2007). Given the coincidence of issues raised by the referendum campaign, it became one of the main issues of Orgogliosamente bloc within the Pride march, with the main slogan being 'An orgasm of Yes!'.[11] In this way, the defence of the commons (like water management) entered the political space of the Pride march, gaining a prominent position amongst other campaigns that were put forward by/at Pride.

Furthermore, the political contention of the bloc also concerned LGBT issues that are usually hidden and underestimated, notably the depathologization of the transsexual condition – that is, the elimination of 'gender dysphoria – from psychiatric diagnostic manuals. Indeed, to obtain access to gender reassignment surgery in Italy it is compulsory to get a diagnosis of 'gender dysphoria'; this is recognized by trans associations and groups as a troubling and discomforting process. Through the engagement of Orgogliosamente with the Pride organization, trans people's access to healthcare became one of the main issues of the demonstration, addressed both in official documentation and public speeches.

These examples reveal how the presence and engagement of LGBTQ, feminist and leftist groups can still make Pride marches queer political spaces by addressing a wide range of social and economic issues, and confronting and overcoming those normalizing, assimilationist and 'complicit' tendencies that feature in part of the LGBT movement. However, further research is needed to study the relations that have been forged through the participation of leftist groups in Pride marches, as there is a need to explore what reflections, tensions and debates arose in the internal organization and working of these groups.

Conclusions: Reaffirming the Place-based Character of Pride Marches

> *Accounts of activisms should be attentive to specific histories and geographies of the areas, which they emerge from and engage with. All activisms are contextually situated, and place is part of the social relations that provide the impetus and resources for action, as well as the means through which social control, hierarchies and inequalities are practiced. (Browne and Bakshi, 2013a, pp. 193–4)*

Following Browne and Bakshi, in this chapter I have challenged widespread, monolithic accounts of Pride marches as merely mainstream and commodified around the Global North through the case of contentious Pride marches in Italy. Likewise, in the case of other social movements, Pride marches have always involved a plurality of positions and issues; thus, 'homonormative' and assimilationist claims and formations coexist with radical and critical ones. This calls into question the need to avoid reductionist accounts of the mainstreaming and depoliticization of the politics of Pride everywhere in the Global North – thinking that because it happened in some countries it will happen also in the others (G. Brown,

---

11   This was the chosen slogan since the referendum presented four propositions and the campaigners promoted a 'yes' vote for all of them.

2012). On the contrary, the contextual, place-based character of Pride marches should be emphasized since this could reveal how the politics of Pride are still perceived as crucial in countries other than the USA, Germany or the Netherlands, and even within these countries in 'ordinary cities' beyond the 'Gay Meccas' (see, for example, G. Brown, 2008; Browne and Bakshi, 2013a; Lewis, 2012a). Future efforts should focus on the tensions inside the LGBT movement – Pride included – and try to follow the insights coming from the literature on social movements. In this respect, it would be worth thinking of LGBT politics as an assemblage (of practices, subjectivities, actors, spaces and so forth) in order to highlight how 'actors within movements construct different spatial imaginaries and practices' (McFarlane, 2009, p. 561). A new emphasis on the interstitial spaces that can be traced inside the LGBT movement and the politics of Pride would avoid reductionist accounts of commodification and mainstreaming. Indeed, we could ask ourselves what we gain by simply denouncing the 'complicit' character of Pride marches without working to open up possibilities within them. Before dismantling the politics of Pride and proclaiming its depoliticization, however, more attention needs to be paid to how hard we still have to fight against social and economic injustice, since it remains the norm for LGBT communities in most parts of the world.

Chapter 13

Radical Activism and Autonomous Contestation 'From Within': The Gay Centre in Tel Aviv

Chen Misgav

From my point of view the idea and aim of the group is to raise awareness and bring into the community discourse things that are not there. Of course it's a political phenomenon, but so is oppression and silencing and what we have been doing is actually a kind of resistance. (Interview, 2011)

This statement was made by Elisha (Shuki) Alexander, an Israeli transgender man and community activist who founded an activist discussion group called 'Trans in the Centre', which operated in the Tel Aviv Gay Centre,[1] The group held 'community meetings focusing on transgender, queer and feminist issues. The meetings [were] *open to the public* and [were] not limited to transgender people. They [took] place twice a month in the Gay Centre in order to encourage inter-communal discourse, raise awareness, and lead to a change' (The Gay Centre Facebook Group, n.d.). These meetings revolved around transgenderhood, queerness and feminism, and addressed specific issues, including body image (for example, transgender bodies, disabilities and queerness, the role of bodies in protests, queer porn and intersexuality) or history, memory and politics (for example, local transgender history and memories, local political issues, such as the Israeli occupation, and queer maternities). Some meetings also revolved around identity categories (for example, queer Russian immigrants, queers and transgender people in the geographical periphery and queer ethnicities). The group first met in July 2009 and came to occupy a central position in the queer and transgender subcommunities within the larger LGBT community in Tel Aviv and in Israel in general.

In this chapter, I argue that this group's activism reconstructs and redefines spatial scales in the city and beyond it. Following Jenny Pickerill and Paul Chatterton's (2006, p. 742) argument that 'there is no place outside the reach of capitalist relations; "new places" have to be created from within, through an attempt – however complicated, contested and fractured – to alter and challenge every-day places', I focus on ways in which reconstruction of space emerges from within the hegemony of the Israeli LGBT community's organized leadership, mostly made up of white gay males). I do so through three spatial–analytic dimensions: discursive space, subversive space and the space of action. My goal is to explore

---

1   The group dissolved after three years. In mid-2013 it re-formed, but with some changes. The research on which the chapter is based refers to the first version of organization, from 2009 to 2012.

whether a radical queer group operating within the space provided by a municipally-funded centre can subvert the hegemony and homonormative space represented by the Gay Centre and create autonomous space within it. Recently there has been growing interest in autonomous geographies and spaces (Chatterton, 2006; Chatterton and Pickerill, 2010; Juris, 2005; Pickerill, 2007; Pickerill and Chatterton, 2006), especially following anarchist approaches and Hakim Bey's (1991) concept of temporary autonomous zones (TAZs) as sites of free expression and experimental short-term uses of space. I begin by defining my conceptualization of autonomy and autonomous space.

Drawing on the conceptualization of autonomy offered by Castoriadis (1991), autonomy, both individual and collective, is closely linked to democracy, freedom and participation in institutions. The current growing appeal of autonomy is a direct result of the crisis of faith in representative democracy (G. Brown, 2007b). Thus, the concept of autonomy is strongly related to autonomous politics and the spaces created by them. In this chapter, I define autonomous spaces as the spaces created and constructed by queer/feminist/transgender politics and activism within the institutional spaces of the Gay Centre, which I discuss as a form of social centre. Autonomous centres are based on a principle of unity in diversity: they are places where anarchist, anti-racist, feminist and queer politics can come together. Created by social movements and social centres, they practise a mix of different types of activity and activism (Wilkinson, 2009b). Autonomous politics and spaces aim to change everyday practices in order to create a better world and spaces (Wilkinson, 2009b), but they are not limited to social movements or social centres only and can occur in other temporary autonomous spaces, such as squats, info-shops, cafes, protest camps and so on (Feigenbaum et al., 2013; Hodkinson and Chatterton, 2006). In this chapter, I focus on the spaces created and constructed by the activities, activism and politics of Trans in the Centre as a radical queer/feminist/transgender group who worked within the mainstream institutional space of the Gay Centre.

Social Centres, Sexual Politics and Autonomous Spaces

Activism is defined as action usually committed by a certain group of people who strive to change a certain reality or to promote certain ideas, to apply political or economic pressure or change existing practices (Takahashi, 2009). Whilst most critical research in the geography of activism deals with ad hoc activities such as protests, parades and demonstrations, recently more attention has been paid to 'ongoing' activities by social centres (see also di Feliciantonio's chapter in this volume). These centres' activism reclaims urban space and reconstructs a social and cultural order and space (Leontidou, 2006).

In recent years social centres have produced and distributed new kinds of regularly occurring community activism that subverts the neoliberal spatial order (Hodkinson and Chatterton, 2006; Mudu, 2004).These social centres, especially in the Italian context, include squatted, occupied buildings run collectively for a range of self-organized social, welfare and political activities. They arose in Italy in the 1970s out of the autonomous Marxist tradition but built upon an older tradition of local working men's clubs linked to trade unions and socialist parties. As Montagna (2006) demonstrates, the social centres have played a particularly important role in the political and cultural world of Italy's autonomous scene. Hodkinson and Chatterton (2006) argue that the concept of social centres has gradually spread across Western Europe with the exception of the UK, where autonomous movements have been weak and the socialist left has generally refused to embrace the practice of physically reclaiming public spaces for political, cultural and community use.

When the phenomena finally arrived in the UK during the 1990s these spaces contributed to the growing urban resistance movement (Hodkinson and Chatterton, 2006) and provided physical and emotional spaces where activists met, sometimes even lived, accessed information and created political groups and movements, and thus challenged capital and the dominant modes of being, communicating and organizing (Lacey, 2005).

Lacey (2005) also highlights the importance of networks that emerge from the interaction of activists in shared spaces. Emotional reflexivity within activist spaces can also contribute to more sustainable individual and collective engagement and resistance over time (G. Brown and Pickerill, 2009) and thus help to build more feminist, queer and open spaces of discussions and greater attachment to the group and its activities. These interactions not only create new patterns of activism that challenge physical and emotional spaces, but also, as Chatterton (2006) notes, create a *third* space in which activists and non-activists meet and interact. Such interactions generate new agendas and can challenge the LGBT community's power structures.

LGBT community centres in the West, unlike the Italian or British social centres, are usually run by NGOs or, as I will show later in the Israeli case, run and partly funded by the municipality. They tend to have a more service-delivery ethos, since they function more as community centres that aim to provide cultural and social services for the local LGBT community – for example, for specified groups within the LGBT community, such as older people. However, not enough attention has been paid to the everyday practices of autonomous activists within them.

Queer geography has devoted very limited attention to autonomous spaces and the activism that creates them, and has almost completely ignored the possibility of creating autonomous activism within the centres run by NGOs or municipalities. Some studies on LGBTQ activism in organizations have focused on the way in which LGBT centres produce queer space and herald themselves as sites of counter-publicity. Drawing on fieldwork in a LGBT centre that is managed by an NGO in the USA, Max Andrucki and Glen Elder (2007) claim that state power is, in fact, constitutive of the material and discursive configurations of queer NGOs, which have come to embody a form of queer space peculiar to advanced liberal democracy. They argue for critical analysis of non-profit organizations' claims of providing autonomous space for queer representation and call for a critical resituating of queer public space. Gavin Brown (2007a) considers a set of alternative, autonomous queer spaces outside the mainstream commercial gay scene, created by radical activist networks to break open the bureaucratically planned spaces of the neoliberal city. Brettina Kohler and Markus Wissen (2003) cited in Brown (2007a, p. 2696) argue that these activist practices open up a discursive space in which social and political alternatives become thinkable. The spaces studied by Brown or Kohler and Wissen are different types of organizations than the one studied by Andrucki and Elder. While the first are autonomous social centres, the second is an NGO and more service-oriented. According to Gavin Brown (2006), queer activist spaces do not exist outside capitalist social relations and the commercial gay scene infrastructure of mainstream service organizations serving gay communities. As I will show in this chapter, even the space provided within the LGBT community centres has the potential to create a subversive autonomous and political space. This has to do with the creation of protest space and social movements.

Both kinds of social centres – the autonomous European version and the LGBT community centres – thus have the potential to create the political conditions for grassroots movements. This is an important issue for the case study discussed here since some feminist and LGBT social movements employ a 'mainstreaming' strategy, which means working for change within an existing institutional order, while others 'disengage' – for example, remain outsiders providing a critique and formulating visions (Berkovitch and Helman, 2005). Some of the movements, especially gay and lesbian movements of the post-Stonewall era or more queer movements from the late 1980s and 1990s AIDS crisis, such as ACT UP, organized around activist protests (M. Brown, 1997b), but not all social movements protest and not all protests are the actions of organized social movements. What is shared between all sorts of movements are the contentious politics activated for the purposes of achieving political goals through non-traditional means (Nicholls, 2007). Although sociologists and political scientists have spent time and effort developing concepts and theories for the study of social movements, geographers have paid little attention to the study of the geographies of these movements (Nicholls, 2007). In this chapter, by pointing to the spaces created, constructed and used by the group 'Trans in the Centre', I pay geographical attention to the spatial dimensions of queer social movements.

Sexual Politics in Israel and the Tel Aviv Gay Centre

Until the late 1980s Israel was a conservative place for LGBTs and in many ways excluded them from the public sphere. The turning-point was the 1988 amendment of the penal code that prohibited homosexual intercourse. This penal code was adopted from the British Mandate and, although rarely applied, its amendment started the local gay legal revolution (Harel, 1999). From this point on, LGBT subjectivities began to be recognized not only legally, but also in the media and even in the Israeli army (Kama, 2011). Tel Aviv became the gay capital of Israel and, unlike the formal capital, Jerusalem, its municipality began to support the LGBT community by producing the biggest gay pride parade and financing the Gay Centre, among other things (Alfasi and Fenster, 2005; Kama, 2011).

Figure 13.1   The LGBT community centre
Source: Misgav, 2011.

108

The Tel Aviv Gay Centre was opened in 2008 in a municipality-owned building at the edge of a park in the city centre (see Figure 13.1). It offered extensive leisure and cultural activities to the LGBT community, and houses an open community-oriented clinic, events hall, cafe, offices, an information centre and various organizations. Financially, it functions as a hybrid organization, operating as an NGO, on the one hand, and receiving municipal support on the other. This enables the municipality to provide the community with high-level services, without necessarily doing so directly (Alfasi and Fenster, 2005). This model proved to be successful as, shortly after opening, the centre achieved a key sociocultural and symbolic position within the local LGBT community. It also became an important power centre, mainly in hegemonic gay male politics.

I started my research process by taking part in the group's meetings as a participant observer. After six months I interviewed 17 of the group's participants. The interviewees' names are pseudonyms except those of Shuki and Yuval Egertt who hold formal positions in the Gay Centre (coordinator for trans people and director of the Gay Centre, respectively) and were chosen by the interviewees themselves, together with gender and sexuality definitions.

The Spatial-Analytical Framework: Discursive, Subversive and Action Space

Discursive Space

Carolyn Whitzman (2007) argues that a discursive space generates community leadership. As the discourse it generates brings about a new and different agenda, and as it may even change norms, opinions, power relations and interactions, this is a space of activism. Gavin Brown (2007b) finds that such spaces, especially of the radical queer sort, deconstruct and destabilize the neoliberal order, allowing a political and social alternative to get to the centre of the discourse. I claim that 'Trans in the Centre' creates such a discursive space.

Unlike other autonomous radical queer spaces, Trans in the Centre operates right in the organizational and geographical centre of the mainstream LGBT community. It is not an anarchist group aiming to bring down the existing institutions. Rather, it is funded by the establishment and works on their terrain. Shuki's description of the group in the opening quote matches what Pickerill and Chatterton (2006, p. 741) say about autonomous spaces in social centres: 'Being interstitial, they incorporate the desire for autonomy as well as the realities of compromise with the state and police. They are laboratories for resistance and creation, being ongoing forums for action and reflection or praxis.'

The discursive space generated in the Trans in the Centre group allows the articulation of sociopolitical alternatives to a broad range of issues, combining feminist and queer views with transgender daily problems. The group members represent ways of life that are not even homonormative, such as genderqueer, intersex, bisexual and transgenders who have changed their minds in the mid-process of gender and bodily change. This discourse brings transgender issues from the margins to the centre:

> Trans in the Centre empowers the community and the trans-queer-feminist identity. It is one of the ways in which the community creates itself, through speaking to itself and about itself. I believe that in many ways the activities of Trans in the Centre are part of the ongoing identity of the community. The subjects discussed ... are the subjects usually left out of the discussion. This is the community discourse. (Karen, 28, genderqueer, bisexual, 2011).

This is activist discourse *par excellence*. It is not locked within group meetings, but trickles out into various social spaces. Trans in the Centre is not merely a consciousness-raising group (in the spirit of 1970s–1980s feminist groups), but also a space for spreading information and changing agendas.[2] As Valery explains:

> *The activities ... have an ongoing effect ... Once there is an effect, and it doesn't have to be a positive one, but merely the fact that people keep on talking about what has been said ... it has a very deep effect, because they are taking those things outside the Gay Centre and into their own social spaces ... In their social spaces there might be people who may never come to the Gay Centre or to a Trans in the Centre meeting, but in this way they are exposed to the ideas and discourse generated by this group ... (Valery, 26, lesbian, butch, woman, 2011)*

The discursive space created in Trans in the Centre is unique not only in the topics it covers and their alterity or radicalness, but also in that it tries to put feminism and queerness into the practice of discussion, in terms of the space and the time dedicated for discussion and questions and answers. Motti elaborates:

> *Trans in the Centre is also somewhat different in that it tries in itself to be a different space. It might not always be 100 per cent successful at that, but the group is definitely trying to create a space that would be more equal and feminist, giving everyone a place to express themselves ... It is even evident in the way the space is organized ... And each and every meeting includes a long part dedicated to discussion. It is not a 90-minute lecture followed by 15 minutes for Q & A. It is more like a 30-minute lecture with one hour for discussion ... Real effort is made to allow people for whom it is usually hard to speak in public to participate, like women, transgender, people with some sort of disability, or people who are merely shy and take longer to participate in discussions, usually ending up not talking, because other people take over. (Motti, 30, gay man, 2011)*

The kind of practices Motti describes can be translated to what Anja Kanngieser calls 'politics of speaking and listening', particularly in terms of the articulations of privilege that underlie our speech (Kanngieser, 2012). Motti also describes the space of the room itself and the contribution of the seating arrangement to the discussion. The discursive space can also facilitate intervention in the public sphere, changing people's opinions or raising their awareness of radical issues. This is what I define as *subversive space*, which is not completely separate from the discursive one, since discursive space is in and of itself subversive, as elaborated in the next section.

Subversive Space

The activism generated by Trans in the Centre creates a subversive space. The subversion is present in the discourse but goes beyond that to affect the character of the venue which hosts and sponsors those meetings, the Gay Centre.

---

2   On the role of feminist consciousness-raising groups, see Eastman (1973) and Shreve (1990). On these groups and their influence on later queer and AIDS activism, see King (1994). On feminist consciousness-raising groups and activism in the Israeli context, see Swirski (1993).

The group's activities are subversive first and foremost of the space where they occur, the Gay Centre. As Lizzie describes it:

> *Trans in the Centre really is a radical group in my opinion, with a broad agenda, that functions with this centre, tilting it a bit towards the margins, and making it less centralized ... Without it [the Gay Centre] will end up being much more mainstream ... Here the margins are beating right at the heart of the mainstream, they shake it up. They are having a queer feminist activity in a place that is neither feminist nor queer. This activity subverts the order of things ... It is important ...*
> *(Lizzie, 50, queer, pansexual woman, 2011)*

Such subversion may be further illustrated by a meeting in May 2011 on the relationship between the LGBT and the BDS (Boycott, Divestment and Sanctions against Israel) movement. In the local context, the very attempt to discuss the BDS movement against Israel as a legitimate political tactic and, furthermore, linking this subject with the LGBT community, was nothing short of revolutionary.[3] The event and its speakers – veteran Israeli and Palestinian anti-occupation activists – drew considerable criticism inside and outside the LGBT community. Before the event, Shuki confided in me as follows:

> *I am going to hold an event on the boycott. I secretly hope that [the Gay Centre's management] would not allow it. It will stir up the community ... What set me up with this idea was an anti-apartheid party that was supposed to take place in the Gay Centre in New York. There they did not allow it. Therefore, I am curious to find out whether here, in our centre, they will let me do it ... If they do, it is cool ... If they do not, it is still cool, because a public discussion will still take place. One way or another we are going to have a discussion. (Shuki, 35, queer and trans man, 2011)*

Eventually, despite many protests to the centre's director and municipal council members, the event took place and attracted a large crowd. I asked the director, Yuval Egertt, why he had allowed it, and he replied:

> *As a member of the establishment, I should have said that it is a public, municipal venue, and there is no way we would allow such an event to take place here. Many people spoke up against me, and called me to cancel the event ... But the greatness about this event was allowing it to happen, and not preventing it. Both because it raised the counter-arguments, and generated a public discourse ... Here, in response to this event many members of the community declared themselves to be Zionists, it created a discourse that asks, what are we above all – gays, Zionists, Israelis, a minority? I don't want to voice my opinion, and I don't want to miss this tsunami that brings to the surface many things which are very important in Israeli society. My personal gain out of it was, again, being in the centre of things. The Gay Centre*

---

3   In the last few years LGBT rights in Israel have been used in the international arena by the government and especially by the Ministry of Foreign Affairs For example, describing tolerance of the LBGT community in Israel – and its lack in Muslim countries – is used as propaganda against the growing global gay resistance to Israeli occupation. Sarah Schulman (2012a) called this process 'pinkwashing' (see also Gross, 2013; Ritchie, 2014). Thus, any critical discussion of these practices used by the government and its institutions is perceived as 'anti-Israeli', 'anti-Zionist' and revolutionary, since it serves the enemies of the state and promotes international critique of Israeli policies. Discussions about the BDS are even more critical and almost forbidden, especially from a perspective that does not negate it completely.

> *became the centre of the discourse in every possible subject. That is what people call*
> *social change, and that's what's happening here. (2011)*

What makes the discussion about BDS within the Gay Centre important and subversive in our context is the fact that beyond 'traditional' LGBT activism, the subversive space of Trans in the Centre served also as a place for raising anti-militarist and anti-nationalist issues and relating them to such activism. This space serves as what Routledge (2003) calls a 'convergence space', used explicitly to allow individual and groups to share ideas and tactics. Through such autonomous actions, it is possible to 'rebuild solidarities and teach about the multi-scalar working of economic globalization'(Routledge, 2003, p. 736), or, in this case, build solidarities with the oppressed Palestinians and raise awareness of tactics of resistance, thereby reconstructing an autonomous space of action from within. Examining this controversial event reveals a complex situation. Sometimes it seems that each part 'plays' a predefined role – one radical and subversive and the other conservative – although eventually everyone wins. The Trans in the Centre activists managed to raise the stakes, to hold a public discussion on a subversive topic and to provoke objection from the heart of the establishment they criticize, while the establishment allowed them to act and was thus perceived as pluralistic and tolerant ('re-centre the centre' as explained by Egertt). Egertt's response also highlights the Gay Centre as a hub of activism, social change and inter-communal discourse – but who serves as the 'gatekeeper' of this activism? Who decides whether to allow any activity? After all, the decision is made by the Centre's administration, representatives of the local queer patriarchy (Nast, 2002) represented by the Gay Centre. Thus it can be said that despite the subversive element of the politics of Trans in the Centre, it is characterized by a certain conventionality stemming from the place where it chooses to operate, and from the way in which it allows the establishment to appear liberal and pluralistic.

Space of Action

This spatial–analytic dimension has a more practical aspect. Although emerging from and feeding back to discursive and subversive spaces, what warrants a separate analytical section on spaces of action is their nature as a one-time event, unlike the group meetings.

To illustrate, Trans in the Centre has held a 'butch–femme bazaar', in which one could get clothes and give away clothes that no longer fit one's gender identity. This is a feminist–environmentalist resistance practice that opposes the popular capitalist, consumerist system which values the new, as opposed to the old and used (Belk, 2007; Gregson and Beale, 2004; Gregson and Crewe, 2003). Here, we can see the construction of autonomous space that is not a kind of direct action or confrontation, but 'perhaps better seen as hard-wired into the productive acts of project building' (Chatterton and Pickerill, 2010, p. 482; see also Carter, 2005).

Other actions in space include demonstrations and protests outside Trans in the Centre, in which Centre members have participated as a group. As Pickerill and Chatterton (2006, p. 737) say, 'Central to autonomy is an explosive combination of making protest part of everyday life, but also making life into workable alternatives for a wider social good'. One example was the Radical Gay Parade in June 2010 (see Figure 13.2) and a year later, which split from the mainstream parade, both organized by group members. The idea was to bring back politics into the parades, which had become increasingly consumerist and had lost the political protest dimension, including controversial issues such as Palestinian LGBTs, racism, transgender and bisexual oppression, and the tendency among some white gay people to privilege their racial and religious identity – what Jasbir Puar called 'homonationalism'

(2007). The Radical Gay Parade used signs in Hebrew and Arabic and, instead of trucks and advertisements, it included drums and megaphones (see Figures 13.2 and 13.3).

Figure 13.2   The Radical Gay Parade, 2011
Source: Misgav 2011.

**Figure 13.3   Signs in Hebrew and Arabic against racism and nationalism on the
            Radical Gay Parade, 2011**
Source: Misgav 2011.

Following Lynda Johnston's argument, Pride politics is entwined with a spatial politics of shame, and both pride and shame are co-constructed and have spatial and embodied effects (Johnston, 2007). Halperin and Traub claim that '[g]ay pride does not even make sense without some reference to the shame of being gay, and its very successes testify to the intensity of its ongoing struggle with shame' (2009, pp. 3–4).What the Radical Gay Parade in Tel Aviv and many worldwide celebrations of gay shame have in common, is their explicit opposition to the takeover of gay pride marches and festivals by municipalities, bourgeois gay organizations, and corporate sponsors. In this sense, gay shame represents an effort to construct a new, grassroots queer collective founded on principles of resistance to normalization (Halperin and Traub, 2009), or to the 'tyranny of assimilation' (Mattilda, 2004, p. 3; see also Probyn, 2008; Shepard, 2010a; Weiss, 2008). The Radical Gay Parade in Tel Aviv can definitely be considered part of the global queer shame movement, but it also has an important local dimension, above all in its focus on opposing the Israeli occupation and the militarization of Israeli society, in addition to LGBT issues or anti-capitalism.[4]

Concluding Remarks

In this chapter, I examined the Trans in the Centre group in terms of three spatial–analytical dimensions of activism which are simultaneously physical, sociocultural, and symbolic–conscious, through the production of discursive, subversive and action space. The construction of queer autonomy through these three dimensions brings me back to the question raised at the beginning of this chapter: can a radical queer group operating within the space provided by a municipally-funded Gay Centre subvert that space and operate autonomously within it? I believe that the answer is 'yes'. I think that the radical and sometimes subversive politics of the group created and constructed an autonomous politics and spaces within the Centre that stands apart from and sometimes against the hegemony of the Centre and the LGBT community – the local 'queer patriarchy' (Nast, 2002). By creating these spaces and offering different and subversive politics, the group expands the range of options open to LGBT people, especially those from relatively marginal groups within the community (such as trangender people, genderqueers, bisexuals and so on), to act and locate themselves in the Gay Centre.

In order to understand how the group creates autonomous queer space within the Centre, thus reconstructing and even subverting the concept of a municipally-funded Gay Centre, we can use Natalie Oswin's conceptualization of 'queer complicity' (2004). Oswin (2004, p. 84), asks: 'might queer radicality still be possible in a state of complicity from which we cannot ever fully be divorced and which we cannot always and everywhere assume to subvert through re-appropriation?' and, in her answer, she suggests that 'instead of thinking complicit space as total and negative, we might reconceptualize it as ambivalent and porous, as an undetermined set of processes that simultaneously enables both resistance and capitulation' (ibid., p. 84). As shown by Farhang Rouhani (2007), the concept of queer complicity is particularly useful in examining the recent florescence of transnational queer movements and activism, such as the Muslim queer movement in the USA. Rouhani (2007) distinguishes between 'gay' and 'queer' within queer activist circles in the USA. He claims that gay represents mainstream organizations and actions, and queer represents radical ones. He uses the concept of queer complicity as the complex political processes through which non-heterosexual Muslim immigrant minorities are seeking to form new spaces and spheres

---

4 For more on the Radical Gay Parade in Israel, see Eisner (2012, pp. 128–31).

of engagement and possibilities to create activist connections. It is also useful in the context of Trans in the Centre and the way in which its activism subverts the Gay Centre's space from within. In this case, radical autonomy has been created within, rather than separately from, a space of hegemony and domination, subverting capitalist and mainstream logics and institutions. This would seem to fly in the face of the often-heard argument that alternative radical spaces of activism cannot be created within the framework of the existing neoliberal order and LGBT hegemony, and shows that such space cannot only grow as counterweight to mainstream community organizations, but out of those very organizations. In other words, the LBGT centre and the hegemony in general actually come to embrace the forces that try to subvert and challenge them, and, in a way, even support them. Following Kath Browne and Leela Bakshi (2013b, p. 235), it might be helpful to view the municipal centre which hosts Trans in the Centre as 'constantly becoming, spatially contingent assemblages', such that 'cooption, deradicalisation and loss of activism are not always, or necessarily, the result of working within and with the state'.

The three spatial–analytical dimensions discussed here also highlight a new type of activism generated and produced routinely in social centres, calling on us to rethink the concept of activism: the activism represented by Trans in the Centre not only embodies unique and single acts such as parades and demonstrations, but is something that occurs continuously, affecting people's opinions and reconstructing the public sphere and space in a variety of ways. This activism, like that created by social movements, takes part in a range of activities in addition to protests, but, unlike most of the social movements and autonomous spaces created in social centres, it takes place within the institutional space (of the LGBT centre) and not outside it. But while Brown (1997b) claimed that the change caused by queer and LGBT activism is shifting from being active in the segregated space of the gay neighbourhood into heteronormative public space, I have demonstrated that it is not only the moving into heteronormative public space that matters, but also, and perhaps more crucially, the fact that activism occurs *inside* homonormative hegemonic space and institutions, such as the Tel Aviv Gay Centre.

The case study highlights the conflict between the municipal centre's politics and the radical and contesting politics represented by the group and its members. These represent contradictory approaches to contemporary local sexual politics and the ways in which the group's politics connected to broader political issues. The group also serves as an example of how to construct autonomous spaces of activism and subversion 'from within', while at the same time collaborating to a certain extent with the establishment and mainstream politics, albeit without being co-opted. The chapter shows how the Gay Centre's politics of service provision, as opposed to the more radical, autonomous contestation of normative politics offered by Trans in the Centre, are not mutually exclusive but rather always entangled and, to a certain extent, mutually facilitative.

Acknowledgements

This chapter is part of a larger PhD project titled 'Spatial Activism in the City: Perspectives of Body, Identity and Memory' supervised by Professor Tovi Fenster at the PECLAB, Department of Geography and Human Environment, Tel Aviv University. First and foremost, I would like to thank the people who agreed to be interviewed for this project. I am also grateful to Professor Lynda Johnston for her help, feedback and support and to Elisha (Shuki) Alexander and Yuval Egertt for sharing their knowledge with me.

Chapter 14

Intersectional Geopolitics, Transgender Advocacy and the New Media Environment

Natasha Vine and Julie Cupples

Introduction

When transgender actress and political activist Laverne Cox appeared on the cover of *Time* at the end of May 2014, the historical moment was described as 'the transgender tipping point'. The article suggests that the struggle for transgender justice as a civil rights movement is beginning to gain traction in terms of both legislative changes and growing social acceptance (Steinmetz, 2014). Indeed, it appears that trans and non-binary struggles in the USA are regaining the significant organizational and sociopolitical foothold that was lost in the mainstreaming of 'gayness' since Stonewall. In diverse media sites, including social media and mainstream entertainment television, transgender and non-gender-conforming people are speaking out in defence of their civil rights and challenging society's entrenched and binarized understandings of gender and sexuality.

Generally speaking, transgender characters very rarely appear in entertainment television and, when they do, they are usually played by cisgender[1] actors. It wasn't until 2007 when Candis Cayne appeared in *Dirty Sexy Money* that a transgender role was played by a transgender actress on network television. Often, storylines featuring transgender characters tend to stigmatize or sensationalize trans lives as aberrations from reified gender norms – representations that tend to affirm the normality and superiority of cisgender identities. Trans and non-binary people who also suffer from additional and intersecting marginalization – women, people of colour, people with disabilities and so on – have been even less likely to receive any media representation at all. There have been a number of feature films and documentaries[2] about the challenges faced by transgender people that have tended to deal primarily with the question of transition and the conflicts this process produces in both the individual and their family members. Whilst these texts often contain humanizing dimensions, as Sender (2006) notes, transition is usually framed as a question of erroneous biology in which a person is born or trapped in the wrong body. The multifaceted aspects of trans and non-binary identities and the question of post-transition

---

1   The term 'cisgender' applies to individuals whose gender identities match those assigned at birth.
2   Examples include *The Crying Game* (1992), *Boys Don't Cry* (1999), *Creature* (1999), *Southern Comfort* (2001), *Normal* (2003), and *Transamerica* (2005).

social acceptance are less present, as are media texts in which the gender identity of the trans person is not the central focus of their character or part of narrative.[3]

In more recent years, however, we have witnessed an important increase in the presence of both transgender advocates and actors on television. Shows such as *Ugly Betty, The L-Word, Glee, Nip/Tuck, Coronation Street* and *Orphan Black* have also included quite complex transgender characters (although in these cases they have all been played by cisgender actors). Laverne Cox described 2011 as a 'notable year' for transgender actors, who appeared in a range of films and television programmes in both trans and non-trans roles. In 2013 and 2014 Laverne Cox appeared in Netflix prison drama *Orange is the New Black*, playing the role of Sophia Burset, an incarcerated African-American transgender woman. Transgender interviewees have also started to appear on news and current affairs shows, talk shows and satirical news shows. These appearances have drawn our attention to the significance of intersectional politics and the ways in which transphobia, homophobia, sexism, ableism, classism and racism reinforce one another.

This chapter discusses the emergence of an intersectional geopolitics on television and in other mediated spaces, as articulated in particular by trans women of colour. We believe that some recent media texts have opened up discursive space for trans and non-binary people to speak to multifaceted constructions of gender and sexual identities that are revolutionary, realistic and, most importantly, humanizing. These texts are particularly important in the context of the discursive turbulence surrounding dominant geopolitical narratives, such as those of freedom, security and democracy. Our chapter explores some of these texts, along with the participatory, convergent and user-driven media activity that surrounds them. We do so through a critical and feminist geopolitical lens in order to consider what an intersectional geopolitics might look like. Whilst acceptable femininities and masculinities are still discursively policed, it is apparent that new and existing political geographies can be queered and destabilized in radical ways as mediated spaces start to overlap with the spaces of queer lived experience. Drawing on debates surrounding media convergence, we assess the extent to which this new televisual visibility might expand both geopolitical and radical queer agendas in significant ways, unravelling heteronormative narratives of queerness and their associated spatialities.

Trans Lives, Trans Struggles

As Laverne Cox frequently acknowledges in interviews, trans and non-binary people suffer disproportionately from marginalization in housing, healthcare, employment, public safety, family acceptance and mental health compared to the cisgender population, and also compared to the rest of the LGB community. Rates of unemployment and homelessness for trans and non-binary people in the USA are twice that of the general public, with rates for people of colour up to four times higher than for the general population. The intersection of race and gender identity is brought into stark resolve by these statistics, the combination of transphobia and structural racism puts trans women of colour in a place of immense vulnerability and danger. A staggering 40 per cent of trans and non-binary people report having attempted suicide, compared with less than 2 per cent of the general population (Grant et al., 2011).

Given these stark realities, it is unquestionably important that trans and non-binary people, especially people of colour, see positive representations of themselves in the media

---

3   One early exception noted by Sender (2006) was the late 1990s style show *The Brini Maxwell Show.*

and popular culture as part of a broader transformative shift towards recognition, acceptance and celebration of diverse gender expressions and identity.

Acknowledging a disheartening framework of systematic violence has a dual and interconnected discursive value. First, acknowledging the marginalization of trans people means that humanizing and accurate representations of this often-erased community is a revolutionary act in and of itself. Media representation has the power to save lives, defend self-esteem and attack pervasive and negative stereotypes. Second, remembering always that discrimination against trans people is rampant can motivate activists and creators of media products to link their struggles. This convergence means a complex trans character has the agency to both reflect and entertain underrepresented groups in a positive way, while denouncing and bringing attention to the unique risks faced by trans individuals.

Most disappointingly, trans and non-binary issues have been not only ignored by the cisgender–heterosexual mainstream, but have been also subject to active discrimination and erasure by much queer activism and scholarship (Namaste, 2000). Stryker (1994, p. 238) notes that the 'attribution of monstrosity remains a palpable characteristic of most lesbian and gay representations of transsexuality'. It seems that the recent 'transgender tipping point' is less of a point of radical inclusion that we have just reached and more representative of a cyclical progression of queer activism that began in the 1960s at Compton's Cafeteria and Stonewall. As Cox has remarked, 'we've been fighting for gender self determination for decades, you know?' (Valdivia Rude, 2014). Those who threw the first bottles at the historic Stonewall riots were women like Sylvia Rivera, Marsha P. Johnston and others whose names have been lost to pervasive erasure by mainstream 'gay rights'. Drag queens and women of colour, many of them trans and genderqueer were the activists who fought the legal battles that ensued after Stonewall, and it was these same activists who, within a few years of the first Stonewall riot, were excluded from the Gay Activists Alliance in New York, in the interests of making 'gay rights' more acceptable to the straight majority (Wilchins, 2002).

These exclusions emphasize not only the diversity of the category queer but also the importance of an intersectional approach – a focus on how oppressions and privileges of race, class, gender, sexuality and geographical location intersect and either compound or mutually constitute one another. Intersectional thinking is important, because as Cho, Crenshaw and McCall (2013, p. 7) write, 'single-axis thinking' weakens struggles for social justice.

The Queering of Critical and Popular Geopolitics

Since the 1990s feminist scholarship in critical geopolitics has challenged the masculinism of the field, disrupting the excessive focus on elite policy actors and texts and reconceptualizing what is considered to be geopolitical subject-matter (Dowler and Sharp, 2001; Hyndman, 2001; Koopman, 2011; Massaro and Williams, 2013; Sharp, 2000; 2007; Staeheli and Kofman, 2005). This scholarship has demonstrated how the formal domestic and foreign policy realms are gendered, that their effects are felt in a range of everyday, institutional and informal spaces, and that geopolitical relations of power, rather than existing in some abstract realm, are situated and embodied. After 9/11, the Bush administration deployed a highly masculine and heteronormative discourse, promoting masculine military aggression in Iraq and Afghanistan while opposing gay rights and exhorting (feminized) shopping at home (Mirzoeff, 2006). It is important, as the edited collection by Rachel Pain and Susan Smith (2008) illustrates, to produce scholarship that connects geopolitics and everyday life and disrupts the hierarchical way in which threats to personal safety are imagined. They note how politicians routinely deploy discourses of fear of Islamic terrorism, while the fear experienced by people seen to be on the margins of, or irrelevant to, global geopolitics is made invisible. More recently, Rachel Pain (2014a) has developed a feminist critical geopolitical analysis of domestic violence as a form of everyday terrorism, noting how both states and political geographers tend to focus disproportionately on global terrorism, even though this form of terrorism is far less common. Noting the differences between public global violence and intimate private violence, she also points to their important similarities in terms of their race and gender politics. In other words, it is important to consider who is perceived to be violent and who is perceived as requiring protection and the modes of securitization put in place to attend to these perceptions and framings. This approach to critical geopolitics is especially important for transgender and non-binary individuals, particularly those of colour, that are exposed to intolerable everyday violence and for whom, as Laverne Cox told Amy Goodman, '[t]he act of merely walking down the street is often a contested act' (Democracy Now, 2014). In 2011 African-American transgender woman, CeCe McDonald, was verbally and physically assaulted while walking from her apartment in Minneapolis to a local store and was subsequently sentenced to 41 months in a men's prison after she fatally wounded her assailant. Her case demonstrates how the political and judicial system along with a cultural environment of racism and transphobia enact an everyday geopolitics of violence so extreme that everyday spaces and actions (going to the local store) are to be feared. It is important not only to critically probe why gender non-conformity provokes anxieties and expressions of violence from the cis population, but also to understand why this everyday violent injustice – both physical and structural – does not garner a decisive formal political response. Why is a violent action motivated by transphobia and racism at home not accorded the same policy attention as the violent action motivated by religious extremism abroad? Why should the everyday insecurities experienced by the transgender and non-binary population remain marginal to the intense securitization of everyday life that current domestic and foreign policy regimes in the USA and elsewhere engender.

In response to the everyday geopolitics of fear, transgender and non-binary activists are enacting what Sara Koopman (2011) calls an alter-geopolitics. Drawing on activist fieldwork accompanying displaced people in Colombia, Koopman uses the term alter-geopolitics to refer to the kind of grassroots, bottom-up and feminist geopolitics taking place outside of academia, to think of geopolitics of being about 'who gets to see, speak, have agency and how we all get to move' (Koopman, 2011, p. 275). Despite the growing literature within feminist geopolitics that deals with the intersections of politics, space, territory, violence, bodies and gender, transgender struggles have not to date been considered through a critical geopolitical lens (although see Hines, 2010), despite a focus on 'the bodies of those at the "sharp end" of various forms of international activity' (Dixon and Marston, 2011, p. 445). Transgender and non-binary struggles are without question the stuff of geopolitics, given the ways in which the US government has deliberately promoted 'heteropatriarchal, nuclear family formations' entangled with 'white supremacist logic' as the basis of good citizenship (McNeil, 2010, pp. 57–60). McNeil's (2010) analysis of the Defense of Marriage Act (now repealed) and the Healthy Marriage Initiative shows how such policies are some of the ways in which heteronormative nuclear families are posited as superior and good for the nation.

Popular geopolitics is the branch of critical geopolitics that deals specifically with the media and popular culture. Like critical geopolitics more broadly, it has suffered from an entrenched masculinist and elitist focus (Sharp, 2000; Glynn and Cupples, 2015). In a critique of popular geopolitics and an analysis of a political drama on network television, Glynn and Cupples (2015) demonstrate how entertainment television can function as an important site of geopolitical engagement and contestation, in which we can detect the queering of US hegemony and foreign policy initiatives. As we demonstrate here, media texts form the basis of important online and offline activism and advocacy, providing forums in which marginalized people are able to highlight issues of social justice and challenge the geopolitical status quo.

Media Convergence and Transgender Politics

The rise in transgender media visibility is in part facilitated by the dramatic transformations that have taken place in the new media environment. The development of bottom-up and user-driven media platforms such as YouTube and Tumblr is enabling ordinary people not only to consume media, but also to produce it and critique it by speaking back to those in the media industry. 'Old' media platforms such as television are converging with 'new' media platforms, such as Facebook, as ordinary people share clips, content and ideas (Jenkins, 2006). Jenkins, Ford and Green (2013) urge us to focus on the spreadability of media – particularly the ways in which people share the media produced by large corporations which can often matter more in terms of citizen engagement than merely focusing on virality or numbers of visits to a particular link. They discuss the ways in which the media landscape and, with it, values and messages are being shaped not only by large companies, but also by ordinary citizens who produce, remix, share and spread media online in order to pursue political or cultural goals, create new communities or participate in broader social networks.

Contemporary television is caught up in these transformations in complex ways. As network television has given way to the rise of cable and subscription TV, we have seen the fragmentation of the mediascape and the emergence of niche programming content. The emergence of premium cable channels such as HBO and Showtime has enabled a greater level of narrative complexity in television drama (Mittel, 2006), encouraging a kind of forensic fandom (Mittel, 2009) as audiences interact in order to debate and theorize about their favourite shows (Cupples and Glynn, 2013). New digital delivery formats such as Netflix, Hulu and Amazon Prime that have brought further disruptions to the regular television broadcast slot are also producing new forms of participation and interactivity. These transformations are producing new relationships between politics and popular culture as discourses rapidly cross media platforms and as television converges with a range of user-driven practices on the internet.

The growth of social media, and in particular Tumblr, Facebook, YouTube and Twitter, has enabled the development of strong transgender activism and advocacy, connecting people who are geographically dispersed but who are confronting similar experiences of isolation and social rejection (see Vivienne, 2011). Online videos and mainstream television appearances which depict familial love and acceptance of transgender children such as Jazz Jennings[4] and Ryland Whittington (*The Whittington Family: Ryland's Story*, 2014) have frequently gone viral and have led to enhanced media visibility and the opportunity to promote more inclusive messages and societal understanding.

---

4 Jazz Jennings' story is covered in the documentary *I am Jazz: A Family in Transition* (2011, dir. Jennifer Stocks) and is the basis of the children's book *I am Jazz* (Herthel, Jennings and MacNicholas, 2014). Jazz has also appeared on 20/20 and Oprah.

Challenging the Liberal Hosts

The rise of Cox's celebrity status has come with an increased visibility not only for the lived experience and humanity of trans and non-binary people, but also for the deeply held preconceptions and preoccupations of mainstream liberalism. In January 2014 Katie Couric conducted a series of interviews with Carmen Carrera and Laverne Cox. Couric's first interview was with Carmen Carrera, a trans woman famous for her role on *Ru Paul's Drag Race*, subsequent publicized transition and modelling career. With a nod to the politics of passing (Kaveney, 1999), Couric opened the interview with an exclamation of Carrera's beauty, surprise laced into her words. She then played into the demeaning and objectifying obsession with trans people's genitalia, asking Carrera about her surgeries and anatomy, referring to her Ru Paul days as '[w]hen you were still a man'. Carrera was visibly offended by the questions and tried to recentre the interview on her modelling career while Couric defended her invasive curiosity with assertions of the 'mystery' of the trans body to the cis public. Couric focused on what Kaveney calls 'conversion narratives' – the assumption that trans and non-binary people have transcended their pre-transition existence and become someone else entirely.

Carmen Carrera appeared on Couric's show again with Laverne Cox only a few days afterwards, when Cox explained the problematic nature of the cis obsession with trans genitalia, and how this preoccupation stops us from talking about the reality of the trans lived experience. Cox then used this platform to bring attention to the case of Islan Nettles, a trans woman of colour who was beaten and killed in an act of hate violence in New York in August 2013. Charges against Islan's attacker were dropped, despite several witnesses identifying the man.

Cox appeared on Couric's show once again, by herself, in June 2014. This time, Couric acknowledged her hurtful comments and asked to learn, giving Cox the interview to show how to have respectful interactions with trans and non-binary people, without fetishizing or objectifying. Cox emphasized the heterogeneity of the trans experience and encouraged us to give individuals space to speak to their own story.

In February 2014 transgender activist and author of *Redefining Realness* Janet Mock appeared on *Piers Morgan Live*. It was a disastrous and highly insulting interview to both Mock and the transgender community, but Morgan's ignorance and the response to it served to raise awareness of the transphobia that exists towards this sector of the population. Like Couric, Morgan was voyeuristically and sensationalistically focused on Mock's transition, her anatomy and the impact of her gender identity on her intimate relationships. Morgan opened the segment problematically stating that Janet 'was born a boy' and in his first question to her said 'had I not known anything about your story, I would have absolutely not a clue that you had ever been a boy, a male' while the chyron along the bottom of the screen stated 'JANET MOCK: Was a boy until age 18' (http://edition.cnn.com/videos/bestoftv/2014/02/05/pml-janet-mock-whole-interview.cnn).

Morgan also offensively stated how Mock 'was formerly a man' and quizzed her on how her boyfriends had responded to her 'news'. Mock was devastated by the treatment she received and, after the interview, responded to Morgan on Twitter, telling him to 'get it the f**k together', asserting that she was not 'formerly a man' and that he had sensationalized her life. Morgan did not take the criticism well and also used Twitter to defend his position. A day later, Mock agreed to return to the show to explain why she had been offended (*Janet Mock rejoins Piers Morgan*, 2014). Morgan continued to arrogantly defend his position, conflating transgender rights with gay rights and repeatedly denying Mock the space to express her position. Rather than being open to learning from his mistakes, he merely reinforced his own transphobia. Mock asserted that she was never 'formerly a man' or 'born a boy', but rather that she was 'born a baby that was assigned male at birth', drawing attention to the serious abuse suffered by the transgender community. Two weeks later, CNN announced that it was cancelling *Piers Morgan Live*, and there is no doubt that Morgan's exchange with Mock was a likely contributing factor (see Poniewozik, 2014).

Two weeks after the disastrous exchanges with Morgan, Janet Mock appeared on *The Colbert Report* (2014). Hosted by Stephen Colbert, *The Colbert Report* is a parodic news and talk show in which Colbert plays the role of a Republican talk show host such as Fox's Bill O'Reilly in order to mock right-wing and Republican political positions through comedy. Colbert, in his introduction on transgender awareness, deliberately and ironically used the problematic language used by Couric and Morgan (such as calling trans people 'transgenders'). The interview with Mock drew attention to the transphobic ignorance of hosts such as Morgan and Couric. Despite the satirical and parodic nature of the show, Colbert has also deeply offended the transgender community in a number of other segments, particularly when he has taken cheap shots at the transgender community in order to satirize a different issue,[5] suggesting perhaps that Colbert can successfully reveal the ignorance of others but cannot always conceal his own. Colbert, along with another satiric news show presenter John Stewart who hosts *The Daily Show*, have become targets of online campaigns by the transgender community (see, for example, the Tumblr site http://yourmomentofhate.tumblr.com/) who accuse them of perpetuating transphobia and violence towards transgender people.

Over a short period there were then a range of media texts in which Mock, Cox and Carrera defended their right to talk about things other than being trans, their careers, success and goals, while they also used their status as celebrities to take control of narratives surrounding trans and non-binary people.

Crossing Platforms: *Orange is the New Black*

Orange is the New Black (OITNB) reflects a shift in television production and consumption, from a traditional once-a-week, network broadcast, to a more user-funded, online release model. *OITNB* is at the forefront of 'a redefinition of television, an extension of what television already is into new domains' characterized by diverse queer modes and messages within participatory culture (Russo, 2013.) Seasons of Netflix original series like *OITNB* and *House of Cards* are released all at once, speaking to the binge consumption television culture of millennials.

The series is based on the true story of a white middle-class woman who finds herself in prison for involvement with her drug dealer ex-girlfriend several years earlier. Piper Chapman is thus pulled from her comfortable, bourgeois, heterosexual existence into a sentence at Lichfield Women's Prison. There is a kind of uncomfortable irony in that one of the most representative shows in terms of race, class, gender and sexuality is set in a prison. The show has one of the most diverse arrays of not only women of colour, queer women, women of all sizes and ages, and women with disabilities, but also various intersections of the above, while also speaking to the structural injustices that lead to the disproportionate imprisonment of these groups. Laverne Cox plays Sophia Burset, a black trans women in

---

5   In April 2012, in a segment about 'pink slime', otherwise known as Lean Finely Textured Beef (LFTB), Stephen Colbert said that 'our beef now has so many hormones, it's a member of the transgendered community' (*The Colbert Report*, 2012).

prison for the credit card fraud she used to fund her transition. Burset is the prison hairstylist, unapologetically trans and, for the most part, accepted by her fellow prisoners.

The show has received significant uptake by communities of intersectional activists online. The diversity of *OITNB* has been extensively embraced and discussed by social media communities like that of Tumblr and Twitter and on fan forums (see, for example, http://www.fuckyeahlavernecox.tumblr.com). Cox outlined to Couric the difference that the Sophia Burset character makes to transgender politics, in particular how it promotes the destigmatization of trans identities for people within and outside the community (*Laverne Cox Opens up about 'TIME' Cover and 'Orange is the New Black'*, 2014).

Queering Political Geographies in Media

The recent appearance of multifaceted characters like *OITNB*'s Sophia means that consumers and actors alike don't have to queer cis–het spaces, but can turn their efforts to activating and radicalizing pockets of queer media space that are already articulated and controlled by queer people – most notably trans and non-binary people – in the first instance.

There exists a tension in the representation of marginalized groups that suffer from the kind of systematic violence experienced by the trans and non-binary community. The contradiction lies in the social and commercial functions of television and the attempt to speak to diverse constituencies, in this case both transgender people and members of the mainstream cis–het public. As previous scholarship on the representation of racial and sexual minorities on television demonstrates, visibility can have highly contradictory outcomes.[6]

For example, the dramatic increase in gay and lesbian characters on television has been accompanied by a sanitized homonormativity (see Duggan, 2002), the tendency to discursively separate the 'good' queers – the generally white, gay sexual subjects who display middle-class practices of consumption and affirm, rather than contest, heteronormativity – from the 'bad' queers (Puar, 2006). On television, this homonormativity is embodied by whitewashed stereotypes that posit queer characters as monogamous, wealthy, comfortable middle-class men, sassy and fashionable, and more than content to pander to heteronormativity, sexism and racism. Examples include Cameron and Mitchell in *Modern Family* (see Doty, 2010) or Bryan and David in *The New Normal*.[7] So, while cheery, idealized narratives might erase the vulnerability of real people or give the impression to uninformed viewers that struggles do not exist, seeing successful, happy, fulfilled trans and non-binary characters is immensely important to the self-esteem of those who so rarely see accurate and complex depictions of their lived experience in televisual spaces. In other words, we need a diversity of (trans) representations.

OITNB has navigated this tension artfully. Burset is glamorous, funny and compassionate. She is open about her gender, even going so far as to talk about her transition and offering the other (cis)women in the prison anatomy lessons. The convergence of Cox's character and her activism surrounding and outside of the show provides a further point of hope and inspiration. She is humble about her success, tirelessly linking it to the strength of

---

6   *The Cosby Show*, for example, both destabilized and reproduced white privilege (see Jhally and Lewis, 1992).

7   This is not, of course, straightforward. Most television texts frequently stage a range of perspectives and facilitate a diverse set of interpretations by viewers (Glynn and Cupples, 2015). As Dhaenens (2014) writes, homonormativity is frequently transgressed, destabilized and called into question in entertainment television.

the community she belongs to, and refuses to let her experience speak immutably to the immense complexity of trans and non-binary lived experiences.

An Intersectional Geopolitics?

Critical geopolitics is concerned with ways in which boundaries and therefore relations of power are made and maintained. It is also concerned with the ways in which political reasoning is constructed to justify particular domestic and foreign policy objectives, including the banning/passing of marriage equality legislation, the articulation of 'stand your ground', the invasion and occupation of sovereign nations and the sending of young lives to fight in distant wars, and the modes of surveillance put in place at airports and in cyberspace. All of these policies are underpinned by dominant modes of understanding race, gender, sexuality and citizenship and would not be in place if the more marginal understandings that constantly challenge and contest them were less marginal.

At the time of writing, US political hegemony is in a state of flux. The militarized masculinism of the Bush administration no longer has the same cultural or political resonance and in recent years we have seen political actions, such as the passing of marriage equality in many US states and the repeal of DOMA and 'Don't ask, don't tell', which would have been unthinkable in the early years of that administration. Political mobilizations such as the Tea Party, the intense debates surrounding reproductive rights and marriage equality, and the failure of Congress to pass urgent immigration reform and to properly attend to the health needs of US veterans result in part from the ways in which white America is struggling with the demographic and cultural changes which repeatedly call white privilege and its concomitant heteronormative gender expressions into question. The discomfort that these cultural changes produce in certain sectors of the population results in an Othering of bodies that are different, not just Muslim religious fundamentalist-terrorist bodies but also non-gender-conforming bodies, immigrant bodies and disabled veteran bodies. Transgender people find themselves caught up in these discursive struggles because of the ways in which they challenge common-sense boundaries, because they appear to constitute a representational threat to the naturalized social order. This challenge is serious, frequently resulting, as we have noted, in incarceration, suicide attempts, unemployment, homelessness and even violent assault. As Sara Smith (2011) writes, bodies are also sites of geopolitics. When CeCe McDonald is attacked not by someone who knows her personally, but because she is a member of marginalized and stigmatized population 'the body itself becomes a geopolitical site' (Smith, 2011, pp. 456–7). The threats to trans people in the USA come from fellow US Americans – neighbours, employers, landlords, colleagues, relatives – rather than from Al-Qaeda operatives or religious fundamentalists in a distant part of the world. In other words, trans people are excluded from the dominant values such as the right to family life, secure employment and freedom from violence that are allegedly the reasons for which the US government goes to war.

The televisual advocacy of transgender activists such as Cox and Mock interrogates geopolitical hegemonies and puts an alternative set of narratives into circulation. This activism should be understood as an alter-geopolitics as it 'works to build and live alternatives to the (in)security of violence' (Koopman, 2011, p. 281), linking corporeal security for trans people to the right to gender self-determination. It engages marginalized trans youth in empowering ways and it calls those with voice in the media to account, forcing them to engage with an alternative set of discourses, to prove that they are teachable (Couric) or face cancellation (Morgan). The media events of 2014 mean that it will not be easy for future interviewers to unthinkingly repeat the transphobia that underpins comments such as 'wow, you're so beautiful' or 'I would never have known you were once/really a man'. They also demonstrate how active online communities can draw upon the media produced by large corporations to debate, endorse (*OITNB*) or challenge (Piers Morgan) views and messages espoused within them and draw attention to injustice. Discourses travel from television to social media and back to television, allowing larger numbers of people to participate in debates about issues that matter to them. As they do so, they begin to constitute themselves as cultural citizens, revealing the exclusions from full citizenship to which they are subjected.

Of course, these shifts do not in themselves end transphobia, and it is important not to be prematurely celebratory. Katie Couric engaged positively with her own transphobia, and online comments across Tumblr and Twitter demonstrate that many trans people feel a palpable sense of possibility as a result of Cox's advocacy. But the internet is also a site of rampant transphobia, racism and misogyny. Many viewers of *The Katie Couric Show* posted extremely hostile comments on the show's website, showing the resilience of transphobia, misogyny and racism in the contemporary USA. The convergent media environment is as much a site for the resecuring of binary gender as it is for its undoing.

But the contemporary discursive terrain has some interesting features. The fact that it is the transphobia of more progressive liberal television hosts such Stephen Colbert, John Stewart, Katie Couric and Piers Morgan, rather than, say, Bill O'Reilly or Anne Coulter, that has been exposed, reveals the hegemonic nature of transphobia. This exposure is a key first step in its dismantling. Furthermore, what is significant about Laverne Cox and *Orange is the New Black* as media texts is the ways in which they keep both diversity and intersectionality at the fore, resisting the kind of sanitized hetero- and homonormativity that has characterized representations of other minorities. In interviews, both Cox and Mock constantly refer to transgender people for whom justice is denied and they retweet the tweets from ordinary transgender people who feel inspired or helped by their visibility. They also refer as much to poverty and racism as well as transphobia, drawing attention to how race, class and gender frequently interact in negative ways. It appears that they are successfully resisting assimilation, struggling to ensure that legislative changes keep pace with cultural changes. In other words, they remain attentive to the everyday spaces that are so hard for transgender people and work to keep them in dialogue with the more spectacular spaces of televisual or cinematic production.

While referring to the transgender community as a key political constituency, they also undermine its easy essentialization through an emphasis on the heterogeneity of this community. Critical geopolitics has stressed the need to disrupt monolithic understandings of the Other. A critical geopolitics would therefore also disrupt the monolithic understandings of gender identity that are frequently applied to trans people. Not all trans people feel trapped in the wrong body, although some do. Not all of them 'pass', although some do. Not all have transitioned or wish to transition, although some do. Some assert identities as men or women and need to be seen as such; others refuse these labels. Some are fighting racism and poverty as well as transphobia. They are gay, straight, bisexual and queer.

Cox's and Mock's articulate mediated activism and the screening of a TV drama such as *OITNB*, which includes a rounded humanized trans character played by a trans actress, are important political interventions that are shifting the discursive terrain surrounding trans rights. Further, the alternative representations they advance provide important building-blocks for those who do not have the media visibility enjoyed by Cox or Mock but are making do with the media resources (Twitter, Tumblr and blogs) that they have available. These resources are creating or expanding spaces of dialogue that previously didn't exist or were marginal and are providing trans and non-binary people with the opportunity to disrupt and reframe how their stories and lived experiences are told in the media.

Acknowledgement

This research is supported in part by the Marsden Fund of the Royal Society of New Zealand: grant number MAU1108.

Chapter 15

Sexual Tensions in Modernizing Singapore: The Postcolonial and the Intimate

Natalie Oswin

When a reform of the Singapore Penal Code was completed in 2007, local gay and lesbian activists seized the opportunity to lobby for the removal of Section 377A, a colonial-era statute prohibiting 'gross indecency' between two men. As public debates ensued, arguments for the repeal of this law focused on its status as a British import that is out of place and out of time in contemporary Singapore. But in a speech detailing the city-state government's rationale for the decision to retain the statute, Prime Minister Lee Hsien Loong (2007) set out a different notion of the relationship between past and present. In his view, the fact that 'we are not starting from a blank slate' is all the more reason to protect the 'heterosexual stable family [as] a social norm' that is 'part of our landscape'. However unwittingly, his dismissal of the argument that being postcolonial entails an outright rejection of the remnants of a colonial past is aligned with postcolonial theory's claim that the postcolonial condition is by no means beyond the colonial. As such, while Prime Minister Lee offered this justification as the last word on these recent debates, I take it as a point of departure for a critical response to this illiberal sexual politics. Following Prime Minister Lee's assertion that Singapore's past valuably shapes its present, I argue that consideration of heteronormativity as a colonial trace is necessary to better understand the politics of its perpetuation in this contemporary global city.

In what follows, a postcolonial queer approach frames empirical evidence drawn from Singapore's late colonial period. I show that although scant mention of homosexuality or the passage of Section 377A is made in the public record, the archive is rich with evidence of the urgent delineation of a proper intimate sphere. By highlighting the efforts of both the colonial administration and members of the colonized elite to transform Singapore from a colonial entrepôt of single male migrant workers into a nation of postcolonial nuclear families, the present-day focus on homosexual versus heterosexual politics gives way to a reading of a much broader politics of intimacy. The establishment of heteronormativity as a central aspect of Singapore's colonial and postcolonial modernization projects has produced sexual exclusion, to be sure. But it also, and inextricably, has constructed an intimate sphere bound up with a relentless progress narrative that has implications for the workings of citizenship along race, class and gender lines. The 'gay issue' that has grabbed the spotlight is therefore only part of the picture of heteronormativity, and there is, despite the Singapore government's contrary assertion, considerable scope for critical response.

Sexuality, Colonial Agency and Postcolonial Governance

Studies of sexuality have brought together intimacy, colonialism and globalization in various ways. For instance, an interdisciplinary body of work has recently emerged to dissect 'the ways in which discourses of sexuality are inextricable from prior and continuing histories of colonialism, nationalism, racism, and migration' (Gopinath, 2005, p. 3). Neoliberalism and desire (Rofel, 2007), gendered diasporic subjectivity (Gopinath, 2005), transnational migration and gay identity (Manalansan, 2003) and biopolitics and terrorism (Puar, 2007) are just some of the topics that have been scrutinized by scholars who innovatively bring queer theory and postcolonial theory together to understand the workings of heteronormativity in an array of contexts. This work goes beyond sexual identity per se to explore the ways in which sexual norms are part of broader constellations of power that situate them in a relationship of mutual constitution with racialized, gendered and classed processes. It also takes us beyond a narrow focus on the prohibition of, or permission for, specific sexual acts and identities to attend to the public construction of an intimate sphere. However, as Anjali Arondekar (2005, p. 12) has pointed out, though informed by postcolonial thought, 'such work focuses overwhelmingly on contemporary issues with colonialism appearing more as a referent than a sustained period of study.' It tends to position colonialism as a backdrop rather than as a still active element in postcolonial place-making. This limits this literature's usefulness in approaching the troubling persistence of mechanisms of colonial sexual regulation and the broader politics of intimacy that such proscriptions participate in shaping.

So we might also turn to literature that puts postcolonial theory to use for somewhat different ends – that is, explicit historical excavations of gender, race, sexuality and empire. The British Empire, of which Singapore was a part, has been particularly well explored in this regard by scholars such as Anne McClintock (1995), Lenore Manderson (1997), Philip Howell (2000) and Richard Phillips (2006). Additionally of course, Ann Stoler (1995, 2002) has provided immensely productive insights on the intimate politics of the colonial Dutch East Indies. A common aim across this work is the disruption of depictions of colonial power relations as somehow stable, fixed and imposed from without. The colonized/colonizer binary is deconstructed to enable analysis of colonial hegemony as the product of constant contest over meanings, ideologies and notions of identity. For these scholars, colonial culture is characterized by dynamism, structure does not overdetermine agency, and boundaries are porous. By challenging perceptions of the distance between metropole and periphery and attending to the myriad relations between these sites, this work interrogates colonial power to demonstrate that 'there was no such thing as a "home base" of British sexuality' (Howell, 2000, p. 336) and calls attention to the 'productivity of the margins' (Phillips, 2006, p. 163) in the establishment of the bourgeois sexuality of the 'centre'. But even these postcolonial examinations of sexuality that concertedly deal with the specific histories and geographies of colonialism take us only a limited way towards understanding the legacy of colonial regulation in postcolonies. For, although the centre is thrown off its axis, attention is still drawn inevitably back to Europe. The crucial undertaking of destabilizing monolithic caricatures of colonial power leads productively to insightful analyses of the constitution of the colonizer. But, given this emphasis, the agency of the colonized, though acknowledged, is not the focal point of study. This is a significant gap since the objects of colonial rule eventually became postcolonial governors who are key actors in the contemporary regulation of sexuality in the era of independence.

I argue that just as colonial governance is the object of study for scholars seeking to understand colonial sexual politics and the broader construction of intimacy of which they are part, a light must be shone on the transition to postcolonial governance when analysing postcolonial sexual and intimate politics. In other words, the post/colony itself can usefully be more firmly located at the centre of study. This chapter therefore extends the insights of histories of the colonial regulation of sexuality to explore the postcolonial regulation of intimacy and its local antecedents. It builds on acknowledgements of the 'tensions of empire' (Cooper and Stoler, 1997) that have enriched understanding of the colonial situation by attending to the significant role that certain colonized actors played in shaping sexual norms as the subsequent ascendance of these actors to positions of power after independence has played an important part in narrowing the imagination of intimacy in contemporary Singapore.

Modern Families for a New Nation

It would be difficult to overstate the importance accorded to the institution of the family in contemporary Singapore. The People's Action Party government that has been in power since the 1965 declaration of independence has vigorously promoted this ideal. Its efforts include policies that tie public housing allotments and subsidies to marriage and a willingness to live in close proximity to one's parents, institutionalization of a national matchmaking agency, aggressive anti-natalist measures that worked all too well and have been followed by pro-natalist initiatives, and constant exhortations to marry and (then) procreate via the state-controlled media, various government ministries and a battery of state-supported organizations. Such initiatives are undoubtedly at least partly responsible for the most recent census data showing that of all households, 82.1 per cent fall into the category 'one family nucleus' and another 5.6 per cent fit into the 'two or more family nuclei' description, leaving only 12.3 per cent to bear the 'no family nucleus' distinction (Leow, 2000). Thus, Prime Minister Lee's assertion, when rejecting the campaign to repeal Section 377A, that the nuclear family is 'part of our landscape' rings exceptionally true.[1] Given Singapore's history as a colonial entrepôt that was overwhelmingly composed of single male migrants, this fact is evidence of a quite remarkable feat of social engineering.

It should also be noted that the state of the nation's families is very well remarked upon. Within both state and popular discourse, the modernization of the family is a key facet of the national progress narrative. Its recognition as an essential element in the city-state's propulsion from 'third world to first' (Lee, 2000) also extends to the substantial social sciences literature on Singapore's political economy, society and culture. Much of this work valorizes a nuclear, heterosexual, middle-class family ideal and makes policy-oriented recommendations that aim to perpetuate it (Quah, 1994; Straughan, 1999). But another strand takes a more critical approach that analyses the state's promotion of this very particular notion of family as an ideological mechanism of social control. Important critiques have been made of the links between Singapore's family policy and gender inequity (Kong and Yeoh, 2003; Teo, 2007), losses of ethnic cohesion (Chua, 1997), the stigmatization of single parents (Wong et al., 2004) and entrenchment of dependence on a market economy (Salaff, 1988). Further, the heterosexual character of the official family ideal is noted as a significant obstacle in commentaries on the status of homosexuality in the city-state (Tan, 2007; Weiss, 2005). So a critical perspective on the role of family norms in contemporary Singapore is well developed, and this literature is a useful reference point for my own interrogation of the sedimentation of heteronormativity across the colonial and postcolonial eras. This range

---

1   For analyses of the ways in which the privileging of the nuclear family norm limits intimate norms in Singapore, see Oswin (2010, 2012).

of work highlights the extraordinary reach of the family ideal and its relationship to the production of a wide variety of social figures. In other words, family norms are involved not only in the production of the heterosexual and the homosexual; they also produce the good mother, the disciplined worker, the filial child and many more identifications.

This insight is exceedingly useful in interpreting the history of sexuality in Singapore as it relates to the contemporary linkage between the official marginality of homosexuality and centrality of the nuclear family. For the archival record actually contains very little mention of the threat of homosexuality. Lenore Manderson (1996) provides evidence that the highly unbalanced sex ratio led colonial officials to advocate female prostitution as a 'necessary evil, to save us from something worse', and James Warren (2003) finds coroner reports of anal syphilis that attest to the existence of male same-sex activity. But records of public attention to the issue are scarce. Three Straits Settlements *Annual Reports* contain brief references to male prostitution. The 1936 report simply states that, 'male prostitution was also kept in check, as and when encountered' (Straits Settlements, 1936, p. 856). The 1937 report goes slightly further:

> Widespread existence of male prostitution was discovered and reported to the Government whose orders have been carried out ... Sodomy is a penal offence; its danger to adolescents is obvious; obvious too, is the danger of blackmail, the demoralizing effect on disciplined forces and on a mixed community which looks to the Government for wholesome governing. (Straits Settlements, 1937, p. 835)

The 1938 report states definitively that 'male prostitution and other forms of beastliness were stamped out as and when opportunity occurred' (Straits Settlements, 1938a, p. 414). In the same year, Section 377A was added to the penal code. Its first reading is noted in the Legislative Council Proceedings. On its second reading, the Attorney General made the following remarks:

> It is unfortunately the case that acts of the nature described have been brought to notice. As the law now stands, such acts can only be dealt with, if at all, under the Minor Offences Ordinance, and then only if committed in public. Punishment under the Ordinance is inadequate and the chances of detection are small. It is desired, therefore, to strengthen the law and to bring it into line with English Criminal Law, from which this clause is taken, and the law of various other parts of the Colonial Empire. (Straits Settlements, 1938b, p. B49)

The only other discussion of its passage is found in the memoirs of a colonial official who states: 'Nor should I fail to mention the social upheaval of the thirties when the diary of a professional Chinese catamite fell into the hands of the police, resulting in an official inquiry, the disgrace of several prominent persons, and the suicide of two of those who were implicated in the matter' (Purcell, 1965, p. 250). But no reports of the passage of this law or the scandal that purportedly precipitated it have been found in any local newspapers or in correspondence with the London Colonial Office. Also, no explicit or even implicit references to homosexuality have been uncovered in any of the numerous publications produced by and for members of the various colonized communities.

This scant public discourse on the prohibition of male same-sex activity is somewhat surprising given that other profound shifts in the management of intimate relations had been occurring in the colony by the time Section 377A was passed. For most of its rule, the colonial administration did not concern itself with transforming the intimate lives of the Straits Settlements' inhabitants. In its view, the combination of an abnormal sex ratio and the cultural 'character' of the colonized population led inevitably to rather different social mores in this corner of the periphery than prevailed in the metropole. For instance, various attempts by British social reformers to counter the social evil of prostitution were rejected by Singapore's colonial officials on the grounds that 'sexual appetite' needed to be filled and that 'the Asiatic regards prostitution and sex generally on a different plane to that of an European' (UK National Archives). There was also a principle of non-interference with the 'customs' of the colonized guided approaches to matters such as marriage, divorce, inheritance and adoption. But from around 1910, shifts in colonial policies that moved away from a narrow emphasis on production and towards a broad approach to social reproduction are evident. Over the remainder of the colonial period, infant and maternal health was prioritized, immigration policies were reconfigured in order to balance the sex ratio and encourage family formation and reunification, the family planning association was founded, the Department of Social Welfare was established, and so on. These changes represent a concerted push toward the socioeconomic development of the Straits Settlements in this late colonial period and, as these efforts centrally entailed the production and promotion of a narrowly defined Singapore family, an integral part of this reorientation was the establishment of heteronormality in place of 'abnormal' population dynamics and 'backward' cultural practices.

The transformation of this colonial entrepôt composed of single, male migrant workers into a modern nation of families was thus well underway by the time Section 377A was deemed a necessary legislative addition. So, although homosexuality is now positioned as a primary threat to the nuclear family, this is a relatively recent narrative. In other words, although it has always been and still remains within the orbit of heteronormativity in Singapore, it did not create it. To understand the provenance of the ideal family that the postcolonial government seeks to protect by upholding Section 377A, we need to look beyond this statute's specific referent to other colonial traces. The remaining pages do this through a brief exploration of debates over Chinese marriages in the late colonial period, as this was one of the ways in which a new heteronormativity was established during this time.

Marrying into Modernity

Ann Stoler, in her work on the Dutch East Indies, exposes intimacy as a central facet of colonial governance. She highlights the ways in which the bodies of colonizers were 'never in fact isolated, but defined by intimate relationships and daily contacts of a special kind' (Stoler, 1995, p. 111). A racialized, gendered and sexualized bourgeois project, she argues, was thus made in the colonies rather than imported to them. The idea of Europeanness was maintained through the negotiation of boundaries between white administrators (and particularly their wives) and their native servants and nursemaids. Also among the 'tensions of empire' that she carefully details are anxieties over mixed marriages and the fate of mixed-race children. Indeed, 'colonial regimes most rigorously controlled marriages that involved elites and "Europeans" because ... these marriages helped regulate who belonged to the ruling class' (Loos, 2008, p. 31). But they much less rigorously controlled unions that did not involve at least one European. In these cases, which constituted the vast majority, the state deferred to the colonized themselves. In the Straits Settlements, marriage within the Indian community was to be administered according to the principles of Hinduism, 'Mahomedan' law guided Malay marriage and Chinese marriage was left to Chinese custom. This neat description is, however, deceptive. For the principle of non-interference worked on a more theoretical than actual level as the colonial government had much to say about the marriage customs of those it ruled, not least because it regarded its own monogamous form of marriage to be the pinnacle of civilized conduct. The legislation of Chinese marriage is exemplary of this fact.

In 1930 an appellate court judge in Penang (another corner of the Straits Settlements) ruled in a case that was brought to determine the legitimacy of a son's claims by a woman other than the wife of his Chinese father's estate. In doing so, he remarked that 'the modifications of the law of England which obtain in the Colony in the application of that law to the various alien races established there, arise from the necessity of preventing the injustice or oppression which would ensure if that law were applied to alien races unmodified' (*Khoo Hooi Leong v Khoo Chong Yeok*, pp. 127–8). After stating this lofty ambition, he went on to assert that 'from the above-mentioned necessity arises the recognition by the Courts of the Colony of polygamous marriages among the Chinese' (ibid., p. 128). This latter statement is common to numerous judgments of colonial courts on matters pertaining to the inheritances of wealthy Chinese men. It had been taken as legal fact that the Chinese were polygamous since the ruling in the precedent setting *Six Widows* case of 1908. But this claim was far from unchallenged within the Chinese community, particularly by members of the Straits Chinese elite.

The appellation 'Straits Chinese' refers to persons of Chinese heritage who were born in the Straits Settlements. Members of this community were English-educated men of a mercantile class who were closely tied to the colonial administration as local informants. For instance, they comprised the Chinese Advisory Board that directly reported to the colonial office of the Chinese Protectorate, and their most well-respected members sat on the Legislative Council as 'unofficials'. As Philip Holden (1999, p. 65) has noted, whilst many communities in the Straits Settlements made efforts to reform their members and enter the public sphere as modern subjects, the Straits Chinese community 'made the most determined effort'. It was duly rewarded with the respect of the colonial administration. Evidence of this respect abounds. One such declaration, made by C.W. Darbishire on the event of the retirement of Tan Jiak Kim from his 'unofficial' position on the Legislative Council, demonstrates the depth of this admiration and is worth quoting at length:

> The Chinese community bulks very largely in the life of these Settlements, and we who are in daily touch with the Chinese cannot fail to realize how overwhelmingly the welfare of these Settlements depends upon their goodwill and upon a mutual understanding. This goodwill, this understanding, this confidence in British rule which we have here is unhesitatingly granted to us, and we recognize that it is so granted to us in no small degree because we have been fortunate in finding men ready to assist us amongst the enlightened members of the Chinese. These leaders are broad-minded enough to grasp the Western point of view and to weld it easily and smoothly with the Eastern point of view. (Straits Settlements, 1915, B30)

Many of the most prominent members of this group made very public their disapproval of the non-requirement of registration of Chinese marriages and the colonial determination that such marriages were customarily polygamous. After years in which successive 'unofficials' raised the issue of Chinese marriage in the Legislative Council, the colonial administration formed a Chinese Marriage Committee to report on the issue in 1926. After consulting with Chinese associations, clan groups and members of the public, the committee reported that opposition to the registration of Chinese marriages was far more widespread than was support. Cited reasons for this stance were 'the dislike of government interference with marriage which has long been managed by the people themselves' and 'fear that registration would be used to enforce monogamy in the future' (*Report of the Chinese Marriage*

Committee, 1926, p. 4). Further, the point is centrally made that opinion was divided between the numerical minority of those born in the colony and numerical majority of those born in China. The report states: 'The District Associations and other societies whose members are composed entirely or in part of Chinese born in China, are almost entirely opposed to registration of Chinese marriages in any shape or form; and this opposition was voiced in most cases by the China-born witnesses' (ibid., p. 5). But by casting the locally born as 'more advanced' members of the community, the committee's report recommends registration on a voluntary basis. Its justification for this recommendation is spelled out as follows: 'We consider that probably in the first instance only Chinese born in the colony or Malaya would make use of the provision, but that as its advantages are recognized, it will become increasingly used' (ibid., p. 7). In discussions of the report in the Legislative Council, Song Ong Siang tried to push this recommendation through by insisting that:

> There is no doubt that the trend of opinion among the educated, intelligent and advanced sections of the Chinese community of this Colony, – both men and women, – is in favour of legislation, in some form, for registration of Chinese marriages, – of a voluntary character to begin with, if compulsory registration should be decried by the Chinese community as objectionable. (Straits Settlements, 1927, p. B27)

The Legislative Council chose not to go forward with the registration of Chinese marriages in any form on the basis that the report had found little desire for it. Yet the Straits Chinese unofficials continued to raise the issue in the Council. The clearest assertion of the motivation behind this continued drive is found in the impassioned speech of Lim Cheng Ean in 1933. He states:

> I have brought up this question because as a father of growing daughters I feel that I must be able to marry off my daughters in the same way as you Europeans marry yours – give them the new freedom and not let them be tied up and at the mercy of brutes … You now exclude the Chinese from China by the Aliens Ordinance, because you want to build a new nationality, a new nation of Straits Settlements people. Give us this then. If other people don't want it, let them not come into it. (Straits Settlements, 1933, p. B107)

He would have to wait until the 1961 passage of the Women's Charter by the People's Action Party government to see this vision of governmental regulation of marriage become reality. With this legislation, polygamy was outlawed and registration of all marriages became a legal requirement. Only then was the law of the former colony that Tan Cheng Lock had described as 'a half-caste offspring resulting from the mating of English law to Chinese law by our Judges' finally made Singaporean (Straits Settlements, 1933, p. B101) as the postcolonial Singapore government purposefully 'upgraded' the family as part of its social engineering and socioeconomic development efforts (see Salaff, 1988).

Conclusion

As Philip Holden (2003, p. 313) notes, 'modern disciplinary power … would be perfected not by the colonialists but by the new nations that emerged from colonialism'. In Singapore, the colonizer/colonized distinction was certainly a core element in the production of a colonial power that was fundamentally divisive. The status of full modern citizen was

135

reserved for those hailing from Europe, the purported centre of civilization. The colonized were associated with tradition or custom and generally treated as objects of rule. As such, the colonial state could never be a representative polity. It could never foster a nation of subjects. Herein is the obvious impetus for the anti-colonial struggle. But to understand both the colonial and postcolonial projects, the stratification of the colonized population ought not to be overlooked. The British administration relied on certain segments of the colonized population to act as interpreters, cultural informants and liaisers with various groups. In addition, business ties, property ownership and educational attainments were elevators of status and created a colonial elite. This elite by no means desired to throw off the mantle of modernity. Rather, they passionately argued for their rightful place within it. They became 'active enunciators of the colonial discourse' who were complicit in the construction of representations of backward colonized others and advocated societal reforms that could civilize the rest of the colonized community (Yao, 1999; see also Hirschman, 1986). With the achievement of independence, the new government embraced the idea of modernization wholeheartedly. Postcolonial Singapore has indeed been shaped by a desire 'to be even *more consistently modern* than the former colonial masters were' (Wee, 2007, p. 20, emphasis in the original). Certain segments of the colonized community were thus important actors in the late colonial drive towards progress and development, and pushed forward an ambitious agenda for the improvement of the people of the postcolonial city-state. They have been, in short, in deep conversation with the ideas that drove colonial rule long before and long after it ended.

As such, a colonial era anti-sodomy law is still on the books in postcolonial Singapore not because the city-state is just not postcolonial enough. Rather, it stands because the establishment of heteronormativity was in fact a key facet of the transition from colonial administration to postcolonial governance. Further, whilst the debates over Section 377A have drawn a line between heterosexuality and homosexuality in Singapore, following Prime Minister Lee's offhand suggestion that this binary is central to the colonial–postcolonial relationship uncovers a much more complex intimate sphere than the sexual binary can capture. Hence the benefit of a postcolonial queer approach that takes the legacy of colonialism seriously and seeks to understand the links between sex, intimacy, citizenship, governance and modernity. Section 377A stands because a specific mode of heteronormativity that was constructed in place during Singapore's late colonial period became an active and influential force and key facet of its development as an independent city-state. The establishment of intimate norms in this past and present have produced convictions regarding the appropriateness of sexual-object choices, to be sure. But they have also rendered family, kinship and domesticity as central areas of governmental intervention in contemporary Singapore. To fulfil desires for modernity, development and progress, it is not just gays and lesbians that have been 'queered' in the city-state. So, too, have the single, the uneducated, the unskilled migrant worker and many others who have been deemed incapable of creating and sustaining a 'quality' population. Prime Minister Lee has called attention to the sedimentation of heteronormativity in the city-state. Critical responses must grapple with the postcolonial politics of intimacy.

SECTION III
Decolonizing Sexualities

Robert Kulpa and Joseli Maria Silva (editors)

Chapter 16

Decolonizing Queer Epistemologies: Section Introduction

Robert Kulpa and Joseli Maria Silva

Since the 1960s and the publication of original works by Kuhn (1996), Feyerabend (1993), Foucault (2002), the Western European and anglophone intellectual hemispheres have been going through a continuous change from positivist to more critical epistemologies (Carr, 1987). In the following decades these parts of the world also lived through rebellious social and cultural mobilizations that are now often called 'new social movements' - feminism, black liberation, black feminism, lesbian and gay liberation, and others. These movements made the issue of 'location' one of their primary objects of critique. For contemporary social initiatives and academic social sciences and humanities, particularly important are feminist debates about 'standpoint theory' in the 1980s (Harding, 1991, 2004; Hekman, 2004) and about 'situated knowledge' in the 1990s (Visweswaran, 1994; Haraway, 1997), along with, and developing since the 1970s, postcolonial studies (Fanon, 1967; Nandy, 1983; Said, 1978; Spivak, 1995). Among other things, they all share an interest in 'self-reflexivity', 'situated knowledge', 'politics of location' and 'critical epistemologies', an interest from which this section of the *Companion to Geographies of Sex and Sexualities* also stems. Although these 'alerting processes' are already decades long, we believe that the contemporary production and circulation of (scientific) knowledge, also within gender and sexuality studies, and geographies, is still affected by the 'coloniality of power' (Quijano, 2000, 2007) related to the (metaphorical *and* physical) place of knowledge enunciation.

As the editors and authors come from a range of geographical contexts, academic traditions and are differently placed in relation to forms of academic privilege, we draw on these rich, diverse positionalities to revisit epistemological practices through geopolitical lenses directed at 'geographies', 'genders' and 'sexualities'. Inspiration is found in the work indicating the Eurocentrism of contemporary 'social sciences' (Bhambra, 2007; Bortoluci and Jansen, 2013; Connell, 2007; Go, 2013; Oommen, 1991; Steinmetz, 2013) and other disciplines (Lal, 2005; Martinez, 2003; Wane et al., 2011; Comaroff and Comaroff, 2012; Hudson and Williams, 2004; Baber, 2002). In particular, we follow geographers, who criticized the anglophone journals for reproducing 'the anglophone' as '*the* canon', thus perpetuating inequality of knowledge (Aalbers, 2004; Aalbers and Rossi, 2006; Garcia-Ramon, 2003; Garcia Ramon et al., 2006; Fall and Rosière, 2008; Kitchin, 2005; Kitchin and Fuller, 2003), those who claimed that anglophone geography is becoming self-centred and thus impoverished (Rodríguez-Pose, 2006; Vaiou, 2004; Whitehand, 2005) and those geographers who have investigated academic neoliberalism as a form of profit-making from the knowledge ownership (Berg, 2012; Best, 2009; Minca, 2000; Paasi, 2005).

The current organization of scientific production is prone to an increasing number of encounters between researchers from around the world, due to the expansion of communication networks, air transport and (supra)national incentives for the internationalization of intellectual labour (but mostly 'quantifiable knowledge outputs'). Consequently, the everyday life of academics is not only intersected by cultural, social or economic dynamics, but is also made accountable to them, especially in terms of the neoliberal economy – consider requirements such as 'a track record of successful grant applications' in the job ads, for example (Bailey and Freedman, 2011; Collini, 2012; Farred, 2003; Raunig, 2013). We urgently need debates about the flux and exchanges between academics, so that we can understand the risks but also the possibilities of rebellion these exchanges and encounters offer to academic communities around the globe. For it is important not only to identify the 'anglophone hegemony' in the scientific world, but – as in the project of 'decoloniality' (Bhambra, 2014; Mignolo, 2011) and 'critical pedagogy' (Freire, 2000; Giroux, 2011) – to also look for alternatives and practices of resistance to these hegemonies. As the section editors, we are convinced that each of the chapters here offers such a two-step approach, and will become important reference points to working in broader 'critical gender and sexuality studies' (not just the geographies of sexualities).

Coloniality and the Decolonial Project

The control of language covers the different forms of colonization of epistemological beings (Fanon, 1967), for language is where knowledge is inscribed (Mignolo, 2003a). Consequently, a mastery of English as a *lingua franca* is a tool for gatekeeping and maintaining an unequal geopolitics of knowledge within academia (Bajerski, 2011; Gutiérrez and López-Nieva, 2001; Lander, 2000, 2005; Short et al., 2001). An alternative can be inspired by the idea of 'decoloniality' (see, for example, Grosfoguel, 2007; Mignolo, 1993; 2000; Lugones, 2007; Tlostanova and Mignolo, 2012; Quijano, 2000, 2007). The argument is that although colonialism is already history, coloniality as complex structures of interlocking economic and social axes continues to perpetuate the contemporary world. It operates on three dimensions of power (Eurocentric systems of economic and other production), knowledge (naturalization of European thought as 'scientific') and being (through, for example, Eurocentric gendered and racialized hierarchies). Coloniality represents the dark and inseparable side of 'modernity' (Mignolo, 2003b; Walsh, 2012): while Europe experienced what it calls 'modernity', the conquered world has been subdued to its opposite, coloniality. In comparison with postcolonial thinkers, decolonial authors suggest that the process began with the 'discovery of Americas' in the fifteenth century, when bonds were formed between formal rationality, the aspiration to dominate the world and the emergence of a world market. These are the links that are the basis for the notion of linear progress, the superiority of white European men over nature, and capitalism as a unique framework to guide and control thought and life. Coloniality is omnipresent and sustains the mechanisms that hinder the possibilities of creating new knowledge-relationships, based on the ideas of the multiplicity and pluri-locality of knowledge(s).

The alternative path begins with an awareness of the effects and affects of the coloniality of being and knowing, hopefully leading to the promotion of social organizations that stand against the persisting inequalities of the modern world (Mignolo, 2000, 2009). Decolonial knowledge must go beyond the simple inclusion of those on the 'academic peripheries' (metaphorical and symbolic, material and geographical). In order to avoid accepting the conditions of inferiority of our knowledge, to avoid accepting the rules of the game that has been imposed on the 'non-Western world' through colonialism and coloniality, the project of decolonial knowledge demands a dedicated space for those hitherto excluded voices – a polyphony of voices – to be enunciated (Tlostanova and Mignolo, 2012), and for the rebuilding of epistemological foundations of contemporary research and teaching practices.

Towards Queer Epistemologies/Epistemologies of Queer

The power shift of epistemic enunciation to produce non-hegemonic relationships between researchers working on genders, sexualities and geographies, who, although they are spread globally, actually coexist on equal terms in the imagined world of academia, is necessary and will only be achieved through/in our everyday practices. We concur with Castro-Gómez (2007) and Walsh (2007) that these encounters will hopefully result in truly intercultural dialogue between scholars from around world, from the places of privilege and periphery, and will result in structures and practices that are truly inter-epistemic. Gender, sexuality and queer studies have, from their inception, offered critical perspectives on inequality, power, and systems of hegemony and subjugation in the 'modern world'. However, dare we play the devil's advocate role and say that the feminist and queer epistemologies we represent across many disciplines have yet to face their colonial legacy and their mostly (Northern) American and Eurocentric and anglophone squint? A proliferation of 'postcolonial queer studies' and works pertaining to geographies 'beyond the West' is not enough if we are to take the decolonial project seriously.

As editors and authors of this section, we feel that as geographers, feminists, queer scholars and all in/out-betweeners, we need not only to look for 'non-Western' examples of the worldwide diversity. Rather, and perhaps foremost, we must reconceptualize our own practices of 'doing knowledge'. We can start by reconsidering our citation policies: how many men over women do we cite? How many white people over other 'races'? How many anglophone authors over those writing in other languages? We can follow by actively reconstituting our 'canons': who and what is left behind? Who is canonized as 'theorist' and who remains a mere 'informant'? As Browne (2014) does, let us think how the conditions of privilege that some producers of knowledge enjoy may be turned into elements of struggle in constructing alternative ways to overcome the cultural, political and economic barriers that prevail in contemporary networks of academic production.

In this spirit, we hope that this introduction, together with the following chapters, will provide an opportunity to open up a dialogue over the epistemic hegemonies in geographies and 'critical gender and sexuality studies', but also possible wilful resistances in our practices of producing ('queer') knowledge. The authors in their individual chapters are exploring a range of issues that are related to the epistemic considerations of what is and who becomes 'a knowledge' within the realms of genders, sexes, sexualities, geographies, activisms and politics. Each author in their own way identifies and names the epistemic hegemonies they struggle with, each also thinks through the possible and already present alternatives and pathways to make them 'partners in dialogue'.

Joseli Maria Silva and Marcio Jose Ornat discuss the economy of knowledge production in geography and sexuality studies – for instance, the financial limitation of access to texts or transformations of universities into for-profit corporations (the latter also highlighted by Borghi, Bourcier and Prieur). Subjecting knowledge to quantifiable outputs under the logic of neoliberal capitalism is also probed, as well as allowing business corporations (under the guise of 'academic publishing houses') to act as gatekeepers of academic credibility and thus employability.

Silva and Ornat also question the dominance of the English language, and a lack of reflection (especially among journal and book editors) that English is not only a means

141

and a vessel of communication knowledge, but also an active component constructing it (remember McLuhan's (1964) idea that 'the medium is the message'). Maria de Rodó Zárate ponders the usefulness of certain English concepts in other linguistic contexts, as well as the process of equivalence of English for 'international' academic debate, emptying it of the local and national, and thus universalizing English in a hegemonic erasure of its particularity.

De Rodó Zárate and Jan Simon Hutta consider how geographical location and (a lack of) institutional affiliation determines who gets to be recognized as a 'knowledge producer' and who is subdued as 'informant and data miner'. This translates onto a range of polarized hierarchies of value: theory/raw data, scientists/lay communities, queer scholars/queer activists, native English speakers/non-native English speakers and so on. Similarly, Niharika Banerjea, Kath Browne, Leela Bakshi, and Subhagata Ghosh pay attention to the overt privileging of institutionalized forms of knowledge. They show how forms of ideas that are written down, are university/institution-attached and thus easy to quantify (and supposedly to reference) – in other words, 'academic texts' – are recognized as 'a (proper) knowledge', whereas the more elusive forms of creating, living, diffusing, collecting, archiving, embodying and imagining of knowledge remain put down as information, examples, cases and empirical data but are hardly ever recognized as actual 'high knowledge' and 'theory'.

Rachele Borghi, Marie Helene Bourcier and Cha Prieur, as well as Banerjea, Browne, Bakshi and Ghosh turn their critical eye on the tensions between academic and activist circles and draw our attention to the alternative modes of 'community engagements' and dissemination practices, envisaging cross-field practices that nurture our hope for the alternatives.

Finally, the viciousness of collegial relations in 'academia' more broadly, as well as within the feminist and queer studies, is of concern for Silva and Ornat. This is exemplified in the case of peer reviewing. Rather than being critical, reviewers could be positively engaged, entering into a dialogue *with* colleagues whose work is being reviewed. It is noted that more often than not peer-reviewing turns out to be a form of policing and gatekeeping of some imagined 'academic standard' (privilege?) that is performed *against* colleagues. Whether works are marked as 'suitable' and 'publishable' is determined by geographical location and linguistic and economic factors that are sites of unrecognized privilege on the part of the reviewing colleagues.

Chapter 17

Queer Affirmations and Embodied Knowledge in the Brazilian Performance Group Dzi Croquettes

Jan Simon Hutta

In its essence, affirmation is itself difference. (Gilles Deleuze, 1968, p. 53)

In 1972, during the most violent phase of the Brazilian military dictatorship, Dzi Croquettes emerged in Rio de Janeiro. Dzi Croquettes were a group of 13 dancers, poets, singers and designers that formed after a smaller circle had started carrying their impromptu living-room performances into night clubs in Rio de Janeiro in the fall of 1972. They were (mostly gay) men from different racial and class backgrounds, living together as a self-declared 'family' in varying amorous and cohabitation arrangements, often together with friends and followers. In their frenetic, multilingual performances, they rescripted poetic verses, interpreted popular Brazilian and international music, staged elaborate dance performances and daily street scenes, and dressed themselves in and out of flamboyant costumes. Their style was marked as much by the use of make-up, glitter and drag as by the experimental mobilization and fusing of vastly differing genres, including vaudeville, *tropicália*, *travesti* shows, underground, carnival or umbanda. While their style resonated with the North Atlantic cultural movements of the 1960s and 1970s, it also connected to Brazilian movements and expressive traditions. Instantly hitting a nerve, especially among young people who suffered from the repressions of the military regime, in 1973–74 the group entered the theatres of São Paulo and Rio de Janeiro, provoking intense public media coverage. While Dzi Croquettes's expressive world gravitated around gender transgression and irreverent eroticism, it simultaneously involved issues of class, race or region and instilled a broader sense of imminent liberation.

Against the backdrop of moral repression that targeted gendered and sexual dissidence, intersecting with postcolonial racialization, Dzi Croquettes invented new ways of publicly enacting the multiply determined body, fashioning a 'queer' expressivity *avant la lettre*. They fabricated their own Dzi-world, which extended from theatre stage to daily interactions. Their world-making was characterized as much by the assertion of a wide range of often incommensurate expressive traditions and repertoires as by the mockery of reigning norms, thus staging a politics of what I call 'paradoxical affirmation'. Although the sheer overabundance of gestures, movements and meanings summoned did not allow for the formation of any coherent political discourse, Dzi Croquettes intervened into the very conditions of knowledge production, pertaining to the body's relationship with the world. Two decades before queer studies galvanized shifting epistemologies around sexuality, gender and the body in the anglophone world, new facets of 'embodied knowledge' were thus being fabricated in Brazil. This was not just knowledge bodily 'positioned', but knowledge bodily *enacted*, subsequently rippling through public debates as well as activist and academic discourses. Engaging with this generation of embodied knowledge, this chapter highlights the ways in which 'Western-centric' queer epistemologies can productively be challenged, as proposed by Silva and Kulpa (this volume).

I want to highlight three key themes in my analysis. First, the singular Dzi-world arising from the midst of contestations over morals and militarism favoured expressive 'becoming-people' over differentiating identities, prefiguring a queer epistemology. Second, this 'universalizing' approach (Sedgwick, 1990) still fostered the creative affirmation of specific (gendered and racialized) capacities residing in a range of expressive traditions. Considering such paradoxical affirmation, I argue, opens new angles on minoritarian politics, as it usefully reworks notions like 'bricolage' or 'disidentification'. Third, Dzi Croquettes's worlding reworked the historical predicament of the body in Brazil, which has persistently been subjected to both violent intrusion and normative closure. Here, I will reconsider, and queer, Teresa Caldeira's (2000) notion of the 'unbounded body', considering queer manners of 'unbounding' the body. Through a discussion of these three themes, I seek to draw attention to what we might call a 'queer epistemology of the body' which, emanating from the Brazilian context, impacted on wider 'imaginary worlds' (Appadurai, 1996), unfolding globally across uneven space.

Throughout the chapter, apart from the documentary *Dzi Croquettes* (2009), I draw on Rosemary Lobert's (2010) ethnographic account, which was originally written as a Master's thesis in the 1970s after the author had followed and partly stayed with Dzi Croquettes over a three-year period. Lobert's ethnography is of particular interest here, as it forms part of a strand of anthropological studies of sexual identities, practices and politics emanating from Brazil in the 1980s (see Fry, 1982; Fry and MacRae, 1983; Perlongher, 1987) that in some ways anticipated later discussions in anglophone queer studies and anthropology (see Boellstorff, 2007) – again serving to multiply queer epistemologies.

Becoming-people

> *Nem senhores, nem senhoras*
> *Gente dali, gente daqui*
> *Nós não somos homens, também não somos mulheres*
> *Nós somos gente … gente computada igual a você.*
>
> *[Neither gentlemen, nor ladies*
> *People from there, people from here*
> *We are not men, we are not women either*
> *We are people … people computed just like you.]*
> (Dzi Croquettes, Opening Monologue, cited in Lobert, 2010, p. 49)[1]

These words opened Dzi Croquettes's 1973 piece *Andróginos: Gente computada igual a você*. Suggesting a transgression of gender binaries ('Neither gentlemen, nor ladies'), the monologue simultaneously asserted fundamentally egalitarian values ('We are people

---

1   The English translations of Portuguese texts are mine.

computed just like you'). While many of the artists identified as *homossexual*[2] and the performances playfully used prevalent terms such as 'androgynous' or *travesti*[3] to offer semantic references for their trans- or multi-gender expressions, Dzi Croquettes persistently undermined differentiating identities, insisting on the universality of being *gente* (people). This posture resonated with the emerging liberation movements known at the time, especially from the USA and Western Europe; but it also signalled a critical distance from their identitarian tendencies. As Seidman (1993, p. 110) argues, early 'gay liberation' based itself on 'a notion of an innate polymorphous, androgynous human nature', aiming at 'freeing individuals from the constraints of a sex/gender system that locked them into mutually exclusive homo/hetero and feminine/masculine roles'. During the 1970s this understanding turned into a narrower 'single-interest-group politic' (ibid., p. 110). Such single-interest politics went against the spirit of Dzi Croquettes's performances. As one performer explained, 'Dzi Croquettes are neither representatives of gay power, nor of the androgynous, neither of men nor of women, neither of the white nor the black, but of all. Because either we represent all, or we don't represent anything' (quoted in Lobert, 2010, p. 245). Whereas a branch of the later Movimento Homossexual Brasileiro questioned the politics of an autonomist 'gay liberation' on behalf of a socialist project of class struggle (Trevisan, 1986), Dzi Croquettes rejected the primacy of *any* overarching *a priori* social category of liberation or revolution. For them, becoming-people was profoundly embodied and subjective, yet never dogmatic or identitarian; or, rather, it emerged from the affirmation and transformation of multiple discourses, expressions and identifications at the same time, as will be further explored below.

By emphasizing the universality of *gente*, Dzi Croquettes asserted a commonality between themselves and spectators, rejecting their own exoticized positioning as deviant 'others'. 'Becoming-*gente*', moreover, had an internal dimension, as Dzi Croquettes cultivated, among themselves, an ethics that privileged the collective process of expressivity over social differences between members. Lobert summarizes:

> *While the group accommodated varying educational or professional experiences and degrees, it did not create barriers, either in terms of age, colour, of traditional Brazilian norms, of nationality, or, more subtly, in terms of place regarding the federal state of origin; nor even in terms of social classes – which concerned both professional status and parents' economic power: while some were the sons of a barber, a pai de santo [religious leader], a primary school teacher, a gambling dealer, a small-town cinema manager, others were the sons of a high-ranking serviceman, a stock exchange investor, not to mention the son of one of the so-called 'traditional families of São Paulo. (Lobert, 2010, p. 27)*

Although this egalitarian ethics did not always neatly translate into practice, it formed a vector along which the group's public and intersubjective activities took shape. Personal histories were decentred both on stage and in daily conversations, the focus being on the dynamics of the group as a whole, and on their interaction with the wider public. At the same time, the variety of affiliations related to class, race or place of origin constituting the

---

2   The term *homossexual* has been used in the Brazilian context generically, not necessarily distinguishing between gay and trans people – even though trans activists have more recently insisted on being identified as trans (*travesti, transsexual*) rather than *homossexual*.

3   *Travesti* refers to individuals who were assigned a male gender at birth and live in a female (or partly female) gender, often using various expressive and body-modifying practices without necessarily aiming to plainly 'pass' as women. In the 1970s drag shows were also referred to as *show de travesti*.

group was seen as a source of creativity and learning, despite some conflicts and tensions that this involved. Subjective growth was considered a main objective, this being conceived as a process of mutual learning and continuous becoming – a process the performers referred to as *'aprender a ser gente'*, 'learning to be people' (Lobert, 2010, pp. 100–102). Thus, while each member possessed vastly differing performative skills and talents, each one was encouraged to *assumir* and *botar fora*, to assume/take on/stand up to, and publicly express their subjectivity, as well as to teach and learn from others. Becoming-people was thus universalizing and singularly situated at the same time. Rather than proposing a generic model for everyone to follow, it was the experimental tracing and development of new expressive capacities and interconnections.

It was precisely this combination of egalitarianism, mutual learning and expressive self-actualization, affectively spanning both group and audience, which became a welcome antidote to the oppressive moralism of the military regime. The dictatorship had, after the coup d'état of 1964, entered its most repressive phase with the issuing of 'AI-5' (Institutional Act Number Five) in 1968, which overruled major constitutional rights. An unprecedented wave of arbitrary imprisonment, torture and killing ensued, as well as the censorship of music, film, theatre, television and the press. Apart from targeting political enemies, generically labelled the 'communist threat', the exceptionalist measures sought to protect 'Brazilian family morals'. It was, in particular, these moral incursions into the arts and people's daily lives that spurred on the Brazilian counter-cultural movements of the 1960s and 1970s. Among the prime targets of the moral policing were gays as well as drag performers, who were known at the time as *travestis* and had emerged in the subcultural scenes of cities like Rio de Janeiro and São Paulo in the late 1950s (Green, 1999; Balzer and Hutta, 2013).

Interestingly, for almost two years Dzi Croquettes managed to fly under the censors' radar, as they eluded the genre of *travesti* and rarely enunciated texts that could be identified as directly attacking the regime. Apart from being popular, extraordinary and bizarre, it was unclear just what they were. This changed only in the summer of 1974, when the 600 seats of Rio de Janeiro's Teatro da Praia were sold out and over 1,000 people stood outside, some banging on the doors. At this point, ruling politicians started perceiving the *banda de viados*, the 'band of faggots' as they called Dzi Croquettes, as a serious threat and censured their piece for several weeks for its use of 'immoral' contents. The group decided to leave the country, continuing their performances in Portugal, France and Italy during their European exile from 1974 to 1975. What constituted this threat was precisely Dzi Croquettes's contagiously queer project of 'becoming-people', as it enfolded inchoate desires for liberation and opened up an arena for anti-authoritarian challenges to identitarian fixations. As is further elaborated in the next section, their performances and associated daily practices thus instigated forms of learning that yielded new kinds of embodied knowledge, knowledge that was paradoxically resistant and affirmative at the same time – and that the military regime feared for its potential spill-over effects with regard to broader fields of life and politics. Considering the traction that civil rights movements and the discourse of *cidadania*, or 'citizenship', would gain from the late 1970s onwards (Dagnino, 2005; Holston, 2011), Dzi Croquettes can moreover be seen as having prefigured, on a performative and affective level, the libertarian edge of this nascent sense of citizenship.

Paradoxical Affirmations

While Dzi Croquettes challenged prevailing norms and discourses, their performances were not only about critiquing and rejection. They rather enacted what I call 'paradoxical affirmation': an invocation of, opening up to and assertion of heterogeneous, often incommensurate, expressions. Attending to such 'affirmative' enactments goes against the grain of those discussions in queer studies that tether radical politics to negativity and equate affirmation with the reproduction of hegemonic norms (see Edelman, 2004; also Halberstam, 2008). By contrast, the understanding I draw from Dzi Croquettes approximates Deleuze's claim that '[i]n its essence, affirmation is itself difference' (1968, p. 52). For Deleuze, this is precisely about affirming 'everything of the multiple, everything of the different, everything of chance *except* what subordinates them to the One, to the Same, to necessity' (ibid., p. 115, emphasis in the original).

The universalizing or 'commoning' project of becoming-people, then, came into being through the affirmation of singular expressive capacities subsisting within gendered and racialized bodies as well as a range of expressive traditions. It was only through such affirmations that gestures of parody and critical distancing gained flesh. On an epistemological level, paradoxical affirmation unsettled hegemonic understandings of body, gender or race, while simultaneously multiplying their respective meanings and senses. This approach is signalled in a monologue recited by an actor with a grave voice to the sound of Richard Strauss's *Thus Spoke Zarathustra*:

> *E eis que surge o novo renascimento*
> *e com ele um novo ser*
> *trazendo toda a força do macho e toda a graça da fêmea.*

> *[And so the new rebirth surges*
> *and with it another being*
> *carrying with itself all the force of the male and all the grace of the female.]*
> (Quoted in Lobert, 2010, p. 63)

While in the Opening Monologue cited above, Dzi Croquettes declared themselves neither men nor women, here, they paradoxically affirmed 'another being' bearing the assumed characteristics of *both* male *and* female – a being, however, that could only be glimpsed in the poetic format of a prophetic, Nietzschean promise, a 'being' only just about to surge and thus present as immanent potential. *Unsettling* normative expectations of both female modesty and male prowess, they simultaneously *affirmed* both 'female grace' and 'male force'. Indexed towards a 'new being', this affirmation of genders can be conceived as an exploration of gendered capacities to affect, through voice, looks and movement – reconfiguring both the affecting body and the body of whoever is enticed by the performance. This doubly eroticized unbounding of bodies had the impact of a 'latent bomb' (Lobert, 2010, p. 121) in the context of the moralist repression of the time.

Beyond gender, Dzi's affirmative approach also concerned the great variety of discourses, genres and expressive traditions they mobilized, spanning popular and bourgeois culture, media representations and daily encounters, vernacular arts and globalized stardom. In text, music, dress and dance, Dzi Croquettes invoked figures ranging from nationalist Brazilian poet Olavo Bilac and Shakespeare to umbanda[4] spirit Exu, *forró* composer Jackson do Pandeiro, and Marlene Dietrich, Billy Holliday or the North American Black Power movement. Interpretations of artistic works were punctuated or accompanied by monologues and scenes written by the performers, and always included considerable improvisation and spontaneous interaction with the audience. In part, what sutured these

---

4   Umbanda is a heterodox Brazilian religion, syncretistically formed from indigenous, African, Catholic and Spiritist traditions.

different elements together was the parodic, camp style of the performance, with its drag, glitter and mix of high- and low-pitched voices. Discussions of bricolage and homology in British post-war subcultures come to mind, where subjects were said to decontextualize heterogeneous elements taken from mainstream consumer culture, replacing them within new ensembles of meaning (see Hebdige, 1979, pp. 100–117). Similarly, Muñoz's (1999) notion of 'disidentification', developed in connection with US-based queer performers of colour, calls attention to a 'working on and against' dominant ideology. Like the scholars from the Birmingham School of Cultural Studies, Muñoz highlighted the complex entanglements of minoritarian subjectivity within dominant culture. For Muñoz, rather than denoting a 'counter-identificatory' opposition, disidentification implies 'a strategy that tries to transform a cultural logic from within' (ibid., p. 11).

This description is particularly resonant with Dzi Croquettes's parodies of public figures, norms and values, in which they juxtaposed and layered vastly heterogeneous expressions. For instance, Olavo Bilac's famous verse 'Ama, com fé e orgulho, a terra em que nasceste!' ('Love your native land with faith and pride!'), recited by a freakish-looking character, was directly preceded by a scene in which a member of the audience was asked to play the role of a *macho* hitting on a performer acting as baroness-cum-whore, only to highlight how the apparently stern and silent baroness-whore-performer-in-drag might actually be the one directing the *macho* and thus the one in charge of the entire scene. The performer from the Opening Monologue then reappeared to remind this character of his 'lesson on proverbs', reciting among others 'A união faz a força' ('Strength comes from union') and, more enigmatically, 'Mais tem Deus para dar do que a porra do diabo para carregar', roughly translating as 'God has more to give than to carry the devil's shit' (Lobert, 2010, pp. 55-56). Nationalist sentiment (conveyed by Bilac's verse), gender roles (in the improvised scene), and religious belief (invoked through the 'proverb'), were thus placed in an odd constellation, stripped of their commonsensical meanings and placed at the performers' and audience's experimental disposal.

Particularly pertinent to such scenes is Hebdige's and Muñoz' emphasis on minoritarian subjects agentially defying consumerism (Hebdige) or racialized heteronormativity (Muñoz) by creatively appropriating and reinvesting signs and objects. Rather than dispelling 'ideological contradictory elements', a disidentifying subject 'works to hold on to this object and invests it with new life' (Muñoz, 1999, p. 12). Engaging with Dzi's performances, however, prompts us to push this line of reasoning further. The range of styles, discourses and traditions summoned in their performances can hardly be captured within the term 'dominant ideology' (around which notions like bricolage or disidentification are framed). While some 'objects' in Dzi's performances – a poem used in national(ist) education, a white movie actress or a soap commercial – easily lend themselves to such an evaluation, directing attention at how they are affectively reinvested 'with new life'; others, like an umbanda spirit or an Afro-Brazilian singer from the country's north-east do not. In such cases, rather than ambivalently 'working on and against' dominant ideology, Dzi's performances mobilized expressive elements so as to affirm particular aspects or intensities subsisting within them, which were conducive to their world-making.

In the scene Ye-Me-Le, for instance, two actors perform a choreography inspired by umbanda rituals. Topless and with their faces still covered in the make-up from previous scenes, they wear umbanda skirts. This performance is particularly striking when considering the repression at the time of heterodox religions like umbanda, which were associated with Africanness. Until 1974 houses of worship were obliged to register with the police and frequently subjected to violent police raids (Nascimento, 2007, p. 61). The music used in the scene is Sérgio Mendes's bossa-rock song Ye-Me-Le, which uses umbanda lyrics and rhythms[5]. Neither bossa nova or rock, nor drag or *travesti* performance, nor umbanda ritual, the performance invokes all of these elements at the same time, affirming and conjoining particular intensities of movement, sound, meaning, visual appearance and bodily performance. Indeed 'reworking' the genres invoked and 'investing them with new life', Dzi Croquettes positively affirm a series of aspects associated with these intensities – umbanda's black and indigenous heritage and animism, drag's gender insubordination, bossa nova's appeal to a vernacular version of modernity. Necessarily, such affirmations remained partial. However, much more than a desire to transform 'dominant ideology', they suggested minoritarian affiliations along lines of class, gender, sexuality and race, as well as an engagement with fragmented projects of modernization, liberation and singularization.

Mockery and parody entwined so intimately with positive affirmation that it seems futile to separate them as distinct performative strategies. What characterized the performances throughout was instead an overabundance of parodic, critical and affirmative gestures, staging a paradoxical simultaneity of apparently incommensurate expressions. Focusing on the use of text, Lobert (2010, p. 78) makes a similar point when she observes: '... [T]he text seemed to both express a continued intention to surprise the spectator, provoking a simultaneity of contradictory affirmations, and to offer a succession of metaphors that broke up without being deepened; without being "resolved".' Instead of 'contradictory affirmations', I speak of 'paradoxical affirmations', as paradox denotes precisely the simultaneous coexistence of heterogeneous elements – it is a logic of 'both ... and ... ' rather than 'either ... or ... ' (Deleuze, 1969; see also Hutta, 2010).

Hebdige (1979, pp. 117–21) comes closest to such a reading in his comments on British punk as 'polysemically' generating 'a potentially infinite range of meanings', placing the very concept of 'meaning' under pressure. As punk subculture, following Hebdige, 'actively *sought* to remain silent, illegible' (ibid., p. 120, emphasis in the original), so Dzi Croquettes systematically stated 'O público não deve entender nada' ('The audience mustn't understand anything') (Lobert, 2010, p. 170). Epitomizing this mystifying gesture, the word 'Dzi' – originally coined by the group's founders to parody the Portuguese pronunciation of the English pronoun 'the' – came to symbolize a 'magic formula': a 'palavra mágica / DZZZIIII!' (Opening Monologue, quoted in Lobert 2010, pp. 20, 49). In Hebdige's reading, however, such polysemic unintelligibility ensues from a fundamental lack, and refusal, of any grounding subject position, producing an elliptic chain of absences, resonating with punk attitude. In Dzi Croquettes's case, by contrast, it was the very overabundance of paradoxical affirmations that made intelligibility collapse, producing a stream of non-sense that signalled, at the same time, a radical multiplication of senses. In this way, Dzi's queer 'knowledge production' was in fact a reworking of the very conditions of knowledge. They affirmed elements within the invoked expressions that, constelled in their non-/multi-sensical scenes, bore a promise, however faint, to assist the projects of becoming-Dzi and becoming-*gente*. In this, the role of the performers' body was paramount, prompting an investigation of the bodily dimensions of such a queer epistemology.

Unbounding the Body

Dzi Croquettes's experimental uses of the body that, apart from drag and dance, often involved eroticism and partial nudity were integral to their performances. Their bodies, including physique, voice and skin as well as make-up, dress and movement, served as the

---

5   The scene is depicted in the film *Dzi Croquettes* at 49'46''.

main medium and substance of expression (an aspect largely neglected by Lobert). This use of the body needs to be considered against the backdrop of post-/colonial power relations that have subjected indigenous and Afro-Brazilian populations to genocide and violent regimes of control (Karasch, 1987; Nascimento, 2007). Invoking this history, Caldeira (2000) has argued that bodies in Brazil have tended to be regarded and treated as 'unbounded'. 'The unbounded body', she notes, 'is a permeable body, open to intervention, on which manipulations by others are not considered problematic' (ibid., p. 368). Providing examples ranging from carnival and the widespread use of caesareans, sterilization and plastic surgery to the popular support of physical punishment and torture, Caldeira argues that this conception of the body permeates Brazilian society as a whole, affecting women and children in particular, as well as Afro-Brazilian and poor (and I would add indigenous and queer) populations. In view of widely naturalized transgressions of bodily integrity, Caldeira sees a particular challenge for the politics of rights and citizenship as they herald from North Atlantic experiences. In order to advance citizenship rights in Brazil, she concludes, a new kind of bounding of bodies is first needed. Such a bounding, however, should not repeat North Atlantic individualization, but should 'leave space for the proximity of bodies and sensuality and yet enforce respect for privacy' (2000, p. 375).

The connection Caldeira makes between acts of violence and a lack of respect for bodily boundaries is striking. In relation to queer and trans politics, it would be worth exploring this issue with regard to pervasive and ongoing manifestations of violence especially against trans people in Brazil (Balzer and Hutta, 2013; Silva et al., 2013). However, the issues of 'proximity' and 'sensuality' Caldeira mentions only in passing would need further exploration. Apart from a *lack* of boundaries, what is at stake in relation to both queer and racial politics are struggles against the *imposition* of bodily norms and boundaries – reaching back to the moral, pathologizing and criminalizing repression of homosexuality around the turn of the last century as well as racist ideologies of the nation's 'whitening' (Green, 1999; Nascimento, 2007). Although Caldeira's analysis usefully directs attention to how such control has been exercised precisely through a violation of certain subjects' bodily boundaries, it is vital to also account for this 'bounding' of bodily expressions and desires itself. Symptomatically, Caldeira neglects particularly queer politics as well as long-existing struggles against different forms of bodily bounding entirely. Against the backdrop of this history of heteronormative and racist incursions on the body, I argue, Dzi Croquettes enacted a radical 'unbounding' of the body, bringing into relief a very different kind of 'unbounded body'-in-the-making.

With the normative bounding of bodies I do not mean a simple repression of an excessive corporeality, but rather, as regards gender and sexuality, the incitation of discourses around the sexualized body and their simultaneous normative regulation, as described by Foucault (1976) and fleshed out with regard to the Brazilian context by Green (1999).[6] The challenge that Dzi's performances posed to ruling conceptions was already signalled by the censorship, which targeted not only their text, but also the smallness of their panty strings. Staging lascivious female and androgynous performances of bodily masculinity, Dzi tested, in particular, the *im*penetratable (and thus bounded), sexually active, male body[7].

Issues of gender and erotic desire were interlaced with racialization in Dzi's performances. In the scene 'James Brown', for instance, three performers (one of them Afro-Brazilian)

---

6 The racializing underpinnings of this dynamic in the postcolonial context, as examined by Stoler (1995), are also relevant here.

7 See Girman (2004), Green (1999) and Parker (1999) for discussions of 'active', impenetrable masculinity in Brazil and Latin America. For a broader discussion in relation to Western culture, see Kemp (2013).

performed a sensual, partly musical-, partly disco-style dance to the music of the Godfather of Soul.[8] Wearing glamorous, funky dresses partly exposing chests and buttocks, as well as black and golden leather boots and stockings, their faces painted in white, silver and rouged carnival make-up, they also wore curly wigs – one red, one black, one white. By coincidence or on purpose, the colours of their wigs corresponded to the three major racial groups composing the Brazilian nation according to the discourse of *democracia racial* (racial democracy) that became hegemonic in the late nineteenth and early twentieth centuries. This discourse, unfolding in the turbulent context of nation-building and modernization, established that racial relations among the indigenous, African and European populations in Brazil were characterized by miscegenation and hybridization, rather than US-style segregation. Asserting the positive value of the nation's multi-racial composition, this discourse at the same time eclipsed the population of white European descent's violence towards and domination of the racialized indigenous and African-descent populations – particularly as it was coupled with a belief in the gradual 'whitening' of Brazilians through miscegenation (Nascimento, 2007; Skidmore, 1989).

Certainly, Dzi Croquettes did not offer any elaborate critique – as articulated by the black movements throughout much of the twentieth century – of the discourse of racial democracy. However, using the music of a black singer who was a prominent figure in the US civil rights movement and asserted a black identity and African culture in many songs, they evoked associations of emancipatory racial politics and indulged in the rhythm of black funk. Far from satisfying fantasies of the nation's whitening, they affirmed blackness while simultaneously presenting an unruly kaleidoscope of hair, skin and facial colours – the darker-skinned performer using silver face colour and wearing a white wig, the two lighter-skinned performers using rouged and white face colour and wearing red and black wigs, respectively. Here, the erotic mobilization of multiply gendered capacities to affect was inseparable from the joyful enactment of multi-racial expressivity, tethering multi-gendered and multi-racial bodily affirmation. Similar approaches could be explored in the umbanda scene mentioned earlier, or in a scene using indigenous clothing. Elements associated with minoritarian cultures were not parodied or exoticized, but rather affirmatively engaged as an unfinished, living heritage, suggesting new affiliations and enabling new kinds of embodied becomings.

Queer Epistemology of the Body

Dzi Croquettes peculiar worlding, I have argued, emerged from their paradoxical affirmation of intensities subsisting within gendered and racialized bodies as well as a range of expressive traditions. Unbounding the body and simultaneously populating it with a cacophonous overabundance of speech acts, songs and dances, Dzi fabricated the kaleidoscopic facets of a new embodied archive – an archive registering dispersed memories of violence as well as the embryonic capacities of a collective becoming-*gente*. Summoning performers, *tietes* (groupies) and audience into an experimental exploration of memories, affects and desires, they fostered new kinds of implicit knowledge, enacting what we might call a queer epistemology of the body.

Geographers and social researchers more broadly have over the last two decades found increasing interest in the role of the body (see, for instance, Longhurst, 2005). Usefully, the body has been viewed in these debates not only as the passive substance for the inscription

---

8   See the film *Dzi Croquettes*, 1h 2'58''. The song used is 'Transmograpfication'.

of discursive power, but also as itself agentially and performatively co-producing subjects' relationships with the world (Haraway, 1991; Grosz, 1994; Mahmood, 2005). These relationships include the generation of knowledge as an always already embodied project (Haraway, 1991). Haraway's discussion of what she calls 'feminist embodiment' is particularly helpful in redirecting engagements with embodied knowledge, which have contemplated the body's phenomenological being-in-the-world (see Tanaka, 2011), towards concrete historical and spatial power formations. Pushing this line of reasoning towards engagements with sexuality in geography, Longhurst (1997, p. 495) wonders: 'What indeed happens to geography if we begin to consider how knowers and subjects can figure as sexually embodied?' Considering Dzi Croquettes helps to flesh out queerly embodied knowledge production.

In Dzi Croquettes, we find subjects not only *embodied* sexually, racially and in terms of class and region, but *bodily enacting* gendered, sexualized, racialized, classed, expressive registers. This helps to reinvigorate the now familiar trope of knowledge being bodily situated by relocating the site of epistemology to a bodily level of knowledge production, following on from Haraway's emphasis on the body's agency.[9] Dzi Croquettes did not, from their embodied position, produce a counter-knowledge in the sense of a propositional discourse, although the tensions arising from such a discursive absence would be worth further investigation. However, tapping and queerly constellating minoritarian expressive archives, they affirmed bodily sensibilities that generated new epistemic relationships with the world. Rhythmic, visual, vocal and physical intensities were extracted from umbanda, *travesti* or funk through bodily performance and were translated into the peculiar, expressive Dzi-world. This embodied world-making, or becoming-Dzi, spanned audience and followers and delivered a sense – or, rather, an overabundant multiplicity of senses – of minoritarian affiliations and imminent liberation. More than the production of propositional counter-knowledge, this was the generation of embodied capacities to know otherwise. It provided rich inspiration for practice, imagination and thought to wander down new pathways. As such, becoming-Dzi also involved transformations in language and discourse, leading, for instance, to new linguistic creations such as the word *tiete*, still in use today for 'groupie'. Gnawing at the edges of propositional knowledge but persistently overflowing any meaningful stability through the paradoxical multiplicity of senses, this embodied worlding could be propositionally captured only in a 'magic formula': DZZZIIII.

The question of embodied positionality remained vital, however. Taking a distance from the joyfully riotous scenario of *Dzi Croquettes* – as it addresses us today, particularly through Tatiana Issa and Raphael Alvarez' 2009 film – thorny questions remain concerning who is enabled, or hindered, to enact what kind of becoming from which embodied subject position (Braidotti, 2003). Dzi's gay male composition certainly predicated their activities. Having been ascribed a male identity at birth, the performers' bodily engagements circulate round the challenging of impenetrable *macho* masculinity whereas a focus on lesbians or trans masculinities would raise different kinds of issues. It is also likely that Dzi Croquettes were able to exploit the relative freedom their male-coded bodies endowed them with, despite homophobic and transphobic repression. Moreover, we know little about the unfolding of race and class relations in the daily life of the group's 'family'. Rather than serving as generic model, then, the kinds of world-making they enacted need to be seen as predicated on the socially, historically and geographically situated subjectivities involved. The impact of this creative and political worlding in Brazil and abroad is remarkable, however, not least in

---

9   'Feminist embodiment', Haraway (1991, p. 195) notes, '… is not about fixed location in a reified body, female or otherwise, but about nodes in fields, inflections in orientations, and responsibility for difference in material-semiotic fields of meaning'.

view of the repeated statements by their (largely female) *tietes* as well as contemporaries from different backgrounds that emphasize Dzi's role in critically nurturing struggles for liberation.

How can we geographically situate Dzi Croquettes's epistemology of the body? International scholars of gender and sexuality engaging with Brazil have repeatedly treated the phenomena observed as genuinely 'Brazilian', thereby risking a repetition of post-/colonial discourses of exoticization, as critics have pointed out recently (for example, Carrara and Simões, 2007; see also G. Brown et al., 2010). To avoid this culturalist trap, it is necessary to investigate how the embodied knowledge generated by Dzi Croquettes interacted with both Brazilian and international movements and discourses. In the Brazilian context, we could, for instance, trace linkages to the modernist cultural movement of the early twentieth century and the notion of 'anthropophagic' hybridization. This movement was, however, itself in dialogue with European modernity and borrowed part of its appeal to local specificity from the reigning discourses of Brazilian nation-building. On the other hand, it would be interesting to compare Dzi's collectivist approach to the contemporary popularization of the (also androgynous, yet highly individualist) figure of David Bowie in the UK or to the California-based performance group The Cockettes (see Tent, 2004; Gamson, 2005), which likely inspired Dzi's name, even though the latter had only vague knowledge of them (Lobert, 2010, p. 24). Rather than trying to identify a genuinely 'Brazilian' kind of epistemology, then, it seems productive to explore connections and ruptures across local and transnational contexts. Constituting a cartography of embodied epistemologies, such an investigation could also shed light on the global ramifications of contestations around the un/bounded body; and on how aspects of the authoritarian, non-liberal power relations that strike us so blatantly in the Brazilian context, can also be found in a range of North Atlantic contexts.

Chapter 18

Feminist and Queer Epistemologies beyond Academia and the Anglophone World: Political Intersectionality and Transfeminism in the Catalan Context

Maria Rodó-de-Zárate

Introduction

The way in which 'queer' is pronounced in English sounds exactly the same as the Catalan word *cuir*. And *cuir* means 'leather'. Pronouncing this word when conducting interviews with young lesbians in a small city close to Barcelona provokes a suspicious reaction: 'What are you exactly asking me about ... ?' In the Catalan context, 'queer' is mainly used in feminist and LGBT social movements and in academia. However, it is not a common word used to identify people or used for self-identification by lesbian, gay, bi or trans people. In the interviews I have conducted in Manresa, Catalonia (Rodó-de-Zárate, 2015), the concept usually came across as unknown. Significantly perhaps, only young lesbian activists were aware of what I was referring to.

In my engagement with the feminist Catalan movement, and as a feminist geographer, I have often felt that some words do not meet the reality – that the words I use to write about young lesbian cultures for the 'international/English journals' do not accurately describe their experience or the activism I (we) practise on the ground. My aim is to show how the production of knowledge that evolves beyond academia and beyond the 'anglophone world' can provide interesting insights into gender and queer practices and theorizations. As Harding (2004, pp. 7–8) puts it, 'standpoint theories map how a social and political disadvantage can be turned into an epistemic, scientific and political advantage'. Following her claim, I argue that the political practices that are being developed in the Catalan and Spanish contexts contribute to feminist theory not only as specific examples of different case studies, but also as different feminist and queer conceptualizations that contest the hegemonic ones.

In this chapter, I will show how the production of knowledge beyond academia and the anglophone world contests and extends some of the existing feminist standpoints. I will evidence this with two examples of Catalan and Spanish feminist and LGBT struggles. The first one relates to feminist and LGBT struggles and their articulation of 'political intersectionality' (Crenshaw, 1991) from the anti-capitalist and pro-independence standpoint. Through a focus on the production of knowledge by activists, I argue that their political discourses challenge hegemonic genealogies and concepts such as 'the West', 'homonationalism' or 'queer'. The second one shows how the development of the 'transfeminist movement' in the Spanish state provides different understandings of how the meanings of 'queer' have travelled and have been reconfigured in context. Generational, linguistic and activist/academic tensions arose as important conditioners for how struggles and ideas are materialized in specific contexts.

As the conceptualizations and proposals that lie behind these two examples mostly come from political movements and not from academia, it is often difficult to give references for some ideas and practices that were developed in collective processes. As Pardo writes, 'the fact that the citation system cannot respond to collective processes shows which forms of work are taken into account by the academy and which ones are made invisible'[1] (Pardo, 2013, p. 168). What counts as knowledge? What kinds of knowledge production are kept and recorded? Where do they come from? The processes and proposals I am going to show have been marked by political events, demonstrations, activist encounters and oral presentations. The production of knowledge, then, has mainly evolved in meetings, gatherings, streets and other collective spaces. When it is possible, I quote them with the aim of providing references that support some of the ideas. And, as there are few academic works that have engaged with these experiences, I also try to bring to bring these other forms of knowledge production into an academic context with the aim of establishing a dialogue between the two.

Free Women in a Free Country[2]: Political Intersectionality in Catalan Countries[3]

In this section I will show how the concept of 'political intersectionality' developed by feminists in the anglophone world takes different forms in the politics of the feminist movements in the Catalan context.

Generally, when looking for the roots of intersectionality as the feminist theory that refers to the interactions between various forms of inequality, theorists point to groups such as the Combahee River Collective (B. Smith, 1983). This was a black lesbian feminist organization from Boston that in 1977 wrote a statement expressing their struggle against different forms of oppression based on race, gender, sexuality and class, and showed how these systems of oppression where interlocked. They argued that their lives were the result of the fusion of social differences (ibid.). This was followed by the influential conceptualization by Kimberlee Crenshaw (1991), who coined the term 'intersectionality'. This was a key step towards the acknowledgement of differences among women and the disruption of homogeneous categories (Davis, 2008). As McCall claims, 'intersectionality is the most important theoretical contribution that women's studies, in conjunction with related fields, has made so far' (McCall, 2005, p. 1771). Crenshaw (1991) distinguishes between two types of intersectionality: the structural and the political. While structural intersectionality refers to how people experience multiple oppressions, the political refers to how it is incorporated in political agendas. In this chapter, I focus on the political agenda of feminist and LGBT movements in the Catalan context.[4]

---

1   If not specified otherwise, all translations into English are my own.
2   This refers to a traditional motto 'Dones lliures en una terra lliure'.
3   The Catalan countries are the territories where the Catalan language is spoken and which share historical and cultural aspects. With a population of around 14 million, they comprise the eastern part of the Iberian Peninsula.
4   For analyses of political intersectionality from an institutional perspective in relation to LGBT policies in this context, see Cruells and Coll-Planas (2013).

While recognizing the importance of the concept of 'intersectionality', I want to show how similar conceptualizations occurred in the Catalan context at the time of the intersectional turn in the 1970s in North America. In 1977, the same year as the Combahee River Collective statement, the Catalan poet Maria Mercè Marçal reflected upon the 'triple oppression' in her poem 'Motto':

> *I am grateful to fate for three gifts: to have been born a woman,*
> *from the working class and an oppressed nation.*
> *And the turbid azure of being three times a rebel.*
>
> *(Maria Mercè Marçal, 1977)[5]*

Maria Mercè Marçal was a teacher, writer and translator. She was also a militant communist, pro-independence supporter, feminist and lesbian. Through her poetry and her politics she struggled against different systems of oppression until she died at the age of 46. Her poem 'Motto' became, and is still, a famous motto that brings together the struggle against national, gender and class oppression understood as multiple forms of inequality. The ideas of her poems were not isolated as many other feminist- and LGBT-related struggles were taking place at that time (VV.AA., 1998; Rodríguez and Pujol, 2008). Historically, the tensions between feminism, class and national struggles have been present in Catalan politics since the beginning of the twentieth century (Capmany, 1973). It was not until Franco's dictatorship (1939–75) had ended that the complex interaction between Catalan, leftist and feminist ideologies emerged in meetings such as the Primeres Jornades Catalanes de la Dona (First Meeting of Catalan Women) in 1976. This was the first popular mass event after the dictatorship, in which more than 4,000 women gathered in Barcelona to discuss their experiences and strategies in relation to gender oppression. Authors such as Maria Mercè Marçal, Maria Aurèlia Capmany and Montserrat Roig defended feminist and leftist positions alongside the defence of Catalan, a forbidden language during the dictatorship (Francés Díez, 2010). In the 1980s, during the 'Second Meeting of Catalan Women' (1982) and thus before Crenshaw theoretically developed the concept of 'intersectionality', some feminists presented a text that indicates their intersectional experience of oppression:

> *Feminism must be a tool for global freedom, one that will break the chain of*
> *interrelated and inseparable oppressions upon which our society is built. Our specific*
> *experience as women that feel oppressed as members of the feminine sex and as part of*
> *a subjugated nation, objects of a cultural and linguistic genocide, has also been very*
> *complex. (Olivares et al., 1982, p. 99)*

They argue that even though there is a tendency to separate oppressions in political struggle, which causes them a constant tension and discomfort, for them there is a single experience of oppression and they contend that for women there must be a project of total liberation against gender, class and national oppression. They argue for the need to struggle from the space where oppressions are interrelated and against those political groups that 'deny that one and the other [oppressions] intersect' (Olivares et al., 1982, p. 99). Such statements point to the heart of intersectional politics and theorizations that can be found in the English literature (see hooks, 1981; P.H. Collins, 1990; Crenshaw, 1991), with conceptualizations such as the 'inseparability of oppressions', the 'specific experience'

---

5   'A l'atzar agraeixo tres dons: have nascut dona, / de classe baixa i nació oprimida. / I el tèrbol atzur de ser tres voltes rebel' (Marçal, 1977, p. 103).

of women crossed by different oppressions or the 'space where oppressions intersect' as a point of departure for the struggle.

LGBT activists also expressed similar claims in relation to sexual identity and sexual practices. The Front per l'Alliberament Gai de Catalunya (FAGC – the Catalan Gay Liberation Front), an association for gay liberation created in 1976 just after the end of the Spanish dictatorship, explained the association's flag in the its 1977 manifesto (1977) as follows:

> *An inverted pink triangle in memory for the gay people killed in Nazi extermination camps, where they were marked with that triangle; from its inside another triangle emerges with the four bars as a reference to our country; and, finally, a closed fist as a symbol of class struggle. (Rodríguez and Pujol, 2008, p. 24)*

This illustrates how LGBT struggles were also taking place from an intersectional perspective in the 1970s. Even though they were not using that specific term, their politics were intersectional. What I want to show here is that some sort of 'Catalan intersectionality' was developed during the 1970s and 1980s, as was also happening in the USA. It is noteworthy that despite the similarities of the discourse and the terms used to refer to the intersection of oppressions, the debate was not centred on race, but on class and cultural and political oppression by the Spanish state. These oppressions pointed towards other kinds of intersectionalities.

Today, this discussion articulating national, class and gender oppressions in Catalan countries is taking place in a hostile situation marked by privatization, cuts in public services and the restriction of civil rights, intensified since the 'crisis' of neoliberal capitalism in the late 2000s[6] and the political limitations imposed by the Spanish government with regard to the Catalan people's right to decide and their claims to sovereignty.[7] Against this background, some feminist anti-capitalist pro-independence groups are currently active agents in the construction of 'national projects'. The following quote is from the 'Independence to change everything' campaign, which aims to show that independence must serve as the opportunity to change the economic system and the social inequalities that currently exist. This fragment of a manifesto illustrates how feminists in the Catalan context articulate different forms of inequality:

> *Our right to decide is being denied in all spheres. We are being denied to decide on our bodies and sexualities, on the future of our country, on the economic model we want. And if we cannot decide, we cannot be free. (Independència per canviar-ho tot, 2013)*

As can be seen here, gender, sexuality, national and class issues are articulated around the same claim: the right to decide. The group 'Feminists for Independence' (created in 2013 arising from the mobilizations for the right to hold a referendum on the independence

---

6   The neoliberal policies deployed by the Catalan government in the last four years have produced dozens of cuts and privatizations that have limited access to public resources. As an indication (Institut Català d'Estadística, 2013), the unemployment rate in 2013 was 23.7 per cent (50.7 per cent for people between 16 and 24 years old) and the risk of poverty for children under 16 was 26.4 per cent. As a response to this situation, a number of social movements and new groups, organizations and popular initiatives have been mobilized to fight against the cuts and build new alternatives.

7   The mobilizations for the independence of Catalonia have been massive during the last four years, with demonstrations of millions of people and many different initiatives from popular organizations, political movements and also institutional parties. The Spanish opposition to the proposal of holding a referendum in Catalonia asking about people's will for independence has been a central concern in Catalan politics.

of Catalonia), would also be an example of how feminist women are active agents in the construction of a political project that sees independence as an opportunity for social, political and economic change. Similarly, in October 2014, 50 prominent LGBTI personalities signed the manifesto 'My country and I want freedom', in which they stated:

> We, with this manifesto, also highlight that it is a historical opportunity to ensure that the new country will celebrate all sexual options, gender identities and gender expressions. We want a country built upon diversity that will take of our rights and our freedoms ... We, lesbians, gays, bisexuals, trans and intersex, with all visibility, state our affirmative vote in favour of starting a new country, with an independent state. (Ara és l'hora, 2014)

What I want to show with these examples is that feminists and LGBT activists are articulating the struggles from an intersectional standpoint, relating gender and sexual freedom to claims for independence. Their claim that there is no freedom for Catalans if women cannot decide on their bodies, or if there is discrimination against LGBT people shows how different inequalities are conceived as 'interlocking'. Many other struggles in different places are conceived in this way too, but the distinctive element here is the presence of the national issue in feminist and LGBT discourses.

Some authors have studied the relation between gender and nation (for example, Yuval-Davis and Anthias, 1989), generally focusing on the representation of women and women's roles in nationalist discourses and the gendered representation of nations. In relation to LGBT groups, it has been argued that nationalism has been used to maintain and consolidate heteronormativity and that nationalist discourses have devalued homosexual practices. It has also been argued that in some cases (for example, Quebec or the Netherlands), however, nationalism is capable of accommodating LGBT claims (Kulpa, 2011). This is possible because, in some cases, lesbian and gay people became 'figures of life' for the capitalist market, a process Duggan defines as 'homonormativity' – that is '[a] politics that does not contest dominant heteronormative assumptions and institutions, but upholds and sustains them, while promising the possibility of a demobilized gay constituency and a privatized, depoliticized gay culture anchored in domesticity and consumption' (Duggan, 2002, p. 179).

Jasbir Puar (2007) elaborated on that argument, writing that the accommodation of LGBT claims responds to a strategy of 'homonationalism', an integration and acceptance of the 'proper homosexuals' into neoliberal citizenship at the cost of rising Islamophobia and the exclusion of the racial 'others'.[8]

In the present context, however, political intersectionality in relation to Catalan identity is not constructed as a 'race' or 'ethnicity', and national identity is not used here as a way of exalting one nation above all others, but as a struggle against the impositions of the state on a territory and culture. As Montserrat Cervera, a feminist activist, stated in a recent article:

> In this process there are pro-independence women and women that are for the right to decide ... autochthonous women and feminist women from other origins that are fed up with hearing that they are migrant women after 20 years living here. We all want

---

8   In the Catalan context, Barcelona's Eixample district called 'Gaixample' is given as an example of a 'gay neighbourhood' that has contributed to the economy of 'pink capitalism' in the city (Brot Bord, 2013). In contrast, feminist and LGBT Catalan movements have been defined by a strong anti-capitalist position while maintaining specific discourses around Catalan identity. For instance, on 8 March 2014 a demonstration marched in Barcelona with the slogan: 'Against the patriarchal and capitalist offensive: feminist disobedience.' On 28 June 2013 another march (celebrated since 1977) used the slogan: 'For a country free of homophobia and transphobia.'

> *to raise our voices. All patriotisms have oppressed and used us ... but we also want to say loudly and clearly that we love our country, our language, our diverse people from diverse origins in a territory damaged by multinational companies and corrupt governments, as other territories in the world. (Cervera, 2014)*

This quote shows how feminist understandings surrounding Catalan independence are based on the right to decide and not on nationalistic discourses in relation to cultural and ethnic supremacies. This conception of national struggle does not fit hegemonic conceptualizations in relation to nationalism, as it destabilizes homogenous identities based on origin. Race, in this sense, is not forgotten in order to give a place to national identity but is configured in a different way. The struggles against racism, in this context, are introduced in feminist discourses through the voices and positions of migrant women. And, as Cervera notes, migrant women's struggles and pro-independence claims are not contradictory but linked through the concept of the right to decide. In this sense, not all alignments with national discourses should imply racist claims. Feminist women and LGBT groups are also active agents in the construction of (emancipatory) national projects. Therefore, concepts such as homonationalism should be used with caution and should take account of the various configurations and uses of different national projects.

Going a step further, understanding that 'queer' is located 'in the radical requirement to question normativities and orthodoxies, in part now by rendering categories of sexualities, genders and spaces fluid' (Browne, 2006, pp. 885–6), could we perhaps say that the struggle of a country for the right to decide its own future in the sense presented above could be conceived as a *queer* struggle? If we understand that Catalan identity destabilizes fixed and imposed categories, such as Spanish nationality and borders, and also contests national projects based on ethnic origins, could some national identities be understood as *queer*? Could we consider such developments queer epistemologies? What implications could this have for theorizations of relations between national identities and LGBT struggles, such as homonationalism?

If, as postcolonial feminists have argued, the 'Third World woman' has been constructed as a homogenous category by 'Western feminists' (Mohanty, 2008), does this vision not construct the 'West' as homogenous while ignoring relations of power within it? Kulpa (2014), in relation to homonationalist discourses, shows how power relations in the West/ Europe are used to differentiate Central and Eastern Europe – that is, to consider CEE as the Other. In this case, I am focusing on power relations not only in relation to the anglophone world, but also in relation to the position of Catalan politics within the Spanish state. Catalan feminisms have occurred within frameworks different to those present in anglophone contexts, producing different epistemic standpoints. It seems counterproductive to 'simply' relate the anti-racist intersectional claims made by black feminists in the USA to this context, as race and slavery have different histories, meanings and connotations, and play different roles in feminist struggles in the Catalan context. Instead, other elements, such as language, play an important role in defining power relations within the Spanish state.[9] Cultural, linguistic and political oppressions occurring within the borders of the EU should also be taken into account when referring to the 'West'. This does not mean that white Western women and LGBT people do not have privileges in terms of race or in relation to the effects of colonization processes but, from an intersectional perspective, the recognition of these

---

9   In some regions of the Spanish state there are languages other than Spanish that are specific to each territory: Catalan, Basque and Galician. The Spanish language is still used as a way of imposing Spanish nationalism in those regions.

privileged positions stands alongside the recognition of the position of subordination in relation to the Spanish state.

In this section I have tried to show how the materialization of political intersectionality in Catalan countries by feminist and LGBT groups arose from rich political debates on the relation between struggles. The way of articulating the national struggle shows the complexity and the diversity of discourses around nations from feminist and LGBT standpoints that challenge hegemonic genealogies and theorizations. This should not only be seen as a specific case where the 'general theory' does not fit, but also as an example of how theories and conceptualizations are context-dependent and may challenge hegemonic assumptions concerning the production of knowledge. These struggles have developed in parallel with anglophone and academic theorizations, and there are other struggles that display tensions over the anglophone influence. In the following section I show how such anxieties have produced new conceptualizations, and how the transfeminist movement serves as a pertinent and current example of these.

Transfeminist 'Sounds' Better than *Cuir*

Gender Trouble (Butler, 1990) was translated into Spanish in 2007, 17 years after its original publication in English. What are the implications of concepts travelling irregular paths? What are the consequences for the local conceptualizations and genealogies of the feminist and LGBT movements? My aim in this section is to show the other side of the coin of the production of queer epistemologies through the presentation of the transfeminist movement as a political and epistemic proposal that arose precisely from the tension between local and anglophone conceptualizations of feminist and LGBT struggles.

The historical evolution of feminisms in the Spanish state is complex and has developed around various debates, differing in every region within the state. Following comprehensive analyses by Gil (2011) and Solá (2011), I revisit some key ideas to understand what 'transfeminism' is, how it differs from queer movements and the concept of 'queer', and what new perspectives it opens. Acknowledging that the word 'transfeminism' has been used in different contexts and with different meanings, here I only refer to 'transfeminism' as it has been used and described in the context of the Spanish state. Miriam Solá, in the introduction of her recent book *Transfeminismo: Epistemes, fricciones y flujos* (Solá and Urko, 2013), writes: '[transfeminism] sounds better in Spanish that the term queer. [It is] something more tangible, more contextualized, more local, full of power [*potencia*] and freshness, [something] that seems to contain an important power of mobilization' (Solá and Urko, 2013, p. 19).

She defends the concept and the word 'transfeminism' versus the word 'queer' as more appropriate in the Spanish context, and the whole book is an excellent anthology of multiple and distinct views on 'transfeminisms' in the Spanish state. This concept first appeared in the *Jornadas Feministas Estatales* (Spanish Feminist Meeting) held in Córdoba in 2000, , where the trans activist Kim Pérez, and the Grup de Lesbianes Feministes de Barcelona (Group of Feminist Lesbians of Barcelona) talked about how sexuality issues and trans people fit into the concerns of feminist movements. During the 1990s many feminist groups questioned the subjects of feminism as being only 'women', and the debates focused on the position of lesbians (Trujillo, 2008; Pineda et al., 2001), sex workers (Garaizábal, 2013) and trans people (Garaizábal, 1994; Pérez and Mónica, 1994) in the movement. It was in 2009, during the Spanish Feminist Meeting in Granada, when young transfeminist activists presented the *Manifiesto para la Insurrección Transfeminista* (*Manifesto for Transfeminist Insurrection*), in

161

which they stated that the feminist subject had become too exclusive and that many bodies were left out:

> *The political subject of feminism 'women' has become too narrow, it is exclusive by itself, it leaves out dykes, trans, bitches, the ones with the veil, the ones that do not earn enough money to go to the university, the ones that shout, the ones without documentation, faggots ...* (Manifesto for Transfeminist Insurrection, 2009)

As can be seen, this manifesto includes within the term 'transfeminism' not only trans issues, but also a critique of the subjects of feminism in relation to sexuality and desire, political practices and the intersection of other identities. Despite the importance of such critique as a way of highlighting exclusions within feminisms, as Solá states, a generational rupture and confrontational logic may not let them realize that 'there were not that many resistances and feminism, in many places, was already "trans" a long time ago' (Solá, 2013, p. 23). Even if this manifesto was written in a new language more similar to queer conceptualizations, such issues were already present in feminist debates decades ago. What does this tell us about the way in which queer theory entered into LGBT and feminist struggles in the Spanish state? Although, as Solá argues, the issues were already present within feminist movement, they were not recognized by younger activists who needed a new 'queer theory' language to address the problems that were already present long before.

Similar disputes occurred more recently in relation to trans struggles. Since the new law on gender identity in 2007,[10] many groups have been created to oppose the pathologization of transsexuality, dichotomies and discourses of normalization (Soley-Beltran and Coll-Planas, 2011). These groups, formed mainly by young people, were strongly influenced by anglophone feminist and queer theories. Their perspectives were different from discourses of transsexuality that sought the normalization of trans people through a clear self-identification of being either men or women and that claimed integration and equality.[11]

Here it is interesting to note that the concepts 'transsexual' and 'transgender' and their connotations are still a battleground of 'trans' rights. For instance, 'whereas the term "trans-gender" in the USA gradually lost its political connotation, in Spain it functions as a more politicized term than "trans", the latter being the preferred umbrella term' (Soley-Beltran and Coll-Planas, 2011, p. 344). This shows how the travelling of concepts has different implications: because of different genealogies and developments, 'trans' and 'transgender' have different meanings for political purposes. Similar issues concern 'queer'. In a non-anglophone context where knowledge of English is a privilege and an issue of social class,[12] the influence of English literature takes place in complex and irregular paths that have political effects. As I have noticed during my fieldwork, in some contexts 'queer' is understood to be a 'classist' and 'elitist' concept used by those who have certain cultural capital (for example, read fluently in English). Since 'queer' has never been used as an insult in Catalan or Spanish, as it was in English, it is not a resignification but an incorporation of the English concept (and a framework for a struggle), and thus in some circles it gains

---

10   Since the approval of this law, in order to apply for a gender reassignment in documents it is not necessary to go through surgical intervention. However, it is necessary to be diagnosed with gender dysphoria and to receive hormonal treatment for at least two years prior to application.

11   Gerard Coll-Planas (2010) argues that there have been two positions in LGBT activism: normalization and transformation. This split can be seen in trans struggles and can be identified in many of the debates around these issues.

12   The necessary skills to be fluent in English are not acquired at school. Normally, it is learned in private academies or during holiday periods in English-speaking countries, which is conditioned by economic possibilities.

these elitist connotations. As such, queer has been widely contested in feminist and LGBT movements, where there are different views on transsexuality in relation to feminist and non-normative perspectives (Cambrollé, 2008; Coll-Planas and Missé, 2013).

> *Self-identifying as transfeminists cannot be an excuse to erase all the marvellous genealogies of radical feminisms that nurture us, because then, transfeminism, dears, will be 'neomachista' [a new form of patriarchal culture]. And we will be making the job for patriarchy, developing anti-feminist propaganda and provoking divisions among ourselves. And, precisely, at this moment of time if we choose to semantically come together as transfeminists more than as queers, it has been, in part and precisely, to banish any anti-feminist tension. And not because queer – or kuir —activisms and multitudes, there where they emerged and where they were passed on, had ever repudiated the feminism that enabled them. (Ziga, 2013, p. 82)*

Ziga's quote expresses the fear that using 'queer' will end up masking gender oppression and making feminist struggles and genealogies invisible. Queer concepts have travelled from the anglophone world to this context in a way that has been used, in some cases, to argue that struggles on women's issues are patriarchal, as they reproduce binary conceptions of gender when speaking about 'women'. Solá states that 'we wonder whether the relativization of identities that queer proposes can conceal the asymmetry between men and women … Here is where the word comes from, a word that, differing from the concept "queer", maintains the term "feminism"' (Solá, 2013, p. 20). This might be a homogenization of a complex and diverse body of work, but what 'queer' means in the anglophone world may not be the same as what 'queer' means or implies in other enclaves.

With the example of transfeminist movements and theorizations, which do not only include trans issues but also a wide array of questions regarding sexualities, intersections and practices, it can be seen how the adoption of a concept other than 'queer' allowed new strategies to be developed and other forms of knowledge to be produced. We have seen how new epistemologies emerge – epistemologies that account for specific realities in a contextualized way and also help us understand that the anglophone queer epistemologies are also situated, partial and local.

Conclusions

In this chapter I have tried to show how the production of knowledge beyond academia and the anglophone world challenges and contests hegemonic conceptualization in relation to gender and sexuality practices. On the one hand, feminist pro-independence politics and theorizations seem to show different productions of knowledge that go beyond hegemonic genealogies. The Anglo-American hegemony in geography establishes the patterns for the intellectual debate (Garcia-Ramon, 2012) and knowledge production in some non-anglophone regions or literature is seen as 'local', as an empirical contribution not capable of producing theory (Silva, 2011). I have tried to show the rich and complex epistemologies developed in Catalan countries based on the need to articulate different struggles. This 'political intersectionality' shows how knowledge production that is developed beyond academia and the anglophone world contests some conceptualizations and opens the debate for other dialogues. Could the conceptualizations made by feminists engaged with national projects be considered as queer epistemologies? Or, maybe, more precisely, could they be considered as transfeminist proposals? As has been seen with the example of transfeminist movements and theorizations, generational divisions and language tensions occur in movements where anglophone influences arrive through irregular paths and produce new conceptualizations. Maybe, 'queer' in some of the ways it is understood in the anglophone world could perfectly refer to what transfeminism seeks to say. But 'queer' is seen in our context as an English concept with imperialist and elitist connotations that has been used, on some occasions, to undermine feminist struggles. However, despite the tensions between transfeminist and queer epistemologies, could we consider transfeminism itself as part of 'queer epistemologies'? With these two examples I hope to have contributed to shedding light into the knowledge productions that come from the margins of academia and the anglophone world, hoping that a dialogue can be established and that these margins could also be seen as a privileged epistemological standpoint that may counter the anglophone/academic hegemony in the production of knowledge on geographies of gender and sexualities.

Chapter 19

Performing Academy: Feedback and Diffusion Strategies for Queer Scholactivists in France

Rachele Borghi, Marie Hélène/Sam Bourcier, Cha Prieur

About 15 years ago, a couple of self-identified queer scholars/activists got into French academia to queer it: they wanted to be there, out as queer subjects, producing queer knowledges and queering university. It was all about épistemopolitique (Bourcier, 2001, 2005), as members of the Zoo Collective[1] would put it. Queering the (straight) university meant countering the existing hierarchical knowledge formations and the politics of *savoir/ pouvoir*, aligned with French universalism and republicanism, which since the eighteenth century have promoted 'equality' as an abstract, exclusive and exceptionalist ideal. French universalism is a self-denying particularism centred on the supposedly unmarked and 'universal subject', which too often translates into hetero, white and male. Within the realm of French republicanism, the only acceptable modalities of citizenship are assimilation and integration. Any (religious, cultural, sexual, racial, class or other) differences must dissolve into the republican ideal of 'neutral universality'; any insistence on group or individual particularity, including recognition of diverse forms of oppression or differences politics are labelled as *communautaire* and framed as a potential threat to the 'national unity' within a republican *une et indivisible* (First Amendment of the 5th French Constitution, 1958). These ideals permeate French academia as well.

Although much work has been done to tackle these exclusionary principles within academic spaces over the last 15 years, queer studies and scholars are still far from victory. The French academic space keeps resisting the development and critical epistemological engagement with its own genealogy. It maintains positivist epistemology as scientific standards, sustaining multiple forms of epistemic violence that prevent the development of epistemological creativity dedicated to social transformation rather than social objectification.

This chapter is co-written by three self-identified 'scholactivists' who work, live and are politically engaged in French academic spaces. Drawing on our auto-ethnographic experiences and previous research projects, our objective is to develop a critique of the normative character of the academy and disciplinary boundaries and to share tactics for overcoming the modalities of control of academic topics and bodies. In the first part, we provide more insight into the mechanisms of the French academic world. In the second part, we present three cases of epistemological practices, which do not conform to

---

1   Founded in 1996, the Zoo was the first French queer collective; it started with a queer seminar held at the Philosophy Department at the Sorbonne, and at the independent Gay and Lesbian Centre (Bourcier, 1998).

the overdominant positivist ideals clouding French academic spaces. These examples concern: 1) pedagogy and teaching; 2) research and methodologies; and 3) dissemination and embodiment.

The French Academic Context

The rise of queer studies and movements in the USA in the early 1990s is often said to be a reaction against the identity politics (Fuss, 1983, 1990) of the 1960s and 1970s (which subsequently developed, academically, into 'women's studies', 'gay and lesbian studies', 'black studies' and 'chicano studies', to name a few examples), as well as the specific impact of the AIDS crisis in the 1980s. The history in France is different. Needless to say that in the French monocultural republic, no minority has yet had a meaningful chance to become part of the academic system, to voice their perspectives, or to offer new and proliferating insights and methodologies that would radically transform the epistemological frame of traditional humanities and social sciences in France. Syllabi made possible in the wake of student, feminist and ethnic movements of the late 1970s never made it in the French context even after the mythic events of May 1968. Thus, it is not by chance that one of the first statements made by the scholactivists from the queer group, Le Zoo, turned upside down US white queer theory's call for an *aufhebung* regarding identity politics. We urged sexual, racial and ethnic minorities to embrace identity politics as a strategy to fight republicanism and universalism by reclaiming 'post-identarian identity politics'. Their implementation, in both the academic field and civil society, would have made visible the exclusionary mechanisms of knowledge production that are disguised in the supposed neutrality and objectivity of academic republican ideals. Needless to say, the rejection of feminist studies in France from the 1980s onwards by academics and by leftist feminist activists themselves (mostly materialist feminists) played a major part in the erasure and the non-dissemination of the feminist knowledges, gender studies and critical epistemological engagements that we deem necessary to destabilize French academic structures of *savoir/pouvoir*. Either they stood up against the institutionalization of feminist and gender studies or they disguised them as *études féminines* (Feminine Studies and Antoinette Fouque's 'feminology') as did the differentialist feminists, such as Helene Cixous and her daughter Anne Emmanuelle Berger at Paris 8 university.

Gender (and sexuality) studies also present several problems and issues. One of them is the hegemony of sociology and history as a disciplinary framework. The institutionalization of gender studies that started in France from the 2000s, under heavy pressure from gender mainstreaming policies implemented by European institutions, borrowed massively from a sociology of gender which relies solely on a mono-paradigm of 'gender as a norm', heavily imbued in the tradition of French anthropology and social constructivism of the 1960s. Over and over, it is reiterated that gender norms matter (as if we did not know), while continuing to measure the 'burden of norms'. To analyse the ways in which people resist gender norms, how they embody and create new genders and what forms of empowerment one may draw from various forms of 'gender embodiment' is not on the research map. Little (if any) intellectual space is left either for queer paradigms of performance and performativity (Butler, 1990, 1993) or for 'gender as technology' (De Lauretis, 1987), for example.

When drawing on auto-ethnographic accounts, we find that the positivist toll in academic research includes not only gender studies but geography as well. Students and scholars are compelled to pursue 'observation' as an academic tool, in its most objectifying and non-collaborative way, in order to gain professional credit and acknowledgement and/

or recognition by colleagues and the academic community. Although people are allowed to be personally out as gay, lesbian, trans or queer within the academy, it appears that they are not allowed to do gay, lesbian or queer research. If they deliberately choose to include self-reflexivity and positionality in our research methods and findings, they will be immediately disqualified as both 'subjective' (not 'objective') and 'militant' (instead of 'universal' and 'neutral').

Geography in the French academic system is most often aligned with its subdiscipline of physical geography (Jégou et al., 2012), deterring geography's engagement with gender and sexuality issues, and leaving them to other disciplines such as sociology, anthropology, or history (Hancock and Barthe, 2005). Marianne Blidon (2008b) builds upon Gagnon (2008) (who analysed the institutional marginalization of researchers working on 'disturbing' and 'controversial' issues) and shows that this lack of interest from geographers towards gender and sexuality studies is linked with the evaluation of the research subject's legitimacy: 'Beyond the embarrassment sexual questions provoke, one of the explanation factors of the lack of interest of French geographers for these themes is the organization in a hierarchy of research subjects, those which are judged more noble than others' (Blidon, 2008b, p. 57). Having explored the broader French academy, we now discuss our individual queering moves.

Tactic 1: How to Queer Academia With Performance – The Spatial–Performative Turn

Marie-Hélène Bourcier

Performance and performativity can be used within the realm of queer pedagogy at university and for queering the university. This is the case when a course combines performance studies as such (already a rather interdisciplinary field) and gender, race, class, ethnic, crip and post-porn performances as a teaching subject and assignment for the students. I have been giving such a course for more than 10 years at the University of Lille III. Part of the course is given to small groups, dedicated to the analysis of performances done either by self-identified performers or by former students who agree to show their work in class. It relies on a performative and a rhizomatic style of teaching that allows crucial dislocations of discursive and spatial boundaries inside and outside the classroom.

One of the main discursive boundaries is the supposed division between theory and practice. The language of gender studies can be very sophisticated, as it is the case of Butler's (1990, 1993) theory of gender as performance and performativity. The question is: how can we ensure that these theory-heavy ideas are grasped by students who may lack sophisticated philosophical vocabulary? In my course, Butler's theory is taught, detheorized and recontextualized, in order to acknowledge its situatedness and connect it to the students' experiences. We read *Gender Trouble* (Butler, 1990) as a text connected to its many outsides. Queer subcultures are one of such contexts, and they are used to both highlight the major role they played in Butler's conceptual elaboration, and to alter the purity of her theory. If one of Butler's major achievements was to bring the drag club culture to the forefront of the straight theoretical horizon in a political and celebratory way, in the classroom we pay attention to how this 'theoretical' shift is also related to her soft butch-lesbian identity, her feminist background and, later in the 1990s, to queer subcultures of genderfucking and drag kinging. Gender as performance is then taught as a knowledge formation – that is, a network of films, gender practices and performances – and does not rely solely on Butler's text. Performance

167

as a paradigm is also reconnected to performance as an artistic and political form and force, coming from the artistic world, which precedes and exceeds Butler's reappropriation of performance. Challenging both the boundaries between disciplines and those between theory and activism produces new knowledge formations – a pedagogical matrix that could be named 'gender power' rather than 'gender theory'.

Gender empowerment is an approach in which gender and performance are understood as process-oriented rather than concept-oriented. For example, students are encouraged to do performances in public spaces, outside the university, so that they have to face the ambivalences of drag and of the repetition of gender quotes. Gender performative repetition is without guarantees; it is not always dissident, dissonant, disloyal in a subversive or parodist way as we may know it. After all, who is to decide that it is the case? How can gender normativity or gender dissidence be meta-performed in public spaces?

Here, spatiality is key to making us understand and feel how doing gender is tied to the binarism of our sex/gender system and how visual landscapes play a major role in gender expression, presentation and doing. Students' first move is always to invert gender expressions in their performances, making them repeat and reify sexual difference, unless they find a way to decontextualize and resignify it. Here are the benefits brought about by the performative and spatial turns in pedagogy, of dislocating the theory/practice boundary and the separation of academic space from the 'outside world'. With the students, we moved from the drag queen scene-made-theory to the public and urban space. Bodies that matter are those who re-matter, bodies involved by and through performance, the bodies of the students who can become acquainted with many gender experiences and identities and explore their own. Teaching, learning and gender performance are all consequently affected and transformed within this spatial frame. Students get to explore the gendered and performative structures of public and private spaces (streets, shopping malls, bathrooms, public transport, university campus or student accommodation halls). Their performance is disseminated back in the university space, in the classrooms, where they show their filmed performances to the rest of group and in front of examining teachers in charge of grading their work. Not only does the theoretical scene become collective, but acknowledging the presence of straight and queer gender identities in a classroom setting becomes a way of queering French universalist and republican academic space. Since French academia is still heavily imbued with positivist, republican universalism (as we have argued above), a distinctively present voice and gesture of subjective reiteration of genders, as experienced and recreated by students as part of their assignment, becomes a mode of queering the scholarly norms of French academia (Bourcier, 2014). Performative courses that engage students' bodies and affects help to question academic norms of knowledge production, as well as the containment of creativity and politics by/within university boundaries.

Another effect of this spatialization and performatization of pedagogic/classroom practice has to do with the regulation of the traffic that takes place between universities and the 'outside world'. French academic disciplinarity and hierarchies hinder possibilities of reconfiguration and de-hierarchization of knowledges, and consequently the prospects of altering the frontier between university and the 'dirty outside world', to borrow from Stuart Hall (Bourcier, 2005; Hall, 1990; 1996). When required and implemented as a side-effect of the corporatization of universities, which are becoming private enterprises since 2007 in France, the so-called porosity of university and civil society translates into a management of equality (between men and women) and anti-discrimination policies that lead to direct attacks against academic freedom and different epistemic practices. During this year, I was accused by the students of pornifying the university by giving a two-hour course on feminist and post-porn pornography, which was part of the theoretical course on performance. In the same academic year, my course on performance was 'neutralized' by the administration, meaning that it would not be graded. Consequently, the professor in charge of the workshop part of the course on performance – who is a performer and former student of the university – was violently delegitimized as a teacher. Most of the students did not show up at his course. He had to go through a violent homophobic campaign on Facebook led by a group of students who portrayed him as doing 'masquerade' instead of 'course' and as a sex pervert, 'ready for anal sex' (he is being portrayed as Spiderman on his all fours, 'his ass ready to go') and willing to fuck the students or to give them good grades if they pose naked for him. Neither the dean of the university nor the different people in charge of my department level nor the person in charge of discrimination took action, even though they had been formally asked to do so. Ironically, all this happened when the university had just adopted a new motto celebrating its involvement against discrimination – 'Lille 3 s'engage' to look more competitive and 'sexy'. Of course, this is nothing but an example of fake management of diversity in a context of privatization of higher education.

Tactic 2: Queering Methodologies – Using Scavenger Methodologies in Queer Research

Cha Prieur

I do not know if I can speak about methodologies which are properly or essentially queer. I would rather speak of the process of queering, which could involve using 'scavenger methodologies' (Halberstam, 1998) on the one hand, and the destabilization of knowledge categories, on the other. 'Scavenger methodologies', at its simplest, is an approach whereby methodology is individually tailored to each research project, to each researcher, each time a new project is conceived. Your positionality, your experiences and your goals guide you towards your own arrangement of methods, the choice of your own methodology (Halberstam, 1998). The latter questions hierarchies of what is, and where is, knowledge, allowing the use of materials which have thus far not been considered academic (militant zines, websites, blogs and so on), not only as sources of information upon which 'knowledge' is built and transferred via academic texts for example, but also as the actual outlets and repositories of knowledge, equal to scientific publications and other repositories.

Queering methods and methodologies lean on feminist-situated knowledges, research positionality and the reflexivity of the researcher on their research (England, 1994), a practice which, in a given context of the French academia, is a bold approach. For example, when your fieldwork covers the places where you socialize and live, you always act two roles in those places: private and professional. When in the 'private' role, if an event occurs, you switch into the 'professional' role of the researcher, because your research is intricately bound with your 'private' person. Sometimes, your friends are speaking about their lives and you realize suddenly that their arguments reinforce or destabilize your own academic argumentation in your study. What kind of relations of power and control are produced in this type of exchange? And what can you do to address such a challenge? In my own research I have tried to think activism and research together ('scholactivism'), which builds on Heckert's '(2010) methodological anarchism' and Liamputtong's (2007) 'sensitive researcher'. Heckert (2010, p. 43) favours the blurring of the hierarchies between the researcher and the researched, accepting and accentuating the co-construction of any research. 'Scholactivism' is also a position of a 'sensitive researcher' who draws on '[q]ualitative research methods [that] are flexible and fluid, and therefore, are suited to understanding the meanings, interpretations and subjective experiences of vulnerable groups' (Liamputtong, 2007, p. 7). Liamputtong

(2007) argues that researchers can hear and give voice to silenced and marginalized groups. She also insists that processes are more important than facts, and since emotions are part of processes, they cannot be separated from facts and behaviours.

For the scholactivist practice, the enactment and the concept of care are also important. How could I do my fieldwork without putting the people I interviewed in danger? How can I ensure a fair exchange with people for the qualitative data they provide me with? What is my place as researcher in taking care of my community? The recognition that researchers' emotions are embodied and linked with our own corporeal memory is important here, as 'emotions are a central part of social research' (Dickson-Swift et al., 2009, p. 61). For example, interviewing people about different types of violence (racism, sexism, sexual or physical abuse) is a very sensitive process, so, in my research, I work on 'active listening' techniques and I have decided more recently to study for a certificate in neuro-linguistic programming: not only am I passively listening to the story, but also engaging with, and acting upon, emotions relived during the interview.

To some readers of this chapter, some of the points raised so far may seem obvious. However, one should bear in mind the French academic setting within which I work and to which I address my concerns. So ethnography that takes into account the researcher's social, cultural and political positionality and power relations also actively acts upon certain ethical principles – 'scholactivism', as I call it. This practice is by no means obvious within the walls of the French university. An approach put forward in several chapters of *Queer Methods and Methodologies* (Browne and Nash, 2010) that insists on the rhizomatic aspect of the research (there are no separate phases between before the fieldwork and after, between gathering materials and writing up results) may also be deemed unacceptable to many French researchers. This rhizomatic approach is a doing, a permanent making, whereby sometimes the researcher develops contradictory or paradoxical re-elaborations and analysis, depending on the phases of their fieldwork. Only *a posteriori* can one recognize the construction of one's discourse, and the choices and arbitrations one makes when the writing phase begins.

Observant participation and, maybe more exactly, participant observation is another way to do activism while staying in the academy. The principal difficulty is the navigation between these two spheres which are not really kind to each other. In the French academy, saying that you are a scholactivist/researcher-militant is a militant action that blurs the academy's norms. Scholactivists fight against the inaccessible French republican ideals of a 'neutral scientist', devoid of subjectivity and emotions. The risk of lack of recognition from their peers in French academia directly translates into the material conditions of researchers' lives (for example, through restricted job opportunities).

Tactic 3: Space Contamination – Rachele aka Zarra Bonheur

Rachele Borghi

In recent years many calls for papers have introduced and opened up new forms of intervention that differ from more usual presentations – for example: 'Beside classical interventions (communications and posters), all sorts of original formats are welcome: workshops based on research in progress, symposium-type workshops, videos and films, sound bites, displays, etc.' (*Sharing Space*, 2014). This coincides with 'the spatial turn' in contemporary art practice and scholarship and its interest in geography: 'Here our main concern is how geographers – as social scientists – are currently addressing the "spatial turn" in contemporary art' (Art and Geography, 2013). But how can geography learn from art, not just the other way round? Or, rather, where does the boundary lie within which the geographer is free to borrow from other disciplines and forms of expression? And what happens if those forms of expression are questioned as 'non-artistic' and not even legitimized by the discourse of art criticism? How much does the university, as a space governed by a set of specific norms, affect and limit different forms of expression? So, how far can a geographer, who does not define themselves as an artist, but who uses performance as a tool for mixing and contaminating different contexts go? What happens if you bring the performance to sites where it is expected least, and if it is produced by the body of a researcher and not by the body of an artist?

Let me use auto-ethnography as a tool of generating information and examples, and as a reference point for further debate. Since 2011, as part of my research, I have been working on post-porno performance in public spaces as a means of space creation and suspending social norms. I instantly clashed with the normative disciplinary discourses in academia that reacted to the embarrassment caused by my 'dirty' topic, insisting that the work was 'non-geographic' and thus delegitimizing my work as valid research. As a part of this research, I reflected upon the uneasy relationship between academic research and activism, and upon the relationship between fieldwork spaces, university spaces and the diffusion spaces for research 'out/in/side' of 'scientific' community. I took up the tool I studied (performance) and the medium (the body) in order to test new (geographical) ways of disseminating research results. In order to do so, I set up the project/character of Zarra Bonheur: 'a perfomer-sexual-queer-feminist-militant-dissident-polytopic-activist-researcher fruit of "do it yourself" contagion and fruit of her friends widespread love' (Zarra Bonheur, 2015). Zarra Bonheur translates 'scientific' researches into performances. The goal is to break the boundaries between contexts (scientific/activist), productions (high/pop culture), places (university, theatre, room, squat, association), expressions (lecture/performance) and to produce spaces of subversion/transgression of the norms. Let me provide two examples.

The performance *Degen(d)erated euphoria* highlights the materiality of thought. In fact, the words allow us to carry forward reflections that deconstruct and rebuild the mind and also transform the body: they become body. The words emerge from the texts. Hovering in the air, they also get rid of their own referents. They lean upon the body and become matter through the bodies. The collective body takes possession of the words; it develops the thought and it creates action. Texts have different origins, such as scientific and philosophical contexts, or militant contexts, breaking up the binarisms that set 'academic' as 'expert and opposed to 'lay/activist' as 'low' cultures. Words emerge from essays, blogs, collective manifestos and fanzines. They alight on bodies and they give rise to construction and deconstruction processes that open new opportunities and euphoric paths that allow the conception of endless chances and identities.

Zarra Bonheur works inside the interstices to create spaces in-between. This is also the case for *Porno Trash*, a performance I created starting from my research (and from my application to the Centre National de la Recherche Scientifique), which deals with the relationship between the body and space, and the representation/perception of nudity in public spaces. *Porno Trash* is a two-stage performance about the body and its oppression and liberation, about social perceptions of nudity, and about the body as a space of practices and relationships. During the first phase, Zarra Bonheur and friends read texts by various authors (such as philosophers and bloggers), academic articles and fanzines that discuss the process of domesticating the body and its political and social control.

During the second phase, the attention moves on to the reappropriation of body by sexuality, by desire and by choice. The reading, accompanied by undressing, ends up by inviting the public to undress and dance with others, creating a 'contagion' of the euphoria

171

of nudity and free body. It is in this way that a space of the suspension and subversion of norms is created. The performance plays with childhood symbols and refers to a time when nudity did not yet have a social value ascribed to it. During this performance, the main message is about the role of the body and of nudity in creative processes, the strengthening of relationships between participants, and the transmission/distribution of the 'bravery' to transgress the norms. Each performance is designed to be specific to the place and people involved, and it changes all the time because Zarra Bonheur, as a character, does not want to represent a person, but is rather a collective project of dissidence, resistance, experimentation and academic pornoactivism.

Zarra Bonheur's performances allow reflection on the weight of epistemological norms, on the (in)visibility of the researcher's body in the (scientific) process of conceiving knowledge, and on the (il)licitness of (non)academic practice. I wanted to experiment with the boundaries and the perception of nudity inside academic environments, and to translate epistemological questions into performance. The goal of each of my porno-activist research-performances is manifold, and includes reflection upon: 1) the relationship between the researcher and space; 2) the voyeurism of research; 3) the non-return of research findings to the context where they were studied or the subjects involved; 4) the formation of a legitimacy for an academic discourse, which often silences the voices of interviewees; 5) the invisibility of the body of the researcher, which is supposed to be represented by its head; 6) a conference as a spectacle and performance; and, finally, 7) the supposed legitimacy of certain tools (a PowerPoint presentation, an academic article), and the supposed inadequacy of others (performance and ritual).

However, at times, there are severe consequences of this approach to doing academic/ geographic research. During the 'Queer Days' conference (7 February 2013), organized at the University of Bordeaux, I was invited to talk about my research on post-porn. I used two sets of tools to deliver my presentation. One was a toolbox of 'academic performance' (PowerPoint, microphone, a pen), and learned languages to create a short circuit between message, referent and code. The other one was my 'theatrical performance', and this involved me undressing as the presentation progressed (*Queer Days*, 2013). Three months later, in May 2013, the video from my presentation/performance provoked a storm of hatred and accusations directly connected to the fact that around that same time I was offered a job contract at the University of Sorbonne: some university professors used my performance/ video to question and undermine my academic credibility, the legitimacy of my research and the appropriateness of my work. They demanded that the university withdrew the job offer (which, in the end, did not happen). Then, many ultra-Catholic and other radical right groups' websites spoke about 'the queer invasion of French universities' and the moral decay of the institution. Finally, it is a sad fact that, in these circumstances, many colleagues remained indifferent to the attack on my person and on my research practice, dismissing these events as 'not serious' or 'not important'. Although it is not yet the time to assess the effects of Zarra Bonheur's work, I hope that the performances and events described above show that she can potentially raise a discussion about the practices of academic knowledge dissemination, and the hegemonic norms of epistemological legitimacy and knowledge production.

Conclusion

How can queer subjects of knowledge and politics, queer bodies and epistemologies exist within French academic and public national space? This is the question we have to answer after 15 years of rejection. In this chapter we have tried to reflect upon the epistemological violence of the French academic system and the possibilities of pedagogies and knowledge creation for researchers and teachers working at the crossroads of geographies, genders and sexualities within that national context. Drawing on auto-ethnographic observations, we have offered examples of alternative ways of conceiving and practising knowledge – practices that work against the unequal power relations between the different subjects involved and practices that benefit the creative exploration of margins, shadows and demi-mondes of the academy.

Marie-Hélène/Sam Bourcier's work and pedagogy deals with the invisible relationship between power and knowledge and ways to counter positivist, republican, modernist and universalist narratives and *espistémé*, especially their arguable quest for neutrality and objectivity, as the ruling principles of the academic system in France. Although the 'hubris of zero degrees' (Castro-Gómez, 2008) which is foundational to the colonial myth of European modernity, objectivity and identity is far from being a French phenomenon, the ongoing promotion of 'a universal point of view', be it by 'true' knowledge as opposed to 'militant's' knowledges or by humanistic sciences and academia, still prevails in a nation allergic to identity and differences politics or multiculturalism and which has become the new cradle of Eurocentrism and civilizationism. He addresses this French monoculturality and the role played by a kind of sociology untouched by the cultural turn and which therefore reinforces disciplinarity.

Cha Prieur insists on the researcher's positionality and reflexivity. Concerning queer methods and methodologies Cha Prieur lends weight to emotions in their studies and in the research process by accepting and recognizing the impact of emotion work in queer research. Rachele Borghi aka Zarra Bonheur, breaks the public/private binary. She promotes the contamination of places and attempts to eradicate the barriers that divide the spaces and spheres of relations. As Michela Baldo (2014, p. 123) explains:

> *Rachele's performative talk at the University of Bordeaux made her naked body visible as integral part of the content of her class, which revolved around queer space and sexuality, and the boundaries between public and private, using it as site of intervention/resistance against those heteronormative ideas of sexuality and space that she was attacking. However, her body troubled academia.*

In the late 1970s US students and teachers fought for and won affirmative action policies and the transformation of the canon in order to challenge human sciences, the so-called *sciences de l'homme* and their master narratives, the national one included. In order to cope with our aspiration to, and estrangement from, institutionalization, we came up with different and maybe less collective answers, strategies and actions in the French context. 'Pornactivism'[2] is one of them and maybe the least expected offspring of the post-porn subculture that emerged around 2000 in France,[3] in itself a very specific and unpredicted translation of 'queer made in France'. As it turned out, 'post-porn' is not disconnected from academia or public spaces; quite the opposite. Nowadays, 'post-porn' stands as a form of sexual disobedience made visible in urban and academic spaces, and this is maybe the reason why we are experimenting with forms of 'porno-scholactivism' by bringing the body and sexuality within the academy where the body is not supposed to be and is not expected. Making bodies present (and visible) highlights and destabilizes the rigid informal expectations for the 'neutrality' of a (body-less, subjectivity-less) researcher, which currently

---

2   The term has been coined by Rachele Borghi.
3   See the chapter 'Post Porn' in *Queer Zones 1*, 2001.

govern French academia. It allows us to work on the contamination among places and context, starting from our position inside academia.

These forms of experimentation bring attention to the relationships between the object and the subject of research, between the observer and the observed and, last but not least, to the academic voyeuristic *dispositif* and the colonial dimension of the 'subject/object' dualism and dynamics (Dussel, 1995b) that informed modern and Eurocentric thought based on asymmetry, exploitation and the elimination of 'epistemic alterity' or difference. Breaking another powerful dichotomy such as theory/practice requires elaborating a new language. To keep talking about 'theoretical' and 'practical' means recognizing the existence of this dichotomy and moving within it. We try to elaborate an experimental language by defining these practices as 'theoractical', going beyond the division between 'who does theory' and 'who does practice'.

However, in discussing the creative ways of producing and disseminating knowledge about space and bodies, we have also identified dangers lurking in the highly hierarchical French academia. The examples we have discussed show that violence is inherent in the production of (hegemonic) knowledges and that academy is no stranger to the violent erasure and devastation of the researcher's body. Putting 'objectivity in parenthesis' (Maturana, 1985), self-identifying as scholactivists – that is, both scholars and activists politicizing the presence of queer researchers in the French academy – comes at a price and with violent 'epistemological expropriations' (Castro-Gómez, 2008). It proved to be a daily fight to be queer, out and proud in the academy, and struggle against transphobia, homophobia and heterosexism. This eventually raises the issue of 'our will to institutionality' (Ferguson, 2012), our ability and political will to address the relationship between the state, capitalism and academia, our determination to destroy the myth of modernity and the fiction of sexual difference and of what it takes to organize an epistemo-political community on a collective and transnational level in order to build the 'epistemic simultaneity of the world' (Castro-Gómez, 2008).

Chapter 20

Writing through Activisms and Academia: Challenges and Possibilities

Niharika Banerjea, Kath Browne,
Leela Bakshi, Subhagata Ghosh

Introduction

Critical writers suggest that academic work, thinking and research can be activist in its motivations, processes and outcomes. Activist-oriented research has a long-standing tradition of engaging legacies of feminist politics and participatory and collaborative research processes (Farrow et al, 1995; Gatenby and Humphries, 2000; Moss, 2002; Ramazanoğlu and Holland, 2002; Sharp, 2005; Thomas, 1993). A body of work has explored the role of the academic-activist, engaged academic, politically purposive researcher, and scholar-activist in furthering social change (Chatterton, 2006; Kindon et al., 2007; Mitchell, 2008; The Autonomous Geographies Collective, 2010). Yet there exist few studies that discuss the actual process of working and writing collaboratively from the perspective of both academics and activists across national contexts in the area of sexualities. This chapter looks at how academics and activists collaborate to produce academic and academic/activist work in two projects concerned with sexualities. One is located in India, where Article 377 of the Indian Penal Code criminalizes certain sexual acts.[1] After a brief reading down in July 2009, this was reinstated in December 2013, the same year that the Marriage (Same Sex Couples) Act was passed in the England and Wales. Putting academics and activists across India and the UK into dialogue, this chapter contests the ways in which some nations are seen as moving 'backwards', and highlights the need to learn from others who are moving 'forward'. Instead, we speak as academics/activists who engage in co-producing useful knowledges with which to intervene in local/national sexuality politics.

In this chapter we share stories about how we came to write together in our respective projects, and the challenges and possibilities of writing across activisms and academia in the UK and India. Speaking together from our different contexts, we discuss the motivations underpinning our collaborations across activist/academic boundaries, the audiences we sought to engage, the complexities of publishing work that refuses the neat boundaries of academic/activist, issues of framing the research findings, and the outcomes of this process. We argue that when considering the politics of sexual geographies, we also need to explore the politics of research and the processes through which we construct knowledges around

---

1   Article 377 of the Indian Penal Code has its origins in an 1860 British colonial law. It was read down by the Delhi High Court in *Naz Foundation vs Government of NCT of Delhi* on 2 July 2009. In the *Suresh Kumar Koushal v Naz Foundation* case, the court reversed the 2009 judgment on 11 December 2013.

marginalized sexualities and sexual lives in different contexts and places. Coming together as academics/activists across geographical and institutional borders in transnational ways, we seek to interrupt hegemonic divides around the politics of sexuality research. These politics include the hegemony of Anglo-American research and activisms. Through our narratives about the thoughts, motivations and journeys that underlie knowledge production about struggles and stories around sexualities we hope to interrupt the popular perceptions about 'backward' and forward' places. We bring activisms and academia in a productive dialogue at the heart of an academic text, interrogate the binaries between theory and practice, and queer the process of knowledge production in geographies of sexualities research.

Queering Participatory Research

Participatory Action Research (PAR), with its roots in feminist challenges to traditional research models, has contested the hierarchies of researcher/researched dichotomies (Kindon et al., 2007). Discussion of this form of research methodology points to how all research is constructed through power relations and suggests other ways of developing research. Participatory research is not necessarily empowering (Kesby, 2007) or transformative (Cooke and Kothari, 2001) and may even reproduce social hierarchies (Banerjea, 2011). Increasingly, this form of research, or at least research that involves its 'end-users' and creates impact, is demanded by funding bodies and assessment exercises, such as the Research Excellence Framework in the UK. What began as a challenge to positivist epistemologies, and specifically to the normativities of distant and objective research and researchers, is increasingly becoming a codified, sanitized and state-required norm in some contexts. The 'impact agenda' has come under some critique (see ACME, 2013). Yet, considerations of usurping the hegemonies within research processes are undoubtedly important in rethinking how our research is and might be political and politicized. The importance of PAR in academic knowledge development is that it has the potential to question and (re)configure researcher/researched hierarchies and points to the ways in which we might queer – that is, disrupt the normativities of research fields (see also Browne and Nash, 2010). We see this chapter as addressing the overlap of queer and PAR critiques, where both seek to contest normativities of knowledge creation and practices.

Practices of reflexivity, positionality and polyvocality are key to unsettling the stable subject/object and researcher/researched distinction. However, by themselves, these practices may not necessarily destabilize the norms of knowledge production based in the dualisms of theory/practice and expert/community. The 'participants' or 'the community' need to be engaged with the research in ways that question academic knowledges in an ethically accountable manner. Richa Nagar (2006, p. xlvii) characterizes accountability as arising out of a recognition that 'knowledge must emerge out of sustained, critical dialogues with those who are the subjects of that knowledge'. It is 'through these dialogues, the subjects of knowledge become the primary evaluator, critics and intellectual partners of those who are seen as experts'. This dialogic act, we argue, is an aspect of queerly produced research practice. A critical dialogue *with* activists needs to be placed in social critique that troubles the 'academic knowledges and vocabularies' (Nagar, 2014, p. 173) through which institutions reproduce their legitimacy. A critique about sexual marginalization, privileges and decolonization has to simultaneously involve an interruption of the processes through which such conversations are produced in the first place.

Collaborative dialogues are complex, involving a movement away from the ethnographic gaze, and co-construct knowledge through a careful and often delicate process of negotiation

(Crick, 1982; Denzin, 1997) These dialogic interactions are not fixed but are meant to be ongoing. Madison (2012, p. 11) points to dialogue as 'situated in multiple expressions that transgress, collide, and embellish realms of meaning' – meaning that also alters as the self's experiences change. Thus, the beautiful paradox about a queer project is that as the dialogic moments of the self and others are created in writing; meaning is brought forth, but one that is resistant to conclusiveness.

However, talking to and across boundaries challenges the ways in which academies operate, and inherent to moving across/between different cultures is a risk of 'missed opportunities':

> *Many times scholars and activists talk past each other: scholars want the 'big picture' and develop a conceptual vocabulary to bring that big picture into focus, whilst activists address immediate concerns and rely on experiential knowledge to make decisions about issues and strategies. Subsequently we miss opportunities to benefit from each other's stock of knowledge. Each purpose is important but there may be ways to reorientate the knowledge produced by each for mutual benefit (Valocchi, 2010, p. 2)*

Valocchi points here to the importance of meaningful dialogues between activists and scholars that can create mutually beneficial knowledges. Yet, whilst Valocchi engages with communities and operates his research 'in dialogue with' activists, the final book is written solely by Valocchi. He is not alone, activist/community outputs and those targeted at academics outputs are often separated, presuming diverse audiences with differing interests (theory versus practice) and abilities (accessibility versus complexity, nuance). Whilst offering different knowledges appropriate to specific contexts can be productive, we question the presumptions that each works to their own separate ends and we question that they work to divergent purposes. Whilst we may 'benefit' from different knowledges, what activists and academics do with these knowledges is often presumed to be for separate ends.

Whereas, authorship for community resources is diffuse and diverse, challenging the boundaries of who 'owns' and created these knowledges, academic authorship in the main is not. Exceptions exist: consider, for example, mrs kinpaisby (2008), The Autonomous Geographies Collective (2010), the Women and Geography Study Group (1997) and Gibson-Graham (1996, 2006). All of these flouted academic conventions of authorship by refusing single-named authorship. Nevertheless, these collectives and pairings still consisted of only academic scholars, and thus the hierarchy of the knowledge producer remained in place. This hierarchy is buttressed by an understanding that theorization by academics is on a higher plane than non-academic activist writings. When incorporated with 'non-academic' forms of writing practices, an academic piece is often labelled as 'methodology', 'activism' or 'atheoretical' (Nagar and Swarr, 2010, p. 8). Our writing practices should perhaps come under the same scrutiny of power relations that we use both to explore our fields of study and critically examine data collection processes. After all, the use of people as research subjects in the conduct of the projects has been roundly critiqued for many years and new ways of working formed. Similarly, neglecting an examination of writing practices reiterates norms that we might well want to critique.

We present this chapter in a dialogic form as a political strategy. We bring academic/activist voices from two different nations in conversation with each other within the pages of an academic output, as a means of further politicizing the processes of writing theory. We do not contest the binary output strategies where 'community' outputs are separate from academic ones, as we don't think that this output will be widely read by activists. However, we are challenging the location of activists writing outside the academy. We see this, often unspoken, dissemination approach as deserving of questioning, critiquing and rethinking. This is not to deny the importance of separate modes of dissemination, but instead to consider what new spaces for the discussion of research may be created by crossing the divides between community/university, activist/academic and Global North/ Global South. These are important concerns, as writing 'with' rather than writing 'about' is a challenge that academics have taken up in recent years in order to redress concerns about marginalization, essentialisms and differences in representation. This chapter seeks to be part of these spaces – spaces that have offered significant innovation, including *Boots of Leather, Slippers of Gold* (Kennedy and Davis, 1994) and *Playing with Fire: Feminist Thought and Activism through Seven Lives in India* (Nagar, 2006). Each text in its own way queered/ crossed the established modes of academic writing by placing oral narratives and journals by working-class lesbians and grassroots development workers at the heart of text, thus questioning what counts as historical analysis and theory.

This chapter draws on a transnational discussion between the authors, undertaken in 2013 over Skype across Brighton and Kolkata, and subsequently edited and updated for this chapter. Leela and Kath worked on the Count Me In Too project (www.countmeintoo.co.uk), in which LGBT activists worked with the public sector and others to improve the lives of LGBT people in Brighton and Hove. This led to a co-authored book, *Ordinary in Brighton: LGBT, Activisms and the City* (Browne and Bakshi, 2013a). Niharika and Subhagata are collaboratively working on a book project on community and spaces of activism in Kolkata. The discussion was transcribed, coded and edited. We present this chapter as an edited version of the conversation. We have followed academic conventions of citation here, whereby the author who has 'led the piece' is the lead author. We have then ordered the authors in relation to contribution and the alphabet. The voice of the introduction, first section and conclusion is an academic one, where Kath and Niharika ensured a properly cited narrative that places this dialogue in appropriate fields. We also edited the narrative into something coherent for Leela and Subhagata to look at and then we all edited our contributions, which reflect other power relations that can be overlooked in participatory research – that is, the ways in which academic research and especially academic writing benefits academic researchers and our careers. In this way, the academic authors of this piece are indeed stabilized as the primary authors of the text. This reiterates certain academic institutional privileges and axes of power. We acknowledge our academic privilege and power as a political act to interrupt this from *within* by centring our thoughts about our respective academic/activist projects in a dialogic form in an academic production. The time commitment that non-academic activists give to research needs to be acknowledged and addressed, with the legwork done by those with institutional support for our time, and recognition of the ways in which benefits accrue differently to those in different positionalities. Our conversations in this chapter are not timeless, but are temporal accounts about dynamic and changing process of collaborative work about queer activism and writing in Brighton and Kolkata in 2013–14.

Tensions, Motivations and Engagements with Activism and Academia

Kath: There is a gap in the literature around writing, with activists and academics writing together. What you have is the discussion of doing the research together. And then academics write up the reports and give activists (and policy-makers) the reports. Or a community activist gets involved and writes the dissemination for community stuff. And then academics write the academic stuff. What Leela and I try to do is something different. Which is we both write the academic stuff.

Niharika: When Sappho for Equality and I began our book project, Subhagata, Sumita (my other writing partner) and I talked about what this book is going to do or achieve outside the academic circle. We decided that after the book is complete, we will have to write a parallel piece which would be useful for dissemination in non-academic circles.

Kath: I think we have to acknowledge that one of the motivations for this work is that it creates good data and writing that is a part of my job. I get paid to do it, but there is a responsibility there as well. If I do a project, I need academic publications that come out of it. However, my work is connected to activisms in ways that might not be possible in other jobs. I think, as academics, we have to acknowledge our privilege there as well.

Niharika: Yes, absolutely. There is a professional demand to publish with an academic publisher especially during the start of one's career. This cannot be discounted.

Leela: I think another motivation is advancing the priorities of the LGBT communities. Activists get clever insight on things we [activists] have been talking about for ages. And that tends to get a bit subsumed into an academic agenda, not in a bad way because the new thinking involves activists as well, but it can pull in a different direction from where activists want to go. I think academic questions become more relevant when they engage with activism and what activists are concerned about. It becomes irrelevant [to activists] when it starts looking at questions that do not have practical application.

Kath: But then we talked about the identities and nuances and the complexities.

Leela: Yes, understanding the complexities helps the activists to be more effective I think.

Subhagata: It is a part of our activism to make a bridge with academia. This has been the motivating factor for this book project. There are not many texts about LBT issues in the Indian context. Also, this city is very important because India is a very big country; it has different cultures in different parts of the country. Therefore the culture of Kolkata is quite different from Delhi. Hence, place-specific studies are needed. Also, as an activist, I perceive this book project as a simultaneous process of documenting activism with some academic feedback or academic analysis. Also, we would like to try to broaden our movement. If we can produce this text, it may help those who are at our stage of activism. Finally, I think that writing and constantly dialoguing and connecting with academics is a continuous learning process for me. My activism is also application of the knowledge thus generated through this learning. I also feel that the lived experience, which creates my activism today is perhaps knowledge for the future.

Leela: I got involved in activism in 2005 with LGBT community groups because of the work they were doing at the time. And I think in some ways I was chased a bit for being the only ethnic representative. That group wanted to have people with disabilities, older people and younger people. And some respectability comes with that … I think that's partly what motivated me to get involved. What motivated me the most was the quality of the work. What motivated me actually was the struggle, and that it was something that felt productive. I think that's when research is really important: to understand what the blockages are and understand what we have to deal with to understand how to move forward … The problem I had there was [what to do with] all the understanding that I didn't have before I started to do activism. And that partly has to do with the political entities and who is taking the power in Brighton at the moment.

Kath: What made you start writing?

Leela: I don't think I could have done it at the same time as the activism, but the activism was winding down in a way and that left me free to do writing. And the question is where to go with this insight … It's like we get a period of activism and now I'm involved with writing the book. So in some ways the knowledge comes a bit late, but we certainly have much more insight into the problems we are working with than before we wrote the book. I think that I really didn't understand, in terms of motivations, the issues that we were dealing with, and there was a lot of tension in the group of activists as we could not explain what the problem was or the issue was. Now, we would be able to explain but we don't have the group of activists anymore … But I guess that where academic writing comes in for activists elsewhere. Maybe reading this text will help people with their own issues in their activism.

Accountability, Audience and Publishing

Niharika: The question of accountability is a key issue framing our book project. We have read about accountability, but what does it mean in practice? I am interested in understanding what accountability means in the process of writing and knowledge production.

Kath: And when you talk about accountability, accountability to whom?

Niharika: Accountability to the people who are being documented and 'written about'. I want to write *with* the activists rather than *about* the activists, as much as is possible within the demands of my profession. Also, as and when I am, let's say, talking about the lives of the people we are working with or the politics and the political vision that we are trying to document, we are thinking who is going to read this, apart from academics in our field? Who is the audience?

Kath: We really struggled with the audience in terms of how we pitch the book and who to pitch it to. Trying to pitch it to both did not work for us at all. We kept trying to write across those boundaries but we ended up pitching to academics.

Leela: Because I think that's what got it published. If we had a publisher who said we would rather have a book for activists, we would have done that.

Kath: When you go to the book publisher, you get a different set of agendas. We had not really considered that; we just did our writing worrying about how those locally might read it, and believing that others would be interested … Even though we tried to write across academic and activists, we had those academic guidelines coming through very strongly. The academic agendas come through because of the structures you have to adhere to.

Subhagata: Is it possible to write a book in a way so that academics and activists can both use it?

Leela: So there was criticism of writing style, and referring to previous academic arguments. But there are sections that refer to academic arguments that I sort of understand but I don't really see the relevance, other than academics insist you do it that way … So in that sense we have gone more the academic route because that is how you get published. When we did the project we wrote for different audiences. We had the detailed findings reports and community summaries ... But I don't know about the activism audience having a particular voice. The activists sort of have to pick from the different styles ... The activists are more interested in having discussions than readings, to be honest. So a lot of the project has been getting people together to work on stuff. Which was then written up.

Subhagata: We have a sexuality resource centre called Chetana, which means consciousness. This is the first of its kind in eastern India. Students doing their Masters or PhD can use our centre for their research and get our book once it is completed. So it is very important to enrich this centre as well. These days the students are very keen to take up the subject of lesbianism or queer politics or LGBT issues or gay politics or transgenderism. All students are not necessarily from the LGBT community. These students, despite their interest, do not have access to much material or text on the contemporary local and national scenario. Therefore, our materials and our sources in Chetana are useful for them. We are the first organization who started LBT rights movement in eastern India. So it is very important to document this journey for both academic and activist purposes. We have been successful in creating a readership for queer politics and queer lives. It is kind of reassuring to know that there is a theoretical back-up for my activism. I am not only demanding rights through my activism, but also creating something which may be useful to the public, the LGBT community, the state, the academia and whoever is connecting with us.

Niharika: Sappho for Equality has also published research reports, newsletters, essays, poetries and other pieces under its own banner. The drive to document and create an archive and a knowledge base is [an] ongoing thing with this collective.

Subhagata: So it is not possible to write this book for both audiences if you want to get an academic publisher?

Kath: We were told that our stuff was not universal or international enough because it was based in a city in the UK. There is something that you have that we didn't have. You might find a publisher because you are read as an 'exotic other'; international is elsewhere. That was infuriating because one the key arguments in our book was 'place matters'. So place plays an importance on how these equalities and issues play out and Brighton is a supposedly equal, accepting, trendy, right-on place, but we still found those issues for LGBT people ... Then they argue, 'How will you internationalize that?' We would say but we don't want to internationalize it, we want to argue that place is important. It quickly became obvious that we needed a publisher who understood the geography of sexualities.

The Journeys, Translations and Relationships of Writing

Subhagata: During the course of this book project, Sumita and I dialogue with each other. We reflect on our past and think about our beginnings 14 years ago; traverse back and forth in time. Today's activism and political understanding is standing on yesterday's beginning of a nascent idea of queer politics. Today we term those ideas as queer politics. But when we started we didn't know that we were doing politics or activism or whatever. That was our day-to-day living at the time. So we never thought that we would be engaged in politics in this way, and that finally, someday, we will be engaged in this transnational academic/ activist collaboration. So today we're reflecting on the past and trying to be as close as possible to yesterday's feelings. For me it is a challenge, because I am being obscured with my present understanding. I feel that the book should reflect a journey. Niharika is using academic terms, terminologies, definitions to theorize this journey. It's my feeling that she is putting practice into theory.

Kath: There is also something to recording those stories that memorializes them or creates passage that celebrates them in a way. Like you tell the stories to people about the activists that came before them and that in itself is activism, in recording what might otherwise get lost. I think that is a really important thing to do. But in terms of the academics making connections with activists, I think there is something of an expectation of what it means to write something in an academic book. Like terminology, class of categories, all that kind of stuff like you said. But in some ways it says 'this is a legitimate study, this is important to academics and it's important to investigate'. Therefore, our group's views are legitimate and our aspects are legitimate.

That's something I think is really important in terms of what that means in the creation of knowledge. Because it could increase our knowledge and that knowledge is legitimate to academics.

Subhagata: So this book will serve that purpose and we personally are being very optimistic. I am thinking of a very long-term usefulness for this book. We have begun to mobilize the youth in universities and colleges as part of our advocacy and awareness. Maybe someday this book will be part of their curriculum; I am just dreaming.

Kath: I think that's what academia can offer. It offers something that is 'real' knowledge. Makes knowledge in a way that isn't known before you put it in an academic book. I mean we have talked about that before; it's the same knowledge, it's just put in a different place. And that makes it different.

Leela: But we have also written about recent history. And if we hadn't, then there is no way to access it. And we have spoken to activists who now are doing different things. Otherwise that would be lost. The work is so partial because we have only written about the bits relevant to our project. There are [*sic*] loads of other stuff we haven't written about that won't get recorded.

Kath: And there is so much more to do and we are hoping that it's a start. It's a beginning rather than an ending and other people will pick it up and do more with it.

Subhagata: We published a book with interviews that were only transcribed and translated, but not analysed. I feel the word analysis is problematic. I feel that who am I to analyse [an] other person's life. Analysis can objectify, which I am uncomfortable with, irrespective of whether I am an activist or an academic. So instead of analysis, we can comment.

Kath: Is it in the interpretation too as well, maybe?

Subhagata: Interpretation, yes.

Niharika: Translating is a challenge. Often when I am using academic concepts, Subhagata stops me, saying, 'make it clear', 'I don't agree with you', 'this doesn't make any sense'.

Subhagata: To me, of course!

Niharika: So I am constantly trying to translate and she is constantly trying to translate as well.

Subhagata: We are actually learning together.

Niharika: Yes, I think we are learning together. I am forced to make things very clear, but not simple. Clear accessible writing is also necessary if we are to reach a wider audience, as we talked about earlier.

Kath: We have spoken about what we will get out of the books, but it's also important to gather what we get out of these kind of collaborations as well. I am thinking around emotional support and having someone else to work with. Just being able to talk things through when you're seven months' pregnant and get a rejection. I think we have a really good friendship.

Leela: I think the basic elements of why it works is very simple, and that is that we are interested in the same thing and we get along well as individuals.

Niharika: For me, the friendship and bonding has been a very big aspect of this work. I have developed some deep friendships. So, along the way, I have begun reading more on friendship and friendship as a way of life. What I ultimately write will also be informed by these friendships.

Subhagata: For me, too!

Success and Costs

Kath: There is something more fulfilling about doing this this type of research when compared to other kinds of research that I might do, The feeling, or hope, of making a difference in the world is very motivating. To know the limitations of that and to know how small a change that might be.

Niharika: But a change nevertheless. How would you define an intangible success of the project?

Leela: I think for activists; a lot of people have called this a success. Activists and marginalized people and practitioners were able to sit and dialogue. In and of itself, this is one of the major successes … I think what is questioned a lot is defining the outcomes of the project because it's very difficult to attribute changes directly to the project. It could have come from somewhere else. I think people want to say that this project caused change or something to happen. And I believe that there have been lots of changes that have happened because of the project, but we can't support that.

Kath: It's really difficult to think through what the successes are, but I think, for this research, that's what we need to do because we don't write about that as much. You put in a lot more of your emotional energy than with other research. It's important for us to see that we are creating and doing something worthwhile given the amount we are putting in. I'm very much invested in this project emotionally and personally.

Leela: I think there is some privilege in there, in being an academic, because they expect everything to go right. But I didn't expect everything to go right because my experience as an activist is that the work we do [at times] doesn't come to anything. It leads to conflicts. But we will try to publish it. Activists also talked about wanting to end homophobia and failing to do that. Again, it's too big of a goal to expect to embrace, but we still have this discussion on how we can end homophobia. So success is really difficult to define would be my honest answer. But I think that we were successful in lots of ways. For me, one of the big things will be having something that lives longer than writing in the newspaper. Because marginalized people have been very badly burnt by the power.

Conclusion

A smug conclusion might note the ways in which this chapter continues to push the boundaries of academic conventions and writing, operating transnationally to explore the issues of working across activist/academic boundaries in ways that do not reiterate presumptions of the progress in the UK versus the move 'backwards' in India. However, instead, we want to note the continued limitations of writing academic texts collaboratively. As we can see from our conversations, there are different priorities that undergird academic and activist writing, including the need to publish and disseminate to a scholarly audience and to advance the needs of a movement in an accessible way. But when academics and activists write together, then the common goal of documenting lives and/or a movement can help further the goals of both academia and activism. These priorities are held together by a sense of accountability for some – accountability in terms of who the audience of the text will be. Further, accountability is not transparent but mediated by the needs of publishing, such as how international and thus marketable the text will be. We nevertheless continue to write together, journey into the motivations and emotions that brought us together to write in the first place. Writing, of course, is not easy, for it involves the challenge of translation. Writing needs to be both conceptual and accessible. Our language and our writing form emerge through practice, experience, and conceptual play. Apart from the tangible successes of getting published and disseminating our work, the multiple intangibles, including the deep friendships that we generate through this process, are invaluable, motivating us to continue this journey and celebrate our small successes along the way. We are not arguing that all PAR or queer research should be written up with activists; what we are asking for is an exploration of these possibilities, recognizing that central to PAR, and indeed queer thinking, is the contestations of normative and potentially exploitative power relations.

Acknowledgement

The transcription was made possible by a small award from the College of Liberal Arts, Faculty Development Award, University of Southern Indiana. This chapter in part arises from research funding from the Economic and Social Research Council, Grant number: ES/M000931/1.

Chapter 21

'Wake up, Alice, This is Not Wonderland!' Power, Diversity and Knowledge in Geographies of Sexualities

Joseli Maria Silva and Marcio Jose Ornat

'Would you tell me, please, which way I ought to go from here?' Alice asked the Cheshire Cat.
'That depends a good deal on where you want to get to' said the Cat to Alice.
Lewis Carroll, *Alice's Adventures in Wonderland* (1865)

Introduction

Thinking about the production of knowledge, how the fruit of our labour is distributed, and exploring the responsibility that we have in reflecting human reality is the task of all social researchers. The title of this chapter includes an expression that is widely used by LGBT groups in Brazil: 'Wake up, Alice!' This expression is used to alert someone that it is necessary to leave a comfortable position of naivety to face the challenges of reality, which, in a globalized world, willingly or not, we all share. This expression is also an invitation to summon up the courage that is necessary to imagine other possible realities in structuring the world, contemplating diversity and the growing intensity of meetings and contacts. After all, as the Cheshire Cat said to Alice in the epigraph to this chapter, it is only possible to find a way out when we know where we want to go. Anglo-American epistemic privilege affects the scientific world and it also silences academic discourses that originate from the peripheries, as argued by Mignolo (2000, 2003a, 2003b) The hegemonic 'truths' that result from power relations between scientists from different contexts have some impact on daily life in a globalized world. Consequently, this chapter aims to highlight some of the elements that underpin the logic of centrality of Anglo-American scientific discourse in global knowledge networks, as well as highlighting the negative effects of the influence of this scientific hegemony in the study of sexualities in Brazil. In the first part of the chapter we reflect on the need for international dialogue between researchers, to form a balance between 'decolonial' Latin American thinking (see Kulpa and Silva's 'Introduction' to this section) and the epistemic principles expressed in the 'Publishing for Non-Native Speakers of English' sessions at the Annual Meeting of the Association of American Geographers (AAG) (2014, Tampa, Florida, USA).[1]

---

[1]   Both sessions are available on YouTube (*Publishing for Non-Native Speakers of English, Session I* (2014); *Publishing for Non-Native Speakers of English, Session II* (2014).

This discussion produces a perspective beyond the Anglo-American view of production and circulation of scientific knowledge and can facilitate collaborative epistemic dialogues that address spatially constituted sexual diversity. In the second section we discuss how the geopolitics of knowledge affects not only the select academic world, but also the everyday experiences and the social and political movements of Brazilian *travestis* and transsexuals. In this section we highlight the idea that anglophone scientific hegemony can result in the silencing of specific sexual groups in the peripheries.

Meetings, Differences and the Geopolitics of Knowledge

As many black feminists have pointed out, personal experiences can be a strong foundation for the production of specific knowledge (Combahee River Collective, 1982; P.H. Collins, 1990; Davis, 1998; hooks, 1981; 1989; Spivak, 1985). As a Brazilian and Latin American respectively, our experiences of anglophone hegemonies highlight broader cultural issues with the production of knowledges.

Our first contact with the anglophone field of geography occurred in the late 1990s and early 2000s. Back then, speaking about gender and sexuality in the context of geography in Brazil was seen by the academic community as a heresy. The isolation we felt and the exclusion of our research were our daily bread (Silva et al., 2013). Coming into contact with the anglophone works in the area helped us to resist the hegemonic relations of academic power at home, and gave us the strength to persist in the struggle to make sexualities a legitimate topic in Brazilian and Latin American geographies. We still remember the excitement of reading texts of Janice Monk, Jon Binnie, William Bell and Gill Valentine. Digital texts were extremely hard to get hold of until the mid-2000s, and a selection of the anglophone journals (paperback) was only available in the library of the Federal University of Rio de Janeiro (UFRJ) – a 12-hour bus ride from our city. To help each other, we were co-buying used books to reduce and spread the cost, and making copious numbers of photocopies of articles whenever some of us managed to make a trip to Rio de Janeiro for a library search.

Publishing about the relationship between space, gender and sexualities in Brazil soon proved to be a difficult task; there were several attempts, and failures were common. The reasons that we were given for not publishing our articles can be organized into two types of argument: first, thematic inadequacy, since gender and sexualities were not considered to be appropriate geographic themes in the hegemonic opinion of the academic field of geography in Brazil; and, second, moral inadequacy, because the contents of the statements of the individuals included in our research was perceived as morally inappropriate for scientific discourse.

Because we were unable to publish our ideas in Brazil we turned to anglophone journals, to share ideas about our own places and knowledge, and to establish scientific exchanges, a relationship. The idea seemed perfect: we already knew that gender and sexualities were a legitimate topic of geographical research and we knew about the importance of the 'situated knowledge'-related discussions (Haraway, 1991), so we believed that the journal editors would surely take into account, and welcome, our social, spatial, temporal and economic position. Disappointingly, our submissions were also rejected by the anglophone journals,[2] this time for different reasons. The recurring justifications were: 'lack of fluency'

---

2   After five attempts, our article was accepted by *Gender Place and Culture*. The role of the editor –
     Lynda Johnston –was instrumental in this process, and we had a broad and open dialogue with
     her that was marked by respect and solidarity.

in the command of English and supposed unfamiliarity with the historical and the latest discussions in the field. We have since realized that in comparison with the Brazilian academia, it was not the topic that put us at a disadvantage, but the specific geographical and epistemic position from which we tried to speak and communicate with the anglophone world. But we did not give up. Having nowhere to go, in 2009 we founded the open-access *Latin American Journal of Geography and Gender* and also the open-access book series *Feminist Geographies*. Both projects are maintained by volunteers from the Latin American Network of Geography, Gender and Sexualities, and economic resources come from monthly donations. In 2013 we merged the Latin American Network with partners from Portugal and Spain, constituting the Ibero-Latin American Network of Geography, Gender and Sexualities.

The organization of the 'Publishing for Non-Native Speakers of English' sessions at the AAG was an important and praiseworthy initiative for opening up dialogue about scientific production. Such meetings enhance the intercultural communication between scientists around the globe and encourage an exchange of epistemic experiences and approaches (Dussel, 1995a; Walsh, 2007; Castro-Gómez, 2007).

However, for us, as Latin American researchers participating at this meeting, it brought with it the harsh realization that the editorial processes regarding the circulation of knowledge increasingly strengthen the central position of anglophone epistemological enunciation. This centrality, achieved through economic and technological dominance, creates the arrogant illusion of the universality of Anglo-American learning. Mignolo (2000) argues that scientific reality is a simultaneous construction of local histories of the production of knowledge. Consequently, for authors, the pretension of local (Anglo-American) knowledge becomes universal, even though it represents nothing more than the expression of a limited and self-centred epistemic perspective.

In addition to technical advice on 'how to publish in an Anglo-American journal' for a distinctly un-anglophone audience, three points were highlighted by the panellists who had experience as journal editors: 1) the reasons for non-English-speaking researchers wanting to publish in an English-language journal; 2) the importance of the theoretical tradition, which has to be taken as a reference; 3) the limits of expression in the English language that need to be overcome. The panellists initially made their own presentations. The presentation by Henry Yeung stood out, in terms of Yeung's experience as an editor of anglophone journals, as well as his involvement in a significant number of those journals (*Publishing for Non-Native Speakers of English, Session II*, 2014). On the basis of the success of his publishing it can be argued that Yeung's ideas (about science and the editorial processes in relation to scientific articles corresponding to the interests of the Anglo-American publishing process) correspond to the interests of the Anglo-American publishing process.

In the hegemonic vision of scientific production, the articles submitted by non-English-speaking researchers to the editing processes of the Anglo-American journals must be closely linked to scientific interests and should be guided by the search for a dialogue with a particular community of researchers – that is, anglophone researchers from the epistemological tradition that gives them support, as can be seen in the excerpt from Yeung's speech that follows:

> So you want to publish in that journal not because of the CIF. Please! Citation impact factor! Please! Don't send them to journals because it's high CIF, or low CIF for that matter. You want to send it because you want to speak to the people who read and publish in that journal ... How do they do a connection? Now this is about how to frame the article. Whatever it is you are writing about, the first thing you should ask yourself is: what kind of literature I want to connect to? ... the ultimate motive of this article that we want to write is to advance knowledge, it's not to get promoted ...

> *Now, the point I wanna read to you is that you've got to ground your paper into some kind of literature. In a way it can't be our native language literature. Because if this is native language literature, you should send it to native language journals, in Chinese, in French, in Italian, in what have you, you get the point? If you wanna publish in this journal, in English, you got to connect to this literature.* (Publishing for Non-Native Speakers of English, Session II, *2014*)

The maintenance of the naive idea that scientific production, a superior educational system and, consequently, a profession of teacher/scientist exists and arises out of a culture dominated by liberal capitalist culture is a subtle and fundamental ideology that serves as an instrument to maintain the order and power of a specific cultural and economic system, as argued by Enrique Dussel (1975) in his book *The Underside of Modernity*. The spread of this perverse idea (that the ultimate goal of the scientist is only to 'advance knowledge') is shaped by factors that are unscientific and economically and geopolitically influenced (Mignolo, 2000; Quijano, 2000).

One of the reasons why researchers feel pressured to publish in anglophone journals and to circulate their research in these places is the fact that these journals can add value to these commodities in the context of the globalization of the field of the production channels and the distribution of knowledge by private interests. It is this power dynamic that has reinforced the place of anglophone scientific enunciation, masked by the noble scientific rationality of 'epistemological advances'. It is this dynamic that still means that an (Anglo-American) regional epistemology is the 'conceptual referent' from which researchers from other regions must start in order that knowledge can 'advance'.

The idea that the scientific communities that use 'native-language literature' should only try to be published in 'native-language' journals, as argued in the excerpt of the transcript of Henry Yeung's speech cited above, is a partial position, whose blind ignorance of who has the privilege of inhabiting the centre separates the current context of the globalization of knowledge from the economic and political bases to which it belongs. The attempt to simplify the academic world that is expressed in Yeung's speech hides the dark side of cultural/scientific subordination and the coloniality of knowledge (Quijano, 2000).

Material conditions mark each researcher, and these conditions insert researchers into a position within the networks of production and circulation of knowledge. However, the relationship between economic and epistemic privilege needs to be hidden (Bhaskaran, 2004) in order to maintain the illusion that it is only intellectual and analytical ability that determines access to the most valued locations of scientific enunciation. The assumption that all scientists start from the same material conditions and that access to scientific product, which is dominated by the private market, is free and depends on the goodwill of the researcher is also a key strategy in the promotion of silencing and excluding those without positions of privilege, as can be seen in the following extract from Henry Yeung's speech:

> *So, please, know your journal. How do you know? Read three recent articles ... I understand there's an access issue. I have had a long-standing debate with publishers [names of publishers] ... So, about this matter, but that is a separate matter. I don't think I can address it here, about how you make journals more accessible or why. That is a separate matter; I can't deal with it here. Assuming it's accessible enough, you really have to read the stuff; because if you don't read it, there's no reason you should publish in that journal, all right?* (Publishing for Non-Native Speakers of English, Session II, *2014*)

The exclusion of access to scientific products of the Anglo-American world is not the only barrier to overcome in order to imagine alternative forms of production and circulation of knowledge. This is not a simple demand for inclusion in the editorial process of scientific production by the 'wretched of science', though. It is so, because the individuals who produce knowledge, and who are not even considered within the geopolitics of knowledge, cannot rely on inclusion, for it only means a new form of assimilation by the Anglo-American hegemonic scientific culture, which will certainly maintain control of enunciation (Mignolo, 2000).

In the following section we discuss the case of *travestis* in Brazil and show how scientific knowledge, which is produced from a hegemonic geopolitical perspective, has profound effects beyond the academy and impacts on the lives of vulnerable groups – a situation that provokes resistance and wilfulness.

Epistemic Disobedience: A Need for *Travesti* Visibility in Brazil

The discussion in the previous section showed that the globalized scientific world, guided by neoliberal logic, has hindered the expression of scientists who are outside the hegemonic domain of the anglophone editorial network and who do not conform to the rules created and maintained by those who inhabit the central positions in the production of knowledge. The decolonial perspective (Mignolo, 2000, 2009; see also Chapter 16 in this volume) emphasizes the idea that coloniality survives through multiple interdependent dimensions of power, knowledge and being. Thus, the dynamics of scientific production affect not only scientists, but also the daily life of other groups who are part of that social reality. To exemplify this reflection, we discuss below tensions around the word *travesti*, and their struggles in maintaining the usage of this particular word as best expressing the reality of their existence and the fight for their social rights.

Travesti is defined as 'disguised; using the dress of another sex' (Michaelis, 2014) and it has been widely contested and discussed during the National Meeting of *Travestis* and Transsexuals Fighting AIDS (Encontro Nacional de Travestis e Transexuais na Luta Contra a AIDS – ENTLAIDS) in Brazil. *Travestis* argue that they experience the world from the female perspective and are not 'disguised' as women, while keeping their male genitals intact. However, their voice is not heard by the academic elites who maintain the official discourses (including dictionary entries). Therefore, when looking at geographies of sexualities, the definitions used by authors do not accord to the experiences of *travestis*. Doan (2007), for example, delineates several distinctions between people who live within a gender spectrum that is focused on Anglo-American cultures. In her 2007 article, 'Queers in the American City', Doan does not address the issue of *travesties*, and they are not part of the cultural realities explored by her. However, the Anglo-American nomenclature, as used by Doan (2007), has been adopted by the Brazilian academy to understand the existence of *travestis*, thereby reinforcing the Anglophone hegemony in defining the realities of 'others'. The word 'transvestite' is often used as the English translation for the word *travesti*. Nevertheless, as used by Doan (2007), the word 'transvestite' does not express the experience of Brazilian *travestis*. Among the nomenclatures used by her, the one that is possibly the closest to the Brazilian *travesti* would be 'transgender'. Having been introduced in Brazil by people who use anglophone literature, this term did not gain any legitimization by *travestis*. For example, during our fieldwork we came across jokes about 'transgender' and the homophone word *transgênico* (genetically modified, as, for example, soya or corn) when *travesties* say, 'I am not *transgênico*, I am a *travesti*!'.

189

The struggle of Brazilian *travestis* for social legitimization also involves recognizing their self-identification. In 2008 the Renascer (Newborn) NGO organized a debate around Don Kulick's (1998) book *Travesti: Sex, Gender and Culture among Brazilian Transgendered Prostitutes*. Ten years after the original English publication, those who were the subject of the text finally had a chance to access the academic knowledge that was produced on them by this Western academic. Although Kulick is aware of the difference between *travestis* and 'transgender', he continued to use the latter term, even though the word is contested by *travestis*. Furthermore, he kept simplifying the identities and existence of Brazilian *travestis* and disregarded the plurality of combinations between sex, gender and desire that they experience. Kulick argues that:

> At every turn, penetration provides explanations and defines identities for travestis. It constitutes the interpretive framework that they draw on in order to be and to act, and in order to understand the being and the actions of others ... The salient difference in such a system, however, is not between 'men' and 'women'. It is between those who penetrate (comer, 'eat') and those who get penetrated (dar, 'give'), in a system where the act of being penetrated has transformative force. Those who only 'eat' and never 'give' in this system are culturally designated as 'men', – those who 'give', even if they also 'eat', are classified as being something else – something that I will call 'not-men', partly for want of a culturally elaborated label and partly to foreground my conviction that the gender system that makes it possible for travestis to emerge and make sense is one that is massively oriented towards, if not determined by, male subjectivity, male desire, and male pleasure, as those are culturally elaborated in Brazil. (Kulick, 1998, p. 229)

This section of the book has generated controversy, especially among those who did not feel that they were included in the model proposed by Kulick. Diamante expressed her outrage in the following way:

> But how can this be? I have spent a lifetime to know that I'm a travesti and now this guy comes along ... What's his name? Whatever! He comes along saying that I am not what I think I am? I'll talk to him, because I am a travesti! How can I tell him this? (Field diary, 29 August 2008)

Although there is a moral category among *travestis* that organizes genders based on penetration (most notably in the situation of sex work), *travesti* identities go beyond this binary and oppositional organization. The daily contact that we had with *travestis* demonstrated that they have diverse arrangements in terms of sex, gender and desire that go far beyond Kulick's simplistic proposals of 1998. There are conjugal-type relationships between *travestis*, between *travestis* and women, and between *travestis* and men, where sexual practices are plural and surpass the binary setting of penetrating/being penetrated.

As well as resisting the semantic categories constructed for them by academics, in recent years *travestis* have also had several conflicts within LGBT movement itself. We have heard some conversations along the lines of 'before I thought I was a *travesti*, but now I think I am transsexual'. These statements could only be possible after the concept of transsexuality[3] arrived in Brazil in the early 2000s, when some people who would have previously self-

---

3   In 1997 the Federal Council of Medicine in Brazil regulated experimental sex-change surgical procedures, but only in university hospitals. In 2008 the Brazilian government formalized these procedures within the Unified Health System. Transsexuality is catalogued in the International

identified as *travestis,* have now self-identified as transsexuals. There is also a noticeable rise in the number of young transsexuals involved in the LGBT movement. Obviously, the processes of identification are relational and situated in space and time. The discussions about transsexuality and widening access to medical techniques must have influenced many subjectivities, intensifying the relations between *travestis* and male/female transsexuals.

At the National Meeting of *Travestis* and Transsexuals Fighting AIDS, held in Brazil in September 2013, a new controversy centred on the term *travesti* occurred. A group of transsexuals suggested eliminating the word *travesti* from the dictionaries on the grounds that it is inadequate. However, rather than insisting on amending the definition, they wanted full erasure, implying that the existence of *travestis* could be described under the dictionary definition of 'transsexual'. The *travestis* at the meeting rejected these proposals, claiming that the transsexuals wanted to 'sanitize' their existence (for it is stereotypically associated with prostitution, poverty and moral deviation). The *travestis* also claimed that because transsexuality is considered a 'disease' in Brazilian society, it is easier to be socially accepted as a transsexual than a *travesti*. The condition of being 'sick' portrays transsexual people as victims and suggests the possibility of a 'cure', while *travesti* remains considered as a degenerate. Ruby addressed the transsexual people at the meeting in these words:

> All of you forget that when the LGBT movement was born in Brazil, while gays were protected in their homes, it was the travestis who were being beaten up in the streets by police and clients. You forget that it was the travestis who fought for citizenship in Brazil. You forget that it was us who literally got punched in the face. I have been beaten up a lot during my life as a travesti and I never wanted to hide behind a term as you want to hide ... If we erase the word 'travesti' from the dictionary we will delete our history. What we have to do is change the meaning of the word, which is not consistent with the reality of travestis. I'm not a transsexual! I'm a travesti! I will never have a sex change! This will die when I do! (making a gesture to show her penis). (Field diary, 27 September 2013)

The tensions that currently exist between *travesti* and transgender people have become more intense in the sense that the idea of transsexuality has become popularized in Brazilian society. When transsexual people gained the right to surgical treatment free of charge through the Unified Health System (SUS), many debates spread across Brazilian media. The medical discourse, which was governed by the pathologization of transsexuality and its inclusion in the International Classification of Diseases (ICD), was an important vector of understanding transsexual lives. The term 'transsexual' was strongly influenced by the North American psychiatric nomenclature gradually adopted in Brazil. Consequently, the hegemony of (anglophone) scientific knowledges penetrates the daily life of Brazilian society and constructs representations (and erasures) of *travestis* in relation to transsexuals. Our ethnographic data strongly suggest that *travestis* do not self-identify with the term 'transsexual' and refuse the medical classification of being 'sick'. Despite many attempts at speaking up, *travestis* have not been heard by discourse gatekeepers, such as linguists preparing dictionaries. The resistance of *travestis* against the nomenclatures imposed on them is a form of struggle to become epistemic agents able to define their own lives. Thus, their epistemic disobedience represents a potential decolonial epistemic project, in which the pluriversality of knowledge overcomes the imposition of universality.

Registry of Diseases (IRD) as a 'disease' for which the only prophylaxis is sex reassignment surgery.

Final Considerations

This chapter has argued that the centrality of anglophone scientific discourse in the global networks of knowledge has hindered dialogue between researchers from different cultures. The epistemological domain, controlled through the economic, political and symbolic mechanisms of the publishing market, has a wide-reaching impact, privileging the 'centre' (anglophone world, 'the West', 'Global North') and muting the 'periphery'. The struggles of Brazilian *travestis* against pathologization and for recognition on their own terms highlight the difficulties that some vulnerable social groups face when their knowledge comes in contact with any form of hegemonic knowledge.

Only the practice of a rebellious scientific approach is capable of confronting epistemic principles that maintain hegemonic relations in the production and circulation of knowledge, both in academia and between science and social movements. Consequently, there is an urgent need to build a scientific interculturality, as well as political and social inter-epistemic projects, in which many worlds can coexist in the logic of mutual respect, in reciprocity and in a collaborative spirit. It is important to note that the liberation of the colonial power matrix entails overcoming bipolar and oppositional ideas that exist between the colonizers and the colonized. The tyranny of colonial power inhabits us all, irrespective of our positions of privilege or oppression. The task of constructing a decolonial project centred on knowledge must be collective in nature. It is necessary to recognize the geopolitics of knowledge and to believe in the possibility of building alternatives to the neoliberal path, which has renewed the practices of creating social, economic and cultural hierarchies. Wake up, Alice! We must learn together to unlearn the epistemic practices that still hinder the understanding of the discourse of the 'other' and destroy the possibilities of meaningful encounters based on differences.

SECTION IV
Mobile Sexualities

Andrew Gorman-Murray and Catherine J. Nash (editors)

Chapter 22

Mobile Sexualities: Section Introduction

Andrew Gorman-Murray and Catherine J. Nash

A Study in Motion

The exploration of the mobility issues and experiences of sexual and gender minorities is a relatively recent addition to geographies of sexualities. Such work arguably found its scholarly catalyst in Kath Weston's 1995 article 'Get Thee to a Big City: Sexual Imaginary and the Great Gay Migration', a (now) highly cited piece that examined the internal migration of lesbians and gay men to San Francisco in the post-Second World War period.[1] Migration is an important dimension of human mobility, but the growing field of 'mobilities studies', which is especially prominent in (and draws together) contemporary geography, sociology, anthropology and cultural studies, encourages researchers to expand their notions of mobility and to consider how different modes of mobility are operable in society and culture (Cresswell and Merriman, 2011). Mobilities studies encompass a diverse range of physical movements and systems of circulation, including, *inter alia*, transport systems, travel, commuting, asylum, locative media, diurnal movements, diaspora and migration (Cresswell, 2010). Mobilities studies also underline the dialectic between fixity and motion, mooring and movement, and ask us to consider the experience and meaning of sites and moments of rest and stillness within mobility systems (Adey, 2006; Bissell and Fuller, 2011).

Geographical, social and cultural research at the nexus of sexualities and mobilities has opened up a range of movements and systems to examination and analysis from the perspective of sexual and gender minorities. Indeed, over the last 20 years scholarship from geography, sociology, anthropology and cultural studies has shown that the life experiences of sexual and gender minorities are arguably underpinned by various experiences of movement, displacement and re-placement within a heteronormative social context (Fortier, 2002; 2003; Puar et al., 2003; Knopp, 2004). This work encompasses migration, tourism, 'cruising', Pride parades, diaspora and urban wayfinding (Gorman-Murray and Nash, 2014). As this is a relatively new research focus there are still many avenues that require conceptual and empirical development. Perhaps most significantly, much work still needs to be done to account for different experiences *within* sexual minorities wrought by gender, gender identity, socioeconomic means, race, ethnicity and disability, along with other cross-cutting social categories. The chapters in this section help address some of these lacunae and encourage further exploration of the diverse experiences of sexualities in motion.

Whilst mobility has become a key theoretical lens in geography and other disciplines interested in understanding the subjectivities, relationships, communities and experiences of sexual and gender minorities, less attention has been given to the mobile sexualities of

---

1   Post-Second World War gay migration to San Francisco was adumbrated in Castells (1983) and D'Emilio (1983), but Weston (1995) catalysed and consolidated the thesis in her article.

the 'dominant category' – that is, heterosexuality. Although there is a lineage of work on marriage migration (Watts, 1983; Willis and Yeoh, 2000), until recently there has been little consideration of sex, sexuality, embodiment and emotion in the mobilities – migration or otherwise – of heterosexual, or straight-identifying, individuals and households. As with most spheres of contemporary society, the assumption of heterosexuality-as-the-norm meant that, on the one hand, 'normal' mobility was heterosexual movement and, on the other hand, given heterosexuality's 'naturalized invisibility', factors other than sex, sexuality, embodiment or emotion were foregrounded in studies of heterosexual mobilities. But work by Walsh et al. (2008), Mai and King (2009) and Noble and Tabar (2014) has trained a critical lens on heterosexual engagements in migration decisions and experiences, demonstrating how heterosexualities vary across regions and between home and host communities, and are refigured in processes of movement. Likewise, scholarship by Johnston (2006) and Frohlick (2013) has drawn attention to how heterosexuality and hetero-sex can inform tourism and travel. Further work is needed to understand how heterosexuality is both normalized and potentially transformed in mobility.

While we acknowledge the need for further scholarship at the intersection of heterosexuality and mobility, the chapters in this section focus on sexual and gender minorities and mobilities. The absence of work on heterosexual mobilities (we did try to solicit contributions) further highlights the paucity of studies in this area. Nonetheless, we argue that it also remains imperative to investigate and better understand the mobilities of sexual and gender minorities, given the ways in which these subjects are both impelled to displacement and movement (Knopp, 2004) and simultaneously encounter barriers that halt or hinder mobility and settlement (Luibhéid, 2008b). We suggest there are several ways to think about and frame the mobilities of sexual and gender minorities – through vectors (the direction of displacement), scales (the scope of movement), temporalities (the duration of the movement, or set of movements, under consideration) as well as 'types' (migration, asylum, travel, commuting and so on). In the following, we draw on these frameworks to briefly review work in this field, demonstrate the contributions of the chapters in this section and suggest ways forward for future research and thinking.

The Nation: Internal Migration

Arguably, the most extensive work to date on the mobilities of sexual and gender minorities is on internal migration – that is, movement within national borders (Binnie, 2004; Wimark, 2014). Within this scale – the nation – several vectors have been distinguished and analysed. Perhaps the most common spatial narrative in popular discourse (though perhaps not in scholarship), is rural-to-urban migration, captured in Weston's 'Get Thee to a Big City'. The push–pull dynamic of classic migration theory is transferred to sexual and gender minorities, though inflected by imperatives of sex and sexuality rather than economic rationalism. Put simply, the 'sexual migrant' flees the constraints of rural and small-town life – seen as conservative, over-familiar and often hostile to non-heterosexuality – where they are ensconced deep in the closet, to find sexual community and to 'come out' in and through the possibilities and anonymity of the 'big city', typically inner cities which are perceived as 'havens' of difference and enabling of diverse sexual and gender subjectivities (Johnson, 2000; Binnie, 2004; see also the chapters in Section II of this volume).

While this vector-cum-narrative is true for some, recent research has begun to examine the diversity of internal migration experiences. This work has queried the empirical prominence and ontological centring of rural-to-urban 'coming out' migration and has instead investigated multiple vectors (Gorman-Murray, 2007). Urban-to-rural migration and rural return migration directly challenge the dominant narrative. Urban-to-rural migration has been documented as a way of refusing the sexual and gender power relations of city life (Smith and Holt, 2005; Gorman-Murray, 2013; Waitt and Johnston, 2013), whereas return migration demonstrates that moving to the city is not the final destination for some rural migrants (Waitt and Gorman-Murray, 2011a; Annes and Redlin, 2012, 2013). Instead, attention has been trained on internal migration as open, peripatetic, episodic and segmented, involving deviations, back-tracking and constant decisions about settling and/or disclosure (Gorman-Murray, 2009a; Waitt and Gorman-Murray, 2011b; Lewis, 2012b, 2013b).

The chapter by Marianne Blidon adds to and extends this scholarship by tracing the complexities of internal migration in France. Drawing on quantitative as well as qualitative data – which is, in itself, a rarity in geographies of sexualities, given the lack of quantitative data on sexual and gender minorities in official sources such as Census counts – Blidon examines the segmented nature of lesbian and gay migration paths, finding they do not fit a neat rural-to-urban vector, sometimes refuse urban settlement and remain open to future possibilities. Blidon highlights the diversity of push–pull factors affecting migrants' decisions and also reveals that internal and international migration intersects in the lives of some. This intersection of scales is an important addition, given that national and international scales of migration for sexual and gender minorities are often considered separately (see below). Elsewhere in the *Companion* (Chapter 32), Nathaniel Lewis also highlights how national and international scales and vectors intersect in his examination of the role of migration itself in gay and bisexual men's sexual health in Canada. These discussions thus draw us to a consideration of international mobilities.

The Globe: International Mobilities

Alongside literature on the internal migration of sexual and gender minorities, though not often intersecting with it, is scholarship on a range of international mobilities, notably international migration, asylum and diaspora (Cant, 1997; Fortier, 2002, 2003; Kuntsman, 2003; Luibhéid, 2008b; Yue, 2008; G. Smith, 2013). These mobilities involve different sets of constraints and possibilities, and sometimes catalysts, than internal migration. International movements entail crossing legal, political and cultural borders, and often require significant economic resources. They are also differentiated from each other. In a world where transnational movements seem commonplace, international *migration* might seem to be a choice, an enactment of freedom, whereas *asylum* might seem to be an act of need, if not desperation. Although these appear to evoke the economic, legal and political factors of international movement, *diaspora* seems to highlight the cultural and familial dimensions wrought by intersections of sexuality, gender and ethnicity. The distinctions are not so clear-cut in lived experience, of course, and three of the following chapters draw attention to the constraints and obstacles of these different types of international movement.

Audrey Yue's chapter introduces new ways to conceptualize 'queer migration' at the international scale, which takes a critical approach to inclusion, mobility and embodiment, and is grounded in two case studies of Chinese migration to Australia. Deploying 'queer' 'as a critical category that challenges normativity', for Yue 'queer migration' enables us to see how 'the regulated norms of migration are constructed as "irregular" by discourses of border protection and its institutions of migration control'. First, examining the history of Chinese migration to Australia, Yue argues that 'regular' migration is queered by institutions of border control concerning race and sexuality, which render Chinese migrants as deviant and

Chinese migration as abnormal. Second, through a case study of contemporary sexuality-based asylum in Australia, Yue shows that these institutions remain operable, simultaneously fetishizing and erasing race through liberal ideals and an appeal to homonationalism.

The chapter by Senthorun Raj similarly applies a critical queer lens to the barriers and problems for (trans)gender bodies and identities in refugee law, which is an area of scholarship and (legal and political) practice still in its infancy. Taking a critical legal studies approach, Raj scrutinizes the complexities around refugee claims and decision-making with respect to gender identity, embodiment and expression. His analysis reveals the disjuncture between legal recognition of sexual orientation and gender identity in refugee law, and the gaps between domestic and international legal geographies regulating (trans)gender claims. These slippages offer possibilities, not only obstacles, and Raj suggests that '[m]obilizing the fissures that emerge between gender and sexuality, domestic law and international law, and recognition and refusal, enables us to think more critically about how to accommodate gender non-conforming bodies into asylum law'.

In his chapter, Farhang Rouhani deploys an approach that is both critical and reparative at several levels. In terms of scholarship, Rouhani argues for a queer intervention in geographical approaches to migration, which could help complicate our understandings of family, nation and nostalgia within diaspora, while also urging for non-geographic queer migration and diaspora researchers to develop nuanced attention to space and place. In terms of the lived experience of international migrants, especially referring to his ongoing research into Iranian and queer Muslim diasporic communities, Rouhani contends that queer approaches to migration politics and diaspora could have a 'significant creative, critical, and positive potential to understanding how migrants placed in impossible situations seek to improve their lives'. Rouhani thus redirects our attention from the global scale of international mobility to the embodied scale of lived experience in everyday spaces. We turn now to this intimate scale.

The Body: Local and Intimate Movements

In considering movement and migration, it is the body that is the vehicle and beneficiary (or victim) of displacement. Yet, the scale of the body is rarely foregrounded in migration studies. While the body has had some consideration as a site and locus of experience in queer migration (Gorman-Murray, 2007, 2009a; Björklund, 2013; Waitt and Johnston, 2013), mobilities studies have been arguably more attentive to embodied experience in movement (see Bissell, 2008, 2014; Cresswell and Merriman, 2011). Similarly, migration research has, understandably, tended to focus on broader scales and vectors of displacement (national, international) rather than more intimate ranges, such as commuting and diurnal or everyday movements. It is precisely such scales of mobility that have been a significant consideration for sexual and gender minorities – that is, the need to resolve how to negotiate the street, neighbourhood, school, workplace or city in a context of heteronormative regulation, potential harassment and threats of sexuality- or gender-based violence (Myslik, 1996; Valentine, 1993c; 1996; Kirby and Hay, 1997; Browne, 2004). Issues of personal safety – of bodily threats – have been a key concern in the everyday mobilities, as well as internal and international migrations, of sexual and gender minorities (Kitchin and Lysaght, 2003; Doan and Higgins, 2009).

The chapter by Petra Doan takes this work forward in pioneering ways. Doan explores 'the ways in which transgender individuals incorporate notions of mobility into their life histories', underscoring and analysing the tight connections between embodiment, movement, lifeworlds and identity transitions. She examines these linkages at several registers, including: trans people's gender journeys as a very visceral mode and experience of mobility; the difficulties of negotiating everyday spaces in a transitioning body; the need trans people have to find spaces of corporeal safety and comfort; and the travels that are undertaken at different scales in the process of gender journeys and locating safe spaces. Doan also explores the segmented and halting non-linearity of these journeys, which involve criss-crossing the gender divide daily and through the life course.

In doing so, and in line with recent work on lesbian and gay migration (Gorman-Murray, 2009a; Waitt and Gorman-Murray, 2011a, 2011b; Lewis, 2012b, 2014a; Wimark, 2014), Doan highlights the importance of the temporal scale of mobility. Migration and other modes of displacement are not discrete, atomized events – they are part of the life course of individuals and households. Different migration decisions, based on different rationales, are made during the life course, as are different experiences of everyday mobilities in neighbourhoods and streets. Marianne Blidon's chapter similarly underscores the way in which migration, movement and mobility at a variety of scales (local, national, international) is entwined in the life courses of sexual and gender minorities. Thus, we need to attend to mobility as an ongoing and shifting experience, not a as singular event.

The chapter by Andrew Gorman-Murray and Catherine Nash seeks to bring these new concerns – embodied mobilities, local scales, everyday engagements and temporal frames – together. This chapter examines and conceptualizes the experience of everyday mobility in different 'queer' inner-city neighbourhoods in Sydney, Australia, and Toronto, Canada. The argument politicizes queer mobility and aligns the politics of mobility with localized politics of visibility and of recognition that are operable in these inner-city neighbourhoods. Beyond mobility over the life course, Gorman-Murray and Nash are concerned with drawing attention to *generational* queer mobilities. These mobilities take several registers: in the material and symbolic mobility of queer neighbourhoods over time (community and neighbourhood change); in the shifting politics of social inclusion at local scales (from visibility to recognition); and in the changing ways queer bodies are able to inhabit and mobilize different inner-city streets and neighbourhoods (across place, time and generations). Social, political, material and embodied mobilities are entwined in this analysis (see Nash, 2013a; Gorman-Murray and Nash, 2014; Nash and Gorman-Murray, 2014).

Moving Along: The Future

While charting new avenues in the exploration of sexual and gender minorities and mobilities, these chapters certainly do not exhaust the work that needs to be done to better understand sexual and gender minorities' experiences and elicit political and social implications. We have not canvassed mobilities such as cruising (Turner, 2003), *flâneurie* (Munt, 2000), Pride parades and marches (Johnston, 2005) or tourism and travel (Waitt and Markwell, 2006). While there is already work developing in these areas (as noted above), there are further additions and new fields to develop.

The affective dimension of mobility, which is central in mobilities studies, is not yet strongly developed in studies of queer mobilities, yet it would seem a useful addition to work that seeks to understand everyday perceptions of safety, violence and comfort while moving through public spaces (see Gorman-Murray, 2009a). Uptake of digital technologies and locative media has been significant in gay communities (especially), with a range of internet sites and apps; however, there is still little work that examines the nexus between physical and digital space in gay communities in relation to mobile practices such as cruising or travel. The vast majority of research remains centred in the Global North and responds to lives, communities and concerns therein. There is a paucity of work about queer mobilities to and within the Global South (tourism aside, arguably – see Waitt and Markwell, 2006), such as internal migration, public transport, public safety, locative media, *inter alia* (but see Parker, 1999, on Brazil). Finally, we would reiterate the call we made in the opening paragraphs of this chapter to examine mobilities in relation to heterosexualities, in order to better understand how mobilities and sexualities are entwined across communities.

Chapter 23

Moving to Paris! Gays and Lesbians: Paths, Experiences and Projects

Marianne Blidon

The city is classically defined as a space with a high density and diversity, in which social and spatial interaction is maximized. In the modern conception, the city carries urban values, such as freedom, emancipation and confronting otherness (Lees, 2004). The attributes deemed characteristic of modern cities – anonymity, consumption, diversity – hence play a role in facilitating a more diverse range of sexual behaviours. Often contrasted with a rurality that is deemed sexually conservative and even backward, the city is thus widely regarded as a site of sexual liberation and emancipation, with key cities such Paris, London, Berlin, Sydney, San Francisco or New York playing host to visible lesbian and gay communities (Knopp, 1998; Podmore, 2006; Hubbard, 2011). Carl Wittman presented San Francisco as 'a refugee camp of homosexuals'. According to him, 'We have fled from every part of the nation, and like refugees elsewhere, we came not because it is so great here, but because it is so bad there' (Wittman, 1970, p. 330). As Henning Bech said, 'The city is the social world proper of the homosexual, his life space; it is no use objecting that lots of homosexuals have live in the country. Insofar as they wish to be homosexual, the vast majority must get out into *'the city'* (Bech, 1997, p. 98). This association between lesbian and gay identities and the metropolis is reinforced by the gay geographical imagination of the migration captured in the title of Weston's (1995) 'Get Thee to a Big City'.

From a scientific point of view, this perspective is problematic as it represents a generalization whose epistemological bases are questionable (Abraham, 2009). It is in fact from the social status of homosexuality and assumed characteristics of the urban environment that the form of the trajectories taken by gays and lesbians is inferred, without these trajectories being studied for what they are precisely (step by step, considering the context and so on). While urban studies are highly present and well documented, the same cannot be said for international and intranational migration. This led Andrew Gorman-Murray (2007, pp. 105–6) to state that 'the nature of queer migration – individual migrants motivations and destinations as well as journeys, paths, patterns and scales of relocation – remains little studied and inadequately conceptualized', thus relaying the call made by Jon Binnie (2004, p. 90) who states that there is a 'need to conceptualize queer migration and to ponder why migration is significant to so many sexual dissidents'. Discussions of the intranational migration of sexual dissidents have focused on rural-to-urban movement and have largely conceptualized queer migration through a symbolic rural/urban binary, consequently normalizing rural-to-urban displacement while eliding the real diversity of queer relocations (Gorman-Murray, 2007; Blidon and Guérin, 2013). Cooke and Rapino (2007) investigate the interregional migration of partnered gays and lesbians between 1995 and 2000 using data from the Public Use Microdata Sample of the 2000 US Census. According to these authors, both partnered gays and lesbians are regionally distributed throughout the USA consistent with the geographical distribution of the entire US population. Partnered gay migration is directed towards moderate-sized urban regions rich in natural amenities without regard for tolerance towards gay lifestyles or the absolute or relative size of the partnered gay community. Partnered lesbian migration is focused on less populous regions with a large, existing, partnered lesbian population. The role of natural amenities, tolerance for lesbian lifestyles and population density are not significant in determining partnered lesbian migration. The only trait partnered gay and lesbian migrations have in common is in their move towards less populous regions.

Again, from a scientific point of view, the theory of rural-to-urban displacement is also problematic as it represents an injunction for mobility, and that is a source of inequality between people who do not have access to the same (economic, cultural, symbolic, social, spatial) resources when it comes to undertaking metropolitan migration.

This chapter consequently proposes to examine the residential mobility of gays and lesbians using an empirically informed study to better understand the socially differentiated ways in which people inhabit and experience urban space. The terms gay and lesbian refer to those who define themselves as such, in terms of identity and self-awareness, in a society where heterosexuality is the dominant standard (Sedgwick, 1990). Geographical mobility is here understood as a movement between spaces of residence and meaning (Creswell, 2006). After introducing the online survey, the analysis will focus on the role played by Paris in the intranational migratory paths of respondents. Then the analysis will focus specifically on the ways in which respondents to this survey objectify their path and their relationship to the city of Paris. In conclusion, the chapter will show the heuristic dimension in order to enrich the geography of sexualities through an approach based on forms of mobility that articulate the analysis of the shape of the paths, the spatial imaginations that inform them and the desires that can potentially transform them.

For a Diachronic Approach to Migration Flows

For some gays and lesbians, the French capital is apparently viewed as a haven and a place where they can hope for durable or even permanent residence. For others, it is just a step along a more complex geographical path. Thus Julien, born in the centre of France in the rural Limousin region, which has a declining population, spent part of his childhood in the countryside, then studied in Bordeaux and later in England. On his return, he settled for a little less than 10 years in Paris before returning to England, where he was living at the time of the survey. Similarly, Jean-Baptiste, born in a village on the island of Corsica, moved with his parents to the mainland in a city of over 200,000 inhabitants and then continued his studies in another city before moving to Paris, where he found work and lived for more than 20 years. Having never severed ties with his family and being very attached to Corsica – the Mediterranean island also known as Ile de Beauté (Island of Beauty) for the quality of its landscapes and its mild climate – he eventually returned there and settled with his partner in a village, despite the very patriarchal, traditional and homophobic reputation of this part of the world. Lastly, Luc, born in Versailles – a town near Paris deemed bourgeois and conservative – moved to a lower-income Paris suburb with his parents. He later began his undergraduate studies in a city of less than 200,000 inhabitants and continued in Paris. When he arrived, he lived in a hostel in the suburbs, and, at the time of the survey, was living in Paris, sharing a flat. These residential choices, which have hardly been long–lasting, portend a new move.

These three cases highlight two central dimensions. On the one hand, there is a diachronic approach that not only considers the place of residence, but also the whole trajectory from childhood; this makes it possible to distinguish individual factors and social rationales. On the other hand, Parisian residential mobility should not be envisaged as only taking place within the limits of the city of Paris (the core city), but in the wider network of the whole metropolitan area, including suburban towns where social housing and low-income habitat are concentrated – whether they are affected by ongoing gentrification or not. These neighbourhoods are often run-down, deemed homophobic and are dangerous because of the concentration of modest households from immigrant backgrounds (Dikeç, 2007).

Certain milestones play an important role in the paths followed, such as the pursuit of graduate studies, entry into active life, professional mobility, inclusion in the gay community, types of relational networks, setting up as a couple or breakdowns of such relationships. Residential choices are not disconnected from housing opportunities, particularly those deriving from available resources, be they economic (capital, level of income and so on) or social (mutual assistance, research and the like). A person's professional and family situation, age, employment status and housing environment are the basis of residential choices. One should therefore be attentive both to the form of the paths and what informs them. To do this, I carried out a survey online.

An Online Survey to Collect Personal Paths

From October 2006 to January 2007, I collected 3,587 responses to an online survey carried out on the site of a French gay magazine (*Têtu*, 2015). Of these questionnaires 239 were not used (heterosexual respondents, people who had never lived in France, minors, inconsistent replies and so on). A database of 16,000 migratory steps was collected from the remaining 2,705 questionnaires, creating holistic personal paths – migration over life course, including the place of birth and the successive towns and/or countries in which people had lived for more than a year up to the time of the survey. In order to understand the characteristics of the paths followed, indicators were established about the location (profile of the urban unit) and the type of path followed ('passing through', number, type and succession of steps), based on data from the 1999 Census (Institut national de la statistique et des études économiques, 1999). These data make it possible to distinguish the paths that take place only in France from those that include time spent abroad, those that pass exclusively through rural or urban (centre or suburban) contexts, or both, and also to find out the duration of the various stages and observe their flows. This brought to light a broad spectrum of highly differentiated migratory behaviours that can be individualized, especially those involving moving away from the family (Blidon and Guérin, 2013). I completed this material with 82 qualitative questionnaires conducted on a sample of Parisian respondents and 60 interviews conducted in Paris, Le Mans and Marseille.

Table 23.1   Sample characteristics

Characteristics	Number	Proportion
Sex		
Female	464	13%
Male	3,106	87%
Sexuality (self-definition)		
Gay	2,952	83%
Lesbian	404	11%
Bisexual	214	6%
Age group		
Less than 25 years old	1,094	31%
26–31	860	24%
31–40	831	23%
Over 40 years old	785	22%
Level of education		
First school level	439	12%
High school diploma	573	16%
Licence	1,015	29%
Master	755	21%
Doctorate	788	22%
Personal status		
Single	1,954	54%
With partner	1,628	46%
Total	3,570	100%

Source: Blidon (2007).

The sample characteristics show several biases (see Table 23.1). Men are overrepresented (87 per cent) with respect to women (13 per cent). This is primarily explained by the fact that the magazine *Têtu*, which published the survey on its website, is aimed principally at gay men. The respondents are much younger, better educated and more urban than the general French population – characteristics which are usually found in press surveys (Schiltz, 1998). Various surveys of male homosexuals use sampling methods (media, meeting places, snowball effect or telephone) allowing the target population to self-select itself for the study on the basis of auto-evaluation and volunteerism. Systemic biases are thus introduced into the surveys, which do not allow us to calculate values or means that are representative of the target population. These selection biases are found in all surveys, transversal or longitudinal, and for all recruitment methods. They have a direct influence on the sociodemographic characteristics of the respondents: the surveys mainly recruit the individuals most integrated into society.

Indeed, in all surveys we find men with similar sociodemographic profiles. They are characterized by a high level of education, belonging to the upper middle classes and living in large urban areas. The 25–45 age bracket is the most represented, and there are great difficulties in recruiting men either at the beginning or at the end of their sexual activity, or those on the margins of the gay community (Lert and Plauzolles, 2003, p. 58).

However, despite these biases, the residential distribution of the respondents is very close to that of the French urban systems (see Figure 23.1). The sample presents a variety of cases from rural districts (6 per cent) to Paris (24 per cent) as well as émigrés (5 per cent) or residents of the French overseas *départements* (2 per cent).

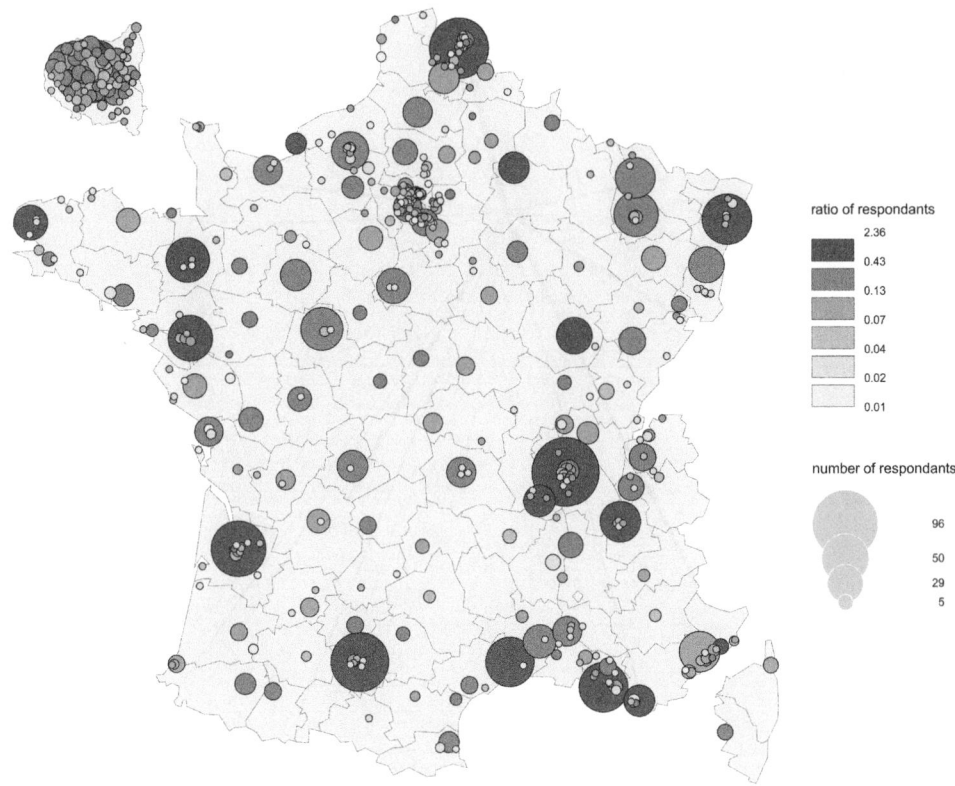

ratio of respondants
2.36
0.43
0.13
0.07
0.04
0.02
0.01

number of respondants
96
50
29
5

Figure 23.1 **Residential distributions of the respondents in terms of the size of districts**
Source: Blidon (2007).

Where do Gays and Lesbians Residing in Paris Originate From?

Starting with the variable 'passing through Paris', we looked at what was the municipality of residence immediately before moving to Paris, in terms of both the size of the urban unit and its location. Contrary to the commonly accepted notion of gays migrating to metropolitan areas from low-density rural and outlying areas, the study reveals the strong metropolitan character of Parisian gay migration. Fully one-quarter of respondents who have resided or reside in Paris come from the Paris conurbation – for example, they leave a municipality in the suburbs to settle in Paris's city centre, and one-third come from a city of over 200,000 inhabitants (Lyon, Toulouse, Lille).

205

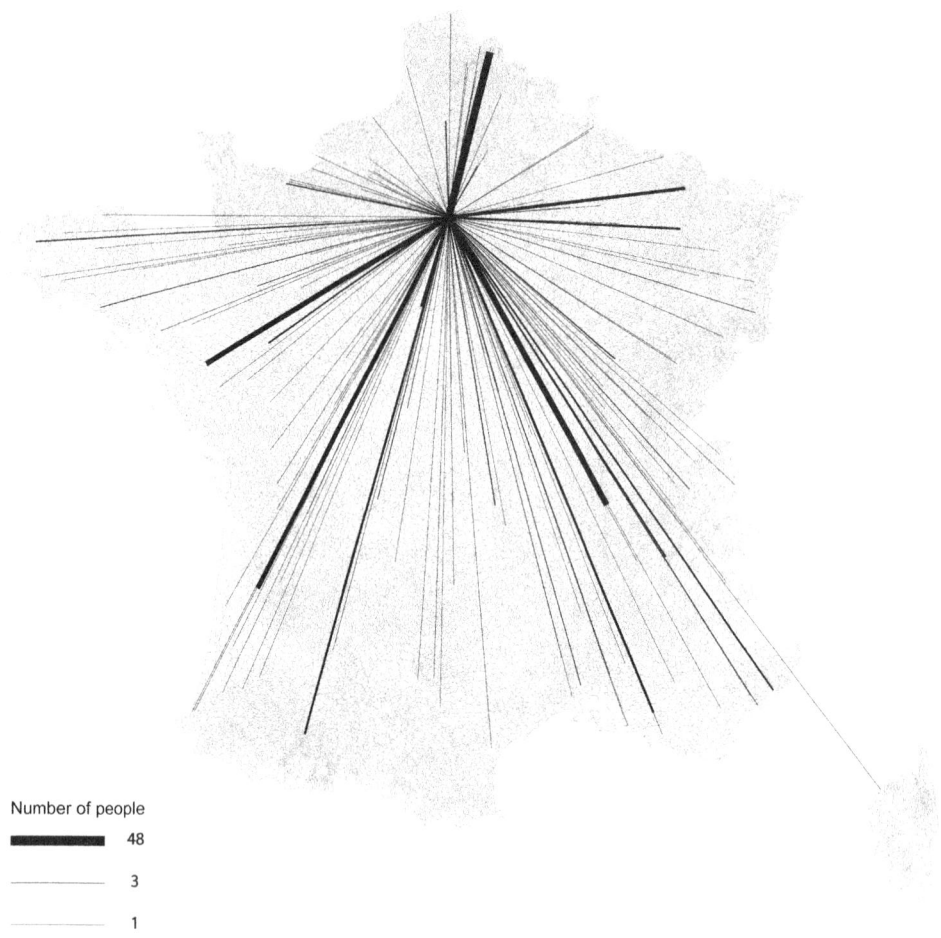

Number of people

———— 48

———— 3

———— 1

Figure 23.2   Map of the municipalities of origin of respondents who have lived or are living in Paris

Notes:
Cohort: It was not possible to identify 17 per cent of municipalities because of homonyms or plural connections to urban units of different sizes. In the majority of cases, they were municipalities that belong at the bottom of the urban hierarchy (rural settlement, village, small town).
Reading: The cohort corresponds to the number of respondents who left a municipality for Paris. For example, 48 respondents came from Lille before arriving in Paris (which does not prejudge that Lille was their town of birth).

Source: Blidon (2007).

    Paradoxically, it is not the cities less well equipped with shops and associations or those that suffer from a homophobic reputation which are the most frequent municipalities of origin of gay respondents who come to settle in Paris. On the contrary, it is those that enjoy a good commercial and associative fabric (Blidon, 2007) and are among the best ranked, by the specialized press, in the ranking of French cities that are the most gay-friendly. Thus, Lyon arrived in first position as a metropolis of emigration, when the city –the second largest city in France in terms of urban area – is presented as benefiting from a policy described by gay magazine *Têtu* as 'ambitious' because 'half of municipal officers were trained in fighting homophobia', the city having set up a 'Charter for the quality of its night life'. Local government aid to associations exceeds €1 million or a fourfold increase. This means that the city offers 'a rich associative life, many places to go out, an LGBT film festival (mixed screens) of very good quality, many gay shops' as well as an archive centre and a free magazine destined for gays and lesbians (Maurice, 2012, p. 87). Conversely, the city of Marseille – the third largest city in France in terms of urban area – is ranked among the large cities from which Parisian gays are least likely to have emigrated, even though the city has an extremely homophobic reputation. Indeed, according to the annual report of the association SOS homophobie (2013), Marseille comes top of large regional cities recording the greatest number of homophobic assaults. Gay visibility in the city – with the exception of the occasional organization of LGBT events – is rare, as reflected in the small number of institutions or associations enabling gays to socialize.

Contrary to what has been written in the literature, it is not the absence of amenities that necessarily constitutes a reason for emigration; in fact, it would appear to be quite the reverse. For those who have benefited from a socialization process in the commercial and/or associative gay community, Paris is an attractive space whose wealth and diversity of resources carry a lot of weight. Another paradox is that among the cities that appear on Figure 23.2 (Lille, Le Mans, Reims), many are close to Paris and are quickly accessible, particularly with the TGV (high-speed train), revealing the residential polarization effect of the French capital (many people prefer to live in Paris than in a town near Paris).

Then, in 13 per cent of cases, respondents come from medium-sized cities or small towns. Towns with less than 10,000 inhabitants and rural towns appear to be very rare (5 per cent of cases) even if these figures are underestimated due to missing data (17 per cent). However, less than 10 per cent of the members of this group have resided at least once in their life in Paris. Their distribution between the different cities of the urban hierarchy is relatively homogeneous. Thus, gays and lesbians who leave the rural town where they grew up do not overwhelmingly settle in Paris; rather, they settle more in intermediate-sized cities. This is a very classic process, often observed in other migration settings – not only in French migrations, but also in African migrations. Few migrants leave a rural town – defined as having fewer than 2,000 inhabitants living within the same boundary, according to the administrative definition in force in France – and move to Paris. In our sample, less than five respondents, for the most part originating from rural villages in the Greater Paris region, moved from their rural setting to Paris. If this migration takes place, it is done via intermediate steps involving university cities of medium size or towns that belong to conurbations. This confirms arguments that it is mainly urban–urban paths that are followed by gays (Gorman-Murray, 2007). In fact, in more than 80 per cent of cases, respondents have never lived in a rural town or village.

Finally, a significant number of respondents come from abroad (17 per cent), whether they were born in France or not. Paris is consequently indeed an attractive city, essentially for gays and lesbians aged over 25. However, this attraction operates mainly for those from a metropolitan background rather than those from the countryside. Finally, it should be noted that, while Paris is undeniably an important stage in the paths, it is not always the final one.

Where do Gays and Lesbians Go When They Leave Paris?

With the variable 'passing through Paris' we looked at the municipality of residence immediately after Paris in the migratory paths of the respondents. This allowed us to understand the dynamic dimension of mobility and evolutions in gay and lesbian life courses.

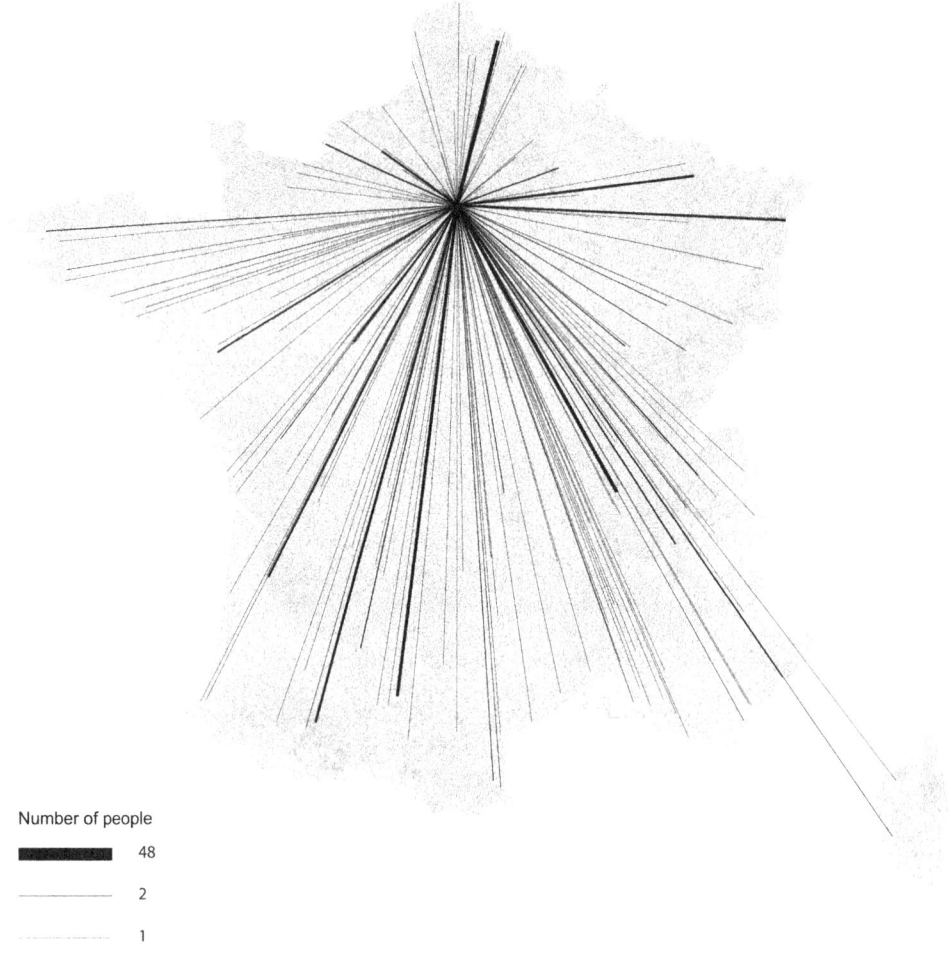

Number of people

— 48

— 2

— 1

Figure 23.3   Map of destination towns of respondents who have resided in Paris

Notes:
Cohort: it was not possible to identify 83 per cent of towns because of homonyms or multiple connections to urban units of different sizes. In the majority of cases, they were towns that belong at the bottom of the urban hierarchy, for example with a population of under 20,000.
Reading: The cohort corresponds to the number of respondents who left Paris for another town.

Source: Blidon (2007).

One in ten respondents who had lived in Paris continued their path abroad, whether in a metropolitan context (Barcelona, London, New York) or not. Depending on the position of the Parisian stage in the person's life cycle, a slight change in migration patterns with regard to destinations, duration and number of stages can be observed. In this case, it is no longer just a question of experiencing life abroad, but of leading an expat life in which the spatial capital mobilized is a resource that can be called upon to offset, to some extent, local constraints. Regarding interviews, the ability to travel far and frequently, to live in a rich and very cosmopolitan environment enables distance from a conservative and homophobic environment. These cases, even though they are limited, offer interesting prospects for studies of the international migration of gays and lesbians who belong to the elite, working in finance, the military or international organizations.

In addition to the case of those who migrate abroad, two major trends can be observed in migrations from Paris. In one-quarter of cases, mobility is more akin to a residential change within the Paris area than a migration away from the city. Fifteen per cent of survey respondents reside in Paris. Among these, 84 were born in Paris and 75 were born in the suburbs. Conversely, 34 respondents born in Paris reside in the suburbs. Their situation shows an anchoring and residential movement in the Paris area, which, in the French context, poses the question of the scale of the analysis and the context (in 2013, the city of Paris had 2,273,300 inhabitants over 105 km^2 and the metropolitan area had 10,516,110 inhabitants over 2845 km^2, divided into 412 districts of Ile-de-France). Thus, the towns of Boulogne, Montreuil, Vincennes, Asnieres, Bagnolet, Issy-les-Moulineaux, Créteil or Colombes appear as preferred destinations after the Paris city stage (see Figure 23.3). Three types of town stand out in this list: those bordering Paris and undergoing gentrification, where gay and lesbian associations are already established (Montreuil, Bagnolet); residential towns bordering Paris with a rather conservative administration, high prices and a predominantly middle-class population (Boulogne, Vincennes, Issy-les-Moulineaux); and, finally, municipalities with a lower-income habitat further from Paris, with lower real estate prices (Asnieres, Créteil, Colombes). The two latter cases are interesting because they correspond to two blind spots in the French research on the geography of sexualities: suburban upper-middle-class housing and suburban low-income housing – two areas considered *a priori* homophobic.

Residential mobility can therefore be a passage from the city centre to the suburbs or a movement within the suburban districts. These changes are related to opportunities (access to home ownership, choosing larger or better located accommodation, setting up as a couple, arrival of a child) or conversely to difficulties (separation, illness, unemployment).

Finally, the majority of respondents who have lived in Paris leave for the provinces. As noted by Alexis Annes and Meredith Redlin (2013, p. 140), despite the city's importance in the initial development of gay identity for most, the city is better identified as a transitional space, rather than one that creates or crystallizes sexual identity. One-third of them choose to live in a big city (Lille, Lyon, Toulouse, Marseille, Montpellier, Strasbourg, Bordeaux, Rouen, Tours) while others are choosing to settle in small and medium-sized towns or even rural communities. As can be seen in Figure 23.1, the spatial distribution of host destinations after a Parisian stage shows a more frequent location in attractive mountain regions (Alps, Pyrenees) or by the sea (Atlantic, Mediterranean). It would be interesting to study the evolution of their social networks, as well as their consumption habits and leisure practices, to see if they remain identical and polarized by Paris or if they undergo a local reconfiguration.

209

Experiences and Projects

A questionnaire with open questions was sent to Parisian respondents who agreed to be contacted after the survey. Of these, 82 people responded, thus allowing me to enrich my understanding of their path and their sometimes ambivalent relationship with the city of Paris.

While the belief that it is easier to live one's life as a gay or lesbian in Paris is fairly unanimously shared by all survey respondents (96 per cent), in line with the spatial imagining of the emancipatory city, those residing in Paris have a more complex and critical discourse, particularly with regard to living conditions and how they envisage their future. Most discourses overlap on several points.

The argument of sexual identity is never put forward as such. It is always entangled with others. What predominates is more the fear of loneliness than homophobia or acceptance. Indeed, many Parisian singles said that they are afraid of not being able to meet someone if they move into sparsely populated or remote areas. Despite available transport, for many distance remains an obstacle. For many gays and lesbians, setting up as a couple is thus seen as a prerequisite for moving to a more attractive environment in terms of housing, home ownership, more space and less pollution.

The environment and reuniting with the family appear as the primary motivations for geographical mobility. Paris is often described as lacking green spaces, as a polluted, stressful and expensive city. Migration, according to the paths actually observed, therefore tends to be oriented towards the larger cities. Montpellier and Bordeaux are frequently presented as alternatives to Paris, both in terms of quality of life, proximity to the sea and for their commercial and associative structures. Thus Antoine notes, 'I would like to live closer to nature in a less stressful, less dense environment and close to the sea. Large provincial towns such as Bordeaux and Montpellier seem perfect because now gay life also exists outside of Paris.' Areas appreciated and frequented during weekends or holidays crystallize fantasies of escape. Martin remarked:

> *I cannot bear the distance from the sea! I need the sea air and open spaces at least once every two months. As for the destination, it could just as well be my native Normandy or the South of France (I love the heat and the older I grow the more I look for it!) or another country, depending on where my next job will be found!*

For many, the range of possibilities is quite wide and motivations intertwine. Thus Daniel wants to leave Paris:

> *... because it's cold, winter is grey, there isn't even the magic of a snowy winter like in the Aisne region [his home region in eastern France, to which he remains very attached]. There are too many people, and those beautiful buildings can be stifling. Paris is too much of a flashy showcase. If I leave Paris it will be to find peace, tranquillity, nature, a house with a garden, and if in addition I have a partner, it will be a paradise. But not too far from a city nonetheless. Take the Lot-et-Garonne département in the South West: Bordeaux and Toulouse aren't far. Yet now that I have my bearings in Paris, it scares me to bury myself in the country.*

Despite dissatisfaction, it is often the fear of change, of leaving one's acquaintances, not to mention just the plain force of habit, that remain a limit to geographical mobility. Marc has no plans to leave Paris and remarks:

I have lived in Paris for a long time. I didn't choose to come, being very young at the time. However, I chose to remain, because it's a very big city, because I'm used to it, and part of my family (mother, grandmother, uncles, aunts, and nephews) is here, as are my friends, and the cultural activity is great. Also, being a homosexual, living here is better than in a village. Personally it [homosexuality] didn't play a large role, I didn't emigrate and I live in the arrondissement next to the one where I went to school!

Change often occurs at the time of separation, or when a couple forms, or for reasons of occupational mobility. The commonly accepted image of the mobile gay needs to be balanced through the notion of rooting and in relation to strong family connections, solidarities and relationships. Data from interviews show that family support may be very important in case of unemployment or disease (Blidon and Guérin, 2013). As Skeggs (2004, pp. 1–2) said, it's important to consider:

... the way some cultural characteristics fix some groups and enable others to be mobile ... The interest here lies in how some forms of culture are condensed and inscribed onto social groups and bodies that then mark them and restrict their movement in social space, whilst other are not but are able to become mobile and flexible.

Conclusion

This chapter empirically enriches the work of Andrew Gorman-Murray, while showing the interest that online surveys and diachronic approach of mobility can provide for enriching the geography of sexualities (Browne and Nash, 2010). In the face of a rural-to-urban perception of gay and lesbian migration patterns, embedded in a social model resulting from the industrial revolution, we see the emergence of more complex and ambivalent types of migratory behaviour and ways of apprehending the capital city. The challenge is not only scientific – that is, to deconstruct the use of reified categories – but also political, as Julie Abraham (2009) points out. For her, by the late twentieth century, 'homosexuals' had become markers of place. By their exclusion, they signal the significance of place, but queers can also signal, by their presence, the insignificance of place. Indeed, the rhetoric that naturalizes the relationship of a social group (gays) and a space (the urban centres of large cities) is not unrelated to the development of a liberal economy based on an essentialized discourse about identity. Revealing the diversity of geographical paths shows that social understanding is produced by different social relations (gender, age, class) that are not reducible to the sexual dimension.

Refusing to reason over fixed entities ... allows us to put the political subject back into the centre of the analysis (and not just the victims of domination), taking into account all its practices, which are often ambivalent and ambiguous. It is an effort to try and think – and provide a method to think – about both the plurality of regimens of power and the alchemy that, sooner or later, transforms this domination, even when it has been internalized in practices of resistance. It is therefore a method for detecting the seeds of utopia in present situations. (Kergoat, 2009, p. 123)

211

To assert a right to complexity thus makes it possible for them to refuse the single place assigned to them, in order to open the field of possibilities, build margins of manoeuvre and open up vistas of freedom.

In conclusion, this chapter invites us to think about gay and lesbian diachronic migration in order to better consider queer experiences; it brings together conceptual and methodological questions that may provide further investigative nuance for understanding the intersection of sexualities with space, imaginaries and mobilities. This chapter also invites us to consider quantitative methods such as online surveys as relevant in queer geography. If queer approaches might contest the possibilities of quantification of subjects, queer approaches should overtly grapple with the contradictions that arise without definitively endorsing one set of methods over another (Browne and Nash, 2010).

Acknowledgements

I sincerely thank Andrew Gorman-Murray and Catherine J. Nash for their trust and support, Kath Browne who has provided helpful and stimulating comments, Gavin Brown for his careful reading and Andrew Wiles for the translation.

The online survey was supported by Thomas Doustaly – *Têtu* editor – and David Alonso, the webmaster. The author also would like to express her gratitude to France Guérin, Arnaud Bringe, Bénédicte Garnier and Raphaëlle Fleureux for their help in data processing.

Chapter 24

Queer Migration: Going South from China to Australia

Audrey Yue

Introduction

Two key contrasting global developments in the last 15 years have shaped the contours of queer migration. The first is the sexual law reform of marriage equality that has witnessed gays and lesbians migrating to countries such as Canada and Sweden with legal same-sex marriage rights. For these potential migrants, international relocation can be motivated by sexuality and the pursuit of a romantic relationship based on public recognition and equality. The second is the rise of heightened border control and increased securitization of cross-border movements. From racial profiling, anti-trafficking policies to the incarceration of those who overstay or seek asylum, refugees, prostitutes, guest workers and international students are increasingly made 'deviant' or 'queer' by the new structures of migration control.

This chapter presents a conceptual overview of these practices of queer migration. The chapter uses the term 'queer' to define 'queer migration' in two ways. First, as an umbrella category to describe a range of gay, lesbian, bisexual and transgender (LGBT) identities, queer migration refers to the migration of LGBTs such as same-sex partner migration and sexual identity-based asylum. Second, as a critical category that challenges normativity, queer migration refers to how the regulated norms of migration are constructed as 'irregular' by discourses of border protection and its institutions of migration control. The chapter begins with a theoretical framing that calls for a critical approach to inclusion and mobility. It further demonstrates its new paradigm of queer migration using two case studies. The first is a historical look back at how Chinese migration to Australia at the turn of the twentieth century provided the impetus for white settler countries to institutionalize their structures of border control. This case study demonstrates queer migration as a literal movement in which regular migration is made irregular or abnormal by the institution of border control.[1] The second is a contemporary investigation into sexual identity-based asylum in Australia. This case study demonstrates queer migration also as a literal movement in which race is both fetishized and erased through homonationalism as a process of progressive sexual reform used to champion the ideals of the liberal nation-state.

These case studies locate practices of queer migration from China to Australia. There are two reasons for this focus. The first is the significance of the Chinese in Australia. The Chinese are the longest non-Asian group to settle in Australia, and also the largest group of those most recently arrived (Australian Bureau of Statistics, 2012). The Chinese community,

---

1 Irregular migration refers to the process where movement occurs outside of the regulations of sending and receiving countries. See International Organization for Migration (2014).

however, is diverse, reflecting different histories and patterns of migration, and includes multigenerational Australian-born Chinese, and migrant groups from East Asia, South-east Asia and Indo-China. It now comprises 4.3 per cent of the country's 22.8 million population, and Mandarin is the second most widely spoken language after English. Chinese migrants are arguably the most significant settler population group in Australia. The second reason is the less discussed north–south trajectory of Chinese migration to Australia. Dominant studies on Chinese and Asian migration have traditionally focused on 'going West', predominantly to North America, the UK and Europe. Even in dominant queer studies of coming out, 'going West' is also always invoked as a rite of passage of leaving the birth home and entering the metropolitan gay communities located in Western cities, such as San Francisco, London and Amsterdam (Sinfield, 1996). By focusing on Australia, this chapter introduces a new trajectory called 'going South'. It highlights the specificity of this geographical travel, the mobility invested in such a movement, as well as the epistemology of Australia located as south of the west and south of Asia (Yue and Hawkins, 2000). Taking 'going South' as a new space of knowledge production, and using 'China' and 'Australia' as methods of analysis, this chapter hopes that the new conceptual paradigm of queer migration presented here will provide a new critical perspective from which to examine the intersection between sexuality, migration and governmentality. In recent times this intersection has become a crucial interface for considering the dimensions of regulated liberties and queer corporealities.

Queer Migration Studies: A Critical Approach to Inclusion

In recent years lesbian, gay, bisexual and transgender (LGBT) migration has emerged as an influential critical discourse in the West as a result of the increasing control of immigration, same-sex marriage activism and new human rights. Synonymous with 'sexual migration', a term coined to refer to the 'international relocation that is motivated, directly or indirectly, by the sexuality of those who migrate' (Carrillo, 2004, p. 59), this framework removes the strict focus on economic motivations that dominate mainstream migration accounts on why people choose to relocate and draws attention to the importance of sexuality in the life goals of gays and lesbians. The decision to migrate may arise from the wish to continue a romantic relationship with a foreign national, explore gender and sexual identities not permitted in home countries, or escape sexual discrimination and persecution (Howe et al., 2008).

Whether through legal or illegal pathways, sexual migration exposes policy regimes that include and exclude homosexuality, and are structured through stratifications of class, gender and race. These contexts are also influenced by different geopolitics of sexual liberation. For some migrants, financial motivations are also equally as important as sexual reasons (Bianchi et al., 2007). Non-Western LGBT migrants in Western gay centres also often confront a new racial hierarchy, as minorities, as people of colour, and through the universalizing tendency of pan-ethnicity.

These issues highlight three concerns central to sexual migration: the regulation of LGBT migration; the intersections of race and sexuality in home and host countries; and changing formations of kinship and community. They find resonance with 'the queer political economy of migration' approach that considers sexuality as an axis of power shaping social relations and institutions, and constituting migratory identities that are imbricated in processes of global capitalism and expansion (Cantú, 2009, p. 21). This approach examines how the marginalization of homosexuality influences immigration discourses and how the institutions of migration have been constituted by heterosexual regimes of social relations and processes (Lubhéid and Cantú, 2005). The term 'queer migration' offers at least three ways of identifying these practices of migration: 1) the sexual migration of LGBTs; 2) the migration of non-normative sexualities such as prostitutes and amoral women (Lubhéid, 2002); and 3) the 'queering' or 'making deviant' of the normative migration patterns of people on the move, such as refugees, guest workers and international students. These practices critically engage the intersections of sexuality, migration and governmentality.

Current theorizations are shaped by three distinctive approaches: using trans studies to rethink queer migration histories, theories and methodologies; historicizing queer migration through slavery, imperialism and exile, and; rethinking how the lives of queer migrants are structured and shaped by the forces of neoliberalism (Luibhéid, 2008a, p. 170). These approaches rework normative theories of migration, provide new empirical accounts of queer migration and show the impact of assimilation on queer migrants. To date there are five seminal collections (Canaday, 2009; Cantú, 2009; Chavez, 2013; Luibhéid, 2002; Luibhéid and Cantú, 2005) that focus on queer migration, and they highlight how queer migrants are excluded from heteronormative migration institutions that are designed to construct the US nation-state. These collections exclusively focus on the US nation-state; they also do not stress the significance of the institution of migration in policies of inclusion and structures of incorporation. In queer geography studies, research also includes intranational migration in Australia (Gorman-Murray, 2009a) and the embodied emotions produced by non-heteronormative migration (Gorman-Murray, 2007). These focus on the structural divisions across the city/rural divide, engage the psychology of displacement and coming-out, and also do not focus on the regulatory logics that shape the institutions of migration control.

This chapter proposes a new conceptual framework that takes a critical approach to inclusion. Rather than highlighting the exclusion of queer migrants from migration laws, this approach shows how they can be included in migration policies and incorporated by the institution of migration. While practices and laws in countries may vary, in general migration policy include all facets of state control over migration, from visa laws to policies on citizenship, naturalization, refugee and asylum, trafficking and border management; it also encompasses incorporation policies and organizations that coordinate internal agencies on health, welfare and language.

Key to migration control is the physical and symbolic border, erected to screen and select those who can enter and those who cannot. The institutionalization of migration has emerged inextricably with such a history of border control (McKeown, 2008). By focusing on migration control through policies of inclusion, this chapter considers borders as 'devices of inclusion' (Mezzadra and Neilson, 2013, p. 7) that have the capacity to filter people in ways that can also be equally violent and exclusionary. Inclusion, in this context, exists differentially, across multiple scales of incorporation along the fault lines of geography, gender, sexuality, class and race, and in a continuum rather than an opposition to exclusion. Such an epistemic perspective, what Mezzadra and Neilson (2013, p. vii) call 'border as method', provides a critical angle to draw out the conflicts and tension that surround the line between exclusion and inclusion, especially in relation to contemporary practices of incorporation, such as social inclusion, and across changing logics of capital, nation-states and people. Rather than simply focusing on laws of exclusion, the emphasis on inclusion also allows a critical examination on techniques of regulation, which include not just laws, but also the broader Foucauldian discourse of policing that takes into account governing and disciplinary systems, as well as practices of subject incorporation and formation. It allows one to confront the tension that takes place between inside and outside, and to be alert to new contingencies of possibilities that make and remake migrant subjects – queer and straight – according to different degrees of subjectivation and subordination. In this context, the singular focus on laws of exclusion in the aforementioned North American studies is limited. Isolating a single function does not allow one to grasp the flexibility and complexity

215

of migration as an institution or understand how the diffusion of practices and techniques of migration control within are bound to spaces and practices of citizenship.

Central to how differential inclusion creates contingencies for new subjects are multiple politics of mobility. Emerging from the mobilities paradigm, the politics of mobility departs from both sedentarist theories that view movement as abnormal and deterritorialization theories that celebrate nomadic travel (Sheller and Urry, 2006). In the context of migration, mobility includes material travel, and movement can be forced or voluntary, stratified according to different scales of power geometry as well as segments of class, race, gender and sexuality. The politics of mobility focuses on how such movements occur and how they are also embedded in practices of rehoming (Brah, 1996) or regrounding (Ahmed et al., 2003). These practices are usually associated with institutional fixity or what has been called 'institutional moorings' (Hannam et al., 2006, p. 3). Often highly immobile, institutional embeddings are usually localized and highly immobile, and have the capacity to reorganize subject-formations and spatial arrangements. The politics of mobility highlight the hybrid combination of movement and containment, what scholars have termed 'materialized mobility', to refer to the friction between materialities and mobilities, a combination of 'objects, technologies, socialities and affects out of which distinct places are produced and reproduced' (Hannam et al., 2006, p. 16). In particular, the 'politics of material movement' stresses the need to examine the ease, frequency and speed of movement, and the discursive representation of mobility as well as the meanings attached to its practices of re-embodiment (Cresswell, 2010, p. 21).

These considerations are especially pertinent when exploring queer migration. Shaped by the border as a physical and symbolic site of mobility and immobility, queer migration crosses geographical, economic, cultural and psychological boundaries. The mobility of queer migrants is inseparable from new forms of heteronormative and homonormative control, from the power of nation-states and their ideologies of inequality, to the multilayered structures of the migration system, and at the level of the social and individual bodies. From material travel, institutional incorporation to individual subjectivity, it is 'about tracking the power of discourses and practices of mobility in creating both movement and stasis' (Sheller and Urry, 2006, p. 211).

The following sections develop the queer migration conceptual approach introduced here. The first case study is historical and the aim is to demonstrate the queering of regular migration. The second case study is contemporary and the aim is to demonstrate the politics of mobility.

Queering Chinese Migration[2]

In the nineteenth century, migration control emerged in the West as part of the business of government to regulate the movement of people. Governments relied on the anthropological understanding of residentialism to rationalize the control of borders using migration laws. Residentialism was a prominent ideology of agrarianism that was part of the theory of socioeconomic evolution at that time. It describes a mode of social organization to refer to 'groups of persons as static, self-sufficient group of settlers who enjoy equal rights of permanent residence', classifies migrants 'as persons with a deviant behaviour' and accords them a lower social status (Kleinschmidt, 2003, p. 10). The core element in this historical definition of migration, as 'the relocation of residence across a border of recognized

---

2   An earlier and shorter version of this section appeared in Yue (2012).

significance', is 'boundary trespass' (Kleinschmidt, 2003, p. 17). This ideology resonates with the framework of sedentarism introduced earlier. A historical and scientific European discourse, sedentarism is a philosophy based on being rooted in a territory. Used to justify Orientalism (Said, 1978), it is associated with civilization and progress whereas its binary other, such as nomadism, is seen as wild and barbaric. Heidegger (2002), in particular, discusses sedentarism using the concept of dwelling as a mode of habitation. Viewing dwelling as normal, stable and bounded, he considers it a practice of being in place, at home and in the world. Dwelling is associated with the authenticity of places and regions. Migration, which uproots dwelling and disrupts the fixity of the home nation-state, is considered abnormal.

The nineteenth century saw the rise of mass Chinese migration – about 50 million people (Lake and Reynolds, 2008, location 134 of 5214) across the Western world. With migrants constructed as 'deviant' and migration 'abnormal', the need to control the Chinese migrant emerged as part of the migration institution, and admission on the basis of race was accepted as a standard part of this procedure. In Australia, these rationales justified a raft of border control procedures that culminated with the institutionalization of the White Australia policy.

Before the 1850s immigration to Australia was not controlled (Jupp, 1998, p. 70). With the discovery of gold in New South Wales and Victoria in 1851, the number of Chinese arrivals started to increase. About 10,000 Chinese, for example, landed in Melbourne in 1854 alone (Lake and Reynolds, 2008, location 260 of 5214[3]). Their visible presence was seen as a threat to the half-million British inhabitants in the country. In 1855 Victoria imposed a landing tax on the Chinese, and confined them to Chinese protectorates in the goldfields under the administration of colonial officers. That same year, the first immigration restriction law, 'An Act to make provisions for certain Immigrants' (Lake and Reynolds, 2008, location 260 of 5214), was passed in Victoria, limiting the number of alien passengers allowed in ships. In 1897 Western Australia followed the Natal formula and introduced a 'dictation test' for immigrants. The law required prospective immigrants to pass a written test in any European language, and the language need not be the one understood by the applicant. New South Wales and Tasmania quickly adopted the Natal formula in 1898 and 1899 respectively. Although nationality, rather than of race, was used as a form of classification, the test was meant to target predominantly Chinese arrivals and 'facilitate exclusion rather than … ascertain whether immigrants were literate' (Jupp, 1998, p. 75). These procedures prevented the Chinese from migration, taking up certain occupations and becoming citizens. These practices were incorporated into the Immigration Restriction Act in 1901 which instituted the country's White Australia policy that remained in place until 1975. Those Chinese already in the country and allowed to remain were not permitted to intermarry or bring their wives and families. These racist laws also sexualized Chinese migrants through emasculation (Ayres, 1999).

Although Australia was one of the first to introduce racial exclusion migration laws, these systems of migration control – the surveillance of Asian indenture, the enforcement of the US Chinese exclusion laws at the turn of the twentieth century and the implementation of the Natal formula across the British empire – were quickly established across other white settler countries. Whiteness was invented as a form of defence against the threat of yellow and black races, and while its methods were nationalist, its ideology was transnational (Lake and Reynolds, 2008). Identity documentation, technologies of documentation and standardization of documentation were introduced to enforce exclusion, deportation and segregation. Together with the literary test, other instruments also included state-based

---

3   Location in reference to an electronic book reader.

217

surveillance, the census and the passport. These basic principles of the modern institution of migration control emerged during this period to justify the control of Chinese migrants to the West: 'The techniques designed to control Asians became the template for practical workings of general immigration laws in the white settler nations, and ultimately around the world' (McKeown, 2008, p. 13).

This history of Chinese migration shows how the institution of migration arose by constructing the Chinese migrant as deviant and Chinese migration as an abnormal practice. Whereas the travel of coolies, rail workers, gold-diggers and shopkeepers at that time was a precursor to contemporary labour migration, this history shows how global border control has emerged through queering regular migration. As a literal movement and discursive practice of queering migration, the critical framework of queer migration demonstrated here reveals how racist structures of incorporation are erected not only to prevent entry but also to configure the migrant subject through sexualized and racialized ideologies of nationalism. These forces have continued to shape border practices up to the present, as is evident in the following case study on queer asylum.

Queer Asylum

The practice of queer asylum is officially referred to as sexual identity-based asylum following the guidelines stated in the 1951 Geneva Convention relating to the Status of Refugees. Although sexual orientation is not identified as one of the grounds for granting refugee status, LGBTs can seek refugee protection on the basis of their membership to 'a particular social group' if they can demonstrate a fear of persecution based on that membership.

Sexual identity-based asylum applicants are based on the construction of a personal narrative that documents an individual's sexual identity, membership of the social group and a history of public persecution. Although applications in countries such as Australia and Canada, for example, do not need to show that they are open about their sexuality or have experienced persecution, their narratives are judged according to a Western-staged model of identity development that assumes applicants, having earlier struggled with self-identity, can now reflect back and tell their coming-out story (Berg and Millbank, 2009). Western homosexual lifestyles and tastes are used as techniques of corroboration and verification. In some instances, applications were rejected because claimants were unable to display intimate knowledge of local gay communities or global gay knowledge, such as the interior layout of bars and saunas or the history of Western gay icons such as Oscar Wilde, gay-themed music and media. The assumption here exposes how gay identity is only recognized according to the accumulation of a normative discourse of gay subcultural capital. These decisions reveal how mobility is constructed to privilege a homogenous Western gay subculture and identity; they also ignore how homosexuality is constructed differently in different countries and how Western homosexual ideals are assimilated and normalized into the values of national citizenship. Applications are also judged according to 'discretion' and 'reasonably tolerable' tests, and can be rejected if claimants reveal that they had previously exercised 'discretion' in their country of origin (Gower, 2010; Millbank, 2009). The argument here is that if they had earlier been discreet about their sexual identity in their home country, they can continue to be discreet on their return. In cases of successful applications, homonationalism, as a process whereby sexual law reform is used to showcase the progressive liberalism of a nation-state, legitimates the hierarchical sexualization and racialization of the refugee other; in unsuccessful cases, it ignores the racial and sexual contexts of home countries that create the persecutory conditions of sexual discrimination.

This logic of legitimating sexual identity-based asylum exposes the queer complicity of homonormativity (Luibhéid, 2008b, p. 180) whereby the discourse used to champion the destination country's progressive sexual reforms is also the same strategy used to orientalize the origin country's primitive sexual laws. The following demonstrates these politics of mobility and complicit homonationalism using Chinese lesbians' applications for asylum in Australia.

Between 1995 and 2008 there were 10 unsuccessful applications from Chinese lesbians seeking asylum. These cases and their narratives of appeals were retrieved from the Refugee Review Tribunal (RRT) Board, and the rationales for rejection are critically analysed here. In nine of these cases, the Australian authorities used the narrative of progressive Chinese queer liberalism to reject their appeals. Evident here are the sources used for corroboration: The *Los Angeles Times* reported that 'China no longer arrests' (RRT, 1995); the *South China Morning Post* noted that 'police no longer arrests homosexuals' (RRT, 1997) and that there were 'flourishing gay bars in China [and] strong LGBT activism' (RRT, 1998a); in two cases, country information verification was sourced from *Third Pink Book*, *Spartacus Gay Guide*, *Campaign*, *The Boston Globe*, *New York Times* and *OG magazine* (RRT, 1998b, 1998c, 1999); and two reports cited China's Ministry of Public Security, stating that 'homosexuality is not a crime' (RRT, 2002) and that there had been 'no arrests of homosexuality' (Federal Magistrates Court of Australia, 2008). Notwithstanding the decriminalization of homosexuality in China in 1997, these sources – from mainstream newspapers outside China, and gay travel guide books and magazines popular in the West and East Asia – reveal how Chinese queer liberalism is constructed according to the post-Stonewall logic of sexual rights and recognition. In this logic, China is treated as equal to Australia in terms of sexual progress, and this is expunged from Australia. Equal because China is seen as having reached the same conditions of sexual emancipation and expunged because the applicants have been denied entry. In a process of what has been called the 'new homonormativity' (Duggan, 2003), the Chinese race is erased and fetishized. It is erased because Chinese queer liberalism is viewed as similar to Australia's, as the sources of corroboration above have identified; it is fetishized because intimacy, when uprooted and regrounded in Australia, has changed in scale as a result of its incorporation by the Australian migration institution, as will be discussed below.

A Chinese lesbian couple were together for a few years when they left China to seek asylum in Australia (RRT, 1998c; see also Millbank, 2002, pp. 166–7). One was divorced and the other still married. The applicant endured beatings by her husband, who discovered her relationship. He threw her out of their home, and she moved with her lover to a hotel room. On the second night at the hotel, a female staff member opened the door to find the two women kissing and touching each other in bed. Two security officers came in, remarked that their relationship was 'not normal' and took them to the local branch of the Public Security Bureau (PSB) where they were detained overnight during which time they were interrogated, beaten and electrocuted. They claimed that they were not in a sexual relationship. The Public Security Bureau explained they were detained because they were 'behaving like hoodlums' and 'their relationship destroyed public order'.

The Australian Asylum Tribunal used the discretion principle to reject their application following verification from aforementioned sources like the *Spartacus Gay Guide*, the US Embassy Report on Beijing and even Amnesty International, stating that there had been no homosexual arrests and there was even a thriving gay scene in Shanghai. It also found the behaviour of the Public Security Bureau consistent with its verification sources and agreed that the couple's detention 'was precipitated by behaviour ... which disturbed others enough to cause them to seek the intervention of authorities' (RRT, 1998c). It believed that their persecution was not caused by their sexual orientation but that their sexual conduct was creating a public nuisance.

This decision reveals how the institutional embedding of a migration institution such as the Refugee Review Tribunal has the capacity to re-arrange the organization of intimacy. Parallel to the decision of the Public Security Bureau, the Refugee Review Tribunal also shares the consensus that private sex in a private space is considered a public offence. Chinese authoritanism – the authoritative and unreasonable way in which Chinese authorities skew perceptions of public disturbances – is singled out in Australia to reveal the changing conditions that regulate intimacy across the Australian migration institution. Although Chinese queer liberalism is supported through the desire to achieve equality with Australia, the same practices of intimacy that are naturalized in Australia (private sex in a private space) are deemed to be anachronistic in Australia. Shifting the focus from sexual orientation to sexual conduct changes the scale of intimacy. Where sexual orientation is usually articulated as a form of self-identity, sexual conduct is often legally mobilized to refer to the demeanour of sexual behaviour in relation to another person or group. What is private, domestic, erotic and interdependent is now reorganized as a form of regulation in a new relationship to the public and nation-state (Berlant, 1998). Rematerialized in the institutional structure of the Refugee Review Tribunal, intimacy has become an instrument of regulation and compliance. On the one hand, it has made visible the subject-position of Chinese lesbian refugees; on the other hand, they have emerged as failed migrants through bad sexual conduct.

Conclusion

This chapter has introduced a new critical framework to consider queer migration. Key here is the approach to inclusion and mobility, and their attendant practices of materiality and embodiment. It has utilized two case studies on literal migration to highlight the two-stage process in such a framework. The first case study returned to the history of Chinese migration to show how queer migration can be formulated as a process by which regular migration is queered or made deviant by the institution of border control. The second examined sexual identity-based asylum to show how queer migration can be formulated as a process by which migrant subjects are made visible by the same regulatory regimes of the migration institution. These processes are symbolic and material, and point to how migration is regulated through policies, structures and institutions of incorporation that constitute the queer migrant subject. Using the north–south axis of China and Australia as an approach towards novel frames of knowledge production, it is hoped that the new trajectory of 'going South' introduced here will highlight not only the specificity of mobility and how such politics are shaped by different histories and locations, but also how such a trajectory can offer an alternative framing of mobility that governs the flows of sexuality.

Chapter 25

Evolving Bodies: Mapping (Trans)Gender Identities in Refugee Law

Senthorun Raj

Introduction

Despite the increasing extension of protection obligations to sexual minorities, the international jurisprudence has yet to resolve the question of recognizing the queer mobilities of asylum claims on the basis of gender identity or expression. While the administrative and judicial decisions in anglophone jurisdictions evince a growing trend towards recognizing transgender or transsexual asylum-seekers, there remains considerable conceptual uncertainty about how this 'particular social group' (PSG) should be defined and about what ought to be considered as a 'well-founded fear of persecution' (UNHCR, 2010, p. 14). Despite the expansive analysis on sexual orientation-related asylum claims, current academic research and policy debates in relation to (trans)gender-identity refugees remain largely in their infancy. While domestic laws governing refugee determinations vary across jurisdictions, there remains little consistency about how the Convention definition is applied. Focusing on the historic US case *Hernandez-Montiel v Immigration and Naturalization Service* [2000], this chapter examines the definition of a PSG; the quantification of persecution; and how the nexus of gender identity-related harms is recognized to consider the queer mobilities possible for both refugees and the laws and processes that govern them.

This chapter opens by examining how the veracity of gender-identity claims is assessed against immutable qualities or personal psychological narratives of gender dysphoria from early childhood. In quantifying persecution, decision-makers' preference for identifying persecution in terms of state actors often obscures the complex domestic and familial contexts in which gender-diverse individuals experience violence and social opprobrium. The chapter concludes by seizing on some of these juridical and administrative limitations, and examines how consideration of gender identity-related asylum claims enables us to rethink the legal mobility of the UN Convention Relating to the Status of Refugees (1951) and the 1967 Protocol to offer protection to displaced individuals Comparing the differing interpretations of the Convention, this chapter reviews a limited number of publicly available administrative and judicial decisions from the USA and Australia to indicate some ways in which refugee jurisprudence and decision-making in this area must grapple with the mobility of migrating bodies and laws in order to offer more appropriate recognition for these complex claims. While the gamut of terms used to describe non-normative gender identities is historically and culturally contested, this chapter adopts the self-identified terminology used by asylum-seekers in their individual cases. In doing so, this chapter seeks to provoke ongoing reflections into the ways in which queer decision-making connects with queer mobilities in refugee law.

Contextualizing International Refugee Law and Gender Identity

International law provides the appropriate starting-point for contextualizing the scope of refugee protection. Under Article 1A(2) of the 1951 Refugee Convention there are no specific categories for persecution on the basis of sexual orientation or gender identity. In order to seek asylum, a person must be outside their country of origin and must face a 'well-founded fear of persecution' owing to their ethnicity, nationality, religion, particular social group or political opinion. International human rights law in recent years has moved to recognize the distinct forms of persecution and discrimination suffered by sexual and gender minorities in the context of asylum. For example, Article 23(A) of the United Nations Yogyakarta Principles (2007) identifies an obligation on states to:

> [r]eview, amend and enact legislation to ensure that a well-founded fear of persecution
> on the basis of sexual orientation or gender identity is accepted as a ground for the
> recognition of refugee status and asylum. (International Commission of Jurists, 2007)

Although the Yogyakarta Principles do not legally bind countries to recognize sexual orientation and gender identity in their domestic application of refugee law, a number of anglophone jurisdictions have come to accept similar recommendations for more two decades. In Australia, this category has taken its legal currency from the *Morato* case in which a person 'belongs to or is identified with a recognisable or cognisable group within a society that shares some interest or experience in common' (*Morato v Minister for Immigration, Local Government and Ethnic Affairs* [1992]). In the USA, *Matter of Toboso-Alfonso* [1990] established the precedent that sexual orientation could constitute a valid social group. Despite the statutory variations relating to refugee recognition in the USA and Australia, sexual identity has largely become reduced to a universal identity that can be attributed to a particular set of shared experiences in both jurisdictions. Thus, clearly delineating sexual orientation within the definition of a particular social group is often essentialist (Millbank, 2003).

Claims for gender-diverse applicants, however, need to be distinguished. Public policy discussions of sex or gender often defaults to assumptions of women and men being delineated by a fixed binary category. Gender, however, is a more elusive concept to define. It can be relationally and hierarchically defined: women are defined in terms of their lack (to men) and are subordinated to men. It is also a porous and performative category. Specifically, gender should be understood as the disparate social practices that constitute the identities, experiences and roles that are typically associated with the binary category of sex (Butler, 1990, pp. 22–34). Gender works as a set of culturally and historically situated expressions that give shape to individual psyches and subjectivities. These dichotomous sexed/gendered identities are also tethered to binary notions of (homo/hetero) sexual orientation and erotic desire – an assumption that excludes intersex bodies that do not conform to these binary expectations. Such a conflation exemplifies the way in which sex, gender and sexual orientation are often rendered co-extensive. In the refugee law, legal scholars Laurie Berg and Jenni Millbank (2013, p. 123) note that the non-conforming gender expressions are often reduced to questions of sexual orientation, at least in the context of understanding the nature of persecution. As Andrew Gorman-Murray (2007, p. 109) suggests, queer bodies often risk having their identities 'aligned' to fit into sedentary categories that deny slippage, movement and contradiction. The proper delineation of gender identity is one that continues to plague refugee law and it is to this to which this chapter now turns.

Scoping the Particular (Transgender) Social Group

Identity is a challenging concept to define in the law. Political scientist Georgia Warnke (2007, p. 87) argues that identity cannot be reduced to a biological reality. Rather, identity should be considered as a historically and culturally contingent phenomenon. More specifically, gender identity adds a further complexity as it is frequently used as an umbrella term to refer to transgender, transsexual and other gender-variant individuals. For example, transgender persons may exhibit characteristics of a gender that may not necessarily correspond to their assigned sex (J. Green, 2004, pp. 2–6). Transsexual is frequently cited as a more specific term to refer to individuals who have undergone some form of medical, hormonal or surgical intervention to affirm their chosen sex or gender identity. Gender identity also incorporates those who may not identify with any particular gender role or sex (Butler, 2004, pp. 85–7). This term is often contested, however, and some prefer the use of 'gender diversity' to capture their non-conforming gender expressions and identifications which do not subscribe to a specific psychological or social sense of identity. Understanding identity requires us to appreciate that bodies are textual surfaces on which social, legal, cultural and biological meaning is inscribed and understood (Butler, 1990, pp. 30–34). Specifically, identity becomes a means by which individuals understand themselves and their relationships to others.

In refugee law, the question of identity and social relationships takes on significant prominence. Justice Gerard La Forest provides an instructive precedential starting-point when defining the 'particular social group' that may qualify for refugee protection. He says that groups defined by an innate or unchangeable characteristics – groups whose members voluntarily associate for reasons so fundamental to their human dignity that they should not be forced to forsake the associated group and groups associated by a former voluntary status, unalterable due to its historical permanence – should be considered for the purposes of asylum law (*Ward v Attorney-General (Canada)* [1993]).

Drawing determinative conclusions on the associated cases that seek to deal with gender identity-based PSG claims is undesirable, if not impossible, given the limited published decisions and the lack of appellate jurisprudence in this particular area. Moreover, the complex transitional and disparate identifications and expressions of some gender-diverse individuals means that some claims for protection fall outside the schema outlined by *Ward*. Some transgender asylum-seekers do not seek sex affirmation/reassignment procedures so lack the 'historical permanence' that comes with surgical interventions whereas others have evolving fluid social or cultural identifications that are not necessarily reducible to 'innate qualities'.

The US Ninth Circuit Court of Appeals in *Hernandez-Montiel* provides one of the more considered judicial opinions on asylum-seekers who seek protection from transphobic persecution. The case concerned an applicant from Mexico who identified as a homosexual man with a feminine identity. The applicant sought asylum in the USA after suffering a brutal history of sexual assault from police and familial ostracism (*Hernandez-Montiel v Immigration and Naturalization Service* [2000], pp. 10488–9). During the initial administrative appeal, the Bureau of Immigration Appeals (BIA) defined the applicant's PSG simply as 'homosexual males who dress as females'. Justice William Schwarzer, however, noted that this was an erroneous PSG on the basis that it conflated sartorial presentation with the question of sexual (or, rather, gender) identity: the passive, feminine role of a same-sex-attracted male (ibid., p. 10482). Instead, the court opted to define the PSG more narrowly: 'gay men with female sexual identities living in Mexico' (ibid., p. 10468). The judicial reasoning placed significant emphasis on academic testimony: the 'female' role performed by a man in a same-sex relationship is subject to heightened level of abuse. Here, personalized country information was used to distinguish a highly specific PSG that incorporated gender expression rather than a more general category of 'homosexuals' that eclipsed gender identity (ibid., p. 10471).

Immutability was central to the formulation of the PSG. Immutability was understood to refer to an innate trait or a shared past experience – it must be an aspect of fundamental significance to personhood. Regardless of element, it was a common characteristic that is unchangeable. *Sanchez-Trujillo* qualifies, however, that the PSG standard is elastic, noting the existence of a voluntary, associational relationship that imparts some common characteristic. However, it must be a small, readily identifiable group (*Hernandez-Montiel v Immigration and Naturalization Service* [2000], p. 10478). In *Hernandez-Montiel*, the judicial idea of immutability was rendered more elastic. The initial BIA decision evinced that the shifting gender presentation/manner (such as moving from male to female dress) was indicative of volition, rather than innate identity. Much of the volition element concentrated on fashion/ dress. Here, the BIA referred to the applicant's presentation as a male sex worker, rather than a homosexual, as the cause for mistreatment (ibid., pp. 10472–3). On judicial review, Schwarzer J chastised the BIA for trivializing the issue of immutability: 'this case is about sexual identity not fashion' (ibid., p. 10485). In narrowing the PSG, the court reiterated the intrinsic relationship between gender identity and sexual orientation in the context of this claim – the applicant would have changed identity if it were volitional after the abuse he endured.

Extending the PSG characterization in *Ward*, Schwarzer J emphasized that gender presentation/identity is crucial to individual personhood, in addition to being related to a person's intimate attractions. In doing so, lawyer Paul O'Dwyer (2008, p. 200) claims that *Hernandez-Montiel* provided a departure-point from current jurisprudence by framing sexual identity in more elastic terms, to include aspects like dress, appearance and other visual typologies. *Hernandez-Montiel* elaborated a more flexible approach for what can constitute an immutable PSG trait. Despite the conflation of gender presentation with sexual orientation here, the references to presentation and dress gesture towards a broader conception of what can count as 'immutable' – including aspects of socialization (O'Dwyer, 2008, p. 205). In doing so, the PSG in relation to sexual minorities was revealed to be porous enough to incorporate minority gender identity.

While the Court in *Hernandez-Montiel* refused to consider whether 'transsexuality' could specifically constitute a PSG for the purposes of refugee law broadly, feminist theorist Anna Kirkland argues that the case provided an encouraging, though somewhat contradictory, framing of sexual/gender identity in the law. Specifically, the shift away from immutability, to the consideration of gender expressions as sites of personhood (despite not necessarily being permanent), provided a much more flexible approach to thinking about PSGs (Kirkland, 2003, p. 32). The idea of 'subordination' was given legal currency: where particularly identity traits should be protected because of the psychological and emotional importance they hold for the individual. We have to question the efficacy of narrowing the PSG in terms of sexual orientation, rather than having it expressed in terms of gender identity. Moreover, there is a possibility of arguing that, for this particular class of person, the choice of dress was not necessarily volitional. That is, deeply felt experiences of gender identity must be negotiated 'discreetly' in heteronormative environments that conflate biological sex with social ideas of gender.

In Australia, while there has been no comparable appellate jurisprudence on the same matter, administrative decisions provide some illuminating examples. The Refugee Review Tribunal (RRT) decisions concerning gender-diverse asylum-seekers exemplify some of the anxieties evident in *Hernandez-Montiel* when it comes to defining the PSG and the inconsistencies in recognizing gender-diverse asylum claims. In an Australian case, an asylum-seeker from Thailand identified as both homosexual and a transvestite. He claimed to be unable to 'practice being gay openly especially in the workplace', and this was linked to being unable to 'dress as a girl to go to work' (RRT, 2003, p. 6). Although the applicant's gender identification as a 'transvestite' was acknowledged by the RRT, no attempt was made to distinguish it from sexuality. Indeed, the claim was collapsed into whether the applicant was a 'practising homosexual' for Convention purposes.

However, another Australian decision evinced a more nuanced approach to the complex question of gender identity. The case concerned a transgender applicant from South Korea who identified 'predominately as male ... [with] a lot of female characteristics' (RRT, 2008, p. 14). In elaborating on the blend between his sexual and gender qualities, the applicant noted that South Korea confused being homosexual and transgender. In response, the RRT defined the relevant PSG as 'male homosexuals with transgender characteristics'. Rather than conflate sexual orientation with gender identity, the RRT clearly distinguished the 'imputed transgender' characteristics from 'homosexuality' through specific references to country information advice provided by an Australian government department (RRT, 2008, p. 14).

While earlier administrative decisions relied on defining the PSG alongside 'homosexuality', in *0902671* [2009], the RRT specifically recognized the validity of 'transsexual' as a PSG. In that case, a Pakistani male-to-female transsexual sought asylum from persecution (RRT, 2009, pp. 2–4). The RRT considered the 'transsexual in Pakistan' constituted a valid social group with a peculiar characteristic common to them. In authenticating the particular social group, the RRT made consistent reference to culturally specific terms of 'third genders' (such as references to '*hijra*') in Pakistan and the medical diagnosis of 'gender dysphoria' (such as the 'wrong body' narrative). While the unique focus on transsexuality was encouraging, the RRT sought to rely on the *Oxford English Dictionary* to define transsexualism narrowly as the dissonance between physical sex characteristics and psychological/emotional gender identifications. In a similar vein to the precedent in *Applicant S* (2004), the decision confined the PSG to transsexuals who have a 'common' experience of a psychological identification of bodily dissonance during early childhood (RRT, 2009, p. 2).

In contradistinction to the above case, the RRT has also demonstrated a preference for extremely parochial constructions of gender-identity claims. A more recent Australian case concerned an applicant who identified as a (heterosexual) post-operative transgender female from Malaysia (RRT, 2010, p. 2). For the purposes of the Convention, the RRT argued that the applicant belonged to the class of a 'Malaysian transgender woman without familial or financial support or protection' (ibid., p. 4). Rendering such a narrow PSG, the RRT expressed considerable concern at accepting 'transgender' as a social group, as it was considered overly broad. In narrowing the PSG, the RRT considered evidence that individuals identified within such a social group lacked employment options and frequently engage in sex work and problematic drug use. No financial or familial support was available to the asylum-seeker either. Elaborating on the culturally specific context of the claim, the RRT made reference to the fact that male-to-female transsexuals or '*mak nyah*' or '*aravanis*' were subject to an Islamic '*fatwa*', and must be subject to policing (ibid., p. 2). Although the culturally specific approach is commendable, the highly specific PSG in this case seems to be determined, at least indirectly, through direct reference to persecution (for example, lack of familial or financial support or protection).

Legal scholar Kristin Bresnahan (2011, p. 661) has suggested that the evolving jurisprudence relating to 'particular social group' has been characterized by analytic and conceptual divisions when considering how approaches in the USA diverge from international refugee law. The USA relies primarily on the test of 'immutability' to determine a PSG (internally focused) whereas Australia evinces a preference for an external social perception test to determine a PSG (externally focused). However, such a neat distinction has been problematized by cases like *0902671* where the issue of 'immutability' (such as gender dysphoria) has been crucial to determining the PSG that transsexuals may belong to. Alternatively, lawyer Joseph Landau (2005, p. 238) indicates that the development of the PSG category in US jurisprudence, like *Hernandez-Montiel*, has ushered in a shift towards 'soft immutability' as the standard to determine what characteristics are protected within the 'particular social group' category. Demographic as well as social identification is included in the formulation – it is not just confined to innate (or bodily) factors. The expansion of the PSG enables transgender bodies greater mobility when seeking recognition before the law. If the PSG is defined in more elastic terms, it invites decision-makers to consider how the thresholds of persecution may change. This consideration demands greater attention to the way in which the 'particular social group' is an entanglement of bodies, places, laws and emotions (Gorman-Murray, 2009a, p. 443). To queer what is meant by the PSG affords greater opportunities for refugee mobility (when seeking asylum) while enabling the mobility of law to navigate disparate gender identities (when granting asylum).

(Trans)gendering Persecution

Considering the conceptual difficulties in defining the PSG, quantifying well-founded fears of persecution unsurprisingly poses juridical challenges. Refugee scholar Kristen Walker (2000, p. 177) reiterates that 'persecution' is defined in international law as a 'serious harm' indexed against a sustained or systemic failure of state protection. What amounts to such 'sustained failure' varies in terms of the kind of harm perpetrated. Barrister Rodger Haines QC (2003, p. 330), in discussing asylum claims made by women, points out that gender-related persecution is often confined to familial circumstances, which do not always attract the concern of the state. Persecution is often annexed to state or government actors of harm (Benson, 2008, p. 27). However, such constructions often mask the more systemic absences or institutional prejudices that enables persecution to persist in a number of countries (Benson, 2008, p. 50).

In *N03/46498* (RRT, 2003), the limited degree of (sexual) harassment/discrimination and teasing faced by the Thai applicant, including family rejection, constituted oppressive conduct. However, this conduct was distinguished from a well-founded fear of persecution. Discrimination or violence against the applicant was reducible to private, rather than state, actors (such as family). In rejecting the idea that such conduct amounted to a 'serious harm' perpetrated by the state, the RRT relied on vague country information reports, which included reference to a gay tourist guide and an informal email from a former RRT member that indicated Thailand was a tolerant place for transgender people. Thus, the RRT inferred that the applicant exaggerated their claims of discrimination. In dismissing the claim, absence of specific legal recognition of transgender people was not sufficient to constitute serious harm.

In contrast, Schwarzer J in *Hernandez-Montiel* held that a history of persecution presumes an inadequacy of state protection. Recognizing the series of sexual assaults perpetrated by the police on the applicant meant no further claims of violence and ostracism need to be considered. The Court acknowledged that there was no evidence to highlight that Mexico had taken effective steps to curb violence motivated on the basis of sexuality (*Hernandez-Montiel v Immigration and Naturalization Service* [2000], p. 10491). The Court chastised the earlier BIA decision for reasoning that implied the applicant 'invited' the persecution by virtue of his appearance.

While the approaches undertaken to determine the PSG and persecution vary between Australia and the USA, the decisions also evince the need for greater clarity in defining the 'nexus' between the two. In the cases discussed above, it is clear that maintaining a broad PSG is not always desirable when attempting to define features of persecution. By narrowing the PSG, *Hernandez-Montiel* broadened the ambit of harm that could qualify as persecution (Neilson, 2005, p. 279). That is, for 'homosexuals' as a general category, the moral opprobrium or reprobation for dressing or presenting a gender in a particular way – as an expression of that identity – would not necessarily constitute a serious harm. However, when that category was framed alongside the 'female sexual identity' component, discriminatory targeting on the basis of how the applicant dressed could amount to persecution.

There is also value in having a flexible PSG so that the nexus of persecution can be understood in context. Strategically, in the cases discussed above, using the 'imputed gay identity' approach can be effective when adjudicating transgender claims. Imputation, rather than immutability, is preferable because it only requires consideration of the persecutor's perception, rather than attempting to locate an essential difference (PSG) peculiar to the person (Landau, 2005, p. 238). In *Hernandez-Montiel*, the Court could have accepted that the applicant's choice of gender presentation was volitional, as opposed to fundamental to their personhood. If it had chosen to do so, and this 'imputed' approach were adopted, the perception that such a person was a transgender in their country of origin could have sufficed to warrant protection.

O'Dwyer (2008, p. 262) also points to the importance of distinguishing malicious intent from the act of persecution. Requiring a punitive dimension to persecution can leave many applicants without protection. In one case, a lesbian asylum-seeker from Russia had her claim initially refused because the attempts to 'cure' her homosexuality through forced conversion therapies were not done punitively (*Pitcherskaia v INS* [1997], p. 645). Although this was overturned on appeal, the administrative decision revealed the way in which a persecutor's intent (for example, lack of malice) can work against the applicant's claim. It can oddly become the determinative test for persecution despite there being no legal precedent to suggest this. In a similar vein, in *Hernandez-Montiel* and *0805932* (RRT, 2008), both the Court and RRT noted that the availability of reparative therapies were used not to 'punish' the applicant, but to 'cure' what was perceived to be illness. In Australia, the High Court has confirmed this underlying principle: persecution need not require enmity of malignity (*Chen Shi Hai v MIMA* [2000], p. 319). However, gender dysphoria, unlike homosexuality, is still pathologized as cognitive discontent (although it is no longer considered a psychiatric disorder). Given this classification, it remains unclear whether non-consensual reparative therapies directed at 'curing' such discontent would constitute a sufficiently serious gender identity-related harm (American Psychiatric Association, 2013, 302.85). This demands further interrogation.

Conclusion

Adjudicating gender-identity refugee claims is an activity that is fraught with legal uncertainty and unpredictability. Yet, as this chapter has suggested, such unpredictability opens up new paths for thinking about (trans)gender identities beyond ideas of immutability or pathology. Even though gender identity has been increasingly recognized in international human rights and refugee law, gender diversity continues to be conflated with sexual orientation. The inconsistencies in the jurisprudence in the USA and Australia highlight the need for new paths to navigate the two without decoupling their slippages or interconnections. Mobilizing the fissures that emerge between gender and sexuality, domestic law and international law, and recognition and refusal, enables us to think more critically about how to accommodate gender-non-conforming bodies into asylum law. Non-normative gender identities are neither necessarily immutable nor universal, yet they remain subject to ongoing violence, harassment and discrimination.

While this chapter does not provide an exhaustive list of recommendations or answers to resolving these tensions, it does signal the need to draw attention to queer mobilities to further a more reflective approach to adjudication. Characterizing 'particular social groups' in relation to gender identity should not be overly broad, but should also not be confined to sexual orientation. Moreover, persecution must be understood in reference to the way in which gender is negotiated, which includes whether the individual is able to move freely in their preferred gender identity (with or without hormonal or surgical interventions) and able to seek appropriate documentation to be able to participate in public life. For litigation and decision-making in this emerging area of refugee law, we must be attentive to how queering mobility can help expand this area of asylum law. In doing so, we can mobilize the law to better recognize the mobile range of gender-identity asylum claims.

Chapter 26

Queer Political Geographies of Migration and Diaspora

Farhang Rouhani

Recent approaches to the study of queer migration politics and diaspora, while appearing to serve only a select set of research interests within geography, have tremendous potential in advancing the study of geographies of migration at large. Most notably, they can: illuminate the impossible positions migrants often occupy; challenge diasporic norms over authenticity; destabilize conventional understandings of gender, nation and home; bring a coalitional understanding of politics to the fore of migration analysis; and situate diasporic experiences within present and future possibilities for new ways of expressing intimacy and kinship beyond the limited scope of nationality and citizenship. Unfortunately, while feminist gender-sensitive approaches to migration now occupy a central place in the geographic study of migration, the often interrelated and overlapping queer approaches to migration continue to be underrepresented. An example is in Michael Samers's *Migration* (2010), from the Routledge Key Ideas in Geography series, a recent key textbook on migration geographies that includes extensive discussions of gender and feminist approaches but hardly a mention of sexuality and queer approaches. Similar omissions exist in a broad set of texts and conference sessions on migration that reveal a critical integration of feminism but not of queer theory.

In this chapter, I argue for a queer intervention on migration studies that critically expands geographic approaches to migration by denaturalizing and complicating approaches to understanding family, nation and nostalgia within the diaspora and by bringing a sensitive, nuanced attention to space and place that non-geographic queer migration and diaspora approaches need. In addition to asserting the vital contributions that queer approaches make to explaining the geographies of migration, I will argue for the usefulness of such approaches in my own ongoing research on debates concerning Iranian and queer Muslim diasporic communities. Ultimately, I see queer approaches to migration politics and diaspora as having significant creative, critical and positive potential in understanding how migrants placed in impossible situations seek to improve their lives.

Sexuality, Migration and Geography

For most of its twentieth-century history, the study of migration has concerned the experiences of men, foregrounded by the notion that most migrants were males travelling for work opportunities or to flee persecution, often without reference to gender. Increasingly, though, especially from the 1980s onwards, feminist scholars began to focus on the complex and differentiated challenges that women face as mothers, labourers and asylum-seekers (see Manalansan, 2006; and Chavez, 2013 for reviews). These studies indicated the need for migration research to become much more sensitive to the situated and differentiated ways in which migrants adapt and survive. Chavez explains, however, that as this feminist body of research grew, 'it became increasingly clear that with rare exception, even within feminist scholarship, women were assumed to be biologically female and all migrants were assumed to be heterosexual' (Chavez, 2013, p. 10). As a result, starting in the late 1990s, a number of scholars such as Eithne Luibhéid, Martin Manalansan, Adi Kuntsman and Lionel Cantu began to examine the ways in which sexuality structures all aspects of migrant life, from the construction of diasporic identities to the ways in which sexuality, like race, gender and other identity aspects, structures national migration policies and procedures.

Similarly, within geography, research on sexuality and migration has built upon advances made by feminist geographers. Rachel Silvey (2004) shows how feminist geographers have brought politicized understandings of mobility, complex questions of subjectivity and identity, and critical theorizations of space and place to the study of migration geographies, and calls for the incorporation of approaches to sex and sexuality that can more fully examine how heteronormativity organizes migration patterns and processes. The geographic research on sexuality and migration, building upon these ideas, has led to at least three important contributions to the study of migration. First, it has argued that the globalizing intersections of love, sexuality and migration impact on practices of movement and settlement in profound ways, urging migration scholars to stop ignoring emotion and sexuality in their research (Mai and King, 2009). Along these lines, Andrew Gorman-Murray (2009a) brings together new work on mobilities and research on emotional embodiment to examine feelings of displacement and re-placement among sexual-minority Australian migrants, ultimately encouraging geographers and others to take emotion seriously in mobilities studies. Second, some scholars have approached the home outside a linear narrative of 'homecoming' and instead have delved into the multiple negotiations with the past and future that queer migrants face within home spaces. In particular, Anne-Marie Fortier's important 2001 work removes a fixed connection among family, comfort and home, thus building upon feminist geographers' criticism of home as refuge, and reveals the complications of home as a fleeting space of disorientation in its connections to migration origins and destinations. As such, these scholars suggest that any simple migration narrative based around nostalgia for the homeland or permanence in the destination home needs to be questioned and probed. And, third, sexuality and migration scholarship has complicated rural/urban coming-out narratives in ways that impact on any preconceived ideas about particular kinds of origins and destinations, no matter what the migrant's sexual orientation may be (Weston, 1995; Brown, 2000; Waitt and Gorman-Murray, 2011b). Nathaniel Lewis (2014a), for example, argues that depending on gay migrants' life-course circumstances and given the changing, uneven landscape of protections for sexual minorities, migration decisions need to be understood in a highly variegated, differentiated way. This insight suggests the need for migration scholars to critically consider changes in the political and economic landscape of opportunities for migrants, as well as life-course needs, in understanding migration processes.

This body of research has brought a sexuality focus to migration studies in geography by revealing the ways in which sexuality and emotion matter to migration research and to the lives of migrants in profound ways. While this research has engaged with queer theory to an extent, there is much room for queer theory to more deeply and critically inspire migration research in geography, in ways that more overtly politicize migration processes and that breathe critical, creative and constructive life into geographic migration research at large. I will argue that a deeper engagement with queer theory helps us advocate for the improvement of migrants' life conditions in the present and the future.

Queering Migration: Terms, Intersections, Methodology

To begin, it is important to clarify what I mean by 'queer' in the context of this chapter. I follow the lead of Samuel Chambers and Nicholas De Genova in criticizing the extent to which 'queer' has become a catch-all inclusive term to refer to all who are now or will someday be non-heterosexual and instead reaffirm the idea of queer politics as a commitment to the impossibility of inclusivity (Chambers, 2009; De Genova, 2010). Queerness, in this sense, refers to all that is opposed to what is considered normal, legitimate and dominant, describing an anti-normative, anti-hierarchical positionality whose extent and possibility cannot be predetermined. This means that, while in much migration literature queerness has become synonymous with research on sexual minorities, it needs to be understood as not limited to sexual orientation, but as having much larger and potentially powerful applications.

De Genova (2010) articulates such an evocation of queerness in his essay on the affinity between the open-ended politics of migrant presence during the 2006 migrant mobilizations in the USA and the similarly destabilizing politics of queer presence. He draws a dynamic comparison, for example, between the chants of 'Here we are, we're not leaving' and 'and if they throw us out, we'll come right back' (in Spanish) with the slogan, 'We're here, we're queer, get used to it!', arguing that they share an 'irreducible spirit of irreverence and dissatisfaction for state power' and 'the intractable challenge of their own intrinsic incorrigibility'. (De Genova, 2010, p. 101) This politics of migrant labour thus became a form of queer migration politics through its defiant visibility, refusal to fit into sanctioned state discourse and denunciation of the abjection of migrants. Bringing queer theory to an examination of the 2006 demonstrations allows De Genova to understand them in a more critical and radical way as opening up the realm of political possibility and visibility. At the same time, it allows him to differentiate between such a queer stance and the compromised stance of other moments in the movement that sought to argue that immigrants are not terrorists or criminals, thus capitulating to the dominant state discursive terrain. De Genova's analysis, as such, expands the uses of queer theory in ways that can inspire any migration research that seeks to advocate for and expand the realm of anti-normative political possibility.

A queer perspective on migration, in this sense, works 'as a methodology, an oppositional mode of reading, interpretive strategy, or critical lens through which to question dominant ideologies of gender, sex, and nation' (Parker, 2011, p. 640). With possible applications to a wide array of discursive realms, this methodology provides a way of critically perceiving dominant and normative understandings, wherever they appear. Moreover, a queer methodology can help to 'foreground the resistant potential of what may initially appear as capitulations to, and collusions with, the dominant' (Gopinath, 2011, p. 636). It acts to highlight the liberating, transformative potential of the impossible spaces that immigrants occupy. Two queer perspectives that can be particularly inspirational for geographers studying migration are queer diaspora studies, influenced particularly by the work of Gayatri Gopinath, and Karma Chavez's recent work on queer migration politics. I will now examine each in depth.

Queer Diaspora Studies

The growth of queer diaspora studies over the past several years has revitalized both queer and diaspora studies. As Gayatri Gopinath posits, 'The concept of a queer diaspora enables a simultaneous critique of heterosexuality and the nation form while exploding the binary oppositions between nation and diaspora, heterosexuality and homosexuality, original and copy' (Gopinath, 2005 p. 11). Queer studies, like diaspora studies, concern disorientation, dislocation and unsettling (Ahmed, 2006). In this way, diaspora studies and queer studies have much to learn from one another when synthesized. A focus on queerness helps to dislocate diaspora studies from a simplified, nostalgic, depoliticized relationship to the family, nation and home, while a focus on diaspora helps to bring questions of race, colonization and globalization to the centre of queer studies. The combined perspective, then, serves as an interpretive framework at the intersection of the two research streams.

Of particular importance to geographers are the works of queer diaspora scholars who unsettle and disturb ideas of attachment, the so-called homing instincts or desires of migrants. Johanna Garvey, for example, uses the concept of 'queer (un)belonging' to refer to spaces of habitation that 'undo belonging while not leading to the destructive behavior of not-belonging' (Garvey, 2011, p. 757). This perspective begins with the impossibility of a queer diaspora, given that there is no such thing as a queer homeland, and instead works critically and creatively towards the building of a reimagined community. This community exists outside of a binary that would have migrants either 'belong' in a way that compromises their identities to the demands of family, nation(s), citizenship and nostalgia, or 'not belong' in a totally disempowered, dislocated way. Instead, queer (un)belonging develops as an embrace of the reality of daily migrant life that does not conform to diasporic nostalgia and, in the process, highlights how migrants can and often do shape a different relationship to time and space. (Un)belonging, then, allows for both a detachment from the confines of existing demands placed on migrants and a reattachment that contains the conditions for renewed intimacy and community on new terms. It also advocates new methods of reading and identifying people that incorporate difference into community. What a queer diaspora approach does above all else is to show the constructive potential of residing within the uncomfortable spaces that disorient normative domestic arrangements. It is, in this way, both a way of seeing and a form of advocating more meaningful, liveable conditions for migrants.

I have found this frame to be particularly useful in my ongoing research on representations of the Iranian diaspora in the West, particularly through the genre of Iranian women's exilic memoirs. In recent years, Iranian studies scholars have conceptualized the idea of an 'Iranian diaspora' in terms of a set of issues that cohere around the complex emotions of nostalgia for Iran, political engagement with both Iran and the destination country, most prominently the USA, and the liminal and syncretic practices of hybrid identity construction (see Elahi and Karim, 2011 for a review). Shakhsari, in her work on queer Iranian subjects in cyberspace, cautions us though against 'the chic of diaspora', given the extent to which diaspora studies have become a popular academic realm in sometimes uncritical ways (Shakhsari, 2012). Any evocation of diaspora, then, needs to be critically qualified within the context in which it is constructed and interpreted. Diaspora, in this sense, is just as constructed as Iranian-ness, and both require critical attention to avoid the simplifications associated with nostalgia and coherence.

The popular consumption of immigrant women's memoirs has been of particular concern and interest within this realm of diasporic Iranian studies. These memoirs include Azar Nafisi's *Reading Lolita in Tehran*, Marjane Satrapi's *Persepolis* series, Azadeh Moaveni's *Lipstick Jihad*, and Firoozeh Dumas's *Funny in Farsi*, among many others, and since the late 1990s they have become a successful genre in themselves within book publishing in North

America and Europe. Some of the main elements of the genre are the emotional recounting of the experiences of expatriation and exile, vivid accounts of the in-betweenness of spaces of immigrant life and the 'homing devices' the authors employ to develop cosmopolitan, hybridized identities and communities (Whitlock, 2008; Malek, 2006). Given the high-profile nature of these memoirs as representations of an 'Iranian diaspora', many prominent Iranian scholars within the diaspora have attacked these authors, particularly on the grounds that they misrepresent Iranian women to a global readership (see, particularly, Mottahedeh, 2004; Dabashi, 2006; Keshavarz, 2007; Akhavan et al., 2007). While some of these scholars' criticisms are valid, other scholars have responded with concern over the 'vituperative' nature of the critiques and for the fact that they seek to replace one representation of what Iranian women are like with another (Motlagh, 2011; Darznik, 2008). The result is an unproductive, divisive struggle over authenticity and authority in the diaspora. Moreover, the critics have very little to say about the actual content of the memoirs or how audiences interpret them. This is one place where the reading practices that queer diaspora scholars advocate are incredibly useful. How can the memoirs be read in an alternative way that, while critical of the disciplining and romanticizing influences of nationalism and nostalgia, works towards the building of new forms of intimacy, kinship and community?

In my analysis of one of the recent books in this memoir genre, *The Good Daughter* by Jasmin Darznik, I argue that it is possible and desirable to engage in an alternative, queer reading practice that, in the context of the Iranian diaspora, challenges concerns about authenticity in representations of Iran and Iranian-ness, and instead looks critically to the past in a way that seeks out meaningful opportunities for building relationships into the future (Darznik, 2011; Rouhani, forthcoming). Such an analysis demands a critical reassessment of the roles of nation and home, and seeks to unearth moments of uneasiness and destabilization as critical opportunities for relationship-building into the diasporic future. It is entirely possible for Darznik's book to be read, through orientalist eyes, as a vilification of the violence of Iranian men and the victimization of Iranian women, and as a linear narrative of immigrant loss, mourning, nostalgia and fulfilment. But Darznik also provides many opportunities for an alternative reading of the multiple disorientations and dislocations of immigrant life, the impossibility of return in any meaningful kind of way, and the possibility for a new kind of critical intimacy and community, as represented through the unconventional, mutually meaningful relationship that unfolds between the author and her mother in the last few chapters of the book. Although the book is not about sexual minority subjects, it is indeed queer, particularly in how it is centred on a mother–daughter relationship, not a reproductive nuclear family relationship, as the inspiration for diasporic community-building, and in its refusal to capitulate to any pre-given understandings of Iranian-ness. Through a queer diasporic lens, it is possible to reveal transformative moments that could be glossed over and the book advocates for the opening of such spaces within diasporic experiences.

Queer Migration Politics

Karma Chavez's recent work, *Queer Migration Politics: Activist Rhetoric and Coalitional Possibilities* (2013), provides another important, more overtly politicized lens from which to approach queer migration studies. She writes in the contemporary context of liberal LGBT advances being made in the USA as organizations direct their attention on issues of rights and inclusion focused on marriage and, in terms of migration politics, on partner and family immigration rights. Perceiving the limits of this movement based on its normative demands and capitulations to state power, Chavez instead focuses on instances where queer politics and migration politics meet in ways that challenge the inclusionary politics of mainstream LGBT activism and shift attention to other sites of activism, which she identifies as being as much about the present as the future. While sensitive to the futurist approaches of people like José Esteban Muñoz, who see the idea of queer futures as the primary way to approach the limits of the LGBT movement in the present, Chavez forcefully argues that such an aesthetic critique based on queer future is no substitute for addressing the activist present (Muñoz, 2009). Her approach advocates a revaluing of the queer present, grounded in even the smallest non-normative moments of community organizing in everyday life, as having much greater potential in advancing queer politics and improving people's life conditions. Instead of something to be hoped for or imagined in the future, an alternative to mainstream lesbian and gay politics is a present practice among activist groups that needs to be highlighted and supported.

Chavez defines her approach, then, as 'activism that seeks to challenge the normative, inclusionary perspectives at the intersections of queer rights and justice and immigration rights and justice' (Chavez, 2013, p. 6). Inspired by feminist scholarship undertaken by queer and women of colour, she views these politics through the lens of a 'coalitional moment', a queer space and time that enables opportunities to re-envision and reconstruct politics in the present. Her approach is particularly salient on a number of levels. It is important to note, as she does, that the queer migrant is 'an inherently coalitional subject, one whose identities and relationships to power mandate managing multiplicity' (Chavez, 2013, p. 9). This means that, because queer migrants live such complex lives in different realms, a coalitional approach is necessary to capture the complications of people's lived experiences on an existential level. Moreover, given the florescence of migration activism in the USA since 2006, a coalitional approach provides the essential means to examine how constructive relationships can be formed among the differential forms and ideologies of activism. These groups may have significant differences in political visions, but many share a common sense of resistance to hegemonic power structures through which it is possible to construct moments of affinity and solidarity. These moments, she argues, may be temporary, or they may great stretched to longer periods of time. Lastly, Chavez's understanding of queer migration politics points out the limitations of state-sanctioned solutions, as those constrained by nationality and citizenship, and instead highlights the work of activists who point to political possibilities other than those bounded by the limited imaginations of state politics.

In my own research on queer Muslim diasporic organizations, I have examined the salience of such coalitional politics, as uncertain and unpredictable as they may be at times, emphasizing the multiple forms of complicity and resistance that exist in the spaces that Muslim diasporic identities inhabit (Rouhani, 2007). Particularly because of the difficulty of discussing sexuality-based issues within the wider progressive diasporic Muslim movement, these organizations actively collaborate with those in other queer Muslim destinations, such as Canada, the UK, Australia, the USA and South Africa, as well as with mainstream liberal human rights organizations such as Amnesty, Human Rights Watch, Human Rights Campaign and the International Gay and Lesbian Human Rights Commission (Grundy and Smith, 2005). The complexities of such coalitions became dramatically evident in response to the 19 July 2005 reporting of two 'gay' teenagers being hanged in Iran, disseminated by both exiled royalist, anti-Islamic Republic of Iran organizations like the National Council of Resistance of Iran and LGBT rights organizations such as the Human Rights Campaign and Outrage!, which called for sanctions against Iran because of the news. As the accusations, accompanied by the final images of teenagers before being hanged, were disseminated through the international gay media, it became increasingly unclear whether the boys were hanged for 'being gay' or for the officially claimed charge of rape. Long shows how these

Western-based organizations misinterpreted the violations in searching for universal gay identities and instances of homophobia in ways that advanced their own liberal political causes in the West but with the result of exposing and endangering the lives of sexual minorities in Iran (Long, 2009). In response to the furore, the US-based Muslim diasporic organization Al-Fatiha released a statement arguing that the accusations by these organizations 'only fed to the growing Islamophobia and hatred toward Muslims and the Islamic world' and that organizations need to work on building stronger ties with on-the-ground activists working within countries like Iran to create new opportunities for social justice at home and asylum abroad (Alam, 2005). As a burgeoning diasporic community, queer Muslims must deal with the question of how to support sexual minorities in predominantly Muslim countries according to the ways in which those minorities want to be supported.

While focused mostly at the intersection of queer and migration politics in the USA, Chavez's work has important implications for understanding and advocating sexual and immigration rights in other contexts as well. She compellingly argues that any effective form of coalitional politics cannot be simplified in the way in which liberal, inclusionary LGBT politics often are. She writes, '[c]oalition features the messiness, the impurity, and the multiplicity of subjectivity, identity, and politics' that other approaches often ignore (Chavez, 2013, p. 147). In the context of the queer Muslim diasporic experiences and exchanges, this means recognizing the impossibility of any universal, simplified fixes, based on Western notions of gay rights and homophobia, and instead advocating approaches that take the identities and experiences of people in multiple and different situations seriously. Such a stance requires a move beyond existing national and transnational imaginaries of what is politically possible in the present. Moreover, a focus on how to improve people's lives in the present calls for the development of coalitions with other kinds of organizations – not specifically queer or LGBT-identified ones – working towards social, economic and environmental justice goals at different scales. Thus, when we are discussing victims of sexual oppression in whatever form, the focus needs to be foremost on how to improve people's living conditions – something that transnational LGBT human rights organizations often overlook because of their universalizing focus on gayness and homophobia.

Queering Migration Politics for Geographers

While the queer diaspora and queer migration politics have some differences in how they approach the politics of migration, they cohere around a set of issues that capture the central tenets of queer anarchism. These include support for autonomy and freedom, a critique of the paternalistic state and its impact on people's lives, a rejection of normative assumptions about sexuality, and a deep respect for pleasure and improving people's life conditions (Shepard, 2010b; Kissack, 2008; G. Brown, 2007b; Rouhani, 2012). Though articulated in different ways, these approaches share a critique of the ways in which migration operates through existing hierarchical arrangements that suppress human expression, and seek out ways to transform them. These approaches offer migration geographers this latter component, in particular, by channelling and supporting the multiple creative and critical ways in which migrants can engage in both a prefigurative politics of how to create new diasporic spaces, relationships and communities on their own terms and an affinity politics of how to survive through coalitions that promote activist alternatives. It is the simultaneously critical, creative and liberatory emphasis shared by these approaches from which migration geographers can significantly gain.

Although migration studies in geography have been effective in explaining the economic, political and cultural structures with which migrants must cope in order to survive, they have been much less effective in examining the ways in which migrants can and do improve their lives, and queer approaches to migration politics and diaspora studies can provide inspiration to that end. In the study of the geographies of labour migration, queer approaches can aid in expanding our existing understanding not just of labour segmentation and migrant survival tactics, but also of how it is possible to subvert and transform those existing structures of segmentation in ways that improve migrants' living and working conditions. Queering the geopolitics of migration can have significant impact on developing other more imaginative and more just systems of migration management outside the repressive transnational, national and local state scales of migration control. And, finally, queer approaches compel us to think of issues of identity and belonging beyond the strict associations with citizenship and nationality in ways that liberate migrants from exclusionary nationalist spaces. Clearly, these are grand, general suggestions that need to be thought through much more carefully, but there is so much that migration scholars can do to both draw inspiration from and give support to 'the ways in which those who occupy impossible spaces transform them into vibrant, livable spaces of possibility' (Gopinath, 2005, p. 194). That is the difference that queer approach to migration and diaspora studies can make.

Chapter 27

You've Come a Long Way, Baby: Unpacking the Metaphor of Transgender Mobility

Petra Doan

Mobility within the LGBT community has not been well studied. A number of authors have explored lesbian and gay migration as a movement from rural to urban areas (Weston, 1995), as a form of an identity quest situated in the body (Knopp, 2004; Gorman-Murray, 2007), and as a series of movements and returns (Waitt and Gorman-Murray, 2011a; Lewis, 2014a). In addition, Nash and Gorman-Murray (2014) argue that a 'new mobilities' approach provides useful new insights about the evolution of LGBT neighbourhoods in Toronto and Sydney. In particular, they suggest that insights into mobility are especially relevant for the analysis of 'LGBT urban migrations and movements since the second world war that contributed to the formation of gay villages, with their economic, political and social influences' (Nash and Gorman Murray, 2014, p. 762). Furthermore, they contend that it is important to analyse not just actual movements, but the ways in which these movements are represented and practised (Cresswell, 2010) to understand the dynamic nature of such migration. This chapter extends Nash and Gorman-Murray's analysis by examining the ways in which transgendered individuals incorporate notions of mobility into their life histories.

The writings of transgendered and transsexual individuals typically describe their gender journey as a sometimes arduous struggle to understand, embody and 'come out' to the world as the gender they know themselves to be (see, for example, Hunt, 1978; Richards and Ames, 1983; Morris, 1986; Bornstein, 1994; Prosser, 1998; McCloskey, 1999; Boylan, 2003; Rubin, 2003; Green, 2004). This voyage of discovery and self-revelation is almost always unidirectional and usually involves crossing a relatively fixed gender binary before finally emerging into new territory on the other side. This metaphorical trope is reproduced in the writings of prominent transgendered individuals and forms a kind of lens through which many trans people have come to view themselves and the gender dichotomy. This chapter also seeks to unpack this travel metaphor and deconstruct its underlying elements. Although the presence of transgendered people is difficult to measure precisely, the chapter argues that recent estimates suggest that they constitute a small but significant proportion of the population of most countries. Following this section is an examination of the ways in which this metaphor of a gender-crossing journey has been visibly displayed through influential autobiographies of transgendered writers. Finally, the chapter seeks to destabilize the underlying assumptions of the movement across the gender divide and towards wholeness and authenticity using a variety of sources, including social science commentary, the author's experience and other narrative accounts of transgender lives.

Transgender Demographics

The usual source of data for analysing the movement of a population or subgroup is the national census. In the USA over the past two decades it has become significantly easier to track the presence of gay and lesbian couples using the 2000 and 2010 Censuses and related demographic products (the American Community Survey) which track the number of same-sex-partner households. However, the transgendered population remains largely invisible because census-takers ask about sex (maleness or femaleness) but never about gender identity. Within this chapter the term 'transgender' will be used as an umbrella term inclusive of a variety of gender-identity subject positions, including cross-dressers, drag kings and queens and transsexuals, where transsexuals are defined as transgendered individuals who have used hormones and/or surgery to transition into and more fully embody their gender identity. Because the census does not ask about gender identity there are no precise measures of the size of this subpopulation. In addition, the lack of population data makes it difficult to track transgender migration patterns on a large scale.

Recent approximations by Reed et al. (2009) of the members of the transgender community who have taken steps towards transition suggest a figure of 0.1 per cent of the adult population in the UK. In New Zealand, Veale (2008) proposes a prevalence rate of 1:6364 or 0.15 per cent on the basis of applications to change the sex markers on New Zealand passports. Olyslager and Conway (2007) suggest a figure of 1 in 500 or 0.2 per cent as a low estimate for the prevalence of transgendered people. In addition, Conron et al. (2011) analysed the Massachusetts Behavioral Risk Factor Surveillance Survey from 2007 and 2009 and found that approximately 0.5 per cent of adults between 18 and 64 identified as transgender. This estimation is significant because it is based on a population-based survey that specifically asks about transgender status. Finally Gates (2011) averages previous estimates (Conron's high estimate of 0.5 per cent, Olyslager and Conroy's 0.2 per cent and Reed et al.'s estimate of 0.1 per cent) and suggests that roughly 0.3 per cent of the US population is transgendered, which in 2011 comes to 697,529 people. Using Gates's estimate, Winter and Conway (2011) suggest there might be 15,324,000 trans people worldwide (assuming 5.1 billion people aged 15+ according to US Census Bureau estimates for 2011), making the transgendered population a significant subpopulation.

The relative invisibility of this community (more than 15 million people) must also be understood within the context of urban areas. Once again using the 0.3 per cent estimate, in New York City (population of 8.3 million) there would be 25,011 trans people; in Sydney (population of 4,39 million) there would be 13,175 trans people; and in Toronto (population of 2.79 million) there would be 8,370 trans people. Understanding the migration and mobility patterns of this population is important because if trans individuals are likely to migrate to large cities, then these numbers could be substantially higher. Although the evidence suggests that transgendered people exist in every country, this research will focus on patterns in the English-speaking world where there is a relatively rich set of bibliographic resources and narratives. Certainly, patterns of mobility in more developed nations may be similar, but it is difficult to extrapolate to lower-income countries and places where cultural values and belief systems may significantly influence mobility patterns and, indeed, the existence of Global North forms of binary gender structures and divisions.

The Journey across the Gender Divide

For many transgendered people, the journey is described as a long and difficult trek to transform one's outward manifestation of gender and bring it into harmony with that which is inwardly experienced. These narrative descriptions are strongly influenced by early accounts of transsexuals whose transition earned them a degree of notoriety. Christine Jorgensen travelled from New York to Copenhagen in search of surgery with very little money and even less of an idea of what would await her, except the certainty that she needed to change. It took Jorgensen three years in Denmark to meet all the requirements for surgery, and when she returned to the USA her transformation created a media sensation. In her case and that of many subsequent transsexuals of the 1960s and 1970s who experienced public notoriety, an overseas journey was necessary because surgeons in the USA were reluctant to commit 'mayhem' by removing or altering otherwise healthy organs (Meyerowitz, 2002). As a result, those with the resources and the need to transform were forced to travel to Europe (Denmark, Belgium), North Africa (Morocco), South-east Asia (Thailand) or, more recently, Canada.

The idea of the gender journey was further cemented by a well-publicized series of transsexual autobiographies that often used metaphorical language to describe the stages of the voyage. Jan Morris (1986) presents her transition as a mystical quest in search of the Holy Grail of her true self. Nancy Hunt (1978) weaves the metaphor of the mirror into telling the story of her gender odyssey to finally become the woman she sees reflected back at her. Sometimes the actual travel to these gender reassignment clinics involved an exhausting voyage overseas. For example, Renee Richards describes the stormy ocean passage aboard the *Michelangelo*, the ship she calls her 'transitional vehicle' that carried her across the Atlantic to the next stage of her life journey (cited in Prosser, 1998, p. 124). Richards's trip was complicated after she was victimized by some local hoodlums in a port in Spain. When she fought back, she was arrested by the local authorities for spying (presumably because she was presenting as a woman, but her passport identified her as a man). It was only after the US consulate intervened to free Richards from jail that she was able to continue her journey to Casablanca.

As the number of people seeking gender reassignment surgery began to rise with the publicity given to transsexuals like Christine Jorgensen, Jan Morris and Renee Richards, the medical community developed a set of 'movement guidelines' that added another level of mobility to the transgender journey. During the 1960s and 1970s doctors routinely told their patients never to reveal their transsexual status, adding that it would be better to change jobs and leave town so that no one would know their prior gender identity. This heteronormative attempt to defuse publicity effectively made a willingness to be mobile a requirement for approval of sexual reassignment surgery. Prominent medical professionals such as Dr Harry Benjamin 'urged post-operative patients to hide, and even to lie about their past lives as the other sex' (Meyerowitz, 2002, p. 166). Kate Bornstein recounts that 'I was told by several counselors that I would have to invent a past for myself as a little girl, that I would have to make up incidents in my girl childhood, that I would have to say things like, "when I was a little girl …". I was told don't *tell* anyone you are transsexual' (Bornstein, 1994, p. 62). Another researcher reports that many of her interviewees were told 'to make a complete break with their pasts and to basically keep their gender transition a secret, even from their intimate partners' (Rudacille, 2005, p. 60). The implicit assumption behind this advice to hide or to move away was that 'normal' people would be unable to accept a known transsexual living in their midst or would be deeply disturbed to be confronted with someone who had publicly transitioned. Mobility in terms of leaving town was seen as essential in preserving heteronormative tranquillity. During this period lesbian and gay mobility often took the form of migration to find a community in which one could discover a gay or lesbian identity, but this form of transgender mobility involved, first, a journey to have surgery and then a second journey to disappear and hide one's newly visible gender from neighbours and acquaintances.

More recent accounts of the journey tell of a process that involves coming to terms with one's whole self and the physicality of one's body that echoes Knopp's (2004) and Gorman-Murray's (2007) understanding of migration that is deeply connected to the scale of the body. Some of these transgender life journeys are consciously framed in terms of the poignancy of the diaspora in a gender crossing that brings great joy combined with a sense of loss for those left behind. These accounts of bodily gender crossings mirror the ambivalence of queer diaspora in Manalansan (2000), Fortier (2001) and Eng et al. (2005).

Many female-to-male transsexuals begin 'a transsexual trajectory by looking for explanations for their feelings of discomfort with their bodies' (Rubin, 2003, p. 178). For example, Jamison Green writes that:

> ... *becoming a visible man has enabled me to find my emotional center and get in touch with my physical body ... for some observers, our journey seems a step outside the boundaries of society; for us, once we have arrived at our balance point – no matter what that looks like to others – we can recognize our humanity and understand our connections with other people. (Green, 2004, p. 216)*

Jennie Boylan adds a rich texture to this diasporic metaphor. She is deeply moved when her Irish friends sing ballads of the Irish emigration to the USA that resonate with her mixed feelings of joy and sadness resulting from by her gender journey:

> *Surely they had me in mind when they sang about leaving the land of their birth because of the Great Hunger. Standing on the deck of a coffin ship, waving farewell to one's sweetheart. Making a difficult ocean crossing. Arriving at last in a new world, the land of promise, the land of freedom. But never quite fitting in, in the new land, always speaking with the trace of a foreign accent. Sometimes I think the best way to understand gender shift is to sing a song of diaspora. (Boylan, 2003, p. 113)*

Movement to Find Support

Given the omnipresent heteronormative gaze, gender survival for transsexuals often requires physical movements to evade the tyranny of gender (Doan, 2010), to avoid unwanted scrutiny and to seek safe havens for gender explorations. Movement as survival strategy cannot be overstated. Transgendered people move away from intolerant locations that are invested in an impermeable gender binary and seek out spaces that permit more active exploration of non-traditional genders. In some cases, just being in a place of relative anonymity can enable individuals to experiment with gender performances that would be too risky closer to home.

Beemyn and Rankin (2011) suggest that it is very common for trans people to travel to support groups and conferences. Prior to her transition Deirdre McCloskey was a well-known professor of economic history at the University of Iowa. In her autobiography she describes her process of coming out not so much as emerging from a closet, but rather as 'lighting candles in a dark cave' (McClosky, 1999, p. 10). McCloskey's position and visibility as a professor made it uncomfortable to explore her emerging gender where she lived. As a result, she used a business trip to Pennsylvania as the occasion for a side visit to Lee's Mardi Gras boutique in Manhattan (ibid., p. 24) to purchase women's clothing for her subsequent trip to Chicago to attend her first-ever support group.

My own experience of attending a transgender support group in Charlotte, North Carolina, for the first time suggests that the difficulty of moving is not always linked to the distance travelled. After travelling three hours by car to attend this meeting, I booked a room in the Red Roof Inn and began my preparations to appear as the woman I knew myself to be. When I had dressed and completed my make-up, I wasn't sure that I had the courage to open the door of my motel room and present myself to the world as a woman. It was only a walk of perhaps 10 feet down the exterior corridor to the room next door where others were gathering, but my fear was palpable and almost overwhelming due to a fierce internal struggle to overcome years of embodied social prohibitions about male-bodied individuals *not* wearing women's clothes under any circumstances. It took the gentle encouragement of a more experienced trans woman to cajole and enable my first public mobilization (about five steps). But once those baby steps had been taken, I felt like a new world had opened. We went to eat at a gay-owned restaurant and later went to a gay bar where we were greeted with an amused tolerance. A subsequent support group outing to Atlanta (an eight-hour drive) brought me to my first live drag show in the wonderful queer world of Midtown, Atlanta. This trip was my first exposure to the apparent safety that a mostly queer neighbourhood provided for transgender experimentation, although it was a lukewarm welcome at best. In each of these excursions the physical distance I travelled was nothing compared to the social distance I had overcome by presenting as a woman in public.

The other major type of physical movement for gender-exploring travellers is attendance at a transgender conference. These occasions include both national events (Fantasia Fair, Southern Comfort, Trans Health Conference, Espirit and the Texas 'T' Party) as well as local and regional gatherings combining an array of educational workshops on gender identity, transition tips and political activism as well as the opportunity to express one's 'true self' in public for an extended time period. Leslie Feinberg recognized the emotional impact of a Texas 'T' Party conference for approximately 350 heterosexual male cross-dressers by observing that:

> ... when this event ends, tears will stream down the cheeks of many of these men. A few will sob because they are going home to a wrenching divorce ... Others will weep because these are the only days out of their entire lives that they could be themselves – and the event is over. (Feinberg, 1998, p. 17)

People are willing to travel considerable distances to attend such conferences. Participants at the Southern Comfort Conference in 2000 were surveyed and asked how far they had travelled to attend the conference. The travel patterns of the 97 respondents (out of a total of more than 600 attendees) are instructive (see Table 27.1), indicating that most of those answering the survey came from the state of Georgia or other nearby states in the south-east. A few people crossed the country to attend, and there were several international attendees. These movements represent a kind of episodic mobility from home to the conference, a return home and on to the next conference in a spiralling journey that is different from the linear 'get thee to a big city' of some gay men and lesbians (Weston, 1995). These movements are a variation of Knopp's (2004) gay identity quest, because for many of these middle-aged trans storytellers, the complex decision to cross the gender divide feels more terrifying than the decision to migrate to a metropolis. The result is a kind of iterative dancing back and forth across the gender divide to build up one's courage to make the final decision to cross over completely.

241

Many of these gatherings take place at a large convention-style hotel in a metropolitan area (Fantasia Fair in Provincetown and Espirit in Port Angeles are two clear exceptions of conferences held in smaller tourist-oriented communities). Attendance requires the payment of a substantial registration fee (often several hundred dollars), lodging at the conference hotel or a nearby substitute and a variety of meals at local restaurants. These costs are sometimes reduced for volunteers and low-income individuals, but the fact remains that they are very expensive outings. The survey from the 2000 Southern Comfort Conference underlines this reality since all the participants had at least middle-level incomes. In addition, the conference was not racially diverse with white attendees far outnumbering all other races and ethnicities.

Table 27.1   **Travel to Southern Comfort Conference in 2000**

South		57
	Georgia	15
	Alabama	8
	Florida	12
	South Carolina	2
	North Carolina	14
	Other	6
North-east		21
Mid-west		9
West		7
International		3

Source: Survey by the author.

Unpacking the Linearity of the Journey

For some people within the transgender community the gender traverse is not unidirectional and can have an episodic character found in migration patterns frequently observed by demographers. The following life narratives are drawn from individuals that I have met in various LGBT groups that illustrate different patterns of movement used to weave a more complex gender pattern. For example, some transgendered individuals' quest to express their gender identity openly involves a life-changing gender transition, then perhaps a change back to the previous gender and sometimes even yet another change, illustrating a kind of embodied circular migration. The journeys of other trans people illustrate a seasonal or episodic style of movement. Finally, other journeys seem more like a reverse commuter flow.

'Kathy' epitomizes this kind of cyclical migration. It took literally years of struggle for her to come to terms with her identity as a male-to-female transgendered person. She had married as a man and fathered two children, but ultimately came out as transgendered and began living as the woman she knew herself to be. When her gender crossing precipitated a strong reaction from her spouse (fleeing with their two children to a distant country), she fell

242

into a deep depression that ultimately led her to sublimate her identity as Kathy and return to presenting in her previous gender as 'Ken'. Ken then gave up his job, sold all his worldly possessions and moved halfway across the world so that he could be closer to his children.

Other people within the transgender community need to 'try out' a different gender presentation for a period of time (a mini Real Life Test) because their fear of making a mistake compels a seasonal migration across the gender divide, with a distinct beginning and end. 'Sally' moved away from her usual residence to a town 500 miles away from home for a six-month consulting job. Because she was married to an unsupportive partner, she was unable to remain in role for any length of time at home, but on her consulting trip she was able to work from her temporary home as Sally. In her new city she also attended the local transgender support group and went to dinner at local restaurants as herself, although she needed to wear heavy make-up to conceal her male beard and two pairs of hose to cover her hairy legs. Her fear of discovery back home prevented her from undertaking electrolysis or even shaving her legs. At the end of her six-month 'season in the sun' Sally migrated back to the reality of her life as a man, or at least a closeted cross-dresser.

'Martha' provides a fascinating example of reverse commuting. Martha also lived for many years as a man, was married and fathered a daughter, but in her 50s she came to terms with her gender identity as a transsexual woman. Her struggles to maintain her family stability led her to quit her government job in favour of work in the service industry where she was able to display an increasingly feminine persona during working hours. For a number of years this employment shift enabled her to work as a woman and return each evening to her home as the 'man' that her wife expected to see. Because her wife was aware of, but not pleased with, Martha's persona at work, this strategy of reverse commuting enabled their marriage to survive for another 10 years. Eventually, the marriage ended, and Martha began living full-time in her preferred gender, ending her long reverse commute across the gender divide. She now lives as the woman she knows herself to be and is a recognized transgender leader in the local LGBT community.

Each of these examples illustrates the complex texture of transgender mobility. Because the journey across the gender divide appears almost impossible to many trans people, mobility enables the discovery of places for role exploration. This movement involves a steady reinvention of self that evokes not placelessness (Knopp, 2004) but an increasing spiral trajectory, centred around the home (Waitt and Gorman-Murray, 2011a). Rather than following the earlier medical advice to leave home towns after surgery, today trans people like Martha have not left town, although, in her case, a period of mobility was required to enable her to transform.

Challenging the Notions of a Binary Gender

Many transgendered people experience the border between genders not as an impermeable barrier, but as a porous and at times indistinct division. Some transgendered individuals swing back and forth across this supposedly fixed divide with great regularity. Although some critics have argued that the early transsexual crossings of the gender binary often reinforced traditional gender roles, repeated movements that traverse a supposedly rigid demarcation slowly wear away the dichotomous logic that sustains it. While cross-dressers as well as drag kings and queens are included under the umbrella of transgender, their regular switching back and forth sometimes causes transsexuals to view them as less serious. However, the repeated act of changing back and forth can also undermine the stability of the gender binary.

Movement across genders requires considerable bodily preparation, including the mastery of gestures, gaits and postures that epitomizes mobility as 'the experienced and embodied practice of movement' (Cresswell, 2010, p. 19). The gender shift permits a highly ritualized process that enables cross-dressers to make a quick change from male to female or vice versa for public or private performance across the gender divide. The transition ritual often involves the application of make-up and costuming for drag queens, or false beards, a binder and a package for drag kings. These small physical additions enable these gender performers to express a gender different from their birth gender. Some of these individuals do such a convincing job that it is only at the end of the stage performance that the traditional doffing of the wig or removal of the false beard reveals their original gender. Other cross-dressers eschew the public performance aspects but may also follow a cosmetic and costuming routine that enables them to privately perform a different gender.

Other transgendered individuals come to reject the notion of gender having a fixed divide and argue that it is a flexible continuum. Kate Bornstein (1994, pp. 51–2) describes gender performance as 'the ability to freely and knowingly become one or any of a limitless number of genders, for any length of time, at any rate of change'. This kind of radical gender fluidity ultimately destabilizes the idea of a gender divide and confounds the gender journey metaphor. Elsewhere, I (Doan, 2010) also emphasize the embodied nature gender such that each performance of gender not only shifts in response to the physical space in which it occurs, but its very expression also changes that space in profound ways. In this way, the journey continues, both as an inward realignment and as an act of transforming the spaces through which transgendered people travel.

The potentially transformative nature of this travel is reflected in Leslie Feinberg's emphasis on the intertwining of transgender liberation with other social and economic justice movements. The question Feinberg asks repeatedly is to what extent does movement across the gender binary also challenge the fundamental nature of that dichotomy? Does all the travelling done by transgendered people – both the physical moves and the performative shifts – coalesce into a social movement that contributes to wider social change? Feinberg notes 'the growth of these movements [union organizing, tenants' rights, and civil rights] helped the Stonewall Rebellion and gay liberation to emerge. Each movement that challenged oppression made more room for another' (Feinberg, 1998, p. 122).

Intersectional Limits on Movement

In order to expand the movement to transgender liberation, it is critical to recognize that the length, degree of difficulty and sheer expense of physical travel may constrain movements for many transgendered people. Moreover, not all urban areas welcome gender differences (Doan, 2007), especially if gender non-conformity is combined with other marginalizing characteristics. A variety of social and economic barriers can have a profound impact on motility, the ability to be mobile in social and geographic space (Kaufman et al., 2004). This lack of access to the means of travel can have an adverse impact on some transgendered people, who may experience mobility quite differently from that described in the relatively privileged autobiographies and anecdotes related above. Certainly, travelling long distances to support groups, shopping for gender-appropriate clothing on business trips and participating in large gender conventions is likely to be out of reach for many transgendered individuals whose intersectional identities may include racial and class differences, as well as age and ability. Gary Bowen, a trans man of Apache and Scotch–Irish heritage, describes the challenges that he faced as 'a journey not only of self-discovery, but of discovery about my family and my culture. Coming out transgendered was easy: grappling with racism, classism, and ableism and other barriers is much harder' (profile in Feinberg, 1998, p. 63).

If travel to another city for a support group is too expensive, movement across the city to a gay neighbourhood may be an attractive alternative. However, sometimes these places have their own expectations of what kinds of people are welcome to move through the area. If you are a person of colour, you may not be welcome, and if you are a trans person of colour, you are even less welcome, and may need to be removed from the area. My research (Doan, 2014) conducted in the Midtown area of Atlanta highlights this lack of welcome because the Midtown Ponce Security Association (MPSA) regularly tracks and photographs gender-non-conforming trans people of colour who visit the area because they are assumed to be engaging in sex work on the fringes of the traditional Midtown gay village. This same kind of harassment appears fairly widespread with similar incidents reported in other predominantly gay neighbourhoods in Toronto (Baute, 2008) and San Francisco (Weinberg et al., 1999; Edelman, 2011).

Such misguided efforts to control sex work can often create zones of immobility for transgendered people, such as in New York City where 'members of the Latina transgender community in Queens experienced being stopped and searched by the police on suspicion of prostitution while walking in their own neighborhoods' (Human Rights Watch, 2012b, p. 4). Similarly, in Los Angeles a Williams Institute Policy Brief recounts that 60 per cent of 220 Latina male-to-female transgendered interviewees reported 'that they had been doing everyday things before being stopped, like "waiting for the bus", "coming back from the grocery store", "walking home" and "shopping"'(Galvan and Bazargan, 2012, p. 7). Clearly, this kind of profiling of transgendered individuals of colour can have a profound impact on their ability to move through an urban area without being hassled, let alone live their lives as the genders they know themselves to be.

Unfortunately, these same social barriers can cause young queer individuals who are actively questioning their sex assigned at birth to feel that there are no options for them except to work as a drag queen or engage in sex work. For instance, Sylvia Rivera, one of the drag queens involved in the Stonewall Rebellion, describes her own coming-out process as an inevitable journey:

> In Spanish cultures, if you are effeminate, you're automatically a fag; you're a gay boy. I mean you start off as a young child and you don't have an option – especially back then – you were either a fag or a dyke. There was no in-between. You have your journey through society the way it is structured ... I was an effeminate gay boy. I was becoming a beautiful drag queen. (Rivera, 2002, p. 69)

Lessons from Transgender Mobility

The stories of transgendered people provide a set of useful insights for geographic theories of mobility. For most trans individuals, mobility involves elements of both physical movements to access a range of support services (information collection at conferences, therapy and perhaps surgery) as well as the internalized bodily mobility needed to 'cross' the gender divide. Autobiographical perspectives illustrate a variety of ways in which this mobility enables and empowers both the spatial journey and the embodied journey of transformation. This queer identity quest is similar to, but has a different pace and rhythm from, the gay and lesbian identity quests frequently cited in the mobility literature (Weston, 1995; Knopp 2004; Gorman-Murray, 2007; Lewis, 2014a).

Gorman-Murray and Nash (2014) have argued that the homophobic violence that occurs in the area of Sydney's Oxford Street may inhibit mobility for some queer-identified individuals. They suggest that the less overtly gay, but still gay-friendly neighbourhood of Newtown may be a safer place for visibly queer people to practise mobility. While this is certainly possible, it remains to be seen whether such mixed places will be the kind of enabling and empowering places needed by many transgendered and transsexual people in their search for information about transition, safe places in which to 'come out' and locations that will enable their long-term quest for wholeness and authenticity. Sometimes, the violence experienced by transgendered people is actually perpetrated by gay residents of gay and possibly gay-friendly neighbourhoods, who equate gender experimentation with prostitution (Doan, 2014). It is vitally important to recognize the ways in which intersectionality can create significant barriers for some transgendered people struggling to discover and embark on their own journeys. It is critical for scholars to recognize the diversity of trans individuals and the kinds of mobility needed to explore their diverse gender identities. Further research is needed on how to protect this most vulnerable segment of the LGBTQ community – the canaries in the coal mine (Doan, 2001).

Chapter 28

LGBT Communities, Identities and the Politics of Mobility: Moving from Visibility to Recognition in Contemporary Urban Landscapes

Andrew Gorman-Murray and Catherine J. Nash

Beyond the Village

Gay villages materialize residential, commercial and organizational concentrations of LGBT – mostly gay male – communities. They manifest *some*, not all, forms of gay social, political and economic life, but have nonetheless become markers of gay visibility and associated identity politics in the post-Second World War era, given that they are integral in the downtown fabric of many cities of the Global North, garnering mainstream attention and participation (Florida, 2002; Collins, 2004a). Over the last decade LGBT and mainstream media, politicians and communities have voiced concern over the 'de-gaying' of some such villages (M. Brown, 2013). Transformations in urban sexual geographies in the Global North include mainstream incorporation of particular gay and lesbian subjects and households, and the coalescence of alternative neighbourhoods and locations mooring and supporting gay, lesbian, bisexual, trans (LGBT) and queer lives (Collins, 2004a; Ruting, 2008). Sexual and gender identity politics are also entwined with a politics of mobility, which has both physical and social dimensions (Nash and Gorman-Murray, 2014). This entails material, representational and behavioural transformations in mobile lives, interwoven with shifting identities, politics and practices.

This chapter therefore deploys ideas of mobility, visibility and recognition to consider how new social and political contexts are experienced and materialized in neighbourhoods *beyond* gay villages. The discussion is largely conceptual, but is grounded in and reflects observations from our current research into changes in LGBT geographies in Sydney, Australia, and Toronto, Canada. We begin with a brief discussion of the changing sexual and gendered landscapes in Toronto and Sydney, including concerns about the future of each city's gay village. We then suggest that as well as the political, social and economic processes at work in these changes, we might also be seeing a shift from a politics of *visibility* to a politics of *recognition* framed within newly emergent social and political mobilities. By a politics of visibility, we mean a politics grounded in an 'out' and 'public' visibility as gay or lesbian. With the term 'recognition' we want to signal a shift to a presence regarded as 'difference' but one that refuses a static (or primary) positioning within LGBT identity politics. We conclude with some final thoughts on what this might suggest about shifting identities, subjectivities and urban landscapes.

The 'Classic' Gay Village

Levine's (1979, p. 364) classic definition of a gay village remains apt for Sydney, Toronto and other cities in the Global North: 'an urban neighborhood [that] contains gay institutions in number, a conspicuous and locally dominant gay subculture that is socially isolated from the larger community, and a residential population that is substantially gay'. This residential, organizational and commercial concentration is enclave-like, and research has described the constitution of villages as territorialization by, primarily, gay men during the post-Second World War era (see Castells, 1983; Lauria and Knopp, 1985; Nast, 2002; Nash, 2006). This commodification and commercialization of gay village life was not necessarily straightforward. For example, in both Toronto and Sydney tensions flared between gay activists and gay business-owners during the 1970s and 1980s. Gay activists regarded villages as sites of regressive self-segregation, with communities exploited by business-owners who profited from the needs and desires of a marginalized group (Nash, 2006; Willett, 2000). Yet, over time, a narrative of the village as the site of consolidated social, political and economic gay territory came to dominate (Elder, 2002; Nast, 2002; Wotherspoon, 1991).

Both Sydney and Toronto have well-known gay villages – Oxford Street, Sydney, and Church-Wellesley Village, Toronto – which observers have suggested are 'de-gaying' (Gorman-Murray and Waitt, 2009; Nash, 2013a, 2013b; Nash and Gorman-Murray, 2014; Reynolds, 2009; Ruting, 2008). At the same time, the last decade has seen the development of alternative 'queer' neighbourhoods in these cities (Gorman-Murray and Waitt, 2009; Nash, 2013a, 2013b). Sydney's Oxford Street is adjacent to the Central Business District, with a nightlife strip of bars, clubs and sex shops, and a concentration of gay venues, community and health services and residents in surrounding suburbs, which coalesced in the 1970s. Oxford Street is associated with gay men, but as the site of the Sydney Gay and Lesbian Mardi Gras it also has significance for a broad LGBT constituency. But since the early 2000s LGBT communities and media have decried Oxford Street's de-gaying, and noted the consolidation of another commercial, residential and service concentration focused on King Street, Newtown, encompassing adjacent suburbs. The congregation of LGBT residents, visitors and organizations in Newtown and the surrounding Inner West (as the area is known locally) suburbs is increasingly palpable in many Sydneysiders' mental maps (as evident in mainstream media commentary and local government planning); indeed, it is now sufficiently embedded for Newtown to be labelled by some as a 'hub' for 'new queer Sydney' (Gorman-Murray, 2006b; Gorman-Murray and Waitt, 2009). In terms of sexual and gender identities, Newtown is more 'mixed' than Oxford Street, with facilities for lesbians and trans folk. Oxford Street has a sex imbalance (59 per cent male to 41 per cent female) while Newtown has a 50:50 residential sex ratio and is seen as inclusive of LGBT groupings.

Toronto's gay village is located downtown, around the intersection of Church and Wellesley Streets. While boundaries are nebulous, the commercial 'strip' is seen to run along Church Street, with a residential population in the surrounding high-rise condominiums and low-rise properties. Gay concentrations originated in the 1960s, and a village materialized in the late 1970s–early 1980s. Church-Wellesley Village remains central to LGBT life as the location of political and social organizations and hub for government-funded social and health services. Yet, in the 2000s concerns surfaced in mainstream and LGBT media about its purported decline (recently contested, too), while a queer presence is increasingly apparent in other downtown neighbourhoods, notably in bars, clubs, cafes, restaurants and dance parties in Parkdale and Leslieville. Several of these Toronto neighbourhoods are also being represented as queer, including the area dubbed 'Queer West' (Parkdale, Queen West and Brockton Village) and Leslieville in the city's east (Nash, 2013a, 2013b).

Gay Villages, Queer Neighbourhoods and the Politics of Mobility

Since the early 2000s long-standing gay villages have been perceived as 'receding in size, scope and function' (M. Brown, 2014, p. 457), including San Francisco's Castro, New York's Greenwich Village, London's Soho, Toronto's Church-Wellesley Village and Sydney's Oxford Street. Some work suggests that, with new legal, social and political gains, sexual and gender minorities are more easily able to be visible as queer in neighbourhoods beyond gay villages (Gorman-Murray and Waitt, 2009; Nash, 2013a, 2013b). Some work suggests that conventional, stable identities such as 'gay' and 'lesbian' are yielding to 'post-gay' and 'queer' sensibilities, with these subjects eschewing the seeming fixity of the historical identities traditionally supported by gay villages (G. Brown, 2006; Nash, 2013a, 2013b). Entwined in this process, new 'alternative' neighbourhoods, distinct from gay villages, are materializing, as we described above with respect to Sydney and Toronto. Researchers have begun to document the development of some neighbourhoods, including Newtown, Sydney (Gorman-Murray and Waitt, 2009), Parkdale, Toronto (Nash, 2013b), Shoreditch and Vauxhall, London (Andersson, 2009, 2011), and Berkeley, Oakland/San Francisco (Compton and Baumle, 2012). We term these 'queer neighbourhoods' not just to distinguish them from gay villages, but because these alternative sites are perceived and experienced as enabling a more expansive range of sexual and gender subjects than gay villages, including differences in terms of gender identity, race, ethnicity and class (Andersson, 2009; Gorman-Murray and Waitt, 2009; Compton and Baumle, 2012).

While these emerging queer locations and neighbourhoods are discrete from gay villages, these sites are relational and well connected through flows of people, ideas, materials and politics. They are linked, compared and contrasted in urban imaginaries (Gorman-Murray, 2006b; Andersson, 2009); people travel between and visit venues across them (Nash, 2013a, 2013b); organizations and services stretch across the sites (Gorman-Murray and Nash, 2014). One way to conceptualize this relational geography is through a mobilities approach, which recognizes that people, ideas and things are in movement, and places are coalesced and moored through the intersections of flows and networks that maintain connections between places (Massey, 1994). Mobilities and moorings are not in untrammelled flow but always contextualized and operable in social power relations. Cresswell's notion of the politics of mobility clarifies this:

> *By politics I mean social relations that involve the production and distribution of power. By a politics of mobility I mean the ways in which mobilities are both productive of such social relations and produced by them. Social relations are of course complicated and diverse. They include relations between classes, genders, ethnicities, nationalities, and religious groups as well as a host of other forms of group identity. Mobility, as with other geographical phenomena, lies at the heart of all of these.* (Cresswell, 2010, p. 21)

Mobility has historical and geographical specificity and is constituted through power relations between social categories – including power relations constraining and impelling sexual and gender minorities. Thinking about the development and appeal of queer neighbourhoods in terms of the politics of mobility, we suggest that these mobile practices and imaginaries are entangled with shifting identity politics – the politics of visibility and of recognition.

Mobilizing Transformation: Moving from Visibility to Recognition

Here, we want to explore how new forms of mobilities, which are potentially reworking the sexual and gendered relational geographies in places such as Toronto and Sydney, are intertwined within a shift from a politics of visibility to one of recognition. Let's start with this comment from a resident of a queer neighbourhood in Sydney:

> *I do not believe that Newtown is a 'gay ghetto'. Granted, it is one of the few places where I can walk hand in hand with my (male) partner and feel relatively safe. However, there is a wide diversity of people here, and the LGBT community is only a part of it. (Harris, 2005)*

This quote is from the *Star Observer*, Sydney's longest-running LGBT newspaper; it is from a Letter to the Editor written by a gay man from Newtown. Using an example of everyday mobility – for example, walking down the street hand-in-hand with his partner – he begins to hint at nuanced differences in same-sex visibility between Newtown and Oxford Street. He can be visible and safe as a gay man on King Street, Newtown, but he intimates that more fine-grained recognition is at work too, whereby the LGBT community is only part of a broader Inner West constituency. LGBT people are visible, acknowledged and accepted, and arguably as 'more than' LGBT people, too.

We suggest that the mobile geographies of changing LGBT urban spaces are informed by, and inform, a partial shift from a politics of *visibility* to a politics of *recognition*. This is enacted in how subjects differently inhabit these neighbourhoods – intimated in the above quote. Let's start with a politics of visibility: historically, this identity politics foregrounds and reifies a specific, usually singular, category of social identity, such as ethnicity, race, gender or sexuality, which is also historically and geographically specific. This politics makes this categorical identity 'visible' by centring it in political claims and making it the basis of identity-formation and community-building. To buttress a presence in the political sphere and advance rights claims, this form of identity politics also stresses visibility and the right to space in the public sphere. Such identitarian and spatial manoeuvres originated in rights movements and associated political changes in the 1960s and 1970s, based on gender (women's rights), race (black rights) or ethnicity (multiculturalism), which was also true for some sexual and gender minorities in terms of 'gay liberation' movements.

These political rights imperatives rendered homosexuality a categorical identity, 'fixing' social identities such as 'gay' and 'lesbian'. For some, especially some gay men, identitarian claims were buttressed through territorialization of certain inner-city neighbourhoods (Knopp, 1998), which gathered pace in the 1970s and 1980s to materialize as gay villages, including Oxford Street and Church-Wellesley Village. While acknowledging constituents' tensions concerning economic and political motives (noted above), alignment of visibility, territory and identity was realized in these spaces. For instance, the refrain of late 1970s gay rights protests in Oxford Street was 'Out of the bars, into the streets!', in which claims to gay identity and rights were manifested in the public visibility and occupation of gay men (and some lesbians), equally bounding Oxford Street as 'gay territory'. Similarly, the 1982 Toronto bathhouse raids brought patrons of village bars and restaurants into the streets in protest, shouting 'Fuck you, 52!' in reference to 'Division 52', the police division responsible for the area where Church-Wellesley Village was located. Gay villages provided secure public access that facilitated a congregation of like others, group identity and political enfranchisement. Certain mobilities were part of this and reinforced a politics of visibility. First, making territory meant gravitational migration *to* the neighbourhood to constitute a visible place-based community; second, this 'safe' territory enabled everyday neighbourhood mobilities *in situ*, fostering public encounters on which individual and group identity, sociality and community could be formed (Nash and Gorman-Murray, 2014).

Alignment of visibility, identity and territory is also evoked, unsurprisingly, in fears of contemporary de-gaying of villages like Oxford Street (Rosser et al., 2008). Loss of territory is decried because of its impact on visibility for sexual and gender minorities, and is linked to place-based political and economic security, particularly for gay men. Yet, we have noted that in Sydney and Toronto it is also evident that some sexual and gender minorities are rejecting this place-based identity politics and eschewing its 'territory' – that is, the gay village. In seeking and enacting other modes of identification and sociality, they are surfacing and 'being recognized' elsewhere in the city, in queer neighbourhoods and other inner-city locales (Gorman-Murray and Waitt, 2009; Nash, 2013b). This 'new' mobility signifies a shifting identity politics - one not founded on a politics of visibility and that might be characterized as a politics of recognition.

Recognition, Legitimacy and Queer Neighbourhoods

A considerable literature, particularly feminist-based work, has discussed (and critiqued) the emergence of a politics of recognition – a politics grounded in the distinctiveness of a particular identity and one claiming recognition for cultural and social difference (see Duggan, 2003; Fraser, 2007; Hines, 2013; McQueen, 2014; Young 1990). For present purposes, we take a slightly different approach, drawing on Noble's (2009) discussion of the politics of recognition and how this both advances, but differs from, the politics of visibility. While acknowledging visibility of sexual and gender identities, a politics of recognition accedes to the complexity and contingency of subjectivity and departs from narrow gay or lesbian identities. Noble (2009, p. 877) contends that while 'sexed or gendered understanding of who we are has profound consequences for the ways we act and are treated … those categories by no means exhaust what we can be said to have or be'. This means acknowledging, first, the multiplicity and intersectionality of diverse categorical identities – that sexual and gender minorities also bear race, ethnicity, class, disability, religion, and so on – which fractures a rigid 'gay' identity or community. Moreover, intersections are situated achievements whereby various social identities borne by individuals are more or less salient in diverse ways in different settings. This also connects with the sociological concept of the agentic 'reflexive self', in which self-understanding is mutable and knowingly reframed across time and place.

But recognition is not only about identities – it is also about situated practices:

> … *much more is at stake in such processes of recognition than what we recognise as the key categories of social identity – class, gender, ethnicity and so on. In any given milieu, participants want to be considered to have a legitimate presence, and so may be more likely to see themselves in terms of the standards of competence within that setting – indeed, they may not even see themselves, at that moment, in terms of categories of identity such as ethnicity or gender. (Noble, 2009, pp. 887–8)*

And thus:

> *... recognition involves complex questions of visibility and legitimacy, but ... it also entails processes that have a temporality and spatiality, because 'social competence' is always something that relates to situated actions. (Noble, 2009, p. 884)*

Competence does 'not just mean whether we are good at something' but whether 'we are seen to be legitimate participants in a specific situation or event' and is thus 'a fundamental aspect of processes of recognition' (ibid., p. 882). The politics of recognition is thus about legibility as a competent, legitimate, fully human actor in public space.

Applying Noble's arguments to LGBT lives, we suggest that a politics of recognition involves:

1. Recognition *as* a LGBT person: the sexuality and gender of individuals must still be acknowledged, or we risk neoliberal mainstreaming or closeting of sexual and gender diversity;
2. Recognition of *intersecting* categorical identities and their effects: class, race, ethnicity, religion and so on are equally salient for LGBT individuals;
3. Recognition of *competence* that exceeds categories: social identities are critical in how people are treated, but other capacities, skills and attributes inform legibility and legitimacy in public settings.

We propose that this politics of recognition has a historical and geographical specificity, arising, as it does now, as a possibility that can emerge beyond the visibility politics of gay village spaces. Lesbians and gay men in Toronto and Sydney have benefited from and gained greater acceptance over the last 20 years or so because of human rights protections and incorporation in national institutions such as family, marriage and the military. As we have argued elsewhere, these legal, social and political changes have opened up the possibilities for greater mobilities across and through inner-city landscapes in both cities (Nash and Gorman-Murray, 2014; Gorman Murray and Nash, 2014). In Sydney and Toronto, it is apparent in the press, social media and conversation that some LGBT people are rejecting an identity politics based on definitional categories and same-sex 'difference', and eschewing spaces associated with such identities, such as the gay village (Nash, 2013a, 2013b). We are suggesting that these new mobilities for some sexual and gender minorities in these cities are generating a new politics of recognition reflected in desires *and capacities* to mobilize in alternative spaces, like Newtown, Parkdale or Leslieville.

There is more work to be done in considering the nature of the relational geographies emerging whereby queer people move across interlinked and related places, including traditional gay villages, and are thereby (re)constituting urban sexual and gendered landscapes. We can characterize these places as more or less queer because LGBT people are *still* acknowledged as such (in affirmative, not derogatory, ways), but are also recognized in terms beyond their sexuality and gender, as composites of social categories and personal attributes, and as legitimate sexual citizens in local settings.

Moving in a Queer Place

A politics of recognition enfolds LGBT identities and intersectional subjectivities with bodily practices and intersubjective relations that underpin 'belonging' in public milieus. Recognition is about acknowledging the composite corporeal categories and capacities that make a LGBT person a competent actor in queer neighbourhoods. This is spatially and temporally contingent on, and enacted in, everyday mobilities and motilities – that is, the sociospatial practices of everyday life that are rendered possible through how we are seen and understood. Contemporary transformations in urban sexual geographies present opportunities for recognition embedded within new formulations of mobilities that presume alternative presences in physical and symbolic landscapes. As we move and act as embodied sexual and gender subjects – and, more than that, within and across the local spaces of queer neighbourhoods like Newtown and Parkdale, inhabiting and mobilizing streetscapes, shops, cafes, pubs, restaurants and houses – social encounters foster 'an awareness of the multifarious dimensions of human experience which make us "fully" human (or deny us this), the forms of connection which make us possible to exist in and move across complex societies (or restrict such movement)' (Noble, 2009, p. 888).

SECTION V
Sexual Health

Andrew Tucker (editor)

Chapter 29

Sexual Health: Section Introduction

Andrew Tucker

Geographical work on the study of sexuality has a long and, at times, complicated relationship to the study of health. Sometimes tangentially and at other times directly, studies with a focus on sexuality within geography have engaged with a variety of health concerns including: mental health (Lewis, 2009); disability (Butler, 1999; Sothern, 2007a; Del Casino, 2007a); migration and its relationships to masculinity and heterosexuality (Elder, 2003; Hunter, 2010a, 2010b); public-health practices and policy (Craddock, 2000; Kesby and Sothern, 2014; MacDonnell and Andrews, 2006), sex work, both contemporary (Hubbard and Prior, 2013; Katsulis, 2009) and in historical settings (Legg, 2014; Howell, 2009); and drug use (Del Casino, 2007b, 2012).

And yet, despite these studies, it is also clear that the relationship within geography between sexualities and health has at times proved to be a rather contentious one. This might seem an unusual situation, considering what would appear to be potentially very important collaborations between studies focused on health and studies focused on sexuality. Nevertheless, this introduction will begin by laying out how exactly these two subdisciplines have sometimes been at odds with each other. It will show that the differing foci of each have sometimes made it difficult for synthesis. It will then go on, by way of introduction to the chapters in this section of the *Companion*, to examine how there may be important ways in which a renewed focus on health as it relates to HIV/AIDS (and other sexually transmitted infections, or STIs) can help highlight how sexuality and health remain directly linked, both in practice and in future research agendas. This is not to suggest that a focus on HIV/AIDS and other STIs is synonymous with all studies that straddle health and sexuality concerns, either within geography or further afield. It is, however, to suggest that HIV/AIDS remains an important lens through which we can appreciate the centrality and tremendous importance of the link between health, sexuality and geography.

Medical Geography and Geographies of Health

When approaching health within the study of geography, it is important to begin by looking at the development of one of the oldest forms of geographical research. Medical geography has been around for a long time. The often cited example of Hippocrates,[1] who lived in the fourth and fifth centuries BC in Greece, was widely considered not only to be the 'father of modern medicine' (Grammaticos and Diamantis, 2008), but also a medical geographer.

---

1   From where we get the modern Hippocratic Oath which medical students, upon completion of their studies, are invited to swear upon.

For Hippocrates there was a desire to understand disease via the close observation and examination of the local environment (Valenčius, 2001). This core belief, through various guises, has remained central to many medical geography studies. For example, the famous case of John Snow in mid-nineteenth-century London shows us how the careful mapping of cholera deaths highlighted how these deaths took place in households that took their water from particular pumps. These pumps were contaminated and so shut down; lives were saved. More recently, too, a variety of studies have explored core issues such as disease ecology and diffusion as well as healthcare access, provision and planning (see Rosenberg, 1998). Such research has been ably assisted by the development of geographical information systems (GIS) (Sui, 2007). However, as various scholars in the 1990s and 2000s highlighted, such studies have very much tended to be quantitative in nature and positivist in their epistemology. In other words, as Gatrell and Elliot explain, there can be a reliance on a particular type of scientific study, closely linked to that deployed with the natural sciences, whereby variation in health outcomes is measured and mapped spatially:

> *In a health context, such approaches seek to uncover causes or "aetiological" factors, though usually the best that can be established is a strong association rather than a "cause". A classically positivist account would have, as its end goal, a search for laws, though weaker versions strive simply to make generalisations. (Gatrell and Elliot, 2015, p. 30)*

This approach therefore, while still viewed as significant in particular contexts – indeed, epidemiologists outside of geography have in part remained very firmly committed to it – has also been critiqued for being overtly focused on *space* rather than *place*. Mirroring elements of key debates within wider geography as to the importance of place vis-à-vis space (Agnew, 2011; Massey, 1994), this argument suggests that a focus on concerns such as diffusion of disease through spatial areas can mean that the study of the actual people involved in the transmission of pathogens become sidelined. Further, factors associated with, for example, differential risk, including representations, lived realities and outcomes of subjectivities such as race, gender and indeed sexuality, also can be inadvertently overlooked (Wilton, 1996). As Robin Kearns in his seminal piece in *The Professional Geographer* in 1993 stated, 'We might ask why medical geography has maintained a detached perspective in analyzing the links between health and place, especially given that the centrality of place as a geographical concern has returned to favor' (Kearns, 1993, p. 140). As a result, an important development occurred within geographical research in the 1990s – a move from medical geography to health geography. While, as some have argued, this shift is not a clear-cut one (Dorn et al., 2010), it does signal an emergent and very important new direction for geographers interested in cultural and social geographies of health, often tied to experiences of place and embodiment (Kearns and Collins, 2010). As Del Casino (2007a) and Parr (2002) highlight, research has therefore covered a very wide range of topics, including the study of therapeutic landscapes (Gesler, 1992) and lively discussions regarding the centrality (or not) of bodies themselves as sites of inquiry, not least as a material entity in addition to a form of representation (Hall, 2000; Sothern and Dyck, 2010; Moss and Dyck, 2002 – see also, below).

Sexuality in Relation to Health

Such concerns and critiques of medical geography also have strong echoes within work more firmly located within the geographies of sexualities literatures. Indeed, Del Casino

(2007a) can be seen to draw his critique of medical geography (and also later some elements of health geography) through an engagement with both gender and sexuality. While others in this *Companion* (for example, see Chapter 1) have explained in detail some of the roots of inquiry which have resulted in the current landscape of studies focused on sexuality and geography, this brief Section Introduction highlights how such studies have emerged in tandem with epistemic critiques of medical knowledge.

Since the 1980s geographers engaged in the study of sexualities have been particularly interested in exploring and destabilizing taken-for-granted categories and hegemonic renderings of power. This work has been especially concerned with understanding and explaining the lives of individuals with same-sex desire in ways that show us both the reasons for particular forms of classification, regulation (and potentially discrimination) and strategies to confront these various forms of subjectification (Tucker, 2009a). This process has been immeasurably enriched since the 1990s by a focused engagement with various forms of *queer theory*. In direct contrast to some of the earlier forms of medical geography, queer theory (and associated poststructuralist approaches to power and the creation and regulation of knowledge) has attempted to question and problematize taken-for-granted stable categories – in particular, those focused around sex, gender, desire, identity and practice (Browne et al., 2007). As Binnie (1997, 2007) has pointed out, the creation of geographical knowledge itself can be seen as a process that can exclude sexual dissidents. A need therefore emerged to reconsider how categories themselves come to be and what power they hold over different groups.

This interest in interrogating the link between knowledge and power is not a new one, especially when looking at medical concerns and the work of the French philosopher Michel Foucault. While his earlier work on madness (Foucault, 1967) is also important for scholars to consider in this regard (see especially Kearns (2007) for a careful consideration of this work in relation to medical geography), it is Foucault's later work on sexuality (1978, 1985, 1986) which is of particular importance here. For Foucault, sexuality is something that is produced historically in the nineteenth century. It is not primordial and it does not exist outside of the social world. For example, when describing the creation of 'the homosexual' as a category of scientific analysis in the nineteenth century – 'the homosexual is now a species' (Foucault, 1978, p. 43) – Foucault wishes us to consider how this was part of a new specification of individuals in Europe, whereby new methods of sexual control became possible (Howell, 2007). This is not to suggest that earlier forms of consideration, such as 'sodomy', were not also defined by various European laws (Halperin, 2002). It is, however, to appreciate that the focus on 'the homosexual' was 'a ruse to power, no longer simply prohibiting behavior but now also controlling, regulating and normalizing embodied subjects' (Halperin, 2002, p. 31). This in turn allows us to appreciate how the very categories we use to describe particular groups or individuals – their identities – have a history and a geography and hence are not fixed. We can thus see here a direct link between the medicalization of a particular bodies and the emergence of identities. Foucault's key move here, for this discussion, was the way in which the development of particular medical knowledge went hand in hand with the development of particular (sexual) subjects brought into being in part by that knowledge.

In a similar fashion also, scholars such as Judith Butler (1990, 1993) have then gone on to argue that discourses are maintained through performance. For Butler, when discussing gender, *performativity* leads to the conclusion that the very idea of an individual's coherent gender identity is nothing more than the result of repetitive acts undertaken to create the impression of a stable and coherent identity. Butler then, in a startling conceptual move, tracks this view on to the very concept of sex itself. While some have argued that sex is the biological underpinning to the socially defined category of gender, Butler suggests something more radical – namely that sex is not a precursor to gender at all. Rather, the very idea of sex is as culturally constructed as gender. What we consider to mean by 'sex' is actually dependent on what we mean by 'gender'. If sex is not a precursor to gender, and if sexual identities such as 'the homosexual' are discursively created, then it becomes possible for scholars to begin to consider radically other ways in which we may want to understand the relationship between medicine/health studies and categories such as 'male', 'female', 'intersex', 'straight', 'bisexual' or 'gay'.

This is something that geographers such as Del Casino (2007a), Philo (2000, 2005) and Sothern (2006, 2007b) amongst others (see below) have called for in various ways. We should interrogate the relationship between research on health and research on sexuality. Put simply, we should move beyond assuming, unproblematically, that identity categories are the starting-point for the analysis of health concerns. We should also explore how particular spaces and places (including the body) actually become medicalized in the first place. This can be viewed as a profoundly democratic process, stepping outside the boundaries deployed by medical workers (and especially epidemiologists) to consider what assumptions are made that allow for those categories to be used in the first place – and how the very process of 'doing' medically focused work can help create the very (often sexualized) categories used for analysis.

Such an approach has been taken up in various quarters by geographers, not least in relation to HIV/AIDS. As mentioned at the start of this introduction, there now exists a very important body of work by geographers that has interrogated the relationships between medical research and sexuality in relation to communicable diseases such as HIV/AIDS. This is not to assume that the study of such diseases is synonymous with all health work undertaken by geographers focused on sexuality. It is, however, important to realize that over 30 years after the first reports of a new disease among gay men in San Francisco and New York, we are still coming to terms with a global pandemic which, as some have argued, has led to a remedicalization of sexuality (Parker et al., 2000). HIV/AIDS can therefore be viewed both as a biological epidemic and, as Paula Treichler (1999) has argued, an epidemic of signification. Geographical work on sexuality has therefore attempted to understand the pandemic and critique some of the ways in which knowledge about it has been created.

Michael Brown (1995b) offered a very powerful exploration and critique of the way in which gay male bodies were rendered by epidemiologists working on HIV/AIDS. Brown here forcefully pointed out that a focus on the spatiality and diffusion of AIDS during the early years of the epidemic in North America rendered the gay male body as solely a vector of transmission. Gerry Kearns (see Chapter 30) takes this idea further. By exploring in depth the historical development of scientific knowledge regarding HIV/AIDS in the 1980s in the USA, Kearns is able to excavate the way in which scientific method (despite its alleged 'objectivity' through positivism) can remain mired in stereotyping and homophobic discrimination about the very individuals it was attempting to understand. He therefore highlights a pressing need to 'queer' epidemiological thinking, to build perception of HIV vulnerability that is truly understanding of sexual diversity. As Del Casino (2006) has also described, such concerns have not been limited to North America (see also Sothern, 2007b; Myers, 2010). In Thailand a powerful and narrowly defined linkage between HIV, homosexuality, urbanization and Western bodies served to reduce the possibility of a solidarity with the wider population in the 1980s (see also Farmer, 1992; Lyttleton, 2000; Kesby and Sothern, 2014). Equally, in a South African context, Stephen Taylor (see Chapter 31) points out how, especially today, medical knowledge is implicated in the regulation of sexual minority groups away from Global North metropolitan centres of privilege. In his critique of scientific method, Taylor describes the possible damage that can be done to men who take part in drug trials for new HIV medications. Drawing on Foucault, Taylor highlights how, through a range of disciplinary technologies, '[m]en who have sex with men' (MSM) have their lifestyles reconfigured so as to create 'docile bodies' subjected to biomedical authority. Similarly, Michael Brown and Larry Knopp (2014) have highlighted the contradictory ways that gay men's health could become regulated through the urban public-health system in a pre-AIDS era (see also Philo, 2000; Foucault, 1973).

Such work and this discussion, however, should not be seen in any way to diminish the crucially important work geographers have undertaken on communicable diseases such as HIV/AIDS with more traditional medical geography techniques. Indeed, quantitative research has examined the linkages between health and the neoliberal hollowing out of inner cities, drawing connections with the material harm that can occur to groups who are left marginalized. Wallace et al. (1999) used such techniques to describe the reasons for the devastating impact of AIDS on the poorest in society in New York (see also Smallman-Raynor et al., 1992; Gould, 1993). Some of this work has also focused on migration and the potential vulnerabilities faced by LGBT groups when they move regionally or internationally. Yet here, too, it is worth discussing the continuing importance of considering the need to interrogate the categories that are deployed. Nathaniel Lewis (see Chapter 32) elucidates the messy connections, identities and power inequalities that can beset especially gay men when they migrate. This work examines how the interaction between place, mobility and changing identities might mediate the causes of HIV infection (see also Craddock, 2000).

Running through much of this work by geographers has also been an overt concern with the political. Geographers focused on sexuality have clearly at times directly engaged with political concerns [see Section II, 'Sexual Politics']. In other instances, access to health has also been framed, by geographers and activists, as an overt and critical political endeavour (M. Brown, 1997a, 2007; Geltmaker, 1992; Kramer, 1989; Shilts, 1987; Kayal, 1993). Tucker (see Chapter 33) goes on to argue that we may want to consider how sexual rights-based activists across sub-Saharan Africa can position their call for human rights and 'gay rights' in relation to health rights. This may help reduce the risk of human rights for sexual minorities becoming bracketed off from the needs of wider populations through erroneous ideas that sexual minorities are alien to the needs of the postcolonial nation-state.

Clearly, this short introduction cannot explore all approaches to the study of health and sexuality undertaken by geographers. And its attention to the links between the work of scholars such as Foucault and geographies of sexuality is not the only history to tell. Equally, however, there remain areas that require future attention by scholars. Most clearly, the majority of research within geography has focused on the health and well-being of gay men. Relatively limited work has taken place from within geography on the health needs of lesbian, bisexual, transgender and intersex groups. Although there does exist a growing wealth of material from within the geographies of sexualities literatures on these groups that have at times touched upon health concerns (see, for example, Valentine, 2000; Hemmings, 2002; Hodge, 2000), a specific focus on the health and well-being of these groups from within geography is still relatively nascent (see, however, important work by Browne and Lim, 2010; Johnson and Browne, 2012; Formby, 2011; Sothern and Dyck, 2010). In a similar light, the possibilities, as outlined by Del Casino (2007a) of queering heteronormative ideas of sexuality and reproduction, through, for example, in vitro fertilization, could also be expanded upon. Further exploration and consideration as to how normative ideas of the family, reproduction and health can be queered is indeed needed. In terms of HIV/AIDS, there is also a need to consider how other groups, beyond gay men or 'MSM', are affected and harmed by the virus. Risk in terms of HIV is often framed in terms of biological risk. Social risk, however, for other groups still requires examination. Recent horrifying reports of the rape of lesbians in parts of sub-Saharan Africa clearly highlights how these women are placed at far higher risk of HIV infection (see Chapter 9 by Lim and Fanghanel for a discussion of the politics of tackling gender-based violence) Work needs to be done to uncover how social inequalities and intersectional anxieties associated with gender, sexuality, race and postcolonial nationalism interact to harm other sexual minority groups. Here, work could also consider how the framing of such attacks can also lead to damaging renderings of individuals. The term 'corrective rape', common in reports of lesbian rape, could be viewed as suggesting the need for some form of 'correction' towards a 'norm'. Left to fully consider is how such extreme violence is not a form of 'correction', but a form of 'punishment' by men who attack that which does not fall into the narrow and misogynistic patriarchy that exists in particular places. Beyond HIV/AIDS also, there is a need to consider further how subgroups within the category of LGBTI experience differential access to healthcare, especially away from the Global North. As epidemiologists begin to explore the health needs of populations such as 'young men who have sex with men' (YMSM), for example, geographers focused on sexuality could also ask how age is associated with vulnerability (not just for YMSM but also for YWSW) across the life course and is dependent on individuals' engagement with particular sexualized and health-oriented spaces.

Chapter 30

Queering Epidemiology

Gerry Kearns

Shame and Stereotypes

Ecofeminism (Silvey, 1998) and queer ecology (Gandy, 2012) highlight relations among gender, sexuality and nature. The agenda of 'queering ecology … opening up … environmental understanding to explicitly non-heterosexual forms of relationship, experience, and imagination as a way of transforming entrenched sexual and natural practices towards … queer … ends' (Mortimer-Sandilands and Erickson, 2010, p. 30), resonates within medical geography and epidemiology. This chapter shows how we might track the effects of entrenched homophobia within the geographical framing of disease by examining one important set of epidemiological writings: those in which AIDS was first registered as a new mortality. I show how homophobic stereotypes shaped scientific writings, and how, in related but different ways, they pervaded the public geographies of AIDS circulating in the mass media. Finally, I will show how activists tried to undo the murderous homophobia of AIDS discourses, building understandings of HIV vulnerability that were accepting of sexual diversity, and effectively queering epidemiology.

Homi Bhabha (1983, p. 18) has highlighted the ambivalence of stereotypes, 'a vacillation between what is always "in place", already known, and something that must be anxiously repeated'. With repetition, the stereotype is confirmed but is never challenged by evidence. Repeatedly, the stereotype gives the unexamined Self the pleasure of feeling superior to the derided Other. The Self obsesses about the Other and yet avoids confronting its own place in a world that includes the subjugation of this Other. This separation has its problems. First, the Self is all too likely to project on to the Other repressed aspects of the Self which conjure the stereotype as a fantasy object (Stallybrass and White, 1986). Alongside the pleasures of superiority and innocence the Self is also able to enjoy disavowed elements of itself by dwelling on the Other's exemplary depravity, but this relish activates the guilty secret of identification. Second, it is terribly difficult for the Self to find in the Other no spark of humanity at all. The stereotype, then, is 'an "impossible" object' (Bhabha, 1983, p. 33). Herein lies the violent energy of abjection, 'the powers of horror' (Kristeva, 1980) that attend any threat to the distinction between Self and Other.

I want to propose that epidemiology makes stereotypes in precisely these ways – through repetition, projection and abjection. Epidemiology is a particularly suggestive vehicle for stereotyping (Craddock, 2000; Sothern, 2007b) because of the ways in which the Other is produced out of the Self's horror and disgust of its own corporeality. Nussbaum (2004, p. 74) has suggested that 'disgust embodies a shrinking from contamination that is associated with the human desire to be nonanimal, it is frequently hooked up with various forms of shady social practice, in which the discomfort people feel over the fact of having an animal body is projected outwards onto vulnerable people and groups'. Disgust, then, 'is typically unreasonable, embodying magical ideas of contamination, and impossible aspirations to purity, immortality, and nonanimality' (Nussbaum, 2004, p. 14). These 'magical' ideas of contamination invite epidemiology as both metaphor and justification. In this way, geography and sociology are collapsed, since the risk is at once both a contagion and a pariah. These discourses of disease are among the most resonant of public geographies, but there have been few studies of their role in reproducing heteronormativity (M. Brown, 1995b; Hubbard, 2000).

The Self's horror of its animality and mortality is paradoxically frequently also expressed as an insistence that the Self, and not the Other, is properly natural (Romanillos, 2011; Barnett, 2012). The harmony between Nature and Self is asserted most strongly with respect to sex for, as Gaard (1997, p. 118) has observed, there is in Western culture, 'a fear of the erotic so strong that only one form of sexuality is overtly allowed'. Among the disallowed sexualities, '[i]n Euroamerican-dominant contexts, two kinds of sex have been (are) said to be toxic to nature: reproductive sex between non-white people, and sex between men' (Gosine, 2010, p. 149). Both sorts of sex were implicated in the epidemiological understanding of AIDS, but it was sex between men that first drew the attention of epidemiologists. The early epidemiological findings about AIDS were understood on the basis of homophobic assumptions, seemingly regardless of contradictions and conflicting results. In epidemiological terms, it seemed that the crucial question was whether AIDS was caused by some distinctive element of a gay lifestyle or, rather, by an infectious agent. Yet, in epidemiological writings, both hypotheses rested on assumptions and invited attitudes that accentuated homophobic prejudice. Public reporting about AIDS rested on multiple iterations of these prejudices in different fora, giving shame and stereotypes many opportunities to adjust the aim of AIDS science back towards its 'homosexual' target. In this it was so successful that AIDS became, for the general public, a marker of homosexual identity, 'outing' as gay those who were infected. I conclude by describing how this dismal science was challenged and devalued by queer activists, queering epidemiology themselves.

Homosexual Diseases?

Pneumocystis carinii pneumonia (PCP) is caused by a protozoa-like organism that is a common infection. It rarely causes sickness unless a person's immune system is seriously compromised. On 5 June 1981 the Centers for Disease Control (CDC) in Atlanta, Georgia, published a communication in their *Morbidity and Mortality Weekly Report*, '*Pneumocystis* Pneumonia – Los Angeles'. The note began: 'In the period October 1980–May 1981, 5 young men, all active homosexuals, were treated for biopsy-confirmed *Pneumocystis carinii* pneumonia' (CDC 1981a). The homosexualization of the disease was evident with this very first sentence, yet the phrase 'active homosexual' is not explicated. Later in the short piece we find that '[t]he 5 did not have comparable histories of sexually transmitted disease', and that only '[t]wo of the 5 reported having frequent homosexual contacts with various partners'. The editorial comment appended to the piece drew a preliminary conclusion: 'The fact that these patients were all homosexuals suggests an association between some aspect of a homosexual lifestyle or disease acquired through sexual contact and *Pneumocystis* pneumonia in this population.' Note that two alternative causes are sketched: lifestyle factors or a sexually transmitted infection (STI). Pariah and contagion were immediately evoked.

In the *Los Angeles Times*, Wayne Shandera, a CDC epidemiologist, explained that '[t]he best we can say is that somehow the pneumonia appears to be related to gay life style' (Nelson, 1981a). Officially, then, the CDC was entertaining both an STI and a lifestyle explanation, but in speculating to a journalist in Los Angeles, this official tilted towards a lifestyle explanation. Crucial in this respect was researchers' puzzlement over the fact that 'there have been no reported cases of this type of pneumonia among gay women or heterosexuals of either sex' (Nelson, 1981a). This article also reported that, in addition to the cases in Los Angeles, there were also '[a]nother half dozen cases … under investigation in San Francisco, along with an undetermined number in New York, Toronto and Florida (Nelson, 1981a). The cases in New York were not written up in the CDC report because an article was in preparation for a medical journal and thus the findings were embargoed (Shilts, 1987, p. 67).

In May, before any CDC report, a gay newspaper, the *New York Native*, had reported on a strange disease among gay men in Manhattan. Seeking confirmation from the New York City Department of Health, Lawrence Mass was told that 'the rumors are for the most part unfounded' (Mass, 1981). 'For the most part', is a strange way to deny a rumour, but the phrasing was perhaps motivated by a wish not to alarm gay men. Shilts learned that, as submitted, the first CDC article on PCP in Los Angeles had borne the title, '*Pneumocystis* Pneumonia in Homosexual Men – Los Angeles', but the CDC was a beleaguered institution in Reagan's America (Harden and Rodrigues 1993) and had no wish to advertise its connection with gay issues. It was also reluctant to fuel prejudice against gay men, especially as gay men had been the main clinical volunteers in the CDC programme to develop a vaccine for hepatitis B. Shilts suggested that, in dropping the reference to 'homosexual men' from the title of the article and placing the article on page two rather than as the cover story, the CDC was animated by twin desires: 'Don't offend the gays and don't inflame the homophobes' (Shilts, 1987, p. 69). Without speculating too far about the motives of the epidemiologists and journalists, it is clear that the 'homosexual' label was handled as a matter more of public relations than of clinical precision. It was the pervasive homophobia that made this seem necessary.

When the research from New York was published in the summer of 1981, it extended the picture of 'exotic' disease in significant ways. The article was about Kaposi's sarcoma (KS), a slow cancer among elderly men, but now manifesting as an aggressive, widely distributed and fatal condition among some young gay men. The authors proposed infection as an explanation: 'This sudden, very high incidence of the condition in male homosexuals suggests an epidemic and raises the possibility of an infectious cause, especially because homosexuals are now known to have high incidence of many infectious diseases, e.g. venereal diseases and viral hepatitis' (G. Gottlieb et al., 1981, p. 111). The known cases of PCP and KS were brought together in a further report from the CDC, this time on the front page of their *Morbidity and Mortality Weekly Report* and referring explicitly to 'homosexual men' in its title (CDC, 1981b). This focus was modified a little in the editorial note appended to the article: 'Although it is not certain that the increase in KS and PC pneumonia is restricted to homosexual men, the vast majority of recent cases have been reported from this group' (CDC, 1981b, p. 307). There was no mention of the infectious agent hypothesis in this summary article, and, in its first report on these new 'homosexual' diseases, the *New York Times* went so far as to assert that 'there is as yet no evidence of contagion' (Altman, 1981). James Curran, head of the Venereal Diseases unit at the CDC and chair of its new Kaposi's Sarcoma and Opportunistic Infections Task Force (KSOI), assured the *Times* that 'there was no apparent danger to nonhomosexuals from contagion. "The best evidence against contagion", he said, "is that no cases have been reported to date outside the homosexual community or in women"' (Altman, 1981).

In its own report, then, the CDC treated the concentration of cases among homosexuals as evidence in favour of an infectious agent, whereas in its comments to the newspaper the same evidence was offered as evidence against contagion. A contagious disease is one that is relatively easily transmitted between persons, so that both statements could be true: the disease is caused by an infectious agent but is not contagious. Nevertheless, the choice of the first statement for the technical epidemiological report and the second for the newspaper is a matter of public relations rather than public health. The second inconsistency is between, on one side, both the reporting only of cases among 'homosexual men' in the CDC article together with the statement to the *Times* that there were 'no cases' outside this group, and, on the other, the editorial note that claimed merely that the 'vast majority' of recent cases of PCP and KS had been among homosexual men. The latter was more accurate because, even at this early stage, the CDC knew of cases that did not fit the homosexual pattern.

The Sickness that is Homosexual Difference

The 'homosexualization' of the disease was relentless and, although (as shown below) it could be served by both the infectious agent hypothesis and the lifestyle hypothesis, the latter carried moral opprobrium more easily while reassuring straight people that they had no cause for anxiety. In its own article on the CDC report, the *Los Angeles Times* admitted that '[r]esearchers are still unable to explain why male homosexuals appear to be especially vulnerable' to PCP and KS, but it added that 'Friedman-Kien [of the New York University Medical Center had] said ... that all of the victims have been exceptionally promiscuous' (Nelson, 1981b). Friedman-Kien himself told the *New York Times* that 'most cases had involved homosexual men who have had multiple and frequent sexual encounters with different partners, as many as 10 sexual encounters each night up to four times a week' (Altman, 1981). Again, 'most' and 'up to' hinted at a diversity that ill served the lifestyle hypothesis.

In contrast, the infectious agent argument did not need to (although it could) pathologize gay sexuality. With a new STI, the majority of the early cases would very likely be among people with the most exposure – people having unprotected sex with many partners, who in turn themselves have unprotected sex with many partners. This is a matter of probability rather than morality. Even among the first five cases of PCP, recall that only two of them self-reported as 'having frequent homosexual contacts with various partners' (CDC, 1981a). Another of the early cases was a 37-year-old man with KS, 'currently in a stable homosexual relationship' and with 'no past history' of STIs (Bokovic and Schwartz, 1981, p. 902). When the author of the very first CDC report, Michael Gottlieb, wrote up the clinical features and blood-work results for four cases of PCP for the *New England Journal of Medicine*, he reported significant diversity within the group: 'Patient 3 was highly sexually active and frequented homosexual bars and bathhouses. Patient 1 had lived with one partner for seven years, and Patients 2 and 4 had regular partners' (M. Gottlieb et al., 1981, p. 1429). Even if one would expect to find 'promiscuous' people among the early cases, one would also expect that focus to fade as an STI became more widely dispersed. Yet the pathologization of gay sexuality led people to project AIDS as a disease of and for the 'promiscuous' gay male, offering false security to all other sexually active people, gay or straight.

Within six months of the first reports there was already significant evidence that this new condition of immune failure was not only associated with gay men. As early as July 1981, one month after its first report, the CDC was investigating cases of PCP among injecting drug-users and, while some researchers assumed that those men must have been lying about not having sex with other men, the field researcher, Mary Guinan, who had conducted the interviews found them credible (Shilts, 1987, p. 83). In December 1981 one study from New York City described 11 men with PCP, of whom seven were injecting drug-users and six were homosexuals, including two reporting themselves as homosexuals who injected drugs (Masur et al., 1981). The profile of the epidemic provided by the CDC in January 1982 likewise noted that of 158 cases of KS, PCP or other serious opportunistic infections with no known cause for immune suppression, 12 were among men understood to be exclusively heterosexual (CDC, 1982a, p. 251). Yet the early researchers continued to try to understand the condition as a manifestation of something specific to gay men; the gay lifestyle hypothesis required nothing less. In 1982 there were reports of '[g]ay-related immunodeficiency' (GRID) (M. Gottlieb et al., 1982; Horowitz et al., 1982). A communication of September 1982 to the *British Medical Journal*, referred to 'gay compromise syndrome' (Oswald et al., 1982) as had a letter published in December 1981 (Brennan and Durack, 1981).

If the condition was not exclusive to gay men, then, forlorn must be the effort to isolate a specific element of gay behaviour as its essential cause. Yet, the search for a gay cause of AIDS continued long after the diversity of the condition was known. Even the earliest letter in the *British Medical Journal* to refer to a 'gay compromise syndrome', had noted in its first paragraph that of the first 108 cases of KS and PCP that were reported, only '94% of the patients were homosexual or bisexual' (Brennan and Durack, 1981, p. 1338). Even as the terminology of the disease evolved, this tension persisted between a gay disease and its non-gay sufferers. Shilts suggested that some epidemiologists thought they might avoid stigmatizing gay people if they referred instead to 'community acquired deficiency syndrome': 'The "community" … was a polite way of saying gay' (Shilts, 1987, p. 138). For example, Arthur Levine reported in June 1982 on the first 300 cases in the USA, of which 242 were identified as gay or bisexual men, ignoring the other 58 to insist that 'the syndrome is occurring mainly in a particular subset of the homosexual male population' and that 'this is the first documented epidemic of community-acquired immune dysfunction' (Levine, 1982, p. 1392).

By focusing only on the gay cases, the question could be posed: what is it about gay men that makes them sick? If the whole population of sufferers was comprehended, the question became: what vulnerability did this group of gay men have in common with this other group of people who are not gay men? But the second was far less efficient as a vehicle for stigma. This representation of a community somehow collectively acquiring a failure of immunity rendered homosexuality dangerously akin to biological suicide, and the hint was taken in such homophobic commentary as that of Patrick Buchanan (1983): 'The poor homosexuals – they have declared war upon Nature, and now Nature is exacting an awful retribution.'

The incoherence that this notion of 'community' is evident even in the titles of some epidemiological articles: 'Opportunistic Infection in Previously Healthy Women: Initial Manifestations of a Community-acquired Cellular Immune Dysfunction' (Masur et al., 1982); 'Community-acquired Opportunistic Infections and Defective Cellular Immunity in Heterosexual Drug abusers and Homosexual Men' (Small et al., 1983). In these examples, it is far from clear which 'community' is being imputed, but the association of gay men with disease was often reinforced even when speaking of the vulnerability of other people. For many newspapers and magazines, the disease only became visible when it affected people who mattered more to the editors than gay men did. Thus, dozens of gay men had died before, in February 1982, the editors at the *Wall Street Journal* finally, in its first piece on AIDS, reported 23 cases among people identifying as heterosexual: 'New, Often-fatal Illness in Homosexuals Turns up in Women, Heterosexual Males' (Bishop, 1982).

Shilts (1987, p. 126) was right: 'The gay plague got covered only because it finally had struck people who counted, people who were not homosexuals.' Yet, the natural home of AIDS among gay men was reinforced even in this early reporting of non-gay cases (Nelson, 1982). Thus the first *Newsweek* article observed that 'the "homosexual plague" has started spilling over into the general population' (Keerdoja and Morris, 1982). It was as if the homosexual community was so saturated with disease that sickness was now moving beyond its natural limits, an impression reinforced in a subsequent *Newsweek* article that warned of AIDS 'creeping out of well-defined epidemiological confines' (Seligmann et al., 1983, p. 74). In its natural form, then, AIDS is made to seem a gay disease, although the deceptively titled 'general population' is warned that it might break out towards them – how unfair. As Jan Zita Grover (1987, p. 23) noted, the 'general population' denoted the part of society that 'is virtuously going about its business, which is not pleasure-seeking (as drugs and gay life are uniformly imagined to be), so AIDS hits *its* members as an assault from diseased hedonists upon hard-working innocents'. This homophobia both produced, and was reproduced by, the homosexualization of AIDS.

A Morbid Lifestyle?

Despite the diversity within the group of people sick with AIDS, the epidemiological focus on gay men was relentless and it directed attention to what was different about gay men, pathologizing that difference. Friedman-Kien, who had spoken to the *New York Times* of the 'exceptionally promiscuous' patients he was seeing (Nelson, 1981b), wrote up the cases in similar terms for a medical journal, describing 19 patients as 'young homosexual men, highly sexually active' (Friedman-Kien et al., 1982, p. 697). This focus likewise directed the search for causes:

> *The recent appearance of this disease may be associated with changes that have occurred over the last 15 years in the lifestyle of homosexual men living in large urban centers. There has been a marked increase in gay bathhouses, bars, and meeting places where multiple anonymous sexual encounters occur ... Use of multiple recreational drugs, especially the inhalation of amyl and butyl nitrite ... is also an important aspect of this changing lifestyle.*

The lifestyle dimension was the preferred focus of epidemiologists, particularly 'nitrite exposure and promiscuity' (Levine, 1982, p. 1394). But once the epidemiologist had identified gay men as the source, then, speculation was unbridled: 'It is also possible that a retrovirus is involved in these malignancies: moreover, as a consequence of intercourse with animals, an animal retrovirus might have been introduced into the homosexual population' (Levine, 1982, p. 1394). No evidence was cited for this observation and yet it was acceptable in a refereed medical journal. Can one imagine such speculation being acceptable in the absence of pervasive homophobia?

Lifestyle was understood as implicated by the clustering of early cases, but, bedevilled by equifinality (Olsson, 1969), such patterns are ambivalent. Thus while one epidemiologist could assert that '[t]he possibility that an infectious agent represents the ultimate cause stems from ... the geographic clustering of cases ... suggesting common sources of possible primary infectious factors' (Quagliarello, 1982, p. 447), others countered that '[t]he geographic clustering of cases suggests causal factors related to lifestyle or environment' (Haverkos and Curran, 1982, p. 335).

One way to establish the significance of various lifestyle elements would have been to frame a case-control study for multidimensional comparisons between the sick and the well. From July 1981, the CDC wanted to conduct such a case-control study of the PCP and KS cases but the National Institutes of Health (NIH) advised that it would take three years to devise, recruit for, and complete such a study (Shilts, 1987, p. 81). Shilts (1987, p. 96) reported that by September 1981 the KSOI had devised a questionnaire and were seeking controls for each KS or PCP case. Selma Dritz (1995, p. 16), an epidemiologist with the San Francisco Department of Health, recalled that she used 'the questionnaire on about 100 of the patients here' but that having 'gathered all the information and sent it all back to CDC ... it took them two years to do a computer analysis of it ... Jim Curran was crazy; he was wild: NIH wouldn't give him the money.' The findings of the case-control study were not published until August 1983 (Jaffe et al., 1983). The delay implied that it was enough to know that gay life was at fault. There was little urgency about facilitating its healthy flourishing.

Yet, the critical evidence against the lifestyle hypothesis was available within months of the first reports. Cases among heterosexual injecting drug-users were published in December 1981 (Masur et al., 1981). In July 1982 the CDC reported cases among Haitian men who denied having had sex with other men, but they also reported cases among Haitian women (CDC, 1982b). In the same month came reports of unexplained PCP among haemophiliacs (CDC, 1982c). In November an article about unexplained PCP, KS and other opportunistic infections reported on 86 heterosexual men and 35 heterosexual women, and noted that of these about three in five reported injecting drugs (Allen and Mellin, 1982). In December 1982 the CDC reported on AIDS transmitted by blood transfusion (CDC, 1982d) and transmission *in utero* (CDC, 1982e). At the start of 1983 the CDC described a set of cases among the female sexual partners of infected males (CDC, 1983). A gay lifestyle could clearly not explain anywhere close to all of these cases. But as the CDC, in reviewing the early years of AIDS with the hindsight of 2011, observed of the reception of these sorts of findings that argued strongly in favour of an infectious agent as the cause of AIDS, 'Nonetheless, whether because of competing hypotheses or merely denial, many scientists and the public were skeptical of the infectious agent causation theory' (Curran and Jaffe, 2011, p. 65).

Curran and Jaffe do not explain the nature of the 'denial' to which they refer. In an oral history of the epidemic, Marcus Conant, who founded the first KS clinic in San Francisco, was asked: 'Why did it take so long to accept the idea that the epidemic was caused by a transmissible agent, and to forget about poppers[1] and all the other things that the CDC and other people were looking at?' His response was almost as evasive as the vague reference to 'denial': 'Well, that's a very good and very complex question, and there's not a simple and easy answer. I guess if there were, this whole terrible epidemic in America would not have happened' (Conant, 1996, p. 144). In other words, focusing on the gay lifestyle was a way of attending to the epidemic that went hand-in-hand with systematic neglect. The implication is that by identifying AIDS as a gay disease, it was not felt to be urgent.

It is not enough to blame this on individual scientists, although one epidemiologist suggested in 1992 that 'Harry Haverkos of the CDC invested his career in [the poppers hypothesis], pushed it very hard. He's still pushing on it' (Moss, 1996, p. 248). He would not be the last, and Peter Duesberg (1987) returned to this hypothesis and from 1990 he promoted it to the South African government (Kalichman, 2009). Another way of putting this question is to ask: why did it seem so easy for scientists, pundits and members of the public to believe that there must be something about a gay lifestyle that was intrinsically harmful to health? With this belief, many people behaved like Pat Buchanan and were content to let nature run its course. Such savage insouciance drove Larry Kramer (1989) to speak of a gay holocaust engineered by an institutional failure to address the epidemic.

---

1   To relax the sphincter prior to anal intercourse, people would snort a concoction derived from alkyl nitrates. These were popularly known as poppers. Their relative novelty on the gay clubbing scene in the early 1980s drew attention as perhaps the novel lifestyle factor that was driving the epidemic. Did they have a toxic effect upon immunity?

Contagion

When the evidence for an infectious agent was overwhelming, the stereotyping and prejudice did not end, but took instead the form of contagion rather than pariah. In early 1982 the CDC's epidemic intelligence service officer assigned to the Los Angeles County Department of Health Services was approached by a local gay man who claimed to know that there had been sexual contact between a number of the earliest cases in southern California (Curran and Jaffe, 2011, p. 65). By June 1982 the CDC felt able to report on a 'cluster' of patients in southern California. Of the 19 reported cases of KS or PCP reported from southern California by 12 April 1982, the eight still alive were interviewed, as were close friends of seven among the 11 already deceased. From these 15 cases, data on aspects of sexual histories were collected for 13 of them. Taking a five-year period preceding the onset of KS or PCP, nine of these 13 had some sexual contact with individuals who either were already diagnosed with KS or PCP or would later be so diagnosed. At this time, very little was known about the latency period between HIV infection and the development of serious opportunistic infections, and the CDC observed three patients who developed KS after sexual contact with someone already diagnosed with KS. In these cases, the intervals were nine months, 13 months and 22 months respectively (CDC, 1982f, p. 305). Among the sexual contacts detailed to the CDC, two KS patients from Orange County and two PCP patients from Los Angeles County were among the sexual contacts detailed by a non-Californian who was also interviewed. In rather low-key reporting, the *New York Times* reported on the cluster study as 'new evidence … suggesting that the outbreak is linked to an infectious agent' (Altman, 1982).

Very quickly, the non-Californian himself became identified as the infectious agent. With these early results from the cluster study, Selma Dritz approached the non-Californian:

> *I told him, 'Look, we've got proof now.' I didn't tell him how scientifically accurate the information was. It wasn't inaccurate, but it wasn't actually scientifically proven. I said, 'We've got proof that you've been infecting these other people. You've got AIDS, you know. We know it's transmissible now, because you're transmitting it.' He was the active partner in all this gay business, anal–genital sex. 'You've just got to cut it out.' 'Don't be silly, I won't cut it out. It's my life. I'll do what I want.' (Dritz, 1995, pp. 35–6)*

Marcus Conant (1996, p. 166) recalled that, as soon as he heard about the cluster study, Randy Shilts, working for the *San Francisco Bay Chronicle*, 'went nuts trying to get the name out of me as to who the patient was'. Someone did leak the name, and Gaétan Dugas, a Canadian airline steward, was soon facing personal threats, 'a group of gay men had decided to drive the "Orange County connection" out of town for so purposefully spreading the disease' (Shilts, 1987, p. 208). At least one of these men, 'a Vietnam veteran, ex-marine medic, who had Kaposi's sarcoma', and who had named Dugas as one of his sexual contacts, claimed that he was 'waiting for Dugas to come back to San Francisco so he could kill him' (Moss, 1996, p. 281). The personification of the disease and attributing base motives to the guilty men spreading it became dominant themes in later press coverage, but they are found here already in the actions of epidemiologists who leaked names and invited mob justice.

The full cluster study would not be published until 1984, but in 1983 fears of contagion were incited by another epidemiological study. A study of AIDS among eight infants in New Jersey established that in each case 'our patients had in common household exposure to one or more persons with known risk factors for AIDS: IV drug abusers (seven), prostitutes (two), Haitians/Dominicans (two), and homosexuals/IV drug abusers (one). There was no evidence that our patients had been sexually abused or given illicit drugs' (Oleske et al., 1983, p. 2347). Of the eight children, six had mothers 'who represented a risk factor' and this suggested 'the possibility of vertical spread of disease' (Oleske et al., 1983, p. 2347). The article, therefore, implied that, for the other two women, having sex with a person with known risk factors was not in itself a putative risk. Thus, while infection within the womb was suggested as a possibility for six of the infants, for the other two, with mothers not themselves in what were thought to be at-risk groups but living with and presumably having sex with men who were in such groups, nothing more specific than 'household exposure' was offered.

In an editorial for this issue of the *Journal of the American Medical Association* (*JAMA*), Anthony Fauci (1983, p. 2375) from the NIH concluded that the widening set of groups presenting with AIDS, meant that 'the evidence for a transmissible agent being the cause of AIDS is about as strong as it can be, despite the fact that, up to this point, no agent has been identified or isolated'. Fauci noted that transmission in the womb was a possibility but he went on to suggest that '[p]erhaps more important is the possibility that routine close contact, as within a family household, can spread the disease' (ibid., p. 2375). This speculation was promoted in a press release from the American Medical Association and, although Fauci later claimed (Shilts, 1987, p. 301) that this sensationalized his speculation, his editorial was certainly inflammatory. The *New York Times* published the Associated Press (1983) piece quoting Fauci's phrase about 'routine close contact' as a possible cause of AIDS. Within a few weeks of the publication of the *JAMA* article, its author was back in the pages of the *New York Times* trying to dampen fears of contagion: 'although the disease can be acquired other than sexually – through blood products or the birth process – Dr. Oleske stresses that "casual contact will not transmit AIDS"' (Gardner, 1983, p. 21).

When the cluster study was finally published in March 1984, Dugas was not named but he still featured, this time as 'Patient 0' who had given the CDC the names of 72 of what he estimated were his 750 sexual partners during three years 1979–81: 'Eight of these 72 named partners were AIDS patients: four from southern California and four from New York City' (Auerbach et al., 1984, p. 489). Patient 0 had marked lymphadenopathy from December 1979 and KS lesions from May 1980, and five of his eight sexual contacts preceded any of these symptoms leading the study to propose the 'existence of an asymptomatic carrier state of AIDS' (Auerbach et al., 1984, p. 490). To estimate the latency (or asymptomatic) period for AIDS, the authors highlighted six cases in which only one other patient was a sexual contact. They then assumed that this must be the occasion of infection and then were able to estimate that the latency period, from infection to diagnosis with an opportunistic infection, was, on average, 10 months. The press reports highlighted Patient 0, the man 'who carried AIDS', 'spreading it across the country' (Associated Press, 1984).

In 1984 it was accepted by most scientists that the retrovirus that caused the failure of the immune system had been identified, and by 1985 there was a blood test available that could detect antibodies to this virus. At this point, a remarkable retrospective study was undertaken (Jaffe et al., 1985). In San Francisco, some 6,875 gay or bisexual men had taken part in a hepatitis B study in 1978–80 and their blood samples had been retained at the CDC. Taking a 50 per cent sample from the earliest part of the hepatitis B study (sera collected January–May 1978) and a 6 per cent sample from the later part of the study (men whose sera was collected June 1978–December 1980), 474 men were selected for follow-up blood tests yielding estimates of HIV prevalence in this cohort for 1978 (4.5 per cent), 1979 (12.6 per cent), 1980 (24.1 per cent) and 1984 (67.4 per cent). Yet in 1984 only 2.4 per cent of the cohort showed evidence of the opportunistic infections that would trigger an AIDS diagnosis. For the men known to have been infected already in 1978–80, the median time thereafter before they developed opportunistic infections was 43 months. By August 1985, then, the cluster study published in May 1984 was known to be highly misleading. The latency periods identified in that earlier study were simply far too short and thus all the sexual contacts listed in the study were between pairs of men already infected with HIV, and that included those attributed to Gaétan Dugas. By the time of the very first report on inexplicable PCP, in June 1981, there was already an appreciable pool of infected men in San Francisco, and probably also in Los Angeles and New York.

This should have been the end of the road for the cluster study, but it was not. When Shilts was writing up his AIDS journalism into the first history of the early years of the epidemic, he retained the focus on Gaétan Dugas. For Shilts, Dugas exemplified one half of the story of AIDS, and that was the half that was about the complicity of gay men in the transmission of the virus. Recent debates over homonormativity (Duggan, 2002; Puar, 2006; Visser, 2008a; Browne and Bakshi, 2011; G. Brown, 2012; Gieseking, 2012; Nash, 2013b) are prefigured in the distinction, suggested by Shilts, between good gays who could restrain their sexuality and bad queers whose unbridled sexuality threatened not only the reputation, but also the lives, of the good gays. Throughout *And the Band Played On*, Shilts (1987) stressed e Dugas's vanity, having him repeatedly look into the mirror to exclaim 'I am the prettiest one' (ibid., p. 21), 'I'm still the prettiest one' (ibid., p. 47), and 'still the prettiest one' (ibid., p. 79). Siding with Apollonian Larry Kramer (1989) rather than Dionysian Michael Callen (Berkowitz and Callen, 1983; Paglia, 1990, 1994), Shilts (1987) used Dugas to make a general point about hedonism, deflating the earlier radicalism of the gay movement: 'Success was spoiling gay liberation' (ibid., p. 15). Shilts implied that indulgence had displaced responsibility within the gay community and that Dugas's promiscuity epitomized the ways in which the gay movement 'had become a victim of its own success' (ibid., p. 15). To present Dugas in this way in 1984 would have been an unfair use of confidential data, but to do so in 1987 was to moralize on the basis of hypotheses long since tested and rejected.

Throughout his book, Shilts presented as fact the discarded guesses of 1983 and 1984. He reported CDC officials discovering that one man developed symptoms 'some ten months after Gaétan spent the weekend with him on Thanksgiving 1980. Another Los Angeles man found his first Kaposi's sarcoma lesions thirteen months after he had slept with the French-Canadian during a trip Gaétan made to southern California in February 1980' (ibid., p. 128). In the light of the science of 1985, these guesses from 1983 were just plain wrong. Both men were almost certainly infected long before 1980. Yet, in 1987, Shilts relies on these speculations to establish his conclusion:

> *Whether Gaétan Dugas actually was the person who brought AIDS to North America remains a question of debate and is ultimately unanswerable. The fact that the first cases in both New York City and Los Angeles could be linked to Gaétan, who himself was one of the first half-dozen or so patients on the continent, gives weight to that theory. (Ibid., p. 439).*

Except that it does no such thing.

When St Martin's Press was trying to ginger press coverage for the book, it found indifference within the media, but decided, in the words of Michael Denneny, Shilts's editor, to descend to 'the worst kind of yellow journalism' and pitch the story to the media that Shilts had uncovered the man who had brought AIDS to America (Babineau, 2001). Dugas became the story, was given a 'key role in spread of AIDS' (Associated Press, 1987), was sensationalized as 'The Appalling Saga of Patient Zero' in *Time* (Henry, 1987), and, even worse, achieved front-page notoriety with the *New York Post* (1987) as 'The Man Who Gave Us AIDS'. Denneny had warned Shilts that '[y]ou're not going to get on the "Today Show" with an attack on the Reagan administration' (Tiemeyer, 2013, p. 175). In other words, the homophobia of the media was insatiable. But, as Crimp (1987) noted, Shilts's own conceptualization of the irresponsibility of promiscuous gay men was easily assimilated into the homophobic agenda. McKay's (2014) study of Shilts's papers shows that the author chose not to use anecdotes about Dugas's consideration for others, including one in which Dugas turned down sex after a dinner date, saying, 'We can't … It won't work out. I can't say any more' (ibid., p. 183). The elision of this story 'removed any ambiguity from Dugas's motivations, and strengthened the image of the flight attendant as a deliberate disease spreader' (ibid., p. 183).

Epidemiology and Stereotypes

As Treichler (1987) remarked, the early association between gay men and the new disease persisted despite the increasing diversity of sufferers. The pervasive homophobia of US society in the early 1980s shaped how epidemiologists communicated their work, producing a vagueness in terminology (bodily fluids, contact) that fed anxiety without developing coherent prevention strategies. The epidemiological obsession with the gay lifestyle that persisted long after the unique focus on gay men had ceased to be a plausible explanation for the dynamics of the epidemic further prejudiced effective prevention policies. It fed such irresponsible reporting as the psychiatrist who, over two years after the CDC had clearly concluded that the virus could be transmitted 'from heterosexual men to their female sexual partners' (CDC, 1985), told the readers of *Cosmopolitan* that that there was no credible threat to heterosexual women from what he described as sex in the 'missionary position' (Gould, 1988). It was activism on the part of the women's group within ACT UP, New York, that challenged this and that eventually forced the CDC (1992) itself to revise its case definition of AIDS so that female conditions such as invasive cervical cancer became recognized as relevant opportunistic infections (Shotwell, 2013).

The presentation of sexual activity as lifestyle made it seem a relatively insignificant consumer choice and it delayed serious consideration of what people invest in sexual expression and of how to accommodate those desires and fears within effective prevention strategies. Here, again, it was activists leading the way in the development of effective epidemiological knowledge, and within two years of the first cases, Berkowitz and Callen (1983, pp. 1–2) had articulated the central theme of practical prevention, insisting that '[s]ex doesn't make you sick – diseases do'. They accepted that the 'challenge is to figure out how we can have gay, life-affirming sex, satisfy emotional needs, and say alive!' Such a pro-sex message was not compatible with the homophobia that treated gay men as sick by virtue of depraved choice.

While epidemiologists debated the relative merits of theories based either on lifestyle or on the presence of an infectious agent, the homophobic context meant that both were grist to the mills of prejudice. If it was lifestyle, this confirmed the dangers of homosexuality. If it was contagion, this confirmed the dangers of homosexual men. Truly, this was a distinction without effective difference. Only this sickening homophobia could so conflate gay men with sickness that when Ryan White, an adolescent with haemophilia, contracted HIV from a transfusion following an operation to remove part of a lung damaged during a bout of pneumonia, not only did other parents try to exclude him from their children's school, but he found his school locker defaced with such graffiti as 'fag' (White, 1988).

Notions of sickness and wellness are irresistible as metaphors for all sorts of social issues. When a new medical crisis erupted in the wealthiest state on earth, epidemiology was so readily colonized by homophobia that the medical response was woeful and public debate toxic. We might speak of epidemiology having been homosexualized when, instead, it needed to be queered.

Chapter 31

'Why Must We Stay in This Cage?' Governing Sexuality in Biomedical Research

Stephen Taylor

Introduction

While an abundance of research has examined sexuality and HIV/AIDS within a discursive or representational frame (Treichler, 1987; Patton, 1990), there has been very little focus on the materiality of life with HIV/AIDS for non-heteronormative subjects (Tucker, 2009a). By materiality, I refer here to those issues of political economy 'that surround, limit and give opportunity to different [non-heteronormative] communities' (Tucker, 2009a, p. 13), including discrimination, spatial segregation and inequalities in access to education and health services (Ross, 2005). In many parts of Africa, for instance, the health needs of non-heteronormative patients remain largely silenced and misrepresented (Johnson, 2007). In many parts of the world, particularly those experiencing concentrated epidemics, gay men and men who have sex with men (MSM) endure widespread stigma, discrimination and constrained access to primary HIV care (Fay et al., 2011; Beyrer et al., 2012).

Despite such barriers to engagement with biomedicine, these men are considered to be a key constituency for research around HIV/AIDS. In the Global North, gay men have actively promoted biomedical agendas through their involvement as research investigators, participants and fund-raisers. Steven Epstein (1996), for instance, documents the campaigns of gay men in the 1980s to press for rapid, responsive and inclusive HIV drug trial protocols and regulations in the USA. However, this active and willing engagement is far from universal. Poorer gay-identified men, whose heterogeneous sexual identities are invariably simplified and collapsed through their biomedical categorization as 'MSM', have largely been subjected to biomedical research in their search for affordable treatment and care. Industry-sponsored trials, for instance, are considered by many to be extractive and largely unresponsive to the needs of MSM in the Global South; indeed, there are discrepancies, and even incompatibilities, between the behavioural norms codified in trial protocols and the lived realities of MSM subjects, most notably around the compulsion to cease risk behaviours – for example, unprotected receptive anal intercourse (Nodin et al., 2008). In light of these concerns, innovative community-based research has sought to overcome histories of neglect and mistreatment by actively involving poorer MSM, especially in the Global South, in the development of research protocols (Tucker et al., 2013a). Without the active engagement of multiple poorer MSM communities in constructing biomedical research agendas, these individuals are unlikely to benefit from the prevention and treatment research that they have been subjected to (AMFAR, 2011).

This chapter focuses on one particular MSM research intervention: the 2010 Phase III NIEMAN (a pseudonym) industry-sponsored anti-retroviral clinical trial in Cape Town, South Africa. While the trial is representative of broader overtures towards the promotion of biomedical research in South Africa (Wemos, 2013), it offers a specific critical window into some of the realities of MSM research participation. Through a suite of disciplinary technologies this chapter argues that MSM subjects were enrolled into a trial machinery that aimed to modify their conduct, attitudes and behaviours towards those considered 'responsible' enough for trial participation. MSM lifestyles were reconfigured with the intention of disciplining and reproducing 'docile bodies' to be subjected to biomedical authority (Foucault, 1977). These technologies of discipline and the self, deployed to control and regulate those deemed sexually other, highlight the inherently political nature of experimental treatment and care (Klein, 2012; Swarr, 2012).

The politicization of biomedical research has several implications for sexuality studies, and it is upon these provocations that I situate this chapter. First, attention must be paid to the ways in which notions of sexuality are scripted into treatment interventions. These interventions reproduce dominant norms about desire and sexual practice, and concomitantly the needs and priorities of 'deviant' groups must be defended. Second, there is a dearth of critical geographical studies focusing on biomedical research on non-heteronormative subjects in the Global South. Critical studies of clinical trials have largely focused on clinical relationships of exploitation, appropriation and accumulation (Rajan, 2007; Petryna, 2009; Cooper and Waldby, 2014). It is not my intention to belittle the appositeness of this focus, but accounts that critique the administration of interventions from the Global North must be wary of obscuring the micro-level political realities that non-heteronormative subjects negotiate in the search for treatment. Finally, we must remain attentive to the role played by sexual subjects in both facilitating and stifling the epistemic ideals of researchers. There is significant unpredictability around treatment interventions, and sexuality should be considered as a key analytical frame through which to examine the connections, frictions and divisions that emerge through biomedical research.

In the rest of this chapter, I first locate the NIEMAN study within a broader history and geography of clinical trials involving gay and MSM subjects, considering these trials as political tools aimed at normalizing the conduct of non-heteronormative bodies. I then draw upon a series of interviews conducted in 2011 with 12 NIEMAN trial participants and 10 coordinators to shed light on the architectures of discipline and normalization that attempt to bring subjects into conformity with trial-specific behavioural norms. Some subjects resist or modify these interventions as their identification with alternative moral economies (most notably around sexuality) conflicts with the rationalities of biomedicine. As such, biomedical processes of normalization do not necessarily fashion the docile research subjects favoured by trial sponsors (Nguyen, 2005, p. 125); rather, unforeseen and unruly subjectivities emerge that disturb biomedical classifications. I conclude by paying particular attention to the experiences of two MSM to highlight the uneasy interplay between trial behavioural norms and the alternative subject positions inhabited by some subjects. Given the sometimes precarious position of MSM within established biomedical research agendas, it is vital that we remain attentive to the ways in which particular MSM subjects are not only produced through technologies of treatment, but also how they actively constitute *themselves* as subjects.

Responsibility In Testing Times

Many critical accounts of drug development focus on the political economies of drug access, regulation and marketing (Abraham, 2002; Dumit, 2012; for an exception, see Petryna, 2009); however, only a fraction focus on the development of drugs for sale and use in clinical practice. Clinical trials, in which experimental drugs are first tested in humans, are necessary to identify the most promising compounds. Recruitment into clinical trials for AIDS in the early years of the epidemic in North America, Europe and Australia emerged from a therapeutic militancy rooted in a decade of gay activism and expanded lay biomedical expertise (Shilts, 1987; Kramer, 1989; Epstein, 1995). The role of gay men in exerting political pressure on the biomedical establishment to make available a cure for AIDS has been rightly celebrated (Epstein, 1996; Comaroff, 2007). However, often neglected is the fact that many also chose to underscore their sincerity as activists, and their responsibility as fellow sufferers, by volunteering as research subjects in the pursuit of AIDS therapies (Chambré, 2006; Nguyen, 2010). Not all gay men and MSM, as I will outline momentarily, shared similar motivations for participation in research.

The assertion of personal and community responsibility for the future trajectory of drug development, a profoundly ethical commitment based around a common will to live, was a key step in rebutting a wider politics of blame around AIDS (Kahn, 1993; Harrington, 2008). Confronted by government and pharmaceutical industry neglect, the dramatist and gay activist Larry Kramer famously called on the gay community to claim power over their own health by offering themselves as subjects in the pursuit of new medicines: 'All power', said Kramer, 'is the willingness to accept responsibility' (Kramer, 1989, p. 136). Gay activists began to frame expedited access to clinical trials as a right and, in doing so, transformed human experimentation from a suspect endeavour into a potentially beneficent one. In the words of one gay subject, 'You're going to die from the disease one way or another so anything you can do to prolong your life is worth a try. It's my body. My choice. I can't wait' (Ervolino, 1993).

In contrast to the active participation of gay men in the development of anti-retrovirals in the Global North, the subsequent scarcity of affordable medicines in other regions – most prominently in Brazil and across Africa – meant that other MSM had to subject themselves to clinical trials in the pursuit of experimental forms of treatment and care (Robins, 2004; Biehl, 2007). In Burkina Faso, Vinh-Kim Nguyen (2005, p. 125) describes the 'fashioning of new identities' as desperate patients, eager to demonstrate their docility and responsibility to a heterogeneous assemblage of treatment providers, competed for access to anti-retroviral clinical trials. Likewise, Didier Fassin (2007, p. 44) details the futile efforts of HIV-positive South Africans to prove themselves both desperate and responsible enough to access the hyped, and subsequently debunked, Virodene AIDS 'cure'. In these instances of treatment scarcity, trial enrolment operated as a form of triage, a political as much as medical technology, in which a privileged few – those deemed responsible enough to conform to behavioural prescriptions – were given access to treatment, while those unable or unwilling to conform to these norms were denied care (Nguyen, 2010).

For Anita Hardon (2012, p. 82), the role of subjects in countenancing the development of industry-sponsored HIV/AIDS cures suggests that 'the hegemony of biomedicine was achieved through consent'. This reading of the history of HIV/AIDS trials potentially ignores instances of subject mistreatment and resistance that complicate efforts to craft a hagiography of research (Washington, 2008). Unlike previous generations of patients, who willingly complied with trial protocols in an effort to altruistically advance science, many early AIDS research subjects were prepared to subvert research to privilege their own survival. One autobiographical account details how one gay subject stockpiled azidothymidine by taking the drug on an alternative schedule to that mandated by the trial protocol. He did so because 'one has to cheat, lie, and who knows what else to obtain what you need to live' ('Wayne', 1989). Such actions remind us of the urgency in examining alternative value structures that govern clinical trial behaviour. These alternative moral economies are simultaneously the object of biomedical discipline while also harbouring the potential to contest and refigure the terrains of biomedical knowledge production.

The Production of Research Subjects

Cape Town's prominent position within emergent geographies of pharmaceutical and biotechnology research is premised in part on the availability of poor, sometimes treatment-naïve subjects-in-waiting (Al-Bader et al., 2009; Wemos, 2013; Pollock, 2014). Their rapid recruitment into trials – in search of financial reimbursement or higher standards of care – expedites the approval of drugs for sale elsewhere in the world. As others have shown, South African subjects themselves can be left with no guaranteed post-trial access to the treatments that they have tested (Wemos, 2013, pp. 28–31; Rajan, 2012).

Included within this pool of subjects-in-waiting are diverse communities of MSM in Cape Town who have developed spatially and racially distinct sexual subcultures within and between the arbitrary racial and residential segregations of the apartheid regime (Tucker, 2009a). High HIV prevalence rates (14–33 per cent) in these communities, particularly in poorer township areas (Sandfort et al., 2008; Lane et al., 2011), may be seen to make recruitment of MSM groups particularly attractive for those seeking to trial new prevention strategies and pharmaceutical products. However, complicating recruitment is the common experience among MSM of stigma and discrimination in healthcare settings, mirroring broader (often violent) expressions of prejudice against non-heteronormative individuals across all sections of South African society, which has been blamed for poor adherence to HIV risk-reduction strategies and a mistrust of healthcare professionals (Lane, et al., 2008; Rispel and Metcalf, 2009). Cape Town's MSM communities, therefore, represent both an opportunity and a challenge to trial recruiters; the materialities of everyday life for these men – that is, their experiences of vulnerability, inequality and discrimination – create an epidemiological niche appropriate for an experimental intervention, and yet these same experiences also foster a widespread unease about the motivations and interests of those conducting research.

It is against this backdrop that 84 MSM were enrolled into the Cape Town arm of the NIEMAN trial at the local facility of a private multinational contract research organization (CRO). The study evaluated a once-daily dose of an experimental integrase inhibitor, an anti-retroviral drug blocking the action of a key viral enzyme involved in retroviral replication (Pommier et al., 2005), versus a twice-daily competitor in self-identified MSM with HIV who were failing on current therapies. Men were recruited from prior studies, sexual health clinics, advertising and referral from other participants. The majority were from poorer socioeconomic backgrounds and were primarily recruited from township sentinel surveillance clinics. Upon enrolment, all participants were required to sign an informed consent document, complete a compliance workshop outlining the trial protocol, and attend risk-reduction counselling. Subsequently, all subjects had to attend the facility once a month to receive new treatments, undergo physical examinations and answer questions about protocol compliance.

The compliance workshop introduced the trial protocol and outlined the responsibilities of subjects in adhering to the treatment regimen. Protocol compliance was encouraged through the enforcement of power structures within the trial facility and through the promotion of a particular subject lifestyle. The importance of everyday 'responsible' behaviour, particularly that deemed 'befitting' of a research subject, was a central theme of staff-led seminars and break-out discussions; some staff went as far as to equate the trial with life itself ('this trial is your life now'). In compliance sessions, subjects were reminded to 'live positively' by acknowledging their HIV infection, adhering to safe-sex practices and avoiding feelings of guilt, shame and blame (Hunter, 2010a). However, the ideal of openness promoted in the workshop sharply contrasted with the very real experiences of homophobia, violence and exclusion that limit MSM health-seeking behaviours in Cape Town (see Tucker et al., 2013b, 2014). In one workshop discussion, a 24-year-old subject recounted losing both of his parents to AIDS, being cast out from a neighbour's house when she discovered his sexuality, and his subsequent life of dependence on a sexually abusive partner. In light of such experiences, it was unsurprising that most subjects were reticent in revealing their seropositivity and sexuality to others, even friends or relatives, who trial staff assumed would support subjects in their compliance with trial protocols.

The subject of sexuality was a key issue in the compliance workshop and subsequent surveillance. All research subjects were encouraged to cease high-risk sexual and lifestyle behaviours. The principal impact of the protocol was the promotion of condom use and abstinence from alcohol or recreational drugs. These ideals are standard practice across most anti-retroviral trials and are considered to be key indicators of subject conformity to protocols. However, the particular prevalence of these behaviours documented in pre-trial screening interviews with NIEMAN subjects, at levels notably higher than among a similar heterosexual trial demographic, meant that compliance would necessitate significant behavioural changes for some subjects. Despite this there was clearly a contrast between what some participants felt was needed and what it was feasibly possible to deliver. As one trial coordinator explained, 'We simply don't have the resources to hold every subject's hand'. The severance of trial behaviour from former risk behaviours proved costly for some subjects who attempted a clean break from these behaviours. As one subject disclosed, 'We were left with no support. The staff said that our relationships would not be affected by involvement. I never used condoms ... telling my partners that I had to use condoms caused me much stress.'

While promised compliance support was sometimes complicated, the policing of behaviour was evident. All subjects were required to complete a coital diary (CD) in which they self-reported all sexual activity during the trial, noting particular sexual practices and the (non-)use of contraceptives. CD entries were examined in detail at each facility visit and formed the basis of a structured case record form (CRF) interview. Through such techniques, individual subjects were incited, through writing and speech, to document intimate details about themselves and self-regulate their sexual behaviour through regular ritual confession (Foucault, 1977). CRF interviews were to be administered in consultation rooms that enabled participants to confidentially disclose personal barriers to consistent behavioural compliance.

Within the same South African treatment context, Steven Robins (2006, p. 321) documents activists' calls for a medical system in which they would be entitled to free anti-retroviral medications but perceptively adds that under such a system 'they would also need to demonstrate that they were "responsibilized clients"'. This 'subtle shaping of subjectivity' (Whyte, 2009, p. 10) was evident through the NIEMAN trial as protocol compliance was vested with significant moral connotations through which the subject's behavioural responsibility could be both benchmarked and policed. However, it is difficult to identify, echoing Robins, responsibilized subjects within the compliance mechanisms outlined above. Once enrolled in the trial, subjects appeared to be inserted into a somewhat inelastic system in which essential treatments and support were only dispensed if subjects complied with defined and carefully controlled norms of sexual behaviour.

Subversive Sexual Subjects

I now turn to the stories of two MSM subjects, Abongile and Lungisile (pseudonyms), who were both involved in the NIEMAN trial and subsequently ejected from the study, according to their discharge letters, for reasons of 'subversive behaviour not befitting responsible trial participation'. These men, the only subjects discharged from the trial, challenged the CRO dictum that absolute adherence to protocol was the only responsible way to behave in the urgent endeavour to create life-saving pharmaceutical cures. These MSM subjects were unable to reconcile a diverse range of sexual identities and practices into the standardized form of sexual behaviour sought by the trial sponsor. Their actions reveal sexual practices to be a prominent influence on compliance priorities.

While discipline and surveillance are effective tools in regulating the production of clinical trial data within facilities, there is an ever-present fear of subversive actions that will create 'friction to the dissemination of biomedical truth' (Robins, 2009, p. 12). Surveillance and retention operations now extend beyond the walls of the trial facility and into the everyday lives of human subjects, ostensibly to follow up on missed appointments but also to capture behavioural information. During house visits by retention operatives, both men were accused of engaging in activities not compliant with the trial protocol and of failing to accurately report sexual behaviour in their CD assessment. A former sexual partner of Abongile disclosed to trial operatives that he was continuing to engage in unprotected anal intercourse with a high number of sexual partners at gay bars in the city. Abongile complained: 'They expect me to leave everything behind when I enrol? How can I live without friends and the people who love me? They love me as a person – a person who is tempted – not as a [blood] sample in a syringe.'

Likewise, a neighbour reported that Lungisile drank heavily and that this was straining his marriage. Lungisile, and at least five other NIEMAN subjects known to him, had not declared a wife to trial staff: 'When I first had sex, I didn't have to ask anyone's permission. So why must I ask now? It angers me that they came looking for gossip about me.' Both men were identified as engaging in risky behaviours that contradicted prohibitions outlined in the trial protocol. They were withdrawn from the study and returned to existing anti-retroviral therapies. In the words of Abongile, 'Why must we stay in this cage? They said it was for our own good. *Our good?* When they make no space for us to speak about our concerns? No. It is for their good that they treated us like caged birds who must sing when commanded.' Abongile and Lungisile's objections against trial behavioural proscriptions can be interpreted as 'a refusal of assuming an AIDS identity, of becoming that biological being that the virus and the regimen of its treatment determine its host to become' (Kistner, 2009, p. 11).

Far from being an irrational response to discipline, the concealment of non-compliance was consistent with the closeting of MSM identity in the townships. For Lungisile: 'My relationships are private to me. That is something that I have had to always have. Privacy. I cannot shout from the rooftops about my love in the townships. So why should I tell them everything in the trial?' Knowledge and acceptability of MSM in Cape Town townships was perceived to be poor and overwhelmingly negative by the men, a judgement corroborated by recent social attitudes research (Cloete et al., 2008; Tucker et al., 2013a). Both men had been victims of societal ostracism because of their sexual behaviours – in the case of

Abongile this had led to his ejection from the family home as a teenager – and this resulted in their unwillingness to disclose their trial responsibilities to anyone. For Abongile: 'What do they know about our [for example MSM] issues? I face many problems here. People call me things and they want to change me, "correct" me. Am I simply meant to reveal myself by saying that I am HIV positive and in a trial?' Both men were traversing discordant moral economies. On the one hand, their involvement in the research necessitated the development of a positive attitude towards compliance and advocated the open disclosure of concealed aspects of their sexuality and selfhood. On the other hand, their continued reliance on both sexual- and kin-centred networks of support outside of the trial necessitated the continued concealment of their sexuality and established patterns of behaviour. The actions of both men are a reminder that responses to the HIV/AIDS epidemic are not wholly predicated on the knowledge, rhetorical conventions and arts of existence promoted by public health authorities; they are also ingrained in the social and moral prerogatives of both individuals and 'sexual communities' confronted by the virus (Binnie and Valentine, 1999; Hubbard, 2001; R. Parker, 2009).

From a research perspective, these subversive subjects 'not only create risks, they ignore ethical responsibilities to observe research agreements and tell the truth' (Dresser, 2013, p. 830). At the same time, however, their subversion could also be viewed as a response to inherent issues in the design and conduct of trials. The actions of Abongile and Lungisile cast light upon the way in which the trial's desire to produce responsible subjects could also have reinforced the closeting of sexual behaviour through 'an excruciating system of double binds' (Sedgwick, 1990, p. 70).

Conclusion

The specific practices deployed in the NIEMAN trial suggest that clinical trials act as political technologies aimed at crafting responsible subjects willing to conform to established behavioural norms. In the context of research on MSM subjects, proscriptions on certain forms of sexual behaviour seek to govern the actions of non-heteronormative bodies. The production of responsible subjects in the trial could be interpreted as not necessarily always a process of empowering individuals to become part of the biomedical research enterprise; rather, compliance could come to be understood for some as inculcated through stringent controls favouring the positioning of subjects through instruments of policing, confession and discipline.

The treatment of subjects in the trial is representative of a wider shift in global health policy away from the advancement of universal rights to health and towards a heightened insistence on security and control (Brown, Craddock and Ingram, 2012; Ingram, 2013). In the NIEMAN trial, stringent disciplinary mechanisms and what was felt by some to be sometimes contrasting ideas of support may have hindered participants openly discussing their compliance difficulties with medical professionals. Absent from the trial was the emancipatory style of politics characteristic of therapeutic and sexual citizenship (Bell, 1995a; Bell and Binnie, 2000; M. Brown, 2006). Instead, the struggle of these MSM may be framed as representative of a biosocial inequality in which poor and marginalized subjects are welcomed into extractive forms of biomedical research and yet systematically excluded from wider participation in the public sphere (Biehl, 2007).

This chapter, however, exposed moments of friction that originated in MSM subject behaviours that did not conform to the normalizing rationality of the clinical trial regime. The actions of Abongile and Lungisile remind us of the agency of research subjects when confronted by technologies of treatment and care that seek to normalize non-heteronormative bodies. Subjects' actions ranged from deliberate subversion to half-hearted compliance as they negotiated the competing demands of the trial protocol, expressions of their sexual identity, the maintenance of support networks and the preservation of their own health. In repoliticizing clinical trials, I have shown that alternative forms of identification and association – notably those emerging around MSM sexual behaviours in this instance – have the potential to contest normalizing treatment practices. The forms of subversion, typified by Abongile and Lungisile, are understandable responses to the scripting of problematic and reductive notions of sexuality into rigid experimental research protocols that are often incompatible with the lived realities of non-heteronormative subjects in the Global South.

This consideration of the entanglements between sexuality and biomedical research should not blind us to the political and socioeconomic determinants of health. Through the above insights into MSM participation in South African clinical trials, and particularly the shaping of responsible and non-responsible subjects, I have demonstrated how socioeconomic circumstances shape MSM trial subjectivities as much as clinical trial protocols. 'Subversive' behaviour can only be understood when the influence of these competing terrains – the social and the biomedical – is recognized. The behaviour of subjects is always already situated in local moral economies, predicated on sexuality, the disciplinary schema of biomedicine and, perhaps most pressingly, the search for care.

Chapter 32

Relocation and Negotiation: Integrating Mobilities in Gay Men's Sexual Health

Nathaniel M. Lewis

Introduction

During the past three decades, geographers have devoted considerable attention to the spatialities of the HIV/AIDS epidemic. Much of their work has focused on the global diffusion of the disease, including its origins, spread, and virological character (Smallman-Raynor et al., 1992; Gould, 1993; Wallace et al., 1999; Barnett and Whiteside, 2003). In line with this diffusionist approach, much of the early work on gay men and other men who have sex with men (MSM) tended to focus on how the behaviours and movements of HIV-positive men might impact on local and regional health service systems (Cohn et al., 1994; Ellis and Muschkin, 1996). During the height of the HIV/AIDS crisis in North America, Michael Brown (1995b) critiqued health researchers for 'medicalizing' gay men as mere disease vectors rather than human subjects whose health and well-being were constructed actively by the social and political environments they inhabited. Geographers have since offered useful interventions into the shrinking life-worlds of HIV-positive men (Wilton, 1996), the regulation of gay men's sexual health through clinics and health promotion campaigns (see M. Brown, 2006, 2009; M. Brown and Knopp, 2014) and the advent of local HIV/AIDS activist movements (M. Brown, 1997a; Tucker et al., 2013a).

Ecological approaches to the HIV/AIDS epidemic offer a particularly useful framing of the relationship between HIV/AIDS and place by outlining the complex ways in which individual experiences and subjectivities intersect with health policies, labour flows and political environments to create conditions under which HIV infection occurs (Farmer, 1992; Barnett and Blaikie, 1992; Kalipeni et al., 2003; King, 2010). Using this more flexible approach, geographers have shown that different populations within the same place experience the epidemic in different ways. In South Africa, for example, divergent histories of opportunity and oppression among white, black, coloured and Asian citizens, including vastly different levels of access to housing, employment, schooling and healthcare, are also associated with differential HIV prevalence rates. Here and in other countries, HIV vulnerability has both a geography and history, defined by the intersection of individual subjectivities and the politics of place (Campbell, 2003; Elder, 2003; Tucker, 2009a).

Despite their significant engagement with the diffusion and governance of HIV/AIDS, geographers have less frequently considered how place and mobility might mediate the causes of HIV infection (but see Lewis, 2015). Even sexualities geographers have only rarely addressed gay men's sexual behaviours, perhaps due to what Del Casino (2007a) has called a 'squeamishness' about sex itself in geography. More frequently, they have focused on the development of gay and lesbian communities in specific cities (Forest, 1995; Podmore,

2001) and on queer identity quests that traverse many different places (Knopp, 2004; Gorman-Murray, 2007, 2009a; Lewis, 2012a). Work in other areas of geography, however, suggests important linkages between mobility and health among gay men/MSM. Mobilities geographers observe that while movement may be empowering or emancipatory, it can also reproduce the vulnerabilities experienced by marginalized populations (Heikkila, 2005; Conradson and McKay, 2007; Bailey, 2009). Studies in epidemiology, psychology and medical sociology have also found that gay men's HIV risk behaviours (for example, frequent, unprotected sex and drug use) are associated statistically with their proximity to the sometimes unfamiliar places (for example, gay neighbourhoods, bar scenes and bath houses) that men encounter after moving to a new city (Egan et al., 2011; Carpiano et al., 2011; Buttram and Kurtz, 2013). At the same time, these quantitative, hypothetico-deductive studies often fall silent on the processes or circumstances that connect mobility and place with HIV exposure. Sexualities geographers therefore have an opportunity to consider more deeply how gay men's mobile *negotiations* of particular geographic and temporal contexts (for example, homophobic communities in adolescence and commercial gay scenes later in life) might precipitate HIV infection and other adverse health outcomes. For example, migration might overcome the ill-effects of homophobia in one place while reinforcing vulnerabilities such as poverty and social upheaval upon arrival in another (Bianchi et al., 2007; Bruce and Harper, 2011; Lewis, 2014a, 2014b).

This chapter sets a research agenda in mobilities and gay men's health by identifying specific elements of the migration–health relationship. Using a study of HIV/AIDS risk and prevention among native-born Canadian gay men moving in and out of Halifax, Nova Scotia, Canada, and a study of sexual health among international immigrants who are gay/ MSM within three cities in Ontario, Canada, this chapter identifies four ways in which both local/regional and international mobilities influence the health of gay men: the conditions of the migration process; relationships with family, ethnic and 'home' communities; relationships with new 'gay communities'; and the dynamics of post-migration encounters with HIV risk. While the Halifax study accounts for within-country migrations, such as those from rural Nova Scotia to Halifax or from Nova Scotia to other Canadian cities (see also Egan et al., 2011; Bruce and Harper, 2011), the Ontario study focuses on international immigrants who have moved to Canada from foreign countries with significant cultural and ethno-racial differences (see also Do et al., 2006; Bedoya et al., 2012). The findings are drawn from eight in-depth interviews conducted with HIV/AIDS service providers in the Halifax, Nova Scotia, region between June 2013 and February 2014 (an additional seven interviews with individual gay men are not included here) and 12 in-depth interviews conducted with settlement and health service providers in Toronto, Ottawa, and London, Ontario, between July 2013 and June 2014. While these service-provider interviews cannot 'speak for' individual stories and subjectivities, they offer a macro-level overview of experiences among the men they work with.

Conditions and Complexities of the Migration Process

There are a wide variety of conditions which can lead gay men to migrate. Such complexity, however, is often overlooked by health researchers and practitioners. It is therefore important here to sketch out the different conditions that lead gay men/MSM to migrate, as well as the challenges associated with different 'types' of migration in this population. Given that much of the research on sexual health and migration (for example, among Latino migrant workers in the American West) does not consider non-normative sexualities, their findings are grounded in presumptive heterosexual and heteronormative family configurations (Levy et al., 2005; Winnett et al., 2012). In these studies, heterosexual men are thought to engage in riskier behaviours as they leave behind monogamous partners and extended families and become acclimated to the transient lifestyle of a manual labourer in the USA. For gay men, too, relocating involves reconciling elements of the place left behind (for example, homophobic social settings, gay-exclusive sexual health education systems), with sexuality-specific desires (coming out, finding first romantic partners) and intervening life events such as education, employment and career development (Bianchi et al., 2007; Lewis, 2012b, 2014a). While migration is therefore an experiential *process* with varied psychosocial implications, much of the work on gay men's sexual health categorizes migration as a single, temporally bounded *event* that either precedes or follows certain health outcomes (Akin et al., 2008; Egan et al., 2011). Biomedical studies of gay migrants frequently collect data on age at time of migration, reason for migrating and time elapsed since migration (Bruce and Harper, 2011; Egan et al., 2011; Frye et al., 2014), as well as country of origin, language, income, immigration status and health coverage (Do et al., 2006; Ramirez-Valles et al., 2008; Bedoya et al., 2012). Unfortunately, these contextual factors tend to simply be measured and then tested for correlations with various health behaviours and outcomes, without looking more deeply at how they influence the intervening migration and resettlement processes.

Studies examining 'sexual migrations', or relocations grounded in concerns about sexual identity and expression, often presume migration to flow from conservative countries and regions with limited sexual-health education programming to liberal places that offer more sexual freedoms and self-care tools (Carrillo, 2004; Bianchi et al., 2007). At the same time, moves to large urban centres with established gay scenes are also associated with increased access to sexual partners and party drugs (Egan et al., 2011; Buttram and Kurtz, 2013). To some extent, the Nova Scotia case affirms both theories. One provider described the unwillingness to acknowledge gay and lesbian sexualities in some of the province's rurally situated schools (see also Preston et al., 2004; Barton, 2010; Bruce and Harper, 2011). 'We all know that HIV is in the curriculum from grade three up', he said. 'However, the teachers … don't have the capacity, they don't have the knowledge … [the sentiment in some locales is] we don't have gay students 'cause it's against our religion' (AIDS service organization director, Colchester County, Nova Scotia). Moving away from small towns and rural areas in regions like Nova Scotia might therefore offer some gay men an opportunity to learn more about HIV and sexual health. At the same time, relocating to a larger city might mean encountering new sexual environments and cultures without having any knowledge of how to negotiate them.

> People come from other parts of … the Maritimes [Nova Scotia, New Brunswick, and Prince Edward Island provinces] to [the Nova Scotia capital city of] Halifax … they're out here to go to [the bath house] and they go back home to the closet. Or they come here to hook up with someone that they met online just for an encounter and then they go back to wherever they go to … and a lot of young men … who were in their early to mid-20s … were coming back home after kind of going and kind of trying to see … another life … they went to Toronto, they were young and they ended up getting HIV and then coming [back] to Halifax. (Gay health liaison, Halifax, Nova Scotia)

On the surface, this account reinforces early work suggesting that gay men and often return to their home regions after contracting HIV (Cohn et al., 1994; Ellis and Muschkin, 1996). But, more importantly, it reveals how childhood and adolescent social marginalization, limited coping skills and unfamiliar sexual environments can all contribute to becoming infected with HIV after relocating (see also Lewis, 2014b).

For men who have moved from other countries, the migration/health nexus can be even more complex. Although some gay men may move to come out or pursue greater sexual freedom, they face the same economic and logistical challenges experienced by all immigrants upon their arrival elsewhere (Carrillo, 2004). Financial difficulties and cultural exclusion (Han, 2007, 2008) can both limit access to the community sites (for example, gay bars and clinics) where gay men's health traditionally has been promoted (Zablotska et al., 2011). As one provider said, 'If somebody is MSM and they're a newcomer to Canada … their first concern is not usually where do I get condoms, it's where do I get housing' (LGBT community development coordinator, London, Ontario). Another added, 'Many newcomers are having to work multiple jobs and not having the time to access those spaces, or [they are in] various precarious working situations where they just do not have the funds to access certain things' (Latino HIV outreach worker, Toronto, Ontario). There may therefore be a significant time lag between arrival and beginning to access gay community infrastructures for either social or healthcare purposes. A settlement agency director agreed: 'I think 'til three years, four years, you have so many other issues than … [generally] enjoying the life … it's hard to say [whether newcomers] are getting included into the gay bar or not' (settlement agency director, Mississauga, Ontario). A lack of immediate involvement with the traditional spaces of sexual encounter, however, does not foreclose migrant men's exposure to risky situations.

The global diffusion of HIV education means that many new immigrants have a baseline knowledge of the disease. However, immigrants from countries where resources are limited or gay men's health is not a policy priority may have difficulty adapting to new sexual health resource regimes (for example, access to free, high-quality condoms and lube) and the notion of planning for sexual health in general. According to one provider, moving to Canada can also create a false sense of security among men who arrive from countries with a much higher HIV prevalence: 'People honestly think they're in the clear when they get here, and we've literally heard that verbatim from clients, and we often have to say "no, more than ever you have to use condoms here"' (LGBT community development coordinator, London, Ontario). Finally, immigration status itself might reinforce insecurity and even discourage health-seeking behaviours such as HIV testing. 'Negotiating … Canadian systems even around immigration and … moving towards citizenship status, it can be such a bureaucratic nightmare for people to negotiate,' said one provider. 'We've definitely been hearing … that guys are more hesitant to get tested, specifically around concerns that HIV status may affect their movement towards citizenship and immigration status' (gay men's health liaison, Toronto, Ontario). The HIV risk for new immigrants who are gay/MSM, then, may be less related to assimilation into 'Western' bar and bath-house 'scenes' than it is to the stressors of relocation and the complex negotiation of *multiple* structures and communities.

Relationships with Family, Ethnic and Home Communities

Migration does not necessarily sever social and cultural ties, and many gay men maintain connections to their place of origin through return trips, family relationships and participation in local expat and ethnic communities within their destination. Attachment to one's home or ethnic community can have divergent and sometimes contradictory effects on sexual health. For example, stressors stemming from relationships with homophobic or unsupportive families have been found to be associated with higher levels of unprotected sex among immigrants moving from Asian and Latin American countries to North America (Diaz et al., 2001; Wilson and Yoshikawa, 2004; Do et al., 2006; Han et al., 2011; Bedoya et al.,

2012). Equally, higher levels of 'acculturation' to one's culture of origin (for example, machismo among Latino immigrants in the USA) have also been found to increase the likelihood of unsafe sex (Poppen et al., 2004; Zea et al., 2008). Conversely, other studies find that the *loss* of family and ethnic community relationships can negatively influence the psychosocial and sexual health of immigrant men. Research on heterosexual Latino migrant workers in the USA shows that those who arrive without family members are more likely to use drugs, pay for sex or have sex with multiple partners (Levy et al., 2005; Winnett et al., 2012). For newcomers who are both gay and racialized, close relationships with family and one's cultural community can also encourage self-care and reduce the dual stressors of racism and homophobia in the destination country (Diaz et al., 2001; Yoshikawa et al., 2004; Akin et al., 2008; Han et al., 2011; Choi et al., 2011). Even in the context of local and regional migration, younger men who leave behind family and community relationships can end up 'operating without a safety net' after moving, particularly if they had been reliant on family or friends for financial and emotional support (Bruce and Harper, 2011, p. 367; Gorman-Murray, 2008; Lewis, 2014b).

In Nova Scotia, many providers indicated that family relationships played a role in clients' decisions to move to other parts of Canada. One provider said:

> Some of them had out-rightly … been kicked out of homes and … told that, you know, you can't be here or we don't want to hear about that. We love you but we don't want to hear about that part of your life, you know. It's having … to keep the secret. (Gay health liaison, Halifax, Nova Scotia)

Moreover, because extended family and community networks are particularly dense in Nova Scotia, men coming out or leaving behind homophobic environments have frequently chosen to travel significant distances rather than settle in familiar cities that have close ties to their towns of origin (see Bulman, 2005; Moreira, 2012). Many providers in Nova Scotia indicated that even in a city the size of Halifax, with a population of over 100,000, 'the six degrees of separation are more like two' (LGBT health liaison, Halifax, Nova Scotia). Some men therefore avoid coming out or using preventive health services (for example, HIV testing) until they leave the province. While men who leave Nova Scotia might emancipate themselves from homophobic home and community environments, they may also have to deal with emotionally challenging processes (for example, coming out and negotiating first sexual relationships) well beyond the familiarity of their home turf (Bruce and Harper, 2011; Lewis, 2014b).

The double-edged nature of post-migration relationships with family and community is also evident in the experiences of men moving to Canada from other countries. One provider, echoing work on the protective effects of filial piety and family responsibility on East Asian gay men (see Wilson and Yoshikawa, 2004; Han et al., 2011), explained, 'there is a connection to family and maintaining expectations and maintaining respect, composure … sometimes maintaining your own health [is akin to] maintain[ing] your family['s] health' (South Asian HIV outreach worker, Toronto, Ontario). At the same time, gay newcomers who rely on family networks for social and financial support might be hesitant to seek out new supports for coming out or sexual health. According to one settlement worker:

> … most of the newcomers will come with the stigma … because they're bringing values of their culture with them here … at the beginning it's very hard to get [disclosure of sexual orientation] from these clients. What is the real reason they are here to see me? … It takes time to make that comfort zone between us as the settlement service providers and the clients. (Settlement counsellor, London, Ontario)

The fact that sexual health resources are made available by settlement counsellors or in gay clinics does not mean that they will be taken up by newcomers Several providers in London, Ontario, observed that the small city's various ethno-cultural communities, much like the small towns in Nova Scotia, were so tightly knit that gay/MSM newcomers became wary of using visible, gay-specific health services. One London provider said, 'From what I gather and I've heard from people, the Latin community in London is really connected and often times it's what happens if I get seen walking in [the HIV and sexual health centre]? So I think we often … lose people that way' (HIV outreach worker, London, Ontario). While being outed can be a worry for any closeted man entering a gay clinic setting, the concern may be even greater for international migrants who rely on local ethnic community support in their daily lives. Meanwhile, finding social support from other gay men within one's own cultural community might also be difficult for newly arrived men. Echoing other providers, one counsellor described a division among gay Asian men in Ottawa:

> [East Asian immigrants] feel more comfortable socializing and they want to socialize with other Asian people, but with guys who were born and raised here it is not necessarily the case. They have, I feel they have different kind of identity struggle. Sometimes they don't want to hang out with the other Asian people because they don't want to be perceived as fresh off boat. (Sexual health counsellor, Ottawa, Ontario)

The affiliations and affinities of gay/MSM newcomers, then, are not unidirectional predictors of risk behaviours, but interdependent, constantly shifting identities that may compound and counteract each other to create or mitigate risk.

Relationships with the 'Gay Community'

Urban gay communities act as loci of both sexual encounters and social support for mobile gay men. A contested term, 'gay community' can involve multiple formations (for example, a neighbourhood, a network), modes of participation (for example, attendance at venues or events, socializing) and inclusions and exclusions based on age, race and sexual or social identifiers (Peacock et al., 2001; Barrett and Pollack, 2005; Han, 2008; Frost and Meyer, 2012). While urban gay communities have long offered potential support networks (Weston, 1995; Bianchi et al., 2007) and concentrated health promotion efforts (Zablotska et al., 2011) that could teach and encourage safer-sex behaviour, a newcomer's connectedness with these communities typically requires being openly gay and having the time and money to spend at social venues such as bars (Barrett and Pollack, 2005; Frost and Meyer, 2012). Others have questioned whether integration into urban gay communities is conducive to sexual health, noting higher rates of unprotected sex and drug use among gay men who move from outlying areas to gay neighbourhoods (Egan et al., 2011; Carpiano et al., 2011; Buttram and Kurtz, 2013). For racialized men, especially those who are recent immigrants, interactions with the 'mainstream' gay community often entail discrimination, rejection and, consequently, lower self-esteem, depression and more risk-taking activities (Diaz et al., 2001; Wilson and Yoshikawa, 2004; Han, 2007, 2008). While the speed, mode and degree of integration into a new gay community all have a potential impact on the sexual health of men, the effects of each are difficult to separate. Some have argued that those who have been in a community longer are more likely to use drugs, use sex venues or have unprotected sex (Mao et al., 2004). Others suggest that the highest-risk activities are more common shortly after arrival, when newcomers may be pursuing sexual encounters despite (or because of) high stress, low self-esteem and lack of familiarity with their local environments (Bianchi et al., 2007; Egan et al., 2011).

For men who move from outlying areas o Nova Scotia to the city of Halifax, interactions with the local gay community are more complex than the linear models of 'integration' or 'connectedness' offered elsewhere (see Barrett and Pollack, 2005; Frost and Meyer, 2012). For these men, the community is often more a source of temporary sexual exchange rather than a sustained source of social support or substantive sexual health education and promotion (Zablotska et al., 2011). As one provider said:

> In [Halifax Regional Municipality] specifically with the gay community there's a lot more transient influx of ... the student population, people who come to attend for example Pride Week ... or you know people from away are coming down because you know even Halifax is becoming more of a well-known LGBT tourist town. You know things like this, all of those things create a kind of transitory interaction between people. (AIDS service organization director, Halifax, Nov Scotia)

For men leaving the Halifax region for larger metropolitan areas, there may also be a time lag between when the possible risks of a large-city environment (for example, proliferation of potential sex partners, more access to alcohol and drugs) are encountered and when its protective elements (for example, friendships, safer-sex education and widespread HIV testing) are accessed. One provider explained:

> I've had many conversations with ... gay men that might be around the 30, 32 age who have spent a number of years ... in the Toronto, Vancouver area, who talk about the minute they got there ... it was like fantasy land right, and they took every advantage they could, of course, and nothing wrong with that, but we're not at all prepared for the emotions, the responsibilities or any of that associated with it. (HIV/AIDS outreach coordinator, Halifax, Nova Scotia)

Another provider discussed the recent proliferation of 'young guys who went to big cities and encountered a whole other realm and level of party scene, of gay party scene'. She continued, 'Well it was like candy, you know, it was like wow, fun but no tools' (gay health liaison, Halifax, Nova Scotia). In the case of both circular, temporary migrations to Halifax and longer-term migrations to other Canadian cities, the adverse circumstances of encountering a new gay community (for example, lack of acceptance or familiarity) may affect newcomers' sexual experiences before coping skills or social supports are developed.

For international immigrants, encounters with gay communities may be further complicated by cultural differences and expectations, as well as the dynamics of the specific cities in which they are located. For some gay newcomers, particularly those settling outside of Toronto, their initial experiences may not reflect the diversity, inclusivity and sexual freedom they were expecting in Canada. Speaking about London, one provider called it 'a more family orientated [sic] city'. He explained, 'If you are identified as LGBTQ – unless you are like ... with a [permanent] job – [you] will start thinking ... maybe in a year or so I will relocate into a bigger city where I will have more opportunity, where there is more services provided for LGBTQ people.' Even within established gay communities and service regimes, newcomers still suffer from past traumas, cultural disconnects and a lack of services geared to men outside the native-born Euro-Canadian mainstream. 'Where do you go to get tested [for HIV]?' one provider in Ottawa asked.

> *Well, it's called Gayzone and that turns [some newcomers] off immediately because it's called that … We had one guy who came [to the centre] quite a bit – he's moved out of town now – he was still struggling with his sexuality because of what he had experienced back home, and he was afraid to go to the gay bar … There are parties I go to where they are playing Indian music and everybody is gay. And that would happen in almost every ethno-cultural community in a city like Toronto but in Ottawa that's a constant struggle … Sometimes I have to resist [telling clients] 'move to Toronto'.*
> *(Ethno-cultural HIV resource coordinator, Ottawa, Ontario)*

Even in Greater Toronto, where men have access to ethno-specific support groups and resources (Catungal, 2013), they experience racism and exclusion in online contexts (for example, cruising site profiles that discriminate by indicating 'no Blacks or Asians'). A gay immigrant's integration into the so-called gay community is therefore not a foregone, linear conclusion, but instead an often fractured process contingent on his location, ethno-racial background and individual life events. As this provider explained:

> *To me there are like two groups, the ones that are very well integrated in the gay community, and they hang out in the same places where white men in the community hang out. There are … many Latin American guys that don't feel engaged [with] the community, attached to the community, and they feel that they don't fit within the community … like they don't know where they need to fit, where they can fit, so for these guys they start feeling like rejection. (Latino HIV outreach worker, Toronto)*

While international immigrants' encounters with gay communities sometimes provide new supports, the estrangement created either by racism or exclusion may increase other risk factors (for example, depression, reduced self-esteem and unprotected sex) for HIV infection or lead men to seek out connections with the gay community by having sex with multiple partners.

Dynamics of Risk Encounters

Both the conditions of a newcomer's migration and his intervening relationships with families, ethno-cultural communities and gay communities inform the contexts in which risk occurs. Although epidemiologic studies often attempt to link risk (most commonly unprotected anal sex) with ostensibly predictive personal attributes (for example, level of acculturation), risk behaviour is as situational as it is knowledge- or value-driven (Diaz et al., 2001). Risk-taking, then, is related to both the immediate sexual situation – including the physical setting, the relationship and whether drugs and alcohol are involved – as well as the individuals' life events, state of mind and motivations for the encounter (Diaz et al., 2001; Bianchi et al., 2007). Unprotected sex and related behaviours like drug use might occur as the result of stressful and precarious work, social isolation), past trauma or seeking out sex in the absence of other social supports (Bianchi et al., 2007; Egan et al., 2011). In addition, newcomer men might be exposed to race-related power dynamics that place them in disadvantaged positions. When 'competing' for white partners perceived as socially superior within the gay community mainstream (Wilson and Yoshikawa, 2004; Han, 2008), immigrants may have difficulty negotiating safer sex. Within North American gay social hierarchies that positions racialized men as less desirable, many immigrant men may feel disproportionate pressure to have sex without a condom (Poppen et al., 2004; Harawa et al.,

2004) or to be the receptive partner during sexual intercourse – which itself carries a greater risk of HIV infection (Han, 2008).

Recent studies have suggested that gay men's migrations – even within countries – produce stress, social upheaval and changing activity patterns that can lead to higher risk profiles after relocating (Bruce and Harper, 2011; Egan et al., 2011; Lewis, 2014b). In Nova Scotia, two HIV nurses linked high levels of risk-taking to the urgency present in sexual encounters among closeted men travelling specifically to Halifax for sex. One said, 'So they flock here ... they may not be out or they may have you know pent up energy or whatever, and they come here and all hell breaks loose sometimes' (HIV nurse #1, Halifax, Nova Scotia). Noting the potential lack of planning and communication in such encounters, another provider said:

> *Depending on where you are ... some people feel like they can't come out so they're doing things that may be riskier because perhaps they don't even want to really talk about it ... if they're not talking, they're not comfortable talking to partners or going and getting condoms ... I suppose you're doing things a little bit more spur of the moment that you hadn't planned on. (HIV nurse #2, Halifax, Nova Scotia)*

As with men migrating internationally, those moving from Nova Scotia to large cities such as Toronto often experience personal traumas (for example, getting kicked out of the family home) before leaving and isolation or poverty after arrival. One provider offered a laundry list of factors involved in a risk encounter:

> *... a lot of stuff around poverty ... I had a lot of men disclose to me that they had been sexually abused as children ... the frustration around there being no services for men in this region ... a good percentage of the men I saw ... had experienced a lot of alienation from family ... a lot of isolation, and they had experienced that before they'd become positive as well. (LGBT health liaison, Halifax, Nova Scotia)*

A second provider explained how these interrelated factors might play out in individual risk scenarios.

> *... I think there's a lot of reasons why [unprotected sex] happens ... there's a lot of gay men who are experiencing poverty ... they're not going to have access to condoms. Do [they] just want to feel better? ... [Are they] going to have a couple of drinks and not think about it 'cause they want to do it? Absolutely. (AIDS service organization director, Halifax, Nova Scotia)*

While migration to new locales can therefore affirm sexual expression and identity, it can also lead to the loss of financial stability, the resurgence of past traumas and other factors associated with higher likelihood of sexual risk-taking.

Men who relocate to Canada from other countries can also experience a loss of self-esteem that, when combined with limited HIV education, can foreground risk behaviour. One health provider spoke about the sexual health implications of racialized immigrants negotiating new gay scenes dominated by Euro-Canadian men (see also Bassi, 2006). 'For some men who aren't empowered, especially around self-esteem and not having the knowledge base,' he said, 'the white man is the superior control, so there's a lot of unprotected sex because of those sorts of relationships' (medical doctor, Toronto, Ontario). Other providers suggested that for newcomers who feel excluded, sexual interactions might emerge as a way of gaining entrance to the local gay community:

If someone is going to put themselves at risk, maybe it's 'I'm going to go to a bath house' and as anxious as I am, I need to connect with people so I might self-medicate to get over the anxiety. Desirability is the same thing right? If this guy who seems to be well-adjusted, really hot is throwing me a bone when I have been rejected from like 10 or 15 people online ... am I going to take it if he [asks for unprotected sex] ... that's a decision that person is going to have to make and it's a difficult one. Is this connection going to happen? What do I have to concede on to make that happen? Because I don't know what my options are, because this might be the only community, the only connection I can access, so if it helps me do that I am going to facilitate it in this way. (South Asian HIV outreach worker, Toronto, Ontario)

Similar to the Nova Scotia case, the insecurity and instability that newcomers experience while seeking sexual encounters in new environments can also result in spontaneous decision-making. 'Well we ask this question to [clients] ... it's always like maybe 80 per cent of the time the heat of the moment ... or it was alcohol or it was maybe once in a while any transgressions are dropped' (Latino HIV outreach worker, Toronto, Ontario). While such situations are not necessarily unique to migrants, they may experience the triggers for particular risk behaviours more acutely because they are less familiar with dominant sexual conventions and are often positioned as less desirable. Both the Nova Scotia and Ontario cases indicate, then, that risk encounters and subsequent decision-making processes are not just driven by individual attributes, but by situations and scenarios that may be common among men negotiating situations and scenes with which they are unfamiliar.

Conclusions

This analysis of the relationships between gay men's sexual health and mobilities at both the regional/national and international scales has introduced four aspects of the migration/health nexus in need of more careful analysis in future research: the conditions and complexities of the migration process, relationships with family and ethnic communities, relationships with the gay community and the dynamics of risk encounters. The epidemiological, hypothetical–deductive research that continues to dominate gay men's health research provides inconsistent results and only basic understandings of concepts such as 'acculturation' and 'community'. In addition, the gay men and MSM being researched are alternately framed as irresponsible sensation-seekers engaging in 'fast-lane' lifestyles or (in the case of international immigrants) as uninformed and oppressed subjects who will either be saved by or corrupted by the countervailing forces of risk, health promotion and potential social support present in 'the gay community'. The narratives presented here, however, show that the relationship between mobility and sexual health is a complex one involving the simultaneous operation of structural factors such as social exclusion and individual choices related to self-esteem, coping and major life changes. While both within-country and international migrations for gay men do not necessarily share the same motivations, many of the post-migration challenges affecting sexual health (for example, isolation, stress, potential depression and instances of unanticipated rejection) are similar. In particular, the results suggest the need for future research on both the geographies and temporalities of gay men's sexual health.

While not the focus of this chapter, the results also suggest major differences between men who had moved to Toronto versus those who had moved to smaller centres in either Ontario or Nova Scotia. While Toronto has a higher concentration of spaces (for example, gay villages, bath houses, bars) that are traditionally associated with higher health risks (Egan et al., 2011; Buttram and Kurtz, 2013), cities such as London, Ottawa and Halifax pose their own sets of challenges. In these environments, the options for building community with other gay men are more limited (especially for men of colour) and family-based or ethno-cultural communities that might be unsupportive or homophobic are also smaller and more dense, causing relocated men to remain closeted or avoid seeking health services like HIV testing. While the social constraints of smaller cities could maintain some separation between newly arrived men and traditionally 'risky' activities or spaces, it might also drive men towards accessing sex with greater urgency, less information or a reduced ability to negotiate safer sex.

Finally, the findings here also raise questions about the timing of migration processes and behavioural trajectories among mobile gay men and MSM. The literatures on both cultural communities and gay communities suggest that there is a shift in the life-worlds of gay men following migration. Exposure to both risk factors (for example, drug use) and protective factors (for example, health education, social support and HIV testing) is assumed to increase over time, whereas sexual exploration is assumed to be greatest shortly after arrival (Bianchi et al., 2007; Egan et al., 2011). But these discussions often ignore the potential for other pressures of migration, such as culture shock and the struggle to find employment, to influence risk behaviour. Future research should consider the relative power and influence of both stressors and protective factors at different points in the post-migration period, and for different ethnic groups and age cohorts. More careful attention to both place and time in the geography of gay men's health will help to identify the populations in need of more targeted resources and campaigns, such as the newly arrived, as well as the interventions needed in different types of urban environments.

Chapter 33

Reconsidering Relationships between Homophobia, Human Rights and HIV/AIDS

Andrew Tucker

Introduction

The recent and dramatic increase in homophobic rhetoric across the African continent has given rise to a variety of responses, both from within the continent and from further afield. On one side of this debate we have seen a range of arguments being marshalled to suggest that 'homosexuality is unAfrican' or that the promotion of sexuality-based rights is a neocolonial imposition on Africa. The recent inhumane treatment of individuals with same-sex desire in places such as Nigeria (*Washington Post*, 2014), Uganda (Tamale, 2007), Tanzania (Kiishweko, 2012), South Africa (Judge, 2008), Zambia (D. Smith, 2013) and Zimbabwe (Brydum, 2014) have all been 'legitimated' through variants of these arguments. Such homophobic arguments should be and are rightly confronted through a variety of means. One of the most powerful and long-standing ways in which such discrimination is challenged (both academically and in civil society) has been, and continues to be, through the argument that sexual minority rights should be protected as a human right (Cock, 2003; Hoad, 1999; Samar, 2000; Sanders, 1996).

This chapter wishes to interrogate how the protection of sexual minorities (and in particular, male sexual minorities[1]) is promoted and challenged through such arguments and how they may relate to HIV. It is split into two sections. The first section will attempt to briefly suggest why the 'human rights' argument to challenge discrimination, while ubiquitous and highly important, may also require some additional support from other types of argument. The second, more exploratory section of this chapter will examine how we might look towards debates surrounding HIV/AIDS as a key way to strengthen and complement the existing human rights argument for the protection of sexual minorities. By way of conclusion this chapter will suggest that linking a challenge to homophobia to the challenge against HIV/AIDS can offer important new avenues for a new wide-ranging solidarity.

---

1   The focus on male sexual minorities here is not to dismiss the centrality of experiences of discrimination on the part of women with same-sex desire in parts of the continent. Indeed, research highlights how lesbians are increasingly becoming a focal point for discrimination, largely due to their intersection at the point of multiple forms of power and discrimination – namely, patriarchy and homophobia (Swarr, 2012). The focus on male sexual minorities is here made due to the biological risk of male same-sex activities with regard to HIV (Patal et al., 2014).

Considering Some of the Current Arguments For and Against Sexual Minority Rights in Africa

It is patently clear that many of the arguments that oppose the protection of sexual minorities in Africa are ill-considered and highly fallacious. Statements by certain 'evangelical' ministers have, for example, attempted to suggest that men with same-sex desire wish only to engage in paedophilic acts (as documented by Reddy, 2002 and Lavers, 2014). Such statements are not only blatantly false; they require a repeated and knowing perversion of peer-reviewed scientific evidence. In the face of overwhelming evidence to counter such views, it is quite simply impossible for such arguments to be sustained without a knowing, and therefore malicious, attempt to peddle lies to the misinformed.

Other statements, too, are also equally misguided. For example, attempts by homophobes to disassociate the continent of Africa from a history of same-sex desire (often through the argument that 'homosexuality is unAfrican') require a complete disavowal of history – both oral and academic (Moodie, 1988; Donham, 1998; Murray and Roscoe, 1998; Murray, 2000; Epprecht, 2007; Hoad, 2007). Statements that suggest that same-sex desire has no history on the continent thus rely on a severely blinkered view of the world.

Nevertheless, once we move beyond such starkly unreliable arguments on the part of homophobes in Africa, the position both of those opposing and those supporting sexual minority rights becomes more complicated. This is not in any way to suggest that sexual minorities should be discriminated against. It is, however, to explore quite why some of the arguments in favour of such discrimination have not gone away.

For example, if we look again at the 'homosexuality is unAfrican' argument, clearly, on one level, when related to same-sex desire, it is empirically incorrect. However, it may also be possible to see how, in two additional ways, its relationship to the struggle against same-sex discrimination becomes more complicated and does in part relate to developments initially outside of the continent. First, on an etymological level, 'the homosexual' has both a history and a geography tied to its emergence in North-west Europe at the end of the nineteenth century. As Michel Foucault (1978) and others have expressed, this was a radically new phenomenon at that time and marked the transition from same-sex sexual practices being something that an individual did to something that defined the individual (Halperin, 2002). This, in turn, allowed individuals (predominantly homosexual men) who were labelled as such to begin a long process of resistance to the power that was used to name individuals as identifiably different to begin with. We can see this most clearly through the various strategies to remove homosexuality as a medical condition (Cain, 1993; G. Smith et al., 2004) and then, later, the granting of 'gay rights' in the Global North (see below). Second, as both Carl F. Stychin (2004) and Dennis Altman (2001) have argued, over the past decade and a half we have been witness to a noteworthy period in history during which same-sex sexualities in various locations have started to become universalized *as identities* – and, in particular, we have become increasingly aware of, associated with and informed by particular forms of 'gay identity' that originate in the Global North (and which themselves therefore relate very closely to the Foucauldian notion of 'the homosexual'). Such globalization, of course, has not eradicated the local or the specific (Binnie, 2004). Cultural flows, as we are well aware, are never simply 'one-way' (Ross, 2005). And as others and I have written previously, it should therefore be remembered that sexual minority groups often very cleverly, strategically and pragmatically deploy local *and* global terms of identification and affinity simultaneously (Manalansan, 1995; Cruz-Malavé and Manalansan, 2002; Tucker, 2009a). But such considerations should not be seen to completely override what is also clearly a shift towards at least a partial adoption of a particular type of language (Leap and Boellstorff, 2004), self-identification (McAllister, 2013; Tucker, 2010a) and legalistic political project (Binnie,

2004). Problematically, each of these shifts can then give impetus to those wishing to suggest that 'homosexuality is unAfrican' (McAllister, 2013). Leading on from this, and of particular importance for the discussion below, this shift (and its concurrent homophobic backlash) has also occurred in parallel to, and gained great traction through, the universalization of 'human rights' (Hoad, 1999; Stychin, 2004).

Indeed, it is important to appreciate here the centrality of rights-based discourses – particularly human rights-based discourses – to the struggles faced by sexual minority groups in parts of Africa (and those opposed to them). For example, the universal language of human rights has helped create a form of solidarity and sharing of information and ideas among sexual minority activists never before possible (Tucker, 2010b). On a practical level, we can see this with the rise of international NGOs such as Human Rights Watch and the International Gay and Lesbian Human Rights Commission (both headquartered in the USA). It is also clear that the deployment of this language, which links human rights and sexual minority rights, has helped to strengthen and legitimate the arguments both for sexual minority rights and for human rights more generally.

We can understand a key way in which this process works by examining some of the language deployed by groups such as Amnesty International. Here, we see a particular type of linkage that is repeatedly made in arguments in support of sexual minority rights (here framed as sexual orientation and gender identity): '... all people, regardless of their sexual orientation or gender identify, should be able to enjoy their human rights' (Amnesty International, 2014).

In its most generalizable form, namely that *everyone* is human and in need of the same protections, this argument remains incredibly powerful. Discursively, however, it also forms part of a political rhetorical argument that forms a particular type of linkage between human rights and sexual minority rights (which is subtly, yet importantly, different from the suggestion that everyone is human). We can understand this, too, as more than a discursive connection between two terms. We can also view it, in relation to what Stuart Hall (1996), Ernesto Laclau (1977) and Antonio Gramsci (1971) might argue, as an *articulation* between sexual minority rights and human rights (see also Featherstone, 2012). Such an articulation in turn leads to the emergence of a particular ideological position. This position, which can be seen to have emerged within the fields of international development and international law, strives to make hegemonic (as 'common sense') an articulation between sexual minorities, their rights and wider universalistic framings of rights (for a recent example, see de Vos, 2014). Human rights, after all, are repeatedly described as inalienable, universal and egalitarian. An articulation between sexual minorities and human rights therefore appears not to be only ascendant but also commonsensical: if everyone is human, then everyone requires rights. And if everyone requires rights, then the inclusion of sexual minorities as a group that is in need of such rights strengthens the idea that human rights are indeed universal. The inclusion of sexual minority rights within the remit of human rights helps to legitimate arguments that spring from each set of rights independently and also together.

Yet as Stuart Hall (1996) might suggest, it is important to appreciate how articulations such as these are not fixed but are instead very much historically (and one might also argue, geographically) contingent. We can see this in the Amnesty International quotation below, which follows on directly from the sentence quoted above. As can be seen here, the rest of this quotation works hard to make an articulation between sexual minority rights (here labelled as LGBT rights) and human rights appear as common sense, despite also having to acknowledge the very fragility of such a link:

> *Although the Universal Declaration of Human Rights does not explicitly mention sexual orientation or gender identity, evolving conceptions of international human*

rights law include a broad interpretation to include the rights and protection of the rights of LGBT people around the world'. (Amnesty International, 2014)

Despite the fact that human rights, by definition, are meant to include everyone, the specifics of sexual orientation are clearly flagged in this quotation as not being included in the 1948 UN Declaration. Such a position is perhaps not surprising, considering the embryonic state of sexuality-based politics immediately after the Second World War. (It is also worth pointing out that the same issue exists for the African Union's Charter of Human and People's Rights.) Yet if human rights are not fixed but changeable (an 'evolving conception') and if, as stated, sexual minority rights (LGBT rights) are not even included in the Universal Declaration, then on one level at least it becomes possible to question the actual power of attempts to link sexuality-based rights and human rights (beyond the more direct argument that everyone is human). As Hall might therefore argue, an articulation between sexual minority rights and human rights, while appearing as 'common sense' and ideologically hegemonic, is in fact anything but that. Both human rights and sexual minority rights are neither universal nor automatically articulated with each other. The very idea of sexual identities tied to sexual minority rights stems from a particular history and geography – as does the development of human rights after the end of the Second World War (Knopp and Brown, 2002).

Once we have shown the fragility of the articulation between sexual minority rights and human rights we are able to see an additional (and in terms of the strength of discursive homophobic attacks on sexual minorities, fundamental) concern. This concern has been variously framed as: the 'communitarian' argument against sexual minority rights by Stychin (2004); the 'post-colonial predicament' by Awwad (2010); and the 'special rights' argument by Roy (2011). What all these arguments have in common is the requirement to see the existence of a different type of articulation between different (yet very closely related) sets of rights. This becomes possible, in part, due to an implicit awareness that the articulation between sexual minority rights and human rights is not necessarily hegemonic and that other types of 'common sense' are feasible when elements are articulated together in different ways.

Here, sexual minority rights are understood to have emerged in the globalized arena and are impacting on the postcolonial nation-state in a way reminiscent of former colonial rule. Indeed, it is telling that, in this variant of the argument against sexual minority rights, such rights are often framed by homophobes not as 'human rights' but as 'special rights'. In this way, sexual minorities are aligned with former (often colonial) rulers – the privileged few – who are both separate from the majority and requiring of 'special' consideration by the majority not for the majority's benefit. (A particular line of this argument highlights the very significant donor aid from the former colonial metropolitan centres in support of sexual minority activists in what would once have been termed the colonial 'periphery' (Kron, 2012)). Because of this, the articulation between human rights and sexual minority rights can potentially be rearticulated so that sexual minority rights become articulated with 'special rights' and human rights become articulated with the rights of the postcolonial nation. As Stychin (2004) in particular has discussed, it becomes important here to realize that any discussion of human rights is politically malleable and, indeed, 'that their deployment is limited only by the imaginations of those who wish to make claims' (ibid., p. 965). The nation, which in this rendering implies the postcolonial heterosexual majority, is framed as under siege by a minority which has aligned itself with foreign (globalized) and neocolonial conceptions of identity. The nation here, rather than sexual minority groups, becomes the element that requires protection against discriminatory forces defined by an articulation between sexual minority rights and the 'special rights' (over and above those available to the heterosexual majority) designed to impact negatively on the majority.

Such homophobic views, which require a disavowal of existing discrimination against sexual minorities by elements of the heterosexual majority, should not, however, be assumed simply to be at the fringes of debate. So powerful has the articulation between 'special rights' and 'sexual minority rights' been, for example, that Hillary Clinton, then US Secretary of State, spent a noticeable portion of her 2011 Geneva speech in 'Recognition of Human Rights Day' attempting to forcibly remove an articulation between 'special rights' and 'gay rights', and instead articulate the link between sexual minority rights (in this instance, 'gay rights') and 'human rights':

> ... *we understood that we are honoring* [sic] *rights that people always had,* rather than creating new or special rights for them. *Like being a woman, like being a racial, religious, tribal, or ethnic minority, being LGBT does not make you less human.* And that is why gay rights are human rights and why human rights are gay rights. *(Clinton, 2011, emphasis added)*

What such a statement by the then US Secretary of State can help us appreciate is just how powerful the rhetoric of special rights can be (and is feared to be). The power of these homophobic articulations requires continual confrontation.

What this very brief discussion has hopefully illustrated are some of the complexities that go to inform arguments both for and against sexual minority rights in Africa that in various ways draw upon a human rights framework. This discussion has clearly *not* been to suggest that the legal, political and social protection of individuals with same-sex desire is not an extremely urgent concern. It is also not to suggest that sexuality minority rights are not themselves important or that an articulation between such rights and human rights does not carry important purchase. It is, however, to suggest that we might want to look at additional ways in which the protection of individuals with same-sex desire can be promoted on the continent, especially in light of the problematic positioning of sexual minorities as 'outside' of the nation, as can sometimes occur with the human rights argument. As the following section will highlight, while a new articulation in the way described by Stuart Hall may not be possible or required, there may still be great benefit in at least seeing a connection between other elements – namely, challenging homophobia and challenging HIV/AIDS.

What We Might Gain from a Deeper Consideration of Homophobia in Relation to HIV/AIDS

A primary benefit, in terms of sexual minority rights struggles, is the way in which it becomes possible through discussions of HIV/AIDS and homophobia to reposition sexual minorities with respect to the nation. The discussion that follows, however, is clearly tentative. For example, it remains uncertain whether the elements discussed below could be anything more than disparate elements, whether they could become linked in some way to each other, or whether they would help form what Hall (1996) might see as ideological elements that could cohere together within a narrative to make a particular historical position intelligible and common sense. Clearly, the latter, whereby contemporary HIV prevention methods and ideas become articulated together with methods and reasons to challenge homophobia would potentially allow the greatest benefit for sexual minority struggles. As discussed below, we do not, however, know what would happen if such links were discursively made or how

299

other elements might relate. This section therefore sets out some tentative suggestions as to what could be gained by more closely aligning calls to challenge homophobia, with broader calls to challenge HIV/AIDS.

To begin with, however, it is noticeable when examining the history of the African AIDS epidemic that the voices of sexual minorities, while included in debate, were not, as in many countries in the Global North, leading the charge to challenge the spread of the virus (Iliffe, 2006). This can readily be explained by a number of reasons. First, countries in Africa have experienced 'generalized epidemics' as opposed to solely 'concentrated' or 'acute' epidemics (Mann and Tarantola, 1996; Stine, 2013). African HIV epidemics have therefore involved larger numbers of heterosexual transmissions than transmissions or infections among sexual minorities. Second, it is also possible to surmise that, compared to gay and lesbian social movements prevalent during the mid- to late twentieth century in the Global North, there have been far fewer and less formalized movements during a similar period in various African countries (Epprecht, 2013). In part this, too, can be rationalized by the fact that the particular formalization and medicalization of, and discrimination around, discrete sexual-identity-based categories such as 'the homosexual', as the above discussion highlighted, emerged in places such as North-west Europe. Third, in places such as South Africa, it is also clear that any specific mobilization of sexuality-based activists that did occur was focused on singular issues such as the granting of legal rights – for example, on the right to gay marriage. Such struggles were very much about an articulation between minority group rights and struggles such as race-based rights and, indeed, human rights. Often, such struggles only paid lip service to more generalizable concerns (Oswin, 2007b). This, it should also be pointed out, occurred while the majority of South Africans had no recourse to the law for the protection of their newly found rights in the first place (Charle, 2009; Nel and Judge, 2008; Verouden, 2007).

While there therefore appears to have been a comparative lack of historical attention to health debates by sexual minority groups, there has also historically been a lack of attention to sexual minorities from those involved in health policy in (especially sub-Saharan) Africa, until recently. We can see this, too, as a consequence of the fact that the majority of HIV transmission in Africa has been heterosexual in nature. Nevertheless, such a statement should not be taken to mean that sexual minorities – and, in particular, men with same-sex desire, or, epidemiologically, 'men who have sex with men' (MSM) – have not continued to become infected and infect each other throughout these generalized epidemics. There are a variety of potential reasons that can help explain why, despite continued infections among MSM, a focus on sexual minority groups has been sorely lacking. As anthropological research from a variety of locations has highlighted, epidemiologists have not, historically, been especially attuned to knowing what or how to ask men questions to do with same-sex sexual behaviour (Chirimuuta, 1997; Farmer, 2006). In addition, institutional inertia and limited funding for studies on the topic may have further hindered the ability of epidemiologists and other scientists to examine African MSM HIV transmission in the 1980s, 1990s and early part of the new millennium (Johnson, 2007). However, it is also clear that, especially during the early years, extremely contentious beliefs emanating from locations in the Global North also hampered a greater understanding of the epidemic. As a variety of social theorists critiqued at the time, racist ideas were deployed by a range of groups to suggest that the African AIDS epidemic was not associated with homosexuality, simply because homosexuality was not found in 'primitive' societies (Austin, 1990; Packard and Epstein, 1991; Patton, 1990; Treichler, 1991; Watney, 1994). Not only were such ideas highly misguided and without doubt racist; they also limited a broader exploration as to how serious the HIV/AIDS epidemic was among MSM across Africa.

What we find therefore is a situation in which sexual minority activists in Africa may not have been in a position to discuss and engage with health and HIV to the same degree as in other parts of the world. We also find a situation in which the plight of groups such as MSM were relatively sidelined within broader struggles about HIV/AIDS occurring on the continent. However, evidence from studies in the past decade from locations including Malawi, Namibia and Botswana (Baral et al., 2009), South Africa (Lane et al., 2011; Tucker et al., 2013b), Tanzania (Dahoma et al., 2011); Lesotho (Baral et al., 2011), Kenya (Sanders et al., 2007) and Senegal (Wade et al., 2005) are starting to uncover the sheer magnitude of the HIV/AIDS epidemic among MSM in Africa. Such figures for HIV prevalence are, in all cases, significantly higher than for the general heterosexual population in each country. Countries such as South Africa are therefore now directly including categories of individual such as MSM in their national plans to confront HIV/AIDS (SANAC, 2011). Recently, groups such as UNAIDS (2009), PEPFAR (2011) and the Global Fund (2009) have also been taking explicit note of the need to engage with particular at-risk key populations such as MSM (see Taylor in this volume). The message from epidemiological data and funding imperatives is therefore clear: MSM are at significant risk of HIV/AIDS, and failing to tackle HIV among MSM groupings limits the efficacy of national HIV/AIDS campaigns.[2]

Yet the need to consider how MSM are affected by HIV goes much further than simply seeing them as a group that should be included within national HIV prevention plans. And it is here that we might want to consider how challenging homophobia itself is key to challenging HIV. Here, we can start to appreciate how there are at least two very important reasons why health policy workers (and associated epidemiologists and activists) would want to explore in greater detail a link between challenging homophobia and challenging HIV. Both of these factors may give important additional justifications as to why states should consider legislating against homophobia (rather than promoting it) beyond debates about the history and geography of 'the homosexual', the applicability of human rights or the separation of sexual minority rights as distant (and dissident) to the rights of the nation. Furthermore, both these factors described below are also at times very closely aligned with existing stigmas that can affect the wider heterosexual population. Thus, not only does homophobia become a mechanism that should be challenged by the majority for the national benefit, but it also emerges that the experiences of homophobia for groups such as MSM are very similar to experiences of discrimination experienced by wider, heterosexual, groups, too.

The first reasons why it may be prudent to examine in greater detail a link between a challenge to HIV and a challenge to homophobia is that homophobia can limit competent medical care. The second reason is that homophobia increases the likelihood of needing competent medical care to begin with. As the rest of this chapter highlights, both these reasons are at times closely aligned to pre-existing forms of discrimination that currently affect wider groups, beyond sexual minorities.

In relation to the first concern, recent work from Kenya and South Africa shows that some workers at public health clinics can sometimes be seen to present as having negative views towards homosexuality, leading MSM to feel stigmatized when visiting facilities (van der Elst et al., 2013; Lane et al., 2008). These issues can in turn lead to MSM feeling unable to visit clinics. Other recent reports, including those published in medical journals such as *The Lancet*, are now also arguing that competent care for MSM in Africa is a prerequisite

---

2   Further, running parallel to these endeavours within the scientific community, we are also seeing early moves among activists in places such as Uganda to link together homophobia and health as they explore diverse ways of confronting state-sponsored discrimination (Mugisha, 2014).

for an effective and comprehensive fight against HIV (Beyrer et al., 2012; Mayer et al., 2012; A.D. Smith et al., 2009).

Such views are, in some ways, very similar to concerns raised by AIDS activists in the very early 1980s, 30 years ago, in the Global North. At that time, activists (and academics) challenged public health services in countries such as the Netherlands, Canada, the UK and the USA to develop better ways of treating men with AIDS. In those instances, homophobia itself was a key – if not *the* key – issue that had to be addressed if the sick were to be treated justly and with dignity (M. Brown, 1997a; Kirp and Bayer, 1992; Kayal, 1993; Kramer, 1989). Unlike the early 1980s, however, discrimination against men with same-sex desire and discrimination associated with AIDS are not wholly synonymous in various countries on the African continent. Instead, a situation has emerged whereby the primary concern has been discrimination and stigma associated with AIDS which, due to a generalized rather than concentrated epidemic, is a manifestation that can potentially affect everyone (Holzemer et al., 2007; Kalichman and Simbayi, 2003; Simbayi et al., 2007).

As a result, a great deal of effort has been put into educating health workers, community groups, traditional healers and politicians to challenge such discrimination. It is thus appreciated that discrimination and stigma can limit visits to clinics and also decrease the overall well-being of people living with HIV (PLHIV) This has the knock-on effect of potentially increasing burdens on families and eventually on healthcare facilities (Barnett and Whiteside, 2006). Of particular interest here is that there therefore exists the very important possibility of seeing how discrimination against groups such as sexual minorities can be understood as a variant of the discrimination and stigma faced by the broader community who may potentially be HIV-positive in spaces such as clinics. This is not to suggest that all sexual minorities or those who visit clinics are HIV-positive. It is instead to suggest that just as members of the general population require competent and non-discriminatory healthcare to reduce HIV in society, so do other groups. This is not because sexual minorities require 'special rights'. It is, rather, because discrimination at clinics can be understood not solely as a factor that only affects sexual minorities.

The second reason is that homophobia is associated with certain risky sexual practices such as unprotected anal intercourse (UAI). Here, research from South Africa has highlighted that MSM who experience homophobia are more likely to engage in UAI. This research also highlights that homophobia is part of a constellation of broader issues, including negative affective states such as depression and a lack of self-efficacy, which must also be acknowledged in HIV prevention work (Tucker et al., 2013b; Tucker et al., 2014). Along a parallel line of inquiry, another correlation has also been found between experiences of human rights abuses (broadly defined) among MSM and having an HIV-positive status (Baral et al., 2009).

Such considerations are, by themselves, not new. Similar research has been conducted in various countries in the Global North, which have also found starkly similar links (Alvy et al., 2010; Crepaz and Marks, 2001). In an African context, however, what is important is understanding what homophobia means for individuals in their day-to-day lives (outside of clinic spaces), beyond the most obvious and harshest reality of physical violence. Research, primarily in North America, has helped develop such a wider perspective on homophobia that effectively links it to the impact it has on longer-term individual health and well-being. Seen as a type of trauma inflicted on the individual, homophobia is understood as a form of discrimination that can have lasting effects on individuals, even if it is not manifested in its most extreme form, through physical violence. The development of similar perspectives in countries such as South Africa – whereby homophobia, clinically defined depression and sexual risk-taking have very recently been found to be linked – could potentially help in the formulation of a broader conceptualization of homophobia as a factor that can lead to negative health outcomes for individuals over the life course (Tucker et al., 2014). This not only broadens the scope in which homophobia can be understood to impact on individuals; it hence also broadens the scope of what needs to be challenged.

In turn, and similar to the above discussion of homophobia in clinics and discrimination associated with AIDS in clinics, there is also a growing body of work that highlights how discrimination linked to AIDS is associated with a far wider range of negative health outcomes. Just as it is now being appreciated that homophobia impacts on a large number of concerns, so too is AIDS discrimination understood to be associated with factors such as a failure to adhere to medication (Rao et al., 2007), and, as with homophobic stigma against MSM) depression (Simbayi et al., 2007). It may therefore be prudent to consider what may be gained from a broader debate about a heterosexual majority struggle against the stigmatization of AIDS and a sexual minority struggle against homophobic stigma – especially when the outcomes of both are at times similar.

A Reconsideration of Solidarity

As discussed at the start of the previous section, it is still uncertain what may be possible when challenging HIV/AIDS and challenging homophobia are discursively linked. Just as the possibility of an articulation of the type Stuart Hall might describe may not be possible, so too should it be accepted that the outcome of possible linkages may serve to increase discrimination. For example, it is possible that an explicit articulation between homophobia and the risks of HIV infection could permit arguments to be put forward that call for the further curtailment of sexual minority rights. After all, it may well be within the remit of homophobes to suggest that a statistical association between homophobia and MSM HIV risk legitimates a curtailment of MSM groups, rather than a curtailment of homophobia.

As Gerry Kearns explores in his chapter in this *Companion*, there has long been a debate as to the possibilities and noticeable problems of developing broad-based solidarities between sexual minority groups and other affected parties (for example, heterosexual groups in relation to epidemiology). Such solidarities, in previous (albeit very different) contexts, have at best been short-lived (Hodge, 2000). This was partly because the actual points of similarity between different groups have been seen (sometimes erroneously) as fleeting. Yet in the context of homophobia in Africa, despite the possibility of negative outcomes, we may still want to consider what can be gained by showing that sexual minority groups are a part of the heterosexual majority in relation to the struggle against AIDS. This connection can now be framed in three interlinked ways. First, HIV prevalence and pressure on resources (families, health facilities and tax) may both remain more severe than they would otherwise be if it is not appreciated that MSM themselves are at risk of HIV. Second, homophobic discrimination at clinics and in terms of broader impacts on individual affective states can lead to increased HIV prevalence. Third, there are sometimes remarkable similarities in the way in which discrimination that affects the majority relates to discrimination that affects sexual minority groups.

As Featherstone (2012) points out in differing contexts, there can exist a great variety of factors which can go together to enable or hinder solidarities. For Featherstone, solidarities are rarely a given, but need to be worked at and produced. Here, I have argued that solidarity with sexual minority groups could be generated or produced by considering the linkages between sexual minorities and the heterosexual majority in relation to health. These linkages may not necessarily be fleeting, but instead may be relatable across the entirety of the AIDS epidemic in Africa. Solidarity then, in this context, may be a means by which sexual minority groups can be more likely to be positioned as part of the nation, rather than outside of it. This may also therefore help give an additional mechanism to activists who articulate a link between sexual minority rights and human rights.

SECTION VI
Commercial Sexualities

Maarten Loopmans (editor)

Chapter 34

Commercial Sexualities: Section Introduction

Maarten Loopmans

Since the pioneering work of geographers like Symanski (1974; 1981), Shumsky and Springer (1981) and Ashworth et al. (1988), sex work has been one of the topical interests in the subdiscipline of geographies of sexualities. Symanski (1981) and Ashworth et al. (1988), inspired by then fashionable social ecology studies and Robert Park's concept of the 'moral region' (places in the city where divergent moral codes prevailed), sought to understand and explain the location of sex work through economic and sociopolitical determinants. Whilst debates in this field continue up to today – for example, in McKewon's (2003), Ryder's (2004, 2010) and Cameron's (2004) writings on the political and economic determinants of the location of sex work venues or in Aalbers and Sabat's (2012) and Weitzer's (2014) discussion of the red-light district as a 'moral region' – geographical research on sex work has now expanded and diverged in various new directions (Hubbard and Whowell, 2008). Contemporary geographical studies on sex work include critical accounts of the relations between, and politics of, urban regeneration, heteronormativity, transnational migration and the policing of sex work as much as approaches giving voice to sex workers and their lived experiences, their spatial tactics of resistance and performances of self. We now also have a wide variety of case studies of cities and sex workers from the Global North to the Global South.

This introductory chapter will discuss the past decade's coming of age of the geographies of sex work, identifying five main fields of research. In the following section we will explore the burgeoning literature exploring the relation between sex work and the politics of urban space. The next section focuses on the global scale, discussing the policing of transnational sex work. The fourth section opens up new avenues of theoretical exploration in discussing the regulation of sex work as a biopolitical endeavour to construct heteronormality. The final two sections are dedicated to micro-level research on the everyday spatial practices of individual sex workers, on the one hand, and the role of places and spatial performances in the construction of identities and subjectivities of sex workers, on the other. In the conclusion, we introduce the four chapters of Section VI by situating them in the five fields described.

Sex Work and the Politics of Urban Space

Since the early discussions on the political and economic determinants of sex work locations (see Ashworth et al., 1988), urban studies on sex work have evolved into a debate on the spatial transformation of urban red-light districts as part of, and related to, wider urban transformation processes, in particular gentrification, touristification and urban regeneration (Papayanis, 2000;

Ryder, 2004; Cameron, 2004; McKewon, 2003; Hubbard, 1997, 1999, 2004a, 2004b; Hubbard et al., 2008; Hubbard and Whowell, 2008; Aalbers and Deinema, 2012; Loopmans and Van den Broeck, 2011; Neuts et al., 2014). Ryder (2004) and Hubbard (2004a) describe how the recent redevelopment of inner cities for gentrification and tourism is pushing up land rent in inner cities, driving profit-maximizing sex entrepreneurs to seek out cheaper sites, or, if possible, upgrade their businesses and integrate them into the wider entertainment and tourism industry (Van Straaten, 2004; Hubbard et al., 2008). Recent policy pressure on the visible presence of the sex industry in inner cities is explained by a reinvigorated conservative sexual morality, intolerant towards public visibility of the sex industry. Consequently, policy-makers aiming to redevelop urban areas have attempted to hide sex work from public view (Papayanis, 2000; Sanchez, 2004; Hubbard, 2004a, 2004b; Löw and Ruhne, 2009; Aalbers and Deinema, 2012). Moreover, as the social geography of cities is changing, red-light districts formerly located in 'working-class' neighbourhoods are now confronted with new populations that generally show less tolerance to non-normative sexual activities (Mathieu, 2011). For instance, immigrant populations that settle in these neighbourhoods sometimes reveal themselves as virulent opponents of overt sex work (Hubbard, 1997). Middle-class gentrifiers might insist on a 'revanchist' kind of cleansing of public space from all sorts of 'nuisance-producing' activities (Papayanis, 2000; Hubbard, 2004a, 2004b). Attempts to close sex businesses or displace street prostitutes are widespread, and, in urban regeneration discourse, quality of life for residents is the antithesis of a visible sex industry. However, the governance of sex work is not only influenced by processes and actors who operate within cities. Increasingly, attention is being paid to global processes affecting the regulation of sex work.

Globalization and the Policing of Transnational Sex Work

In addition to a long-standing interest in the local (mainly urban) politics of sex work, geographers have now also started to pay more attention to the connection between sex work and globalization. Historical geographers have considered the relation between imperialism and the policing of prostitution (Kumar, 2005; Howell, 2004, 2009; Legg, 2012). The apparent globalization of sex work today has gained increasing attention (see Kempadoo and Doezema, 1998; Sassen, 2002; Agathangelou, 2004), some authors having begun to disentangle its geographies (Sanchez, 2004; Hubbard and Whowell, 2008; Hubbard, 2012). Two mutually related 'global' processes are emphasized in geographical studies: first, a growing international mobility of sex workers and clients; second, the way in which the globalization of sex work has affected the national and local regulation of sex work.

In 1981 Symanski was already contending that the 'demand for diversity has been a significant reason for the [interurban and international] mobility of prostitutes' (Symanski, 1981, p. 184). Since then, international migration and tourism has expanded in both scale and scope. This increase in migration and tourism includes growing numbers of sex tourists and migrating sex workers (Agustin, 2007; Laidler et al., 2007; Chang and Chen, 2013), giving a new boost to the sex industry and to the development of new local and national policy approaches to sex work. Constituting new spaces of action and erotic/exotic pleasures for sex buyers, these transnational sex markets greatly stimulate demand (Wonders and Michalowski, 2001; Marttila, 2008) and have given rise to the development of 'world cities of sex work' (Hubbard, 2012; Deinema and Aalbers, 2015). Places like Amsterdam and Cuba have been promoting themselves as sex-tolerant places (Pope, 2005; Deinema and Aalbers, 2015; Neuts et al., 2014) as part of a struggle for geopolitical prominence and capital flows, thereby actively contributing to the construction of 'real and imagined' global geographies of sexualities.

The increasingly transnational character of sex work has also stimulated other policy initiatives. Comparing recent reforms in EU countries, Hubbard et al. (2008) and Crowhurst et al. (2012) explain how recent policy reforms relating to prostitution within individual nation-states cannot be disentangled from the discursive equation of sex workers with trafficked women and the moral panic in society over rising migration, as 'legislative reform is deemed necessary to maintain the integrity of nation-state' (Hubbard et al., 2008, p. 148). Indeed, O'Neill et al. (2008) emphasize how residents' reactions to street sex work are increasingly informed by media discourses about their ethnic and racial 'Otherness', whereas FitzGerald (2013) explores the geographic identity politics of Western feminists in organizing their discourse on the female trafficked migrant, increasingly eclipsing earlier political struggles for both sex workers' and migrants' rights (Chapkis, 2003; Agustin, 2007). Crowhurst et al. (2012) also point to the role of supranational government bodies such as the EU or the UN in universalizing discourses on trafficking and potential policy answers. How this moral panic affects national and local policy-making is debated among geographers. Hubbard et al. (2008) see strong similarities in otherwise very different policy models of legalization, abolitionism and prohibitionism, as all tend to expel prostitutes out of sight from 'respectable' places, and from legal protection. Loopmans and Van den Broeck (2011), on the other hand, emphasize how a globalizing discourse on trafficking translates into different local policy reactions because it is mediated by specific local cultures, institutions and actors (see also Di Ronco, 2014).

Heteronormative Sexual Politics

A powerful critique of the policing of sex work builds on the works of Michel Foucault, Jacques Derrida, Gilles Deleuze and Giorgio Agamben to reveal the connections between the regulation of sex work as 'deviant' and the construction of heterosexuality. In these studies, sex work and heterosexuality are presented as an effect of knowledge and discourse production, as a normative and regulatory fiction embedded in wider biopolitical urges. The sex worker is described as a *homo sacer*, excluded and segregated from 'the normal' (Sanchez, 2004; Hubbard et al., 2008) to serve as a rightless antipodal 'Other' necessary for the construction of heteronormality (and, increasingly, homonormality – see Ross and Sullivan, 2012). In such discourse, a moral geography is constructed 'in which sex work is deemed incompatible with family occupation' (Hubbard and Prior, 2013, p. 145). The policing and control of sex work and sex-work spaces is exposed as functional to the biopolitical regulation of the wider population (Howell, 2004; M. Brown and Knopp, 2010; Evered and Evered, 2013). However, empirical studies reveal how this control is produced through geographically unevenly distributed governmental networks and diverse mundane practices of politicians, planners, policemen and licensing officers. Consequently, such biopolitical regulation of sex-work spaces remains incomplete, contradictory and open at the level of its effects on the ground (Loopmans and Van den Broeck, 2011; Laing, 2012; Legg, 2012; Prior et al., 2013).

Everyday Spatial Practices of Sex Workers

In the past decades geographers have also turned to an understanding of the lived experiences of sex workers, centring the voice and highlighting the agency of sex workers, rather than the structural and spatial constraints they face. This introduced a whole set of alternative theories and methods to the geographic literature on sex work.

In discussing the micro-geographical tactics sex workers deploy to avoid harassment and marginalization by police, punters and protesters, Hubbard and Sanders (2003) reveal how sex workers tactically negotiate societal constraints by navigating and reshaping 'pre-inscribed' spaces and policies of marginalization. The struggles against societal constraints and social and spatial marginalization in cities has since been discussed in various ways. Central to these interventions is the degree of agency sex workers reveal in co-producing the spatial ways in which sex work is regulated and organized. At the micro-spatial level of the sex work venue, Whowell (2009) and Atkins and Laing (2012), studying male sex work in Manchester's Gay Village, explain how places for sex work are as much produced by the spatial and bodily performances of sex workers and clients, as by the regulatory strategies of government bodies. Similarly, Laing (2012) emphasizes the way in which exotic dancers in Canada expand the spaces available to them in clubs, in order to make additional income. Subverting the stereotypical conception of male dominance in a sex-work relationship, Aalbers (2005), in an exploration of the 'unwritten rules' of the Amsterdam red-light district, describes how sex workers control and manipulate the behaviour of clients. However, in a study on 'bar girls' in Ethiopia, Van Blerk (2011) emphasizes how such 'autonomous performative tactics' take place within the boundaries set by bar owners and customers, and the agency of bar girls remains fragile and bound up in micro-power relations beyond their control.

At the wider level of the city, Becki Ross (2010) describes the strategies of resistance against displacement deployed by sex workers during the gentrification of Vancouver's West End. Similarly, Williams (2014) describes how the development of the historic centre of Salvador de Bahia into a tourist place has inscribed itself in the city's rigid and hierarchical racial and class structure, with black and poor citizens considered as 'out of place' in the historic centre. Resisting being exiled from such 'whitened' spaces, black sex workers carve out particular places in the inner city as 'sex work spots'. Whereas Williams (2014) marks this as a clear example of reclaiming agency by marginalized subjects, she asserts that the presence of black sex workers in the historic centre simultaneously reinforces the geographical and racial discourses stimulating sex tourism and the domination of black people in the city. Emphasizing the social construction of sex workers' identities, her work ties in with studies deploying feminist theories of performativity to explore the construction of identities in place.

Identity and Performance

Everyday geographies of sex work have also turned to the construction of identities and subjectivities in relation to places and performances of sex work. Much of this work demonstrates how heteronormativity is at the same time challenged and reproduced through the repeated construction and performance of subjectivities (following Butler, 1990, 1993; Gregson and Rose, 2000). Such an approach has proven useful in problematizing and transcending the binaries of passive/active, victimization/empowerment, sex worker/ prostitute often mobilized in public debate (Frank, 2003; Yea, 2012).

Collins (2012) discusses the practices of 'hosts' to gay tourists in a transnational gentrifying district in Malate, the Philippines. Malate's development into a popular gay urban enclave relies on host work to facilitate the movement of tourists among Malate's gay venues., Hosts simultaneously develop and perform their knowledge of the place, but performing hospitability involves much more, including enacting desire or the specific sexual roles visitors imagine them to play. At the same time, hospitability is also desirable to hosts, as it involves not only economic rewards, but also cultural capital and access to desired gentrified gay spaces. As Collins (2012, p. 515) writes, 'hosts explore their own capacity for self-transformation through desire'. Ding and Ho's (2013) study of rural-to-urban migrant female sex workers in the Pearl River Delta equally stresses the potential for self-transformation, describing how sex work offers female migrants a way out of the stigma of poverty and rurality. Allowing them to perform a sophisticated urbanity, sex work offers an escape from traditional gender and sexual roles, and provides them with emotional satisfaction and a more liberated sexuality. Ding and Ho (2012) emphasize how such identities are not crafted by individuals in isolation, but result from the interactional relations with particular spaces, clients, mamasans,[1] husbands, boyfriends and themselves. This point is taken up by Faier (2014) in her analysis of the mobilization of 'the prostitute stigma' by Filipina migrant women in a rural Japanese village against fellow migrant women. She describes how this occurs not so much to categorize a sexual–economic relationship, but to distinguish themselves in a strategy to strengthen their own position as respectable mothers and partners. She shows how Filipina migrant women in Japan are always at risk of being stigmatized, as they are often considered poor and hence sexually available to Japanese men, whereas, in the Philippines, they are believed to be immoral and willing to do anything for money. As Silvey (2010) in a case study of Indonesian women explains, the discursive interpretation of migration is heavily gendered, and, whereas migration might be a way of evading moral scrutiny (Van Blerk, 2011; Ding and Ho, 2013), female mobility itself is often at risk of being linked to immorality and the stigma of prostitution (see Sörensson, 2012 on the sexualization of female tourist guides in Indonesia).

Yea (2012) demands attention to the way in which trajectories of migration or trafficking affect subject positions of sex workers, their tactics and performances (see also Mai, 2009). Yea explains how performances as sex workers or trafficking victims in one place and time cannot be understood in isolation from experiences and performances in other places and times along this trajectory. On a somewhat smaller scale, Spanger (2013a) also detects 'infections' between spaces and performances, between performances and between different spaces. She emphasizes the negotiation of various social positions with each other and with the places in which they are performed. In her work with Thai sex workers in Denmark, she understands how gender performances play a part in sex work and how sex work relates to their gendered subject positions in spaces away from sex work, like home.

Conclusion and Section Overview

New directions in geographies of sex work have given rise to improved and more nuanced understandings of the spatialities of sex work and have introduced a number of theoretical and methodological innovations. Geographers of sex work have been influenced by critical urban political economists in understanding the role of capitalist urbanization (and most notably gentrification) in unsettling the urban geographies of sex work, and by Foucault and Agamben in understanding the biopolitical urge behind many national and local prostitution policies. Queer and postcolonial theorists have had their influence on debates on the lived experiences of sex workers. They have stimulated geographers to reject unfruitful binary

---

1   Mamasan is a term sometimes used in East Asia to refer to a woman in a position of authority in a geisha house, bar, nightclub, massage parlour or brothel.

interpretations of sex work. Moreover, in a number of instances, fruitful theoretical cross-overs between various theories have been established (see Collins, 2012; Hubbard, 2013; Williams, 2014). These theoretical innovations have been accompanied by the introduction and expansion of novel methodologies such as discourse analysis, visual anthropology (see Atkins and Laing, 2012), time–spatial life-course analysis (Yea, 2012) or multi-sited ethnographies (Yea, 2012; Spanger, 2013a). This methodological expansion has allowed for increased attention and access to less publicly visible forms of sex work, so that we now have a rather good understanding of private bars, massage parlours, closed brothels and their relations with other lived spaces in the lives of sex workers.

Notwithstanding great progress in the recent past, gaps in the geographies of sex work remain, particularly when compared to the literature on sex work in other disciplines. While now clearly centring on the voices of sex workers, the experiences of other individual actors with whom they relate and interact (police officers, brothel owners, traffickers, planners, partners, punters and so on), though important in the making of sex work, still remain relatively understudied in geography. And although a turn has been made to pay attention to the lived experiences of sex work, a fleshy, embodied understanding of sex work remains underdeveloped. Similarly, the focus is mainly on female sex workers catering to male clients in urban space, while LGBTQI sex workers and rural or cyberspace – and the methodological opportunities and challenges these have to offer – are still given too little attention (but see the special issue of *Sexualities* coordinated by Smith and Laing (2012)).

The chapters in this section have been selected to offer insights into the variety of approaches in contemporary geographies of sex work. In the first chapter Phil Hubbard addresses the intricate web of governmental strategies which shapes the urban geographies of sex work in the Global North. He discusses the way in which the practices of licensing, zoning, policing and surveillance can be linked to revanchist gentrification, sexual normativity and the gendering of urban spaces.

Next, Magaly Rodríguez García opens up our perspective on sex work and its discursive construction by providing a global history of commercial sexualities. She shows how throughout space and time, moral, cultural and legal definitions overlap and reinforce each other. Rodríguez García explains how such definitions have always served to simultaneously condemn and commodify sexual practices in an attempt to tame the socially disruptive character of desire. Conscious of the power of discourse, she warns against binary interpretations of commercial sexualities, emphasizing its ineffectiveness in encompassing the complexities of commercial sexualities.

In a third chapter, Joseli Maria Silva and Marcio Jose Ornat contribute to the literature on the intricate identity performances of migrant sex workers to disrupt the binary conception of domination and resistance. Introducing the concept of 'tropicalization', the authors discuss the corporeal and sexual production of Brazilian sex workers in Spain as resulting from a complex interplay between a hegemonic European gaze and the subversive reactions of Brazilian women engaged in commercial sex. In a highly relational account, they explain how Spanish men and women construct and legitimize their own sexuality in relation to geographical imaginations of 'Brazilianness', whereas Brazilian women appeal to and reproduce these imaginations to claim sexual power as sex workers in Spanish society.

Finally, Marlene Spanger mobilizes Butler's theory of performativity in exploring the connections between places and subject positions in her story of a Thai migrant sex worker in Denmark. She discusses how her performances of the gendered subject positions of sex worker, wife and migrant intersect in different ways, in relation to and navigating the heteronormative discourses which set the boundaries of performances in particular places.

Chapter 35

Sex Work, Urban Governance and the Gendering of Cities

Phil Hubbard

Introduction

While the buying and selling of sex has never been a solely urban phenomenon, it has arguably been most visible in 'red-light' districts – for example, De Wallen in Amsterdam, Soho in London, the Reeperbahn in Hamburg, King's Cross in Sydney, Pigalle in Paris and Patpong in Bangkok (Hubbard and Whowell, 2008; Ryder, 2004). In most cases, these 'hot districts' are particularly associated with street or window prostitution by female or trans workers. In some instances, they are also home to commercial sex in the form of 'adult-oriented' businesses, 'gentleman's clubs', sex shops, massage parlours, theatres and peep shows. Geographical literature concludes that this clustering is not simply a simple response to (economic) patterns of supply and demand, but is also shaped by the moral codes, legal strictures and police strategies that push sex work towards particular spaces (see especially Symanski, 1981; Hubbard, 1998; Howell, 2009). It is, in effect, the outcome of a social production of space that involves the entwining of dominant representations of red-light districts (as sites of 'irregular' or even 'perverse' sexuality) with the spatial practices of a variety of actors, including sex workers, clients, police, outreach workers, city bureaucrats, residents, businesses and so on (Hubbard and Sanders, 2003; Mathieu, 2011; Kingston, 2013). This produces the distinctive choreography of many red-light districts, typified by particular rhythms of inhabitation, tactical ways of looking and being, and the creation of sights and sounds that might be viewed as 'out of place' elsewhere in increasingly sanitized cities (Aalbers, 2005; Cook and Whowell, 2011; Weitzer, 2014).

Beyond the fact that red-light areas provide urban geographers with a fertile environment in which to examine the corporeality of metropolitan life and to document the emergence of a distinctive 'subcultural' space, there is much that can be learnt about the wider relations of society and space through examination of such overt spaces of sex work. For example, considered in the context of social norms of comportment and behaviour, the location of sex work in the city can be revealing of the dominant moral geographies that reproduce both social and spatial norms (Symanski, 1981; Hubbard, 1999). As far back as the work of the pioneering Chicago School sociologists, zones of 'vice' have been read as revealing the wider social ecology of the city, with the social 'disorganization' characterizing the red-light area being juxtaposed with the social order found elsewhere. Reckless (1933, p. 252), for example, argued that 'vice concentrates in those tracts of the city which showed the highest rate of community disorganization', which he measured through a variety of indicators, including rates of poverty, divorce and poor health. Subsequent analyses have challenged the characterization of red-light districts as necessarily typified by high crime rates and deprivation (see Edwards, 2010; Weitzer, 2014), yet it is clear that areas with publicly visible erotic businesses and sex work remain known through particular place myths that 'distance' them from more desirable, wealthier and whiter urban neighbourhoods.

Locating sex work districts within wider urban contexts accordingly involves more than simply 'mapping' their occurrence; it requires an exploration of how their manifestation reflects, and reproduces, dominant social and spatial orders. In this chapter, I hence consider some of the principal ways in which studies of red-light landscapes have helped enrich ongoing geographical debates concerning urban governance, the relations of sexuality, and space and geographies of gender. In doing so, I draw primarily on studies carried out in a Western context: while this comes with certain dangers, this focus helps steer the chapter towards a set of distinctive debates in Anglo-American geography concerning the remaking of sex and gender in the contemporary 'revanchist' city. What this reveals is that although national laws surrounding prostitution can be highly variable (with approaches ranging from prohibition through to outright decriminalization), there are often remarkable similarities and resonances between cities in terms of how policies of spatial containment, exclusion and surveillance construct geographies of sex work (Laing and Cook, 2014).

Urban Governance, Gentrification and the Revanchist City

In many accounts, the red-light district is seen to emerge through a coincidence of different factors that have centripetal or centrifugal effects on the location of prostitution in the city:

> The specific locations of prostitution are determined by history and geopolitics: where it began and where people came to accept it; where prostitutes helped blight a neighbourhood in establishing a niche and where public opinion, financial interests and those who enforce laws that have pushed prostitution or permitted it to remain. (Symanski, 1981, p. 38)

The implication here is that the emergence of red-light zones cannot be understood without reference to wider processes of urban governance, with the creation of a visible but contained area of 'vice' being a common strategy for imposing urban order (see also Aalbers and Deinema, 2012). Traditionally, policing has been to the fore in this process (Laing and Cook, 2014), with the criminal law posited as the chief means by which forces of law and order can exercise some control over the location of street sex work in the city. In most jurisdictions, this has been driven by a clear anxiety that spaces of visible street prostitution should be off-limits to children, as well as being distanced from groups who object to such activities on cultural or religious grounds. Moreover, it is motivated by the notion that street sex work constitutes a form of nuisance that is associated with obscenity, littering, noise and petty crime. This given, the use of police powers to contain street sex work in specific urban neighbourhoods or 'tolerance zones' allows the forces of law and order to ensure that these provide controlled environments for commercial sex via an enclosure of the bodies of sex workers and their clients that prevents such nuisance 'spilling' out into other neighbourhoods. Surveillance of such spaces by state agents (for example, the police, but also the judiciary, doctors and social workers) hence constitutes a form of *biopower*, given that this allows a level of monitoring and control to be exercised over those populations who buy and sell sex on the street.

Viewed from a Foucauldian perspective, the policing of street sex work and the creation of sites of surveillance are suggestive of the logic of panopticism and a control society in which prostitution is effectively disciplined through an ongoing regulation of space. While such control is rarely total, with many forms of sex work evading the gaze of the state and the law, this means that prostitution – at least in the form of female and trans street sex working – is effectively contained and policed. The zones accordingly created hence serve both as spaces of legal censure as well as pragmatic spaces where sex is permitted to be sold under state surveillance. The police thus take on a key role as enforcers of urban order, maintaining the bounded order of the red-light district through forms of place-making and urban territoriality (Hubbard, 2004a; Sanders, 2004). At times, this policing can take punitive forms, with many street sex-work areas having witnessed periodic 'sweeps' or 'crackdowns'. Although these may be prompted by the complaints of local residents or businesses about anti-social behaviour (Mathieu, 2011), a noted trend here is the implication of muscular and punitive 'zero tolerance' policing in the 'revanchist' (literally, *revenging*) cleansing of inner urban spaces which are becoming oriented towards middle-class sensibilities and modes of comportment (Kunkel, 2012). First noted in New York in the late 1990s, where Bill Bratton's adoption of the logic of 'broken windows' figured prostitution as a form of incivility prefiguring more serious criminality (Papayanis, 2000), 'zero tolerance' approaches to street sex work were quickly adopted elsewhere (see Hubbard, 2004a).

That said, recent attempts to bring prostitution within the ambit of 'municipal law' in many jurisdictions suggest an important shift in its regulation from coercive control via the police to a more diffuse social control enacted through a bureaucratic regulation of space:

> *Recent regulation operates by reference to the control of the space in which the activity of prostitution takes place, and by reference to community public health and amenity standards. In effect, it requires the disciplining and self-disciplining of the 'body' within the spatial and public health parameters defined by the bureaucratic state. In this transformation of regulatory control, the instrumental 'technology' of the law has shifted from an embodiment of the moral force of the sovereign state via a criminal law ... to a statutory framework that seeks to make safe: to contain the 'vice' by imposing on the body a system of constraints and privations, obligations and prohibitions. (Godden, 2001, p. 78)*

This implies that muscular policing can go only so far in effecting the control of prostitution, with off-street sex work less susceptible to 'zero tolerance' policing than street-working. While there have been few societies – past or present – in which prostitution has been fully legalized, premises where sexual services are sold are not necessarily illegal in societies in which prostitution itself is not a crime (for example, where it is not a crime to pay for sex). This means that many cities have enacted pragmatic strategies of control over such premises, seeking to limit them to designated areas through the exercise of municipal law. Here, it is important to note that civic leaders and urban governments have a rich diversity of 'command-and-control' techniques – including licensing, zoning and planning powers – at their disposal to exercise control over off-street sex premises (Prior, 2008). For instance, while brothels remain illegal in most US states, licensing and zoning ordinances have been used to control other sexually-oriented businesses (for example, strip clubs, sex shows, shops and cinemas). While licensing places limits on the way in which a premise advertises, opens and admits customers, zoning ordinances typically prevent such businesses from operating within a certain distance from residences, schools and religious facilities, characteristically pushing adult businesses towards non-residential areas and away from middle-class neighbourhoods (Kelly and Cooper, 2000).

While restricting sex premises to specific locales has apparent advantages for both customers and non-customers (who can avoid such areas if they are offended by the sight and sounds of the sex industry), in some instances these districts have become something of an embarrassment to city governors when they are seized upon by the media as spaces of sleaze and depravity. A much-discussed example concerns the Times Square precinct in New York, which by the mid-1990s had become a no-go area for many because of its concentration of (poorly managed) sex cinemas and 'girly' shows. Mayor Giuliani subsequently introduced a radical rezoning forbidding the co-location of sexually-oriented businesses within 1,000 feet of one another on the basis that clusters of such businesses were associated with nuisance and criminality (Papayanis, 2000). Such ordinances have since become widespread in the USA, dispersing and making invisible erotic businesses in the townscape, with varying degrees of success, through policies designed to disperse rather than cluster sex working (Kelly and Cooper, 2000). Such policies are also evident elsewhere, with the licensing of sexual entertainment venues and striptease clubs in much of England and Wales mirroring the zoning regulations evident in much of the USA by insisting that venues are not located within 50 metres of existing clubs to prevent any perception that a 'red-light district' is emerging (Hubbard et al., 2008).

What is notable is that such strategies can, inadvertently or otherwise, encourage investment in particular areas by displacing forms of commercial sex that appear to stand in the way of corporate property development (Papayanis, 2000). This highlights the fact that strategies to displace sex work need to be understood in the context of entrepreneurial governance and the formation of coalitions of interest between city authorities, developers and home-owners alike (Aalbers and Deinema, 2012; Neuts et al., 2014). Recent geographic analyses of sex work accordingly 'zoom in on the concrete political struggles through which new sexual geographies unfold' (Loopmans and Vandenbroecke, 2011, p. 559).

For example, Neuts et al. (2014) note the use of local licensing, accountancy and planning laws to dramatically reduce the overall number of sex premises in Amsterdam's red-light district, with select sex businesses sacrificed in the attempt to reimagine the Wallen as a hip, fashionable district that is now depicted as edgy, but free from criminal influence. Here, the description of sex businesses as criminogenic – and of sex workers as involved in a criminal subculture of drug abuse, coercion and trafficking – appears to have been a justification for excluding 'adult businesses' from the central city, to the mutual benefit of developers, local landowners and the city council (see also Aalbers and Deinema, 2012). This type of outcome has been noted in other instances where new municipal powers have been deployed to plan sex work 'out of existence' (see Papayanis, 2000; Hubbard, 2004a; B.L. Ross, 2010; Sanchez, 2004). The use of zoning and planning powers to displace sex businesses, when viewed through the lens of Marxist urbanism, thus amounts to a form of revanchism via stealth, with militarized policing of visible street sex work accompanied by an insidious bureaucratization of off-street working spaces.

Sexing the City and the 'New Normal'

Revanchist discourse positions the sex worker as an illiberal subject, standing in the way of capital accumulation in potentially profitable inner-city locations. The consequences of this are repeated across the urban West, with visible spaces of sex work at the heart of the city making way for gentrified businesses and residential developments (see Kerkin, 2003; B.L. Ross, 2010; Sasijimi, 2012) –although in some instances these gentrified businesses remain connected to the sex industries (for example, independent brothels giving way to corporate 'gentlemen's clubs'). Importantly, this process can be related to other shifts in the way in which sexuality has been enrolled in the making of urban political economies. Here, it is worth noting the work of globalization 'guru' Richard Florida (2002). According to Florida, for a city to become a magnet for the 'creative class', it must be an example of 'the three Ts', providing Talent (have a highly talented, educated and skilled population), Technology (have the technological infrastructure necessary to fuel an entrepreneurial culture) and Tolerance (having a diverse community with a 'live and let live' ethos). One way in which Florida operationalizes the latter is by a diversity index based on the proportion of coupled gay households in a region, this being seen as a good predictor of creativity and urban productivity. Although this theory has been criticized both conceptually and empirically (Ward, 2003; Wimark, 2013), the idea that gay male populations are particularly creative and/or artistic persists as a widespread myth that feeds into numerous policy initiatives designed to market 'wannabe' world cities as hip and happening gay capitals, notably through the promotion of 'gay villages'.

Examining the commodification and marketization of 'gay villages', geographers have noted that these often normalize affluent, white homonormative consumer values. Such villages have accordingly been described as exclusionary towards women and trans people (Doan and Higgins, 2011), people of colour (Elder, 2005) and working-class gays and lesbians (Lewis, 2013a). This points to a number of contradictions, with the seeming diversity signalled by the presence of a gay village effacing the exclusions and displacements required to secure that gay village as an ordered site of consumption and capital accumulation. Elaborating, Binnie and Skeggs (2004) argue that the use of the white gay man to mark out diversity has depended on them remaining in the position of the safe, usable Other, with other 'queer' expressions of sexuality depicted as threatening or abject. As such, the promotion of white, gay, male consumer spaces can occur at the expense of spaces associated with 'perverse' sex, whether it be public, promiscuous or paid sex. A notable example is provided by Soho, London, which is becoming a highly sanitized and consumerist space marketed as a cosmopolitan gay village, yet has been characterized by repeated raids and closures of flats used by sex workers, especially in the run-up to the 2012 Olympics (Hubbard, 2004b; Hubbard and Wilkinson, 2014). In such instances, it is apparent that while sexual diversity can be promoted in the global marketplace, this does not extend to the promotion of sex work itself, which remains difficult to represent as a legitimate tourist or consumer attraction given continuing discourses of stigma and shame surrounding the sale of sexual services.

The marketing of gay villages has thus fuelled debates about the colonization of indigenous, queer and diverse sexual scenes by a Western-inflected homonormative culture (Bell and Binnie, 2004). Classic studies of gay residence postulate that the incipient gentrification associated with gay inner-city residency results from childless, single (and partnered) gay-identified individuals seeking affordable apartments and flats (rather than houses) in inner-city locations (Knopp, 1995). Here, the idea that inner cities are more diverse, cosmopolitan and accepting of different sexualities than suburbia seems to be a major factor in encouraging gay gentrification. As Neil Smith (1996) has noted, young, mobile gentrifiers characteristically identify themselves as being 'streetwise', claiming to be attracted to the inner city because it offers a contrast to the mundane and unsexy nature of suburban living. This tendency is thought to be particularly pronounced among gay male populations (Collins, 2004a). Yet, simultaneously, members of this population seem remarkably anxious about individuals whom they regard as an unaesthetic presence in 'their' urban space. A notable example here is the street sex worker. As Sanders (2009, p. 511) argues, by being labelled as 'anti social' – unclean, unwanted and a symbol of decay – 'the iconic whore figure is entirely out of step with gentrified notions of modern city living and leisure' and becomes 'an easy target for removal'. Ross (2010, p. 212) similarly talks of the eradication of street sex work from specific landscapes which become imbued with the 'potent ideology of forgetting', indicative of the 'gentrification of the mind' (Schulman,

2012b) that so often accompanies the sanitation of space. Vibrant, mixed communities of sex work are eradicated, both physically and mentally.

Hence, in many instances, an influx of affluent home-owners, surprised to find themselves sharing their neighbourhood space with sex workers (and their clients), launches a prolonged and high-profile campaign of exclusion against prostitution (see, for example, Bondi, 1998; O'Neill et al., 2008; Mathieu, 2011). While not all of these instances of opposition are associated with gay gentrification, time and again spaces once shared by sex workers and LGBT communities (for example, Soho, London, Greenwich Village, New York, or the West End of Vancouver) are becoming more homogeneous spaces of gay consumption where sex working retains only a tenuous presence. What appears to be happening here is that the dominance of normative sexual values (and an associated investment in property) based on notions of love, futurity and sexual privacy is prompting the removal of visible sex work (whether male, trans or female). Hence, whereas domesticized gay sex can be accommodated within the emergent geographies of gentrified inner-city living, sex work appears increasingly out of place. Therefore, whilst idealized gay consumers are being welcomed as a civilized presence in the city, the dangerous queer Other (in the form of the sex worker) is displaced (Sanchez, 2004). This poses important questions about the sexual normativities that are reproduced by dominant urban processes, and demands further scrutiny of the ways in which previously marginal sexualities are being centred in the city, colonizing previously 'disordered' spaces.

Gendering the City: Reinforcing Patriarchal Urbanism

Although the idea of sexual diversity can be important in prompting gay gentrification, sexual freedom is also played up in the marketing of flats and condos to young straight-identified men and, increasingly, women. Lloyd (2008) demonstrates this in her study of the marketing of inner-city housing in Sydney to single career women. She focuses on the advertising of the Lumina Apartments, inner Sydney, which sold a sexy Sydney lifestyle in which single women were depicted as using the space of the home not as a space for housework, but for consumption – especially sexual consumption. Using appropriate sexy models, these adverts hinted at a *Sex and the City* lifestyle, knowingly implying that these types of lifestyle are an inversion of 'normal' gendered relations, but also, Lloyd (2008) argues, that these lifestyles are easily within reach. In her studies of gentrification in Canadian cities, Kern (2010) likewise notes that condominiums have been marketed as offering access to the social and economic advantages of home ownership from which single women have often been excluded, with inner-city dwelling allowing them to combine work and leisure in an environment rich with urban spectacle (and sex).

Reinvented as spaces of gentrified consumption, contemporary inner cities accordingly feign to be safe and seductive spaces for middle-class solo residents, whether female or male (Day, 1999). Again, the removal of sex work appears a precondition for this to occur, the presence of street prostitution being described as particularly problematic for non-sex-working women residing in inner cities (Bondi, 1998). In some instances, gentrification appears predicated on *genderfication* (van den Berg, 2013) with the making of 'child-friendly' urban spaces also suggesting a strong connection between class, gender and urban regeneration strategies that imply that central cities need to be free from sex work. Nevertheless, the animated public spaces of inner cities remain dramatized settings for *flânerie* (the process by which urban space is consumed as a visual spectacle by a voyeuristic, wealthy, observer). Although some commentators have suggested *flânerie* was a short-lived phenomenon of the nineteenth century, the figure of the *flâneur* remains crucial in understanding the gendering of contemporary urban space because the *flâneur's* right to look gratuitously now irradiates the spaces of the consumer society. And while *flânerie* can theoretically be performed by women, it remains profoundly gendered. For the 'man about town' – whether straight or gay – women are to be looked at, becoming part of the urban spectacle; being looked at is passive and female whereas looking (and returning the gaze) is deemed active and male. Accordingly, for the man on the street, the spectacle of being gazed on by sex-working women can provoke profound anxiety (Aalbers, 2005). Prostitution disturbs.

Accordingly, while prostitution legislation designed to curtail the visibility of feminine sexuality on the streets is typically claimed to be necessary to protect 'public morals', taking this type of perspective suggests that sex workers embody a transgressive identity that must, from the *flâneur's* perspective, remain invisible (Hubbard, 1999). Though undoubtedly overused as a metaphor for the gendering of the city, the relationship between the male *flâneur* and female prostitute continues to crystallize the gendered inequalities that characterize the contemporary city – a city where men display their activities of exchange and consumption for others to look at. To paraphrase Nast (2002, pp. 896–7), it seems that all the systems of exchange characterizing the contemporary city – including the modalities of consumption – remain men's business. Interestingly, this seems to mean that while visible sex work in the form of street prostitution is often repressed, off-street working in corporate spaces of 'adult entertainment' is being normalized, allowing men to access women's bodies in a space of homosociality that is essentially privatized (Hubbard and Whowell, 2008).

Contemporary *flânerie*, central to the playful forms of consumption played out in the gentrified city, accordingly marginalizes the female (and trans-identified) street sex workers who challenge men's mastery of public space (Hubbard, 2004b; Sanchez, 2004). This gendering of space is, however, obscured by policy-makers' references to 'community safety' or the creation of 'child-friendly' cities, with legislation designed to curtail the visibility of feminine sexuality on the streets usually claimed to be necessary to protect general 'quality of life' (Papayanis, 2000). City fathers frequently claim to act in the interests of those women and children who might feel disturbed or upset by the presence of sex work in the city, with the removal of visible sex work from Western cities accordingly being hailed by some as an important step in the creation of more gender-equal cities, challenging long-standing assumptions that women's access to nightlife can only be on men's terms (Listerborn, 2003). Yet it is general notions of nuisance, safety and public order, and not women's rights per se, that are in play here, with the claim that women need equality with men being subsumed beneath a discourse that proclaims women's vulnerability and inability to negotiate the sexual city on their own terms. Unfortunately, this gendering is also obscured in many accounts of prostitution in the revanchist city, which argue that this involves a colonization of urban space by (global) capital without pointing out that this continues to value male virility – whether straight or gay – in ways that recreate patriarchal stereotypes of women's sexual vulnerability. Hence, although geographers are becoming increasingly attentive to 'concrete' manifestations of revanchism in different temporal, institutional and spatial contexts, it appears that further studies of the repression of (female) sex work are required to explore how the contemporary urban process reproduces 'phallic cities'.

Conclusion

In this chapter, I have considered the urban geographies of prostitution as the outcome of diverse processes that render sex work more, or less, visible in particular neighbourhoods.

These include the forms of licensing and zoning control that shape spaces of off-street prostitution as well as the more obviously coercive strategies of policing, anti-social behaviour legislation and surveillance that circumscribe spaces of street sex work. In this context, it appears that the general quest for hospitable, safe and sanitized inner cities has led to the effective disappearance of street sex working in many contexts, as well as the gradual evisceration and gentrification of areas of off-street sex working: despite the best efforts of sex-worker advocate organizations, contemporary discourses of sexual diversity do not seem to have extended to the figure of the sex worker, who continues to occupy a marginalized role in debates concerning rights to the city. Noting the range of scholarship linking the shifting geographies of sex work to deliberative policies of urban gentrification and 'regeneration', this chapter has placed this literature in the context of wider debates concerning: first, urban revanchism; second, the perpetuation of sexual normativity; and, finally, the changing gendered identities of the city. Overall, it can be concluded that the changing character of red-light districts reflects the increasing influence of corporate developers on urban politics, the gradual replacement of queer and rebellious sexual cultures by normative consumer cultures, and the continuing marginalization of women in the 'man-made' city. While there remains much more that could be said about the shifting relationality of gender, sex and capital accumulation as it is manifest in the forms of sex work that characterize the 'internet age', it is clear that such analyses of the place and space of sex work in the city are both productive and revealing, speaking to some of the pressing geographical debates of our times.

Chapter 36

Defining Commercial Sexualities, Past and Present[1]

Magaly Rodríguez García

Introduction

This chapter offers a historical overview of the notions that have been used in different times and societies to refer to the sex trade. In so doing, I attempt not only to provide an etymological review, but also to unravel the moral, cultural and legal constructions of commercial sexuality and to map the intersection between sexual exchange, intimacy and so-called deviant behaviour. As Amalia Cabezas (2009, p. 4) compellingly argues, 'the exchange of goods and money for sexual services is not an unambiguous commercial endeavour but a discursive construction that is contested and in motion, changing across time and space'. A broad geographical and long historical perspective allows us to identify the commonalities and differences between terms, the purposes they served, the continuities or discontinuities in their use, their limitations and their internal contradictions.

Of all the terms used, 'prostitution' is perhaps the most ubiquitous. The online Cambridge dictionary (2015) defines prostitution as 'the work of a prostitute', and the latter as 'a person who has sex with someone for money'. Although commonly accepted, these definitions do not permit the identification of the immense range of remunerated sex activities. Moreover, if taken literally, these definitions can include practices that have most often been accepted as mainstream and very different from prostitution. Marriages or other forms of intimate relationships, for example, have often involved sexual exchange for livelihood, gifts or privileges but society – except for radical feminists – has never linked them to commercial sex. Perhaps the metaphorical definition of prostitution provided by the Oxford online dictionary (2015) gives us a clearer clue to its symbolic meaning across time and space: prostitution is 'the *unworthy* or *corrupt* use of one's talents for personal or financial gain' (my emphasis). Indeed, it is the moral or status connotation attached to it, and not, per se, the exchange of sexual favours for money or in kind that has characterized the understanding of prostitution in many societies.

In what follows, I aim to take the reader on a conceptual tour from antiquity to the present and to demonstrate that 'prostitution' was and is but one among many ways to describe the commodification of sex. I argue that the terminology for prostitution has always encompassed more than the exchange of sex for money or goods, and that the introduction of alternative terms has not fully served the purpose of reducing the negative connotation of commercial sexual services. This study relies heavily on recent literature on prostitution and

---

1   I am indebted to Kath Browne and Maarten Loopmans for their constructive comments on an earlier version of this chapter.

on some of the overviews collected for the project 'Selling Sex in the City', organized by the author in cooperation with Elise van Nederveen Meerkerk and Lex Heerma van Voss. These academic works allow for the development of a geographical exploration of the way in which the sex trade was understood in cities as varied as Amsterdam, Berlin, Buenos Aires, Istanbul, Lagos, London, Mexico City, Moscow, New York, Paris, Potosí, St Petersburg, Stockholm and Tel Aviv. The focus on females and urban settings is justified, on the one hand, by the fact that commercial sex has nearly always been a city phenomenon involving women servicing men and, on the other, by the availability of information. Qualitative and quantitative data on the involvement of men, homosexuals and transvestites, as well as on commercial sex activities in rural areas, is – particularly for past times – very scarce.

Not the Oldest Profession

Various authors have accepted the interpretation of the Sumerian word *kar.kid* as the first mentioning of the word 'prostitute' in a list of professions dating back to c. 2400 BC (Lerner, 1986; Roth, 2006). According to Gerda Lerner (1986, p. 245), the term *kur-garru* referred to a male prostitute or a transvestite and appeared in the same list, but was placed together with entertainers. She goes on to explain that prostitutes continued to appear on other lists of professions in the Middle Babylonian period, and that they were listed as *kar.kid* or by its Akkadian equivalent, *harimtu*. Julia Assante (1998, 2007), on the other hand, claims that there were no words for 'prostitute' in cuneiform texts. In her view, *kar.kid* or *harimtu* was a legal status that referred to a single woman without patriarchal status. It could be that some prostitutes came from the *kar.kid/harimtu* class, but this does not mean that these terms were synonyms for 'prostitute'. Furthermore, she accuses some scholars of mistranslating cuneiform words for 'tavern', 'ale house' or 'brewery' into 'brothel'. Neither of these terms has, in Assante's opinion, an inherent sexual meaning.

Despite this ongoing debate, scholars seem to agree on two issues: prostitution did exist in the ancient world (but, for Assante, prostitution in societies without currency was of a different nature from that in coin economies), and, although very old, prostitution is not the oldest profession. Several occupations, including those of priest, tavern owner, doctor, scribe, barber and cook are as old, if not older. There also seems to be a consensus on the negative perception of prostitution in the ancient world (Lerner, 1986; Glazenbrook, 2006; Assante, 2007). Generally, extramarital sex was not perceived as a moral problem but rather as a threat to the economic and social stability of the patriarchal system (Roth, 2006). Perhaps this helps to explain why many authors have often translated ancient words for 'fornication' into 'prostitution'. In his recent study on prostitution in ancient Israel, Phyllis Bird (2006, pp. 42, 57) explains that the Hebrew verb *zanah* meant 'to engage in extramarital sex' or 'to fornicate', and translates its feminine participle form *zonah* as 'fornicator-woman'. But he further argues that *zonah* was often used by ancient authors to refer to a professional prostitute. Also, the authors of an essay on Tel Aviv and Jaffa for the 'Selling Sex in the City' project state that a woman who associated with a man foreign to the Jewish collective in the twentieth century was often referred to as a 'whore' or *zona*, irrespective of whether sex was exchanged for cash or goods (Bernstein et al., 2013).

Another scholarly debate revolves around the distinction between the *hetaira* and *pornē* in ancient Greece. The term *hetaira* appeared first in the sixth century BC and is related to *hetairos*, a man's war companion. This explains the interpretation of *hetaira* as sexual companion or courtesan, who would have provided more than pure sexual services. According to some authors, *hetairai* were free prostitutes working independently and in much better conditions

322

than *pornai* or 'common prostitutes', who were of slave status and confined in brothels (Cohen, 2006). Other authors question this strict taxonomy of prostitution and the idealized view of the *hetaira*. Allison Glazenbrook (2006, 2011) argues that the ancients did not make a clear differentiation between *hetairai* and *pornai*, or between *hetairai* and adulteresses or women in atypical relationships. *Pornē* was, in any case, the more pejorative term. The word probably derives from the verb *pernēmi*, which means 'to sell'. Other ancient nicknames also emphasize the material nature of the prostitute–client relationship and the (female) prostitute's 'innate immorality'. For male prostitutes, not the noun *pornoi* but the verb form for prostitution, *pornos*, was commonly used. This suggests that, for males, prostitution was simply perceived as a trade, while for women it was considered an identity. In Rome, both adulteresses and women in prostitution were required to wear a toga suggesting that female prostitutes were licentious by nature (Glazenbrook, 2011).

In republican and imperial Rome, the most common terms for prostitute were *meretrix* and *scortum*. *Meretrix* derives from *mereo*, meaning 'to earn' or 'to merit', and stresses the economic aspect of prostitution. Since it also implied an affectionate relation with clients, it was not used for brothel prostitutes only, but for more sophisticated ones, too. The terms *meretrix* and *amica* were preferable to *scortum* and less insulting than *puella*, which referred to a woman of easy virtue, or *lupa*, a 'she-wolf', a predatory, wild woman (Glazenbrook, 2011). Interestingly, derivatives from the Latin *meretrix* are preferred in some contemporary societies. In Bolivia, for example, prostitutes like to be called *meretrices*, as the word highlights the labour aspect of prostitution and depicts them as working women (Absi, 2013).

Less common words for prostitute in the ancient world referred to the methods or places of solicitation: sitting or standing in front of a brothel (*sellaria, prostituta, prostibulum*) or walking the streets (*spodēsilaura, circulatrix*). Pejorative terms like *chalkiditis* (penny whore) in Greek, or *publica* in Latin referred to the presumed indiscriminate access to, and lack of virtue of, prostitutes (Glazenbrook, 2011). As will become clear in the following pages, many of these understandings of commercial sexuality travelled across time and space.

Fallen Women and Evil Men

Until more or less the eighteenth century, prostitution was dealt with via a combination of toleration and repression (Mechant, 2013). In cities like Amsterdam, Bruges, Florence, Mexico City and Shanghai, local authorities undertook measures to identify, regulate and segregate prostitutes. However, early regulations always encompassed more than mercenary sex and, as in antiquity, a conflation between adultery and prostitution was often made. Medieval and early-modern intellectual elites, jurists and theologians focused on the promiscuity of women, rather than on the commercial aspect of prostitution. The twelfth-century jurist Gratian argued, for example, that what marked a prostitute was that she took many lovers (Mummey, 2011). Hence, premarital sex, adultery or 'indiscriminate availability' (Karras, 1996, p. 17) were included in the more commonly used terms 'whoredom', 'fornication' or 'adultery'. In places as diverse as Amsterdam, Bruges, Istanbul, London, Paris, Mexico City, Shanghai and Stockholm there was no clear distinction between 'whores', 'harlots', 'mistresses', 'woman of the streets', 'loose', 'kept', 'unchaste' or 'unruly woman'. In Germany, the term *Kokette* was used in eighteenth-century literature to mean 'prostitute-like' or 'lustful woman'. Since the second half of the nineteenth century, *cocotte* and *Kokotte* became words for 'prostitute' in Paris and Berlin, although their elegant appearance and mannerism of respectability 'blurred the lines between flirtatious, fashionable women and women for hire' (J.S. Smith, 2013, p. 11; Guigon, 2012). In the rest of Europe, the notions of 'prostitute' and 'prostitution' became more widely used only after the mid-eighteenth century to differentiate the sale of sex from simple fornication and adulterous sexual behaviour.

Another analogy between the ancient and modern eras was the link made between prostitution and entertainment. In Shanghai (or generally in China), Buenos Aires, Havana, Cairo and New York, actors, singers and dancers were often perceived or did actually double as prostitutes. In colonial territories, women who in precolonial periods had provided more spiritual than sexual services to men (for example, the *devadasi*, or dancing girls in India, or courtesans in China, Japan and other parts of Asia), without necessarily participating in the commercial sex trade, were automatically identified as prostitutes by European colonialists. Despite the different prostitution policies in various colonial settings (for example, the system of regulation, official red-light districts and migration of 'white' prostitutes was more common in French colonies than in British ones), discourses around sexuality, prostitution and 'indigenous degeneracy' (Frances, 2011, p. 165) contributed to the so-called civilizing mission of imperial powers throughout the colonial world. Moreover, prostitution was also linked to marginality, and prostitutes were frequently arrested under regulations against disorderliness and vagrancy until well into the twentieth century. This explains the use of the terms 'scrounging' or 'wandering woman' as synonyms for prostitution and prostitute in different times and places (Gronewold, 2013; Gilfoyle, 1992; Mummey, 2011; Schettini, 2013; White, 1990).

During the nineteenth century, with the installation of the French system of regulation in many world cities (except London and New York), which required a clearer categorization of prostitution, the economic aspect of sexual exchange became more prominent. However, promiscuity continued to function as an important definition of prostitution in most contexts. Hence the identification of 'real' prostitutes in regulationist cities (or *de facto* regulationist in Rio de Janeiro, for example) remained problematic; any sexually active woman risked being registered as a prostitute. And as in antiquity, female prostitution was not regarded as an act among others or as an activity for making a living, but as an identity. Prostitution was perceived as essentialist: women involved in prostitution were labelled 'prostitutes' inside and outside their places of work (Blanchette, 2013). This helps to explain why cases of rape in prostitution frequently went and still go unpunished. As Barbara Sullivan (2000, p. 1) argues, 'sex workers were [and still are] legally constructed as women who were [or are] "always consenting" and incapable of non-consent'.[2]

It seems that increasingly throughout time, the idea of prostitution came to be defined as a female activity, while procuring and pimping became linked to men. Although some terms could refer to men and women, the most common nouns and nicknames for prostitute referred to women only. Despite the fact that some regions in the world had a rich tradition of male and transvestite prostitution (in, for example, Berlin, Cairo, London, New York and Shanghai), most legal contexts defined prostitution as female. In some contemporary societies this is still the case. In Istanbul, for instance, the law prescribes that all sex workers in licensed brothels need to be female by birth or by gender reassignment surgery. In present-day Bolivia and Mexico, transvestite prostitutes are not allowed in brothels and are usually confined to street prostitution (Absi, 2013; Gronewold, 2013; Laite, 2011; Nuñez and Fuentes, 2013; Wyers, 2013).

In Christian societies, the understanding of prostitutes as 'fallen women' evolved throughout time. Before the eighteenth century, religious interpretations of prostitution

---

2   In nineteenth-century Brazil, the Imperial Criminal Code of 1830 stipulated that the maximum penalty for the rape of a prostitute would be one year; the rape of 'honest' victims led to a sentence of up to 12 years (Blanchette and Schettini, 2013).

dominated. Following Judeo-Christian traditions, prostitution was perceived as sinful behaviour in Europe and the Americas. This led to the proliferation of seclusion institutions and asylums (for example, Magdalen homes), which aimed at reforming and controlling women's sexuality. Also, in the Ottoman Empire prostitution was considered as an act that ran contrary to Islamic law, and for hundreds of years in precolonial India common prostitutes formed part of the mainstream labour population but were considered sinners (Frances, 2011; Wyers, 2013). In parallel to being associated with the language of sin, the view of prostitution as a social or pathological condition became increasingly popular from the late eighteenth century onwards, probably as a result of Enlightenment rationalization. Although some authors pointed to the pauperization of the working class in industrial societies as the main cause of prostitution, many authorities, doctors and scientists understood the sex trade in terms of deviancy. Writing in a period during which public transgressions were perceived as potential threats to the social order and as a problem that called for intervention, the ideas of Cesare Lombroso, the Italian founder of positivist criminology, reinforced the perception of prostitutes as deviants and offenders. This led to the prohibition of prostitution and the (*de facto*) criminalization of prostitutes in some countries – for example, in the USA, the USSR and China (Rodríguez García, forthcoming).

Yet the idea of prostitutes as 'feeble-minded' or as outright criminals in the nineteenth and twentieth centuries was not universal. The notion of the fallen woman could refer not only to sinful or unruly behaviour for which she was responsible, but also to situations of vulnerability in which women fell prey to malevolent men. From the second half of the nineteenth century, women involved in prostitution became increasingly perceived as victims in Western countries where the feminist movement gained ground. In the UK, feminists and libertarians helped publicize a series of sexual scandals in the 1880s, which ended with the reporting of Jack the Ripper and the murder of five prostitutes. William Stead's newspaper publication on the abduction of English girls sold to continental brothels, as well as the media attention given to the Ripper murders rendered all men suspect and strengthened the notions of urban danger and female fragility (Walkowitz, 1982). The link between (migration for) prostitution, male violence and traffic was established then; by the end of the nineteenth century a movement for the suppression of 'white slave traffic'[3] had emerged in Britain and had been disseminated internationally. From the early twentieth century onwards, national and international initiatives to curtail the traffic for prostitution rose to a crescendo[4] (Limoncelli, 2010; Rodríguez García, 2012).

The perception of prostitution as a harmful activity in which women are the main victims has become increasingly influential since the last decades of the twentieth century. In the USA, certain feminists view prostitution as the sexual oppression of women and demand the decriminalization[5] of prostitutes as a short-term solution and the radical transformation of the socioeconomic structure of society to eliminate prostitution in the long run. Kathleen Barry and some other authors refuse to understand prostitution in terms of labour. Many radical feminists define prostitution as 'sexual slavery' and prefer to speak of 'prostituted women' instead of 'prostitutes', as the former term 'brings the perpetrator into the picture' (Jeffreys, 1997, p. 5) and emphasizes, in their view, the male sexual violence involved in it (Barry, 1979).

---

3   The term 'white slavery' was used at the early 1800s, to denounce the plight of sailors of 'white' nations captured by pirates in the North of Africa. Only by the end of the nineteenth century did the term become feminized and linked to the traffic of women for prostitution.

4   In 1921 the League of Nations replaced the racialized term 'white slavery' by 'traffic in women and children'.

5   Advocates of decriminalization are not in favour of legalizing prostitution. Many radical feminists oppose legalization because it would normalize prostitution.

In Sweden, a similar logic but a new strategy has been applied. Focusing on the demand side of prostitution, some Swedish feminists called for the criminalization of clients. After a long debate, the purchase of sex has been illegal in Sweden since 1999 (Svänstrom, 2004). Prostitution is, then, viewed as a crime, but one committed by men on women. Hence the idea of women as victims and men as predators is strengthened. With some variations, the so-called Swedish model has spread to several European countries. As at the turn of the nineteenth century, supporters of this interpretation of prostitution are of the opinion that commercial sex fuels human traffic. In February 2014 the European Parliament approved a non-binding resolution, which recommends that EU countries re-evaluate their sex-work policies and to reduce the demand for prostitution and trafficking by punishing the clients. Since commercial sex is seen as inherently exploitative and as a violation of human rights, supporters of the Swedish model make no distinction between voluntary and forced prostitution. In their view, women are forced into prostitution by third parties, poverty or both, even though an increasing number of women openly defend the right to use their body and sexuality to obtain financial or other benefits. As noted below, the involvement of the men and women concerned in debates around the sale or bartering of sex led to the development of parallel ways of looking at commercial sexuality.

Work, Barter or Transaction?

'Prostitute' and 'prostitution' were words commonly applied by officials in Europe, the Americas and colonial territories during the nineteenth and twentieth centuries to the activities of selling sex in exchange for money. However, more insulting words like 'whore' and its equivalents in non-English-speaking contexts were and still are widely used in common parlance. Official and unofficial abuse of prostitutes led to protests not only by feminists but also by affected women themselves. Although most formal organizations appeared only in the second half of the twentieth century, prostitutes' protests have occurred since the late 1800s. In British territories, Indian prostitutes protested against the harsh regulation system; in imperial Russia, they demanded the health inspection of clients and not only of women; and in the 1930s, Argentinean women involved in prostitution used the printed media to call for better working conditions and respect for prostitutes as workers (Guy, 1991; Hetherington, 2013; Levine, 2003). Then, as the cultural changes brought about by the 1960s led to a further strengthening of the feminist movement and to a freer sexual morality, prostitutes from different parts of the world became more vocal and began to organize themselves.

With the emergence of the prostitutes' rights movement in the USA and France during the 1970s, pejorative names and the stigma around prostitution came under attack. A restructuring of the sex trade's language took place and prostitution came to be defined as 'sex work'. The new usage of the terms 'sex work' and 'sex worker' was an important semantic shift, signifying the strengthening of a movement that understood prostitution in terms of labour and attendant human rights (Delacoste and Alexander, 1988; Pheterson, 1989). Those terms encompass the whole industry, so that not only prostitutes, but also all women, men and transgendered people and transvestites active in striptease, pornographic film-making, phone sex, lap dancing, erotic massage and so on are described as sex workers. Hence, contrary to previous periods, these terms are gender-neutral and can, according to some historians, be used completely appropriately for all forms of commercial sex in past times.[6] Interestingly, there seems to be a consensus among American and British historians who treat prostitutes as 'workers and agents in history' and who interpret prostitution as a form of labour, not necessarily 'noble or dignified labor, but labor nonetheless' (Walkowitz, 2014).

But although the labour perspective has received much support from (some) state and non-state actors in various countries, the notion of 'sex work' and, generally, the understanding of commercial sexualities in terms of labour, have been increasingly criticized in recent years. Historically, sexual barter has always defied easy categorization. As noted above, Julia Assante argues that prostitution in ancient, pre-coinage societies meant something different from prostitution in coin economies. In those societies, 'individual bartering for sexual favors might have been culturally too normative to be regarded as an official profession' (Assante, 2007, p. 129). The exchange of sex for material or non-material benefits was basic to arranged marital alliances, and prostitution among slaves and captives was probably accepted as part of the natural social order in the ancient world. In later periods too, sexual barter seems to have been common. In seventeenth-century Mexico, for example, slaves could buy their freedom through sexual services (Nuñez and Fuentes, 2013). In late nineteenth- and early twentieth-century New York, 'charity girls' exchanged sex for entertainment expenses or small gifts, but made a clear distinction between what was called 'treating' and prostitution, which they considered immoral. In past and contemporary African and Asian cities, sexual bartering for material goods or privileges was, and is, evenly widespread (Clement, 2006; Ekpootu, 2013; Gronewold, 2013). In contexts of abject poverty, the notion 'survival sex' is used to describe the exchange of sexual services for shelter, food or clothing. Other situations in which an upfront monetary transaction does not always take place are sex tourism and relationships with teenagers or young men and women, in which gifts such as trips, meals, phones, drugs or school tuition are seen as compensation for the sexual services rendered (Kempadoo, 2009).

These various forms of commodified sexuality have motivated scholars to introduce new terms to the lexicon of sexual arrangements. According to Kamala Kempadoo, the notion 'transactional sex' is more useful to describe activities of individuals who are located outside the sex industry. Transactional sex can be read as 'the umbrella term for all acts, including but not limited to sex work, where sexuality is exchanged for material and other non-sexual benefits' (Kempadoo, 2009, p. 14). Contrary to conventional prostitution, transactional sex would be more oriented towards consumption and personal betterment than towards pure subsistence (Leclerc-Madlala, 2003).

Similarly, Amalia Cabezas (2009) challenges the concept of sex work as the only viable tool for understanding interactions between tourists and locals in Cuba and the Dominican Republic. These authors argue that like 'prostitute', the term 'sex worker', presupposes a fixed identity; hence, prostitution or sex work are perceived as a way of life, not just a job (Kempadoo and Doezema, 1998; Cabezas, 2009). In their view, other important issues that are absent in the terms 'prostitution' and 'sex work' are affection, companionship and intimacy. If prostitution is understood as 'an institution that promotes sexual relations without emotional attachment, [one that] detaches love from sex' (J.S. Smith, 2013, p. 3), then a whole range of sexual arrangements that involve not only monetary considerations but also affective and spiritual ones are discarded. For this reason, Cabezas (2009, p. 120)

---

6   This was an issue of debate during the conference 'Selling Sex in the City: Prostitution in World Cities, 1600 to the Present', Amsterdam, 25–27 April 2013. While some researchers thought that the term 'sex work' would be an anachronism for the period before 1970, others contended that 'prostitution' is also a relatively recent concept. The latter reasoned that since men and women active in prostitution before 1970 were part of the (broadly understood) working class, they should also be called 'sex workers'.

chooses to use the term 'tactical sex', which serves to better convey the 'complex circulation of sex and affect'. The importance of gifts is then emphasized, as they represent an 'important feature of exchange and solidarity' and can transform the sexual relationship into one of courtship and love (Cabezas, 2009, p. 122). Indeed, gifts are crucial in sexual barter, not only in contemporary societies but also in the recent and not so recent past. In the Inanna-Dumuzi literature of ancient Mesopotamia, there are descriptions of marriage based on love but also various references to the negotiation of gifts during courtship (Assante, 2007). Another interesting parallel with the ancient world is that transactional sex between men in the Caribbean region is not claimed or understood as identity-forming but rather as a mere strategy to obtain material and non-material benefits (Kempadoo, 2009).

Through these new terms, authors seek to stress the self-perception of the participants in 'sexual–affective–economic activities' (Kempadoo, 2009, p. 15). As with 'charity girls', people involved in transactional or tactical sex do not define themselves as 'prostitute' or 'sex worker' but rather as 'escort', 'entertainer', 'business girl', 'beach boy', 'friend' and so on. Whether these euphemistic neologisms alter the essence of commercial sexualities, and above all the stigma around them, is doubtful.

Conclusion

A geohistorical overview of the conceptualization of commercial sexualities shows that moral, cultural and legal definitions have often overlapped. Throughout time and space the notions used have nearly always involved a condemnation of atypical sex acts. Despite the geographical and time differences in how the sex trade was practised and policed, the available literature demonstrates that sexual desire has been deemed disruptive in most cultures. As it became increasingly commodified with the rise of industrial societies, the nation-state and globalization, commercial sex became a constant preoccupation of elites and the bourgeoisie (Foucault, 1976; Barker and Elliston, 1984). In particular, women using sex for purposes other than (future) procreation were (and still are, in many places) openly or less openly incriminated. The increasing commercialization of sexual activities in capitalist societies seems to have run parallel to an increased sense of moral opprobrium, either because it is associated with promiscuity, disorderliness and backwardness or because it is understood as a violation of human rights – particularly those of women. Neither the decline in religion and the spread of secularism nor the diffusion of liberal attitudes toward sex since the second half of the twentieth century have changed societal attitudes towards prostitution, sexual barter, sex work, transactional sex or whatever people choose to call it.

This 'simultaneous commodification and condemnation of unusual sexualities and practices' (Peršak and Vermeulen, 2014, p. 15) has, from antiquity to the present, led to a mushrooming of concepts meant to either disguise the nature of the activities or to distinguish between 'good' and 'bad' sexual behaviour. Discourses on commercial sexualities have only recently become more considerate of the people directly involved. Yet the new terminology has its own limitations. As Kamala Kempadoo (2009, p. 15) admits, 'the notion of tactical sex closely approximates what has been described ... as transactional sex, even while the definitions of both remain fuzzy'. Furthermore, the boundary between transactional/tactical sex and prostitution/sex work is very blurred. According to Amalia Cabezas, the term 'tactical sex' permits us to acknowledge that commodification and affect are not mutually exclusive, but this can also be said of unequivocal sex work. Sufficient empirical evidence exists testifying that prostitutes in past and present societies have often offered much more than fast and unceremonious sexual intercourse, and that their relations with loyal clients frequently involved friendship and even affection. Transactional sex is said to respond to the interest of new needs (the 'commodities of modernity'), rather than basic ones (Leclerc-Madlala, 2003). However, past and contemporary sex workers have often justified their involvement in prostitution in terms other than pure economic survival. Case studies of cities as varied as Lagos, London, Moscow, Nairobi, Potosí, Rio de Janeiro or Shanghai provide evidence of thousands of women making use of sex work to evade the limitations of the patriarchal order and to enter the consumption society independently. Proponents of new terms also aim at avoiding the so-called essentialism of words like prostitution and sex work. They correctly point out that since ancient times these activities (particularly when practised by women) have been understood in terms of identity, not mere occupations. Yet this is not inherent in prostitution. As John Budd (2011) notes in his study on the thought of work, there are numerous (past and present) cultures in which there is a strong link between one's job and identity.

This conceptual overview demonstrates that there is no single word that encompasses the complexity of commercial sexualities. The new lexicon is a welcome warning against the myths, generalizations and oversimplifications that abound whenever commercial sex is discussed. This has been achieved through the bottom-up approach of research initiatives that include the points of view of the people directly involved in these activities. Yet the danger in deconstructing the use of sexuality in exchange for material or non-material benefits is that some 'sexual–affective–economic activities' become romanticized as feelings or companionship are stressed at the expense of economic considerations. After all, we should keep in mind that authorities, jurists, doctors or social workers were and are not the only ones who aim to construct commercial sexualities under single terms such as 'fornication', 'whoredom' or 'prostitution'. Many of the actors involved often seem to contribute to discursive constructions, which attempt (but often fail) to draw a radical distinction between prostitution, sex work, sexual barter and transactional or tactical sex.

Chapter 37

Sexualities, Tropicalizations and the Transnational Sex Trade: Brazilian Women in Spain

Joseli Maria Silva and Marcio Jose Ornat

Introduction

The door opened and a woman of about sixty years of age, with a beautiful smile, appeared. She asked if we were the people recommended for the job of a maid and we said yes. She invited us to come in and immediately started to show us around her four-bedroom apartment while speaking about the demands of the job she was offering; cleaning, cooking, washing and ironing for her three male adult children, herself and even her mother, an older lady who required special care. She offered a wage that was below the minimum salary in Spain, justifying this because of the extra expenses she said she would have by having one more person in her home; the job entailed sleeping in the apartment because of the need to care for her mother at night. Before we left, the lady also warned: 'I don't care if you are illegal, I know the difficulties of being Brazilian. If you do not speak Spanish well, no problem, it is just important to understand very well what we tell you. Another thing is that with three sons at home, you will have to learn to behave like a respectable person so that there won't be any kind of problem OK?' (Excerpt from field diary, Madrid, 31 May 2008)

This extract from a field research diary is the record of an experience that was shared with Cassiopeia,[1] a female Brazilian prostitute[2] living in Madrid, in one of her attempts to leave commercial sexual activity and, in her own words, 'make an honest living' because her children were growing up and would soon know the real nature of her occupation in Spain. Leaving the apartment, there were a few minutes of silence. A sense of revulsion had permeated the thoughts and voice of that elderly woman, and it expressed the colonial

---

1   This research would never have been possible without the generosity and intelligence of Cassiopeia, a Brazilian female sex worker who lives in Madrid and who became a good friend, with whom I shared knowledge, adventure and above all, great affection and admiration. All names used in the text are fictitious.

2   There is a general provision of the Ministry for Employment, as well as global human rights for the use of the term 'sex professional'. The DAVIDA group, a Brazilian organization that fights for the civil rights of people who sell sexual practices prefer to use the word 'prostitute' in an attempt to redefine this term. The women who were interviewed in Madrid referred to themselves as 'whores'. Consequently, in an attempt to follow these different positions, various forms of nomenclature will be used, depending on their context in the text.

violence that still underpins Eurocentric thinking about the value of women from Latin America. Apart from the demeaning exploitation of labour, two elements stood out in her words: the female colonized body, understood as a threat to order, and the imposition of silence as a normality of imposed power relations. Although a feminist outlook might have increased the level of outrage about this experience, Cassiopeia, in all her wisdom, said 'I think it better to be a whore! As a whore, I feel more important here!' We looked at each other, laughed complicitly, and I fully agreed with her.

The aim of this chapter is to understand how the corporeality[3] and sexuality of Brazilian women is produced under the hegemonic Eurocentric outlook, as well as examining the subversive capacity of prostitutes, who develop strategies to take advantage from a structure that is strongly exclusionist, and which forces these women into a position of vulnerability in Spain. The approach that has been adopted is an intersectional perspective that considers class, gender and race.

This chapter is based on a 2008 survey about the illegal immigration by Brazilian women to Spain to work in the sex industry.[4] Joseli met Cassiopeia in Madrid; she was a Brazilian sex professional with whom I developed a deep friendship that has lasted to this day. Through knowing her, for the eight months I lived in Madrid, I became part of her social networks, which were composed of other Brazilian prostitutes, their clients, friends and boyfriends.

Thus, it was possible to create a natural approach to this research, in which 14 in-depth interviews were conducted with female Brazilian sex workers, aged from 23 to 30, and six interviews with Spanish men aged between 35 and 62, who regularly frequented locations where commercial sex activities took place. The Brazilian women reported that they had finished secondary school, earned a low income in Brazil, and that they had children. Of the male respondents, 66.7 per cent claimed to have a higher educational level and 33.3 per cent an average level of education. They all claimed to earn an average salary in Spain. In addition, field observations were carried out at four upmarket nightclubs that offer sexual services in Madrid. These interviews explored the representations of Brazilian women in Spanish society and their role in the sexual market. The interviews were transcribed in full and interpreted using content analysis (Bardin, 1977).

The first part of this chapter explores the hegemonic representations created about Brazilian women in Spain, which are marked by the exoticization of their nationality in that context. The second part explores the representations created by female Brazilian sex workers who, recognizing their exclusion and marginalization, create forms of subversion of their social and economic condition in Spain.

Tropicalization under the Hegemonic Gaze: The Presence of Brazilian Women in Spain and the Geopolitics of Desire

The first decades of the twenty-first century have been marked by an intensification of discussions about transnational movements involving gender, sexuality and economic interests. Brazil is one of the countries that is globally recognized as the source of flows to

---

3   The idea of corporeality is used to express the fluidity of the human body. The notion of the body goes beyond that of a fixed and finished entity, to incorporate the concept of something that is malleable, constantly changing, and dependent on the relationship between space and time (McDowell, 1999).

4   The eight months of fieldwork were conducted jointly. While one of us (author 1) investigated the networks established in Spain, the other (author 2) explored the connections of these networks in Brazil.

so-called 'central countries', particularly Portugal and Spain (see Fernandes and Nunan, 2008; Masanet and Padilla, 2010). Data from the National Statistics Institute of Spain (INE) for 2010 indicated that Brazilian immigration was largely feminine, composed of 60.9 per cent women and 39.1 per cent men.[5] In addition, the worsening economic crisis in many European countries receiving immigrants, as well as the intensification of anti-immigration policies, has increasingly prompted the Brazilian government to act against transnational movement for sexual purposes.[6]

The debate about international mobility promoted by desire, sexuality and financial advantages involving Brazil has aroused the interest of researchers such as Pelúcio (2010, 2011), Piscitelli (2007, 2009) and Piscitelli et al. (2011). The intensification of policies to combat people trafficking, both in Brazil and in other countries receiving flows of people from peripheral countries, has drawn the attention of the media, which identifies the transnational movement for sexual purposes as dangerous and criminalized, generating much controversy. (Grupo Davida, 2005; Hynes and Raymond, 2002; Kempadoo et al., 2005; Schauer and Wheaton, 2006).

The media is an important tool in the creation and circulation of hegemonic ideas, and Brazilian women in Spain and in Portugal are presented in two ways: first, in marriages between Brazilian women and Portuguese or Spanish men; and, second, as Brazilian prostitutes working in those countries. Advertisements regarding the provision of sexual services are notably marked by references to Brazilian nationality, which appears to be an important attribute to be marketed.[7]

The names used by sex workers in their adverts make direct reference to Brazilian nationality, and their bodily images explore the colours and symbols associated with Brazil. Apart from this, there are also reports of Brazilians as victims of 'people trafficking'. In reports about marriage and prostitution there is often mention of Brazilian corporeality and the 'natural' ability of Brazilian women to seduce.

The cover of the magazine the Portuguese magazine *Focus* in 2010 showed a female body with a bikini in the colours of the Brazilian flag and the following caption: 'The secrets of Brazilian women. Worshiped by men, hated by women; the fact is that Brazilian women are successful and of all nationalities they are the ones who most marry Portuguese men' (Lopes and Simões, 2010, pp. 116–17) Another magazine, *Activ*, published the following in an article in 2011: 'After all, what is it that Brazilian women have that we don't?'(Fonseca, 2011). This article contained a discussion of a book titled *The Secrets of Brazilian Women: How to Keep Men Madly in Love* written by Nelma Penteado (2010).

Another article, published by the BBC in 2009, addressed the issue of the large numbers of Brazilian women in Spain and the position they have achieved in Spanish society through marrying Spanish men: 'Brazilians top the preferences of Spanish men among foreigners, in terms of marriage' (Infante, 2009).

The presence of Brazilian women in Spain creates 'contact zones' in which people have different positions of power (Pratt, 1991). In addition to the disadvantages in terms of material conditions that Brazilian women experience, they mostly provide badly paid labour for domestic services and hotels, as pointed out by Fernandes and Nunan (2008); they

---

5   In 2010 the INE data indicated a population of 146,941 Brazilian immigrants living in Spain (INE, 2010).

6   The Brazilian National Justice Secretariat of the Ministry of Justice, in conjunction with the Department of Human Rights and the Secretariat of Policies for Women, prepared the National Policy to Combat Trafficking in Persons in 2006. In 2008 the Ministry of Justice in Brazil established the first National Plan to Combat Trafficking in Persons, and in 2011 the second plan was released.

7   See national newspapers such as *El País* and *El mundo*.

also suffer disadvantages in the production of discourses about their own reality and their position as colonized individuals (Spivak, 1988; hooks, 1990).

The situation of invisibility of Latin American women and the hegemonic discourses that are produced about them in Spain were investigated by Echezarrieta and Leyva (2008). According to these writers, the hegemonic articulation of Spanish society characterizes itself using terms such as 'advanced', 'working', 'rational', 'modern', 'democratic', 'egalitarian', while representing Latin American women from a notion of opposition, creating the usual imaginary of opposition between 'self' and 'other' (Said, 1978).

Discourses about Latin American women in Spain produce a political fiction which involved those women and which also justifies colonial attitudes towards them. Aparício and Chávez-Silverman (1997) created the concept of 'tropicalization'[8] which means:

> ... to trope, to imbue a particular space, geography, group, or nation with a set of traits, images. These intersecting discourses are distributed among official texts, history, literature, and the media, thus circulating these ideological constructs throughout various levels of the receptor society ... the sort of tropicalization we are considering here would be a mythic idea of Latinidad based on Anglo (or dominant) projections of fear. It is intricately connected to the history of political, economic and ideological agendas of governments and social institutions. (Aparício and Chávez-Silverman, 1997, p. 8)

Tropicalization involves power relations and the position of the individual who enunciates the hegemonic discourse, but, according to Aparício and Chávez-Silverman (1997), representations produced from the perspective of the 'tropicalized' individual produce potential assimilation, but also potential subversion (Danielson, 2009).

In an attempt to move beyond the dichotomy between hegemonic and subversive tropicalization, this chapter presents other forms of power relations, involving intersections between different categories of identities, which complicate those power relations and the organization of tensions between individuals. The hegemonic discourse of Spanish society about Brazilian women, for example, is not hegemonic in relation to gender because men and women have different experiences with Brazilian women, which may create alliances or oppositions.

Echezarrieta and Leyva (2008) discuss the notion of *Latinidade* that is constructed by the dominant outlook of Spanish women in relation to immigrant women from Latin America. According to these writers, Spanish women have a clear discourse of racialization towards immigrant Latin American women in order to constitute a 'naturalization' of the existing asymmetrical power relations and the inferiority of Latin American women in relation to Spanish women. Latin American women are frequently described as 'submissive', 'coming from underdeveloped countries', 'poor', 'hypersexualized', 'backward', 'docile', and as having 'uncontrolled reproduction'.

When the discourse of Spanish women about Latin American women identified by Echezarrieta and Leyva (2008) is compared with the results of the interviews with Spanish men in our research, there is some convergence of ideas on the representations of Latin American women between Spanish women and men, but also some opposition. It is precisely in this opposition of views between Spanish men and women that Brazilian women find cracks in the structures of power, and in that context they are able to gain some possible advantages, which will be addressed in the following section.

---

8   The authors use Edward Said's notion of 'Orientalism'(1978) to analogously construct the idea of 'tropicalization'.

Table 37.1 shows that Spanish men also construct ideas about the docility, hypersexuality and poverty of Brazilian women. However, their views about such characteristics of Brazilian femininity appear to complement the construction of their views about their own masculinity and also serve to reduce conflict over issues such as immigration and rejection.

Table 37.1   Discourses of Spanish men about themselves and about Brazilian women

Discursive categories % of utterances	Attributes of 'us' (Spanish men)	Attributes of 'them' (Brazilian women)
Sexuality (35%)	Necessity/biological instinct/ nature	Hot/uninhibited/available/feel pleasure/ know what to do to please a man
Corporeality (30%)	No direct reference	Beautiful/sensual/attractive/big ass
Immigration for prostitution (21%)	Greater opportunities for sexual services/variety/ novelty	Overcoming poverty/poverty/ opportunity for advancement/family support/temporary situation
Affection (14%)	Need/loneliness/ dissatisfaction	Tender/sweet/sensitive/ generous/liars

Source: Interviews conducted between February and September 2008 in Madrid, with six men who frequented places offering commercial sex activities in Spain.

The discourses of Spanish men about Brazilian women are structured in relational form. They represent their own sexuality as something instinctive, a natural need. Because Brazilian women are considered to be available for sex and 'hot', they are considered to be desirable partners for them.

Another discursive axis expressed with intensity by Spanish men was in relation to corporeality; this was linked overwhelmingly positively in relation to Brazilian women and was non-existent in their discourse about themselves. The absence of discussion of their own corporeality was guided by the masculine position of being an active agent in the definition and characterization of the bodies of 'others', while their own bodies were not categorized. Although the Spanish men who participated in this research were not questioned about their statements regarding Spanish women, the latter were sometimes compared unfavourably to Brazilian women: Spanish women were generally described as cold, unsexy, unfeminine, bossy and coarse.

In the discourses of Spanish men who were interviewed in this study, immigration to work as a prostitute appeared to be a calamity for the women involved. The poverty of the Brazilian women, and their quest to overcome this condition, is a representation that puts the Spanish men into a position of 'aiding needy women'. Thus, while ridding themselves of the negative moral connotation of being users of sexual services, they were also able to enjoy the diversity of bodily fulfilment of desire by immigrant women:

> *In that subcontinent, many people live in absolute poverty and it is very usual to have a family consisting of a woman with several children. They might be her children or nephews and they might be living with a man who is not the father of their children. Very often in these places women have their first child at the age of 15. The practice of sex in these societies is more uninhibited, more natural there than in Europe. And when a woman realizes that she is attractive to many men here, of course they want to use it to get out of poverty, and that is normal. (Ares, Spanish man, aged 51)*

The Spanish men justified their use of sexual services as more than merely a 'natural necessity', and as a way of meeting their needs, which are associated with the inability of Spanish women to match their emotional–sexual expectations. Brazilian women, whom they consider to be caring, sensitive and sweet, are considered to complement their needs. Even though the discourses of Spanish men and women about Latin American women have many profound similarities there are also paradoxes that emerge from the position of the view of each group (men and women), who develop different experiences in relation to those Latin American women (Sánchez, 2006).

For example, for those who were interviewed in this study, hypersexuality was a negative attribute from the viewpoint of Spanish women, and positive from the point of view of the Spanish men, even though both groups are hegemonic and Eurocentric in nature. Submission, associated with docility, appeared as an attribute of 'backward and traditional' women in the discourses of the Spanish women, while the same attributes from the perspective of the Spanish men were extremely positive and were associated with the idea that 'a Brazilian woman knows how to please a man' (Hermes, Spanish man, aged 42). The attributes that produce the representations of Brazilian women in Spain, even though they are commonly shared by Spanish men and women, acquire different meanings.

Tropicalization from the Margins: 'Yes, We Have Booties, Pussies, Bananas, Tambourines and Bangles'

> *A Brazilian woman in Spain has no value outside the nightclub. At the club, my clients pay for every minute to be with me. Outside, some former customers call me and want to fuck for free, without even giving me a pack of cigarettes. What's more, it is a common thing for the boss of a restaurant or bar to want to fuck for free too, so as not to sack you. In the end, they cap your salary and still threaten that they will report you to immigration if you cause a fuss. So, it is inside the club that my pussy has power! (laughs). This little body outside the club is worth nothing here in Spain. But inside the club, Ah! There it is really an advantage to be a Brazilian. (Cassiopeia, Brazilian woman aged 30)*

This excerpt from an interview highlights the recognition on the part of Brazilian women of the intersections between class, gender and race/nationality, and their direct relationship with spatiality. Spatiality is an important element in intersectional analysis (M Brown, 2012; McDowell, 2008; Valentine, 2007), which is capable of creating advantages or disadvantages in the composition of power relations.

Hegemonic tropicalization, marked by the stereotype of the hypersexualized, submissive and poor Brazilian woman, is permeated by the actions of Brazilian women who, even though they are mediated by strong colonial discourse, develop the capacity for cultural, social and economic action, recognizing cracks within power structures and acting to subvert the process of marginalization. Thus, tropicalization is constructed not only by the macro-narrative of the nationality of Brazilian women in Spain, but also by their own resistance and transgressions (Bhabha, 1990b).

Brazilian women providing sexual services in Spain are tropicalized, but they themselves also tropicalize Spanish society. Moreover, they represent themselves using the same attributes found within the hegemonic discourses. However, they use these hegemonic representations as tools of power for their own ends (Aparício and Chávez-Silverman,

1997). Their statements about these attributes, about themselves, Spanish men and Spanish women, were organized into four categories and are shown in Table 37.2.

Table 37.2 Discourses of Brazilian women about themselves and about Spanish men and women

Discursive categories % of utterances	Attributes of 'us' (Brazilian women)	Attributes of 'them' (Spanish men)	Attributes of 'them' (Spanish women)
Sexuality (45%)	Hot/uninhibited/ available/feel pleasure/	Promiscuous/ uninhibited/ effeminate/ drug-users/ married	Cold/regulated/ don't feel pleasure/ conservative/ inaccessible
Corporeality (30%)	Beautiful/polite/ elegant/feminine/ sensual	Lack of personal hygiene/physically attractive	Masculine/sloppy/ unfeminine
Affection (18%)	Tender/sweet/ emotional/generous	Needy/silly/gentle/ emotional	Rude/authoritarian/ selfish/rational/ money-orientated
Conjugality (7%)	Passion/love/giving	Respect for social stability	For financial and social stability

Source: Interviews conducted with 14 female Brazilian sex workers in Spain between February and September 2008.

The Brazilian women in this study capture the hegemonic representations about their sexuality and physicality and, as sex workers, use tropicalization to their own advantage. Green (2008) defines the quality and quantity of attributes that a person possesses, which cause an erotic correspondence with another person, as 'erotic capital'. Sexual attraction involves the sexualization of the body, sex and affection, which can take many forms, depending on the time, space and social groups that are involved in the erotic relationship. Thus there is no single form of erotic appeal, but different configurations of the organization of desire, in which resources are distributed in varying proportions among people involved in the erotic game.

A comparison of the structures of the statements shown in Tables 37.1 and 37.2 reveals some similarity with regard to the attributes associated with the representations of Brazilian women regarding their sexuality and corporeality. The attributes in these categories pervade the representations of Spanish women (Echezarrieta and Leyva, 2008) and the representations of Spanish men about Brazilian women, as well as the representations of Brazilian women about themselves. However, in the groups of Spanish men, the attributes of Brazilian women are considered to be positive, and in the group of Spanish women they are considered to be negative.

In order to put themselves in a position of advantage in social relationships in Spain, female Brazilian sex workers, construct discourses in which Spanish men and women are represented in a negative way, or in opposition to themselves. For example, the Brazilian women reported sexual practices that were unusual in their cultural universe, cocaine addiction as a major component of sexual activity and the intensive use of unusual erotic instruments.

Although they do not highly rate the masculinity of Spanish men, they do recognize their economic power. However, they consider themselves capable of manipulating men through their sexual superiority, assigning the characteristics of being 'fools' and 'needy' to their clients. They claim to use hegemonic representations about themselves to take economic advantage of their male clients:

> *The men here think that we in Brazil we live in the Amazon rainforest, that we are impoverished. So I make the face of a sweet, unprotected woman, and I tell a sad story about my kids and then they help me. Wow, you can't believe how many gifts I have sent to Brazil to my family, which these men have bought to help me. (Gaia, Brazilian woman aged 26)*

These tropicalized Brazilian women understand how power structures operate and they are able to play with the attributes that mark their representation within Spanish society, as well as to identify spaces that give them greater or lesser opportunities to use their Brazilianness, as in the spaces of prostitution. However, they also reported using their representations as sensual, sexy and 'easy' to take advantage of situations of interaction with men in other places, beyond the limits of the nightclubs.

On the other hand, these Brazilian women hide their nationality in spaces in which these same attributes of corporeality and sexuality could be considered to be a disadvantage, as reported by Valentine (2007) in relation to the spatial dynamics in the analysis of intersectionality. They are skilled at recognizing particular places and the power relations that prevail in those places. They disguise their nationality in situations where it is not advantageous to them. Among the Brazilian women who were interviewed in this study, it was clear that many of them avoided speaking aloud when they were outside the confines of the club, as shown in this excerpt:

> *Because I am very light-skinned I can easily pass as a Spanish woman. I prefer to go into stores where you can pick up the merchandise, have a look at it, pay and leave. I can pass unnoticed in these places and it is better than being recognized as a Brazilian. (Xanta, Brazilian woman aged 30)*

This game is supported by the recognition of the existence of advantages and disadvantages in interactions with men and women. The Brazilian women recognize that the same attributes that characterize their corporeality and sexuality, which are seen as positive from the point of view of the erotic desire of Spanish men, can be negative from the point of view of Spanish women. They reported that in shops, streets and restaurants where they interact with Spanish women, they seek to disguise their nationality, as in this excerpt: 'The Spanish women hate us. It is horrible; they think that we are always ready to steal their men from them. It is obvious; their faces and attitudes change once they realize that I am Brazilian' (Morea, Brazilian woman aged 28).

In order to justify their opposition to Spanish women, these Brazilian women produce a discourse that attributes to them characteristics of being cold, sexually, conservative, unfeminine, sloppy, rude, selfish and authoritarian. Consequently, they construct a Spanish feminine stereotype that is the complete opposite of their own stereotype (sexually liberated, very female, beautiful, generous and sweet).

The stereotypes produced by female Brazilian prostitutes about Spanish women are a way of simultaneously assimilating the hegemonic representations of themselves and subverting them by using them as tools of power (Aparício and Chávez-Silverman, 1997; De la Peña et al., 2009). If Spanish society attributes the characteristic of hypersexuality to Latin American woman in a pejorative manner, then these Brazilian women turn this same characteristic into an advantage for them in the sexual market, while at the same time deriding the sexuality of Spanish women.

Moreover, the attributes attributed by the Brazilian women in relation to Spanish women help them to justify their role as prostitutes. Spanish men are considered by these Brazilian prostitutes to be victims of their own cold, arrogant, authoritarian women, who need Brazilian women to meet their needs and sexual fantasies. Here, it is the creation of a discourse by these Brazilian women that forms an opposition between their representation of Spanish men and women, creating a binomial between debauched/emotional/needy men and conservative/rational/selfish women.

It is through the complementarity of their relationship with Spanish men that these Brazilian women justify their position in Spanish society. However, as clients, Spanish men still occupy an inferior position in comparison with the seductive power of the Brazilian women in the relationship between prostitute/client. These Brazilian women judge that they are fulfilling a role (the failure to provide sexual services desired by Spanish men) that is not provided by Spanish women, and therefore the latter are to blame for their husbands seeking the services of prostitutes.

Conclusion

Despite the hegemonic tropicalization, which establishes a discourse that exoticizes their corporeality and sexuality, the Brazilian women in this study recognize the power structures within which they operate, and they are able to find cracks within those power structures in order to counteract the processes of their marginalization. One of the most striking fissures in the hegemonic power structure recognized by these female Brazilian sex workers is the organization and distribution of erotic resources within Spanish society. The stereotypes that associate Brazilianness with hypersexuality are widely used by Brazilian women sex workers to their advantage in the competitive process of commercial sexual activity. The recognition of this organization transforms itself into subversive actions centred on the meanings of the attributes that sustain their representations of sexuality and corporeality. The Brazilian women produce alliances with hegemonic individuals through the use of erotic conquest of Spanish men as well as oppositional relationships with Spanish women. These Brazilian sex workers establish games, concealing and exaggerating their 'Brazilianness' according to the interactions and spatialities that they consider to be advantageous or disadvantageous for the conquest of power. In this sense, tropicalization does not have a linear and oppositional axis between colonizers and colonized. However, the tropicalization process, which has been produced by the Eurocentric hegemonic viewpoint, as well as by subversive actions of Brazilian women sex workers in Spain, has helped to maintain the structure of the social and economic hierarchies that exist between the groups analysed in this study.

Chapter 38

Beyond Dichotomies of Victimization versus Agency: Bringing in Gendered Spatial Subject Positions Related to Intimacy

Marlene Spanger

Introduction

Men and women selling sexual services have been articulated as 'victims of trafficking', 'modern female slaves', or alternatively as 'empowered women' or 'entrepreneurs' both in the media and in the public debates emanating from feminist scholarly studies on prostitution (Davidson, 1998; Chapkis, 2002; Agustín, 2007; Doezema, 2010). In particular, feminist scholars (Agustín, 2005; Doezema, 2010), cooperating closely with sex-worker rights activists draw attention to sex workers' labour rights as another feminist strategy for deconstructing both the whore stigma and the modern female slavery stigma. Another body of literature understands the sale of sexual services as a structural and symbolic result of a patriarchal society always limited by particular social, political and economic conditions, which subordinate women selling sexual services. Despite the different voices and views on sex sale, they all spring from a dichotomous thinking that refers to a question of victimization versus agency, prostitution versus sex work or trafficking versus labour migration. This conceptual framework was established during the 1980s and since then has dominated international political debates on human trafficking, migrant-related prostitution and global sex work (Kempadoo et al., 2005; Doezema, 1998). The dichotomous thinking also permeates the scholarly field of sex commerce. Third, a number of scholars propose approaches that overcome this dichotomous thinking (see Cheng, 2010; Sanders, 2008; Nencel, 2001; Trautner, 2005). This chapter can be situated within this third way by demonstrating how attention to spatial performances of sexuality and gender is a relevant perspective within studies of commercial sex and intimacy. In particular, I am inspired by Butler's theory on gender performativity and how this theory can be applied within studies on spatial relations.

On the basis of experiences from a study on female migrants selling sexual services in Denmark, I realized at an early stage in my research process that romance, marriage and mothering as the intimacy aspects of female Thai migrants' lives in Denmark somehow relate to their sale of sexual services (Spanger, 2010). Sea-Ling Cheng (2010) stresses similar scholarly experiences studying Thai migrants in South Korea. Using a critical approach to the dichotomous thinking, I argue that this entanglement cannot be reduced to understanding the women as either victims or entrepreneurs. Rather, the subject positions of these female migrants are rather complex and ambiguous.

Thus, this chapter provides an introduction to the theoretical perspective of gendered subject positions and spatial acts in order to understand the complexity of migrants selling sexual services. Moreover, I argue that the identity of migrants selling sex is produced through the discourse of heterosexuality and their navigation of different places and environments. Anchored in a study of Thai migrants married or having intimate relationships with Danish men, as well as selling sexual services in Denmark full time or occasionally, this chapter demonstrates how the gendered subject positions of sex worker, wife and migrant entangles in such ways that it is difficult to position them as either victims or empowered women. A new, growing body of literature (see Cabezas, 2006; Faier, 2007; Cheng, 2010; Spanger, 2013b) that has emerged from the scholarly fields of migration and sex work questions the concepts of 'sex work' and 'prostitution' as well as the way in which previous studies have compartmentalized sexual services from other social and intimate relations and activities. Thus, it is argued that the sale of sexual services cannot be perceived as an isolated activity. Instead, this new emerging literature opens up an entanglement of money, sex and love, introducing concepts like 'transactional relationships', 'intimate migrations', 'flexible intimacy' and so on.

The empirical example springs from fieldwork undertaken from September 2005 to April 2006. I conducted participant observations and interviews of female Thai migrants living in Denmark comprising female-born subjects, transgendered subjects (male-to-female) and cross-dressers, as well as social workers.

Once or twice a week I followed a counselling programme targeting migrants selling sexual services, participating in a coordinating meeting for all the actors involved in the counselling programme and in meetings with social workers and consultants involved in policy work within the field of prostitution.[1] Moreover, I visited massage parlours, strip bars, places and events (Thai concerts, the annual Thai festival, Thai clubs and bars and so on) that constitute the Thai migrant culture in Denmark. During my fieldwork I realized that female Thai sex workers are not an isolated social group within the Thai migrant community. During my interviews I worked with two interpreters, since the Danish and English language skills of my interviewees were poor, and I cannot speak Thai. Due to the sensitive nature of the subject, the interviewees were unwilling to talk with any other interpreter than the social worker, whom they trusted. This meant that the social worker also functioned as an interpreter during the interviews with those who spoke only Thai and were connected to the programme. I suggested using an interpreter from outside the Thai migrant community, but the migrants rejected my idea. However, despite the fact that from the outset I made my aim and position (as an academic) clear when I introduced myself to the interviewees at the counselling programme both the social worker and the interviewees had difficulties distinguishing between interview situations and social work. Consequently, in some interview situations, as in Nook's case story discussed below, the social worker, took over my role when I conducted the interviews. Seeing that she had a very clear opinion on sex work I was uncertain how to read her translation when she disagreed with the interviewees. Later, the second interpreter checked and transcribed the taped interviews. The second interpreter, who also assisted me at night, has no connections to the Thai migrant sex worker milieu in Denmark.

Inspired by Nencel's (2001) ethnographic fieldwork on women selling sex in Lima, I structured my participant observations and interviews in a day and night rhythm. Visiting bars and participating in various events in the Thai migrant community at night and following the counselling programme and visiting massage parlours during the daytime

---

1 Referring to the policy field of prostitution, I apply the term 'prostitution' since in Denmark this policy field is dominated by a view of women selling sexual services as in need of social and psychological assistance (Spanger, 2011; Bjønness, 2008).

gave me an opportunity to meet Thai migrant sex workers in different everyday situations and spaces, resulting in different kinds of narrative. Together, the female Thai migrants' narratives paint a complex picture of their everyday lives.

The next section will introduce Butler's (1990, 1997b) theories on gender performance and the theoretical concept of spatial acts proposed by Gregson and Rose (2000). In the subsequent sections I analyse how the Thai migrant Nook, who lives and works in Denmark, navigates between home and workplace, and how she and the social worker negotiate gender in the space of domesticity. I was introduced to Nook through a social counselling programme. Through her everyday life and migratory trajectory the figure of Nook represents the majority of the female Thai migrants selling sexual services in Denmark. The final analytical section concentrates on how she performs and negotiates gender in the space of sexual consumption. Thereafter, the chapter concludes how gendered subject positions and spatial acts challenge the dichotomy of victimization versus agency.

Subject Positions and Spatial Acts

The literature that investigates sex work from a spatial perspective is dominated by studies on street prostitution and red-light districts that focus on how sex work is regulated within public space (Hubbard, 2001; Sani, 2002; Hubbard and Sanders, 2003). I take a different stance, concentrating on the example of Nook and her spatial acts by paying attention to how she performs and navigates between various spaces in order to represent intelligible gendered subjects in these spaces. Other poststructuralist empirically-driven studies on sex work (see Trautner, 2005) that draw on Butler's theory focus solely on the level of subject formations. Such studies explicitly leave out physical surroundings and the ways in which the societal context affects the subject's gender performances. By contrast, I focus on the nexus of discourse and materiality when analysing how gendered subject positions are constituted within spaces. Inspired by Judith Butler, Gregson and Rose (2000) approach gender performance as 'spatial acts'. Feminist geography scholars (see McDowell, 1999; Massey, 1994) demonstrate how a binary gender hierarchy is deeply implicated in the social production of space through an association with dichotomies of spaces: public (man)/private (woman), home (woman)/work (man). I analyse how they perform and negotiate the subject positions of mother and sex worker through their spatial acts, transgressing the dichotomy of victimization versus empowerment.

Gender Performativity

Butler's critical poststructuralist gender theory has generated studies of the multiplicity of unstable gender categories. Their purpose has often been to question naturalized heterosexualities (Hawkes, 1995; Eng et al., 2005; D. Richardson, 1996b; Wilson, 2002). Butler (1990) focuses on how the subject is culturally intelligible within specific Western epistemological and philosophical discourses. In contrast, I investigate how the subject *becomes* culturally intelligible within everyday life discourses through multiple spaces. To do so, I find Gregson and Rose's (2000, p. 434) interpretation of Butler (1990, 1993) rather useful. They extend Butler's version of performativity[2] by introducing the concept of space

---

2   Performance is subsumed within, and is also connected to, performativity (Gregson and Rose, 2000, p. 441).

drawn from a critical human geography approach; this then leads to the notion of 'performed spaces'. In particular, within human geography, Butler's concept of performativity is crucial for understanding not only how subject formations take place, but also difference and power relations and the way in which space articulates these (Butler, 1990). Before elaborating on the synthesis of Butler's theory and space, I outline how her (1990, 1993, 1997b) concepts of performativity and subjection are relevant when analysing how Thai migrant sex workers understand heterosexuality and femininity/masculinity, how gender plays a part in sex work and how sex work affects the migrant sex workers' understanding of their gendered subject positions in spaces away from their sex work.

Butler (1990, 1993) challenges the naturalized heterosexual matrix by questioning how gender, based on a sex/gender distinction, is constituted. According to Butler, the sex/gender distinction relies on the idea that sex is prediscursive and prior to gender. Thus, sex poses as 'the authentic': 'the corporeal ground (the body) upon which gender operates as an act of cultural inscription' (Butler, 1990, p. 186). This entails practices, speech, gestures, appearances and so forth being construed as signs of two genders, 'woman/femininity' and 'man/masculinity', assumed to result from the sex (ibid., p. 173). Through the heterosexualization of desire, the two genders and the two bodies are consolidated as binary opposites in a power system in which 'woman' is seen as inferior to 'man' (ibid., p. 23). Within the heterosexual matrix, the two genders become intelligible, while other types of gendered subject positions are rendered impossible when gender does not follow body, and when sexual practices and desire do not follow gender (ibid., p. 24).[3] However, homosexuality and bisexuality that transgress the heterosexual matrix are intelligible within this matrix, though positioned in a hierarchical order (Hawkes, 1995, pp. 265–6). Thus, the heterosexual matrix regulates the possible ways of signifying gender. In the case of the Thai migrant sex workers who are transgendered or cross-dress, they subvert this heterosexual matrix and its assumption of there being just two genders. The subversion, as well as the reproduction of the heterosexual matrix, depends on the citational practices of this social group. The transformation of their bodies through hormones and/or surgery introduces a realigning within or, a reconstruction of, the heterosexual matrix. Some keep their penis and have breast operations, others have undergone a complete change, and others again do not have any surgical procedure or take hormones, but only cite femininity through dress and gesture.

By deconstructing the heterosexual matrix, Butler analyses how intelligible gender institutes and reproduces the cohesion between the four components: body, gender, sexual practices and sexual desire (Butler, 1990, p. 23). In this way, 'man' and 'woman' are established through specific relations between body and gender, as well as sexual desire and gender that require specific sexual practices. In relation to this, I argue that the limit of gender configurations depends on the particular space that offers possibilities and sets constraints. Focusing on these components as performed within Nook's narrative, I will investigate how she, through her agency, became an intelligible gendered subject in different spaces. Butler (1997b, p. 2) argues that becoming a subject is an ambivalent never-ending process which she terms 'subjection' that 'consists in this fundamental dependency on a discourse we never choose but that, paradoxically, initiates and sustains our agency'. Simultaneously, this process of subordination constitutes the subject. Thus, the subject is produced within a process of power relations, compulsion and reproduction conditioned by the heterosexual discourse that simultaneously constitutes and dissolves the very same subject. The ambivalence becomes the premises of the subject's existence, which is captured

---

3   By 'follow' Butler (1990, p. 24) refers to cultural laws and norms that establish and regulate the meaning of sexuality.

by the tension between what Butler (1997b, p. 18) calls 'already there and the yet-to-come'. The gender performativity of the subject takes place within this process.

Spatial Acts

Addressing Butler, Gregson and Rose (2000, p. 441) stress that performances must always be connected to the citational practices (reiterations of norms, bodily practices, gestures, appearance and words) that simultaneously reproduce and subvert discourse – in this case, the heterosexual discourse. At the same time, citational practices enable and construct the subjects and their performances. For the subject it is not a question of citation or not, rather it is a question of how the subject does citational practices (Butler, 1990, p. 185). These practices are not mechanical, but 'produced and compelled by regulatory practices of gender coherence' in terms of the heterosexual discourse (ibid., p. 33). The possibilities for disruption or realigning rely on how the subject cites, and 'there is no guarantee … that its repetition will be successful' (Gregson and Rose, 2000, p. 437). Subversion of the two genders or of heterosexuality is a consequence of the realignment that is inherent in citation. Thus, gender performativity creates a tension between an institutionalization of gender and the possibility of disputing gender.

Against the background of Gregson and Rose's (2000, p. 437) assertion that 'the discourse of heterosexuality is always threatened with its own instability', I analyse how Nook's gender performances subvert the heterosexual matrix. In Nook's case, it is a matter of doing the 'right' femininity in various spaces. I argue that the way in which realignments or disruptions take place when Nook performs gender depends on a number of factors, one of which is performative space. Thus, the heterosexual matrix functions as a mechanism that seeks to discipline the subject, and, in the very same process, multiple gendered subject positions are (re)constituted – for example, female sex worker and single mother. Not all are intelligible.

Gregson and Rose's (2000, p. 325) concept of 'performed spaces' refers to the fact that power relations reproduce both the gender performances of the subjects and space. However, the places in which performances occur (massage parlours, bars, hairdressing salons and so on) cannot be said to pre-exist these performances; they merely wait to be mapped out by them. Places like the massage parlour, the strip bar or Nook's home are not just places for sexual consumption or leisure. Rather, specific performances bring spaces into being (Gregson and Rose, 2000, pp. 441–2). Understanding space as multiple, relational, unfinished and as always in the process of being made, rather than just a passive backdrop to social relations or identity work, derives from a poststructuralist tradition (see McDowell, 1999; Gregson and Rose, 2000; Massey, 2005; Green et al., 2010; Murdoch, 2006). In particular, Gregson and Rose (2000, p. 442) explore 'the social relations of performances and the relationality of their spaces' by suggesting that 'another source of performative instability is the blurring of clear distinction between positions and spaces' and that 'performed spaces are not discrete, bounded stages, but threatened, contaminated, stained, enriched by other spaces; as are the performers'. Addressing space as performative allows me to analyse precisely how Nook's various gender performances within this case story constitute various gendered subject positions. At the same time, the performativities bring the spaces into being in rather different ways. Moreover, all spaces are dominated by a heterosexual discourse.

Having outlined the poststructuralist framework of performativity, subject position and spatial acts, the next sections delves into the analysis of Nook's narratives, emphasizing how the gendered subject positions, performed by Nook, are constituted within spaces.

The Case Story of Nook: Navigating Between Home and the Strip Bar

Nook is 34 years old and has lived in Denmark for more than six years. She works as a dancer and as a hostess in a strip bar. When I interviewed Nook she was taking a break from the strip bar due to the birth of her child. When Nook became pregnant, she needed a place to live and she approached a social counselling programme to procure a flat for her. Before this, when she worked at the bar, Nook rented a room from the bar owner, located in the same building as the bar in a neighbourhood dominated by a mixture of ethnic restaurants, cafés, porn shops, go-go bars, massage parlours, street prostitution and restored old dwellings. Nook's felt she belonged to this area. Her everyday life revolved around the strip bar. The social worker had difficulties persuading Nook to accept the suburban flat eight kilometres from the strip bar. Since her move to the outskirts of Copenhagen, no one passes by or visits Nook anymore. As another Thai migrant from the strip bar noted, 'I don't know where the area is located!' Following her move to the suburbs, Nook became isolated and experienced a loss of community. She did not want to live so far away from the nightlife and the strip bar where she worked, but the social worker had convinced her that living on the outskirts would be good for her and her daughter – a nice flat with a good view, surrounded by small squares of lawn! The strip bar constitutes a space of sexual consumption associated with nightlife, sex work and making money, whereas the new home in the periphery of Copenhagen constitutes a space of domesticity. The negotiations between the social authorities and Nook about 'proper' motherhood bring this space into being. The two contrasting spaces organize Nook's life: motherhood/sex work, day/nightlife and in/out.

The Space of Domesticity

As she has difficulties with the father of her daughter, Nook intends to apply for full custody. Besides interviewing Nook, I followed one of the social workers who are in weekly contact with Nook, which is how I came to attend one of the meetings at Nook's flat, where the social worker dealing with her case, a health visitor and another social worker were visiting Nook and her daughter. At this meeting they encouraged Nook to apply for custody. At such meetings, the function of the first social worker is to support Nook, and, if necessary, translate for her. Self-support, self-discipline and self-help are goals of social work, and Nook is seen as a 'strong client', a single 'foreign' mother who wants to commence a Danish-language course, a good caregiver towards her daughter and someone who creates a home. In particular, the social worker emphasizes to the other two social authorities how happy Nook is about the flat, stating how wonderfully she has created a home, pointing at the new furniture and the curtains. During the meeting they praise Nook for doing a good job with her daughter.

Living on the outskirts of Copenhagen, creating a home and devoting her time to her daughter signify practices that constitute Nook's motherhood within the space of domesticity. The way in which Nook performs motherhood around the social workers makes her gendered subject position intelligible. By applying for custody, she displays the 'will' to become a responsible mother to the social authorities. This is important to Nook as the performance of acceptable and unacceptable femininity is a delicate balance. Among social workers in Denmark, selling sex is solely signified as a social problem whereby the construction of the prostitute relies on the discourse of victimization (Spanger, 2011). According to the social worker, sex work is a social problem, which is why she was very keen on helping Thai migrants who sell sexual services to find a job outside the sex industry as cleaners. Nook is one of the Thai migrants that for whom the social worker is trying to help in finding another job. She wants to discuss Nook's job plans after her maternity leave is over in order to help Nook out of prostitution. The following extracts are from my interview with Nook in which the social worker (SW), who functioned as interpreter, slightly took over the interview. Before the interview I asked Nook to choose between two interpreters: the social worker she already knew and a Danish final-year student, who speaks fluent Thai. However, she wanted to use the social worker she already knew beforehand.

> SW: Yes, we have to be prepared that Nook has to be in employment when she applies for custody. You have to find a job in the daytime.

> Nook: Do I have to find a job?

> SW: You have to find a job. If you want to be awarded custody on your own, then they [the social authorities] look at ...

> Nook: They have written that I have to attend a language course next year.

> SW: It is good, it is really good. Then you can tell them [the social authorities] that you receive social security, attend school, you are home at night ... you take care of your child ...

> Nook: Yes ... but in reality ... in my heart I want to work as before [at the strip bar]. But it's just that that it's at night.

> SW: But who can take care of Stella at night?

> Nook: That is the problem!

> Researcher: But can't you find a babysitter? If you make good money you can pay a babysitter. Other people work at night.

> SW: Yes, it's a bit of a slippery downward path as it won't work in the long run. And how can she do it [sell sex at night], and when ... and when is Stella old enough for somebody else to take care of her ...

> Nook: Yes, I am tired of thinking about the future ...

> SW: [addressed to me in Danish while Nook was present] Mmm, if she [Nook] was a cleaner at night, then it would be fine, but she is not ...

Discourses of motherhood, including ideas of home and having a 'proper' job, constitute the space of 'proper' domesticity. This space establishes the premises for performing intelligible femininity, such as the subject position of single mother which becomes a counter-construction to the subject position of the female sex worker who prefers to sell sex or does not recognize herself as a victim. Consequently, when Nook talks about how she sells sex in the space of domesticity, her femininity becomes unintelligible. In this way, the space of domesticity is 'contaminated' by the space of sexual consumption; the last-mentioned space creates instability within the space of domesticity.

Nook explains her view on selling sex to the social worker (SW):

> Nook: *When you ask me what I want to work with – but you have to know that it is not necessary to wriggle. It is not necessary just to lie down on the bed with legs apart. It is not like that. All who work have their skills. It depends on how you speak, on your style and charm, how you play up to them. It is what you say that determines the sum of money. It is the words that decide! …*

> SW: *[translating] It's not that, it's the way you act, act your role. Then you earn a lot of money.*

> Nook: *But Phi bum [means older sister[4]] the work with the guests … if you want something from them, then you have to show consideration for the guests. Not just fool them all the time. Then they notice it.*

The simplification of Nook's explanation, in the translation process of the social worker, reflects how the social worker attempts to communicate another picture of Nook. The social worker's interpretation that Nook 'acts a part' when selling sex reflects a distinction between a 'real' self and a 'false' self. This distinction made by the social worker is an example of how Nook's narrative about performing femininity within the space of sexual consumption contaminates the space of domesticity where the social worker seeks to project her as a 'good' mother *and* a 'good' woman.

Through her detailed explanation of how she understands her sex work – attitude, flirtation, conversation and the sex practices – Nook tries to position herself as an intelligible gendered subject within the space of domesticity. This succeeds as performing the 'good single mother'. Put differently, by talking about her job as a dancer and selling sexual services she becomes non-intelligible in the gaze of the social workers because they view sex workers as subjects who need psychological and social help. Nook tells us in detailed account of her bar work reflects how gender is communicated through appearance. She dresses up and performs body language that connects gender, body, sexual desire and practices by way of citational practices constituting a feminine subject position that meets the idealized heterosexually desirable object within the space of sexual consumption. Moreover, Nook narrates the encounter with the guests as a professional skill. With the combination of her (female) body, dress and body language and flirtation with the male clients, her sexual desire and practices addressed to men, Nook lives up to certain cultural norms of citing the 'right' femininity as a heterosexual sex worker in the space of sexual consumption. While talking about her job as sex worker in the space of domesticity she does not become intelligible.

The Space of Sexual Consumption

Together with my research assistant, I undertook participant observation at strip clubs that are owned and run by Thai people. One night, after performing a strip show, one of the dancers enters the bar, ready to flirt with the guests. Very soon one of the men addresses her. Another woman, working as a hostess, has already engaged in small talk with the guests. Seduction and attractiveness are important assets in order to perform intelligible femininity that brings the space of commercial sex into being. The dancers, hostesses and bartenders

---

4   *Phi bum* has a double meaning. It refers to an older sister in a familiar sense, or, as *Phi Bum*, it refers to a specific way of addressing another woman who is positioned higher in the social hierarchy.

are Thai female migrants, ciswomen[5] and transwomen. Only the bouncers are white Danish men. I was told by the bar staff that those frequenting the strip bar are Danish men and male tourists. It is not unusual for friends of the hostesses and the dancers to pass by in their spare time to have a 'fun time' and a drink.

The strip bar is a place where notions of the 'exotic other', employed by the categories of race, gender and sexuality, are remade and played out by the social groups of female Thai migrants and Danish men through sexual exchange and the profit economy. Studies of commercial sex performances (Manderson, 1992; Trautner, 2005; Brott, 2006) point out that desire, lust and imagined sex are constructed within such a space. As Trautner (2005, p. 772) argues, a central premise for such bars is a 'consumption of women's bodies and the presence of those bodies in hegemonic male fantasies'. Not only the choice of clothes and make-up, but also how the women address the guests, move or gesticulate are spatial acts that perform a particular form of intelligible heterosexual femininity. Within the space of sexual exchange, this seeks to be constituted as attractive and 'the perfect seduction'. Brott (2006) underscores that physical appearance is directly related to profitability within lap dancing. This condition is present at the Thai strip bar, too. On the basis of my observations at this strip bar, the sex workers very rapidly estimate whether the guest is interested in buying sex.

The space of the strip club relies on a complex gender hierarchy that exceeds the heterosexual matrix. Power relations between the transwomen and ciswomen, who sell sex, and between masculinity and femininity institute the hierarchy. Profit, consumption and commercial interests determine this relation. Both female groups vie for the male guests' favour. Such relations reproduce an extreme heterosexual gender hierarchy caused by the ways in which femininity is evoked through the components of gender, body, sexual desire and practices. Talking about work at the strip club, Nooks stresses how transwomen and ciswomen compete:

> They [kathoeys a Thai word for male-to-female transgendered individuals] outnumber us and they are much pushier. We women do not dare to do the same. When we sit, we put our legs together. When it is a kathoey, they have to show off. There is a clear difference. I sit next to the men, a kathoey sits on the men's lap.

Making a clear demarcation between 'us and them', the 'normal versus abnormal' femininity, statements such as 'we are women' and 'they [kathoeys] can't compete with a woman' demonstrate that the space of sexual consumption is also created through gendered performance. Here Nook essentializes biologically born women by signifying that only they can posses an inherent femininity. According to Nook, the two genders depend solely on the genitals the person is born with (penis, vagina) or what kind of bodily parts the person has developed (breasts, hips and so on) later on.

Drawing on the idea of 'the original body' when asserting that '… they can't compete with a woman, a real pussy', Nook does not recognize *kathoeys* as 'real women'. From Nook's perspective, the gendered citational practices of the *kathoeys* reflect realignments that disturb her performance of femininity. Simultaneously, she is challenged by how the *kathoeys* reshape their bodies through surgery in combination with their height and build (often tall and slim), since transwomen may perform forms of ideal femininity as sexual objects in spaces of sexual consumption. Following Nook, the spatial acts of the *kathoeys* subvert the heterosexual discourse. 'Who can compete with silicone? Simply the way they

---

5   This term is used to recognize women who were assigned female at birth and continue to live as women.

stick out. It has to be in this way! And then their cunts – ooh fuck … "My pussy is giant" something like that they [*kathoeys*] say. The guests like when it [genitalia] is voluminous …'

Nook regards *kathoeys*' social acts towards the guests as a sign of '… inferiority because they are men. They have to be more courageous. They have to show off for the guests, so the men want them.' Nook depicts as overly feminine certain social acts and practices that are performed by the *kathoeys*. She is disturbed by the *kathoeys* because of how they perform female bodies that ideally meet the norms of femininity in this space because their performance to a certain extent fits into the hierarchical binary gender system that refers to a sex/gender distinction, even if Nook rejects *kathoey* as a gender category that performs 'real' femininity. Nook's statement reflects how she feels threatened by the existence of the *kathoeys*. By demarcating between 'real' woman and 'non-real' women, characterizing their practices as aggressive, as well as the *kathoeys*' need to work harder to make 'men want them', she constitutes a gender hierarchy that confirms a particular heteronormative discourse.

Conclusion

Nook's story demonstrates how the gendered subject positions of mother and sex worker imply specific spaces such as the space of domesticity and sexual consumption. Nook performs the various subject positions through the way in which she navigates in these spaces through power relations. For instance, in the space of domesticity she tries to negotiate the way in which she is positioned as a victim of prostitution by the social workers, wanting them to approach her as a sex worker with agency. However, she does not succeed. By contrast, in her narratives related to the space of sexual consumption, she demonstrates her agency through the way in which she struggles for power with the *kathoeys*, also positioning them as acting towards the sex clients. Coined by the heterosexual discourse, the narratives of how Nook and the *kathoeys* perform gender reflect a process of how heterosexual femininity is both subverted by the transgendered women (the *kathoeys*) and confirmed by the ciswomen (in this case, Nook). Within this process of Nook's and the *kathoeys*' gendered performances, calling for attention from the male guests brings the space of sexual consumption into being, which exactly reflects the agency of the Thai migrants selling sexual services. In both spaces – the space of sexual consumption and the space of domesticity – gender and sexuality seem to be performed as strategic subjectivities that reflect the complexity of the migrants selling sexual services. The spatial performativities of the Thai migrant sex workers demonstrate how identity work, agency and space are inseparable, and thus it is not a question of either agency or victimization.

SECTION VII
Digital Sexualities

Catherine J. Nash and Andrew Gorman-Murray (editors)

Chapter 39

Digital Sexualities: Section Introduction

Catherine J. Nash and Andrew Gorman-Murray

New technologies, including the internet, new media and mobile apps, appear to be fomenting a new 'sexual revolution', one that is rewriting how we understand what our bodies can 'do' and how we comprehend ourselves as sexual beings.[1] In fact, at this historical juncture, it would not be an overstatement to argue that we are in 'the midst of a technologically mediated reorganization of the social relations of sexuality' (Garlick 2011, p. 223; see also Bargh and McKenna, 2004; Lasén, 2005). As Chris Brickell (2012, p. 28) suggests, the 'internet is an important enabler and mediator of sexual relations in society', the depth and breadth of which we are just beginning to explore. Not surprisingly, these technologically mediated transformations in sex and sexualities are not without their proponents and detractors. Various factions in both popular media and academic research paint the internet as a place of danger, deviancy and untenable risk, where access to sexual materials, partners and knowledges are wreaking havoc on sociosexual relations (see Cooper et al., 2000; Griffiths, 2001; Grov et al., 2008). For others, cyberspace offers a place of liberation, celebration and triumph as human beings are untangled from outmoded constraints on their honest explorations and experimentations of what it means to be a sexual being (see Chiou, 2006; Kendall, 2000, 2002; Turkle, 1999).

This burgeoning online activity has spawned the notion of 'internet sexuality' as an area of academic study, focusing on 'sexual-related content and activities observable on the internet', as well as various forms of 'cybersexuality' (Döring, 2009, p. 1090). The online journal *Medium* recently published an article by Emily Witt exploring the implications of the website Chaturbate, a live-cam site, launched in 2011. Witt represents the site as a place of 'total sexual anarchy' and as an example of how the internet and social media 'has created a whole new sexual persuasion', that of the 'internet sexual', suggesting the advent of new sexual identities, mediated by new and emergent technologies (Witt, 2015).

Nicola Döring (2009), in her critical review of the literature on aspects of internet sexuality since 1993, lays out an argument charting the potentially broad impact (both positive and negative) of new technologies:

> *Internet sexuality can have impacts on sexual attitudes and identities, the sexual socialization of children and adolescents, gender relations, the social position and political activism of sexual minorities, the inclusion of people with disabilities, the spread of sexually transmitted infections, sexual satisfaction in couple relationships,*

---

1   The term 'new technologies' encompasses a broad range of information and communication technologies (ICTs) overland in the digital age. These include the internet and Web 2.0, ICTs, digital media, new media, location-based services (LBS), social networking applications and locative mobile social networks (LMSN).

the promotion of sexual health, the development of sexual disorders, and the occurrence of sexual victimization. (Döring, 2009, p. 1090)

Döring's (2009) review led her to argue that scholarship on internet sexuality could be grouped into six broad categories (while recognizing the limitations of attempts at cataloguing research). These are: 1) pornography, 2) sex shops online, 3) online sex work, 4) sexual education, 5) sex contacts and 6) sexual subcultures. As geographers interested in the implications of places and meanings in understanding human experiences, we can study the nature of the places being created and used online (their meanings, social relations, normative frameworks, possibilities/limitations) as well as how new technologies alter or transform our offline experiences. For example, seeking sexual contacts online has implications for our offline lives given that an increasing number of people utilize the internet to make sexual connections. As van Doorn (2011, p. 532) argues, online and offline interactions highlight how 'articulations of gender, sexuality and embodiment are intricately interwoven with people's physical embedding in everyday life as well as the new technologies they employ to extend daily experiences into digital locales'. In North America, by 2009 some 20 per cent of heterosexual couples had met online, while the number of same-sex attached individuals was estimated at 60 per cent. By 2013 research suggested that some 30–40 million North Americans used online dating services (an estimated 1,500 sites), including Match.com, OKCupid.com, eHarmony.com (Engelhart, 2013) and hook-up apps such as Tinder.

While cyberspace facilitates innumerable sexual and gendered possibilities, geographers are increasingly attentive to the ways in which online and offline worlds connect, reconstituting or reformulating material social relations through the remediation or intertwining of on online/offline lives (see Crang et al., 2007). The online dating scene is radically changing how people meet, offering opportunities to connect with others across great distances or maintain long-distance relationships in ways that fundamentally alter human intimacies (Brickell, 2012; Constable, 2009; Duncan and Phillips, 2010). Online sex work can have offline implications for urban places – for example, through the (re)creation, facilitation and promotion of sex tourism places, and locations for prostitution, strip clubs and other sexual venues (see Hubbard, 2008, 2011).

Sexual subcultures have also found the internet a liberating and empowering space – a place to connect with others of similar interests or persuasions, offering the opportunity to foster community, reduce social isolation and marginalization, and encourage political activism (Döring, 2009; Hillier and Harrison, 2007; McKenna and Bargh, 1998). As Döring (2009, p. 1097) notes, the internet is an important place of refuge 'for individuals who do not have access to urban subcultures by virtue of social restrictions or their place of domicile'. A plethora of sexual subcultures have found their voice (and perhaps community) through internet blogs, websites, bulletin boards, chat rooms and dating services. Prominent groups including LGBT people (Usher and Morrison, 2010; Wakeford, 1999), cross-dressers (Hegland and Nelson, 2002), and those interested in BDSM, polyamory or various fetishisms (Barker, 2005; Newman, 1997; Palandri and Green, 2000).

New Media and the Undoing of Sexuality and Place?

For geographers, social commentators and media scholars, there is little doubt that new technologies are having a profound effect on our experiences of, and engagement with, our everyday lived places, suggesting that any seeming dichotomy between our online and offline life is artificial. Graham (2013, p. 179) argues that concepts such as 'cyberspace' and 'virtual reality' are 'distracting metaphors' that seem to 'claim an aspatiality for the collective hallucination of internet; a disembodied place, but a place nonetheless' (see also Morgan, 2004). As new mobile technologies evolve, we are increasingly able to take our social networks with us. No longer confined to our desktops, smart phones, wireless networks and mobile social networking applications have rendered our online life portable, mobile and connected – a state of affairs that 'alters our relationship to and experience of place' (Ito, 2005; Ito and Okabe, 2005). Conceptualizing interwoven online/offline spatialies is becoming increasingly more complicated given that 'the space we inhabit is at an "intersection of two worlds" where cyberspace and place are intricately connected in a dynamic and mutually constitutive process' (Zook and Graham, 2007, p. 468). Rather than eradicating physical spaces, new mobile technologies challenge geographers to reconceptualize notions of 'place'. Wilken (2009, p. 40) argues that we need to rework our understandings of place, noting that 'how this concept is conventionally understood is inadequate for understanding contemporary mobile media'.

Perhaps one of the clearest examples of new online engagements that are potentially reconfiguring offline locations is reflected in the current debates about the apparent demise of gay villages in many cities in the global north (see Ghaziani, 2014). One of the key historical narratives embedded in LGBT and queer political and social life has been the importance of creating and defending LGBT physical places (bars, baths, cafes, community centres and neighbourhoods) (see Binnie and Skeggs, 2004; Castells, 1983; Gorman-Murray and Waitt, 2009; Knopp, 1990; Nash, 2006; Podmore, 2013a). As research suggests, the increasing use of new technologies raises important questions about the constitution of LGBT identities and subjectivities, and the transformative processes implicated in the (re)production of social space. As Nash and Gorman-Murray's chapter suggests, a substantial body of scholarship claims that the internet, ICTs and new mobile social media are reworking LGBT social life, thereby rendering actual material space irrelevant to developing LGBT identities and social networks. Worries about the loss of these political and economic strongholds are prominent in many cities, such as Toronto, Sydney, New York and San Francisco (Nash, 2013a; Gorman-Murray and Nash, 2014; Ghaziani, 2014). While new social and legislative gains ensure that LGBT and queer people have greater protections and therefore opportunities to be visible in a broad range of locations, there is also evidence to support the contention that new technologies are diminishing the need for LGBT and queer material spaces. A generational divide seems to be emerging whereby a new generation of LGBT and queer people no longer regard gay spaces, including gay villages, as necessary to their social or political life. This generational divide is exacerbated by an emerging digital divide where older LGBT and queer individuals are increasingly distanced from more technologically adept LGBT and queer youth and their online engagements (Nash, 2013a). Nevertheless, research suggests that older adults (LGBT, queer and heterosexual) are increasingly engaging with new technologies to find new opportunities for gendered and sexual expression (Adams et al., 2003; Alterovitz and Mendelsohn, 2013; Rowan, 2009).

So while a substantial body of geographical scholarship on sexual minorities suggests that non-normative sexual (and gendered) identities require access to physical (and often urban) locations to meet and mingle and form community, more recent research claims that new technologies seemingly reduce the need for physical space as LGBT and queer individuals meet others, experiment with new gendered and sexual identities and belong to a variety of communities in cyberspace (see Nash and Gorman-Murray in this section). Long-standing LGBT and queer physical locations, such as gay villages, may no longer be necessary as LGBT and queer people increasingly move online (Collins, 2004a; Ruting, 2008; Usher and Morrison, 2010; Nash, 2013a).

Geographical research is deeply implicated in broader debates about geographies of sex and sexualities as they are developing within and through new technologies. This will require the creation of new conceptual frameworks that can provide insights into the complexities of our experiences of place as we increasingly occupy online and offline worlds simultaneously. Arguably, these shifting experiences of place will vary across space and time, and across cultural and social divisions. Geographers will need to explore how new meanings are being constituted in and through the use of various spaces and what this means for how we currently demarcate space, such as the divisions between 'home' and 'work' (which are already breaking down), between work and leisure spaces, urban and rural spaces, as well as potential changes in the meaning of our humanness – being 'alone', experiencing silence, tuning in or tuning out.

About this Section

It should go without saying, then, that geographical scholarship has much to contribute to debates about how sex, sexuality and gendered experiences are increasingly being constituted in and through new technologies. The chapters in this section do much to advance this project, making an important contribution to research on the complex ways in which technologies are interweaving our online/offline lives.

In her chapter on school and 'sexting', Kath Albury positions her work within the spaces of the Australian classroom to consider how the carefully defended boundary between student sexuality (expected to be 'outside' the school both temporally and materially) and the 'spaces of learning' are being eroded by student use of laptops, mobile phones and social networking applications. Albury examines the emerging tensions arising from educators' attempts to regulate and control such activities and students' strategies to challenge such attempts through the reworking of mediated sexual cultures across spatial boundaries. She suggests that educators 'might productively engage with mediated sexual practices … in order to explore and promote ethical cultures of learning and teaching regarding sex, gender and relationships' in ways that grapple with the fact of 'mobile media practice as an ordinary part of young people's experiences of both sexuality and schooling'.

Gary Downing's chapter explores how non-heterosexual youths use the internet to explore and negotiate identities, social networks and sociosexual relations in order to 'supplement their virtual and material sociosexual relations'. His work demonstrates how online activities allow youth to examine questions about sexual identity and sexual health in a safe, peer-based environment while concurrently arranging to find offline support networks, social space and perhaps professional assistance. Downing argues that 'LGBT sociosexual networking on the internet has offline foundations' and that 'online and offline realities were also mutually constitutive in non-heterosexual young people's everyday sociosexual lives'. This work nicely highlights the need to (re)conceptualize notions of space and place in light of fluid and overlapping online/offline interweaving (Wilken, 2009).

Online gaming constitutes an important social environment, and, in her chapter, Cherie Todd examines how certain offline heteronormative values and norms are embedded and reinforced in online environments and identities. Online spaces are arguably constituted as heterosexual, so non-normatively gendered and sexualized avatars (as self-representations in the game) are often 'marginalized' and made to feel 'out of place'. Despite the fact that offline discriminatory practices and behaviours are visible in the online world, various modes of resistance and contestation are also present, and the chapter examines the role of virtual corporealities, modes of play and acts of resistance deployed in the online game World of Warcraft.

Sharif Mowlabocus's chapter considers two very distinctive examples of how mobile applications can remap space in ways that might open up public spaces to some users while closing down that same space to other users. His broad goal is to demonstrate how digital technology can 'serve to regulate and shape the spaces of our everyday lives', and perhaps not always for the best. A distinctive aspect of this work is a consideration of the 'politics' embedded in the use of various technologies – a point often overlooked in the research on new technologies.

Finally, Catherine Nash and Andrew Gorman-Murray consider how LGBT and queer engagements with new technologies contribute to the ongoing transformations in and of LGBT and queer urban landscapes in the Global North, particularly the ongoing change in many North American and Australian 'gay villages'. They consider the current literature about LGBT and queer adoption of new technologies, and suggest that a 'new mobilities' approach might be one way of reconceptualizing sexual and gendered urban landscapes that incorporates new media, new experiences in urban spaces and the emergence of new urban social networks that have mutually constitutive virtual and material aspects.

Chapter 40

Sexting, Schools and Surveillance: Mediated Sexuality in the Classroom

Kath Albury

Introduction

Carrie Paechter (2004) has proposed that sexuality education occupies an inherently 'problematic' space within the broader secondary school curriculum, because it troubles the implied Cartesian split within schooling. By extension, students' use of media (particularly mobile media), can be seen to further erode the boundaries between sexuality (which belongs 'outside', in the realm of bodies) and schooling, in which 'the space of learning' is understood as a realm of the mind (Paechter, 2004, p. 315). While students' bodies can be contained and regulated within classrooms, their ubiquitous access to laptops and mobile phones allows them to sustain friendships and intimate relationships, and to co-inhabit other (sexual) spaces and places.

As Browne et al. (2007) observe, the past 20 years have seen a proliferation of literature exploring the interrelationship of space, place and sexuality, including a focus on sites where sexuality is implicitly or explicitly surveilled or regulated (Brown et al., 2007, p. 3). At the same time there has been an emerging interest in the ways in which media technologies, such as mobile phones, are implicated in this relationship, particularly in relation to mobility and urban space [see Nash and Gorman-Murray in this volume]. A number of scholars have explored the interplay between media technologies (particularly social media) and sex and gender diversity of young people's experience of sexuality, considering ICT's role in facilitating 'alternative' places and spaces for exploring sexual identity (for example, Crowley, 2010; Hillier et al., 2012; Fink and Miller, 2013). Recently, scholars in the fields of cultural geography and media and cultural studies have explored the ways in which young people's everyday mobile-media practices shape, and are shaped by, their experiences of gender, their intimate and familial relationships, and their perceptions of risk and safety in urban public spaces (for example, Pain et al., 2005, Thompson and Cupples, 2008; Evers and Goggin, 2012; Lasén and Casado, 2012; Leyshon et al., 2013).

Beyond the sphere of educational research and curriculum development, however, there has been little focus on the ways in which emerging mobile-media cultures might impact on the more 'disciplined' space of young people's formal sexual learning, particularly the sex-education classroom. This chapter draws on focus groups with young people, as well as interviews and group discussions with educators, as part of two Australian studies: Young People and Sexting in Australia and Young People, Sex, Love and the Media[1] Both projects

1   Young People and Sexting in Australia was funded by the Australian Research Council (ARC) Centre of Excellence in Creative Industries and Innovation, and Young People, Sex, Love and the

aim to better understand a range of practices and spaces that can be considered as 'young people's mediated sexual cultures'.

While mediated sexual cultures may include the production and distribution of professional and amateur pornography (including user-generated images and written texts), participation in social networking sites, online dating or hook-up apps, and engagement with 'traditional' media texts such as popular music, magazines, television programmes, films and advertisements, this chapter focuses not on media content, but on the use of mobile-media technologies, such as phones, tablets and laptops. Within the Australian context, neither educators nor young people are currently well supported to engage with the implications of mobile media in relation to learning and teaching, particularly in relation to sex and relationships education (SRE). By exploring the ways in which media practices such as sexting and selfies render student sexuality visible within the space of schooling, I seek to move away from framing these activities as intrinsically risky and problematic, and consider instead *why* mobile-media practices provoke concern (and, in some cases, anxiety) within school communities. Following boyd (2014), I suggest that teachers might positively reframe mobile-media practice, allowing for classroom engagements that acknowledge young people's 'desire to be seen and be part of a broader conversation [and] … a broader social world' (boyd, 2014, p. 206).

Background

Recent research conducted by the Australian Communication and Media Authority (ACMA, 2013) indicates that 86 per cent of Australians aged 14–17 own smartphones. Access to smartphones (and the data-plans required to use them) is far from universal and is contingent on socioeconomic conditions and mobile carrier coverage. However, those young people with access to a smartphone gain personalized access to apps, websites and social networking sites and, by extension, privatized access to sexual information and communication. Smartphone users have the means to produce and distribute sexual self-representations in the form of selfies (or digital self-portraits) and sexting – a term that is not generally used by young people when describing their own practices (Albury et al., 2013), but widely understood within popular and academic discourse to refer to the production and sharing of sexually suggestive messages and pictures. Since 2009 popular and academic discussions of sexting (and selfies) in Australia, North America and the UK have focused on the potential sociolegal risks to young people – most often framed as a risk to young women's sexual reputations (Albury and Crawford, 2012; Hasinoff, 2012; Ringrose et al., 2013). These concerns have led to an increasing focus on sexting (and mediated sexual cultures in general) within the space of schooling and education. However, a recent study

Media was funded by Australian Research Council Discovery grant, DP120102594. The formal interview processes for these projects were approved by the UNSW Human Ethics Research committees (HC12043 and HC12050), and we received additional permission to record notes at our stakeholder consultation forums in 2012. While both projects aim to foreground young people's views on the ways in which contemporary media practices, such as sexting, are represented within 'adult' discourses of education and the law, the research team also sought to understand adult stakeholders' perspectives. This stakeholder consultation process was both formal and informal, involving interviews with school- and community-based educators and policy officers from the fields of education and health. Additionally, I was invited by a number of school and community education groups to present work-in-progress findings to staff and participate in question-and-answer sessions. My discussion here is informed by these formal and informal discussions about sexting, sex education and schools.

of Australian SRE teachers found that they struggle with 'content surrounding the more contemporary issues of sexting, online pornography and sexuality. Many of the teachers stated that their peers invariably privileged the delivery of *the plumbing* [for example, body parts and functions] to avoid the "messiness" of these topics' (Leahy and McCuaig, 2013, pp. 17–18).

This ambivalence among educators is unsurprising. While mobile devices can be framed primarily as communications devices, or a means of delivering online content, mobile-media scholars are increasingly suggesting that these technologies impact on users' experiences of space, time and intimacy in complex ways (Lasén, 2004; Hjorth and Lim, 2012). Consequently, engaging with mobile practices in the classroom also requires educators to engage with students' affective and embodied experiences across multiple online and offline spaces.

Intimate Technologies and the 'Doubling of Place' in the Classroom

In his pioneering analysis of the impact of electronic media on everyday life, Meyrowitz argues that they 'affect us ... not primarily through their content, but by changing the "situational geography" of social life' (Meyrowitz, 1985, p. 6). Moores (2004) extends Meyrowitz's conceptualization of media practices by drawing on Scannell's (1996) phenomenological study of broadcast media audiences. Extending Scannell's concept of the 'doubling of place' to mobile-media users, he suggests that rather than untethering us from our sense of place, mobile-media practices promote the *pluralization* of our experience of time, space and place.

Whereas Meyrowitz (1985) argues that media users have 'no sense of place', Moores (2004, 2006) suggests that the use of online and mobile media does not remove us from space or place, but issues a layering of one's sense of place via relationality, allowing users to be co-present in multiple spaces simultaneously. In the case of high-school students, use of a mobile device (or Department of Education laptop) can permit them to inhabit multiple places at once. Students may simultaneously engage in an asynchronous exchange via email and a real-time conversation on MSN Messenger while remaining physically present in the physical boundaries of the classroom-as-container (Leander et al., 2010). However, as Moores (2004, pp. 29–30) notes in his discussion on doubling of place, such co-location is not seamless. It relies on an implicit agreement by those who are physically co-present (teachers and other students) to not draw attention to any interruptions and distractions that leak through from other mediated spaces.

This capacity of technology to facilitate the doubling of place is not necessarily exclusive to digital media. As de Souza e Silva and Frith (2012) note in their study of geo-locative media, books are also portable handheld devices. Reading a novel or magazine instead of a textbook, or silently writing and passing notes, are time-honoured modes of classroom resistance, and these practices also allow students to inhabit other places while their bodies remain contained. Similarly, Morgan (1995) has argued that 'traditional' forms of media, specifically television, have served as 'cartographic technologies', allowing young people to overlay other places and spaces (including spaces of informal sexual learning) on to the space of formal schooling.

However, mobile phones seem to play a starring role in contemporary adult anxieties around media practices such as sexting and the production and distribution of selfies (digital self-portraits) via social media, precisely because they are central to young people's everyday cultures. Several scholars have noted the intimate practices of mobile-phone users, drawing attention to a metaphorical merging of bodies, emotions and phones, creating

361

affective assemblages of individuals, machines and social networks (Lasén, 2004; Allen, 2015). As Lasén notes:

> ... *the way mobile phones are held and touched is one of the aspects that make this relationship different to other ICT devices. The attachment to mobile phones is revealed by the transformation from being an object always at hand, to being almost always in the hand and close to the body. (Lasén, 2004, p. 4)*

I suggest that it is this merging of bodies and technologies that makes sexting so 'messy' for teachers and schools. Drawing on Deleuzian concepts of assemblages as 'more than human', Allen (2015, p. 124) reflects on her study of young people's narrative and photographic accounts of sexual cultures in school, concluding that 'sexuality-as-assemblage is the grouping, mobile phones/young people/school'. This assemblage does not necessarily sit comfortably within the space of schooling, however, and it is unsurprising that mobile/mediated practices of sexting (and, to a lesser extent, the production and distribution of selfies) is so problematic for teachers. In the Young People and Sexting in Australia study, one group of 16–17-year-old women protested what they saw as a continuum of adult surveillance of their sexualities, on- and offline. One participant states:

> *It's the whole issue of teen sexuality in general. You get told not to have sex. At school you get told to pull our skirts down because that's seen as provocative if you have them too high. And it just – I think it makes the older generation uncomfortable, because they don't understand. Because it's all moving so fast with technology and it's just much more accessible I guess.*

These young women can be seen to position adult concerns regarding sexting and selfies within the context of a broader cultural anxiety regarding the role of media in the sexualization of children – an anxiety that has been the subject of intensive popular and scholarly debate in Australia since 2008 (see Egan, 2013; Hasinoff, 2014; Lumby and Albury, 2010). It is clear that despite Paechter's (2004) observation of an inherent Cartesian split in schooling, high-school students are indeed understood as bodies, and not just minds – and both their bodies and minds can be troubling and troublesome to the space of schooling. As Holloway and Valentine (2003, 2005) have noted, children and young people's access to both 'private' and 'public' spaces can be framed as problematic within a range of contexts and settings, both on- and offline. Media practices make students' sexuality visible to not only their peers, but also teachers and other authority figures. They also facilitate student resistance to formal teaching strategies and enable them to transgress the temporal and spatial boundaries of 'school business'.

This transgression is not intrinsically emancipating, however, and this chapter should not be read as a utopian celebration of sexting and associated media practices. As Moores (2004, p. 29) observes, both online and offline spaces can facilitate overtly (and sometimes aggressively) sexed and gendered modes of communication. Indeed, the warmth or belonging that constitutes a 'sense of place', both on- and offline, can depend on the exclusion of those deemed to be outsiders (Moores, 2006). As in adult-mediated sexual cultures, young people's negotiation of mobile and online sexuality can be unethical, coercive and abusive (Ringrose et al., 2013). However, unethical media practices are not inevitable, nor are they easily avoided by abstaining from media practice. Further, I suggest that adults who adopt an abstinence approach to mobile and online media are not likely to be seen as a source of support by those young people who are at risk. It is more appropriate for educators to: a) seek to understand or engage with young people's own understandings of ethical and unethical media practices; and b) be prepared to offer practical support and/or access to means of redress to young people who have suffered exploitation, bullying or abuse on- or offline (Albury and Crawford, 2012; Albury et al., 2013). However, both these responses are far more challenging than promoting a 'just say no' approach, for a range of reasons.

Teaching Sex and Mobile Media: Educational Challenges

Between 16 and 20 per cent of respondents in the First National Survey of Australian Secondary Teachers of Sexuality Education identified a lack of support in terms of training, resources or school management/policy as reasons to avoid teaching a 'controversial' topic altogether (A. Smith et al., 2011, p. 27).[2] While there is a tradition in Australian education of encouraging 'critical reading' of commercially produced depictions of gender and sexuality (such as magazine covers, music videos and advertising billboards), there is increasing concern among educators that current SRE resources for in-service teachers do not adequately address young people's contemporary media practices (such as sexting), which involve the production and distribution of user-generated images (Leahy and McCuaig, 2013). This partly reflects legal constraints in that Australian Commonwealth laws may define any 'sexually suggestive' text or image relating to a person under 18 as 'child pornography' (Albury et al., 2013).[3]

Additionally, where parents (and not young people) are perceived as a school's primary clients, educators are understandably sensitive to public debates regarding the content of 'controversial' topics such sex and relationships education. In both formal consultations and informal discussions, educators frequently raised concerns about overcrowded curriculums and timetables, suggesting that teachers and schools are made responsible for addressing all social ills but are still required to deliver a full range of 'traditional' content in the time they have with students.[4] Yet, as one adult interviewee observed, it is commonly agreed that education on sexual media cultures *should* take place in schools, since, as she described, home life can be 'random', chaotic or even unsafe for many young people, and further, school students are a 'captive audience'.

Considering Sexting, Schools and Space

While teachers are understandably reluctant to squeeze additional content into overcrowded timetables, there may also be other reasons for their resistance to discussing mediated sexuality in school. The draft Australian National Health and Physical Education

---

2   This finding resonates with Preston's (2013) study of North American sex education teachers' perceptions of sexuality education as 'risky' and Kehily's (2002) observation that British sex education teachers tend to self-censor (or 'teach defensively') when approaching controversial or uncomfortable topics (Kehily, 2002, p. 217).

3   Educators interviewed for the Young People and Sexting in Australia project indicated that teachers may be uncertain about their mandatory notification obligations in relation to child pornography laws and consequently may be reluctant to engage in conversations addressing mediated sexuality (Albury et al., 2013). A recent study by the National Children's and Youth Law Centre (Tallon et al., 2012) also found a significant gap between young people's media practices and their knowledge of criminal laws pertaining to media use.

4   This response echoes a sentiment expressed by educational researchers Alldred and David (2007, p. 51) as NABI or 'Not Another Bloody Initiative' syndrome.

Curriculum (2013) notes the increased role of online and mobile media in young people's lives, and foregrounds a need to support young people's ethical use of information and communication technologies (ICT) 'as key tools for communicating, collaborating, creating content, seeking help, accessing information and analysing performance in the Health and Physical Education field' (ACARA, 2013 p. 20). However, where Australian educational resources are available, they tend to address mobile and online practices (including sexting) primarily from the perspective of bullying and/or technological 'risk to reputation', promoting what can be considered an 'abstinence' approach (Albury et al., 2013).

Although 'mobile phones [are] inconspicuously everywhere, constituting part of the mundane landscape of schooling' (Allen, 2015, p. 124), many Australian schools attempt to ban their use in classrooms. As one interviewee (a community nurse/educator) states, 'I'm sure it's [in] most schools you aren't allowed … I'm pretty sure in some of the schools, parents sign – co-sign – with their son or daughter, an agreement around the phones not to be seen in class – that sort of stuff. Which doesn't always work.'

In an informal discussion with urban teachers (following a formal research presentation), I encountered an almost gleeful support for rules banning the use of mobiles at school and permitting teachers to confiscate them. The teachers' antipathy to mobiles seemed to support Alldred and David's (2007, p. 95) observation that young people's engagement with online and mobile media demands a renegotiation of boundaries for entire school communities, blurring the temporal and spatial lines between 'school business' and 'personal' or 'family business'. These teachers spoke of the difficulty of negotiating student, community and school expectations regarding mobile use. This issue was also raised in a formal interview with an educator based in rural Victoria, who observed that sexting 'always becomes the school's problem, even though it's happened … out of school hours'. She further states:

> *The schools have got a difficult position because, in many ways, they see the parents as the client. There lies a lot of problems. I think there is always a fear – and I'm sure this happens everywhere. But even in a smaller town, there's a fear that if we're not seen to be doing the right thing – and of course in a smaller town, word gets out to the adult population that this has happened. I think schools really, really struggle, and then it becomes a knee-jerk reaction.*

This observation raises an interesting question regarding the often invoked notion of the 'digital footprint' (for example, see NSW Government, 2008). While the concept is often presented in discussions of sexting and bullying in a common-sense way, this interviewee suggests that online activity may have quite different resonances in different geographical and social settings and contexts. Further, the interviewee's account suggests that not only the local young people, but also local schools, were disadvantaged by their rural location. She believed that this leads both to increased embarrassment for young people whose images or texts are digitally shared without their consent and to increased risk of excessive or 'knee-jerk' reactions from schools who become involved. As she put it:

> *I'm sure it's full on everywhere, but there's something a bit more intimate about a smaller town when that stuff happens … We have … four secondary schools … in the council area. That photo can spread through those whole four schools. But everybody knows everybody, so it's not just this sexy photo getting sent or whatever. It's actually 'oh, we know this girl' or boy, or whatever.*

This observation presents an interesting contrast to the position of 16–17-year-old women in one of our Sydney focus groups, who were dismissive of the suggestion (promoted in anti-sexting educational resources) that the circulation of a naked picture among their peers would be emotionally devastating. This group argued that while having a picture exposed to teachers or parents would be 'mortifying', peer-to-peer exposure in school wouldn't have the same impact (Albury et al., 2013). A 17-year-old participant states: 'I think the most mortifying thing would be your family found out, because teenage kids, you can sort of go I'll never see you again in three years, or whatever, but family is like always there.'

The adult interviewee's perspective, however, indicates that this avenue of resilience is not equally available to rural and regional young people. This connection between the *offline* temporality and spatiality of the 'mortifying' digital event (in this case, the non-consensually shared text or image) has not been explored to date within scholarship addressing sexting. It resonates, however, with studies of gender and sexuality in rural contexts (such as Bryant and Pini, 2011). Such studies emphasize the 'spatial contingency' of sexed and gendered experience, where, for example, rural women's performance of femininity and heterosexuality may be subject to critical scrutiny by extended family and community well into adulthood (Pini et al., 2014, p. 1).

Mobile Technologies as a Challenge to Containment

Although the preceding discussion of sexting's impact on schools suggests that young people's digital and social media practices offer an unprecedented challenge to the boundaries between school and non-school business, Allen (2005, pp. 495–6) observes that high-school students' open expression of sexual desires, or disclosure of sexual activity outside of school, has been interpreted by teachers as evidence of resistance to formal learning or a repudiation of schooling itself. As Leander et al. (2010, p. 329) found in their review of research on schooling and mobilities, the metaphor of 'classroom-as-container' dominates educational research. Similarly, Allen (2005) observes that the physical space of the classroom (including the positioning of furniture, whiteboards and other teaching technologies) exert, in Foucauldian terms, a 'disciplinary power' on teachers, students and researchers alike (Foucault, 1979; Allen, 2005, p. 493). Yet, as Collins and Coleman (2008, pp. 287–89) have noted, other school spaces, such as school buses and playgrounds, can house informal sexual and social learning that trouble or disrupt the disciplinary control of the classroom.

I suggest that educator discomfort regarding mobile-media use in classrooms does not simply relate to concerns regarding the production or distribution of inappropriately sexual content, but reflects an unease provoked by digital media's challenge to spatial boundaries. One adult interviewee recounted her experiences of teaching Personal Development, Health and Physical Education at a girls' high school in a socioeconomically disadvantaged outer suburb of Sydney. In response to the question 'has there been a time when use of media has actually hindered or held back your education work?', she offered this energetic account of ways in which her students used their Department of Education-issued laptops:

> ... we [teachers] have teaching strategies in place where, okay, while the teacher's talking you need to turn your laptop to the front of the classroom. Or you'll get a teacher who has a board at the front, yet her desk, or his desk, is at the back of the class so you can view all the laptops ... But [students are] very clever and trying to get away ... I don't know, they're so clever ... As soon as they find one person with a password or an unlocking code or whatever it is to get over that they use it and it spreads virally. Like, all of a sudden you find everyone's been able to access this porn

site and you're like, 'oh my gosh, how the heck did this happen?' They're meant to be secured. We can't even get through [to] it on the teachers' computers.

Despite the teacher's strategies for manipulating the classroom space and technologies, the students' minds ('they're very clever') were not contained. Instead, the students were able to breach the classroom-as-container by breaching the school's firewalls, spreading passwords 'virally' and gaining access to pornography, games and social media sites.

This anecdote was offered in the context of discussing the role of media in sex education, which had previously focused on the teacher's appraisal of sexualized media content, such as music videos. In this event, however, the educator did not discuss the *content* of the pornography that was accessed in the classroom, and there was no explicit concern regarding media *effects*. Rather, it was young people's engagement with digital media practices that disrupted the classroom space. Couldry's (2012) taxonomy of media practices is useful here as a means of conceptualizing young people's media *use*, rather than their relations to particular images or texts. It includes:

- *Searching and search enabling* (a process that includes 'liking' Facebook posts)
- *Showing and being shown* (a loosely defined set of practices that might involve posting selfies on Instagram)
- *Presencing* (or 'managing presence-to-others across space' (Couldry, 2012, p. 49) – again, selfies and sexting might fit in this category)
- *Archiving* (or 'presencing's equivalent in time' (ibid., pp. 51–2) – for example, a Tumblr page or Facebook's timeline)
- *Complex media-related practices* – including 'keeping up with the news', 'commentary', 'keeping all channels open' via 'continuous connectivity and 'screening out' (for example, going offline or deleting social media profiles).

These practices represent forms of digital literacy that exceed the boundaries of classrooms and school timetables. As Gershon (2010) observes in her study of relationship break-ups and Facebook, participating in everyday practices of presencing, archiving and 'keeping up with the news' may mean that details of young people's friendships and intimate relationships are made visible to peer groups and adults in immediate and lasting ways. Over the course of my research, several teachers observed that mobile and online media facilitated young people's continuous involvement in ongoing 'playground dramas' (ranging from flirtations and playful teasing, to gossip, public break-ups and bullying) within the space of the classroom (see boyd and Marwick, 2011). As one interviewee (a legal educator) states, 'offline life is very much mirrored online [for young people]. The same dramas that happen in real life face-to-face are happening there as well with friends and break-ups and loyalties and so on.' This interconnection of online and offline life can make it difficult for students to maintain strict boundaries between intimate (or personal) relationships and the public space of school and family life, although they may manage these boundaries by coding or encrypting their online communication to evade adult surveillance, a process boyd and Marwick (2011) have dubbed 'social steganography'.[5]

---

5   While a detailed discussion of this practice is beyond the scope of this chapter, the process of coding or encrypting intimate communications is also important for same-sex-attracted, gender-variant and/or questioning young people for whom online and mobile-media practices offer both a site for building support networks and a site for inadvertent exposure and outing. See, for example, Albury and Byron (2014), Gray (2009) and Robinson et al. (2014).

Conclusion

Like other recent Australian research, the Young People and Sexting in Australia and Young People, Sex, Love and the Media studies indicate that teachers and community educators consider young people's media practices (including sexting) as both highly relevant and highly problematic for schools and schooling. In this chapter, I have sought to explore the inherent tensions that young people's mediated sexual cultures present within the spatial boundaries of schools and classrooms. Through an engagement with the work of educational and media researchers, I have suggested that media practices allow young people to challenge the ways in which their minds and bodies are regulated by the spaces of schools and classrooms.

Participation in media practices allows for a doubling (or multiplication) of place and space, facilitating continuing parallel engagements with friends and intimates *within* the disciplinary space of the classroom. While this participation allows young people to evade classroom discipline, it simultaneously renders their desires and bodies visible to their peers, and to adult surveillance. Rather than seeking to police these visible relationships and bodies, educators might productively engage with mediated sexual practices, such as selfies, in order to explore and promote ethical cultures of learning and teaching regarding sex, gender and relationships. These engagements would require a whole-school (and whole-community) approach that both acknowledges mobile-media practice as an ordinary part of young people's experiences of both sexuality and schooling[6] and supports teachers in overtly engaging with the presence of mediated intimacies within the classroom. Although this is not likely to be a straightforward or simple process, I suggest that formal recognition of the merger of online and offline intimacies would not only allow teachers to integrate formal educational content with students' alternative forms of mediated learning and literacy, but would also permit sex and relationships educators to expand their teaching beyond the constraints of 'the plumbing'.

---

6   The Fifth National Study of Australian Secondary Students and Sexual Health (2013) found that more than half of all students surveyed had received an explicit text message, and more than 20 per cent had sent one themselves. These figures increased 84 per cent and 72 per cent respectively among students who reported being sexually active. This suggests that while sexting is not ubiquitous among young people, it is a frequent enough activity to be considered ordinary (Mitchell et al., 2014).

Chapter 41

Youth Online: Non-heterosexual Young People's Use of the Internet to Negotiate their Identities, Support Networks and Sociosexual Relations

Gary Downing

Introduction

This chapter investigates how non-heterosexual[1] youth are using the internet to construct and maintain their identities, support networks and sociosexual relations in the UK. In particular, this research explores the role of social networking websites that have been designed for non-heterosexual users, and examines young people's negotiation of these to supplement their virtual *and* material sociosexual relations. This responds to Vanderbeck's (2008) call for discussion of young people's access to particular kinds of media and contributes to the growing body of literature which understands online and offline realities as interconnected in young people's everyday lives (Holloway and Valentine, 2003). This chapter focuses on non-heterosexual youth, who negotiate an increasingly individualized range of sociosexual trajectories (Valentine et al., 2003; Beck and Beck-Gernsheim, 2002). Non-heterosexual young people's identities have been traditionally bound by essentialist identity categories (for example, gay, lesbian) (Wysocki, 1998), and also constrained by the dominance of heterosexual discourses in spaces such as schools and homes (Holloway et al., 2000). Moreover, in contrast to those who made their transition to a non-heterosexual identity in previous decades, young people in the UK are making their transition to a non-heterosexual identity in a society that recognizes same-sex relationships and has a greater visible presence of homosexuality in the media. Therefore, following a brief overview of previous research in this area and related methodology, this chapter will explore how non-heterosexual young people negotiate their identities, support networks and sociosexual relations online, and will analyse the connections between virtual and material realities.

---

1   I employ the term 'non-heterosexual' to encompass the variety of ways in which the participants defined their sexual identities. This was not limited to LGBT, but also included queer, asexual and some who felt uncomfortable identifying with any one label due to the fluidity of their sexuality. Moreover, for many young people, discourses of heterosexuality were critical in the performance of their identities – being 'not' heterosexual. Although I acknowledge that this could be seen as a negative term, by highlighting the ongoing significance of heterosexuality I hope to continue to problematize this as a presumed 'norm' in society.

Non-Heterosexual Youth and the Internet

Traditionally, geographers have focused on the connections between the identities of young people who define as LGBT (lesbian, gay, bisexual and transgender) and the 'spatial manifestations' (Browne, 2007b, p. 996) of their experiences. Studies have highlighted the sociofamilial impacts of sexual disclosure in the home (Gorman-Murray, 2008; Valentine et al., 2003) and the effects of negative stereotypes on young people's identity construction in gay scene venues (Barron and Bradford, 2007; Valentine and Skelton, 2003). However, even within geographies of sexualities, recent research makes little reference to non-heterosexual young people's use of virtual spaces (see Browne et al., 2007).

Despite the recognition that online and offline interactions are interlinked and actively managed by young people (Wellman and Gulia, 1999), the ways in which internet technologies are used to facilitate specific sociosexual relations in virtual *and* material realities remains under-researched. In particular, the ways in which non-heterosexual youth use an increasing array of specialized online media platforms[2] has been overlooked. Although young people's use of the internet may have some intrinsic characteristics, a specific type of use has emerged amongst non-heterosexual users. This is a result of the significance attached to LGBT self-representation in predominantly heterosexual discourse (Mowlabocus, 2010b; Whitesel, 2010), and the geographical dominance of urban gay venues in comparison to rural locations (Valentine and Skelton, 2003). A recent collection (Pullen and Cooper, 2010) has begun to explore the broad range of reasons why non-heterosexual people value online communication platforms. These include the provision of opportunities for sexual encounters and social networking, as well as the opportunity to perform alternative identity narratives and construct virtual communities.

To date there has been little research exploring the recent growth and uses of social networking websites designed for non-heterosexual users. Hillier and Harrison's (2007) study in Australia found that online platforms are used by non-heterosexual young people to *rehearse* new sexual identities, same-sex friendships and intimate relationships. Similarly, Addison and Comstock (1998) argue that LGBT-oriented social networking websites are a space of relative safety, where young people can *practise* important turning-points, such as sexual disclosure, before telling friends and family. Although these studies argue that the 'internet and immediate physical world' (Hillier and Harrison, 2007, p. 86) are mutually constitutive, the specific ways in which virtual and material spaces are connected is overlooked, and the links between these realities only appear to be unidirectional (for example, from online to offline). Therefore, this chapter aims to explore non-heterosexual young people's experiences of constructing identities, support networks and sociosexual relations on the internet, and revisit the connections between online and offline realities.

Embodiment and Performativity

Theorizations of performativity and embodiment are important in this research. From a social constructionist viewpoint, Butler (1990) argues that gender and sexuality are socially produced and performed, which refutes biologically determinist interpretations of social

---

2   Pullen and Cooper (2010, p.1) use the term 'online new media' to emphasize the diverse uses of the internet, which are concerned with 'identity, representation, production, consumption … [and] self-regulation'.

difference (Alsop et al., 2002). Social scientists have used this notion of performativity, or the 'rituals and social processes which help constitute an identity' (Sherry, 2004, p. 780), to analyse the gendered and sexualized performances that young people enact within schools to maintain peer relations (Gagen, 2000; Hyams, 2000). Moreover, Butler (1990, p. 140) argues that performativity is produced 'through the stylization of the body', which results in specific embodied performances in different sociospatial contexts (Oswin, 2008). For example, research has identified that the performance of feminized bodily comportment amongst gay young men can lead to exclusion in schools (Barron and Bradford, 2007). Valentine and Skelton (2003) also highlight the significance of dancing within the gay scene, which allows young people to express their non-heterosexual identities through actively performing the body (Malbon, 1999).

The concepts of performativity and embodiment are also relevant to online interactions. This contests the notion that the internet only produces disembodied relations (Lupton, 1995). As Lazzara (2010, p. 60) argues, exploring human interaction in virtual reality exposes 'the complex performative aspects of online identity'. For example, courtship rituals established through video blogging involved a negotiation between romantic meta-narratives and norms of online communication, which blurred private and public spheres during the performance of virtual sociosexual relations. Mowlabocus (2010b, p. 210) also suggests that non-heterosexual young men enact a particular performance of age when online, which 'tends to lean towards more "mainstream" sexual acts'. In this way, virtual performances are embodied, since identifying as a 'twink' (young non-heterosexual man) aligns the user with a specific corporeality (slim and hairless body) and a set of preferred sexual practices. This chapter will draw on these concepts to investigate the ways in which virtual and material realities are interconnected in non-heterosexual young people's embodied performance of their identities and sociosexual relations.

Research Design and Methods

This chapter is based on a small-scale research project that aimed to explore how non-heterosexual young people (aged 16–25) negotiate virtual and material identities in the UK. The methodological approach taken aligned with the new social studies of childhood, which positions young people as active agents who shape their own lives depending on specific spatial and temporal contexts (Holloway and Valentine, 2000). This research also recognizes that young people do not follow fixed transitions to adulthood, but experience trajectories that are complex, fluid and individualized (Valentine and Skelton, 2007).

Semi-structured interviews/focus groups were conducted with 34 young people and seven LGBT youth workers. Of the young people, 14 took part across three focus groups (two offline, one online), and 20 took part in interviews (10 offline, 10 online). Participants were purposively recruited from five youth groups in London and the south-west of England, and through five popular LGBT social networking websites. Although the sample was not statistically representative, this research recruited young people across the age range of 16 –25 years. Participants also had a variety of sexual orientations, diverse levels of education and lived in different geographical locations. However, the sample does contain a bias towards white gay males. This is attributable to the high proportion of white young males in comparison to females and other ethnicities within the youth groups sampled. A full examination of the strategies that were used to facilitate data collection/ analysis, ethical protocols[3] and the role of positionality can be found in Downing (2013).

The Interconnected Online and Offline Experiences of Non-heterosexual Young People

Linking Virtual and Material Support

For the young people in this research, the internet was often used to seek support relating to a range of sexuality-related issues, which included sexual disclosure, sexual health and non-heterosexual identities. As Philip[4] (aged 23) typifies:

> It was one of the most essential parts of me coming out to be honest. When I had the kind of curiosity about my sexuality, I searched the internet ... without me doing that research I would always be curious ... there would always be a big question mark hanging over me ... thinking 'is it just because I'm young' ... or 'is this really because I do actually like men'.

Although Cline and Haynes (2001) argue that using the internet to access health-related content is now commonplace, especially amongst non-heterosexual people in relation to HIV/ AIDS concerns (Clift, 2010; Weatherburn et al., 2003), the participants in this investigation sought online support about a broader range of issues. In particular, young people said that they had searched for information about the range of non-heterosexual identities and niches within the 'LGBT community' (Wysocki, 1998). This support must be understood within the context of a predominantly heterosexual familial, educational and peer culture offline, in which guidance about sexual diversity was limited (Hillier and Harrison, 2007; Addison and Comstock, 1998). As one participant expressed about school sex education, 'in all the millions of hours I've had being lectured about sex (and why you shouldn't do it) I never had something that even CONSIDERED the possibility of anyone being gay ... completely useless, most of it' (Hannah, female, age 18).

As a result, the participants used a variety of online platforms targeted at LGBT youth seeking support (Lazzara, 2010; Alexander, 2004). Many young people identified the importance of LGBT social networking websites on account of the high proportion of non-heterosexual users and the focus on relevant discussion topics. As Rachel (female, age 16) said, 'Each site will have its own target audience which will change what is discussed on it. All the features can be the same but it's more about the other people who will be using it and the other people it will connect you to.' Although some online platforms were only deemed useful for 'hooking up'/dating, a number of LGBT social networking websites were classified as information/support-oriented. Within this category, the virtual identity of each website was considered different depending on where it originated geographically and the political affiliation of its users. As Wakeford (2000, p. 408) argues, virtual spaces are 'necessarily embedded within both institutional and cultural practices, and are a means by which the lesbian/gay/transgendered/queer self can be read into the politics of representation'.

---

3   Ethical approval was granted by the University of Reading's Research Ethics Committee in 2010. This research conforms to the ethical protocols of the British Sociological Association and Social Research Association.

4   Participants were given pseudonyms in order to protect their identities.

Moreover, several youth workers explained that dedicated websites are used to advertise the services provided by LGBT youth groups. They thought that professional support is enhanced through a range of increasingly interactive online information platforms. Young people also said that they used these websites to foster friendship with other members before going to the youth group, as well as to find out about future offline meetings. Similarly, LGBT networking websites are used to organize collective offline sociopolitical and support events, as these participants explained:

> QYN [Queer Youth Network] members have linked up before at NUS [National Union of Students] events, anti-BNP/EDL [British National Party/English Defence League] protests, at Prides and punk gigs ... (Ryan, male, age 25)

> Those who ... often blog on 'ladslads' ... they discuss events online and sometimes organize events that brings the offline and online worlds together ... I think they organized a camping trip online that a lot of the 'ladslads' community went to. (Tim, male, age 21)

For many of the participants, these events provided an alternative way to seek advice and guidance, in a 'community' within which young people already felt comfortable in virtual reality. Some also commented that they may have never attended a 'face-to-face' event without previously having spoken online to other young people planning to attend. Therefore, events and youth group activities that were organized online afforded non-heterosexual young people greater opportunities to access sexuality-related support offline.

LGBT Sociosexual Networking on the Internet: Offline Foundations

Many non-heterosexual youth also visit LGBT networking websites to construct and maintain sociosexual relations (Hillier and Harrison, 2007). Although online social networking creates opportunities for dating and engaging in sexual activities, establishing friendships is a greater priority for most people (Hardie and Buzwell, 2006). This was echoed by a number of the participants, who said that LGBT networking websites provided an effective medium in which to develop sustained virtual friendships with other non-heterosexual youth. Some young people appeared more hesitant about using online interaction as a means of engaging in dating or establishing a relationship, as exemplified by Rachel:

> I would say the internet can be a useful tool for creating friendships as it allows you to get in to contact with many people very quickly. I think as far as relationships go it can be useful but it depends on the individuals involved and whether they would be comfortable with it. (Rachel, female, age 16)

This hesitation was linked to a stigma understood to be aligned with 'the "lonely hearts" columns in the newspaper' (Sandra, youth worker), which was based on a perceived failure to meet sexual partners in material spaces. For example, Olivia recalls discussing with her friends how she arranged to go on a date:

> They were like 'oh right, where did you meet her', and I was like 'hmmm, on the internet'. And I felt uncomfortable saying it, even though I knew that there was nothing in it. I don't think that internet dating is unacceptable, but I do think ... there's a little bit of stigma attached to it. (Olivia, female, age 22)

This narrative suggests that the offline stigma relating to the use of the internet for online dating (Couch and Liamputtong, 2008) persists for some non-heterosexual young people. This can be linked to normative discourses of romance, which prioritize 'face-to-face' interaction in offline settings (Anderson, 2005) and mark other types of relationship as deviant. However, a number of the participants reported that through online dating they had met someone with whom they had constructed a serious and long-lasting romantic relationship. Therefore, for the young people in this research, LGBT networking websites afforded opportunities to develop sociosexual relations that were highly valued. This supports the findings of Hillier and Harrison (2007), who found that the safety and anonymity provided by virtual networking platforms enabled young people to negotiate worthwhile same-sex friendships and romantic relationships.

Furthermore, for some of the participants, online sociosexual relations were only possible in the context of the 'communities'[5] that had been established on LGBT networking websites. As Toby (aged 24) typifies:

> There is a sense of community … seeing lists of gay guys' profiles is almost like walking into a virtual club. You see the guys you like the look of, but instead of just judging them on their looks, you can see a little more about them before you have even spoken to them.

In this example, opportunities to interact with other LGBT people within the community were valued. This was particularly important to participants who lived in rural areas where there was a limited physical community of LGBT people in geographical proximity (Gray, 2010; K. Robins, 2007). Moreover, some young people felt that the marginalization they had experienced within their local gay scene on the basis of ethnicity, age or sexual orientation had heightened the need to achieve a sense of belonging online. As Valentine and Skelton (2008) argue, virtual communities are constructed by specific groups in order to escape some of the limitations of community space offline. Therefore, online LGBT communities should not only be understood as a reaction to the exclusion of non-heterosexual young people in material spaces that are coded as heterosexual (Valentine et al., 2003), but also as a consequence of young people's dissatisfaction with offline LGBT venues. However, despite the liberating potential of online communities amongst marginalized groups (Willson, 2007), several participants warned that these are contributing to a decline of physical gay spaces (Pullen, 2010; Usher and Morrison, 2010). As one youth worker said, 'Pubs and clubs with an LGBT clientele have declined since social networking has taken off … it has reduced the social interaction of some people … where it is easier to talk to someone on a computer screen than in real life'. This suggests that the continued growth of LGBT networking websites could potentially limit opportunities for young people to express their identities and develop friendships/ sexual relations in offline spaces. However, this must be understood in the context of normative discourses that (re)produce the superiority of face-to-face interactions (Anderson, 2005). These overlook the positive effects of online sociosexual relations within non-heterosexual young people's everyday lives.

---

5   This article conceptualizes 'community' as a diverse term that extends beyond bounded territories (K. Robins, 2007). Although young people primarily equated notions of community with physical spaces, such as gay scene venues, they felt that these were in small urban clusters. As a result, many participants considered LGBT networking websites as virtual communities that provided comparable sociosexual opportunities and a similar sense of belonging to physical LGBT spaces (Valentine and Skelton, 2008).

Online-Offline Interconnections in Young People's Sociosexual Lives

The complex relationship between virtual and material realities was also apparent in young people's negotiation of their online sociosexual relations (Drushel, 2010; Addison and Comstock, 1998). Virtual interactions were frequently embodied by the participants through phone conversations, profile photography and webcams. This contests conventional discourses relating to communication technologies, which suggest that humans can transcend their corporeality (Lupton, 1995). Themes of embodiment were especially evident during conversations with gay young men, who may be more concerned with aesthetic appearance and the condition of their physical body than heterosexual youth (Whitesel, 2010). As Philip stated:

> Talking about relationships … it [online communication] is a good way to start because it is kind of like a brief introduction to each other … sharing pictures … and a lot of people go on the camera [webcam] to see each other. I would say that people want you to go on camera just to have the kind of verification that you are the person who you say you are. (Philip, male, age 23).

As this narrative illustrates, images act as 'a stabilizing force for identity formation' (Mowlabocus, 2010b, p. 201) through embodying the virtual self using the physical body (Wolmark, 1999). Using webcams, young people actively performed their gendered and sexualized bodies, and authenticated the identities of others. For example, gay young men often wanted to verify the relative masculinity and femininity of their own bodily comportment (Farr, 2010). Participants also had concerns about whether those they were interacting with were too 'butch', 'camp' or 'ugly' in relation to gay bodily expectations. In this way, technology, corporeality and social interaction were mutually constitutive in young people's virtual lives and were interconnected through the performances of a range of social identities (Barber, 2010; Mowlabocus, 2010b).

Some young people's comments also suggest that processes of inclusion and exclusion in offline LGBT environments were (re)produced by the interactions which took place on LGBT networking websites. As Hillier and Harrison (2007, p. 87) argue, 'virtual reality is coded as "normal reality"', and this connects online and offline spaces in non-heterosexual young people's everyday lives. As Robert (male, age 21) explains, 'The guys at the top of the scene's social status will be the ones most active. They have a lot to say … generally speaking, the guys you will see most actively in a gay bar, the popular ones … you see most frequently blogging and commenting'. Inclusion and exclusion were also understood to be dependent on the length of time each user had been registered on each website, on level of activity and on sexual orientation. Newer members, and those who identified as transgendered and asexual, were perceived to be marginalized in virtual reality, as Ryan (male, age 25) elaborated: 'I think there does tend to be a cliquey thing going on too, with people who have been on there ages and have met each other loads, versus new members who haven't borne [sic] into the "in" crowd yet.' This mirrors the significance that participants felt was attached to time spent socializing in gay scene venues and the limited offline support facilities available for those who did not identify as gay, lesbian or bisexual. Therefore, although virtual environments are often considered 'less exclusionary or repressive' (Willson, 2007, p. 213), online interactions sometimes marginalized groups of non-heterosexual young people in parallel with exclusion in offline LGBT spaces. Furthermore, although Valentine and Skelton (2003) argue that marginalization within gay scene venues is a consequence of the dominance of sexuality over other social differences (for example, ethnicity, disability), there were also more nuanced exclusions in online and offline non-heterosexual realities.

These were rooted in a 'politics of recognition' (Noble, 2009), which valued contingent and contextual subjectivities such as the performance of a 'competent' sexuality based on dominant ideals about 'gay' identities (Noble, 2009). For example, gay young men often mentioned the significance of having a certain musical taste, aspiring to be 'body beautiful' (tanned, skinny and sexually desirable) and being 'bitchy' to others, which made their identities more legitimate. This demonstrates that the construction of a normative gay identity revolved around a range of embodied performances and discourses apparent in physical gay venues *and* LGBT networking websites.

Finally, many participants reported that they had developed individual friendships and sexual relations in physical spaces following virtual interactions, as Toby (male, age 24) typifies: 'I guess meeting my partner from Liverpool, found we had a very good rapport chatting online ... moved on to chatting on the phone ... after 9 months talking I went up to Liverpool for a weekend ... we ended up making a go of things.' In this way, online and offline realities were mutually constitutive in the performance of sociosexual relations (Holloway and Valentine, 2003). As Livingstone (2008, pp. 393–4) argues, 'the simple distinction between offline and online no longer captures the complex practices associated with online technologies as they become thoroughly embedded in the routines of everyday life'. Moreover, the notion of a virtual 'rehearsal', or one-dimensional relationship *from* online *to* offline interactions (Hillier and Harrison, 2007), masks a more complex array of sociosexual negotiations in which the young people engaged. As these participants expressed:

> *I talk to people who I've met in real life already, online. I do it the other way around, so I like to meet people first in person and then add them to my Skype list. (Joel, male, age 21)*

> *I went to Brighton with my family, and I saw one there, and I was speaking to him and he lives in London as well ... I met him online as a friend ... but that's the second time I've seen him out and about. (Oscar, male, age 18)*

LGBT networking software that allowed users to search for potential contacts according to geographical distance also structured the virtual interactions that took place (Drushel, 2010; Barber, 2010). As Rachel (aged 16) reflects, 'I would say that the majority of people will look for someone in their local area ... distance is definitely a factor. I think if two people who meet on the internet live far away there is always the feeling that they will only ever talk online.' Therefore, non-heterosexual young people's sociosexual relations involve a multidimensional dialogue between online and offline realities (Gray, 2010). Young people not only 'rehearse' their offline identities on the internet, but also blur the boundaries between virtual and material spaces as they negotiate new sociosexual trajectories during their everyday lives.

Conclusion

In this chapter, I have examined young people's experiences of using the internet to negotiate their non-heterosexual identities, support networks and sociosexual relations, and explored the connections between online and offline realities. The internet afforded young people access to a variety of platforms which they used to seek support about issues such as sexual disclosure, sexual health and non-heterosexual identities. This must be understood within the context of a predominantly heterosexual familial, educational and peer culture offline. LGBT youth groups are also using the internet to supplement the peer/professional support which is provided during face-to-face meetings, and LGBT networking websites are used to organize offline support events. Furthermore, LGBT sociosexual networking on the internet has offline foundations. For example, the online 'communities' established on LGBT networking websites were particularly important to participants who lived in rural areas where there was a limited offline community of LGBT people. Young people who had been marginalized in local gay scene venues also valued opportunities to establish sociosexual relations online. However, although LGBT networking websites were often used to construct and maintain friendships, young people were more hesitant about using virtual spaces to develop romantic relationships. This hesitation was linked to an offline stigma that continues to measure online sociosexual relations against romantic heterosexual discourses.

Online and offline realities were also mutually constitutive in non-heterosexual young people's everyday sociosexual lives. For example, the interactions which took place on LGBT networking websites were embodied, and non-heterosexual youth attached significance to performing the body during virtual interactions. Normative discourses of being 'body beautiful' were also significant to the sociosexual relations and processes of exclusion within both LGBT online and offline contexts. Moreover, although there were parallels between a 'politics of recognition' (Noble, 2009) within gay scene venues *and* on LGBT networking websites, many participants recognized that virtual reality had afforded new opportunities for the development of their sociosexual relations offline. However, the relationship between online and offline relations was not a one-way 'rehearsal', but a multidimensional process that blurred the boundaries between virtual and material realities. Non-heterosexual youth moved fluidly within and between online and offline spaces/contexts during their everyday lives, in order to negotiate new sociosexual relations.

Further research could continue to explore these connections, alongside the rise of new technologies such as the smartphone applications Grindr and GayCities, which facilitate mobile sociosexual networking across space. Additionally, in an era of economic austerity and cutbacks in youth services for LGBT young people in the UK, the role of the internet in facilitating support for this group of young people may become increasingly important. How non-heterosexual young people construct positive identities and new sociosexual trajectories from this virtual support in rural and urban areas may also provide new avenues for research in the future.

Acknowledgements

I wish to thank all the participants who shared their experiences during interviews and focus groups. Particular thanks must go to Lukasz Konieczka, Andrew Wilson and their respective youth groups for their invaluable support and enthusiasm for this investigation. The research on which this chapter is based was supported by an FSS Studentship from the University of Reading.

Chapter 42

'Male Blood Elves Are So Gay': Gender and Sexual Identity in Online Games

Cherie Todd

Introduction

I don't like playing as a blood elf because they are male, yet super feminine, and I just cannot identify with a man that looks like a 10 year old girl with a big sword. (Steve, online discussion, 31 May 2014)

Steve's comment shows how identifying with an online avatar can be a serious affair for some gamers.[1] Virtual re-presentations of 'self' in an online environment are for some, a liberating experience; however, as demonstrated above, they can also be problematic. Steve, for example, identifies as a masculine, heterosexual man, but the race[2] of male blood elves in *World of Warcraft* (WoW) are constructed as flamboyant with egotistical personalities, and are portrayed with bodies that could be described as elegant and feminine. In massive multiplayer online role-playing games (MMORPGs) such as WoW, it is common practice for both game creators and the majority of players to reinforce heteronormative values and norms. As a result, players who identify as lesbian, gay, bisexual, transgender or queer (LGBTQ) are often marginalized and made to feel 'out of place'. While there is intolerance and discrimination, however, there is also resistance. Therefore, it is relevant to examine the ways in which the spaces of online games serve as sites of resistance to authority and inequality (Del Casino, 2009).

In this chapter, I discuss findings from interviews with online gamers, as well as highlighting experiences of auto-ethnography fieldwork. I also draw on a range of literature to inform discussion related to issues of body politics, gender and sexuality in online games. First, I begin with a brief overview of the methods used in conducting the research. Second, I discuss the role of avatars' virtual bodies, which play an integral part in WoW where virtual characters are often viewed as extensions of gamers' identities. Third, I consider online gender and sexuality, paying particular attention to performances of gender that enable new ways of experiencing identity, and which problematize notions of masculine and feminine subjectivity. In particular, I examine the practice of gender-switching, and discuss the ways in which gender and sex are both contested and accepted within the spaces of online games.

---

1   All participants are 18 years or older and reside in various countries. Pseudonyms are used for all participants.
2   Rather than 'ethnicity', the term 'race' is a central concept of avatar construction in MMORPGs, as it distinguishes between various character templates, such as troll, orc and elf. The topic of race, however, is very relevant to many contemporary studies that examine the effects of racialized discourse within gaming cultures (see, for example, Nakamura, 2009, 2011).

Finally, I draw attention to the cultural discourse of online gaming, what this means for players with LGBTQ identities, and how dominant discourses concerning sexuality and queer identity are negotiated, resisted and challenged. In all of the above areas, I look critically at how online games are fraught with discriminatory and oppressive discourses regarding non-heterosexual identities.

During the course of this research I employed various recruiting and data-gathering methods, including the developing methodology of auto-ethnography. Butz (2010, p. 139) explains that auto-ethnography 'is an epistemological orientation to the relationships among experience, knowledge, and representation that has a variety of methodological implications'. As an 'epistemological orientation', autho-ethnography has emerged as a powerful tool for highlighting the ways in which particular marginalized identities negotiate spaces of power and control. Not only does it offer an in-depth perspective from which to examine particular phenomena, but it also serves as a form of self-narrative that works to place the 'self' within a given social context.

Methods of recruitment involved 'snowballing', from handing out flyers to local game retailers to sending email flyers across online social media networks, including Facebook. Posting within online gaming forums such as GamePlanet.co.nz, DSLreports.com and MMOsite.com proved to be the most effective, as these postings attracted the majority of participants and led to much conversation and debate in online discussion threads. Forum discussions ranged from people asking questions about the research, including my own online gaming experience, to people posting stories about their own or others' experiences. In each forum, users were invited to take part in an online questionnaire. If interested, they had to click on a hyperlink contained within the post that directed them to the research questionnaire. This method proved to be very successful, and approximately 40 per cent of questionnaires were completed,[3] with several questionnaires consisting of pages of 'rich' data where participants openly discussed their experiences and any other relevant issues. Included in this material were accounts of online identities and connections with avatars, which I go on to discuss in the following section.

Online Bodies at Play

The current depth of player choice and avatar customization in WoW allows gamers to experiment and role-play with online identities in ways that are impossible in an offline world. Such experimentation provides evidence of the potential for online spaces to be utilized as places where people are free to express themselves and gain a sense of liberation from the 'real' world. Places are recognized by geographers as socially constructed with sexualized dimensions. Furthermore, geographers have highlighted the reproduction of heterodominant spaces and critically examined how sexual 'others' negotiate and experience these spaces on a daily basis. Work by Oswin (2008), for example, brings to attention the active production of space as heterosexualized and the often implicit heterosexual bias of much geographical theorizing. Johnston and Longhurst (2010) also provide an insightful critique of sex and sexuality, from the body to the globe and, in doing so, they bring attention to the ways in which sex and sexuality are connected to both online and offline spaces and places. Furthermore, McGonigal (2011) highlights how hundreds of millions of people worldwide

---

3   While completing the questionnaire, participants were also invited to take part in a follow-up email questionnaire. Approximately 10 per cent of participants opted to do this. This also resulted in the gathering of photographic (screenshot) research data.

are choosing to spend more of their time gaming and socializing within virtual landscapes (McGonigal, 2011). As such, there is growing evidence that supports an understanding of online games as 'new worlds'. For example, MMORPGs, such as WoW come complete with their own social structures, communities and economies. Gunkel and Gunkel (2009, p. 105) argue that the intricate and expansive worlds of online games are commonly perceived to be a viable alternative to the world that we currently live in:

> MMORPG is not only difficult to pronounce but identifies a technology that is perhaps even more difficult to define. And expanding the acronym, massively multiplayer online role playing game, does not necessarily provide much help. Although these things are routinely called 'games', research has demonstrated that they are much more than fun and games. (Gunkel and Gunkel, 2009, p. 104)

Furthermore, the internet can be understood as a new 'queer space', where people can express a diverse range of gendered and sexed identities while participating in online games – changing their identities as easily as they change their clothes, and doing so without the degree of criticism that would otherwise occur in real world/offline situations (Todd, 2012). As promising as this sounds, it is not entirely accurate. Performances of gender and sexuality online continue to be affected by archaic heteronormative value systems, transported into virtual worlds via game design and the players themselves. Nonetheless, similar to offline life, there are numerous examples of resistance that challenge these dominant values and norms. These acts of resistance (such as gay-friendly guilds and gay pride parades/marches) bring attention to the taken-for-granted, privileged positioning of heterosexual identity within online games. According to Del Casino (2009), resistant spaces contest dominant narratives of what is in place/out of place spatially. Thus, space is a 'performed space of both power and resistance. As such, social identities are tied to how people perform where and who they are as individuals, community members, and social beings' (Del Casino, 2009, p. 24).

Ideas around 'gender performance' in relation to online games offer new and intriguing areas of examination. Butler (1993), for example, views sexual distinction as being 'performed' through a vast number of institutionalized social practices that invoke, materialize and naturalize sexual identity. Earlier discourses surrounding corporeality and the internet tended to be utopian in nature, claiming that the disembodied nature of online spaces created an experience aligned with egalitarian values (Sundén, 2009). As Brophy argues, however, this viewpoint 'denies the situated and lived experiences of individuals, and reinforces the mind/body dualism'. It also tends to minimize the 'inequalities that exist in "real" space, as well as ignore the reification of gender and sexuality norms in cyberspace' (Brophy, 2010, p. 933). Feminist theorists were some of the first to point out the possibilities for experimenting with online identities, such as gender-bending. Some were, however, sceptical about the internet as a utopian medium and, as such, were not so quick to dismiss 'the body' from online experiences (Featherstone and Burrows, 1996).

In online role-playing games such as WoW, players assume the role of an avatar. Avatars are typically fantasy-based creations, and it is usual for role-playing games to have a large selection of avatar templates.[4] It is also standard practice for the bodies of avatars to be designed in a hypersexualized manner, in that they often tend to be more feminine or more masculine than offline, 'flesh and blood' bodies. Graphic designers for role-playing games, in particular, have been consistent in their efforts to expand the selections available for avatar customization. In MMORPGs like WoW and *City of Heroes*, for example, there

---

4   Avatar templates are influenced by various forms of being, often portraying bodies from myth and
      fantasy, such as elves, dwarves, magic users, machines, cyborgs, animals and necro (dead) bodies.

are literally millions of possible unique avatar and costume combinations available to players (Ochoa, 2012). Consequently, gamers are able to shape their avatars according to their own preferences, across a range of avatar templates with varying ages and degrees of attractiveness.[5]

My experience of shaping my own avatar's look has helped me to feel increasingly connected with my online identity (for example, I am her, she is me). Similarly, Rose's examination of fantasy and desire in films shows that the 'key point about fantasy is that the subject need not only be the audience of a fantasy. The subject may also imagine that they participate in the fantasy as well' (Rose, 2012, p. 1). In this sense, Rose's statement is undoubtedly applicable to gamers who connect with their online avatars: 'There's an awful lot of hype around "the visual" these days. We're often told that we now live in a world where knowledge as well as many forms of entertainment are visually constructed, and where what we see is as important, if not more so, than what we read' (ibid.). Unsurprisingly, the visual is a crucial element of game design, so much so that the virtual representations of online bodies often remain linked to offline body politics and sexual identity. This link has also been shown to affect the choices that gamers make in virtual environments. Lee and Hoadley's (2006) study, for example, examines the responses of students participating in the online role-playing game *Second Life*. Several students opted to play as opposite-sex characters, while others chose to make their avatars unattractive. The latter reported being socially excluded from interactions with other gamers, who would move away from them when they tried to approach and participate in conversations. In this way, the students were able to experience the ways in which real-world phenomena such as stereotypes, social status, attractiveness and other discriminations are transferred into virtual worlds. In this context, being 'ugly' was a disempowering experience for the students involved. Avatar appearances and the performances of one's gender within an online gaming environment offer a different experience for each person. In many instances, avatars affect not only a player's sense of self, but also the way in which they play the game and interact with others, as well as how others perceive them (Todd, 2012).

With this in mind, it is easy to understand how certain performances of gender in online games can become exaggerated. Rosier and Pearce (2011), for example, argue that gamers communicate in a deliberate manner to better portray their sexuality. Men gamers, for instance, might act in a manner more aligned with hypermasculinity in order to establish their identity as male/heterosexual.

'Playing' with Gender and Sexuality in World of Warcraft

Yee's (2008) research with WoW gamers shows that most people prefer to create virtual avatars that reflect their own stereotypical or 'ideal' traits. For example, tall players typically prefer taller avatars, women prefer feminine avatars, and men prefer masculine avatars.

---

5   As such, an avatar's image can be altered across a range of features, such as gender, race, age, body shape and size (but also) skin colour, facial features (eyes, nose, chin, cheekbones and so on), hair colour, body piercings and tattoos (Taylor, 2003). The current racial selection of avatars offered by WoW includes: human, dwarf, night elf, gnome, draenei (human/goat), worgen (human/wolf), and pandaren (human/panda), orc, undead (necro/human), tauren (human/bull), troll, blood elf and goblin. As well as choosing a race and gender, each avatar must have a specific class. These include: warrior, paladin, hunter, rogue, priest, shaman, mage, warlock, monk, druid and death knight (with some classes only being available to certain races).

This was certainly true for Steve, a guild member,[6] whose offline body is over 6ft (183cms) tall. Steve ended up changing the 'race' of his online character from a blood elf to a tauren because he did not like the slender build and shorter stature of the blood elf avatar. In WoW, the race known as 'blood elf' is widely considered to be one of the more 'attractive' races and, compared to other races, male blood elves have a build that closely resembles the bodily construction of female blood elves. As a result, the body, face and hair selections for male blood elves do little to distinguish them from the females of their race.[7] In most games there are female avatars that are portrayed as strong and masculine. Effeminate male avatars, however, are rarely seen. In an online gaming culture where homophobic language is commonplace and widespread, and where game design purposely sets up the sexual dynamics of male blood elves as effeminate, it is not surprising that they are often ridiculed for being too 'pretty' or 'girly' looking.

The title of this chapter, 'male blood elves are so gay', is an often heard phrase in WoW, and there have been several instances where Steve has pointed out to me and other guild members how ridiculous he thinks his avatar looks when performing actions like running with two huge swords at either side of his waist or when dancing. Overall, dancing is not typically considered to be a masculine activity, but some of the male races in WoW, such as the undead, have aggressive or masculine dances that involve jumping up and down or head-banging. The male blood-elf dance, however, is often joked about and cannot be defined as masculine. Rather, it appears to be more like a striptease performance, involving hip gyrations and wide 'air guitar' arm swings. While male blood elves commonly receive derisive comments, there are some who appreciate their design. Sundén (2009, p. 1), for example, states that 'male blood elves are routinely read along the lines of male femininity – or "gay" – and as such [are] cherished among queer gamers'. For Steve, however, this was not the case. He found it difficult to identify with his blood-elf character and so he began altering his avatar through different tactics, such as changing the hairstyle, the armour, and weapons. Unfortunately, none of these worked; the changing of armour had minimal effect and the swords appeared too large for the blood elf's slight stature. Eventually, Steve felt he had little choice but to pay (real money) for a racial change, from a blood elf to the more masculine appearance of a tauren.

During my five years gaming in WoW there have been several elements of online play (which revolve around avatar appearance, customization and socialization) that have worked to enhance the sense of connectedness with my avatar, and over time I have come to view my avatars as extensions of my offline self. Ducheneaut et al.'s (2009, p. 1157) findings support this view, with the authors noting that 'as one's tenure in a given VW [virtual world] increases, their offline and online personalities become more congruent, perhaps to the point of becoming identical'. While some gamers prefer their online avatars to portray their offline sexuality, the majority of gamers (including those involved in this study) have experienced playing as the opposite gender and are well versed in the practice of gender-switching in online environments. This gives credence to Butler's (1990) argument that sees gender as a performance unencumbered by the restrictions of sex, in that masculinity is not just restricted to men and being male, nor is femininity restricted to women and being female. Kennedy's (2002) examination of the game *Lara Croft: Tomb Raider* highlights how the act of

---

6   Guilds or clans are common in online games and they are made up of a group of players who play together on a regular basis.

7   These image templates work to reinforce a stereotype of male blood elves as being elegant and effeminate. Currently, the templates for male blood-elf avatars offer 10 hairstyle options, and it is notable that eight of these consist of long, straight hair styles.

switching gender can present a new way of examining the fusion between avatar and gamer. She argues that relationships between players and their avatars can be viewed as:

> ... a kind of queer embodiment, the merger of the flesh of the (male) player with Lara's elaborated feminine body of pure information. This new queer identity potentially subverts stable distinctions between identification and desire and also by extension the secure and heavily defended polarities of masculine and feminine subjectivity. (Kennedy, 2002, unpaginated)

While there is a steadily growing body of work that enriches understanding of gender and virtual reality (see Hansbury, 2011; Kennedy, 2002), it is important to note that gamers have been experiencing different genders and ways of being since the advent of full-bodied avatars in popular games in the 1990s. As such, the gender-switching that occurs in games is typically viewed as a 'normal' activity within gaming culture, and it has done little to challenge the dominant status of heteronormativity within these spaces (Todd, 2012).

One research participant, Jenny (37), identifies as a bisexual woman, and she spoke to me about her experiences of gaming as a virtual man – one who meets, flirts and forges relationships with other women. She comments: '[I]t was completely different. Interacting with girls was easy but with guys, I had to have a certain restraint. I had to be almost sort of impersonal.' Jenny shows that notions of gender and sexuality play an important role in the social spaces of online games, and she was careful to maintain a heteromasculine presence. It is in instances such as these that both the complexities of gender performance and the constraints of cyberspace become realized. Utilizing game avatars can, and does, afford people new ways of experiencing different types of being. Yet, even these can become fraught with complexities, while at the same time subjected to varying degrees of surveillance.[8] In Jenny's case, she initially revelled in her online identity as a masculine character and although she enjoyed this new embodiment and the company of new online friends, she also tired of having to constantly think about her gendered performance.

Jenny's experience demonstrates how performances of gender in online spaces are often subjected to the same sociocultural norms as offline spaces. Jenny, however, belongs to a minority group, in that she is one of the few women gamers who play as a virtual man. Research shows that men participate significantly more in gender-switching activities than women, with recent reports showing that 53 per cent of men playing WoW have at least one avatar that is female, in comparison to only 9 per cent of women with male avatars (Yee, 2014). Another recent study conducted by Martey et al. (2014) found that gender-switching can influence gendered behaviours in an online environment. They state, for example, that men who play as virtual women often, without intending to, adopt more 'feminine' speech patterns (Martey et al., 2014, p. 288). They also point out that 'in a digital world, Butler's (1990) distinction between what is perceived as the "natural" gender of a specific body and performances of gender conventions can be made literal'(cited in Martey et al., 2014, p. 288). An increasing amount of research connects people's online personas to their offline identities, especially in relation to sex and gender. During the course of this research, I had the opportunity to discuss various aspects of gender-switching with Jim (39), a man who games predominantly as a virtual woman. In response to my question as to why he chooses to game as a woman, Jim replied:

---

8   Several theorists highlight the ways in which the 'panopticon' is present in, and affects, online spaces. See, for example, Taylor (2008).

Well if I'm going to be staring at a screen for several hours, I want something nice to look at and if a guy tells you otherwise, he's lying. In most games there's no difference now between men and women avatars. Women [avatars] are just as strong, if not stronger than men. So why not play as a woman? It just makes better sense – I've got something nice to look at and I kick ass. (Fieldnote entry, online discussion via TeamSpeak[9] while playing Diablo 3, 9 April 2014).

Here, Jim's comment not only defends his preference for using female avatars, but also reinforces his identity as heterosexual. MacCallum-Stewart (2008, p. 35) argues that 'players are absolutely unrepentant about the fact that they find the female avatars more attractive'. Yee (2014) also states that the most common explanation provided by male gamers as to why they choose to play as virtual women is that they enjoy looking at the image of their female avatar's body from behind while playing in a third-person perspective. It is important to note, however, that while these accounts are valid, there is the potential for them to detract from the extent of blurring that occurs across the heavily defended borders which work to distinguish men/masculinity from women/femininity.

'Gaymers' and Guilds: Online Gaming Communities

In mainstream games, homosexual or 'queer' identities exist within a derogatory discourse of 'put-downs' and humour. As such, the public arena of online games is not typically a 'safe' or supportive space. Therefore, it is not surprising that very few game designers have made the effort to include lesbian, gay, bisexual, transgender and queer (LGBTQ) characters as a serious design component:

Among the factors affecting the representation of the GLBT community are the attitudes of those in the video game development community, the construction of the gamer audience, the expected backlash for having GLBT content, whether the structure of the industry allows it to face this backlash, and the potential for representing sexual and gendered identities in the medium. (Shaw, 2009, p. 229)

While MacCallum-Stewart (2008, p. 38) states that video games, more than any other media, allow players to 'revel in their own embodiment as alternative beings', it is also important to note that, in many online role-playing games, homophobic discourse is prevalent and the 'everyday norm'. For example, in WoW, the level of homophobic language in-game is evident and widespread. Matt and Regina are two participants who managed a guild together in WoW and welcomed people regardless of their sexual orientation. Regina states: '[W]e've known gay people and it has never been an issue simply because we had a policy of not having anything against someone's sexuality.' She adds:

If there was any carry-on about two of the male guild characters getting together, they'd carry on just as much as anyone else just because it was funny ... there was never anything said in a particularly serious way ... It was a joke ... Girls don't seem to be quite so hung-up about making a joke of their sexuality, whereas guys will be like

---

9   TeamSpeak is a voice-over IP software that allows users to speak on a chat channel with other users, much like a telephone conference call. Users typically wear a headset with an integrated microphone. There can be multiple users on one channel simultaneously.

'no, no, no' ... and the number of times I've seen girls kissing each other just because it's funny, or to tease guys ... but you'd never see two guys doing that.

Regina highlights how some performances of sexuality are more taboo than others, with lesbian and female bisexuality constructed as being more socially acceptable. Past studies examining bi-negativity highlight how those who identify as LGBTQ are also affected by stereotypes and negative attitudes (see, for example, Rubinstein et al., 2013). Sundén (2009, p. 6) notes that guilds act as a 'safe haven of sorts, a home away from home in World of Warcraft, a place with warm hearts and sharp tongues. It is a place with plenty of room for queerly playing up against, or transgressing the implied or ideal player.' Similarly, my research findings and auto-ethnographical experiences of belonging to several heterodominant (and LGBTQ-inclusive) guilds have shown that a similar style of humour also occurs within these guilds. Not many guilds, however, utilize any formal type of guideline policy regarding sexual politics. Therefore, guild leaders like Matt and Regina are exceptional as they make a point of outlining guild policies regarding sexual difference and, in doing so, attempt to create a welcoming and safe space for all gamers.

Challenging and Resisting Heteronormative Values in Mainstream Gaming Culture

Walmsley (2000, p. 17) notes that 'cyberspace might have annihilated distance, but not place'. Clearly, cyberspace is an important place for gaming communities. While cyberspace is often viewed as a continually developing place of exploration, it also has many of the same dominant social cues that exist within the real world, transported there by the very people who enter into it. Therefore, many negative elements of offline life, such as racism and homophobia, also exist within cyberspace. There are, however, also groups of like-minded people who resist and challenge heteronormative values in the spaces of online games. This has seen the formation of many new friendships and virtual communities. In online games, guilds are one example – communities that allow players to recruit other gamers who have similar interests. In WoW it is standard practice for players to join a guild at some point.[10] In order to recruit players into a guild, most people use WoW's chat channels to advertise their guild's aims and/or philosophy. While guilds offer gamers a space to create their own sense of belonging, there is still the wider public arena of online gaming to consider:

> *Virtual community spaces, like other spaces, are subject to social relations of power, to pressures to conform to certain socialized norms, and to sanctioned rules appropriate to a particular community. The practices of virtual spaces can be highly regulated, and they can produce knowledge that targets particular populations within the community. (Del Casino, 2009, p. 137)*

Del Casino's comment is particularly relevant to Sara Andrews' story. In 2006 Andrews, a 25-year-old transsexual, was the leader of a LGBTQ friendly guild in WoW.[11] One particular

---

10   This is not surprising as the game is designed to encourage the growth of guilds. For example, belonging to a guild affords players certain perks that aid their avatars, as well as accessing other various in-game materials, such as armour and weapons.

11   Andrews is not a participant in this research; however, her story is only one of a few that has received public attention.

day, Andrews was performing her guild recruitment call-out and, as usual, she added that her guild was 'GLBT (gay/lesbian/bisexual/transsexual) friendly' (Peckham, 2006). This time, however, Blizzard (the creator of WoW) received a complaint from another player and, shortly after, Andrews received a warning email from a game master (GM).[12] The email informed Andrews that she had been temporarily banned from playing WoW due to a violation of the terms of use (TOU) agreement, under the section 'Harassment – Sexual Orientation'. In short, Andrews was warned that the continued use of 'both clear and masked sexual language which … insultingly refers to any aspect of sexual orientation pertaining to themselves or other players' would result in further action being taken (Jennings, 2008, p. 104).

Andrews argued with Blizzard, stating that she did not want to 'recruit any other way, because there are WAY too many people on WOW that use REAL antigay terms, and I do not want those people in my guild' (Andrews, cited in Peckham, 2006, emphasis in original). Andrews also stated that the word GLBT was not being used in a derogatory fashion and explained to Blizzard that it had made a 'HUGE mistake … [Oz] is a place where GLBT players can come without being harassed or insulted for their sexual orientation with phrases such as "That's so gay!" and "That horde just ganked me![13] What a fag!"' (Andrews, cited in Peckham, 2006). Blizzard eventually removed Andrews' ban but did not recant its position, stating that its rationale for the warning was in fact to protect Andrews from the expected backlash that would ensue from other players whose stances were anti-GLBT.

Andrews' argument highlights how words such as 'gay' and 'fag' are derogatory and commonplace in WoW. Yet, there are no repercussions for the players who use these terms. Hence, the familiar privileged positioning of heterosexuality as the invisible, yet dominant, norm. Andrews, however, chose to circulate her story more publicly, and over the ensuing weeks her story was picked up by multiple online forums, blogs and news sites.[14] In a particularly apt response, Chonin (2006) questions Blizzard's rationale, asking how the TOU applies to Andrews' post, stating:

> The answer is simple. The policy doesn't apply. Andrews' post contained neither clear nor masked insults. Hence, no infraction. … If I parse [comprehend] correctly, what the folks at Blizzard are really saying is this: Forget the guidelines. By being openly inclusive of GLBT players, Andrews is inviting harassment. By inviting harassment, she is herself a harasser. Extend the logic and this means that, according to Blizzard, anyone who is openly gay is to blame for inciting homophobia. … In essence, Blizzard Entertainment is taking a policy intended to protect sexual minorities and using it against those same minorities. (Chonin, 2006)

Shortly after the emergence of these critical commentaries Blizzard issued a statement of apology and termed the actions of the GM who dealt with the original complaint as an 'unfortunate mistake'. It stated further that 'it has always been, and will remain Blizzard's policy that LGBT-friendly guilds are allowed to announce their existence, and to recruit members in the same manner as any other guilds' (Fahey, 2009).

Blizzard's admission of error did not, however, have a significant impact on the dominant positioning of heteronormative discourse within online gaming, as queer identities and uses

---

12   Game masters (GMs) have the authority to act as senior account administrators within WoW.
13   To be 'ganked' is to be killed, without mercy, for sport by other players. This can also occur in most game settings, but is more common in player versus player game environments.
14   The following are just a few of the online sites that reported on Andrews' story: WoW Insider; lawgeek.com; bbs.stardestroyer.net; news.bbc.co.uk; joystick.com; Kotaku.com; and 1up.com.

of anti-gay language continue to be synonymous with things 'lesser than'. Valentine (2007, p. 19) asserts that the identity of particular spaces is 'produced and stabilized through the repetition of the intersectional identities of the dominant groups that occupy them … such that particular groups claim the right to these spaces'. Furthermore, when non-conforming identities are '"done" differently in particular temporal moments they rub up against, and so expose, these dominant spatial orderings that define who is in place/out of place, who belongs and who does not' (ibid.). In Andrew's experience, WoW was not only being produced, but also regulated and maintained, as a heteronormative (and homophobic) space where non-conforming 'queer' identities are marginalized and oppressed. Andrews' enduring conflict and eventual win, however, shone a much needed spotlight on an issue that was, up until that point, being swept under the proverbial rug:

> *Andrews' win was more of an ideological victory for gay rights in the game. The knowledge that there is a viable means of recourse for players who have an interest in protecting the ability of GLBT 'friendly' players to enjoy the game – that those players are not totally marginalized is a result of Andrews and her sympathizer's ability to effectively navigate the lingual landscape and draw attention to their cause.*
> *(Jennings, 2008, p. 105)*

Other game developers have also been recipients of critical feedback concerning their management of sexual politics. In response to player demand, for example, the game developer BioWare announced its decision to include same-gender romance (SGR) in the expansion of *Star Wars*: *Rise of the Hutt Cartel*, which would be located on one particular planet – Makeb. This information was met with criticism by both pro- and anti-SGR groups. Anti-SGR groups protested because of concerns about being forced to interact with SGR content, whereas pro-SGR groups were worried that SGR content was being 'quarantined' to one location within the game. As such, BioWare received much negative feedback and was accused of attempting to marginalize and segregate non-heterosexual romance (Pearson, 2013), with media sources referring to the expansion update as 'The Gay Planet', or 'The Gay Ghetto'. BioWare responded to these critiques by stating that SGR would be occurring in several different areas of the game, not just on Makeb, and that all players would have a choice as to whether or not they engage with the game's various NPCs and the SGR storyline dialogues. Regardless of the negative backlash, BioWare's efforts to be more inclusive of same-sex relationships were well intended, and this example not only demonstrates that a fundamental shift in the design of mainstream games is occurring, but also highlights the level of debate surrounding identity politics in the spaces of online games.

Conclusion

Over the past two decades geographers have effectively demonstrated that space is a social construct with sexualized dimensions. Particular attention has been paid to the active production of heterosexualized space and how sexual 'others' live and experience particular spaces on a daily basis (Johnston and Longhurst, 2010; Oswin, 2008). The current depth of player choice and avatar customization in WoW allows gamers to experiment and role-play with online identities, in ways that would otherwise be impossible in an offline world. It is in these ways that we see the potential for online spaces to be utilized as places where people are free to express themselves and gain a sense of liberation from the real world.

Consequently, on the one hand, people are finding amazing ways of living, experiencing and enhancing their lives through online games. It is now possible to meet new people from all over the world and form complex and cooperative groups that are motivated to work together to achieve incredibly difficult and multifaceted goals – all of this is occurring within the dynamic environments of online games. On the other hand, those who do not conform to dominant norms are often subjected to varying degrees of oppression and prejudice, especially within the public arena of gaming. As outlined in this chapter, I have discussed several facets of online gaming culture and, overall, one thing is clear: online games are much *more* than just games because they comprise diverse communities that continue to evolve and grow. Advances in video-game design not only make it possible for gamers to experience social connections in very real and emotional ways, but also continue to open up new avenues for exploring different kinds of identities, connections and interactions.

Chapter 43

Horny at the Bus Stop, Paranoid in the Cul-de-sac: Sex, Technology and Public Space

Sharif Mowlabocus

In this chapter, I explore the relationship between technology, space and sexuality within the context of Western culture – a culture that is increasingly experienced as digitally immersive. I shall draw upon two specific examples from contemporary digital culture to examine aspects of this relationship. Both examples are mobile applications that serve to remap space. The first example demonstrates the ways in which technology can be used to 'open up' public space by creating sexual networks, while the second illustrates the ways in which technology can be deployed as a method of 'closing down' and regulating our use of public spaces. These examples allow me to explore the ways in which digital technology can serve to regulate and shape the spaces of our everyday lives, and the role that sexual discourses play within these shaping practices.

While the two examples I employ are discrete, they are connected in two specific ways. First, they both rely on GPS-enabled smartphones, and the vast technological infrastructure that situates and facilitates the operation of these palm-sized technologies. Second, they both draw upon the same reservoir of representational strategies, in particular the user profile, a digital form that I have discussed extensively elsewhere (Mowlabocus, 2010b) and which has become a ubiquitous form of (self) representation in digital culture.

Before I turn my attention to these two platforms, however, I want to begin by signposting the long historical relationships that have been established between sex and space and sex and technology. I do so primarily because, in our rush to study web forms and techno-sexual practices, it is all too easy to lose sight of the fact that these new objects of desire are in fact not new, but instead represent the latest iteration of a much older – indeed, in some cases, ancient – set of relations between sex, technology and space. Thus, it is to the first of these relationships – the one between sex and space – that I now turn my attention.

Barracks, Bedrooms and Bathhouses: Tense Relationships of Sex and Space

As has been identified in other chapters in this collection, sex and space have a long and complex relationship. Foucault's (1976) work on sexuality acknowledges the disciplinary mechanisms brought to bear on sex during the Victorian era. Much of this disciplining work carried with it a spatial dimension. The architecture of *homosocial* spaces (such as the prison, the boarding school dormitory, the military barracks), together with the organization of life in those spaces, inferred a disciplining – a regulation – of sexuality. Most often, this regulation was in fact a curbing of (homo)sexual practice, although masturbation – scourge of the eighteenth- and nineteenth-century boarding school – was also heavily policed (Hunt, 1998). Such policing was aided by the careful organization of living and sleeping quarters, allowing a single supervisor to be able to monitor – to *survey* – their charges during nocturnal hours: 'The fear of children's sexuality elicited several pedagogical interventions, from dormitory architecture to bathroom-monitoring practices, as adults focused on preventing sexualized contact, including limiting opportunities for privacy and seeing other children's genitals' (McLelland and Hunter, 2013, p. 64). It was not only 'deviant' sexual practices that were subjected to spatial organization. The 'correct' form of sex, a heteronormative form of sexual relations (undertaken primarily for procreative purposes), was also subject to spatial regulation. Such sex, when it had to take place, should be confined to the intimate spaces of private bedrooms. Indeed, at one point in history, deviant and immoral behaviour was thought to proliferate among the 'lower classes' because children and parents shared sleeping accommodation, causing a warping of the former's impressionable minds (Crook, 2008). It seems that sex, of whatever kind, needs to be *located*.

Today, such locative work continues to shape our understanding of sex. We need only look the 'sex zones' (Califia, 2000, p. 217) of a city to see how particular forms of sex are relegated to particular areas of the urban environment. Hence prostitution is understood as occurring within the red-light *district* of a city. Gay sex has historically been aligned with semi-public spaces (Humphries, 1970; Leap, 1999), and entire cities have been understood in the public imagination as the site of illicit sexual practice. Brighton, on the south coast of England, is the most obvious example that comes to mind (see Browne and Bakshi, 2013a), but Las Vegas in the USA and Amsterdam in the Netherlands can also be read in this way (see Duyves, 1992; Pritchard and Morgan, 2006). This is not to suggest that prostitution (to take one example) has been confined to the red-light district, or that it is tolerated and accepted within that district. If anything, red-light districts serve to highlight the tense spatial politics at work in discussions of public sexual cultures, as sex workers, clients and 'legitimate' members of the local community all seek to claim ownership of – or at least access to – a given space (see Hubbard, 1998 for discussion).

Of course, battles over space *can* be won by sexual minorities and sexual outsiders. Califia (2000, p. 217) cites American gay male subculture as an example of how one sexual minority has succeeded in creating 'legitimate' zones in which dissident sexual identities can be expressed and where same-sex practices are, to a degree, tolerated (see also Hubbard, 2001). The commercial dimension of these 'success stories' should not be overlooked (Binnie and Skeggs, 2004). However, when sexual cultures spill out on to the street, then it becomes a 'problem' (see Buckingham, 2009). Sex and space remain (uncomfortable) bedfellows and have a long and complicated history.

Technology and Sex: History Repeating Itself?

At the same time, technology and sex also have a complex relationship. If we think of technology in its broadest sense, this relationship goes back several millennia. In museums around the world one can find examples of ancient sex aids and prophylactics scattered among collections of antiques (Lieh-Mak et al., 1983; Simmons, 2002; Laichen, 2007). I am reminded here of the 'secret museum' – another spatial regulation of sex (Kendrick, 1987) – where men of letters were granted access to sexualized objects and sexual materials. Ancient dildos and condoms are sexual technologies; they either heighten sexual pleasure or reduce the chances of pregnancy. Then there are those technologies designed to censure pleasure: the chastity belt, the anti-masturbatory belt, the mittens that stop individuals stimulating themselves. In this electronic age it is too easy to think of technology as requiring silicon or radio transmitters, but technology is far broader than this narrow definition. The condom, the contraceptive pill and Viagra, for instance, are all sexual technologies (see Loe, 2004; Watkins, 2007; Maddison, 2007; Del Casino, 2007b; Marks, 2010).

However, technology is rarely singular in its use[1] and the co-opting of 'benign' technologies for sexual purposes is also a regular feature of our recent (and not so recent) history. Pornography, for example, is largely the result of a technological co-optation (Coopersmith, 1998, 2000). Whether in the form of the written or typed word, the photographic image, the moving picture or the webcam, our desire to witness sex has led to the appropriation of technology in the service of sexual desire. The telephone is a great example of an interpersonal communication technology that became sexualized. Since the 1980s one has been able to dial up and listen to a panoply of prerecorded pornographic stories (see Hall, 1995). Around the same time, live sex-chat lines began to appear, allowing the caller to engage in a sexual fantasy of their own choosing with (in effect) a call-centre worker. These continue to exist today, and the origins of internet-based webcam sex work can be located in these pre-digital forms and practices (see O'Toole, 1999).

It is important to note these historical relationships when considering more recent iterations of the sex–space–technology triad. Doing so allows us to understand both the differences and similarities that are afforded by these new technologies. It also allows us to identify the ongoing tensions and anxieties that surround issues relating to both the location of sex and the mediation of sexual practice. With these ideas in mind I now turn to my first case study.

Bored and Horny @ the Bus Stop: The Case of Digital Cruising

Gay male culture in the West developed an affinity with digital and social media early on in the history of domestic internet use. As I have discussed elsewhere (Mowlabocus, 2010a), long before it became socially acceptable for heterosexual folk to use (or at least admit to using) online dating services, gay, bisexual and 'non-identifying' men incorporated digital platforms into their sex-searching practices. This integration has been so great that some have lamented the 'death' of gay male public sexual cultures (P.L. Brown, 2007; Dean, 2009). Since 2007, around the same time as the first iPhones went on sale, gay men's digital practice has been extended to include mobile platforms and applications.

These applications are continually evolving, and, at the time of writing this, the UK market is dominated by one application in particular – Grindr. We might think of Grindr as a general 'all-purpose' social/sex app for gay men; other applications have differentiated themselves by targeting niche groups, focusing on particular body types and particular sexual practices. Examples of these include Scruff, Growlr, Squirt, Recon, Jack'd and BoyAhoy. These applications share a similar design and *modus operandi*, allowing users to create basic image-centric profiles through which they can be seen on the application. Users can also scroll though a list of other users currently online and contact them in various ways. Crucially, these applications also provide information on the location of other users or, more specifically, a measurement of how far away they are from the user who has looked them up.

---

1   Indeed, Viagra, the drug developed for erectile dysfunction, is today being used by those who do not suffer from impotence as an enhancement to their sexual repertoires.

I broadly define the practices engendered by these applications as a form of 'digital cruising' and I use this label in order to acknowledge not only the methods by which these communicative acts take place, but also the rich subcultural history that such acts draw upon. Cruising remains a powerful and recognizable trope within gay male culture (see Humphries, 1970; Healy, 1996; Tattelman, 1999; Flowers et al., 2000; Tomsen, 2006 for discussion) and digital cruising relies on existing social norms that have hitherto been established within gay male culture. Digital cruising underscores a difference between 'earlier' forms of Internet-enabled interaction and more recent forms of communicative practice. This difference relates to the mobility of the latter – the live, 'on the go', opportunistic and serendipitous facet of digital cruising. Digital cruising also realizes Bratton's (2009, p. 93) claim that the mobile device 'enables physical, communicative and thereby social mobility' and 'dramatically reinserts specific location into digital space'.

Digital cruising, like its analogue 'physical' predecessor (which, of course, remains alive and well today) does not always result in sexual contact. Whether it takes place on the street or on your phone, cruising does not necessarily signal more than an acknowledgement, perhaps an appreciation, of the (possibly) queer other. This is not to say that men don't 'hook up' via apps, but the act of browsing – of looking – does not always result in sex, at least not immediately. However, while digital cruising does not always result in sex, it is nevertheless *framed* by sex, by which I mean that sexual discourse is often deployed by users of these technologies as a method of communicating with one another during these episodes. Messages that typically get exchanged on such services range from sexual flirtation – 'nice pic' or 'hot mate' – through to more direct forms of sexual solicitation – 'wanna fuck?' or 'up 4 it?' or 'top or bottom?'. A recent video on YouTube (*Grindr in Real Life*, 2013) in which two men act out three typical Grindr conversations, offers a useful and humorous overview of life on the app.

If digital cruising relies on sexualized discourse, that discourse is *located*. Such a focus on rearticulating space through digital interventions builds on and extends earlier work on mobile-phone use, mobile internet uptake, laptop use and mobile gaming (see Bull, 2004; Garcia-Montes et al., 2006; Daliot-Bul, 2007; Bittman et al., 2009; Bassett, 2009). Much of this work was developed in response to the ubiquity of the mobile phone, a perceived 'unshackling' of the internet (from fixed landlines, desktops and Ethernet connection points), and the mobilizing of web access via Wi-Fi, WiMax and 3G networks.

If cruising has a relationship to space, particularly the spaces that we move through, that relationship is almost always 'tactical' (De Certeau, 1984, p. xix). By this I mean that not only does such digital cruising take place within (physical) contexts that are avowedly heterosexist, but also that the notion of looking at another man is fraught with anxieties in Western culture. Cruising opens up transitory spaces that articulate homosexual desires and identifications, and I want to suggest that digital cruising approaches this queering of space through the creation of 'hybrid spaces', which exploit the tension between physical and digital environments. In this respect, *all* cruising can be thought of as a response to the sense of 'placelessness' that queer people contend with in societies that privilege and normalize heterosexuality: 'We [queer people] are keenly aware of the hybrid nature of our existences, and of the highly contingent nature of both our power and the constraints on it. Hence our ambivalent relationships to place and identity, and our affection for placelessness and movement' (Knopp, 2004, p. 129). I use the term 'hybrid space' to refer to the work of de Souza e Silva (2006), whose work on space and mobile culture is useful in helping us think beyond the outmoded binaries of offline/online and physical/digital and understand social (and sexual) interactions as they become manifest via mobile-locative platforms. She defines hybrid spaces thus: 'Hybrid spaces are mobile spaces, created by the constant movement of users who carry portable devices continuously connected to the Internet and to other users' (de Souza e Silva, 2006, p. 262).

We can think of digital cruising as creating such hybrid spaces. As men move around the city or the suburbs (or rural areas), as they look up, hook up, chat and connect with other men, they form loose, ephemeral connections. These connections can be thought of as 'queer' pathways and the queerness of these pathways is twofold. They are queer in that they 'queer' space – they allow for the articulation of gay male desire in spaces that are 'public' – and they are queer in that such pathways span both the physical and the digital – they are neither fully one nor the other.

I am reminded here of a line from Berlant and Warner's essay, 'Sex in Public'. They describe the queer world as 'a space of entrances, exits, unsystematized lines of acquaintance, projected horizons, typifying examples, alternate routes, blockages, incommensurate geographies' (Berlant and Warner, 1998, p. 558). In comparison to heterosexual culture, queer cultures appear to be far more 'transitory', and the popularity of mobile applications such as Grindr can, in part, be understood as acknowledging the pleasures (as well as the politics) of such 'transitory' gay presence.

Digital cruising operates at an intersection where physical space encounters freedom of manoeuvrability as it is rendered through digital communications. This intersection is not only a site for pleasurable exploration; it is also fragile and contested. In his ethnographic study of American cruising sites Hollister (2002, p. 134) remarks that 'men who cruise a rest area experience a very different place, albeit with the same buildings, pavement, and foliage, than those who just stop to rest, use the facilities, and move on'. These different experiences of space are rarely equally weighted, and this inequality reflects the fact that public spaces (whether physical or digital) are more often than not coded as heterosexual. Hillis notes that:

> With respect to gay/queer experiences of material public space, belief or desire that the Web might constitute not only mobility but also some form of actual space grows in tandem with the reality that it remains taboo, for example, to hold hands with one's same-sex partner at the mall. (Hillis, 2009, p. 234)

The hybrid spaces of digital cruising bring together and hold the 'belief' and 'reality' that Hillis identifies in tension, causing physical space to be subjected to acts of queer digitalization and recoding. As de Souza e Silva (2006, p. 270) notes, 'in the hybrid-spaces logic, cell phones do not take users out of physical space' as perhaps the static web might be seen to do, but rather, 'strengthen users' connections to the space they inhabit, because the connection to other users depends on their relative position in space'. Considering the relatively small amount of information often transmitted during encounters on gay male apps, (often nothing more than 'hi mate' or 'hot!' or 'wot u in2?'), it would seem that, like other forms of 'phatic' communication (Malinowski, 1923), digital cruising demonstrates how 'social contacts are often maintained through the mere act of communicating' (Provine et al., 2007, p. 305). This notion of strengthening connections within physical space is arguably most keenly felt by those who are regularly perceived as existing (to paraphrase Hillis) somewhere 'over there' rather than ever fully 'here' (Hillis, 2009, p. 234).

Fearful in the Cul-de-sac: The Strange Case of Sex-Offender Applications

However, at the same time that mobile-locative technologies and 'app culture' are opening up space through discourses of sex and sexuality, they are also being utilized to regulate our movements within those same spaces. I want to move on to consider a manifestation of mobile-locative technology that operates in stark contrast to services such as Grindr but through the same triple lens of sex–technology–space. In particular, I want to focus on a different genre of applications: sex-offender location apps.[2]

Like Grindr, the Sex Offender Search app relies on mapping and location technologies. Like Grindr, it uses the location of the user to organize the information in its database and then uses a familiar GUI[3], in this instance a map, to visualize that data. Finally, both applications use profiling practices that look unnervingly like one another.

But what is the Sex Offender Search? What does it do? This application belongs to a genre of software currently only usable in the USA. They offer users (often framed as concerned parents[4]) the opportunity to 'see' where registered sex offenders in their local neighbourhood live. More precisely, these apps mine data from sex-offender registers and translate it into a 'user-friendly' map. In the USA, convicted sex offenders are required to register with their local police department and while the terms of that registration (including what information is required) varies dramatically from state to state, registry entries always include the home address of the offender and a list of the crimes they have been convicted of.

Importantly, this data is available, for free, to the public. Anyone who wishes to can log on to (for instance) the Massachusetts sex-offender registry[5] and perform a search on the database. Applications such as Sex Offender Search, Sex Offender Tracker and Offender Locater do not produce any new data on sex offenders. They simply reproduce – they *re*present – what was recorded on the relevant sex-offender register the last time the developers updated the application. One could be forgiven for thinking that this was not the case. The marketing material used to promote this genre of applications often misleadingly connotes 'liveness', using radar imagery reminiscent of war and science-fiction films, as well as augmented reality tropes to instil a sense of immediacy in the data represented.

A cursory exploration of such technology might lead one to believe that this genre of applications builds upon Bentham's Panopticon, the prison model that Foucault (1977) used as a metaphor for a society obsessed with (self-)surveillance. The offender application offers us the illusion that the perpetrator is always visible, that *he* (the databases are overwhelmingly populated by men) cannot escape the interrogative light shone on him by technology, and that we can undertake the role of the policing agent at our will. As previously stated, this visibility is tied to the offender's (last recorded) location, and all the applications in this genre represent nearby offenders on a rendering of Google maps, with individual offenders represented as 'pins' dropped on to the map and the user represented by a different coloured dot that moves across the map as we move through physical space. In fact, the constant visibility implied by these apps is patently untrue – it is a 'false light'. To repeat, these applications have no access to real-time feeds produced by (for instance) the GPS ankle bracelets worn by some offenders.

However, we might look at the locative aspects of these 'services' from a different perspective in order to consider the ways in which these applications speak to themes of sex and space. Or, to phrase this in Foucauldian language, we might consider who becomes the subject of surveillance via such technologies – who becomes the subject of such disciplining.

---

2   I am grateful to the work of Annany (2011) which brought my attention to this class of applications.
3   Graphical User Interface
4   The figure of the concerned parent simultaneously raises the spectre of the child and of a (heteronormative) understanding of futurity. Edelman's (2004) queer anti-social thesis, as well as the intergenerational work of Vanderbeck (2007) and the sexual geography work of Hubbard and Lister (2015) provide useful avenues for a further discussion of how the concept of the (heterosexual) family – especially the child – is invoked in discussions of 'public' and 'community' space, with the effect of sidelining anyone considered 'deviant'.
5   See Massachusetts SORB (2014).

While the immediacy of the sex-offender data feed might be an illusion, the liveness of where *we* are located certainly is real. *We* are the glowing blue dot that moves around our mobile screen and appears to be surrounded by red dots. It is *us* who are tracked in real time. It is not the offender but the user who becomes the object of such mobile-locative techno-practice. Indeed, rather than surveying and regulating the sex offender, these applications invite the user to survey and regulate *themselves* and, more precisely, their own movements within public space. In other words, this genre of applications appropriates the publicly available data on sex offenders in order to recode it through the *individualized* language of app culture. In doing so, our relationship to this data – and to the spaces that we move through – becomes reorganized. We become the 'moving targets' that have to 'dodge' the sexual predators lurking in our environment.

My mention of moving targets and of manoeuvring out of harm's way is intentional here and highlights the processes by which these forms of data visualization should be understood as part of an ongoing *gamification* of various aspects of contemporary life – economic, social, cultural, health, financial (see Gazzard, 2009; Harwood, 2012; Valiaho, 2014; Fuchs, 2014). Sex-offender locater apps are one more illustration of an ongoing discussion about the representation of data and of the blurring of the lines between fiction and reality, information and entertainment. This discussion also includes the work of Stallabrass (1996), Burston (2003), Stockwell and Muir (2003) and Huntemann and Payne's edited collection (2009). Read through the lens of critical political economy, these applications fit into an ongoing critique of data representation and the politics of its aesthetics.

Most offender applications invest in the belief that knowing who is 'out there' is both useful and important (particularly to parents and families). We should remember that in the USA laws govern the use of sex-offender data, and information gleaned from such databases must not be used to perpetrate violence against offenders or to otherwise intimidate them: vigilantes are not sanctioned by these applications. Indeed, quite what users are supposed to do with the information available via these applications remains unclear.

While the software developers are largely mute in this regard, the common deployment of a game aesthetic does point towards an answer to this question. I would argue that these visualizations of data support two complementary readings of this information. The first reading is that, through these applications, users are somehow safer – the apps operate as a preventive tool (Staples, 1994) similar to an early warning system or a personal sensor. Second, and building on my previous point, these applications support the creation of zones of sexual safety and sexual danger within the environments the user moves through. Just as the computer game allows us to build up a cartography defined by spaces of conflict, of risk and of safety, so these applications serve to remap the user's space (typically their local space) according to the logic of the sex-offender database. Given that we are not allowed to forcibly 'engage' the offender who resides down the street, it appears that our only option is to run for cover.

My argument here is that we are invited by such apps to renegotiate (and restrict) our use of public space in order to avoid the offender. The spaces of our everyday lives become coded according to sexual risk and (by implication) sexual safety. We might declare a certain park as a no-go area because an offender lives nearby. We might choose to go to another park, further away, so as to minimize a perceived risk. We might suggest that friends visit our kids rather than vice versa, because they live near an offender. There are multiple ways in which this app can serve to inscribe restrictions on our movements.

Here, we see an altogether different configuration of the technology, sex and space relationship from that found in gay male subculture. This relationship trades on pre-existing discourses of sex (primarily of sex as fearful and predatory) in order to regulate

397

the movement of citizens and to (re)inscribe public space as a site of sexual danger and sexual deviance.

Of course, the great irony here is the fact that sex offenders are positioned as dangerous 'others'. They may well be dangerous (I do not wish to downplay the horrific nature of sex crimes), but 80 per cent of the time they aren't 'others'; 80 per cent of the time sex offenders are known by their victims and include parents, caregivers, family friends and significant others (Colorado Bureau of Investigation, 2014). Mapping sex offenders within our local community obscures the fact that many offenders actually live under the same roof as their victims. Meanwhile sex-offender apps reinscribe prevailing cultural fears about both public space and sex and, in doing so, further regulate the spaces through which we permit ourselves to move through (see Valentine and McKendrick, 1997; Day, 2001).

Conclusion

Taken together, these two case studies feed back into the discussion that opened this chapter, regarding the relationship between technology, space and sex. In different ways, these two examples illustrate how technologies can serve to recode and 'map' space through the lens of sexuality. To repeat the declaration I made in the introduction, these examples of contemporary digital culture do not so much reveal changes to the way in which we view sex, space and technology, but rather point towards the ongoing tension that exists between these three concepts. That the technologies we are discussing today are themselves caught up in a complex relationship with space, being geo-locative examples of a converged mobile-media platform only serves to further complicate this ongoing discussion. To paraphrase Langdon Winner (1986), we might ask whether technologies have politics (or, indeed, whether the built environment has a politics). The answer to this is, of course, 'yes, they do'. Those politics are not necessarily new, even if the technology we hold in our hands today is. Exploring how we understand space through discourses of sexuality and technologies of mediation simultaneously provides us with an opportunity to see how our sexual identities, practices and even fears have a spatial dimension, and how technology continues to frame our experience of (perhaps even the construction of) sexuality today.

Chapter 44

Digital Technologies and Sexualities in Urban Space

Catherine J. Nash and Andrew Gorman-Murray

Introduction

In this chapter we explore how lesbian, gay, bisexual, trans and queer (LGBTQ)[1] people's engagement with the internet and new media might be implicated in contemporary transformations in LGBT and queer urban landscapes in the Global North, particularly in ways that rework sexual and gendered sociospatial relations across urban space. Substantial scholarship details LGBT and queer people's distinctive relationship with urban locations, especially in cities in the Global North where highly visible and vibrant gay villages are important inner-city landscapes (Castells, 1983; Lauria and Knopp, 1985; Adler and Brenner, 1992; Florida, 2002; Nash, 2005, 2006, 2010, 2013a; Podmore, 2006, 2013b; Mowlabocus, 2010b; Gorman-Murray and Waitt, 2009; see also Section I, 'Urban Sexualities'). Contemporary scholarship suggests that many well-established locations are undergoing some sort of transformation, variously described as a 'decline' or 'degaying', and suggesting a diminishing economic, social and political importance in queer lives (see Collins, 2004a; Ruting, 2008; Nash, 2013a, 2013b). At the same time, alternative sexual and gendered landscapes are emerging for some queer people who, as a result of legal, social and political changes, are increasingly integrated into urban residential neighbourhoods and entertainment districts, and have greater opportunities to be visible across a variety of queer-friendly landscapes (Visser, 2008a; Gorman-Murray and Waitt, 2009; Nash, 2013a, 2013b).

While some might suggest that gay villages are in decline (or disappearing altogether) and that alternative queer landscapes emerging (see G. Brown, 2004; Collins, 2004a; Ruting, 2008; Visser, 2008a), here we want to suggest an alternative conceptualization that positions restructured gay villages within new sets of relational and networked geographies (see Podmore, 2013b). These evolving landscapes not only reflect new (and admittedly uneven) LGBTQ mobilities, driven by legal, political and social changes (Nash and Gorman-Murray, 2014; Gorman-Murray and Nash, 2014), but are also facilitated, we suggest, by queer engagements with evolving information and communication technologies (ICTs). How this unfolds and the particular form that it might take depends very much on the social, historical and geographical peculiarities of place (see, for example, Nash and Gorman-Murray, forthcoming).

---

1   We use the term queer as a broadly inclusive phrase for gender and sexual minorities. Where required, we use specific categories such as LGBT, 'gay men' or 'lesbians' as used in the scholarship cited.

We begin with a consideration of the current literature on queer engagements with ICTs that allude to (albeit somewhat peripherally) the possible implications of these for material places. While some work suggests that ICT use means the end of gay villages as we know them, other literature recognizes a more complex interrelationship between online and offline life (see Ito, 2003; Ito and Okabe, 2005; Yoon, 2003; Galloway, 2004; Dourish, 2006). We then draw on the work of theorists such as Rowan Wilken (2009), as well as Sheller (2004) and de Souza e Silva (2006), to develop conceptualizations of place that can 'illuminate the complexities of human–technology–environment interactions' (Wilken, 2009, p. 39). While much of this work is focused on the way in which ICTs are integrated into, and reshape, place and the experiences of everyday life, we want to sketch out how this might provide a starting-point to begin thinking through how queer engagements with new technologies might be playing a role in the reorganization of urban life both within and beyond gay villages.

LGBTQ People and New Technologies

ICTs, particularly new media, are transforming the material, social, political and economic organization of cities as well as how we, both as individuals and collectively, interact with and experience urban spaces (Graham and Marvin, 2001; Graham, 2004; Wilken, 2009; de Souza e Silva and Frith, 2010). Contemporary scholarship portrays gays and lesbians as early adopters of new technologies within somewhat romanticized and utopian notions of cyberspace as facilitating the formation of alternative identities, subjectivities and communities unbounded by the constraints of the physical world (Wakeford, 2002; Tudor, 2012). As Aslinger (2010, p. 113) argues, engaging in life online overcomes the 'tyranny of geography', thereby enabling 'new forms of queer cultural flows'. Queer life online demonstrates that, for sexual minority groups, the internet provides invaluable opportunities for self-exploration and community-building (Barnhurst, 2007; Florida, 2002; Gross, 2003, 2007; Tudor, 2012; Cassidy, 2013). But, almost from the outset, claims about the unbound characteristics of virtual communities and the potential for limitless connections unhindered by geography were countered by concerns about the potential for isolation and disconnectedness, and suggestions that online social relations might not be as 'real' or meaningful as face-to-face interaction (G. Brown, 2007a; Wellman et al., 2001; Baym, 2010).

Queer scholarship in the early 1990s positioned queer subjects, queer theory and 'cyberspace' as a 'natural fit'. The online or virtual world was a libratory space, offering unlimited potential to break free from the limits of physical embodiment and dominant social forms of representation (Rheingold, 1993; Munt and Medhurst, 1997; Bell and Kennedy, 2000; Alexander, 2002; Berry et al., 2003; Yep et al., 2004). This thinking was premised on the notion that cyberqueer spaces offered a degree of anonymity that encouraged the participation of previously inaccessible communities across geographical locations (Cassidy, 2013; McKenna and Bargh, 1998; Morahan-Martin, 1999; Tyler, 2002; McIntosh and Harwood, 2002). The internet and related technologies seemed capable of overcoming the social and political limitations of offline racialized, gendered, classed and sexualized categories, presenting new possibilities for greater participation in the public sphere and potentially improved forms of democracy (Rheingold, 1993). Not surprisingly, the potential of this 'disembodiment thesis' (Campbell, 2004) was compromised by anxieties about deceptions, misrepresentations and the authenticity of online personae. Despite such optimistic beginnings, subsequent scholarship highlights how social categories such as gender and race continue to matter across various online communities (Nakamura, 2002; see also Todd, 2012; Vries and Peter, 2013).

Cyberqueer studies not only focused on the potential for new identities and (dis)embodied self-representation, but also critiqued the ways in which LGBT media online (newspapers, magazines and tourist businesses, for example) worked to increasingly commodify and/ or reify particular sorts of LGBT identities. Research on the development of online LGBT media examined how, in their quest for investment through marketing and advertising, LGBT media groups in the USA (for example, Gay.com, PlanetOut and The Advocate) developed a specific set of narratives about LGBT people in order to fit comfortably into mainstream investors' notions of an LGBT market (Chasin, 2000; Gamson, 2003; Campbell, 2005; O'Riordan and Phillips, 2007). Gramson (2003, p. 258) argues that cyberspace, far from offering a 'breeding ground ... for evolving cybercultures of sexual dissidents' actually encouraged the 'already-existing conservative trends in sexual identity politics', particularly those driven by an assimilationist, neoliberal politic (see also Duggan, 2002; I. Richardson, 2005; Aslinger, 2010). This suggests additional avenues of research that might explore the linkages between the commodification impulse of online LGBT commercial enterprises and the increasing commodification of LGBT identities and neighbourhoods during the same period (see Rushbrook, 2002; Binnie, 2004; I. Richardson, 2007).

New social networking sites, such as Facebook, and mobile applications such as Grindr, offer additional opportunities to (de)construct identities. As Cooper and Dzara (2010, p. 100) note, new social media sites such as Facebook allow LGBT people to 'employ, construct, maintain and sometimes hide their identities', highlighting the possibilities for new and alternative forms of identity management. Conversely, others argue that most queer social networking sites actively constrain identity formation and management through 'menu-driven' dropdown boxes that restrict self-representation within categories geared to mainstream marketing investors and advertising (O'Riordan, 2005; Light, 2007; see also Fletcher and Light, 2007; Light et al., 2008; Cassidy, 2013). Light (2007), for example, argues that users on Gaydar, a gay male social networking site, are required to 'shoehorn' themselves 'into very specific masculinities' if they wish to participate in Gaydar's social networking activities (see also Fletcher and Light, 2007; Light et al., 2008; Mowlabocus, 2008, 2010b; Nakamura, 2002).

New technologies and new media have been taken up by queer populations in different ways. Young LGBT and queer people, in particular, were early adopters, making use of social networking sites to explore different sexual and gendered identities and to make connections with other sexual and gendered minorities (Hillier and Harrison, 2007; Addison and Comstock, 1998). Fleischer (2005), for example, explores how the internet overcame the limitation of geography in her work on how isolated married lesbian women were able to connect online to others in similar situations, finding support and community where connections with a local LGBT community were unlikely (see also Bryson, 2006, for discussion of queer women). Cyberspace is an invaluable site, offering trans people access to social and support networks, a political community and opportunities to explore and experiment with gendered identities and subjectivities (Whittle, 2001; see also Stone, 1995; Stryker, 2000; Farr, 2010).

Conceptualizing the Online/Offline Divide: Rethinking LGBTQ Places

Preliminary scholarship conceptually separated online and offline life, imagining offline social life as being radically transformed by the unlimited potentialities of virtual communities (Cassidy, 2013; see also Balsamo, 2000; Branwyn, 2000; Tsang, 2000; boyd,

2001). Campbell (2004) argues, for example, that computer-mediated communications, including online gay men's chat rooms, dating sites and message boards, function as 'virtual gay bars' offering intimacy, connection and support, thereby diminishing the importance of offline physical spaces. Similarly, work on gay teens in the USA argues that many will 'come out' in, and find support through, involvement in an online community before doing so in their offline life (Holloway and Valentine, 2003; Alexander, 2002; Downing, 2013). More recently, conceptualizations such as 'online' and 'offline' no longer seem relevant given the increasingly seamless integration of 'actual' and 'virtual' experiences and how 'the deeply contextual, multi-site experiences of new media use … shape our everyday lives' and its geographies (Livingstone, 2008, pp. 393–4).

This online/offline intersection has received considerable attention given how new locative, mobile technologies have unchained users from their desktops, placing the internet in the palm of an ever-mobile hand. These new technologies enable individuals to interact across a range of communities, social networking sites, chat rooms and blogs, thoroughly embedding technologies into everyday routines and practices (Choi, 2006; Lampe et al., 2006; Ellison et al., 2007; Kuntsman, 2007; McLelland, 2002; Berry et al., 2003). Mowlabocus (2010b, p. 79), in examining gay male digital culture, highlights how historically (and geographically) specific gay male (offline) cultural norms are incorporated into, reworked and deployed in online environments. He proposes the concept of 'cybercarnality' to conceptualize how gay male culture manifests through digitally and physically entwined spaces, and that these 'multiple manifestations occur simultaneously and shape one another continuously' (ibid., p. 56). Arguably, online and offline life are now so thoroughly intertwined that conceptualizing urban spaces requires understanding the embeddedness of technologies in our everyday lives. For many gay men at least, the internet is the main facilitator of gay cruising, generating debates about the extent to which online activities are superseding activities and practices in traditional offline locations such as parks and bars (Tsang, 2000; Campbell, 2004; G. Brown et al., 2005; Cassidy, 2013).

New Mobilities: Technologies and Conceptualizations of LGBTQ Places and Social Relations

While little empirical work considers how new technologies might be affecting the existence of traditional gay villages, scholarship nevertheless seems quite certain that such technologies are a significant contribution to transformations in gay villages. Usher and Morrison (2010, p. 281) declare that San Francisco's Castro District is currently 'in decline', a state of affairs that will continue, they speculate, as the 'gay community' increasingly moves online. Further, online information for LGBT people in larger cities is less likely to reference a specific downtown district as LGBT venues are increasingly found city-wide. As a result, they claim, LGBT people no longer have the same sense of attachment to a physical neighbourhood even though the mainstreaming of LGBT rights has not necessarily meant the end of discrimination and inequalities. Given LGBT people are now located 'both globally and locally', 'gay sites online represent an alternative space for political engagement where gays regardless of location could come together to organize around common issues' (ibid., p. 276).

In a similar study, Pullen and Cooper (2010, pp. ii–iii) argue that LGBT communities are being transformed through new online practices – a transformation that is 'increasingly distanced from the need for physical social space, in the mediation, and evocation of its messages, politics and textures'. Yet while the internet might free LGBT people from the specificities of the local, there is perhaps the potential to 'contribute to the reconstruction of everyday physical living space' closer to democratic ideas (ibid., p. 11). For contemporary scholarship, the question remains open as to whether the gay village is 'necessary' for LGBTQ people, given online possibilities.

Contemporary urban life is increasingly mediated by engagement with ICTs, challenging geographical scholarship to conceptualize how new technologies are reworking urban sexual and gendered landscapes (Tsang, 2000; Campbell, 2004; Nash, 2013a, 2013b). Development of conceptual frameworks that consider online and offline life (or technology and space) as co-constitutive, rather than separate and determining, seems the better approach. Current scholarship on the transformations of traditional gay villages 'has tended to focus on either "place-making" and "territories" or "movement" and "mobility", largely overlooking the interconnections and mutually-constitutive processes between fixity and movement, migration and place-making' (Gorman-Murray and Nash, 2014, p. 623). As we have argued elsewhere, a 'new mobilities approach' offers critical perspectives for thinking about the processes currently transforming gendered and sexual landscapes in places such as Toronto, Canada and Sydney, Australia (Nash and Gorman-Murray, 2014; Gorman-Murray and Nash, 2014). However, our preliminary work does not expressly deal with new technologies, and we would like to conclude this chapter by suggesting how mobilities scholarship might prove a useful starting-point for thinking about traditional gay villages and new queer spaces – scholarship that links mobile technologies, relational geographies and conceptualizations of place.

Mobile technologies are reconstituting our experiences and understandings of place as well as how we organize, negotiate and engage with physical space. Wilken (2009, p. 40) argues that, given the ubiquitous nature of ICTs, we need 'a better model of place that is sensitive to the complexities of human–technology–environment interactions'. Drawing on Wilken (2009), we understand place as constituted through a recursive relationship between physical location and social relations, such that place is 'both the outcome of embodied social interactions' (Berland, 2005, p. 258) and 'integral to the very structure and possibilities of experience' (Malpas, 1999, p. 32). Place is shaped by the social relations that transpire in that location, while social relations (their form and substance) are enabled and constrained by the meanings and power relations embedded in a place. LGBTQ experiences in place are shaped by what is possible in a place, including visibility and safety as queers, and place is in turn shaped by the uses made of that place by queers.

This raises intriguing questions about queer people's embrace of new technologies in light of new queer sociospatial organization in inner-city neighbourhoods (Nash, 2013b; Gorman-Murray and Waitt, 2009). A new generation of queer people is now largely connecting online, arguably reducing the need for physical locations – such as gay bars, baths, restaurants, community centres and gay villages – to meet other queer people. With changing political, social and legal circumstances, queer people are utilizing new technologies to become increasingly visible as queers in a wider range of locations in inner-city areas. This dovetails with what some might argue is a new 'queer cache' where specific sorts of businesses, catering to a hip urban crowd, advertise their queer-friendly credentials on Facebook and other social media sites, again linking queer(ness) to consumer culture and commodified landscapes. Certain commercial streetscapes in both Toronto, Canada, and Sydney, Australia, encourage a queer presence to signal a specific political affiliation coupled with the desire to tap into a queer consumer market (Nash and Gorman-Murray, 2014; Gorman-Murray and Nash, 2014). Further, the 'older' meeting places have not disappeared since, for example, gay men still utilize well-known physical locations, such as parks, baths and commercial establishments, to connect with others using new media and social networking sites (Mowlabocus, 2010b; Cassidy, 2013). In other words, everyday mobile practices have reconfigured existing urban spaces and places, and queers, in particular, use new technologies to '"appropriate" existing urban spaces in different ways' (Wilken, 2009, p. 46) – a sociospatial activity that queer people have been employing for some time.

Therefore, we would need to (re)conceive of 'place' in ways that account for these myriad interactions that occur within, between and across specific places as queer social relations stretch across inner-city locations. One such conceptualization linked to location-based mobile technologies is the notion of 'hybrid spaces' developed by de Sousa e Silva. For de Sousa e Silva (2006), hybrid spaces come into being in temporary and fluid ways as mobile devices ensure people are constantly connected as they move through urban spaces. In this way, 'hybrid spaces merge the physical and the digital in a social environment created by the mobility of the users connected via mobile technology devices' (ibid., p. 263; see also Mowlabocus in this volume). Queer users of mobile technologies (as well as social networks such as Facebook, IRC, blogs, BBS and new media) are reconstituting the spatial imaginaries of movements through urban locations that include queer nodes, pathways and locations with varying spatial and temporal resonance. And, arguably, when such places come into existence as queer people move through and inhabit particular locations (and as these places become more stable), a set of relational geographies is created between newly constituted queer locations and traditional gay spaces, including gay villages. As Ek (2012, p. 42) argues, 'relational places are events that are folded into existence or "actualized"' and can be understood as forming across multiple vectors, comings and goings and across temporal moments (Doel, 2000; Thrift and Massey, 2003). This speaks to the workings of new queer mobilities (more available for some) that, in turn, rework networked relationships amongst and between more stable locations, such as the gay village, and emergent alternative locations (unstable, temporary or permanent), as well as new linkages (of varying strengths) stretched across inner-city locations. LGBTQ people have often understood urban spaces in this way – that is, as networked locations, unstable, sometimes temporary and sometimes permanent. However, identities, experiences and the constitution of place is distinctively different when mediated by new technologies (Gorman-Murray and Waitt, 2009; Podmore, 2006, 2013b; Nash, 2010, 2013b).

In trying to understand these stretched, fluid and unstable interconnections between nodes, networks and ethereal hybrid places, we find the concept of 'relational geographies' particularly useful. The notion of relational geographies draws together time, space and place as 'constituted, folded together, situated, mobile and multiple' (Ek, 2006, p. 53). As Doreen Massey (2005, p. 181) argues, a relational understanding of space highlights that 'not only is space a process, something produced, so is place' and, furthermore, places are 'worked out through social action in ways that ceaselessly change over time' (Ek, 2006, p. 51). Moreover, we need to attend to the 'power geometries' produced through the activities, processes, actors and structures in the articulation and transformation of space. Space, therefore, not only is a product of complex internal relations, including social interactions, but is also constituted through its 'connectedness to other places' (Wilken, 2009, p. 46).

Given this, and without denying that gay villages are perhaps 'declining' in certain ways, we would argue that we can understand the rise of alternative queer places and neighbourhoods in terms of an emergent formulation of relational geographies. In understanding the instability and fluidity of hybrid spaces, we can argue that, as places, they are 'articulated moments of networks of social relations and understandings' (Wilken, 2009, p. 46). New technologies facilitate the constitution of these hybrid relational geographies as users of Gaydar or Grindr move through urban locations, discovering the presence of other queers and arranging to meet, perhaps in queer-friendly locations, reinforcing that designation (Mowlabocus, 2008). As lesbians seek to make connections through online social networks, offline locations advertise their queer-friendliness, offering places to meet and socialize (Nash, 2013b). Events such as Pride and Mardi Gras continue to operate in traditional gay villages, bringing people together, even while venues for events spread across the city to different, queer-identified locales. Facilitated by new technologies and new social acceptances, gendered and sexual landscapes are being transformed.

To conclude, we argue that framing the impact of new technologies as something leading to the demise of gay villages is somewhat too simplistic (and deterministic) in terms of sociospatial reorganizations. Second, how this plays out depends on the histories and geographies of the gay villages under consideration (Nash and Gorman-Murray, forthcoming). Conceptualizations such as hybrid space, relational geographies and 'power geometries' allow us to envision a much more complex, unstable and temporally and spatially interconnected set of networks and nodes reflecting LGBTQ everyday experiences in urban spaces. LGBTQ people, as early adopters of new technologies, particularly mobile technologies and new media, are in a unique position to proffer distinctive understandings of how new technologies are transforming our relationship with urban spaces in ways that are fundamentally changing our understandings of the relationship between place, identity and social relations.

Bibliography

Aalbers, M.B. (2004) 'Creative Destruction through the Anglo-American Hegemony: A non-Anglo-American View on Publications, Referees and Language', *Area*, vol. 36, no. 3, pp. 319–22.

Aalbers, M.B. (2005) 'Big Sister is Watching You! Gender Interaction and the Unwritten Rules of the Amsterdam Red-light District', *Journal of Sex Research*, vol. 42, no. 1, pp. 54–62.

Aalbers, M.B. and Deinema, M. (2012) 'Placing Prostitution: The Spatial–Sexual Order of Amsterdam and its Growth Coalition', *City*, vol. 16, nos 1–2, pp. 129–45.

Aalbers, M.B. and Rossi, U. (2006) 'Beyond the Anglo-American Hegemony in Human Geography: A European Perspective', *GeoJournal*, vol. 67, no. 2, pp. 137–47.

Aalbers, M.B. and Sabat, M. (2012) 'Re-making a Landscape of Prostitution: The Amsterdam Red Light District', *City*, vol. 16, nos 1–2, pp. 112–28.

Abraham, J. (2002) 'Transnational Industrial Power, the Medical Profession and the Regulatory State: Adverse Drug Reactions and the Crisis over Halcion in the Netherlands and the UK', *Social Science and Medicine*, vol. 55, no. 9, pp. 1671–90.

Abraham, J. (2009) *Metropolitan Lovers: The Homosexuality of Cities*, Minneapolis, University of Minnesota Press.

Absi, P. (2013) 'The Future of an Institution from the Past: Accommodating Regulationism in Bolivia, from the Nineteenth to the Twenty-First Century', paper presented at Selling Sex in the City: Prostitution in World Cities, 1600 to the Present Conference, Amsterdam, 25–27 April.

ACARA (2013) *Australian Curriculum Health and Physical Education Consultation Report Version 1.2*, Sydney, ACARA [Online]. Available at http://www.acara.edu.au/verve/_resources/HPE-F-10-Draft_Consultation_Report-July_2013v2.pdf (accessed 1 March 2014).

ACMA (2013) *Communications Report 2011–2012 Series Report 3 – Smartphones and Tablets Take-up and Use in Australia Summary Report*, Canberra, Australian Government [Online]. Available at http://www.acma.gov.au/webwr/_assets/main/lib310665/report-3-smartphones_tablets-summary.pdf (accessed 1 March 2014).

ACME (2013) *Special Issue*, vol. 13, no. 1 [Online]. Available at http://www.acme-journal.org/volume13-1.html (accessed 2 April 2015).

Acquistapace, A. (2011) *Relazioni senza nome. Reti di affetti, solidarietà, intimità e cura oltre la 'coppia eterosessuale obbligatoria'*, University of Bologna [Online]. Available at http://smaschieramenti.noblogs.org/files/2013/07/Relazioni-senza-nome_Alessia-Acqui stapace_cc_web1.pdf (accessed 2 April 2015).

Adam, B. (2009) 'How Might We Create a Collectivity That We Would Want to Belong to?', in Halperin, D. and Traub, V. (eds) *Gay Shame*, Chicago, University of Chicago Press, pp. 301–11.

Adam, B., Duyvendak, J.M. and Krouwal, A., (eds) (1992) *The Global Emergence of Gay and Lesbian Politics: National Imprints of a Worldwide Movement*, Philadelphia, Temple University Press.

Adams, M., Oye, J. and Parker, T. (2003) 'Sexuality of Older Adults and the Internet: From Sex Education to Cybersex', *Sexual and Relationship Therapy*, vol. 18, no. 3, pp. 405–15.

Addison, J. and Comstock, M. (1998) 'Virtually Out: The Emergence of a Lesbian, Bisexual and Gay Youth Subculture', in Austin, J. and Willard, M. (eds) *Generations of Youth: Youth Cultures and History in Twentieth–Century America*, New York, New York University Press, pp. 367–78.

Adey, P. (2006) 'If Mobility is Everything Then It is Nothing: Towards a Relational Politics of (Im)mobilities', *Mobilities*, vol. 1, no. 1, pp. 75–94.

Adkins, L. (2002) *Revisions: Gender and Sexuality in Late Modernity*, Buckingham, Open University Press.

Adler, S. and Brenner, J. (1992) 'Gender and Space: Lesbians and Gay Men in the City', *International Journal of Urban and Regional Research*, vol. 16, no. 1, pp. 24–33.

Agamben, G. (1998 [1995]) *Homo Sacer: Sovereign Power and Bare Life* (trans. D. Heller–Roazen), Stanford, CA, Stanford University Press.

Agathangelou, A. (2004) *The Global Political Economy of Sex, Desire, Violence and Insecurity in Mediterranean Nation States*, London, Palgrave Macmillan.

Agenda 21 (1992) *UNCED* [Online]. Available at http://sustainabledevelopment.un.org/content/documents/Agenda21.pdf (accessed 10 April 2014).

Agender NZ (n.d.) [Online]. Available at http://agendernz.matrx.co.nz/ (accessed 5 March 2015).

Agustín, L.M. (2005) 'Migrants in the Mistress's House: Other Voices in the "Trafficking" Debate', *Gender, State and Society*, vol. 12, no. 1, pp. 96–117.

Agustin, L.M. (2007) *Sex at the Margins: Migrations, Labour Markets and the Rescue Industry*, London, Zed Books.

Agnew, J.A. (2011) 'Space and Place', in Agnew, J.A. and Livingstone D.N. (eds) *The Sage Handbook of Geographical Knowledge*, London, Sage, pp. 316–31.

Ahmed, S. (2006) *Queer Phenomenology: Orientations, Objects, Others*, Durham, NC, Duke University Press.

Ahmed, S., Casteneda, C., Fortier, A-M. and Sheller, M. (eds) (2003) *Uprootings/Regroundings: Questions of Home and Migration*, New York, Berg.

Akhavan, N., Bashi, G., Kia, M. and Shakhsari, S. (2007) *A Genre in the Service of Empire: An Iranian Feminist Critique of Diasporic Memoirs* [Online]. Available at http://www.payvand.com/news/07/feb/1007.html (accessed 1 July 2013).

Akin, M., Fernandez, M.I., Bowen, G.S. and Warren, J.C. (2008) 'HIV Risk Behaviors of Latin American and Caribbean Men Who Have Sex with Men in Miami, Florida', *American Journal of Public Health,* vol. 23, no. 5, pp. 341–8.

Alam, F. (2005) 'Gay Media's Failure to Accurately Report Stories Adds to Growing Islamophobia and Hatred Toward Islamic World', press release, Al-Faitha Foundation, 1 August.

Al-Bader, S., Frew, S.E., Essajee, I., Liu, V.Y., Daar, A.S. and Singer, P.A. (2009) 'Small but Tenacious: South Africa's Health Biotech Sector', *Nature Biotechnology*, vol. 27, pp. 427–45.

Albury, K. and Byron, P. (2014) 'Queering, Sexting and Sexualisation', *Media International Australia, Incorporating Culture and Policy*, no. 153, November, pp. 138–47.

Albury, K. and Crawford, K. (2012) Sexting, Consent and Young People's Ethics: Beyond *Megan's Story, Continuum*, vol. 26, no. 3, pp. 463–73.

Albury, K., Crawford, K., Byron, P. and Mathews, B. (2013) *Young People and Sexting in Australia: Ethics, Representation and the Law*, Sydney, ARC Centre for Creative Industries and Innovation and Journalism and Media Research Centre at The University of New South Wales.

Aldrich, R. (2004) 'Homosexuality and the City: An Historical Overview', *Urban Studies*, vol. 41, no. 9, pp. 1719–37. DOI: 10.1080/0042098042000243129.

Alexander, J. (2002) 'Queer Webs: Representations of LGBT People and Communities on the World Wide Web', *International Journal of Gay and Lesbian Studies*, vol. 7, nos 2–3, pp. 77–84.

Alexander, J. (2004) *In Their Own Words: LGBT Youth Writing the World Wide Web*, New York, GLAAD Center for the Study of Media and Society.

Alfasi, N. and Fenster, T. (2005) 'A Tale of Two Cities: Jerusalem and Tel Aviv in an Age of Globalization', *Cities*, vol. 22, no. 5, pp. 351–63.

Aljazeera (2014) 'Ethiopia Groups to Stage Anti-gay Protest', *Aljazeera*, 11 April [Online]. Available at http://www.aljazeera.com/news/africa/2014/04/ethiopia-groups-stage-anti-gay-protest-20144111342549830.html (accessed 5 May 2014).

Alldred, P. and David, M. (2007) *Get Real About Sex: The Politics and Practice of Sex Education*, Milton Keynes, Open University Press.

Allen, J. and Mellin, G. (1982) 'The New Epidemic', *American Journal of Nursing*, vol. 82, no. 11, pp. 1718–22.

Allen, L. (2005) 'Concrete and Classrooms: How Schools Shape Educational Research', *British Journal of Sociology of Education*, vol. 26, no. 4, pp. 491–504.

Allen, L. (2015) 'Sexual Assemblages: Mobile Phones/Young People/School', *Discourse: Studies in the Cultural Politics of Education*, vol. 36, no. 1, pp. 120–32.

Alsop, R., Fitzsimmons, A. and Lennon, K. (2002) *Theorising Gender*, Cambridge, Polity Press.

Alterovitz, S.S. and Mendelsohn, G.A. (2013) 'Relationship Goals of Middle-aged, Young-old, and Old-old Internet Daters: An Analysis of Online Personal Ads', *Journal of Aging Studies*, vol. 27, no. 2, pp. 159–65.

Althusser, L. (1971) 'Ideology and Ideological State Apparatus (Notes Toward an Investigation', in Althusser, L., *Lenin and Philosophy and Other Essays*, Delhi, Aakar Books, pp. 85–126 (this edition 2006).

Altman, D. (2001) *Global Sex*, Chicago, IL, University of Chicago Press.

Altman, L. (1981) 'Rare Cancer Seen in 41 Homosexuals', *New York Times*, 3 July, A20.

Altman, L. (1982) 'Clue Found on Homosexuals' Precancer Syndrome', *New York Times*, 18 June, B8.

Alvarez, W. (2013) 'Finding "Home" in/through Latinidad Ethnography: Experiencing Community in the Field with "My People"', *Liminalities: A Journal of Performance Studies*, vol. 9, no. 2, pp. 49–58. Available online at http://liminalities.net/9-2/ (accessed 15 April 2015).

Alvy, L.M., McKirnam, D.J., Mansergh, G., Kolbin, B., Colfax, G.N., Flores, S.A. and Hudson, S., Project MIX Study Group (2010) 'Depression is Associated with Sexual Risk among Men who Have Sex with Men, But is Mediated by Cognitive Escape and Self-efficacy', *AIDS and Behavior*, vol. 15, no. 6, pp. 1171–9.

Amar, P (2013) *The Security Archipelago: Human-Security States, Sexuality Politics, and the End of Neoliberalism*, Durham, NC, Duke University Press.

American Psychiatric Association (2013) *Diagnostic and Statistical Manual of Mental Disorders* (5th edn), Arlington, TX, APA.

AMFAR (2011) *Respect, Protect, Fulfill: Best Practices Guidance in Conducting HIV Research with Gay, Bisexual, and Other Men Who Have Sex with Men (MSM) in Rights-constrained Environments*, New York, AMFAR.

Amnesty International (2014) 'About LGBT Rights', *Amnesty International* [Online]. Available at http://www.amnestyusa.org/our-work/issues/lgbt-rights/about-lgbt-human -rights (accessed 30 March 2014).

Anacker, K.B. and Morrow-Jones, H.A. (2005) 'Neighborhood Factors Associated with Same-sex Households in US Cities', *Urban Geography*, vol. 26, no. 5, pp. 385–409.

Anderson, B. (1983) *Imagined Communities: Reflections on the Origin and Spread of Nationalism*, New York, Verso.

Anderson, T. (2005) 'Relationships among Internet Attitudes, Internet Use, Romantic Beliefs, and Perceptions of Online Romantic Relationships', *CyberPsychology and Behavior*, vol. 8, no. 6, pp. 521–31.

Andersson, J. (2009) 'East End Localism and Urban Decay: Shoreditch's Re-emerging Gay Scene', *London Journal*, vol. 34, no. 1, pp. 55–71.

Andersson, J. (2011) 'Vauxhall's Postindustrial Pleasure Gardens: "Death Wish" and Hedonism in 21st Century London', *Urban Studies*, vol. 48, no. 1, pp. 85–100.

Andrucki, M.J. and Elder, G.S. (2007) 'Locating the State in Queer Space: GLBT Non-profit Organizations in Vermont, USA', *Social & Cultural Geography*, vol. 8, no. 1, pp. 89–104.

Annany, M. (2011) 'The Curious Connection between Apps for Gay Men and Sex Offenders', *The Atlantic* [Online]. Available at http://www.theatlantic.com/technology/archive/2011/04/the-curious-connection-between-apps-for-gay-men-and-sex-offenders/237340/ (accessed 20 March 2014).

Annes, A. and Redlin, M. (2012a) 'Coming Out and Coming Back: Rural Gay Migration and the City', *Journal of Rural Studies*, vol. 28, pp. 56–68 [Online]. DOI: 10.1016/j.jrurstud.2011.08.005 (accessed 15 April 2015).

Annes, A. and Redlin, M. (2012b) 'The Caseful Balance of Gender and Sexuality: Rural Gay Men, the Heterosexual Matrix and "Effeminophobia"', *Journal of Homosexuality*, vol. 59, pp. 256–88.

Annes, A. and Redlin, M. (2013) 'Conceptual and Spatial Migrations: Rural Gay Men's Quest for Identity', in Gorman-Murray, A., Pini, B. and Bryant, L. (eds) *Sexuality, Rurality and Geography*, Lanham, MD, Lexington Books, pp. 129–41.

Aparício, F.R. and Chávez-Silverman, S. (eds) (1997) *Tropicalizations: Transcultural Representations of Latinidad*, Dartmouth, NH, Dartmouth/University Press of New England.

Appadurai, A. (1996) *Modernity at Large: Cultural Dimensions of Globalization*, Minneapolis, University of Minnesota Press.

Applicant S v MIMA (2004) HCA 25.

Ara és l'hora (2014) *El meu país i jo volem viure en llibertat* [Online]. Available at https://actua.araeslhora.cat/page/content/lesbianes-gais-bisexuals-trans-i-intersex-per-la-independencia/ (accessed 2 April 2015).

Armstrong, E.A. (2002) *Forging Gay Identities: Organizing Sexuality in San Francisco, 1950–1994*, Chicago, University of Chicago Press.

Arondekar, A. (2005) 'Without a Trace: Sexuality and the Colonial Archive', *Journal of the History of Sexuality*, vol.14, pp. 10–27.

Art and Geography (2013) 'Call for Papers', Art and Geography Conference, Lyon, 11–13 February [Online]. Available at http://artgeographie.sciencesconf.org/ (accessed 2 April 2015).

Ashworth, G., White, P. and Winchester, H. (1988) 'The Red Light District in the Western European City: A Neglected Aspect of the Urban Landscape', *Geoforum*, vol. 19, pp. 201–11.

Aslinger, B. (2010) 'PlanetOut and the Dichotomies of the Queer Media Conglomeration', in Pullen, C. and Cooper, M. (eds) *LGBT Identity and Online New Media*, New York and London, Routledge, pp. 113–23.

Assante, J. (1998) 'The kar.kid/*harimtu*. Prostitute or Single Woman? A Critical Review of the Evidence', *Ugarit-Forshungen*, vol. 30, pp. 5–96.

Assante, J. (2007) 'What Makes a "Prostitute" a Prostitute? Modern Definitions and Ancient Meanings', *Historiae*, vol. 4, pp. 117–32.

Associated Press (1983) 'Family Contact Studied in Transmitting AIDS', *New York Times*, 6 May, A21.

Associated Press (1984) 'U.S. Medical Study Singles Out a Man Who Carried AIDS', *New York Times*, 27 May, A25.

Associated Press (1987) 'Canadian Said to Have Had Key Role in Spread of AIDS', *New York Times*, 7 October, B7.

Atkins, M. and Laing, M. (2012) 'Walking the Beat and Doing Business: Exploring Spaces of Male Sex Work and Public Sex', *Sexualities*, vol. 15, no. 5–6, pp. 622–43.

Auerbach, D.M., Darrow, W.M., Jaffe, H.W. and Curran, J.W. (1984) 'A Cluster of Cases of the Acquired Immune Deficiency Syndrome: Patients Linked by Sexual Contact', *American Journal of Medicine*, vol. 76, March, pp. 487–92.

Austin, S. B. (1990) 'AIDS and Africa, United States Media and Racist Cantasy', *Cultural Critique*, vol. 14, pp. 129–41.

Australian Bureau of Statistics (2012) *Reflecting a Nation* [Online]. Available at http://www.abs.gov.au/ausstats/abs@.nsf/Lookup/2071.0main+features902012–2013 (accessed 28 November 2012).

Author Janet Mock joins Piers Morgan (2014) YouTube video, added by CNN [Online]. Available at www.youtube.com/watch?v=btmMVM23Ekk (accessed 9 August 2014).

Awwad, J. (2010) 'The Postcolonial Predicament of Gay Rights in the Queen Boat Affair', *Communication and Critical/Cultural Studies*, vol. 7, no. 3, pp. 318–36.

Ayres, T. (1999) 'China Doll: The Experience of Being a Gay Chinese Australian', in Jackson, P. and Sullivan, G. (eds) *Multicultural Queer: Australian Narratives*, New York, Haworth Press, pp. 87–97.

Azione gay e lesbica (ed.) (2004) *Gay, Lesbiche, Trans e Neoliberismo*. Florence, Azione Gay e Lesbica.

Baber, Z. (2002) 'Orientalism, Occidentalism, Nativism: The Culturalist Quest for Indigenous Science and Knowledge', *The European Legacy*, vol. 7, no. 6, pp. 747–58.

Babineau, G. (2001) 'The Prettiest One: Gaétan Dugas and the "AIDS Mary" Myth', *Xtra West*, 29 November, pp. 13–15 [Online]. Available at http://dailyxtra.com/ottawa/news/gaétan-dugas-and-the-aids-mary-myth (accessed 1 April 2014).

Bailey, A. (2009) 'Population Geography: Lifecourse Matters', *Progress in Human Geography*, vol. 33, no. 3, pp. 407–18.

Bailey, M. and Freedman, D. (eds) (2011) *The Assault on Universities. A Manifesto for Resistance*, London and New York, Pluto Press. Available online at http://search.ebscohost.com/login.aspx?direct=true&scope=site&db=nlebk&db=nlabk&AN=434975 (accessed May 12, 2013).

Bailey, M.M. and Shabazz, R. (2014) 'Editorial: Gender and Sexual Geographies of Blackness: Anti-black Heterotopias (Part 1)', *Gender, Place and Culture*, vol. 21, no. 3, pp. 316–21.

Bain, A.L. and Nash, C.J. (2007) 'The Toronto Women's Bathhouse Raid: Querying Queer Identities in the Courtroom', *Antipode*, vol. 39, no. 1, pp. 17–34 [Online]. DOI: 10.1111/j.1467–8330.2007.00504.x (accessed 15 April 2015).

Bajerski, A. (2011) 'The Role of French, German and Spanish Journals in Scientific Communication in International Geography', *Area*, vol. 43, no. 3, pp. 305–13.

Baldo, M. (2014) 'When the Body of the Queer Researcher is "Trouble"', *Lambda Nordica*, vol. 2, pp. 118–32.

Balsamo, B.A. (2000) 'The Virtual Body in Cyberspace', in Kennedy, D. and Kennedy, B.M. (eds) *The Cybercultures Reader*, London, Routledge, pp. 489–503.

Balzer, C. and Hutta, J.S. (2013) 'Identities and Citizenship under Construction: Historicising the "T" in LGBT Anti-violence Politics in Brazil', in Taylor, Y. and Addison, M. (eds) *Queer Presences and Absences*, Basingstoke, Palgrave Macmillan, pp. 69–90.

Banerjea, N. (2011) 'Voluntary Participation and Poor Women's Work: A Critical Examination of a Community Health Improvement Initiative in a Kolkata Slum', *Contemporary South Asia*, vol. 19, no. 4, pp. 427–40.

Baral, S., Adams, D., Lebona, J., Kaibe, B., Letsie, P., Tshehlo, R., Wirtz, A. and Beyrer, C. (2011) 'A Cross-sectional Assessment of Population Demographics, HIV Risks and Human Rights Contexts among Men Who Have Sex with Men in Lesotho', *Journal of the International AIDS Society*, vol. 14, no. 36 [Online]. DOI: 10.1186/1758–2652–14–36 (accessed 15 April 2015).

Baral, S., Trapence, G., Motimedi, F., Umar, E., Lipinge, S., Dausab, F. and Beyrer, C. (2009) 'HIV Prevalence, Risk for HIV Infection, and Human Rights among Men Who Have Sex with Men (MSM) in Malawi, Namibia, and Botswana', *PLoS one*, vol. 4, no. 3 [Online] e4997. DOI: 10.1371/journal.pone.0004997 (accessed 15 April 2015).

Barber, T. (2010) 'Stephanie is Wired: Who Shall Turn Him On?', in Pullen, C. and Cooper, M. (eds) *LGBT Identity and Online New Media*, New York, Routledge, pp. 245–57.

Bardin, L. (1977) *Análise de Conteúdo*, **Lisboa, Edições 70.**

Bargh, J.A. and McKenna, K.Y. (2004) 'The Internet and Social Life', *Annual Review of Psychology*, vol. 55, pp. 573–90.

Barker, M. (2005) 'This is My Partner, and This is my … Partner's Partner: Constructing a Polyamorous Identity in a Monogamous World', *Journal of Constructivist Psychology*, vol. 18, no. 1, pp. 75–88.

Barker, R. and Elliston, F. (1984) *The Philosophy of Sex*, New York, Buffalo University Press.

Barnett, C. (2012) 'Geography and Ethics: Placing Life in the Space of Reason', *Progress in Human Geography*, vol. 36, no. 3, pp. 379–88.

Barnett, T. and Blaikie, P. (1992) *AIDS in Africa: Its Present and Future*, London, Guilford Press.

Barnett, T. and Whiteside, A. (2003) *AIDS in the Twenty-first Century: Disease and Globalization*, Basingstoke and New York, Palgrave Macmillan.

Barnett, T. and Whiteside, A. (2006) *AIDS in the Twenty-first Century: Disease and Globalisation* (2nd edn), Basingstoke, Palgrave Macmillan.

Barnhurst, K.G. (ed.) (2007) *Media Q: Media/queered: Visibility and its Discontents*, New York, Peter Lang.

Barrett, D.C. and Pollack, L.M. (2005) 'Whose Gay Community? Social Class, Sexual Self–Expression and Gay Community Involvement', *The Sociological Quarterly*, vol. 46, pp. 437–56.

Barron, M. and Bradford, S. (2007) 'Corporeal Controls: Violence, Bodies and Young Gay Men's Identities', *Youth and Society*, vol. 39, no. 2, pp. 232–61.

Barry, K. (1979) *Female Sexual Slavery*, Englewood Cliffs, NJ, Prentice Hall.

Barton, B. (2010) '"Abomination" – Life as a Bible Belt Gay', *Journal of Homosexuality*, vol. 57, no. 4, pp. 465–84.

Bassett, C. (2009) 'Up the Garden Path: Or, How to Get Smart in Public', *Second Nature: International Journal of Creative Media*, vol. 1, no. 2, pp. 42–63.

Bassi, C. (2006) 'Riding the Dialectical Waves of Gay Political Economy: A Story from Birmingham's Commercial Gay Scene', *Antipode*, vol. 38, no. 2, pp. 213–35.

Bassi, C. (2010) '"It's New But Not That New": On the Continued Use of Old Marx', *Feminist Legal Studies*, vol. 18, no. 1, pp. 69–76.

Bassi, C. (2012) '"Shanghai Goes West": Reflections on the City's Gay Political Economy', in Hines, S. and Taylor, Y. (eds) *Sexualities: Past Reflections, Future Directions*, London, Palgrave Macmillan, pp. 226–45.

Baum, D. (2006) 'Women in Black and Men in Pink: Protesting Against the Israeli Occupation', *Social Identities*, vol. 12, no. 5, pp. 563–74.

Baute, N. (2008) 'Take a Walk on Someone Else's Wild Side', *The Star*, 6 September [Online]. Available at http://www.thestar.com/news/2008/09/06/take_a_walk_on_someone_elses_wild_side.html (accessed 15 May 2013).

Baym, N. (2010) *Personal Connections in the Digital Age*, Malden, MA, Polity.

Bech, H. (1997) *When Men Meet: Homosexuality and Modernity*, Chicago, University of Chicago Press.

Beck, U. and Beck-Gernsheim, E. (2002) *Individualisation*, London, Sage.

Bedoya, C.A., Mimiaga, M.J., Beauchamp, G., Donnell, D., Mayer, K. and Safren, S.A. (2012) 'Predictors of HIV Transmission, Risk Behavior and Seroconversion among Latino Men Who Have Sex with Men in Project EXPLORE', *AIDS and Behavior*, vol. 16, pp. 608–17.

Beemyn, B. (ed.) (1997) *Creating a Place for Ourselves: Lesbian, Gay, and Bisexual Community Histories*, London, Routledge.

Beemyn, G. and Rankin, S. (2011) *The Lives of Transgender People*, New York, Columbia University Press.

Belk, R. (2007) 'Why Not Share Rather than Own?', *Annals of the American Academy of Political and Social Science*, vol. 611, pp. 126–40.

Bell, D. (1994) 'In Bed with the State: Political Geography and Sexual Politics', *Geoforum*, vol. 25, pp. 445–52.

Bell, D. (1995a) 'Pleasure and Danger: The Paradoxical Spaces of Sexual Citizenship', *Political Geography*, vol. 14, no. 2, pp. 139–53.

Bell, D. (1995b) 'Perverse Dynamics, Sexual Citizenship and the Transformation of Intimacy', in Bell, D. and Valentine, G. (eds) *Mapping Desire: Geographies of Sexualities*, London, Routledge, pp. 304–17.

Bell, D. (2000) 'Farm Boys and Wild Men: Rurality, Masculinity and Homosexuality', *Rural Sociology*, vol. 65, pp. 547–61.

Bell, D. (2001) 'Fragments for a Queer City', in Bell, D., Binnie, J., Holliday, R., Longhurst, R. and Peace, R. (eds) *Pleasure Zones: Bodies, Cities, Spaces*, Syracuse, NY, Syracuse University Press, pp. 84–102.

Bell, D. (2006) 'Bodies, Technologies, Spaces: On "Dogging"', *Sexualities*, vol. 9, pp. 387–407 [Online]. DOI: 10.1177/1363460706068040 (accessed 15 April 2015).

Bell, D. and Binnie, J. (2000) *The Sexual Citizen: Queer Politics and Beyond*, Cambridge, Polity Press.

Bell, D. and Binnie, J. (2004) 'Authenticating Queer Space: Citizenship, Urbanism and Governance', *Urban Studies*, vol. 41, pp. 1807–20.

Bell, D., Binnie, J., Cream, J. and Valentine, G. (1994) 'All Hyped up and No Place to Go', *Gender, Place and Culture*, vol. 1, no. 1, pp. 37–47.

Bell, D. and Kennedy, B. M. (eds) (2000) *The Cybercultures Reader*, London, Routledge.

Bell, D. and Valentine, G. (eds) (1995a) *Mapping Desire: Geographies of Sexualities*, London, Routledge.

Bell, D. and Valentine, G. (1995b) 'Queer Country: Rural Lesbian and Gay Lives', *Journal of Rural Studies*, vol. 11, no. 2, pp. 113–22.

Benson, C.J. (2008) 'Crossing Borders: A Focus on Treatment of Transgender Individuals in U.S. Asylum Law and Society', *Whittier Law Review*, vol. 30, pp. 41–66.

Berg, L.D. (2012) 'Knowledge Enclosure, Accumulation by Dispossession, and the Academic Publishing Industry', *Political Geography*, vol. 31, no. 5, pp. 260–2.

Berg, L. and Millbank, J. (2009) 'Constructing the Personal Narratives of Lesbian, Gay and Bisexual Asylum Claimants', *Journal of Refugee Studies*, vol. 22, no. 2, pp. 195–223.

Berg, L. and Millbank, J. (2013) 'Developing a Jurisprudence of a Transgender Particular Social Group', in Spijkerboer, T. (ed.) *Fleeing Homophobia*, London, Routledge, pp. 121–53.

Berkovitch, N. and Helman, S. (2005) 'Global Social Movements', in Esseed, P., Goldberg, D.T. and Kobayashi, A. (eds) *A Companion to Gender Studies*, Oxford, Wiley-Blackwell, pp. 266–78.

Berkowitz, R. and Callen, M. (1983) *How to Have Sex in an Epidemic: One Approach*, New York, News From the Front.

Berland, J. (2005) 'Place', in Bennett, T., Grossberg, L. and Morris, M. (eds) *New Keywords: A Revised Vocabulary of Culture and Society*, Oxford, Blackwell, pp. 256–8.

Berlant, L. (1998) 'Intimacy: A Special Issue', *Critical Inquiry*, vol. 24, no. 2, pp. 281–8.

Berlant, L. and Freeman, E. (1993), 'Queer Nationality', in Warner, M. (ed.) *Fear of a Queer Planet: Queer Politics and Social Theory*, Minneapolis, University of Minnesota Press, pp. 193–229.

Berlant, L. and Warner, M. (1998) 'Sex in Public', *Critical Inquiry*, vol. 24, no. 2, pp. 547–66.

Berlant, L. and Warner, M. (2002) 'Sex in Public', in Warner, M. (ed.) *Publics and Counterpublics*, New York, Zone Books, pp. 187–208.

Bernstein, D., Shamir, H., Levenkron, N. and Amir, D. (2013) 'Sex Work and Migration: The Case of Tel Aviv and Jaffa, 1918–2000', paper presented at Selling Sex in the City: Prostitution in World Cities, 1600 to the Present Conference, Amsterdam, 25–27 April.

Berry, C., Martin, F. and Yue, A. (eds) (2003) *Mobile Cultures: New Media Inquiry on Asia*, Durham, NC, Duke University Press.

Bertone, C., Casiccia, A., Saraceno, C. and Torrioni, P. (eds) (2003) *Diversi da chi? Gay, lesbiche, transessuali in un'area metropolitana*, Milan, Guerini.

Best, U. (2009) 'The Invented Periphery: Constructing Europe in Debates About "Anglo Hegemony" in Geography', *Social Geography*, vol. 4, no. 1, pp. 83–91.

Betsky, A. (1997) *Queer Space: Architecture and Same-sex Desire*, New York City, William Morrow & Company.

Bey, H. (1991) *T.A.Z.: The Temporary Autonomous Zone, Ontological Anarchy, Poetic Terrorism*, Brooklyn, NY, Autonomedia.

Beyrer, C., Baral, S.D., van Griensven, F., Goodreau, S. M., Chariyalertsak, S., Wirtz, A.L. and Brookmeyer, R. (2012) 'Global Epidemiology of HIV Infection in Men Who Have Sex with Men', *The Lancet*, vol. 380, no. 9839, pp. 367–77 [Online]. DOI: http://dx.doi.org/10.1016/S0140-6736(12)60821-6 (accessed 15 April 2015).

Bhabha, H.K. (1983) 'The Other Question … ', *Screen*, vol. 24, no. 6, pp. 18–36.

Bhabha, H.K. (1990a) 'The Third Space: Interview with Homi Bhabha', in Rutherford, J. (ed.) *Identity: Community, Culture, Difference*, London, Wishart and Lawrence, pp. 207–21.

Bhabha, H.K. (1990b) *Nation and Narration*, London, Routledge.

Bhabha, H.K. (1994) *The Location of Culture*, London, Routledge.

Bhambra, G.K. (2007) *Rethinking Modernity: Postcolonialism and the Sociological Imagination*, London, Palgrave.

Bhambra, G.K. (2014) 'Postcolonial and Decolonial Dialogues', *Postcolonial Studies*, vol. 17, no. 2, pp. 115–21.

Bhaskaran, S. (2004) *Made in India: Decolonizations, Queer Sexualities, Trans/national Projects*, New York, Palgrave Macmillan.

Bianchi, F.T., Reisen, C.A., Zea, M.C., Poppen, P.J., Shedlin, M.G. and Penha, M.M. (2007) 'The Sexual Experiences of Latino Men Who Have Sex with Men Who Migrated to a Gay Epicentre in the USA', *Culture, Health and Sexuality*, vol 9, no 5, pp. 505–18.

Biehl, J. (2007) *Will to Live: AIDS Therapies and the Politics of Survival*, Princeton, NJ, Princeton University Press.

Binnie, J. (1994) 'The Twilight World of the Sadomasochist', in Whittle, S. (ed.) *The Margins of the City: Gay Men's Urban Lives*, Aldershot, Ashgate, pp. 157–71.

Binnie, J. (1995) 'Trading Places: Consumption, Sexuality and the Production of Queer Space', in Bell, D. and Valentine, G. (eds) *Mapping Desire: Geographies of Sexualities*, London, Routledge, pp. 166–81.

Binnie, J. (1997) 'Coming Out in Geography: Towards a Queer Epistemology', *Environment and Planning D: Society and Space*, vol. 15, pp. 223–37.

Binnie, J. (2004) *The Globalization of Sexuality*, London, Sage.

Binnie, J. (2007) 'Sexuality, the Erotic and Geography: Epistemology, Methodology and Pedagogy', in Browne, K., Lim, J. and Brown, G. (eds) *Geographies of Sexualities: Theory, Practice and Politics*, Farnham, Ashgate, pp. 29–38.

Binnie, J. (2014) 'Relational Comparison, Queer Urban and Worlding Cities', *Geography Compass*, vol. 8, no. 8, pp. 590–99.

Binnie, J., Holloway, J., Millington, S. and Young, C. (2006) *Cosmopolitan Urbanism*, New York, Routledge.

Binnie, J. and Klesse, C. (2012) 'Solidarities and Tensions: Feminism and Transnational LGBTQ Politics in Poland', *European Journal of Women's Studies*, vol. 19, no. 4, pp. 444–59.

Binnie, J. and Skeggs, B. (2004) 'Cosmopolitan Knowledge and the Production and Consumption of Sexualized Space: Manchester's Gay Village', *The Sociological Review*, vol. 52, no. 1, pp. 39–62.

Binnie, J. and Valentine, G. (1999) 'Geographies of Sexuality: A Review of the Progress', *Progress in Human Geography*, vol. 23, no. 2, pp. 175–87.

Bird, P. (2006) 'Prostitution in the Social World and Religious Rhetoric of Ancient Israel', in Faraone, C.A. and McClure, L. (eds) *Prostitutes and Courtesans of the Ancient World*, Madison, University of Wisconsin Press, pp. 40–58.

Bishop, J.E. (1982) 'New, Often-fatal Illness in Homosexuals Turns up in Women, Heterosexual Males', *Wall Street Journal*, 25 February, p. 8.

Bissell, D. (2008) 'Comfortable Bodies: Sedentary ffects', *Environment and Planning A*, vol. 40, no. 7, pp. 1697–712.

Bissell, D. (2014) 'Encountering Stressed Bodies: Slow Creep Transformations and Tipping Points of Commuting Mobilities', *Geoforum*, vol. 51, pp. 191–201.

Bissell, D. and Fuller, G. (eds) (2011) *Stillness in a Mobile World*, London, Routledge.

Bittman, M., Browne, J. E. and Wajcman, J. (2009) 'The Mobile Phone, Perpetual Contact and Time Pressure', *Work, Employment and Society*, vol. 23, no. 4, pp. 673–91.

Björklund, J. (2013) 'Coming Out, Coming In: Geographies of Lesbian Existence in Contemporary Swedish Youth Novels', in Gorman-Murray, A., Pini, B. and Bryant, L. (eds) *Sexuality, Rurality, and Geography*, Lanham, MD, Lexington, pp. 159–71.

Bjønness, J. (2008) 'Between Emotional Politics and Biased Practices – Prostitution Policies, Social Work, and Women selling Sexual Services in Denmark', *Sexuality Research and Social Policy*, vol. 9, no. 3, pp. 192–202.

Blanchette, T. (2013) '"Seeing beyond Prostitution": Work, Agency and the Organization of Sex Workers', paper presented at Selling Sex in the City: Prostitution in World Cities, 1600 to the Present Conference, Amsterdam, 25–27 April.

Blanchette, T. and Schettini, C. (2013) 'Sex Work in Rio de Janeiro: "More than Tolerated, Effectively Managed"', paper presented at Selling Sex in the City: Prostitution in World Cities, 1600 to the Present Conference, Amsterdam, 25–27 April.

Blidon, M. (2007) 'Ville et homosexualité, une relation à l'épreuve de la cartographie', in Mattei, M-F. and Pumain, D. (eds) *Données urbaines 5*, Paris, Anthropos, pp. 67–76.

415

Blidon, M. (2008a) 'La casuistique du baiser – L'espace public, un espace hétéronormatif', *EchoGéo*, vol. 5 [Online]. Available at http://echogeo.revues.org/5383 (accessed 15 April 2015).

Blidon, M. (2008b) 'Géographie de la sexualité ou sexualité du géographe? Remarques sur le sexe de l'enquêteur', Symposium 'À travers l'espace de la méthode: les dimensions du terrain en géographie', Arras, France, June [Online]. Available at http://hal-paris1. archives-ouvertes.fr/halshs-00422392/fr/ (accessed 13 April 2015).

Blidon, M. (2013) 'Analyser les trajectoires géographiques des gays. Présupposés et données disponibles', *Regards Sociologiques*, vol. 45–46, pp. 71–82.

Blidon, M. and Guérin, F. (2013) 'Un rêve urbain? La diversité des parcours migratoires des gays', *Sociologie*, vol. 2, no. 4, pp. 119–38.

Blunt, A. and Dowling, R. (2006) *Home*, London, Routlege.

Boellstorff, T. (2007) *A Coincidence of Desires: Anthropology, Queer Studies, Indonesia*, Durham, NC, Duke University Press.

Bokovic, S.P. and Schwartz, R.A. (1981) 'Kaposi's Sarcoma Presenting in the Homosexual Man – A New and Striking Phenomenon!', *Arizona Medicine*, vol. 38, no. 12, pp. 902–4.

Bolding, G., Davis, M., Hart, G., Sherr, L. and Elford, J. (2005) 'Gay Men Who Look for Sex on the Internet: Is There More HIV/STI Risk with Online Partners?', *Aids: Official Journal of the International AIDS Society*, vol. 19, no. 9, pp. 961–8.

Bondi, L. (1992) 'Gender and Dichotomy', *Progress in Human Geography*, vol. 14, no. 3, pp. 438–45.

Bondi, L. (1998) 'Sexing the City', in Fincher, R. and Jacobs, J. (eds) *Cities of Difference*, New York, Guilford.

Bordo, S. (1986) 'The Cartesian Masculinization of Thought', *Signs*, vol. 11, pp. 239–56.

Bornstein, K. (1994) *Gender Outlaw: On Men, Women, and the Rest of US*, New York, Routledge.

Bortoluci, J.H. and Jansen, R.S. (2013) 'Toward a Postcolonial Sociology: The View from Latin America', *Political Power and Social Theory*, vol. 24, pp. 199–229.

Bourcier, M-H. (1998) *Q comme Queer*, Lille, GayKitschCamp.

Bourcier, M-H. (2001) *Queer Zones 1, Politiques des identités sexuelles et des savoirs*, Paris, Éditions Amsterdam [Online]. Available at www.academia.edu/4478733/Queer_Zones _1_Politiques_des_identit%C3%A9s_sexuelles_et_des_savoirs_Paris_Editions_ Amsterdam_Poche_2011_3rd_edition_(accessed 2 April 2015).

Bourcier, M-H. (2005) *Queer Zones 2, Sexpolitiques*, Paris, La Fabrique [Online]. Available at www.academia.edu/4478214/Sexpolitiques._Queer_Zones_2_Paris_La_Fabrique_2005 (accessed 2 April 2015).

Bourcier, M-H. (2011) *Queer Zones 3, Identités, Cultures, Politiques*, Paris, Éditions Amsterdam [Online]. Available at www.academia.edu/4482086/Queer_Zones_3_Identit%C3%A9s_ Cultures_Politiques_Paris_Editions_Amsterdam_2011(accessed 2 April 2015).

Bourcier, M-H. (2014) '50 nuances de genres (et de sexes) ou plus? Entre karaoké de la différence sexuelle et politiques multisexgenres', in Leduc, G. (ed.) *Comment faire des études genres avec de la littérature, Masquereading*, Paris, L'Harmattan [Online]. Available at www.academia.edu/10060263/50_nuances_de_genres_et_de_sexes_ou_plus_Entre_kar aok%C3%A9_de_la_diff%C3%A9rence_sexuelle_et_politiques_multigenres (accessed 2 April 2015).

Bouthillette, A-M. (1997) 'Queer and Gendered Housing: A Tale of Two Neighbourhoods in Vancouver', in Ingram, G.B., Bouthillette, A-M. and Retter, Y. (eds) *Queers in Space: Communities, Public Spaces, Sites of Resistance*, Seattle, Bay Press, pp. 213–32.

boyd, d. (2001) 'Sexing the Internet: Reflections on the Role of Identification in Online Communities', paper presented at Sexualities, Medias, Technologies, University of

Surrey, 21–22 June [Online]. Available at www.danah.org/papers/SexingTheInternet. conference.pdf (accessed 21 March 2008).

boyd, d. (2014) *It's Complicated: The Social Lives of Networked Teens*, New Haven, CT, and London, Yale University Press.

boyd, d. and Marwick, A. (2011) 'Social Privacy in Networked Publics: Teens Attitudes, Practices, and Strategies', in the proceedings of A Decade In Internet Time: Oxford Internet Institute Symposium on the Dynamics of the Internet and Society, Oxford, 21–24 September.

Boyd, N.A. (2006) 'Bodies in Motion: Lesbian and Transsexual Histories', in Stryker, S. and Whittle, S. (eds) *The Transgender Studies Reader*, New York, Routledge, pp. 420–33.

Boylan, J. (2003) *She's Not There: A Life in Two Genders*, New York, Broadway Paperbacks.

Brah, A. (1996) *Cartographies of Diaspora: Contesting Identities*, New York, Routledge.

Braidotti, R. (2003) 'Becoming Woman: Or Sexual Difference Revisited', *Theory, Culture & Society*, vol. 20, pp. 43–64.

Braidotti, R., Charkiewicz, E., Häusler, S. and Wieringa, S. (1994) *Women, the Environment and Sustainable Development: Towards a Theoretical Synthesis*, London, Zed Books.

Brandzel, A. (2005) 'Queering Citizenship? Same-Sex Marriage and the State', *GLQ: A Journal Of Lesbian and Gay Studies*, vol. 11, no. 2, pp. 171–204.

Branigan, T. (2011) 'Chinese Hit Talent Show to be Replaced with Housework Programme', *The Guardian*, 18 September [Online]. Available at http://www.theguardian.com/world/2011/sep/18/chinese-talent-show-housework-programme (accessed 16 March 2012).

Branwyn, G. (2000) 'Compu–sex: Erotica for Cybernauts', in Bell, D. and Kennedy, B.M. (eds) *The Cybercultures Reader*, London, Routledge, pp. 396–402.

Bratton, B.J. (2009) 'iPhone City', *Architectural Design*, vol. 79, no. 4, pp. 90–97.

Brennan, R.O. and Durack, D.T. (1981) 'Gay Compromise Syndrome', *The Lancet*, vol. 318, no. 8259, pp. 1338–9.

Bresnahan, K.A. (2011) 'The Board of Immigration Appeals's New "Social Visibility" Test for Determining "Membership of a Particular Social Group" in Asylum Claims and its Legal and Policy Implications', *Berkeley Law Review*, vol. 29, pp. 649–79.

Bretherton, C. (1998) 'Global Environmental Politics: Putting Gender on the Agenda?', *Review of International Studies*, vol. 24, no. 1, pp. 85–100.

Brickell, C. (2000) 'Heroes and Invaders: Gay and Lesbian Pride Parades and Public/Private Distinction in New Zealand Media Accounts', *Gender, Place and Culture*, vol. 7, no. 2, pp. 163–78.

Brickell, C. (2012) 'Sexuality, Power and the Sociology of the Internet', *Current Sociology*, vol. 60, no. 1, pp. 28–44.

Brickell, K. (2008) '"Fire in the House": Gendered Experiences of Drunkenness and Violence in Siem Reap, Cambodia', *Geoforum*, vol. 39, pp. 1667–75.

Brickell, K. (2012) '"Mapping" and "Doing" Critical Geographies of Home', *Progress in Human Geography*, vol. 36, pp. 225–44.

Brooks, O. (2011) '"Guys! Stop Doing It!" Young Women's Adoption and Rejection of Safety Advice when Socializing in Bars, Pubs and Clubs', *British Journal of Criminology*, vol. 51, no. 4, pp. 635–51.

Brophy, J.E. (2010) 'Developing a Corporeal Cyberfeminism: Beyond Cyberutopia', *New Media & Society*, vol. 12, no. 6, pp. 929–45.

Brot Bord (2013) 'Somewhere under the Rainbow: Mercantilización y asimilación de la disidencia sexual', in Solá, M. and Urko, E. (eds) *Transfeminismos: Epistemes fricciones y flujos*, Txalaparta, Tafalla, pp. 153–66.

Brott, E. (2006) 'Migrant British Women Producing "Selves" through Lap Dancing Work', *Feminist Review*, vol. 83, pp. 23–41.

Brown, G. (2004) 'Sites of Public (Homo)sex and the Carnivalesque Spaces of Reclaim the Streets', in Lees, L. (ed.) *The Emancipatory City? Paradoxes and Possibilities*, London, Sage, pp. 91–107.

Brown, G. (2006) 'Cosmopolitan Camouflage: (Post-)gay Space in Spitalfields, East London', in Binnie, J., Holloway, J., Millington, S. and Young, C. (eds) *Cosmopolitan Urbanism*, New York, Routledge, pp. 130–45.

Brown, G. (2007a) 'Mutinous Eruptions: Autonomous Spaces of Radical Queer Activism', *Environment and Planning A*, vol. 39, no. 11, pp. 2685–98.

Brown, G. (2007b) 'Autonomy, Affinity and Play in the Spaces of Radical Queer Activism', in Browne, K., Lim, J. and Brown, G. (eds) *Geographies of Sexualities: Theory, Practivces and Politics*, Aldershot, Ashgate, pp. 195–205.

Brown, G. (2008) 'Urban (Homo)sexualities: Ordinary Cities and Ordinary Sexualities', *Geography Compass*, vol. 2, no. 4, pp. 1215–31.

Brown, G. (2009) 'Thinking Beyond Homonormativity: Performative Explorations of Diverse Gay Economies', *Environment and Planning A*, vol. 41, no. 6, pp. 1496–510 [Online]. DOI: 10.1068/a4162 (accessed 16 April 2015).

Brown, G. (2012) 'Homonormativity: A Metropolitan Concept that Denigrates "Ordinary" Gay Lives', *Journal of Homosexuality*, vol. 59, no. 7, pp. 1065–72.

Brown, G. (forthcoming) 'Marriage and the Spare Bedroom: Exploring the Sexual Politics of Austerity in Britain', *ACME: An International E-journal for Critical Geographies*.

Brown, G., Browne, K., Elmhirst, R. and Hutta, S. (2010) 'Sexualities in/of the Global South', *Geography Compass*, vol. 4, no. 10, pp. 1567–79.

Brown, G., Kraftl, P., Pickerill, J. and Upton, C. (2012) 'Holding the Future Together: Towards a Theorisation of the Spaces and Times of Transition', *Environment and Planning A*, vol. 44, no. 7, pp. 1607–23.Brown, G., Maycock, B. and Burns, S. (2005) 'Your Picture is Your Bait: Use and Meaning of Cyberspace among Gay Men', *Journal of Sexual Research*, vol. 42, no. 1, pp. 63–73.

Brown, G. and Pickerill, J. (2009) 'Space for Emotion in the Spaces of Activism', *Emotion, Space and Society*, vol. 2, no. 1, pp. 24–35.

Brown, M. (1995a) 'Sex, Scale and the "New Urban Politics": HIV-prevention Strategies from Yaletown, Vancouver', in Bell, D. and Valentine, G. (eds) *Mapping Desire*, London, Routledge, pp 245–63.

Brown, M. (1995b) 'Ironies of Distance: An Ongoing Critique of the Geographies of AIDS', *Environment and Planning D: Society and Space*, vol. 13, no. 2, pp. 159–83.

Brown, M. (1997a) *RePlacing Citizenship: AIDS Activism & Radical Democracy*, New York, Guilford.

Brown, M. (1997b) 'Radical Politics out of Place? The Curious Case of ACT UP Vancouver', in Pile, S. and Kieth, M. (eds) *Geographies of Resistance*, London, Routledge, pp. 152–67.

Brown, M. (2000) *Closet Space: Geographies of Metaphor from the Body to the Globe*, London, Routledge.

Brown, M. (2006) 'Sexual Citizenship, Political Obligation and Disease Ecology in Gay Seattle', *Political Geography*, vol. 25, no. 8, pp. 874–98.

Brown, M. (2007) 'Working Political Geography through Social Movement Theory: The Case of Gay and Lesbian Seattle', in Cos, K.R., Low, M. and Robinson, J. (eds) *The Sage Handbook of Political Geography*, London, Sage, pp. 285–304.

Brown, M. (2009) '2008 Urban Geography Plenary Lecture – Public Health as Urban Politics, Urban Geography: Venereal Biopower in Seattle, 1943–1983', *Urban Geography*, vol. 30, no. 1, pp. 1–29.

Brown, M. (2012) 'Gender and Sexuality I: Intersectional Anxieties', *Progress in Human Geography*, vol. 36, no. 4, pp. 541–50.

Brown, M. (2014) 'Gender and Sexuality II: There Goes the Gayborhood?', *Progress in Human Geography*, vol. 38, no. 3, pp. 457–65.

Brown, M. and Knopp, L. (2006) 'Places or Polygons: Governmentality, Scale, and the Census in *The Gay and Lesbian Atlas, Population, Space and Place*, vol. 12, no. 4, pp. 223–42.

Brown, M. and Knopp, L. (2010) 'Between Anatamo- and Bio-politics: Geographies of Sexual Health in Wartime Seattle', *Political Geography*, vol. 29, no. 7, pp. 392–403.

Brown, M. and Knopp, L. (2014) 'The Birth of the (Gay) Clinic', *Health and Place*, vol. 28, pp. 99–108.

Brown, P.L. (2007) 'Gay Enclaves Face Prospect of Being Passé', *New York Times*, 30 October, p. 17.

Brown, T., Craddock, S. and Ingram, A. (2012) 'Critical Interventions in Global Health: Governmentality, Risk and Assemblage', *Annals of the Association of American Geographers*, vol. 102, no. 5, pp. 1182–9.

Browne, K. (2004) 'Genderism and the Bathroom Problem: (Re)materialising Sexed Sites, (Re)creating Sexed Bodies', *Gender, Place and Culture*, vol. 11, no. 3, pp. 331–46.

Browne, K. (2006) 'Challenging Queer Geographies', *Antipode*, vol. 38, pp. 885–93.

Browne, K. (2007a) 'A Party with Politics? (Re)making LGBTQ Pride Spaces in Dublin and Brighton', *Social & Cultural Geography*, vol. 8, no. 1, pp. 63–87.

Browne, K. (2007b) '(Re)making the Other, Heterosexualising Everyday Space', *Environment and Planning A*, vol. 39, no. 4, pp. 996–1014.

Browne, K. (2008) 'Imagining Cities, Living the Other: Between Gay Urban Idyll and Rural Lesbian Lives', *The Open Geography Journal*, vol. 1, pp. 25–32.

Browne, K. (2011) 'Beyond Rural Idylls: Imperfect Lesbian Utopias at Michigan Women's Music Festival', *Journal of Rural Studies*, vol. 27, no. 1, pp. 13–23.

Browne, K. (2013) 'Special Issue: New Sexual and Gendered Landscapes', *Geoforum*, vol. 49, pp. 203–5.

Browne, K. (2014) 'Contestando O Privilégio Anglo-Americano Na Produção Do Conhecimento Em Geografias Das Sexualidades E De Gênero', in Silva, J.M. and Nascimento e Silva, M.G. (eds) *Interseccionalidades, Gênero e Sexualidades na Análise Espacial*, Ponta Grossa, Todapalavra, pp. 135–56.

Browne, K. and Bakshi, L. (2011) 'We Are Here to party? Lesbian, Gay, Bisexual and Trans Leisurescapes beyond Commercial Gay Scenes', *Leisure Studies*, vol. 30, no. 2, pp. 179–96.

Browne, K. and Bakshi, L. (2013a) *Ordinary in Brighton? LGBT Activisms and the City*, Aldershot, Ashgate.

Browne, K. and Bakshi, L. (2013b) 'Insider Activists: The Fraught Possibilities of LGBT Activism From Within', *Geoforum*, vol. 49, pp. 253–62.

Browne, K. and Ferreira, E. (eds) (forthcoming) *Lesbian Geographies: Gender, Place and Power*, Aldershot, Ashgate.

Browne, K. and Lim, J. (2010) 'Trans Lives in the "Gay Capital of the UK"', *Gender, Place and Culture*, vol. 17, no. 5, pp. 615–33.

Browne, K., Lim, J. and Brown, G. (2007) 'Introduction, or Why Have a Book on Geographies of Sexualities?', in Browne, K., Lim, J. and Brown, G. (eds) *Geographies of Sexualities: Theory, Practice and Politics*, Farnham, Ashgate.

Browne, K. and McGlynn, N. (2013) 'Rural Lesbian, Gay, Bisexual and Trans Equalities: English Legislative Equalities in an Era of Austerity', in Gorman-Murray, A., Pini, B. and Bryant, L. (eds) *Sexuality, Rurality and Geography*, Lanham, MD, Lexington Books, pp. 35–49.

Browne, K. and Nash, C.J. (2009) 'Lesbian Geographies', in Kitchin, R. and Thrift, N. (eds) *International Encyclopaedia of Human Geographies*, London, Elsevier, pp. 187–92.

Browne, K. and Nash, C.J. (2010) *Queer Methods and Methodologies: Intersecting Queer Theories and Social Science Research*, London, Ashgate.

Browne, K. and Nash, C.J. (2014a) 'Transnational Resistances to Lesbian, Gay, Bisexual and Trans Equalities', *Journal of Human Rights*, vol. 13, no. 3, pp. 322–36.

Browne, K. and Nash, C.J. (2014b) 'Resisting LGBT Rights Where "We Have Won": Canada and Great Britain', *Journal of Human Rights*, vol. 13, no. 3, pp. 322–36.

Browne, K., Nash, C.J. and Hines, S. (2010) 'Introduction: Towards Trans Geographies', *Gender, Place and Culture*, vol. 17, no. 5, pp. 573–7.

Brown-Saracino, J. (2011) 'From the Lesbian Ghetto to Ambient Community: The Perceived Costs and Benefits of Integration for Community', *Social Problems*, vol. 58, no. 3, pp. 361–88.

Bruce, D. and Harper, G. (2011) 'Operating Without a Safety Net: Gay Male Adolescents and Emerging Adults' Experiences of Marginalization and Migration, and Implications for Theory of Syndemic Production of Health Disparities', *Health Education & Behavior*, vol. 38, no. 4, pp. 367–78.

Brundtland, G. (1987) *Our Common Future: The World Commission on Environment and Development*, Oxford, Oxford University Press.

Bryant, L. and Pini, B. (2011) *Gender and Rurality*, London, Routledge.

Brydum, S. (2014) 'Zimbabwe's President Threatens to Deport LGBT-supportive Diplomats' Advocate. com, 18 April [Online]. Available at http://www.advocate.com/world/2014/04/18/zimbabwes-president-threatens-deport-lgbt-supportive-diplomats (accessed 4 May 2014).

Bryson, M. (2006) 'New Media and Sexual Subcultures: Critical Perspectives on Research Problematics, Possibilities, and Practices', *Journal of Gay and Lesbian Issues in Education*, vol. 3, no. 4, pp. 109–18.

Buchanan, P. (1983) 'AIDS Disease: It's Nature Striking Back', *New York Post*, 24 May, p. 31.

Buckingham, C. (2009) 'Kvetching for some Cruising' [Online]. Available at http://homopop.com/taxonomy/term/106 (accessed 11 October 2009).

Budd, J. (2011) *The Thought of Work*, Ithaca, NY, Cornell University Press.

Bull, M. (2004) 'Automobility and the Power of Sound', *Theory, Culture and Society*, vol. 21, no. 4/5, pp. 243–59.

Bulman, D.E. (2005) 'A Constructivist Approach to HIV/AIDS Education for Women within the Maritime Provinces of Canada', *International Journal of Lifelong Education*, vol. 24, no. 6, pp. 475–87.

Bumiller, K. (2008) *In an Abusive State: How Neoliberalism Appropriated the Feminist Movement Against Sexual Violence*, Durham, NC, Duke University Press.

Burston, J. (2003) 'War and the Entertainment Industries: New Research Priorities in the Era of Cyber-patriotism', in Thussu, D.K. and Freedman, D. (eds) *War and the Media: Reporting Conflict 24/7*, London, Sage, pp. 163–75.

Busarello, R. (2011) 'Untitled', in Pustianaz (ed.) *Queer in Italia. Differenze in movimento*. Pisa, Edizioni ETS, pp. 52–9.

Buss, D. and Herman, D. (2003) *Globalizing Family Values: The Christian Right in International Politics*, Minneapolis, University of Minnesota Press.

Butler, J. (1990) *Gender Trouble: Feminism and the Subversion of Identity*, New York, Routledge.

Butler, J. (1992) 'Contingent Foundations: Feminism and the Question of Postmodernism', in Butler, J. and Scott, J.W. (eds) *Feminists Theorise the Political*, New York and London, Routledge, pp. 153–70.

Butler, J. (1993) *Bodies That Matter: On the Discursive Limits of Sex*, New York, Routledge.

Butler, J. (1997a) 'Merely Cultural', *Social Text*, vol. 15, no. 3/4, pp. 265–77.

Butler, J. (1997b) *The Psychic Life of Power: Theories in Subjection*, Stanford. CA, Stanford University Press.

Butler, J. (2004) *Undoing Gender*, London and New York, Routledge.

Butler, R. (1999) 'Double the Trouble or Twice the Fun? Disabled Bodies in the Gay Community', in Butler, R. and Parr, H. (eds) *Mind and Body Spaces: Geographies of Illness, Impairment and Disability*, London, Routledge.

Buttram, M. and Kurtz, S. (2013) 'Risk and Protective Factors Associated with Gay Neighbourhood Residence', *American Journal of Men's Health*, vol. 7, pp. 110–18.

Butz, D. (2010) 'Autoethnography as Sensibility', in DeLyser, D., Herbert, S., Aitken, S., Crang, M. and McDowell, L. (eds) *The Sage Handbook of Qualitative Geography*, London, Sage, pp. 138–55.

Cabezas, A.L. (2006) 'The Eroticization of Labor in Cuba's All-inclusive Resorts: Performing Race, Class and Gender in the New Tourist Economy', *Social Identities*, vol. 12, no. 5, pp. 507–21.

Cabezas, A.L. (2009) *Economies of Desire: Sex and Tourism in Cuba and the Dominican Republic*, Philadelphia, PA, Temple University Press.

Cain, P.A. (1993) 'Litigation for Lesbian and Gay Rights: A Legal History', *Virginia Law Review*, vol. 79, no. 7, pp. 1551–41.

Caldeira, T.P.R. (2000) *City of Walls: Crime, Segregation, and Citizenship in São Paulo*, Berkeley, University of California Press.

Califia, P. (2000) *Public Sex: The Culture of Radical Sex*, San Francisco, CA, Cleis Press.

Cambridge Online Dictionary (2015) 'Prostitute' [Online]. Available at http://dictionary. cambridge.org/dictionary/british/prostitute (accessed 14 April 2015).

Cambridge Online Dictionary (2015) 'Prostitution' [Online]. Available at http://dictionary. cambridge.org/dictionary/british/prostitution (accessed 14 April 2015).

Cambrollé, M. (2008) *La transexualidad no es queer* [Online]. Available at http://archivo. dosmanzanas.com/index.php/archives/5697 (accessed 5 March 2014).

Cameron, D. (2014) 'Straight Talking: The Socioliguistics of Heterosexuality', *Langage et Société*, vol. 148, pp. 75–93.

Cameron, S. (2004) 'Space, Risk and Opportunity: The Evolution of Paid Sex Markets', *Urban Studies*, vol. 41, no. 9, pp. 1643–57.

Campbell, C. (2003) *Letting Them Die: How HIV Prevention Programs Often Fail*, Oxford, James Currey.

Campbell, J.E. (2004) *Getting It Online: Cyberspace, Gay Male Sexuality and Embodied Identity*, New York, Harrington Park Press.

Campbell, J. (2005) 'Outing PlanetOut: Surveillance, Gay Marketing and Internet Portals', *New Media and Society*, vol. 7, no. 5, pp. 663–83.

Canaday, M. (2009) *The Straight State: Sexuality and Citizenship in Twentieth-Century America*, Princeton, NJ, Princeton University Press.

Cant, B. (ed.) (1997) *Invented Identities? Lesbians and Gays Talk about Migration*, London, Cassel.

Cantú, L. (2009) *The Sexuality of Migration: Border Crossings and Mexican Immigrant Men*, New York, New York University Press.

Capmany, M.A. (1973) *El Feminsme a Catalunya*, Barcelona, Editorial Nova Terra.

Carpiano, R., Kelly, B., Easterbrook, A. and Parsons, J. (2011) 'Community and Drug Use among Gay Men: The Role of Neighbourhoods and Networks', *Journal of Health and Social Behavior*, vol. 52, no. 1, pp. 74–90.

Carr, E.H. (1987) *What is History?*, London, Penguin Books.

Carrara, S. and Simões, J.A. (2007) 'Sexualidade, cultura e política: a trajetória da identidade homossexual masculina na antropologia brasileira', *Cadernos Pagu*, vol. 28, pp. 65–99.

Carrillo, H. (2004) 'Sexual Migration, Cross-cultural Sexual Encounters and Sexual Health', *Sexuality Research and Social Policy*, vol 1, pp. 58–70.

Carroll, L. (1865) *Alice's Adventures in Wonderland*, London, Macmillan & Co.

Carter, A. (2005) *Direct Action and Democracy Today*, London, Polity Press.

Casa (2011) 'Call for Submissions: Cabinet of Queeriosities' [Online]. Available at http://bowmanartscentre.blogspot.ca/2011/01/call-for-submissions-cabinet-of-queer.html (accessed 7 May 2014).

Casey, M. (2004) 'De-dyking Queer Space(s): Heterosexual Female Visibility in Gay and Lesbian Spaces', *Sexualities*, vol. 7, no. 4, pp. 446–61.

Casey, M. (2007) 'The Queer Unwanted and their Undesirable Otherness', in Browne, K., Lim, J. and Brown, G. (eds) *Geographies of Sexualities*, Farnham, Ashgate, pp. 125–36.

Cassidy, E. (2013) 'Gay Men, Social Media and Self-presentation: Managing Identities in Gaydar, Facebook and Beyond', unpublished PhD thesis, Brisbane, Queensland University of Technology.

Castelli Gattinara, P. and Froio, C. (2014) 'Discourse and Practice of Violence in the Italian Extreme Right: Frames, Symbols, and Identity–Building in CasaPound Italia', *International Journal of Conflict and Violence*, vol. 8, no. 1 [Online]. Available at http://www.ijcv.org/earlyview/339.pdf (accessed 16 April 2015).

Castells, M. (1977) *The Urban Question: A Marxist Approach* (trans. A. Sheridan), London, Edward Arnold.

Castells, M. (1983) *The City and the Grassroots: A Cross-cultural Theory of Urban Social Movements*, Berkeley, University of California Press.

Castells, M. and Murphy, K. (1982), 'Cultural Identity and Urban Structure: The Spatial Organization of San Francisco's Gay Community', in Fainstein, N. and Fainstein, S. (eds) *Urban Policy under Capitalism*, Beverly Hills, CA, Sage, pp. 237–59.

Castoriadis, C. (1991) *Philosophy, Politics, Autonomy: Essays in Political Philosophy*, Oxford, Oxford University Press.

Castro-Gómez, S. (2007) 'Decolonizar La Universidad. La Hybris Del Punto Cero Y El Diálogo De Saberes', in Castro-Gómez, S. and Grosfoguel, R. (eds) *El Giro Decolonial: Reflexiones Para Una Diversidad Epistémica Más Allá Del Capitalismo Global*, Bogotá, DC, Siglo del Hombre Editores: Universidad Central, Instituto de Estudios Sociales Contemporáneos, IESCO-UC: Pontificia Universidad Javeriana, Instituto de Estudios Sociales y Culturales, Pensar, pp. 79–91.

Castro-Gómez, S. (2008) '(Post)Coloniality for Dummies: Latin American Perspectives on Modernity, Coloniality, and the Geopolitics of Knowledge', in Moraña, M., Dussel, E. and Jauregui, C.A. (eds) *Coloniality at Large*, Durham, NC, Duke University Press, p. 259–85.

Cattan, N. and Clerval, A. (2011) 'Un droit à la ville? Réseaux virtuels et centralités éphémères des lesbiennes à Paris', *Justice Spatiale*, vol. 3 [Online]. Available at http://www.parisgeo.cnrs.fr/spip.php?article5178 (accessed 10 September 2012).

Cattan, N. and Vanolo, A. (2014) 'Gay and Lesbian Emotional Geographies of Clubbing: Reflections from Paris and Turin', *Gender, Place & Culture*, vol. 21, no. 9, pp. 1158–75.

Catungal, J.P. (2013) 'Ethno-specific Safe Houses in the Liberal Contact Zone: Race Politics, Place-making and the Genealogies of the AIDS Sector in Global–Multicultural Toronto', *ACME: An International E–Journal for Critical Geographies*, vol. 12, no. 2, pp. 305–30.

CAWI–ITVF (2014) *Equity & Inclusion in Our Cities (2013–2016)* [Online]. Available at www.cawi-ivtf.org/equity-inclusion (accessed 30 September 2014).

CDC [Gottlieb, M.S. et al.] (1981a) '*Pneumocystis* Pneumonia – Los Angeles', *Morbidity and Mortality Weekly Report*, vol. 30, no. 21, pp. 250–52 [Online]. Available at http://www.cdc.gov/mmwr/preview/mmwrhtml/june_5.htm (accessed 1 April 2014).

CDC [Friedman-Kien, A. et al.] (1981b) 'Kaposi's Sarcoma and *Pneumocystis* Pneumonia among Homosexual Men – New York City and California', *Morbidity and Mortality Weekly Report*, vol. 30, no. 25, pp. 305–7.

CDC [Curran, J.W. et al.] (1982a) 'Task Force on Kaposi's Sarcoma and Opportunistic Infections: Epidemiologic Aspects of the Current Outbreak of Kaposi's Sarcoma and Opportunistic Infections', *New England Journal of Medicine*, vol. 306, no. 4, pp. 248–52.

CDC [Hensley, G.T. et al.] (1982b) 'Opportunistic Infections and Kaposi's Sarcoma among Haitians in the United States', *Morbidity and Mortality Weekly Report*, vol. 31, no. 26, pp. 360–61 [Online]. Available at http://www.cdc.gov/mmwr/preview/mmwrhtml/00001123. htm (accessed 1 April 2014).

CDC [Ehrenkranz, H.J. et al.] (1982c) '*Pneumocystisis carinii* Pneumonia among Persons with Hemophilia A', *Morbidity and Mortality Weekly Report*, vol. 31, no. 27, pp. 365–7 [Online]. Available at http://www.cdc.gov/mmwr/preview/mmwrhtml/00001126.htm (accessed 1 April 2014).

CDC [Ammann, A. et al.] (1982d) 'Possible transfusion-associated Acquired Immune Deficiency Syndrome (AIDS) – California', *Morbidity and Mortality Weekly Report*, vol 31, no. 48, pp. 652–4 [Online]. Available at http://www.cdc.gov/mmwr/preview/ mmwrhtml/00001203.htm (accessed 1 April 2014).

CDC [O'Reilly, R. et al.] (1982e) 'Unexplained Immunodeficiency and Opportunistic Infections in Infants – New York, New Jersey, California', *Morbidity and Mortality Weekly Report*, vol. 31, no. 49, pp. 665–7 [Online]. Available at http://www.cdc.gov/mmwr/ preview/mmwrhtml/00001208.htm (accessed 1 April 2014).

CDC [Fannin, S., et al.] (1982f) 'A Cluster of Kaposi' Sarcoma and *Pneumocystis carinii* Pneumonia among Homosexual Male Residents of Los Angeles and Orange Counties, California', *Morbidity and Mortality Weekly Report*, vol. 31, no. 23, pp. 305–7 [Online]. Available at http://www.cdc.gov/mmwr/preview/mmwrhtml/00001114.htm (accessed 1 April 2014).

CDC [Harris, C. et al.] (1983) 'Immunodeficiency among Female Sexual Partners of Males with Acquired Immune Deficiency Syndrome (AIDS)', *Morbidity and Mortality Weekly Report*, vol. 31, no. 52, pp. 697–8 [Online]. Available at http://www.cdc.gov/mmwr/ preview/mmwrhtml/00001221.htm (accessed 1 April 2014).

CDC [Handsfield, H. et al.] (1985) 'Heterosexual Transmission of Human T-Lymphotropic Virus Type III/Lymphadenopathy-Associated Virus', *Morbidity and Mortality Weekly Report*, vol. 34, no. 37, pp. 561–3 [Online]. Available at http://www.cdc.gov/mmwr/ preview/mmwrhtml/00000610.htm (accessed 1 May 2014).

CDC [Castro, K.G. et al.] (1992) '1993 Revised Classification System for HIV Infection and Expanded Surveillance Case Definition for AIDS among Adolescents and Adults', *Morbidity and Mortality Weekly Report*, vol. 41, RR-17, pp. 1–17 [Online]. Available at http://www.cdc.gov/mmwr/preview/mmwrhtml/00018871.htm (accessed 1 May 2014).

Cervera, M. (2014) *Desde Catalunya con Amor: Feminismos, 9-N y Derecho a Decidir* [Online]. Available at http://www.feministas.org/desde-catalunya-con-amor.html (accessed 20 November 2014).

Chambers, S.A. (2009) 'A Queer Politics of the Democratic Miscount', *Borderlands E–journal*, vol. 8, no. 2 [Online]. Available at http://www.borderlands.net.au/ (accessed 10 May 2014).

Chambré, S.M. (2006) *Fighting for Our Lives: New York's AIDS Community and the Politics of Disease*, New Brunswick, NJ, Rutgers University Press.

Chang, C.F. and Chen, M.H. (2013) 'Dependency, Globalization and Overseas Sex-related Consumption by East Asians', *International Journal of Tourism Research*, vol. 15, no. 6, pp. 521–34.

Chapkis, W. (2002) 'The Meaning of Sex', in Williams, C.L. and Stein, A. (eds) *Sexuality and Gender*, Malden & Oxford, Blackwell Publishers.

Chapkis, W. (2003) 'Trafficking, Migration, and the Law Protecting Innocents, Punishing Immigrants', *Gender and Society*, vol. 17, no. 6, pp. 923–37.

Charle, J. (2009) 'Gays Can Marry, But They Can't Kiss in Public', *Pretoria News*, 19 August.

Chasin, A. (2000) *Selling Out: The Gay and Lesbian Movement Goes to Market*, New York, Palgrave.

Chatterton, P. (2006) '"Give up Activism" and Change the World in Unknown Ways: Or, Learning to Walk with Others on Uncommon Ground', *Antipode*, vol. 38, no. 2, pp. 259–82.

Chatterton, P. (2010) 'So What Does It Mean to be Anti-capitalist? Conversations with Activists from Urban Social Centers', *Urban Studies*, vol. 47, no. 6, pp. 1205–24.

Chatterton, P. and Pickerill, J. (2010) 'Everyday Activism and Transitions Towards Post-capitalist Worlds', *Transactions of the Institute of British Geographer*, vol. 35, pp. 475–90.

Chauncey, G. (1994) *Gay New York: Gender, Urban Culture, and the Making of the Gay Male World, 1890–1940*, New York, Basic Books.

Chavez, K. (2013) *Queer Migration Politics: Activist Rhetoric and Coalitional Possibilities*, Chamapign, University of Illinois Press.

Chen Shi Hai v MIMA (2000) 201 CLR 293.

Cheng, S. (2010) *On the Move for Love. Migrant Entertainers and the U.S. Military in South Korea*, Philadelphia, Pennsylvania University Press.

Chetcuti, N. (2010) *Se dire lesbienne. Vie de couple, sexualité, representation de soi*, Paris, Éditions Payot & Rivages.

Chiou, W-B. (2006) 'Adolescents' Sexual Self-disclosure on the Internet: Deindividuation and Impression Management', *Adolescence*, vol. 41, pp. 547–61.

Chirimuuta, R. (1997) *AIDS, Africa and Racism*, London, Free Association Books.

Chisholm, D. (2005) *Queer Constellations: Subcultural Space in the Wake of the City*, London, University of Minnesota Press.

Cho, S., Crenshaw, K.W. and McCall, L. (2013) 'Toward a Field of Intersectionality Studies: Theory, Applications, and Praxis', *Signs: Journal of Women in Culture and Society*, vol. 38, no. 4, pp. 785–810.

Choi, J.H. (2006) 'Living in Cyworld: Contextualising Cy-ties in South Korea', in Bruns, A. and Jacobs, J. (eds) *Uses of Blogs*, New York, Peter Lang, pp. 173–86.

Choi, K.H., Han, C., Paul, J. and Ayala, G. (2011) 'Strategies for Managing Racism and Homophobia among U.S. Ethnic and Racial Minority Men Who Have Sex with Men', *AIDS Education and Prevention*, vol. 23, no. 2, pp. 145–58.

Chonin, N. (2006) 'MMORPG! WOW! TOS! GLBT! Sexual Harassment!' [Online]. Available at http://www.sfgate.com/entertainment/article/MMORPG-WOW-TOS-GLBT-Sexual-Har assment-2505160.php (accessed 17 April 2012).

Chua, B.H. (1997) *Political Legitimacy and Housing: Stakeholding in Singapore*, New York, Routledge.

City of Lethbridge (2013) *Lethbridge Census: Count Yourself in 2013 Census Results*. City of Lethbridge, Lethbridge, Alberta [Online]. Available at: www.lethbridge.ca/census (accessed 17 March 2014).

Clémençon, R. (2012) 'Welcome to the Anthropocene Rio+ 20 and the Meaning of Sustainable Development', *The Journal of Environment & Development*, vol. 21, no. 3, pp. 311–38.

Clement, E. (2006) *Love for Sale. Courting, Treating and Prostitution in New York City, 1900–1954*, Chapel Hill, University of North Carolina Press.

Clift, J. (2010) 'Health Information, STDs, and the Internet: Implications for Gay Men', in Pullen, C. and Cooper, M. (eds) *LGBT Identity and Online New Media*, Abingdon, Routledge, pp. 258–68.

Cline, R. and Haynes, K. (2001) 'Consumer Health Information-seeking on the Internet: The State of the Art', *Health Education Research*, vol. 16, no. 6, pp. 671–92.

Clinton, H.R. (2011) 'Remarks in Recognition of International Human Rights Day', Human Rights Day Speech presented at Palais des Nations, Geneva, Switzerland [Online]. Available at http://www.state.gov/secretary/20092013clinton/rm/2011/12/178368.htm (accessed 1 May 2014).

Cloete, A., Simbayi, L.C., Kalichman, S.C., Strebel, A. and Henda, N. (2008) 'Stigma and Discrimination Experiences of HIV-positive Men Who Have Sex with Men in Cape Town, South Africa', *AIDS Care*, vol. 20, no. 9, pp. 1105–10.

Cloke, P. and Johnston, R. (2005) 'Deconstructing Human Geography's Binaries', in Cloke, P. and Johnston, R. (eds) *Spaces of Geographical Thought: Deconstructing Human Geography's Binaries*, London, Sage, pp. 1–20.

CMARD Team Lethbridge (2011) *Building Bridges: A Welcoming and Inclusive Lethbridge Community Action Plan 2011–2021*, Lethbridge, Alberta, City of Lethbridge.

Cobbina, J.E., Miller, J. and Brunson, R.K. (2008) 'Gender, Neighborhood Danger, and Risk-avoidance Strategies among Urban African-American Youths', *Criminology*, vol. 46, no. 3, pp. 673–709.

Cock, J. (2003) 'Engendering Gay and Lesbian Rights: The Equality Clause in the South African Constitution', *Women's Studies International Forum*, vol. 26, no. 1, pp. 35–45.

Cohen, E. (2006) 'Free and Unfree Sexual Work: An Economic Analysis of Athenian Prostitution', in Faraone, C.A. and McClure, L. (eds) *Prostitutes and Courtesans of the Ancient World*, Madison, University of Wisconsin Press, pp. 95–124.

Cohn, S.E., Klein, J.D., Mohr, J.E., van der Horst, C.M. and Weber, D.J. (1994) 'The Geography of AIDS: Patterns of Urban and Rural Migration', *Southern Medical Journal*, vol. 87, vol. 6, pp. 599–606.

Collard, A. and Contrucci, J. (1988) *The Rape of the Wild: Man's Violence against Animals and the Earth*, London, The Women's Press.

Collini, S. (2012) *What are Universities For?*, London, New York, Penguin.

Collins, A. (2004a) 'Sexual Dissidence, Enterprise and Assimilation: Bedfellows in Urban Regeneration', *Urban Studies*, vol. 41, pp. 1789–806.

Collins A. (2004b) 'Sexuality and Sexual Services in the Urban Economy and Socialscape: An Overview', *Urban Studies*, vol. 41, no. 9, pp. 1631–41.

Collins, A. (2006) 'Sexual Dissidence, Enterprise and Assimilation: Bedfellows in Urban Regeneration', in Collins, A. (ed.) *Cities of Pleasure: Sex and the Urban Socialscape*, London, Routledge, pp. 159–76.

Collins, D. (2012) 'Gay Hospitality as Desiring Labor: Contextualizing Transnational Sexual Labor', *Sexualities*, vol. 15, nos 5–6, pp. 538–53.

Collins, D. and Coleman, T. (2008) 'Social Geographies of Education: Looking within, and beyond, School Boundaries', *Geography Compass*, vol. 2, no. 1, pp. 281–99.

Collins, P.H. (1990) *Black Feminist Thought: Knowledge, Power and the Politics of Empowerment*, Boston, MA, Unwin Hyman.

Coll-Planas, G. (2010) *La voluntad y el deseo. La construcción social del género y la sexualidad: el caso de lesbianas, gays y trans*, Barcelona, Egales.

Coll-Planas, G. and Missé, M. (2013) 'El papel de la transformación corporal en el activismo trans', presentation at International Congress of Critical Social Psychology: Discourse, Materiality and Politics, Universitat Autònoma de Barcelona, Barcelona, 6–8 February.

Colomina, B. (1992) *Sexuality and Space*, New York, Princeton Architectural Press.

Colorado Bureau of Investigation (2014) *Convicted Sex Offender Search* [Online]. Available at: http://sor.state.co.us/?SOR=home.youshouldknow (accessed 20 March 2014).

Comaroff, J. (2007) 'Beyond Bare Life: AIDS, (Bio)politics and the Neoliberal Order', *Public Culture*, vol. 19, no. 1, pp. 197–219.

Comaroff, J. and Comaroff, J.L. (2012) 'Theory From the South: Or, How Euro-America is Evolving Toward Africa', *Anthropological Forum*, vol. 22, no. 2, pp. 113–31.

Combahee River Collective (1982) 'A Black Feminist Statement', in Hull, G., Scott, P.B. and Smith, B. (eds) *All the Women are White, All the the Blacks are Men, But Some of Us are Brave*, New York, The Feminist Press, pp. 13–22.

Compton, D.L.R. and Baumle, A.K. (2012) 'Beyond the Castro: The Role of Demographics in the Selection of Gay and Lesbian Enclaves', *Journal of Homosexuality*, vol. 59, no. 10, pp. 1327–55.

Conant, M.A. (1996) 'Founding the KS Clinic, and Continued AIDS Activism', an Oral History Conducted in 1992 by Sally Smith Hughes, in *The AIDS Epidemic in San Francisco: The Medical Response, 1981–1984, Volume II*, Berkeley, CA, Regional Oral History Office, The Bancroft Library, University of California, pp. 93–238.

Connell, R. (2007) *Southern Theory: The Global Dynamics of Knowledge in Social Science*, Cambridge, Polity.

Conradson, D. and McKay, D. (2007) 'Translocal Subjectivities: Mobility, Connection, and Emotion', *Mobilities*, vol. 2, pp. 167–74.

Conron, K. J., Scott, G., Stowell, G.S. and Landers, S. (2011) 'Transgender Health in Massachusetts: Results from a Household Probability Sample of Adults', *American Journal of Public Health*, vol. 102, pp. 118–22.

Consoli, M. (2000) *Independence Gay. Alle origini del Gay Pride*, Bolsena, Massari.

Constable, N. (2009) The Commodification of Intimacy: Marriage, Sex, and Reproductive Labor, *Annual Review of Anthropology*, vol. 38, pp. 9–64.

Convention Relating to the Status of Refugees 1951 (1951) SI: 1951, Geneva, United Nations.

Conway, L. (2002) 'How Frequently Does Transsexualism Occur?', December 2002 [Online]. Available at http://ai.eecs.umich.edu/people/conway/TS/TSprevalence.html (accessed 10 May 2014).

Cook, I.R. and Whowell, M. (2011) 'Visibility and the Policing of Public Space', *Geography Compass*, vol. 5, no. 80, pp. 610–22.

Cooke, B. and Kothari, U. (eds) (2001) *Participation: The New Tyranny?*, London, Zed Books.

Cooke, T.J. and Rapino, M. (2007) 'The Migration of Partnered Gays and Lesbians between 1995 and 2000', *The Professional Geographer*, vol. 59, no. 3, pp. 285–97.

Cooper, A., McLoughlin, I.P. and Campbell, K. (2000) 'Sexuality in Cyberspace: Update for the 21st Century', *CyberPsychology and Behavior*, vol. 3, pp. 521–36.

Cooper, F. and Stoler, A. (eds) (1997) *Tensions of Empire: Colonial Cultures in a Bourgeois World*, Berkeley, University of California Press.

Cooper, M. and Dzara, K. (2010) 'The Facebook Revolution: LGBT Identity and Activism', in Pullen, C. and Cooper, M. (eds) *LGBT Identity and Online New Media*, New York, Routledge, pp. 100–12.

Cooper, M. and Waldby, C. (2014) *Clinical Labor: Tissue Donors and Research Subjects in the Global Bioeconomy*, Durham, NC, Duke University Press.

Coopersmith, J. (1998) 'Pornography, Technology and Progress', *Icon*, vol. 4, pp. 94–125.

Coopersmith, J. (2000) 'Pornography, Videotape and the Internet', *Technology and Society Magazine IEEE*, vol. 19, no. 1, pp. 27–34.

Conner, S. (2013) 'Selling Sex in the City: Paris', paper presented at Selling Sex in the City: Prostitution in World Cities, 1600 to the Present Conference, Amsterdam, 25–27 April.

Corlouer, M. (2013) 'Quelles places pour les lesbiennes?', in Alessandrin, A. and Raibaud, Y. (eds) *Géographie des homophobies*, Paris, Editions Armand Colin, pp. 1954–5.

Cornwall, R. (1997) 'Queer Political Economy: The Social Articulation of Desire', in Gluckman, A. and Reed, B. (eds) *Homo Economics: Capitalism, Community, and Lesbian and Gay Life*, London, Routledge, pp. 89–122.

Correa, S. and Parker, R. (2004) 'Sexuality, Human Rights and Demographic Thinking: Connections and Disjunctions in a Changing World in Sexuality Research and Policy', *Journal of NSRC*, vol. 1, no. 1, pp. 15–39.

Corteen, K. (2002) 'Lesbian Safety Talk: Problematizing Definitions and Experiences of Violence, Sexuality and Space', *Sexualities*, vol. 5, no. 3, pp. 259–80.

Couch, D. and Liamputtong, P. (2008) 'Online Dating and Mating: The Use of the Internet to Meet Sexual Partners', *Qualitative Health Research*, vol. 18, no. 2, pp. 268–79.

Couldry, N. (2012) *Media, Society, World: Social Theory and Digital Media Practice*, Cambridge, Polity.

Cowen, D. (2003) 'From the American Lebensraum to the American Living Room: Class, Sexuality, and the Scaled Production of "Domestic" Intimacy', *Environment and Planning D: Society and Space*, vol. 22, pp. 755–71.

Cox, L. (2011) 'Acting while Trans: A Look Back at 2011 for Transgender Actors in the Media', *The Huffington Post*, 23 December [Online]. Available at www.huffingtonpost.com/laverne-cox/transgender-actors-2011_b_1162279.html (accessed 5 July 2014).

Craddock, S. (2000) 'Disease, Social Identity, and Risk: Rethinking the Geography of AIDS', *Transactions of the Institute of British Geographers*, vol. 25, pp. 153–68.

Crang, M., Crosbie, T. and Graham, S.D.N. (2007) 'Technology, Timespace and the Remediation of Neighbourhood Life', *Environment and Planning A*, vol. 39, no. 10, pp. 2405–22.

Crepaz, N. and Marks, G. (2001) 'Are Negative Affective States Associated with HIV Sexual Risk Behaviours? A Meta-analytic Review', *Health Psychology*, vol. 20, pp. 291–9.

Crenshaw, K. (1991) 'Mapping the Margins: Intersectionality, Identity Politics, and Violence against Women of Colour', *Stanford Law Review*, vol. 43, pp. 1241–99.

Cresswell, T. (2006) *On the Move: Mobility in the Modern Western World*, London, Routledge.

Cresswell, T. (2010) 'Towards a Politics of Mobility', *Environment and Planning D: Society and Space*, vol. 28, no. 1, pp. 17–31.

Cresswell, T. and Merriman, P. (eds) (2011) *Geographies of Mobilities: Practices, Spaces, Subjects*, Farnham, Ashgate.

Crick, M. (1982) 'Anthropological Field Research, Meaning Creation and Knowledge Construction', in Parkin, D. (ed.) *Semantic Anthropology*, London and New York, Academic Press, pp. 15–37.

Crimp, D. (1987) 'How to Have Promiscuity in an Epidemic', *October*, vol. 43, pp. 237–71.

Crimp, D. and Rolston, A. (1990) *AIDS DemoGraphics*, Seattle, WA, Bay Press.

Crook, T. (2008) 'Norms, Forms and Beds: Spatializing Sleep in Victorian Britain', *Body & Society*, vol. 14, no. 4, pp. 15–35.

Crowhurst, I., Outshoorn, J. and Skilbrei, M.L. (2012) 'Introduction: Prostitution Policies in Europe', *Sexuality Research and Social Policy*, vol. 9, no. 3, pp. 1–5.

Crowley, M.S. (2010) 'how r u??? Lesbian and Bi-identified Youth on MySpace', *Journal of Lesbian Studies*, vol. 14, no. 1, pp. 52–60.

Cruells, M. and Coll-Planas, G. (2013) 'Challenging Equality [olicies: The Emerging LGBT Perspective', *European Journal of Women's Studies*, vol. 20, no. 2, pp. 122–37.

Cruz-Malavé, A. and Manalansan, M.F. (eds) (2002) *Queer Globalizations: Citizenship and the Afterlife of Colonialism*, New York, New York University Press.

Cupples, J. and Glynn, K. (2013) 'Postdevelopment Television? Cultural Citizenship and the Mediation of Africa in Contemporary TV Drama', *Annals of the Association of American Geographers*, vol. 103, no. 4, pp. 1003–21.

Curran, J.W. and Jaffe, H.W. (2011) 'AIDS: The Early Years and the CDC's Response', *Morbidity and Mortality Weekly Report. Supplement*, vol. 60, no. 4, pp. 64–9 [Online]. Available at http://www.cdc.gov/mmwr/preview/mmwrhtml/su6004a11.htm (accessed 1 April 2014).

Dabashi, H. (2006) 'Native Informers and the Making of the American Empire', *Al-Ahram Weekly*, 1–7 June [Online]. Available at http://weekly.ahram.org.e.g./2006/797/special.htm (accessed 1 July 2013).

da Costa, B.P. (2010a) 'Espaço social, cultura e território: o processo de microterritorialização homoerótica', *Espaço e Cultura*, vol. 27, pp. 25–37.

da Costa, B.P. (2010b) 'Geografias das interações culturais no espaço urbano: o caso das territorializações das relações homoeróticas e/ou homoafetivas', *Revista Latino Americana de Geografia e Gênero*, vol. 1, no. 2, pp. 207–24.

da Costa, B.P. (2010c) 'Geografias das Representações Sobre o Homoerotismo', *Revista Latino Americana de Geografia e Gênero*, vol. 1, no. 1, pp. 21–38.

da Costa, B.P. (2012a) 'As microterritorialidades nas cidades: reflexões sobre as convivências homoafetivas e/ou homoeróticas', *Terr@ Plural*, vol. 6, no. 2, pp. 257–71.

da Costa, B.P. (2012b) 'Pequenas cidades e diversidades culturais no interior do Estado do Rio Grande do Sul: o caso das microterritorializações homoeróticas em Santo Ângelo e Cruz Alta–RS', *Revista Latino Americana de Geografia e Gênero*, vol. 3, no. 1, pp. 37–53.

da Costa, B.P. (2012c) 'Pequenas cidades e diversidades culturais no interior do Estado do Rio Grande do Sul: o caso das microterritorializações homoeróticas de Santa Maria, Bagé, Alegrete, Uruguaiana e Itaqui', *Revista Latino Americana de Geografia e Gênero*, vol. 3, no. 2, pp. 125–37.

Dagnino, E. (2005) '"We All Have Rights, But ... ": Contesting Concepts of Citizenship in Brazil', in Kabeer, N. (ed) *Inclusive Citizenship: Meanings and Expressions*, London, Zed Bbooks, pp. 149–63.

Dahoma, M., Johnston, L.G., Holman, A., Miller, L.A., Mussa, M., Othman, A., Khatib, A., Issa, R., Kendall, C. and Kim, A.A. (2011) 'HIV and Related Risk Behaviour among Men Who Have Sex with Men in Zanzibar, Tanzania: Results of a Behavioural Surveillance Study', *AIDS and Behaviour*, vol. 15, pp. 186–92.

Daly, M. (2013) 'The Meth-Fuelled, Week-Long Orgies Ravaging London's Gay Sex Party Scene' [Online]. Available at http://www.vice.com/en_uk/read/the-week-long-meth-fuelled-sex-parties-taking-over-londons-gay-scene (accessed 1 September 2015) .

Daliot-Bul, M. (2007) 'Japan's Mobile Technoculture: The Production of a Cellular Playscape and its Cultural Implications', *Media, Culture and Society*, vol. 29, no. 6, pp. 954–71.

Danielson, M.T. (2009) *Homecoming Queers: Desire and Difference in Chicana Latina Cultural Production*, New Brunswick, NJ and London, Rutgers University Press.

Darznik, J. (2008) 'The Perils and Seductions of Home: Return Narratives of the Iranian Diaspora', *MELUS*, vol. 33, no. 2, pp. 55–71.

Darznik, J. (2011) *The Good Daughter*, New York, Grand Central Publishing.

da Silva, F.B. (2011) *Turismo e Lazer Sexual na Cidade de São Paulo*, São Paulo, Universidade de São Paulo.

Davidson, J. (1998) *Prostitution, Power and Freedom*, Cambridge, Polity.

Davis, A. (1998) 'I Used to be Your Sweet Mama: Ideology, Sexuality and Domesticiy', in David, A. (ed.) *Blues Legacies and Black Feminism*, New York, Vintage Books, pp. 3–41.

Davis, K. (2008) 'Intersectionality as Buzzword: A Sociology of Science Perspective on What Makes a Feminist Theory Successful', *Feminist Theory*, vol. 9, no. 1, pp. 67–85.

Day, K. (1999) 'Introducing Gender to the Critique of Privatized Public Space', *Journal of Urban Design*, vol. 4, no. 2, pp. 155–78.

Day, K. (2001) 'Constructing Masculinity and Women's Fear in Public Space in Irvine, California', *Gender, Place and Culture*, vol. 8, no. 2, pp. 109–27.

Day, K. (2006) 'Being Feared: Masculinity and Race in Public Space', *Environment and Planning A*, vol. 38, pp. 569–86.

Dean, T. (2009) *Unlimited Intimacy: Reflections on the Subculture of Barebacking*, Chicago, University of Chicago Press.

De Certeau, M. (1984) *The Practice of Everyday Life* (trans. S. Rendall), Berkeley, University of California Press.

De Genova, N. (2010) 'The Queer Politics of Migration: Reflections on "Illegality" and Incorrigibility', *Studies in Social Justice*, vol. 4, no. 2, pp. 101–26.

Deinema, M. and Aalbers, M.B. (2015) 'A Global Red-Light City? Prostitution in Amsterdam as a Real-and-Imagined Place', in De Waard, M. (ed.) *Imagining Global Amsterdam*, Amsterdam, Amsterdam University Press, pp. 273–87.

Delacoste, F. and Alexander, P. (1988) *Sex Work: Writings by Women in the Sex Industry*, London, Women's Press.

Delany, S.R. (1999) *Times Square Red, Times Square Blue*, New York, New York University Press.

De la Peña, T., Serna, C., Negrón-Muntaner, F., Troyano, E. and Tropicana, C. (2009) 'Complicating Community', in Danielson, M.T. (ed.) *Homecoming Queers: Desire and Difference in Chicana Latina Cultural Production*, London, Rutgers University Press, pp. 92–120.

De Lauretis, T. (1987) *Technologies of Gender*, Blomington, Indiana University Press.

Del Casino, V.L. Jr (2006) 'NGOs and the Reorganization of "Community Development": Mediating the Flows of People Living with HIV and AIDS', in Sleigh, A.C., Leng, C.H., Yeoh, B.S.A., Hong, P.K. and Safman, R. (eds) *Population Dynamics and Infectious Diseases in Asia*, Singapore, World Scientific Publishing.

Del Casino, V.L. Jr (2007a) 'Health/Sexuality/Geography', in Browne, K., Lim, L. and Brown, G. (eds) *Geographies of Sexualities: Theory, Practice and Politics*, Farnham, Ashgate, pp. 39–52.

Del Casino, V.L. Jr (2007b) 'Flaccid Theory and the Geographies of Sexual Health in the Age of Viagra', *Health and Place*, vol. 13, no. 4, pp. 904–11.

Del Casino, V.L. Jr (2009) *Social Geography: A Critical Introduction*, Chichester, John Wiley & Sons.

Del Casino, V.L. Jr (2012) 'Drugs, Sex, and the Geographies of Sexual Health in Thailand, Southeast Asia', *Social and Cultural Geography*, vol. 13, no. 2, pp. 109–25.

Deleuze, G. (1968) *Difference and Repetition*, London and New York, Continuum (this edition 2001).

Deleuze, G. (1969) *The Logic of Sense*, London, Athlone (this edition 2004).

Della Porta, D. and Diani, M. (2006) *Social Movements: An Introduction* (2nd edn), Malden, Oxford and Carlton, Blackwell Publishing.

D'Emilio, J. (1983) *Sexual Politics, Sexual Communities: The Making of a Homosexual Minority in the United States, 1940–1970*, Chicago, University of Chicago Press.

D'Emilio, J. (1993) 'Capitalism and Gay Identity', in Abelove, H., Barale, M. and Halperin, D. (eds) *The Lesbian and Gay Studies Reader*, London, Routledge, pp. 467–78.

Democracy Now (2014) *'Black Trans Bodies are Under Attack': Freed Activist CeCe McDonald, Actress Laverne Cox Speak Out* [Video online]. Available at http://www.democracynow.org/2014/2/19/black_trans_bodies_are_under_attack (accessed 26 March 2015).

Denzin, N.K. (1997) *Interpretive Ethnography: Ethnographic Practices for the Twenty-first Century*, Thousand Oaks, CA, Sage.

de Souza e Silva, A. (2006) 'From Cyber to Hybrid: Mobile Technologies as Interfaces of Hybrid Spaces', *Space and Culture*, vol. 9, no. 3, pp. 261–78.

de Souza e Silva, A. and Frith, J. (2010) 'Locative Mobile Social Networks: Mapping Communication and Location in Urban Spaces', *Mobilities*, vol. 5, no. 4, pp. 485–505.

de Souza e Silva, A. and Frith, J. (2012) *Mobile Interfaces in Public Spaces: Locational Privacy, Control and Urban Sociability*, London, Routledge.

De Vivo, B. and Dufour, S. (2012) 'Omonazionalismo. Civiltà prodotto tipico italiano?', in Marchetti, S., Mascat, J. and Perilli, V. (eds) *Femministe a parole. Grovigli da districare*, Rome, Ediesse, pp. 203–9.

de Vos, P. (2014) 'Uganda: Why Quiet Diplomacy is a Devastating Betrayal of Gay Men and Lesbians on the Continent', *Daily Maverick*, 4 March [Online]. Available at http://www.dailymaverick.co.za/opinionista/2014–03–04-uganda-why-quiet-diplomacy-is-a-devastating-betrayal-of-gay-men-and-lesbians-on-the-continent/#.U2i3F175nnc (accessed 30 April 2014).

Dhaenens, F. (2014) 'Articulations of Queer Resistance on the Small Screen', *Continuum: Journal of Media and Cultural Studies*, vol. 28, no. 4, pp. 520–31.

Diaz, R.M., Ayala, G. and Bein, E. (2001) 'Sexual Risk as an Outcome of Social Oppression: Data from a Probability Sample of Latino Gay Men in Three U.S. Cities', *Cultural Diversity and Ethnic Minority Psychology*, vol. 10, no. 3, pp. 255–67.

Dickson-Swift, V., James, E.L., Kippen, S. and Liamputtong, P. (2009) 'Researching Sensitive Topics: Qualitative Research as Emotion Work', *Qualitative Research*, vol. 9, no. 1, pp. 61–79.

Di Feliciantonio, C. (2014a) 'Por uma análise interseccional (e materialista) da migração queer: levando em consideração o papel dos regimes de bem-estar social', in Silva, J.M. and Nascimento e Silva, M. G. (eds) *Interseccionalidades, Gênero e Sexualidades na Análise Espacial*, Ponta Grossa, Todapalavra, pp. 57–78.

Di Feliciantonio, C. (2014b) 'Exploring the Complex Geographies of Italian Queer Activism', *Lambda Nordica*, vol. 2014, no. 2, pp. 27–52.

Dikeç, M. (2007) *Badlands of the Republic. Space, Politics and Urban Policy*, Oxford, Blackwell Publishing.

Ding, Y. and Ho, P.S.Y. (2013) 'Sex Work in China's Pearl River Delta: Accumulating Sexual Capital as a Life-advancement Strategy', *Sexualities*, vol. 16, nos 1–2, pp. 43–60.

Di Ronco, A. (2014) 'Regulating Street Prostitution as a Public Nuisance in the "Culture of Consumption": A Comparative Analysis between Birmingham, Brussels and Milan', in Vermeulen, G. and Peršak, N. (eds) *Reframing Prostitution: From Discourse to Description, From Moralisation to Normalisation?*, Antwerp, Maklu, pp. 145–71.

Dixon, D. and Marston, S. (2011) 'Introduction: Feminist Engagements with Geopolitics', *Gender, Place and Culture*, vol. 18, no. 4, pp. 445–53.

Do, T.D., Hudes, E.S., Proctor, K., Han, C. and Choi, K. (2006) 'HIV Testing Trends and Correlates among Young Asian and Pacific Islander Men Who Have Sex with Men in Two U.S. Cities', *AIDS Education and Prevention*, vol. 18, no. 1, pp. 44–55.

Doan, P.L. (2001) 'Are the Transgendered the Mine Shaft Canaries of Urban Areas?', *Progressive Planning*, vol. 146, nos 1–4 [Online]. Available at http://www.plannersnetwork.org/publications/2001_146/Doan.html (accessed 5 May 2014).

Doan, P.L. (2007) 'Queers in the American City: Transgendered Perceptions of Urban Space', *Gender, Place and Culture*, vol. 14, no. 1, pp. 57–74.

Doan, P.L. (2009) 'Safety and Urban Environments: Transgendered Experiences of the City', *Women & Environments International Magazine*, vol. 78/79, pp. 22–5.

Doan, P.L. (2010) 'The Tyranny of Gendered Spaces – Reflections from beyond the Gender Dichotomy', *Gender, Place and Culture*, vol. 17, no. 5, pp. 635–54.

Doan, P.L. (ed) (2011) *Queerying Planning: Challenging Heteronormative Assumptions and Reframing Planning Practice*, Aldershot, Ashgate.

Doan, P.L. (2014) 'Regulating Adult Business to Make Spaces Safe for Heterosexual Families in Atlanta', in Maginn, P. and Steinmetz, C. (eds) *(Sub)Urban Sexscapes Geographies and Regulation of the Sex Industry* London, Routledge.

Doan, P.L. and Higgins, H. (2009) 'Cognitive Dimensions of Wayfinding: The Implications of Habitus, Safety, and Gender Dissonance among Gay and Lesbian Populations', *Environment and Planning A*, vol. 41, pp. 1745–62.

Doan, P.L. and Higgins, S. (2011) 'The Demise of Queer Space? Resurgent Gentrification and the Assimilation of LGBT Neighbourhoods', *Journal of Planning Education and Research*, vol. 31, no. 1, pp. 6–25.

Dodds, K. (2014) *Geopolitics: A Very Short Introduction*, Oxford, Oxford University Press.

Doel, M. (2000) 'Un-glunking Geography: Spatial Science after Dr. Seuss and Gilles Deleuze', in Crang, M. and Thrift, N. (eds) *Thinking Space*, London, Routledge, pp. 117–35.

Doezema, J. (1998) 'Forced to Choose: Beyond the Voluntary v. Forced Prostitution Dichotomy', in Kempadoo, K. and Doezema, J. (eds) *Global Sex Workers: Rights, Resistance, and Redefinition*, New York, Routledge, pp. 34–50.

Doezema, J. (2010) *Sex Slaves and Discourse Masters: The Construction of Trafficking*, New York, Zed Books.

Donham, D.L. (1998) 'Freeing South Africa: The "Modernisation" of Male–Male Sexuality in Soweto', *Cultural Anthropology*, vol. 13, no. 1, pp. 3–21.

Döring, N.M. (2009) 'The Internet's Impact on Sexuality: A Critical Review of 15 Years of Research', *Computers in Human Behavior*, vol. 25, no. 5, pp. 1089–101.

Dorn, M.L., Keirns, C.C. and Del Casino, V.J. Jr (2010) 'Doubting Dualisms', in Brown, T., McLafferty, S. and Moon, G. (eds) *The Companion to Health and Medical Geography*, Chichester, Wiley-Blackwell, pp. 55–78.

Doty, A. (2010) '*Modern Family, Glee,* and the Limits of Television Liberalism', *Flow 24*, September [Online]. Available at http://flowtv.org/2010/09/modern-family-glee-and-limits-of-tv-liberalism/ (accessed 9 August 2014).

Dourish, P. (2006) 'Re-space-ing Place: Place and Space Ten Years On', paper presented at *CSCW'06*, 4–8 November, Banff, Alberta, Canada.

Dowden, C. and Brennan, S. (2012) 'Police-reported Hate Crime in Canada, 2010 [Juristat No. 85–002-X]', Statistics Canada [Online]. Available at http://www.statcan.gc.ca/pub/85–002-x/2012001/article/11635-eng.pdf (accessed 29 April 2013).

Dowler, L. and Sharp, J. (2001) 'A Feminist Geopolitics?', *Space and Polity*, vol. 5, no. 3, pp. 165–176.

Downing, G. (2013) 'Virtual Youth: Non-heterosexual Young People's Use of the Internet to Negotiate their Identities and Socio-sexual Relations', *Children's Geographies*, vol. 11, no. 1, pp. 44–58.

Dresser, R. (2013) 'Subversive Subjects: Rule-breaking and Deception in Clinical Trials', *Journal of Law, Medicine and Ethics*, vol. 41, no. 4, pp. 829–40.

Dritz, S.K. (1995) 'Charting the Epidemiological Course of AIDS, 1981–1984', an Oral History Conducted in 1992 by Sally Smith Hughes, in *The AIDS Epidemic in San Francisco: The Medical Response, 1981–1984*, Volume I, Berkeley, CA, Regional Oral History Office, The Bancroft Library, University of California, pp. 1–106.

Drucker, P. (2000) 'Introduction: Remapping Sexualities', in Drucker, P. (ed) *Different Rainbows*, London, Gay Men's Press, pp. 9–42.

Drushel, B. (2010) 'Virtually Supportive: Self-Disclosure of Minority Sexualities through Online Social Networking Sites', in Pullen, C. and Cooper, M. (eds) *LGBT Identity and Online New Media*, Abingdon, Routledge, pp. 62–72.

Ducheneaut, N., Wen, M.H., Yee, N. and Wadley, G. (2009) 'Body and Mind: A Study of Avatar Personalization in Three Virtual Worlds', in *Proceedings of the SIGCHI Conference on Human Factors in Computing Systems*, ACM, pp. 1151–60.

Duesberg, P. (1987) 'Carcinogens and Pathogens: Expectations and Reality', *Perspectives in Cancer Research*, vol. 47, pp. 1199–220.

Duggan, L. (2002) 'The New Homonormativity: The Sexual Politics of Neoliberalism', in Castronovo, R. and Nelson, D.D. (eds) *Materialising Democracy: Towards a Revitalized Cultural Politics*, Durham, NC, Duke University Press, pp. 175–94.

Duggan, L. (2003) *The Twilight of Equality: Neoliberalism, Cultural Politics and the Attack on Democracy*, Boston, MA, Beacon Press.

Dumit, J. (2012) *Drugs for Life: How Pharmaceutical Companies Define our Health*, Durham, NC, Duke University Press.

Duncan, N. (ed.) (1996) *BodySpace*, London, Routledge.

Duncan, S. and Phillips, M. (2010) 'People Who Live Apart Together (LATs) – How Different Are They?', *The Sociological Review*, vol. 58, no. 1, pp. 112–34.

Dussel, E. (1975) *The Underside of Modernity: Apel, Ricoeur, Rorty, Taylor and the Philosophy of Liberation*, Atlantic Highlands, NJ, Humanities (this edition 1996).

Dussel, E. (1995a) *The Invention of the Americas: Eclipse of 'the Other' and the Myth of Modernity*, New York, Continuum.

Dussel, E. (1995b) *Introduccion a la Filosofia de la Liberacion*, Bogota, Editorial Nueva America.

Dutton, M. (2007) 'An All-Consuming Nationalism', in Denoon, D. (ed.) *China: Contemporary Political, Economic, and International Affairs*, New York, New York University Press, pp. 172–81.

Duyves, M. (1992) 'Framing Preferences, Framing Differences: Inventing Amsterdam as a Gay Capital', paper presented at the Sexuality and Space Network Conference, London, September, 1992.

Dzi Croquettes (2009) Dir. Raphael Alvarez and Tatiana Issa [Film]. Brazil, Canal Brasil, TRIA Productions.

Eastman, P.C. (1973) 'Consciousness-raising as a Resocialization Process for Women', *Smith College Studies in Social Work*, vol. 43, no. 3, pp. 153–83.

Eaves, L. (2013) 'Space, Place, and Identity in Conversation: Queer Black Women Living in the Rural U.S. South', in Gorman–Murray, A., Pini, B. and Bryant, L. (eds) *Sexuality, Rurality and Geography*, Lanham, MD, Lexington Books, pp. 111–26.

Echezarrieta, V.S. and Leyva, M.J.S. (2008) 'Latinoamericanas em España: encarnación de un estereotipo ambivalente', in Rodriguez, I. and Martínez, J. (eds) *Postcolonialidades históricas: (in)visibilidades hispanoamericanas / colonialismos ibéricos*, Barcelona, Anthropos, pp. 169–86.

Edelman, E.A. (2011) '"This Area Has Been Declared a Prostitution Free Zone": Discursive Formations of Space, the State, and Trans "Sex Worker" Bodies', *Journal of Homosexuality*, vol. 58, pp. 848–64.

Edelman, L. (2004) *No Future: Queer Theory and the Death Drive*, Durham, NC, Duke University Press.

Edwards, M. (2010) 'Gender, Social Disorganization Theory, and the Locations of Sexually Oriented Businesses', *Deviant Behaviour*, vol. 31, pp. 135–58.

Egan, J., Frye, V., Kurtz, S., Latkin, C., Chen, M., Tobin, K., Yang, C., Koblin, B. (2011) 'Migration, Neighborhoods, and Networks: Approaches to Understanding How Urban Environmental Conditions Affect Syndemic Adverse Health Outcomes among Gay, Bisexual, and other Men Who Have Sex with Men', *AIDS and Behaviour*, vol. 15, pp. S35–S50.

Egan, R.D. (2013) *Becoming Sexual: A Critical Appraisal of the Sexualisation of Girls*, Cambridge, Polity.

Eisner, S. (2012) 'Love, Rage and the Occupation: Bisexual Politics in Israel/Palestine', *Journal of Bisexuality*, vol. 12, no. 1, pp. 80–137.

Ek, R. (2006) 'Media Studies, Geographical Imaginations and Relational Space', in Falkheimer, J. and Jansson, A. (eds) *Geographies of Communication, The Spatial Turn in Media Studies*, Nordicom, Göteborg, pp. 45–66.

Ek, R. (2012) 'Topologies of Human–Mobile Assemblages', in Wilken, R. and Goggin, G. (eds) *Mobile Technology and Place*, London, Routledge.

Ekpootu, M.U. (2013) 'Sexualizing the City: Female Prostitution in Nigeria's Urban Centers in Historical Perspective', paper presented at Selling Sex in the City: Prostitution in World Cities, 1600 to the Present Conference, Amsterdam, 25–27 April.

Elahi, B and Karim, P (2011) 'Introduction: Iranian Diaspora', *Comparative Studies of South Asia, Africa and the Middle East*, vol. 31, no. 2, pp. 381–7.

Elder, G. (2002) 'Response to "Queer Patriarchies, Queer Racisms, International"', *Antipode*, vol. 34, no. 5, pp. 988–91.

Elder, G.E. (2003) *Hostels, Sexuality and the Apartheid Legacy*, Athens, Ohio University Press.

Elder, G. (2005) 'Love for Sale: Marketing Gay Male P/Leisurespace in Contemporary South Africa', in Nelson, L. and Seager, J. (eds) *A Feminist Companion to Geography*, Oxford, Blackwell, pp 578–97.

El Feki, S. (2013) *Sex and the Citadel: Intimate life in a Changing Arab World*, New York, Pantheon Books.

Ellis, M. and Muschkin, C. (1996) 'Migration of Persons with AIDS – A Search for Support from Elderly Parents?', *Social Science & Medicine*, vol. 43, pp. 1109–18.

Ellison, N., Steinfield, C. and Lampe, C. (2007) 'The Benefits of Facebook "Friends:" Social Capital and College Students' Use of Online Social Network Sites', *Journal of Computer-Mediated Communication*, vol. 12, no. 4, pp. 1143–68.

El-Tayeb, F. (2012) '"Gays Who Cannot Properly Be Gay": Queer Muslims in the Neoliberal European City', *European Journal of Women's Studies*, vol. 19, no. 1, pp. 79–95.

Eng, D.L., Halberstam, J. and Muñoz, J.E. (2005) 'What's Queer About Queer Studies Now?', *Social Text*, vol. 23, nos 3–4, pp. 1–17.

Engelhart, K. (2013) 'Online Dating and the Search for True Love – or Loves' [Online]. Available at http://www.macleans.ca/society/life/true-loves (accessed 24 January 2015).

Engels, F. (1890) 'Letter to Joseph Bloch', in Storey, J. (ed) *Cultural Theory and Popular Culture: A Reader*, London, Prentice Hall (this edition 1998), pp. 71–72.

England, K. (1994) 'Getting Personal: Reflexivity, Positionality, and Feminist Research', *Professional Geographer*, vol. 46, no. 1, pp. 80–89.

England, M. and Simon, S. (2010) 'Scary Cities: Urban Geographies of Fear, Difference and Belonging', *Social & Cultural Geography*, vol. 11, no. 3, pp. 201–7.

Ensor, S. (2012) 'Spinster Ecology: Rachel Carson, Sarah Orne Jewett, and Nonreproductive Futurity', *American Literature*, vol. 84, no. 2, pp. 409–35.

Epprecht, M. (2007) *Hungochani: The History of Dissident Sexuality in Southern Africa*, London, McGill-Queen's University Press.

Epprecht, M. (2008) *Heterosexual Africa? The History of an Idea from the Age of Exploration to the Age of AIDS*, Athens, OH, Ohio University Press.

Epprecht, M. (2010) 'The Making of "African" Sexuality: Early Sources, Current Debates', *History Compass*, vol. 8, no. 8, pp. 768–79.

Epprecht, M. (2013) *Sexuality and Social Justice in Africa: Rethinking Homophobia and Forging Resistance*, London, Zed Books.

Epstein, S. (1995) 'The Construction of Lay Expertise: AIDS Activism and the Forging of Credibility in the Reform of Clinical Trials', *Science, Technology and Human Values*, vol. 20, no. 4, pp. 408–37.

Epstein, S. (1996) *Impure Science: AIDS, Activism and the Politics of Knowledge*, Berkeley, University of California Press.

Ervolino, B. (1993) 'Club Medicine: Underground Pharmacies Dispensing Experimental Drugs to Patients who Cannot Wait', *The Record*, 11 January, D1.

Escoffier, J. (1997) 'The Political Economy of the Closet: Notes Toward an Economic History of Fay and Lesbian Life before Stonewall', in Gluckman, A. and Reed, B. (eds) *Homo Economics: Capitalism, Community, and Lesbian and Gay Life*, London, Routledge, pp. 123–34.

Ettorre, E.M. (1978) 'Women, Urban Social Movements, and the Lesbian Ghetto', *International Journal of Urban and Regional Research*, vol. 2, nos 1–4, pp. 499–520.

European Journal of Ecopsychology (2012) *Special Issue: Queering Ecopsychology* [Online]. Available at http://eje.wyrdwise.com/ojs/index.php/EJE/issue/view/6, (accessed 17 September 2014).

Evans, D. (1993) *Sexual Citizenship: The Material Construction of Sexualities*, London, Routledge.

Evered, E.Ö., and Evered, K.T. (2013) '"Protecting the National Body": Regulating the Practice and the Place of Prostitution in Early Republican Turkey', *Gender, Place and Culture*, vol. 20, no. 7, pp. 839–57.

Evers, C. and Goggin, G. (2012) 'Mobiles, Men and Migration: Mobile Communication and Everyday Multiculturalism in Australia', in Fortunati, L., Pertierra, R. and Vincent, J. (eds) *Migration, Diaspora, and Information Technologies in Global Societies*, New York, Routledge.

Fahey, M. (2009) 'How Not to Address Homosexuality in Gaming' [Online]. Available at http://www.kotaku.com.au/2009/04/how-not-to-address-homosexuality-in-gaming/ (accessed 12 March 2012).

Faier, L. (2007) 'Filipina Migrants in Rural Japan and their Professions of Love', *American Ethnologist*, vol. 34, no. 1, pp. 148–62.

Faier L. (2014) 'Everyday Articulations of Prostitution: How Some Filipina Migrants in Rural Japan Describe Sexual–Economic Relationships', *Gender, Place and Culture*, vol. 21, no. 8, pp. 979–95.

Fall, J. and Rosière, S. (2008) 'On the Limits of Dialogue Between Francophone and Anglophone Political Geography', *Political Geography*, vol. 27, no. 7, pp. 713–16.

Fanghanel, A. (2013) 'On Going Too Far: Safe-keeping, Public Space and the Discursive Limits of being a Slut', *The Howard League for Penal Reform ECAN Bulletin*, vol. 21, October, pp. 10–15.

Fanghanel, A. (2014) 'Approaching/Departure: Effacement, Erasure and "Undoing" the Fear of Crime', *Cultural Geographies*, vol. 21, no. 3, pp. 343–61.

Fanon, F. (1967) *Black Skin, White Masks*, New York, Grove Press (this edition 2008).

Farmer, P. (1992) *AIDS and Accusation: Haiti and the Geography of Blame*, Berkeley, University of California Press.

Farmer, P. (2006) *AIDS and Accusation: Haiti and the Geography of Blame* (2nd edn), Berkeley, University of California Press.

Farr, D. (2010) 'A Very Personal World: Advertisement and Identity of Trans-persons on Craigslist', in Pullen, C. and Cooper, M. (eds) *LGBT Identity and Online New Media*, Abingdon, Routledge, pp. 87–99.

Farred, G. (2003) 'Reconfiguring the Humanities and the Social Sciences in the Age of the Global University: Introduction', *Nepantla: Views from South*, vol. 4, no. 1, pp. 41–50.

Farrow, H., Moss, P. and Shaw, B. (1995) 'Symposium on Feminist Participatory Research', *Antipode*, vol. 27, pp. 71–4.

Fassin, D. (2007) *When Bodies Remember: Politics and Experiences of AIDS in South Africa*, Berkeley, University of California Press.

Fauci, A.S. (1983) 'The Acquired Immune Deficiency Syndrome: The Ever-broadening Clinical Spectrum', *Journal of the American Medical Association*, vol. 249, no. 17, pp. 2375–6.

Fay, H., Baral, S.D., Trapence, G., Motimedi, F., Umar, E., Iipinge, S., Dausab, F., Wirtz, A. and Beyrer, C. (2011) 'Stigma, Health Care Access and HIV Knowledge among Men Who Have Sex with Men in Malawi, Namibia and Botswana', *AIDS and Behaviour*, vol. 15, no. 6, pp.1088–97.

Featherstone, D. (2012) *Solidarity: Hidden Histories and Geographies of Internationalism*, London, Zed Books.

Featherstone, M. and Burrows, R. (1996) *Cyberspace/Cyberbodies/Cyberpunk: Cultures of Technological Embodiment*, vol. 43, London, Sage.

Federal Magistrates Court of Australia (FMCA) (2008) *SZLFZ v Minister for Immigration & Anor*, FMCA 192, 28 February [Online]. http://www.austlii.edu.au/au/cases/cth/FMCA/2008/192.html (accessed 12 November 2012).

Feigenbaum, A., Frenzel, F. and McCurdy, P. (2013) *Protest Camps*, London and New York, Zed Books.

Feinberg, L. (1996) *Transgender Warriors: Making History from Joan of Arc to Dennis Rodman*, Boston, MA, Beacon Press.

Feinberg, L. (1998) *Trans Liberation: Beyond Pink and Blue*, Boston, MA, Beacon Press.

Ferguson, A.R. (2012) *The Reorder of Things, The University and its Pedagogies of Minority Difference*, Minneapolis and London, University of Minnesota Press.

Fernandes, D. and Nunan, C. (2008) 'O imigrante brasileiro na Espanha: perfil e situação de vida em Madrid', paper presented at Encontro Nacional de Estudos Populacionais, Belo Horizonte, Brazil, 29 September–3 October.

Ferrante, A.A. (2014) 'Homo Skin, Hetero Masks: A Representation of Italian Homonationalism', *LES Online*, vol. 6, no. 1, pp. 114–21.

Ferreira, E. (2011) 'Geographies of (In)equalities: Space and Sexual Identities', in Salvador, R., Firmino, A., Ponte, C. and Ferreira, E. (eds), *Proceedings of Geographies of Inclusion: Challenges and Opportunities*, Lisboa, e-GEO.

Ferreira, E. and Salvador, R. (2015) 'Lesbian Collaborative Web Mapping: Disrupting Heteronormativity in Portugal', *Gender, Place and Culture*, vol. 22, no. 7, pp. 954–70. Available online at http://dx.doi.org/10.1080/0966369X.2014.917276 (accessed 19 April 2015).

Feyerabend, P.K. (1993) *Against Method: Outline of an Anarchistic Theory of Knowledge* (3rd rev. edn), London, Verso Books.

Fink, M. and Miller, Q. (2013) 'Trans Media Moments: Tumblr, 2011–2013', *Television & New Media*, pre-print [Online]. DOI: 10.1177/1527476413505002 (accessed 19 April 2015).

Firrincielli, S. (2005) 'Le pelli del Pride glbt. Frammenti di auto/etero rappresentazione', degree dissertation, Rome, Sapienza – University of Rome.

First Amendment of the 5th French Constitution (1958) [Online]. Available at http://www.conseil-constitutionnel.fr/conseil-constitutionnel/francais/la-constitution/la-constitution-du-4-octobre-1958/texte-integral-de-la-constitution-du-4-octobre-1958-en-vigueur.5074.html#preambule (accessed 6 April 2015).

Fiske, J. (1996) *Media Matters: Race and Gender in US Politics*, Minneapolis, University of Minnesota Press.

FitzGerald, S.A. (2013) 'Putting Traficking on the Map: The Geography of Feminist Complicity', in Munro, V. and Della Giusta, M. (eds) *Demanding Sex: Critical Reflections on the Regulation of Prostitution*, Aldershot, Ashgate, pp. 99–120.

Fleischer, J. (2005) *Married to a Man and in Love with a Woman*, Los Angeles, Alyson Publications.

Fletcher, G. and Light, B. (2007) 'Going Offline: An Exploratory Cultural Artifact Analysis of an Internet Dating Site's Development Trajectories', *International Journal of Information Management*, vol. 27, no. 6, pp. 422–31.

Florida, R. (2002) *Rise of the Creative Class*, New York, HarperCollins.

Flowers, P., Marriott, C. and Hart, G. (2000) 'The Bars, the Bogs and the Bushes: The Impact of Locale on Sexual Cultures', *Culture, Health and Sexuality*, vol. 2, no. 1, pp. 69–86.

Fluri, J. (2011), 'Bodies, Bombs and Barricades: Geographies of Conflict and Civilian (In) security', *Transactions of the Institute of British Geographers*, NS 36, pp. 280–96.

Fonseca, C. (2011) 'Afinal, o que é que a mulher brasileira tem … que nós não temos?', *Activa* [Online]. Available at http://activa.sapo.pt/sexo/2011–07–31-afinal-o-que-e-que-a-mulher-brasileira-tem … -que-nos-nao-temos (Accessed 9 October 2014).

Forest, B. (1995) 'West Hollywood as Symbol: The Significance of Place in the Construction of a Gay Identity', *Environment and Planning D: Society and Space*, vol. 13, pp. 133–57.

Formby, E. (2011) 'Lesbian and Bisexual Women's Human Rights, Sexual Rights and Sexual Citizenship: Negotiating Sexual Health in England', *Culture, Health and Sexuality*, vol. 13, no. 10, pp. 1165–79.

Forsyth, A. (1997a) 'NoHo: Upscaling Main Street on the Metropolitan Edge', *Urban Geography*, vol. 18, no. 7, pp. 622–52.

Forsyth, A. (1997b) '"Out" in the Valley', *International Journal of Urban and Regional Research*, vol. 21, no. 1, pp. 38–62.

Fortier, A-M. (2001) '"Coming Home": Queer Migrations and Multiple Evocations of Home', *European Journal of Cultural Studies*, vol. 4, no. 4, pp. 405–24.

Fortier, A-M. (2002) 'Queer Diaspora', in Richardson, D. and Seidman, S. (eds) *Handbook of Lesbian and Gay Studies*, London, Sage, pp. 183-97.

Fortier, A-M. (2003) 'Making Home: Queer Migrations and Motions of Attachment', in Ahmed, S., Castañeda, C., Fortier, A-M. and Sheller, M. (eds) *Uprootings/Regroundings: Questions of Home and Migration*, Oxford, Berg, pp. 115–35.

Foster, E.A. (2011) 'Sustainable Development: Problematising Normative Constructions of Gender within Global Environmental Governmentality', *Globalizations*, vol. 8, no. 2, pp. 135–49.

Foster, E.A. (2013) 'Deconstructing International Sustainable Development and Population Policy Directives: The (Re)production of Sexual Norms through Environmental Discourses', *Gender, Place and Culture* [Online]. Available at http://www.tandfonline.com/doi/full/10.1080/0966369X.2013.810593 (accessed 15 June 2014).

Foucault, M. (1967) *Madness and Civilization: A History of Insanity in the Age of Reason*, London, Tavistock.

Foucault, M. (1973) *The Birth of the Clinic*, New York, Vintage.

Foucault, M. (1976) *The History of Sexuality, Vol. 1: The Will to Knowledge*, London, Penguin (this edition 1998).

Foucault, M. (1977) *Discipline and Punish*, London, Penguin.

Foucault, M. (1978) *The History of Sexuality, Vol. 1: The Will to Knowledge*, London, Allen Lane.

Foucault, M. (1979) *Discipline and Punish: The Birth of the Prison*, New York, Vintage Books.

Foucault, M. (1985) *The History of Sexuality, Vol. 2: The Use of Pleasure*, New York, Pantheon.

Foucault, M. (1986) *The History of Sexuality, Vol. 3: The Care of the Self*, New York, Pantheon.

Foucault, M. (2002) *The Order of Things: An Archaeology of the Human Sciences*, London, New York, Routledge.

Foucault, M. (2007) *Security, Territory, Population: Lectures at the Collège de France 1977–1978*, Basingstoke, Palgrave Macmillan.

Frances, R. (2011) 'Prostitution: The Age of Empires', in Beccalossi, C. and Crozier, I. (eds) *A Cultural History of Sexuality in the Age of Empire*, Oxford and New York, Berg, pp. 145–70.

Francés Díez, M.Á. (2010) '"La llengua sóc jo": identitat nacional i de gènere en Montserrat Roig', *Anuari de l'Agrupació Borrianenca de Cultura: revista de recerca humanística i científica*, Special Issue: *Pensar la nació en femení. Una construcció inacabada*, vol. 21, pp. 47–62.

Frank, K. (2003) 'Just Trying to Relax: Masculinity, Masculinizing Practices, and Strip Club Regulars', *Journal of Sex Research*, vol. 40, no. 1, pp. 61–75.

Fraser, N. (1995) 'From Redistribution to Recognition? Dilemmas of Justice in a "Post–Socialist" Age', *New Left Review*, vol. 212, pp. 68–93.

Fraser, N. (1997) 'Heterosexism, Misrecognition, and Capitalism: A Response to Judith Butler', *Social Text*, vol. 15, nos 3–4, pp. 279–89.

Fraser, N. (2007) 'Feminist Politics in the Age of Recognition: A Two-dimensional Approach to Gender Justice', *Studies in Social Justice*, vol. 1, no. 1, pp. 23–35.

Freire, P. (2000) *Pedagogy of the Oppressed*, London and New York, Continuum.

Friedman-Kien, A E., Laubenstein, L.J., Rubinstein, P., Buimovici-Klein, E., Marmor, M., Stahl, R., Spigland, I., Kim, K.S. and Zolla-Pazner, S. (1982) 'Disseminated Kaposi's Sarcoma in Homosexual Men', *Annals of Internal Medicine*, vol. 96, no. 6/1, pp. 693–700.

Frohlick, S. (2013) *Sexuality, Women, and Tourism: Cross–border Desires Through Contemporary Travel*, New York, Routledge.

Frost, D.M. and Meyer, I.H. (2012) 'Measuring Community Connectedness among Diverse Sexual Minority Populations', *Journal of Sex Research*, vol. 49, no. 1, pp. 36–49.

Fry, P. (1982) *Para inglês ver: identidade e política na cultura brasileira*, Rio de Janeiro, Zahar.

Fry, P. and MacRae, E. (1983) *O Que É Homossexualidade*, São Paulo, Brasiliense (this edition 1991).

Frye, V., Egan, J., Van Tieu, H., Cerdá, M., Ompad, D. and Koblin, B. (2014) 'I Didn't Think I Could Get Out of the Fucking Park: Gay Men's Retrospective Accounts of Neighborhood Space, Emerging Sexuality and Migrations', *Social Science & Medicine* [Online]. DOI: 10.1016/j.socscimed.2013.12.002 (accessed 19 April 2015).

Fuchs, M. (2014) 'Gamification as Twenty-first Century Ideology', *Journal of Games and Virtual Worlds*, vol. 6, no. 2, pp. 143–57.

Fuss, D. (1983) *Essentially Speaking: Feminism, Nature and Difference*, London, New York, Routledge.

Fuss, D. (ed.) (1990) *Inside/Out, Lesbian Theories, Gay Theories*, London, New York, Routledge.

Gaard, G. (1997) 'Toward a Queer Ecofeminism', *Hypatia*, vol. 12, no. 1, pp. 137–55.

Gabb, J., Klett-Davies, M., Fink, J. and Thomae, M. (2013) *Enduring Love? Couple Relationships in the 21st Century: Survey Findings Report*, Milton Keynes, The Open University [Online]. Available at http://knowledgebank.oneplusone.org.uk/wp-content/uploads/2014/05/Enduring-Love.pdf (accessed 23 March 2015).

Gagen, E. (2000) 'Playing the Part: Performing Gender in America's Playgrounds', in Holloway, S. and Valentine, G. (eds) *Children's Geographies: Playing, Living, Learning*, Abingdon, Routledge, pp. 213–29.

Gagnon, J. (2008) *Les scripts de la sexualité: Essais sur les origines culturelles du désir*, Paris, Payot.

Galloway, A. (2004) 'Intimations of Everyday Life: Ubiquitous Computing and the City', *Cultural Studies*, vol. 18, no. 2/3, pp. 384–408.

Galvan, F.H. and Bazargan, M. (2012) 'Interactions of Latina Transgender Women with Law Enforcement', *Los Angeles: Williams Institute Policy Brief* [Online]. Available at http://williamsinstitute.law.ucla.edu/wp-content/uploads/Galvan-Bazargan-Interactions-April-2012.pdf (accessed 27 April 2014).

Gamson, J. (2003) 'Game Media, Inc.: Media Structures, the New Gay Conglomerates, and Collective Sexual Identities', in McCaughey, M. and Ayers, M.D. (eds) *Cyberactivism: Online Activism in Theory and Practice*, New York, Routledge, pp. 255–78.

Gamson, J. (2005) *The Fabulous Sylvester: The Legend, the Music, the Seventies in San Francisco*, New York, H. Holt.

Gandy, M. (2012) 'Queer Ecology: Nature, Sexuality and Heterotopic Alliances', *Environment and Planning D: Society and Space*, vol. 30, pp. 727–47.

Garaizábal, C. (1994) 'Me llamo Pepe, me siento María', in *Jornadas Feministas 1993: Juntas y a por todas*, Madrid, Federación de Organizaciones Feministas del Estado Español, p. 197.

Garaizábal, C. (2013) 'Feminismos, sexualidad y trabajo sexual', in Solà, M. and Urko, E. (eds) *Transfeminismos: Epistemes fricciones y flujos*, Txalaparta, Tafalla, pp. 59–72.

Garcia-Montes, J.M., Caballero-Muñoz, D. and Pérez-Álvarez, M. (2006) 'Changes in the Self Resulting from the Use of Mobile Phones', *Media, Culture and Society*, vol. 28, no. 1, pp. 67–82.

Garcia-Ramon, M-D. (2003) 'Globalization and International Geography: The Questions of Languages and Scholarly Traditions', *Progress in Human Geography*, vol. 27, no. 1, pp. 1–5.

Garcia-Ramon, M-D. (2012) 'Las diferencias que crea el lugar. Una mirada crítica a la hegemonía angloamericana en geografía', *Documents d'Anàlisi Geogràfica*, vol. 58, no. 2, pp. 307–19.

Garcia Ramon, M-D., Simonsen, K. and Vaiou, D. (2006) 'Guest Editorial: Does Anglophone Hegemony Permeate Gender, Place and Culture?', *Gender, Place & Culture*, vol. 13, no. 1, pp. 1–5.

Gardner, C.B. (1995) *Passing By: Gender and Public Harassment*, Berkley and Los Angeles, University of California Press.

Gardner, S. (1983) 'AIDS and Herpes Fomenting Fears', *New York Times*, 29 July, pp. 1, 21.

Garland, D. (1996) 'The Limits of the Sovereign State: Strategies of Crime Control in Contemporary Society', *British Journal of Criminology*, vol. 36, no. 4, pp. 455–71.

Garlick, S. (2011) 'A New Sexual Revolution? Critical Theory, Pornography and the Internet', *Canadian Sociology Association*, vol. 48, no. 3, pp. 221–39.

Garvey, J. (2011) 'Spaces of Violence, Desire, and Queer (Un)belonging: Dionne Brand's Urban Diasporas', *Textual Practice*, vol. 25, no. 4, pp. 757–77.

Gasparini, A., La Torre, C., Gorini, S. and Russo, M. (2012) 'Homophobia in the Italian Legal System: File not Found', in Trappolin, L., Gasparini, A. and Wintemute, R. (eds) *Confronting Homophobia in Europe: Social and Legal Perspectives*, Oxford and Portland, Hart Publishing, pp. 139–70.

Gatenby, B. and Humphries, M. (2000) 'Feminist Participatory Action Research: Methodological and Ethical Issues', *Women's Studies International Forum*, vol. 23, pp. 89–105.

Gates, G. (2011) 'How Many People are Lesbian, Gay, Bisexual, and Transgender?', *Los Angeles: Williams Institute Briefing Paper* [Online]. Available at http://williamsinstitute. law.ucla.edu/wp-content/uploads/Gates-How-Many-People-LGBT-Apr-2011.pdf (accessed 27 April 2014).

Gates, G.J. and Ost, J. (2004) *The Gay and Lesbian Atlas*, Washington, DC, The Urban Institute.

Gatrell, A.C. and Elliott, S.J. (2015) *Geographies of Health: An Introduction* (3rd edn), Chichester, Wiley.

Gazzard, A. (2009) 'The Avatar and the Player: Understanding the Relationship beyond the Screen', 2009 Conference in Games and Virtual Worlds for Serious Applications, pp. 190–93.

Geltmaker, T. (1992) 'The Queer Nation Acts Up: Health Care, Politics and Sexual Diversity in the County of Angels', *Environment and Planning D: Society and Space*, vol. 10, no. 6, pp. 609–50.

Geltmaker, T. (1997) 'The Queer Nation Acts Up: Health care, Politics, and Sexual Diversity in the County of Angels, 1990 – 92', in Ingram, G.B., Bouthillette, A. and Retter, Y. (eds)

Queers in Space: Communities/Public Places/Sites of Resistance, Seattle, WA, Bay Press, pp. 233–74.

Gentile, P. (2010) 'Capital Queers: Social Memory and Queer Place(s) in Cold War Ottawa', in Opp, J. and Walsh, J.C. (eds) *Placing Memory and Remembering Place in Canada*, Vancouver and Toronto, UBC Press, pp. 187–214.

Gershon, I. (2010) *The Breakup 2.0: Disconnecting over New Media*, Ithaca, NY, Cornell University Press.

Gesler, W. (1992) 'Therapeutic Landscapes: Medical Issues in the Light of New Cultural Geographies', *Social Science and Medicine*, vol. 34, no. 7, pp. 735–46.

Ghaziani, A. (2011) 'Post-Gay Collective Identity Construction', *Social Problems*, vol. 58, no. 1, pp. 99–125.

Ghaziani, A. (2014) *There Goes the Gayborhood*, Princeton, NJ, Princeton University Press.

Gibson-Graham, J.K. (1996) *The End of Capitalism (As We Knew It): A Feminist Critique of Political Economy*, Minneapolis, University of Minnesota Press.

Gibson-Graham, J.K. (2006) *A Post-capitalist Politics*, Minneapolis, University of Minnesota Press.

Gieseking, J.J. (2012) 'Living in an (In)Visible World: Lesbians' and Queer Women's Spaces and Experiences of Justice and Oppression in New York City', PhD thesis, New York, The Graduate Center of the City University of New York.

Gieseking, J.J. (2013) 'Queering the Meaning of "Neighbourhood": Reinterpreting the Lesbian–Queer Experience of Park Slope, Brooklyn, 1983–2008', in Taylor, Y. and Addison, M. (eds) *Queer Presences and Absences*, Basingstoke, Palgrave Macmillan, pp. 178–200.

Gieseking, J.J. (2015) 'Crossing Over into Neighbourhoods of the Body: Urban Territories, Borders and Lesbian–Queer Bodies in New York City', *Area* [Online]. DOI: 10.1111/ area.12147 (accessed 19 April 2015).

Giffney, N. (2004) 'Denormatizing Queer Theory More Than (Simply) Lesbian and Gay Studies', *Feminist Theory*, vol. 5, no. 1, pp. 73–8.

Gil, S.L. (2011) *Nuevos Feminismos. Sentidos comunes en la dispersión: Una historia de trayectorias y rupturas en el estado español*, Madrid, Traficantes de suenos.

Gilfoyle, T. (1992) *City of Eros: New York City, Prostitution and the Commercialization of Sex, 1790–1920*, New York, Norton & Company.

Giraud, C. (2014) *Quartiers Gays*, Paris, Presses Universitaires de France.

Girman, C. (2004) *Mucho Macho: Seduction, Desire, and the Homoerotic Lives of Latin Men*, New York, Harrington Park Press.

Giroux, H.A. (2011) *On Critical Pedagogy*, London, New York, Continuum.

Giwa, S. and Greensmith, C. (2012) 'Race Relations and Racism in the LGBTQ Community of Toronto: Perspectives of Gay and Queer Social Service Providers of Color', *Journal of Homosexuality*, vol. 59, no. 2, pp. 149–85.

Glazenbrook, A. (2006) 'The Bad Girls of Athens: The Image and Function of *Hetairai* in Judicial Oratory', in Faraone, C.A. and McClure, L. (eds) *Prostitutes and Courtesans of the Ancient World*, Madison, University of Wisconsin Press, pp. 125–38.

Glazenbrook, A. (2011) 'Prostitution', in Golden, M. and Toohey, P. (eds) *A Cultural History of Sexuality in the Classical World*, Oxford and New York, Berg, pp. 145–68.

Global Fund (2009) 'The Global Fund Strategy in Relation to Sexual Orientation and Gender Identities', Geneva: The Global Fund [Online]. Available at http://www.theglobalfund. org/documents/core/strategies/Core_SexualOrientationAndGenderIdentities_Strategy_ en/ (accessed 30 April 2014).

Gluckman, A. and Reed, B. (eds) (1997) *Homo Economics: Capitalism, Community, and Lesbian and Gay Life*, London, Routledge.

Glynn, K. and Cupples, J. (2015) 'Negotiating and Queering US Hegemony in TV Drama: Popular Geopolitics and Cultural Studies', *Gender, Place and Culture*, vol. 22, no. 2, pp. 271–87.

Go, J. (2013) *Postcolonial Sociology*, Bingley, Emerald Group Publishing.

Godden, L. (2001) 'Bounding of Vice: Prostitution and Planning Law', *Griffith Law Review*, vol. 10, pp. 77–91.

Gopinath, G. (2005) *Impossible Desires: Queer Diasporas and South Asian Public Cultures*, Durham, NC, Duke University Press.

Gopinath, G. (2011) 'Foreword: Queer Diasporic Interventions', *Textual Practice*, vol. 25, no. 4, pp. 635–8.

Gorman-Murray, A. (2006a) 'Homeboys: Uses of Home by Gay Australian Men', *Social & Cultural Geography*, vol. 7, pp. 53–69.

Gorman-Murray, A. (2006b) 'Imagining King Street in the Gay/Lesbian Media', *M/C Journal*, vol. 9.3 [Online]. Available at http://journal.media-culture.org.au/0607/04-gorman-murray.php (accessed 19 April 2015).

Gorman-Murray, A. (2007) 'Rethinking Queer Migration through the Body', *Social & Cultural Geography*, vol. 8, no. 1, pp. 105–21.

Gorman-Murray, A. (2008) 'Queering the Family Home: Narratives from Gay, Lesbian and Bisexual Youth Coming Out in Supportive Family Homes in Australia', *Gender, Place & Culture*, vol. 15, no. 1, pp. 31–44.

Gorman-Murray, A. (2009a) 'Intimate Mobilities: Emotional Embodiment and Queer Migration', *Social & Cultural Geography*, vol. 10, no. 4, pp. 441–60.

Gorman-Murray, A. (2009b) 'What's the Meaning of ChillOut?: Rural/Urban Difference and the Cultural Significance of Australia's Largest Rural GLBTQ Festival', *Rural Society*, vol. 19, no. 1, pp. 71–86.

Gorman-Murray, A. (2013) 'Documenting Lesbian and Gay Lives in Rural Australia', in Gorman-Murray, A., Pini, B. and Bryant, L. (eds) *Sexuality, Rurality, and Geography*, Lanham, MD, Lexington, pp. 95–109.

Gorman-Murray, A. and Nash, C.J. (2014) 'Mobile Places, Relational Spaces: Conceptualizing Change in Sydney's LGBTQ Neighborhoods', *Environment and Planning D: Society and Space*, vol. 32, no. 4, pp. 622–41.

Gorman-Murray, A., Pini, B. and Bryant, L. (eds) (2013) *Sexuality, Rurality and Geography*, Plymouth, Lexington Books.

Gorman-Murray, A. and Waitt, G. (2009) 'Queer-friendly Neighbourhoods: An Interrogation of Social Cohesion across Sexual Difference in Two Australian Neighbourhoods', *Environment and Planning A*, vol. 41, no. 12, pp. 2855–73.

Gorman-Murray, A., Waitt, G. and Gibson, C. (2008) 'A Queer Country? A Case Study of the Politics of Gay/Lesbian Belonging in an Australian Country Town', *Australian Geographer*, vol. 39, no. 2, pp. 171–91.

Gorman-Murray, A., Waitt, G. and Gibson, C. (2012) 'Chilling Out in Cosmopolitan Country? Urban/Rural Hybridity and the Construction of Daylesford as a "Lesbian and Gay Rural Idyll"', *Journal of Rural Studies*, vol. 28, pp. 69–79.

Gosine, A. (2010) 'Non-white Reproduction and Same-sex Eroticism: Queer Acts against Nature', in Mortimer-Sandilands, C. and Erickson, B. (eds) *Queer Ecologies: Sex, Nature, Politics, Desire*, Bloomington, Indiana University Press, pp. 149–72.

Gottlieb, G.J, Ragaz, A., Vogel, J.V., Friedman-Kien, A., Rywlin, A.M., Weiner, E.A. and Ackerman, A.B. (1981) 'A Preliminary Communication on Extensively Disseminated Kaposi's Sarcoma in Young Homosexual Men', *American Journal of Dermatopathology*, vol. 3, no. 2, pp. 111–14.

Gottlieb, M.S., Schroff, R., Schanker, H.K., Weisman, J.D., Fan, P.T., Wolf, R.A. and Saxon, A. (1981) '*Pneumocystis carinii* Pneumonia and Mucosal Candidiasis in Previously Healthy Homosexual Men: Evidence of an Acquired Cellular Immunodeficiency', *New England Journal of Medicine*, vol. 305, no. 24, pp. 1425–31.

Gottlieb, M.S., Schroff, R., Fligiel, S., Fahey, J.L. and Saxon, A. (1982) 'Gay-related Immunodeficiency (GRID) Syndrome: Clinical and Autopsy Observations', *Clinical Research*, vol. 30, no. 2, p. A349.

Gould, R.E. (1988) 'Reassuring News about AIDS: A Doctor Tells Why You May Not be at Risk', *Cosmopolitan*, no. 204(1), January, pp. 146–147, p. 204.

Gould, P. (1993) *The Slow Plague: A Geography of the AIDS Pandemic*, Oxford, Blackwell.

Gower, M. (2010) 'Asylum: Claims Based on Sexual Identity', *July Home Affairs Section Standard Note SN/HA/5618 9*, House of Commons, UK.

Graham, M. (2013) 'Geography/Internet: Ethereal Alternative Dimensions of Cyberspace or Augmented Realities?', *The Geographical Journal*, vol. 179, no. 2, pp. 177–82.

Graham, M., Zook, M. and Boulton, A. (2013) 'Augmented Reality in Urban Places: Contested Content and the Duplicity of Code', *Transactions of the Institute of British Geographers*, vol. 38, no. 3, pp. 464–79.

Graham, S. (2004) 'Introduction', in Graham, S. (ed) *The Cyber Studies Reader*, London and New York, Routledge, pp. 1–29.

Graham, S. and Marvin, S. (2001) *Splintering Urbanism: Networked Infrastructures, Technological Mobilities and the Urban Condition*, London and New York, Routledge, pp. 1–36.

Grammaticos, P.C. and Diamantis, A. (2008) 'Useful Known and Unknown Views of the Father of Modern Medicine, Hippocrates and his Teacher Democritus', *Hellenic Journal of Nuclear Medicine*, vol. 11, no. 1, pp. 2–4.

Gramsci, A. (1971) *Selections from the Prison Notebooks of Antonio Gramsci* (trans. Q. Hoare and G. Nowell Smith), London, Lawrence and Wishart.

Grant, J.M., Mottet, L.A., Tanis, J., Harrison, J., Herman, J.L. and Keisling, K. (2011) *Injustice at Every Turn: A Report of the National Transgender Discrimination Survey*, Washington, DC, National Center for Transgender Equality and National Gay and Lesbian Task Force.

Gray, M. (2009) *Out in the Country: Youth, Media and Queer Visibility in Rural America*, New York, New York University Press.

Gray, M. (2010) 'From Websites to Wal–Mart: Youth, Identity Work, and the Queering of Boundary Publics in "Small Town", USA', in Pullen, C. and Cooper, M. (eds) *LGBT Identity and Online New Media*, Abingdon, Routledge, pp. 288–98.

Green, A.I. (2008) 'The Social Organization of Desire: The Sexual Fields Approach', *Sociological Theory*, vol. 26, no. 1, pp. 25–50.

Green, A.I., Follert, M., Osterlund, K. and Paquin, J. (2010) 'Space, Place and Sexual Sociality: Towards an "Atmospheric Analysis"', *Gender, Work & Organization*, vol. 17, no. 1, pp. 7–27.

Green, J. (2004) *Becoming a Visible Man*, Nashville, TN, Vanderbilt University Press.

Green, J.N. (1999) *Beyond Carnival: Male Homosexuality in Twentieth-century Brazil*, Chicago, University of Chicago Press.

Gregory, D. (1994) *Geographical Imaginations*, Malden, MA, Wiley-Blackwell.

Gregson, N. and Beale, V. (2004) 'Wardrobe Matter: The Sorting, Displacement and Circulation of Women's Clothing', *Geoforum*, vol. 35, no. 6, pp. 689–700.

Gregson, N. and Crewe, L. (2003) *Second-hand Cultures*, Oxford, Berg.

Gregson, N. and Lowe, M. (1995) '"Home"-making: On the Spatiality of Daily Social Reproduction in Contemporary Middle-class Britain', *Transactions of the Institute of British Geographers*, vol. 20, pp. 224–35.

Gregson, N. and Rose, G. (2000) 'Taking Butler Elsewhere: Performativities, Spatialities and Subjectivities', *Environment and Planning D: Society and Space*, vol. 18, pp. 433–52.

Grewal, I. and Kaplan, C. (2001) 'Global Identities: Theorizing Transnational Studies of Sexuality', *GLQ: A Journal of Lesbian and Gay Studies*, vol. 7, no. 4, pp. 663–79.

Griffiths, M. (2001) 'Sex on the Internet: Observations and Implications for Internet Sex Addiction', *Journal of Sex Research*, vol. 38, pp. 333–42.

Grindr in Real Life (2013) YouTube video, added by Will Means [Online]. Available at https://www.youtube.com/watch?v=B0ec7C7_9lY (accessed 9 April 2015).

Gronewold, S. (2013) 'Selling Sex in Shanghai, 1600 to the Present', paper presented at Selling Sex in the City: Prostitution in World Cities, 1600 to the Present Conference, Amsterdam, 25–27 April.

Grosfoguel, R. (2007) 'The Epistemic Decolonial Turn', *Cultural Studies*, vol. 21, no. 2, pp. 211–23.

Gross, A. (2013) 'The Politics of LGBT Rights: Between (Homo) Normality and (Homo) Nationalism and Queer Politics', *Ma'aseiMishpat*, vol. 5, pp. 101–42.

Gross, L. (2003) 'The Global Gay Village in Cyberspace', in Couldry, N. and Curran, J. (eds) *Contesting Media Power: Alternative Media in a Networked World*, New York, Rowman and Littlefield, pp. 259–72.

Gross, L. (2007) 'Foreword', in Phillips, J., David, J. and O'Riordan, K. (eds) *Queer Online: Media, Technology and Sexuality*, New York, Peter Lang Publishing Inc.

Grosz, E. (1993) 'Bodies and Knowledges: Feminism and the Crisis of Reason', in Alcoff, L. and Potter, E. (eds) *Feminist Epistemologies*, New York, Routledge, pp. 187–215.

Grosz, E. (1994) *Volatile Bodies: Toward a Corporeal Feminism*, St Leonards, Allen and Unwin.

Grov, C., Bamonte, A., Fuentes, A., Parsons, J., Bimbi, J. and Morgenstern, J. (2008) 'Exploring the Internet's Role in Sexual Compulsivity and Out of Control Sexual Thoughts/Behaviour: A Qualitative Study of Gay and Bisexual Men in New York City', *Culture, Health, and Sexuality*, vol. 10, pp. 107–25.

Grover, J. Z. (1987) 'AIDS: Keywords', in Crimp, D. (ed) *AIDS: Cultural Analysis, Cultural Activism*, Cambridge, MA, MIT Press, pp. 17–30.

Grundy, J. and Smith, M. (2005) 'The Politics of Multi-scalar Citizenship: The Case of Lesbian and Gay Organizing in Canada', *Citizenship Studies*, vol. 9, no. 4, pp. 389–404.

Grupo Davida (2005) 'Prostitutas, "traficadas" e pânicos morais: uma análise da produção de fatos em pesquisas sobre o 'tráfico de seres humanos', *Cadernos Pagu*, vol. 25, pp. 153–84.

Guigon, C. (2012) *Les Cocottes: reines du Paris, 1900*, Paris, Parigramme.

Gunkel, D.J. and Gunkel, A. H. (2009) 'Terra nova 2.0 – The new world of MMORPGs', *Critical Studies in Media Communication*, vol. 26, no. 2, pp. 104–27.

Gupta, A. and Ferguson, J. (1997) *Anthropological Locations: Boundaries and Grounds of a Field Science*, Berkeley, University of California Press.

Gutiérrez, J. and López-Nieva, P. (2001) 'Are International Journals of Human Geography Really International?', *Progress in Human Geography*, vol. 25, no. 1, pp. 53–69.

Guy, D.J. (1991) *Sex & Danger in Buenos Aires: Prostitution, Family, and Nation in Argentina*, Lincoln, University of Nebraska Press.

Haines, R. (2003) 'Gender-related Persecution', in Feller, E., Turk, V. and Nicholson, F. (eds) *Refugee Protection in International Law*, Cambridge, Cambridge University Press, pp. 230–350.

Halberstam, J. (1998) *Female Masculinity*, Durham, NC, Duke University Press.

Halberstam, J. (2005) *In a Queer Time and Place: Transgender Bodies, Subcultural Lives*, New York, New York University Press.

Halberstam, J. (2008) 'The Anti-social Turn in Queer Studies', *Graduate Journal of Social Science*, vol. 5, no. 2, pp. 140–56.

Hall, E. (2000) '"Blood, Brains and Bones": Taking the Body Seriously in the Geography of Health and Impairment', *Area*, vol. 32, no. 1, pp. 21–9.

Hall, K. (1995) 'Lip Service on the Fantasy Lines' in Hall, K. and Bucholtz, M. (eds) *Gender Articulated: Language and the Socially Constructed Self*, New York, Routledge, pp. 183–216.

Hall, S. (1985) 'Signification, Representation, Ideology: Althusser and the Post-Structuralist Debates', *Critical Studies in Mass Communication*, vol. 2, no. 2, pp. 91–114.

Hall, S. (1990) 'The Emergence of Cultural Studies and the Crisis of the Humanities', *October*, vol. 53, pp. 11–23.

Hall, S. (1996) 'On Postmodernism and Articulation: An Interview with Stuart Hall', *Journal of Communication Inquiry*, vol. 10, no. 2, pp. 45–60.

Halperin, D.M. (2002) *How To Do the History of Homosexuality*, Chicago, IL, University of Chicago Press.

Halperin, D.M. and Traub, V. (2009) 'Beyond Gay Shame', in Halperin, D.M. and Traub, V. (eds) *Gay Shame*, Chicago and London, University of Chicago Press, pp. 3–40.

Hamilton City Council (2011) *About Hamilton* [Online]. Available at http://hamilton.co.nz/page/pageid/2145832768/City_Info (accessed 1 May 2011).

Hamilton Pride Incorporated Society (n.d.) [Online]. Available at www.hamiltonpride.co.nz (accessed 5 March 2015).

Han, C. (2007) 'They Don't Want to Cruise Your Type: Gay Men of Color and the Racial Politics of Exclusion', *Social Identities*, vol. 13, no. 1, pp. 51–67.

Han, C. (2008) 'A Qualitative Exploration of the Relationship between Racism and Unsafe Sex among Asian Pacific Islander Gay Men', *Archives of Sexual Behavior*, vol. 37, pp. 827–37.

Han, C., Operario, D. and Choi, K. (2011) 'If I was Infected with HIV, I Would Be Letting my Family Down: Family Influences on Risk and Protective Factors for Unsafe Sex among Gay Asian Pacific Islander Men', *Health, Risk & Society*, vol. 13, no. 4, pp. 373–88.

Hancock C. and Barthe F. (eds) (2005) 'Le genre. Constructions spatiales et culturelles', *Géographie et cultures*, no. 54, Paris, L'Harmattan.

Hanhardt, C. (2013) *Safe Space: Gay Neighborhood History and the Politics of Violence*, Durham, NC, Duke University Press.

Hannam, K., Sheller, M. and Urry, J. (2006) 'Mobilities, Immobilities and Moorings', *Mobilities*, vol. 1, no. 1, pp. 1–22.

Hansbury, G. (2011) 'Trans/Virtual: The Anxieties of Transsexual and Electronic Embodiments', *Journal of Gay & Lesbian Mental Health*, vol. 15, no. 3, pp. 308–17.

Harawa, N.T., Greenland, S., Bingham, T.A., Johnson, D.F., Cochran, S.D., Cunningham, W.E., Celentano, D.D., Koblin, B.A., LaLota, M., MacKellar, D.A., McFarland, W., Shehan, D., Stoyanoff, S., Thiede, H., Torian, L. and Valleroy, L.A. (2004) 'Associations of Race/Ethnicity with HIV Prevalence and HIV-related Behaviors among Young Men Who Have Sex with Men in 7 Urban Centers in the United States', *Journal of Acquired Immune Deficiency Syndrome*, vol. 35, no. 5, pp. 526–36.

Haraway, D. (1991) *Simians, Cyborgs and Women: The Reinvention of Nature*, New York, Routledge.

Haraway, D.J. (1997) *Modest-Witness@Second-Millennium.FemaleMan-Meets-OncoMouse: Feminism and Technoscience*, New York, Routledge.

Harden, V.A. and Rodrigues, D. (1993) 'Context for a New Disease: Aspects of Biomedical Research Policy in the United States before AIDS', in Berridge, V. and Strong, P. (eds) *AIDS in Contemporary History*, Cambridge, Cambridge University Press, pp. 182–202.

Hardie, E. and Buzwell, S. (2006) 'Finding Love Online: The Nature and Frequency of Australian Adults' Internet Relationships', *Australian Journal of Emerging Technologies and Society*, vol. 4, no. 1, pp. 1–14.

Harding, S. (1991) *Whose Science? Whose Knowledge? Thinking from Women's Lives*, Ithaca, NY, Cornell University Press.

Harding, S. (ed.) (2004) *The Feminist Standpoint Theory Reader*, New York and London, Routledge.

Hardon, A. (2012) 'Biomedical Hype and Hopes: AIDS Medicines for Africa', in Geissler, P.W., Rottenburg, R. and Zenker, J. (eds) *Rethinking Biomedicine and Governance in Africa: Contributions from Anthropology*, Bielefeld, Transcript Verlag, pp. 77–96.

Harel, A. (1999) 'The Rise and Fall of the Israeli Gay Legal Revolution', *Columbia Human Rights Law Review*, vol. 31, pp. 443–71.

Haritaworn, J., Kuntsman, A. and Posocco, S. (2013) 'Murderous Inclusions', *International Feminist Journal of Politics*, vol. 15, no. 4, pp. 445– 52.

Harrington, M. (2008) 'AIDS Activists and People with AIDS: A Movement to Revolutionize Research and for Universal Access to Treatment', in da Costa, B. and Philip, K. (eds) *Tactical Biopolitics: Art, Activism and Technoscience*, Cambridge, MA, MIT Press, pp. 323–40.

Harris, S. (2005) 'Not a Gay Ghetto', *Star Observer*, 21 January, issue 749, p. 9.

Harry, J. (1974) 'Urbanization and the Gay Life', *Journal of Sex Research*, vol. 10, no. 3, pp. 131–56.

Harvey, D. (1973) *Social Justice and the City*, Baltimore, MD, Johns Hopkins University Press.

Harvey, D. (1989) 'The Condition of Postmodernity: An Enquiry into the Origins of Cultural Change', Oxford, Blackwell.

Harvey, D. (2004) 'The "New" Imperialism: Accumulation by Dispossession', *Socialist Register*, vol. 40, pp. 63–87.

Harvey, D. (2005) 'The Sociological and Geographical Imaginations', *International Journal of Politics, Culture & Society*, vol. 18, nos 3/4, pp. 211–55 [Online]. DOI: 10.1007/s10767–006–9009–6 (accessed 19 April 2015).

Harvey, D. (2007) *A Brief History of Neoliberalism*, Oxford, Oxford University Press.

Harwood, T. (2012) 'Emergence of Gamified Commerce: Turning Virtual to Real', *Electronic Commerce in Organisations*, vol. 10, no. 2, pp. 16–39.

Hasinoff, A. (2012) 'Sexting as Media Production: Rethinking Social Media and Sexuality', *New Media & Society*, vol. 15, no. 4, pp. 449–65.

Hasinoff, A. (2014) 'Blaming Sexualisation for Sexting', *Girlhood Studies*, vol. 7, no. 1, pp. 102–20.

Haverkos, H.W. and Curran, J.W. (1982) 'The Current Outbreak of Kaposi's Sarcoma and Opportunistic Infections', *CA-A Cancer Journal for Clinicians*, vol. 32, no. 6, pp. 330–39.

Hawkes, G. (1995) 'Dressing Up: Cross-dressing and Sexual Dissonance', *Journal of Gender Studies*, vol. 4, no. 3, pp. 261–70.

Hays Gries, P. and Rosen, S. (2004) 'Introduction: Popular Protest and State Legitimation in 21st-Century China', in Hays Gries, P. and Rosen, S. (eds) *State and Society in 21st-century China: Crisis, Contention, and Legitimation*, London, Routledge, pp. 1–23.

Healy, M. (1996) *Gay Skins: Class, Masculinity and Queer Appropriation*, London, Continuum.

Heaphy, B. (2011) 'Gay Identities and the Culture of Class', *Sexualities*, vol. 14, pp. 42–62.

Hebdige, D. (1979) *Subculture: The Meaning of Style*, London, Routledge.

Heckert, J. (2010) 'Intimacy with Strangers/Intimacy with Self: Queer Experiences of Social Research', In Browne, K. and Nash, C.J. (eds) *Queer Methods and Methodologies: Intersecting Queer Theories and Social Science Research*, Farnham and Burlington, Ashgate.

Hegland, J. and Nelson, N. (2002) 'Cross-dressers in Cyber-space: Exploring the Internet as a Tool for Expressing Gendered Identity', *International Journal of Sexuality and Gender Studies*, vol. 7, nos 2–3, pp. 139–61.

Heidegger, M. (2002) 'Building, Dwelling, Thinking', *Basic Writings*, London, Routledge, pp. 347–63.

Heikkila, E. (2005) 'Mobile Vulnerabilities: Perspectives on the Vulnerabilities of Immigrants in the Finnish Labour Market', *Population, Space and Place*, vol. 11, pp. 485–97.

Hekman, S. (2004) 'Truth and Method: Feminist Standpoint Theory Revisited', in Harding, S. (ed.) *The Feminist Standpoint Theory Reader: Intellectual and Political Controversies*, New York, Routledge.

Held, N. (2015) 'Comfortable and Safe Spaces? Gender, Sexuality and "Race" in Night-time Leisure Spaces', *Emotion, Space and Society*, vol. 14, pp. 33–42 [Online]. DOI: 10.1016/j. emospa.2014.12.003 (accessed 19 April 2015).

Hemmings, C. (2002) *Bisexual Spaces: A Geography of Sexuality and Gender*, London, Routledge.

Henry, W.A. (1987) 'The Appalling Saga of Patient Zero', *Time*, 19 October, p. 40.

Herman, R.D.K. (2007) 'Playing with Restraints: Space, Citizenship, and BDSM', in Browne, K., Lim, J. and Brown, G. (eds) *Geographies of Sexualities: Theory, Practices and Politics*, Aldershot, Ashgate, pp. 89–100.

Hernandez-Montiel v Immigration and Naturalization Service (2000) 225 F.3d 1084.

Herring, S. (2010) *Another Country: Queer Anti-urbanism*, New York, New York University Press.

Herthel, J., Jennings, J. and McNicholas, S. (2014) *I am Jazz*, New York, Dial Press.

Hetherington, P. (2013) 'Selling Sex in the City: St. Petersburg and Moscow, Russia', paper presented at Selling Sex in the City: Prostitution in World Cities, 1600 to the Present Conference, Amsterdam, 25–27 April.

Hille, K. (2011) 'Censors Kill off China's "Super Girl"', *Financial Times* [Online]. Available at http://www.ft.com/cms/s/0/8ba5b642-e1c1–11e0–9915–00144feabdc0.html#a xzz3BsN4HBJv (accessed 16 March 2012).

Hillier, L. and Harrison, L. (2007) 'Building Realities Less Limited Than Their Own: Young People Practising Same Sex Attraction on the Internet', *Sexualities: Studies in Culture and Society*, vol. 10, no. 1, pp. 82–100.

Hillier, L., Mitchell, K.J. and Ybarra, M.L. (2012) 'The Internet as a Safety Net: Findings From a Series of Online Focus Groups with LGB and Non-LGB Young People in the United States', *Journal of LGBT Youth*, vol. 9, no. 3, pp. 225–46.

Hillis, K. (2009) *Online a Lot of the Time: Ritual, Sign, Fetish*, Durham, NC, Duke University Press.

Hines, S. (2007) *TransForming Gender: Transgender Practices of Identity, Intimacy and Care*, Bristol, Policy Press.

Hines, S. (2010) 'Queerly Situated? Exploring Negotiations of Trans Queer Subjectivities at Work and within Community Spaces in the UK', *Gender, Place and Culture*, vol. 17, no. 5, pp. 597–613.

Hines, S. (2013) *Gender Diversity, Recognition and Citizenship: Towards a Politics of Difference*, London and New York, Palgrave Macmillan.

Hines, S. and Sanger, T. (eds) (2010) *Transgender Identities: Towards a Social Analysis of Gender Diversity*, London, Routledge.

Hines, S. and Taylor, Y. (2011) *Sexualities: Reflections and Futures*, London, Palgrave Macmillan.

Hines, S., Taylor, Y. and Casey, M. (eds) (2010) *Theorising Intersectionality and Sexuality*, London, Palgrave Macmillan.

Hirschman, C. (1986) 'The Making of Race in Colonial Malaya: Political Economy and Racial Ideology', *Sociological Forum*, vol. 1, pp. 330–61.

Hjorth, L. and Lim, S.S. (2012) 'Mobile Intimacy in an Age of Affective Mobile Media', *Feminist Media Studies*, vol. 12, no. 4, pp. 477–84.

Hoad, N. (1999) 'Between a White Man's Burden and the White Man's Disease: Tracking Lesbian and Gay Human Rights in Southern Africa', *GLQ: A Journal of Lesbian and Gay Studies*, vol. 5, no. 4, pp. 559–84.

Hoad, N. (2007) *African Intimacies: Race, Homosexuality and Globalisation*, Minneapolis, University of Minnesota Press.

Hodge, G.D. (2000) 'Retrenchment from a Queer Ideal: Class Privilege and the Failure of Identity Politics in AIDS Activism', *Environment and Planning D: Society and Space*, vol. 18, pp. 355–76.

Hodkinson, S. and Chatterton, P. (2006) 'Autonomy in the City? Reflections on the Social Centers Movement in the UK', *City*, vol. 10, no. 3, pp. 305–15.

Hofer, G. and Ragazzi, L. (2008) *Improvvisamente l'inverno scorso* [Online]. Available at https:// vimeo.com/ondemand/33355 (accessed 20 April 2015).

Holden, P. (1999) 'The Beginnings of "Asian Modernity" in Singapore: A Straits Chinese Body Project', *Communal/Plural*, vol. 7, pp. 59–78.

Holden, P. (2003) 'Rethinking Colonial Discourse Analysis and Queer Studies', in Holden, P. and Ruppel, R.J. (eds) *Imperial Desire: Dissident Sexualities and Colonial Literature*, Minneapolis, University of Minnesota Press, pp. 295–321.

Holleran, A. (1978) *Dancer from the Dance: A Novel*, New York, Penguin.

Hollister, J.W. (2002) 'Reconstructing Social Theory at a Cruising Site', unpublished dissertation, Binghamton, State University of New York.

Holloway, S. and Valentine, G. (eds) (2000) *Children's Geographies: Playing, Living, Learning*, Abingdon, Routledge.

Holloway, S.L. and Valentine, G. (2003) *Cyberkids: Children in the Information Age*, London, Routledge.

Holloway, S.L. and Valentine, G. (2005) 'Children's Geographies and the New Social Studies of Childhood', in Jenks, C. (ed.) *Childhood: Critical Concepts in Sociology*, London, Routledge. pp. 163–88.

Holloway, S., Valentine, G., and Bingham, N. (2000) 'Institutionalising Technologies: Masculinities, Femininities, and the Heterosexual Economy of the IT Classroom', *Environment and Planning A*, vol. 32, no. 4, pp. 617–33.

Holmes, C. (2012) 'Violence Denied, Bodies Erased: Towards an Interlocking Spatial Framework for Queer Anti-Violence Organizing', PhD thesis, Vanvouver, University of British Columbia.

Holston, J. (2011) 'Contesting Privilege with Right: The Transformation of Differentiated Citizenship in Brazil', *Citizenship Studies*, vol. 15, nos 3–4, pp. 335–52.

Holt, M. and Griffin, C. (2003) 'Being Gay, Being Straight, and Being Yourself: Local and Global Reflections on Identity, Authenticity and the Lesbian and Gay Scene', *European Journal of Cultural Studies*, vol. 6, pp. 404–25.

Holzemer, W.L., Uys, L., Makoae, L., Stewart, An., Phetlhu, R., Dlamini, P.S., Greeff, M., Kohi, T. W., Chirwa, M., Cuca, Y. and Naidoo, J. (2007) 'A Conceptual Model of HIV/ AIDS Stigma from Five African countries', *Journal of Advanced Nursing*, vol. 58, no. 6, pp. 541–51.

hooks, b. (1981) *Ain't I a Woman? Black Women and Feminism*, Boston, MA, South End Press.

hooks, b. (1989) *Talking Back: Thinking Feminist, Thinking Black*, Boston, MA, South End Press.

hooks, b. (1990) 'Marginality as a Site of Resistence', in Ferguson, R., Gever, M., Minh-ha, T.T. and West, C. (eds) *Out There: Marginalization and Contemporary Cultures*, Cambridge, MA, MIT Press, pp. 241–3.

Horowitz, S.L., Benson, D.F., Gottlieb, M.S., Davos, I. and Bentson, J.R. (1982) 'Neurological Complications of Gay-related Immunodeficiency Disorder', *Annals of Neurology*, vol. 12, no. 1, pp. 80–88.

Horton, J. and Kraftl, P. (2009) 'Small Acts, Kind Words, and "Not Too Much Fuss": Implicit Activisms', *Emotion, Space and Society*, vol. 2, no. 1, pp. 14–23.

Houlbrook, M. (2005) *Queer London: Perils and Pleasures in the Sexual Metropolis, 1918–1957*, Chicago and London, University of Chicago Press.

Howe, C., Zaraysky, S. and Lorentzen, L. (2008) 'Transgender Sex Workers and Sexual Transmigration between Guadalajara and San Francisco', *Latin American Perspectives*, vol. 35, no. 1, pp. 31–50.

Howell, P. (2000) 'Prostitution and Racialised Sexuality: The Regulation of Prostitution in Britain and the British Empire before the Contagious Diseases Act', *Environment and Planning D: Society and Space*, vol. 18, pp. 321–39.

Howell, P. (2004) 'Race, Space and the Regulation of Prostitution in Colonial Hong Kong', *Urban History*, vol. 31, no. 2, pp. 229–48.

Howell, P. (2007) 'Foucault, Sexuality, Geography' in Crampton, J.W. and Elden, S. (eds) *Space, Knowledge and Power: Foucault and Geography*, Aldershot, Ashgate.

Howell, P. (2009) *Geographies of Regulation: Policing Prostitution in Nineteenth-century Britain and the Empire*, Cambridge, Cambridge University Press.

Hubbard, P. (1997) 'Red-light Districts and Toleration Zones: Geographies of Female Street Prostitution in England and Wales', *Area*, vol. 29, no. 2, pp. 129–40.

Hubbard, P. (1998) 'Sexuality, Immorality and the City: Red-light Districts and the Marginalisation of Female Street Prostitutes', *Gender, Place and Culture*, vol. 5, no. 1, pp. 55–76.

Hubbard, P. (1999) *Sex and the City: Geographies of Prostitution in the Urban West*, Aldershot, Ashgate.

Hubbard, P. (2000) 'Desire/Disgust: Mapping the Moral Contours of Heterosexuality', *Progress in Human Geography*, vol. 24, pp. 191–217.

Hubbard, P. (2001) 'Sex Zones: Intimacy, Citizenship and Public Space', *Sexualities*, vol. 4, no. 1, pp. 51–71.

Hubbard, P. (2002) 'Sexing the Self: Geographies of Engagement and Encounter', *Social & Cultural Geography*, vol. 3, no. 4, pp. 365–81.

Hubbard, P. (2004a) 'Cleansing the Metropolis: Sex Work and the Politics of Zero Tolerance', *Urban Studies*, vol. 41, no. 9, pp. 1687–702.

Hubbard, P. (2004b) 'Revenge and Injustice in the Neoliberal City: Uncovering Masculinist Agendas', *Antipode*, vol. 36, no. 4, pp. 665–86.

Hubbard, P. (2007) 'Between Transgression and Complicity (Or, Can the Straight Guy have a Queer Eye)', in Browne, K., Lim, J. and Brown, G. (eds) *Geographies of Sexualities: Theory, Practices and Politics*, Aldershot, Ashgate, pp. 151–6.

Hubbard, P. (2008) 'Here, There, Everywhere: The Ubiquitous Geographies of Heteronormativity', *Geography Compass*, vol. 2, no. 3, pp. 640–58.

Hubbard, P. (2011) *Cities and Sexualities*, London, Routledge.

Hubbard, P. (2012) 'World Cities of Sex', in De Rudder, B., Hoyler, M., Taylor, P.J. and Witlox, F. (eds) *International Handbook of Globalization and World Cities*, Cheltenham, Edgar Elgar, pp. 295–305.

Hubbard, P. (2013) 'Response – Phil Hubbard', *Gender, Place and Culture*, vol. 20, no. 3, pp. 407–10.

Hubbard, P., Campbell, R., O'Neill, M., Pitcher, J. and Scoular, J. (2007) 'Prostitution, Gentrification and the Limits of Neighbourhood Space', in Atkinson, R. and Helms, G. (eds) *Securing an Urban Renaissance*, Bristol, Policy Press, pp. 203–17.

Hubbard, P. and Colosi, R. (2015) 'Taking Back the Night? Gender and the Contestation of Sexual Entertainment in England and Wales', *Urban Studies*, vol. 52, no. 3, pp. 589–605.

Hubbard, P. and Lister, B. (2015) 'Sexual Entertainment, Dread Risks and the Heterosexualisation of Community Space', in Maginn, P.J. and Steinmetz, C. (eds) *(Sub)urban Sexscapes: Geographies and Regulation of the Sex Industry*, London, Routledge, pp. 141–58.

Hubbard, P., Matthews, R., Scoular, J. and Agustin, L. (2008) 'Away from Prying Eyes? The Urban Geographies of "Adult Entertainment"', *Progress in Human Geography*, vol. 32, no. 3, pp. 363–81.

Hubbard, P. and Prior, J. (2013) 'Out of Sight, Out of Mind? Prostitution Policy and Health, Well-being and Safety of Home-based Sex Workers', *Critical Social Policy*, vol. 33, no. 1, pp. 140–59.

Hubbard, P. and Sanders, T. (2003) 'Making Space for Sex Work: Female Street Prostitution and the Production of Urban Space', *International Journal of Urban and Regional Research*, vol. 27, no. 1, pp. 75–89.

Hubbard, P. and Whowell, M. (2008) 'Revisiting the Red Light District: Still Neglected, Ommoral and Marginal?', *Geoforum*, vol. 39, no. 5, pp. 1743–55.

Hubbard, P. and Wilkinson, E. (2014) 'Welcoming the World? Hospitality, Homonationalism, and the London 2012 Olympics', *Antipode* [Online]. DOI: 10.1111/anti.12082 (accessed 19 April 2015).

Hudson, R. and Williams, A.M. (2004) 'European Voices: Towards the Internationalization of Academic Discourse', *European Urban and Regional Studies*, vol. 11, no. 4, pp. 355–6.

Human Rights Watch (2012a) 'Police Practices Fuel HIV Epidemic: Sex Workers at Risk From Condom Policy' [Online]. Available at http://www.hrw.org/news/2012/07/19/us-police-practices-fuel-hiv-epidemic (27 April 2014).

Human Rights Watch (2012b) 'Sex Workers at Risk: Sex Workers at Risk from Condom Policy', 19 July [Online]. Available at http://www.hrw.org/node/108771/section/5 (accessed 27 April 2014).

Humphries, L. (1970) *Tearoom Trade: A Study of Homosexual Encounters in Public Places*, London, Duckworth.

Hunt, A. (1998) 'The Great Masturbation Panic and the Discourses of Moral Regulation in Nineteenth- and Early Twentieth-Century Britain', *Journal of the History of Sexuality*, vol. 84, pp. 575–615.

Hunt, N. (1978) *Mirror Image: The Odyssey of a Male to Female Transsexual*, New York, Holt.

Huntemann, N.B. and Payne, M.T. (eds) (2009) *Joystick Soliders: The Politics of Play in Military Video Games*, New York, Routledge.

Hunter, M. (2010a) *Love in the Time of AIDS: Inequality, Gender and Rights in South Africa*, Bloomington, Indiana University Press.

Hunter, M. (2010b) 'Beyond the Male-migrant: South Africa's Long History of Health Geography and the Contemporary AIDS Pandemic', *Health and Place*, vol. 16, pp. 25–33.

Hutchings, J. and Aspin, C. (eds) (2007), *Sexuality & the Stories of Indigenous People*, Wellington, Aotearoa New Zealand, Huia Publishers.

Hutta, J.S. (2010) 'Paradoxical Publicness: Becoming-imperceptible with the Brazilian Lesbian, Gay, Bisexual and Transgender Movement', in Mahony, N., Newman, J. and Barnett, C. (eds) *Rethinking the Public: Innovations in Research, Theory and Politics*, Bristol, Policy Press, pp. 143–61.

Hyams, M. (2000) '"Pay Attention in Class … [and] Don't Get Pregnant": A Discourse of Academic Success among Adolescent Latinas', *Environment and Planning A*, vol. 32, no. 4, pp. 635–54.

Hyndman, J. (2001) 'Towards a Feminist Geopolitics', *The Canadian Geographer*, vol. 45, no. 2, pp. 210–22.

Hynes, H.P. and Raymond, J.G. (2002) 'Put in Harm's Way: The Neglected Health Consequences of Sex Trafficking in the United States', in Silliman, J. and Bhattacharjee, A. (eds) *Policing the National Body: Race, Gender and Criminalization*, Cambridge, MA, South End Press, pp. 197–230.

ILGA (2014) *State Sponsored Homophobia. A World Survey of Laws: Criminalization, Protection and Recognition of Same-sex Love* [Online]. Available at http://old.ilga.org/Statehomophobia/ILGA_SSHR_2014_Eng.pdf (accessed 14 December 2014).

Iliffe, J. (2006) *The African AIDS Epidemic: A History*, Oxford, James Currey.

Independència per canviar-ho tot (2013) *Si no podem decidir no podem ser lliures! Avortament lliure i gratuït!* [Online]. Available at http://percanviarhotot.cat/blog/si-no-podem-decidir-no-podem-ser-lliures-avortament-lliure-i-gratuit (accessed 2 April 2015).

INE (2010) *Instituto Nacional de Estadística* [Online]. Available at https://www.ine.es/jaxi/menu.do?type=pcaxis (accessed 30 May 2014).

Infante, A. (2009) 'Espanhóis preferem noivas brasileiras entre as estrangeiras, diz pesquisa', BBC, 16 April [Online]. Available at http://www.bbc.co.uk/portuguese/noticias/2009/04/090416_espanahabrasileiras_fp.shtml (accessed 10 September 2014).

Ingram, A. (2013) 'After the Exception: HIV/AIDS beyond Salvation and Scarcity', *Antipode*, vol. 45, no. 2, pp. 436–54.

Ingram, G.B., Bouthillette, A-M. and Retter, Y. (eds) (1997) *Queers in Space: Communities/Public Places/Sites of Resistance*, Seattle, Bay Press.

International Commission of Jurists (2007) *The Yogyakarta Principles: Principles on the Application of Human Rights Law in Relation to Sexual Orientation and Gender Identity* [Online]. Available at http://www.yogyakartaprinciples.org/principles_en.pdf (accessed 2 April 2015).

International Organization for Migration (2014) 'Key Migration Terms' [Online]. Available at http://www.iom.int/cms/en/sites/iom/home/about-migration/key-migration-terms-1.html#Irregular-migration (accessed 15 November 2014).

Institut Català d'Estadística (2013) *Idescat*, [Online]. Available at www.idescat.cat (accessed 15 September 2014).

Institut national de la statistique et des études économiques (1999) *Le recensement de 2009, France* [Online]. Available at http://www.insee.fr/ (accessed 31 March 2015).

Isoke, Z. (2014) 'Can't I Be Seen? Can't I Be Heard? Black Women Queering Politics in Newark', *Gender, Place & Culture*, vol. 21, no. 3, pp. 353–69.

Itaborahy, L.P. and Zhu, J. (2014) *State-Sponsored Homophobia: A World Survey of Laws: Criminalisation, Protection and Recognition of Same-sex Love*, Geneva, ILGA.

Ito, M. (2003) 'Mobiles and the Appropriation of Place', *Receiver*, vol. 8 [Online]. Available at http://www.receiver.vodafone.com (accessed 19 April 2015).

Ito, M. (2005) 'Mobile Phones, Japanese Youth, and the Re-placement of Social Contact', in Ling, R. and Pedersen, P.E. (eds) *Mobile Communications: Re-negotiation of the Social Sphere*, London, Springer.

Ito, M. and Okabe, D. (2005) 'Technosocial Situations: Emergent Structurings of Mobile Email Use', in Ito, M., Okabe, D. and Matsuda, M. (eds) *Personal, Portable, and Pedestrian: Mobile Phones in Japanese Life*, Cambridge, MA, MIT Press, pp. 257–73.

Jacobs, J.M. and Fincher, R. (1998) 'Introduction', in Fincher, R. and Jacobs, J.M. (eds) *Cities of Difference*, New York, The Guilford Press, pp. 1–25.

Jaffe, H.W., Choi, K., Thomas, P.A., Haverkos, H.W., Auerbach, D.M., Guinan, M E., Rogers, M.F., Spira, T.J., Darrow, W.W., Kramer, M.A., Friedman, S.M., Monroe, J.M., Friedman-Kien, A.E., Laubenstein, L.J., Marmor, M., Safai, J., Dritz, S.K., Crispi, S.J., Fannin, S.L., Orkwis, J.P., Kelter, A., Rushing, W.R., Thacker, S.B. and Curran, J.W. (1983) 'National Case Control Study of Kaposi's Sarcoma and *Pneumocystisis carinii* Pneumonia in Homosexual Men: Part I, Epidemiologic Results', *Annals of Internal Medicine*, vol. 99, no. 2, pp. 145–51.

Jaffe, H.W., Darrow, W.M., Echenberg, D.F., O'Malley, P.M., Getchell, J.P., Kalyanaraman, V.S., Byers, R.H., Drennan, D.P., Braff, E.H., Curran, J.W. and Francis, D.P. (1985) 'The

Acquired Immunodeficiency Syndrome in a Cohort of Homosexual Men: A Six-year Follow-up Study', *Annals of Internal Medicine*, vol. 103, no. 2, pp. 210–14.

Jakes, S. (2005) 'Li Yuchun', *Time* [Online]. Available at http://content.time.com/time/world/article/0,8599,2054304,00.html (accessed 16 March 2012).

Jakes, S. (2006) 'China's Super Girl Needs a Rescue', *Time* [Online]. Available at http://content.time.com/time/magazine/article/0,9171,1176987,00.html (accessed 16 March 2012).

Janet Mock Rejoins Piers Morgan (2014) YouTube video, added by CNN [Online]. Available at www.youtube.com/watch?v=0F8WiuxYoE4&feature=kp (accessed 9 August 2014).

Jeffreys, S. (1997) *The Idea of Prostitution*, North Melbourne, Spinifex Press.

Jégou, A., Chabrol, A. and De Bélizal, E. (2012) 'Rapports genrés au terrain en géographie physique', *Géographie et culture*, vol. 83, no. 1 [Online]. Available at http://gc.revues.org/2027#tocto1n1 (4 January 2015).

Jenkins, H. (2006) *Convergence Culture: Where Old and New Media Collide*, London, Routledge.

Jenkins, H., Ford, S. and Green, J. (2013) *Spreadable Media: Creating Value and Meaning in a Networked Culture*, New York, New York University Press.

Jennings, B. (2008) 'WTFpwned by Chinese Gold Farmers: Translating "Otherness" into Synthetic Worlds through Culture and Language Hierarchies', in Leino, O., Wirman, H. and Fernandez, A. (eds) *Extending Experiences: Structure, Analysis and Design of Computer Game Player Experience*, Rovaniemi, Lapland University Press, pp. 93–109.

Jhally, S. and Lewis, J. (1992) *Enlightened Racism: The Cosby Show, Audiences, and the Myth of the American Dream*, Boulder, CO, Westview Press.

Jian, M. and Liu, C. (2009) '"Democratic Entertainment" Commodity and Unpaid Labor of Reality TV: A Preliminary Analysis of China's Supergirl', *Inter-Asia Cultural Studies*, vol. 10, no. 4, pp. 524–43.

Joffe-Walt, B. (2005) 'Mad about the Girl: A Pop Idol for China', *The Guardian*, 7 October [Online]. Available at http://www.theguardian.com/media/2005/oct/07/chinathemedia.broadcasting (accessed 16 March 2012).

Johnson, C.A. (2007) *Off the Map: How HIV/AIDS Programming is Failing Same-sex Practicing People in Africa*, New York, International Gay and Lesbian Human Rights Commission.

Johnson, K. and Browne, K. (2012) 'Trans and Intersex Issues in Health and Care', *Diversity and Equality in Health and Care*, vol. 9, pp. 235–57.

Johnson, L. (2000) *Placebound: Australian Feminist Geographies*, South Melbourne, Oxford University Press.

Johnston, L. (2005) 'Man: Woman', in Cloke, P. and Johnston, R. (eds) *Spaces of Geographical Thought: Deconstructing Human Geography's Binaries*, London, Sage. pp. 119–41.

Johnston, L. (2006) '"I Do Downunder": Naturalizing Landscapes and Love through Wedding Tourism in New Zealand', *ACME: An International E-Journal for Critical Geographies*, vol. 5, no. 2, pp. 191–208.

Johnston, L. (2007) 'Mobilizing Pride/Shame: Lesbians, Tourism and Parade', *Social & Cultural Geography*, vol. 8, no. 1, pp. 29–45.

Johnston, L. (2009) *Queering Tourism: The Paradoxical Performances of Gay Pride Parades*, London, Routledge.

Johnston, L. and Longhurst, R. (2010) *Space, Place, and Sex: Geographies of Sexualities*, Lanham, MD, Rowman & Littlefield.

Johnston, L. and Valentine, G. (1995) 'Wherever I Lay my Girlfriend, That's my Home: The Performance and Surveillance of Lesbian Identities in Domestic Environments', in Bell, D. and Valentine, G. (eds) *Mapping Desire: Geographies of Sexualities*, London, Routledge, pp. 99–113.

Jordan, J. (2004) 'Beyond Belief: Police, Rape and Women's Credibility', *Criminal Justice*, vol. 4, no. 1, pp. 29–59.

Jordan, S.R. (2011) 'Un/Convention(al) Refugees: Contextualizing the Accounts of Refugees Facing Homophobia or Transphobic Persecution', *Refuge*, vol. 26, no. 2, pp. 165–82.

Jorgensen, C. (1967) *Christine Jorgensen: A Personal Autobiography*, San Francisco, CA, Cleis Press.

Judge, M. (2008) 'Exploring Homophobic Victimisation in Gauteng, South Africa: Issues, Impacts and Responses', *Acta Criminologica*, vol. 21, no. 3, pp. 19–36.

Jupp, J. (1998) *Immigration*, Melbourne, Oxford University Press.

Juris, J.S. (2005) 'Social Forums and their Margins: Networking Logics and the Cultural Politics of Autonomous Space', *Ephemera: Theory & Politics in Organization*, vol. 5, no. 2, pp. 253–72.

Kahn, A. (1993) *AIDS: The Winter War*, Philadelphia, PA, Temple University Press.

Kalichman, S. (2009) *Denying AIDS: Conspiracy Theories, Pseudoscience, and Human Tragedy*, New York, Copernicus Books.

Kalichman, S.C. and Simbayi, L.C. (2003) 'HIV Testing Attitudes, AIDS Stigma, and Voluntary HIV Counselling and Testing in a Black Township in Cape Town, South Africa', *Sexually Transmitted Infections*, vol. 79, pp. 442–7.

Kalipeni, E., Craddock, S., Oppong, J. and Ghosh, J. (2003) *HIV & AIDS in Africa: Beyond Epidemiology*, London, Wiley-Blackwell.

Kama, A. (2011) 'Parading Pridefully into the Mainstream: Gay & Lesbian Immersion in the Civil Core', in Ben-Porat, G. and Turner, B. (eds) *The Contradictions of Israeli Citizenship: Land, Religion and State*, New York, Routledge, pp. 180–202.

Kanai, J. M. (2014) 'Whither Queer World Cities? Homo-entrepreneurialism and Beyond', *Geoforum*, vol. 56, pp. 1–5.

Kanai, J.M. and Kenttamaa-Squires, K. (2015) 'Remaking South Beach: Metropolitan Gayborhood Trajectories under Homonormative Entrepreneurialism', *Urban Geography*, vol. 36, no. 3, pp. 385–402.

Kanngieser, A. (2012) 'A Sonic Geography of Voice: Towards an Affective Politics', *Progress in Human Geography*, vol. 36, pp. 336–53.

Karasch, M. (1987) *Slave Life in Rio de Janeiro 1808–1850*, Princeton, NJ, Princeton University Press.

Karras, R. M. (1996) *Common Women: Prostitution and Sexuality in Medieval England*, New York, Oxford University Press.

Katsulis, Y. (2009) *Sex Work and the City: The Social Geography of Health and Safety in Tijuana, Mexico*, Austin, University of Texas Press.

Kaufmann, V., Bergman, M.M., Joye, D. (2004) 'Motility: Mobility as Capital', *International Journal of Urban and Regional Research*, vol. 28, pp. 745–56.

Kaveney, R. (1999) 'Talking Transgender Politics', in More, K. and Whittle, S. (eds) *Reclaiming Genders: Transsexual Grammars at the Fin de Siècle*, London, Cassell, pp. 146–58.

Kawale, R. (2004) 'Inequalities of the Heart: The Performance of Emotion Work by Lesbian and Bisexual Women in London, England', *Social & Cultural Geography*, vol. 5, no. 4, pp. 565–81.

Kayal, P.M. (1993) *Bearing Witness: Gay Men's Health Crisis and the Politics of AIDS*, Oxford, Westview.

Kearns, G. (2007) 'The History of Medical Geography after Foucault', in Crampton, J.W. and Elden, S. (eds) *Space, Knowledge and Power: Foucault and Geography*, Aldershot, Ashgate, pp. 205–22.

Kearns, R. (1993) 'Place and Health: Towards a Reformed Medical Geography', *The Professional Geographer*, vol. 45, no. 2, pp. 139–47.

Kearns, R. and Collins, D. (2010) 'Health Geography', in Brown, T., McLafferty, S. and Moon, G. (eds) *The Companion to Health and Medical Geography*, Chichester, Wiley-Blackwell, pp. 15–32.

Keerdoja, E. and Morris, H. (1982) 'Homosexual Plague Strikes New Victims', *Newsweek*, 23 August, p. 10.

Kehily, M. J. (2002) 'Sexing the Subject: Teachers, Pedagogies and Sex Education', *Sex Education: Sexuality, Society and Learning*, vol. 2, no. 3, pp. 215–31.

Kelly, E.D. and Cooper, C. (2000) *Everything You Always Wanted to Know About Regulating Sex Businesses*, Chicago, IL, American Planning Association.

Kemp, J. (2013) *The Penetrated Male*, New York, Punctum.

Kempadoo, K. (2009) *Prostitution, Sex Work and Transactional Sex in the English-, Dutch- and French-Speaking Caribbean: A Literature Review of Definitions, Laws and Research*, Greater Georgetown, Pan Caribbean Partnership Against HIV and AIDS.

Kempadoo, K. and Doezema, J. (eds) (1998) *Global Sex Workers: Rights, Resistance, and Redefinition*, London, Psychology Press.

Kempadoo, K., Sanghera, J. and Pattanaik, B. (2005) *Trafficking and Prostitution Reconsidered: New Perspectives on Migration, Sex Work, and Human Rights*, London, Paradigm Publishers.

Kendall, L. (2000) '"Oh No! I'm a Nerd!": Hegemonic Masculinity on an Online Forum', *Gender and Society*, vol. 14, pp. 256–74.

Kendall, L. (2002) *Hanging Out in the Virtual Pub: Masculinities and Relationships Online*, Berkeley, University of California Press.

Kendrick, W. (1987) *The Secret Museum: Pornography in Modern Culture*, Oakland, University of California Press (this edition 1997).

Kennedy, E. and Davis, M. (1994) *Boots of Leather, Slippers of Gold: The History of a Lesbian Community*, New York, Penguin.

Kennedy, H.W. (2002) 'Lara Croft: Feminist Icon or Cyberbimbo? On the Limits of Textual Analysis', *Game Studies: International Journal of Computer Games Research*, vol. 2, no. 2, unpaginated.

Kenney, M.R. (1998) 'Remember, Stonewall Was a Riot: Understanding Gay and Lesbian Experience in the City', in Sandercock, L. (ed.) *Making the Invisible Visible: A Multicultural Planning History*, Berkeley, University of California Press, pp. 120–32.

Kenney, M.R. (2001) *Mapping Gay L.A.: The Intersections of Place and Politics*, Philadelphia, PA, Temple University Press.

Kentlyn, S. (2008) 'The Radically Subversive Space of the Queer Home: Safety House and Neighbourhood Watch', *Australian Geographer*, vol. 39, no. 3, pp. 327–37.

Kergoat, D. (2009) 'Dynamique et consubstantialité des rapports sociaux', in Dorlin, E. (ed.) *Sexe, race, classe. Pour une* épistémologie *de la domination*, Paris, La dispute, pp. 111–25.

Kerkin, K. (2003) 'Re-placing Difference: Planning and Street Sex Work in a Gentrifying Area', *Urban Policy and Research*, vol. 21, no. 2, pp. 137–49.

Kern, L. (2010) 'Selling the "Scary City": Gendering Freedom, Fear and Condominium Development in the Neoliberal City', *Social & Cultural Geography*, vol. 11, no. 3, pp. 209–30.

Kesby, M. (2007) 'Spatialising Participatory Approaches: The Contribution of Geography to a Mature Debate', *Environment and Planning A*, vol. 39, no. 12, pp. 2813–31.

Kesby, M. and Sothern. M. (2014) 'Blood, Sex and Trust: The Limits of the Population-based Risk Management Paradigm', *Health and Place*, vol. 26, pp. 21–30.

Keshavarz, F. (2007) *Jasmine and Stars: Reading More than Lolita in Tehran*, Chapel Hill, University of North Carolina Press.

Khoo Hooi Leong v Khoo Chong Yeok [1930] Straits Settlements Law Reports, Singapore, Government Printing Office.

Kiishweko, O. (2012) 'Tanzania: Views United in Trashing Same-sex Marriage', *AllAfrica*, 18 October [Online]. Available at http://allafrica.com/stories/201210180288.html (accessed 5 May 2014).

Kindon, S., Pain, R. and Kesby, M. (eds) (2007) *Participatory Action Research Approaches and Methods: Connecting People, Participation and Place*, New York, Routledge.

King, B. (2010) 'Political Ecologies of Health', *Progress in Human Geography*, vol. 34, pp. 38–55.

King, K. (1994) *Theory in Its Feminist Travels: Conversations in U.S. Women's Movements*, Bloomington, Indiana University Press.

Kingston, S. (2013) *Prostitution in the Community: Attitudes, Action and Resistance*, London, Routledge.

Kirby, S. and Hay, I. (1997) '(Hetero)sexing Space: Gay Men and "Straight" Space in Adelaide, South Australia', *The Professional Geographer*, vol. 49, no. 3, pp. 295–305.

Kirby, V. (1997) *Telling Flesh: The Substance of the Corporeal*, New York, Routledge.

Kirkey, K. and Forsyth, A. (2001) 'Men in the Valley: Gay Male Life on the Suburban–Rural Fringe', *Journal of Rural Studies*, vol. 17, no. 4, pp. 421–41.

Kirkland, A.R. (2003) 'Victorious Transsexuals in the Courtroom: A Challenge for Feminist Legal Theory', *Law and Social Inquiry*, vol. 28, no. 1, pp. 1–37.

Kirp, D.L. and Bayer, R. (1992) *AIDS in the Industrial Democracies: Passions, Politics and Policies*, New Brunswick, NJ, Rutgers University Press.

Kissack, T. (2008) *Free Comrades: Anarchism and Homosexuality in the United States, 1895–1917*, Oakland, CA, AK Press.

Kistner, U. (2009) 'Adversities in Adherence: Paralogisms of "Biological Citizenship" in South Africa', paper presented at AEGIS, 3rd European Conference on African Studies, Leipzig, Germany, 4–7 June.

Kitchin, R. (2005) 'Commentary: Disrupting and Destabilizing Anglo-American and English-language Hegemony in Geography', *Social & Cultural Geography*, vol. 6, no. 1, pp. 1–15.

Kitchin, R. and Fuller, D. (2003) 'Making the "Black Box" Transparent: Publishing and Presenting Geographic Knowledge', *Area*, vol. 35, no. 3, pp. 313–15.

Kitchin, R. and Lysaght, K. (2003) 'Heterosexism and the Geographies of Everyday Life in Belfast, Northern Ireland', *Environment and Planning A*, vol. 35, no. 3, pp. 489–510.

Klein, T. (2012) 'Configuring Trans* Citizens in South Africa: Somatechnics, Self-formation and Governmentality', in Geissler, P.W., Rottenburg, R. and Zenker, J. (eds) *Rethinking Biomedicine and Governance in Africa: Contributions from Anthropology*, Bielefeld, Transcript Verlag, pp. 43–74.

Kleinschmidt, H. (2003) *People on the Move: Attitudes toward and Perceptions of Migration in Medieval and Modern Europe*, Westport, CT, Praeger.

Klesse, C. (2007) *The Spectre of Promiscuity: Gay Male and Bisexual Non-Monogamies and Polyamories*, Aldershot, Ashgate.

Klesse, C. (2014a) 'Polyamory – Intimate Practice, Identity or Sexual Orientation?', *Sexualities*, vol. 17, nos 1–2, pp. 81–99.

Klesse, C. (2014b) 'Poly Economics – Capitalism, Class, and Polyamory', *International Journal of Politics, Culture, and Society*, vol. 27, no. 2, pp. 203–20.

Knopp, L. (1987) 'Social Theory, Social Movements and Public Policy: Recent Accomplishments of the Gay and Lesbian Movements in Minneapolis, Minnesota', *International Journal of Urban and Regional Research*, vol. 11, pp. 243–61.

Knopp, L. (1990) 'Some Theoretical Implications of Gay Involvement in an Urban Land Market', *Political Geography Quarterly*, vol. 9, no. 4, pp. 337–52.

Knopp, L. (1992) 'Sexuality and the Spatial Dynamics of Capitalism', *Environment & Planning D: Society and Space*, vol. 10, pp. 651–69.

Knopp, L. (1995) 'Sexuality and Urban Space', in Bell, D. and Valentine, G. (eds) *Mapping Desire: Geographies of Sexualities*, London, Routledge, pp. 149–61.

Knopp, L. (1998) 'Sexuality and Urban Space: Gay Male Identity Politics in the United States, the United Kingdom and Australia', in Fincher, R. and Jacobs, J. (eds) *Cities of Difference*, New York, Guilford Press, pp. 149–76.

Knopp, L. (2004) 'Ontologies of Place, Placelessness, and Movement: Queer Quests for Identity and their Impacts on Contemporary Geographic Thought', *Gender, Place, and Culture: A Journal of Feminist Geography*, vol. 11, no. 1, pp. 121–34.

Knopp, L. (2007) 'On the Relationship between Queer and Feminist Geographies', *The Professional Geographer*, vol. 59, no. 1, pp. 47–55 [Online]. DOI: 10.1111/j.1467–9272.2007.0 0590.x (accessed 20 April 2015).

Knopp, L. and Brown, M.P. (2002) 'We're Here! We're Queer! We're Over There Too! Queer Cultural Geographies', in Anderson, K., Domosh, M., Pile, S. and Thrift, N. (eds) *The Handbook of Cultural Geography*, New York, Sage, pp. 313–24.

Knopp, L. and Brown, M.P. (2003) 'Queer Diffusions', *Environment and Planning D: Society and Space*, vol. 21, no. 4, pp. 409–24.

Kohler, B. and Wissen, M. (2003) 'Globalizing Protest: Urban Conflicts and Global Social Movements', *International Journal of Urban and Regional Research*, vol. 27, pp. 942–51.

Kong, L., Yeoh, B.S.A. (2003) *The Politics of Landscape in Singapore: Constructions of 'Nation'*, Syracuse, NY, Syracuse University Press.

Konrad, C.L. (2014) 'This is Where We Live: Queering Poor Urban Spaces in the Literature of Black Gay Men', *Gender, Place and Culture*, vol. 21, no. 3, pp. 337–52.

Koopman, S. (2011) 'Alter-geopolitics: Other Securities are Happening', *Geoforum*, vol. 42, no. 3, pp. 274–84.

Korinek, V. (2012) '"We're the Girls of the Pansy Parade": Historicizing Winnipeg's Queer Subcultures, 1930s–1970', *Histoire sociale*, vol. xlv, pp. 117–55.

Koskela, H. (1997) '"Bold Walk and Breakings": Women's Spatial Confidence versus Fear of Violence', *Gender, Place and Culture*, vol. 4, no. 3, pp. 301–19.

Koskela, H. (1999) '"Gendered Exclusions": Women's Fear of Violence and Changing Relations to Space', *Geografiska Annaler B*, vol. 81, no. 2, pp. 111–24.

Kramer, J.L. (1995), 'Bachelor Farmers and Spinsters: Gay and Lesbian Identities and Communities in Rural North Dakota', in Bell, D. and Valentine, G (eds) *Mapping Desire: Geographies of Sexualities*, London, Routledge, pp. 200–13.

Kramer, L. (1978) *Faggot*, New York, Grove Press.

Kramer, L. (1989) *Reports from the Holocaust: The Making of an AIDS Activist*, New York, St Martin's Press.

Kristen (2013) 'A Few Anti-Gay Apples Ruin the Bunch in Manitoba, Help Make the Case for Bill 18', *autostraddle*, 4 April [blog]. Available at: http://www.autostraddle.com/a-few-antigay-apples-ruin-the-bunch-in-manitoba-help-make-the-case-for-bill-18–171526/ (accessed 20 April 2015).

Kristeva, J. (1980) *Powers of Horror: An Essay on Abjection* (trans. L.S. Roudiez), New York, Columbia University Press (this edition 1982).

Kron, J. (2012) 'Resentment toward the West Bolsters Uganda's New Anti-Gay Bill', *New York Times*, 28 February [Online]. Available at http://www.nytimes.com/ 2012/02/29/world/afri ca/ugandan-lawmakers-push-anti-homosexuality-bill-again.html?_r=0 (accessed 3 April 2014).

Kuhn, T.S. (1996) *The Structure of Scientific Revolutions* (new edn of 3rd rev. edn), Chicago, IL, Chicago University Press.

Kulick, D. (1997) 'A Man in the House: The Boyfriends of Brazilian Travesti Prostitutes', *Social Text*, vol. 52, no. 3, pp. 133–60.

Kulick, D. (1998) *Travesti: Sex, Gender, and Culture among Brazilian Transgendered Prostitutes*, Chicago, IL, University Of Chicago Press.

Kulpa, R. (2011) 'Nations and Sexualities –"West" and "East"', in Kulpa, R. and Mizielińska, J. (eds) *De-centring Western Sexualities*, Farnham, Ashgate, pp. 43–62.

Kulpa, R. (2014) 'Western Leveraged Pedagogy of Central and Eastern Europe: Discourses of Homophobia, Tolerance, and Nationhood', *Gender, Place & Culture: A Journal of Feminist Geography*, vol. 21, no. 4, pp. 431–48.

Kulpa, R. and Mizielinska, J. (eds) (2011), *De-centring Western Sexualities: Central and Eastern Perspectives*, Farnham, Ashgate.

Kumar, M.S. (2005) '"Oriental Sore or Public Nuisance": The Regulation of Prostitution in Colonial India, 1805–1889', in Proudfoot, L.J. and Roche, M.M. (eds) *(Dis)Placing Empire: Renegotiating British Colonial Geographies*, Aldershot, Ashgate, pp. 155–74.

Kunkel, J. (2012) 'Community Goes German: The Displacement of Sex Work in the Name of a Neoliberal Concept', *Social Justice*, vol. 38, nos 1–2, pp. 47–70.

Kuntsman, A. (2003) 'Double Homecoming: Sexuality, Ethnicity and Place in Immigration Stories of Russian Lesbians in Israel', *Women's Studies International Forum*, vol. 26, no. 4, pp. 299–311.

Kuntsman, A. (2007) 'Belonging through Violence: Flaming, Erasure, and Performativity in Queer Migrant Culture', in O'Riordan, K. and Phillips, D.J. (eds) *Queer Online: Media, Technology and Sexuality*, New York, Peter Lang, pp. 101–20.

Kuntsman, A. (2009) 'The Currency of Victimhood in Uncanny Homes: Queer Immigrants' Claims for Home and Belonging through Anti-homophobic Organising', *Journal of Ethnic and Migration Studies*, vol. 35, no. 1, pp. 133–49.

Lacey, A. (2005) 'Networked Communities: Social Centers and Activist Spaces in Contemporary Britain', *Space and Culture*, vol. 8, no. 3, pp. 286–301.

Laclau, E. (1977) *Politics and Ideology in Marxist Theory*, London, New Left Books.

Laichen, S. (2007) 'Burmese Bells and Chinese Eroticism: Southeast Asia's Cultural Influence on China', *Journal of Southeast Asian Studies*, vol. 38, no. 2, pp. 247–73.

Laidler, K.J., Petersen, C. and Emerton, R. (2007) 'Bureaucratic Justice: The Incarceration of Mainland Chinese Women Working in Hong Kong's Sex Industry', *International Journal of Offender Therapy and Comparative Criminology*, vol. 51, no. 1, pp. 68–83.

Laing, M. (2012) 'Regulating Adult Work in Canada: The Role of Criminal and Municipal Code', in Johnson, P. and Dalton, D. (eds) *Policing Sex*, London, Routledge, pp. 166–84.

Laing, M. and Cook, I. R. (2014) 'Governing Sex Work in the City', *Geography Compass*, vol. 8, pp. 505–15 [Online]. DOI: 10.1111/gec3.12144 (accessed 20 April 2015).

Laing, M., Smith, N. and Pilcher, K. (eds) (2015) *Queer Sex Work*, London, Routledge.

Laite, J. (2011) *Common Prostitutes and Ordinary Citizens: Commercial Sex in London, 1885–1960*, New York, Palgrave Macmillan.

Lake, M. and Reynolds, H. (2008) *Drawing the Global Colour Line: White Men's Countries and the International Challenge of Racial Equality*, Cambridge, Cambridge University Press.

Lal, V. (2005) *Empire of Knowledge: Culture and Plurality in the Global Economy* (2nd rev. edn), New Delhi, Vistaar.

Lam, T. (2000) 'Identity and Diversity: The Complexities and Contradictions of Chinese Nationalism', in Weston, T. and Jenson, L. (eds) *China beyond the Headlines*, Lanham, MD, Rowman & Littlefield, pp. 147–70.

Lampe, C., Ellison, N. and Steinfield, C. (2006) 'A Face(book) in the Crowd: Social Searching vs. Social Browsing', *Proceedings of CSCW – 2006*, Banff, Alberta, Canada.

Landau, J. (2005) '"Soft Immutability" and "Imputed Gay Identity": Recent Developments in Transgender and Sexual Orientation-Based Asylum Law', *Fordham Urban Law Journal*, vol. 32, no. 2, pp. 237–64.

Lander, E. (2000) 'Eurocentrism and Colonialism in Latin American Social Thought', *Nepantla: Views from South*, vol. 1, no. 3, pp. 519–32.

Lander, E. (2005) 'Ciências Sociais: Saberes Coloniais E Eurocêntricos', in Lander, E. (ed.) *A colonialidade do saber: Eurocentrismo e ciências sociais*, Buenos Aires, Consejo Latinoamericano de Ciências Sociais, pp. 21–54.

Lane, T., Mogale, T., Struthers, H., Mcintyre, J. and Kegeles, S. (2008) '"They See You as a Different Thing": The Experiences of Men Who Have Sex with Men with Healthcare Workers in South African Township Communities', *Sexually Transmitted Infections*, vol. 84, pp. 430–33.

Lane, T., Raymond, H.F., Dladla, S., Rasethe, J., Struthers, H., McFarland, W. and McIntyre, J. (2011) 'High HIV Prevalence among Men Who Have Sex with Men in Soweto, South Africa: Results from the Soweto Men's Study', *AIDS and Behavior*, vol. 15, no. 3, pp. 626–34.

Lasén, A. (2004) 'Affective Technologies – Emotions and Mobile Phones', *Receiver*, vol. 11, Vodaphone {Online]. Available at https://www.academia.edu/472410/Affective_Techno logies._Emotions_and_Mobile_Phones (accessed 2 September 2015).

Lasén, A. (2005) 'History Repeating? A Comparison of the Launch and Uses of Fixed and Mobile Phones', in Hamill, L. and Lasén, A. (eds) *Mobile World: Past, Present and Future*, London, Springer, pp. 48–9.

Lasén, A. and Casado, E. (2012) 'Mobile Telephony and the Remediation of Couple Intimacy', *Feminist Media Studies*, vol. 12, no. 4, pp. 550–59.

Lasker, S. (2002) 'Sex and the City: Zoning Pornography Peddlers and Live Nude Shows', *UCLA Law Review*, vol. 49, no. 4, pp. 1139–86.

Lauria, M. and Knopp, L. (1985) 'Towards an Analysis of the Role of Gay Communities in the Urban Renaissance', *Urban Geography*, vol. 6, no. 2, pp. 152–69.

Laurier, E. (2001) 'Why People Say Where They are During Mobile Phone Calls', *Environment and Planning D: Society and Space*, vol. 19, pp. 485–504.

Laverne Cox Opens up about 'TIME' Cover and 'Orange is the New Black' (2014) YouTube Video, added by Katie Couric [Online]. Available at https://www.youtube.com/ watch?v=3mgBwCxTRDY (accessed 9 August 2014).

Lavers, M.K. (2014) 'LGBT Ugandans Dying in "Crimes against Humanity"', *Washington Blade*, 30 April [Online]. Available at http://www.washingtonblade.com/2014/04/30/lgbt-ugandans-dying/ (accessed 6 May 2014).

Lazzara, D. (2010) 'YouTube Courtship: The Private Ins and Public Outs of Chris and Nickas', in Pullen, C. and Cooper, M. (eds) *LGBT Identity and Online New Media*, Abingdon, Routledge, pp. 51–61.

Leach, M. (2007) 'Earth Mother Myths and Other Ecofeminist Fables: How a Strategic Notion Rose and Fell', *Development and Change*, vol. 38, no. 1, pp. 67–85.

Leander, K.M., Phillips, N.C. and Taylor, K.H. (2010) 'The Changing Social Spaces of Learning: Mapping New Mobilities', *Review of Research in Education*, vol. 34, no. 1, pp. 329–94.

Leahy, D. and McCuaig, L. (2013) *Supporting Teachers to Teach Relationships and Sexuality Education: FPA Queensland Workforce Development Scoping Paper*, Brisbane, FPA Queensland.

Leap, W. (1999) *Public Sex/Gay Space*, New York, Columbia University Press.

Leap, W. and Boellstorff, T. (eds) (2004) *Speaking in Queer Tongues: Globalisation and Gay Language*, Chicago, University of Illinois Press.

Leclerc-Madlala, S. (2003) 'Transactional Sex and the Pursuit of Modernity', *Social Dynamics: A Journal of African Studies*, vol. 29, no. 2, pp. 213–33.

Lee, H.L. (2007) *Speech to Parliament on Reading of Penal Code (Amendment) Bill*, Singapore, 22 October.

Lee, J.J. and Hoadley, C.M. (2006) 'Ugly in a World Where You can Choose to be Beautiful: Teaching and Learning about Diversity via Virtual Worlds', *Proceedings of the 7th International Conference on Learning Sciences*, Indiana University, Bloomington, 27 June–1 July, International Society of the Learning Sciences, pp. 383–9.

Lee, K.Y. (2000) *From Third World to First: The Singapore Story, 1965–2000*, New York, HarperCollins.

Lees, L. (2004) *The Emancipatory City?*, London, Sage.

Lefebvre, H. (1968) *Le droit à la ville*, Paris, Éditions Anthropos.

Lefebvre, H. (1974) *La production de l'espace*, Paris, Éditions Anthropos.

Lefebvre, H. (1991) *The Production of Space* (trans. D. Nicholson-Smith), Oxford, Blackwell.

Legg, S. (2009) 'Governing Prostitution in Colonial Delhi: From Cantonment Regulations to International Hygiene (1864–1939)', *Social History*, vol. 34, no. 4, pp. 447–67.

Legg, S. (2012) 'Stimulation, Segregation and Scandal: Geographies of Prostitution Regulation in British India, between Registration (1888) and Suppression (1923)', *Modern Asian Studies*, vol. 46, no. 6, pp. 1459–505.

Legg, S. (2014) *Prostitution and the Ends of Empire: Scale, Governmentalities, and Interwar India*, Durham, NC, Duke University Press.

Legg, S. and Roy, S. (2013) 'Neoliberalism, Postcolonialism and Hetero-sovereignties: Emergent Sexual Formations in Contemporary India', *Interventions*, vol. 15, no. 4, pp. 461–73.

Leontidou, L. (2006) 'Urban Social Movements: From the "Right to the City" to Transnational Spatialities and Flaneur Activist', *City*, vol. 10, no. 3, pp. 259–68.

Leow, B.G. (2000) *Census of Population 2000: Households and Housing*, Singapore, Department of Statistics.

Lerner, G. (1986) 'The Origin of Prostitution in Ancient Mesopotamia', *Signs*, vol. 11, no. 2, pp. 236–54.

Leroy, S. (2009) 'La possibilité d'une ville. Comprendre les spatialités homosexuelles en milieu urbain', *Espaces et sociétés*, vol. 139, pp. 159–74.

Lert, F. and Plauzolles, P. (2003) 'Apports des enquêtes quantitatives dans la connaissance des comportements sexuels et préventifs chez les homosexuels et bisexuels masculins', in Broqua, C., Lert, F. and Souteyrand, Y. (eds) *L'homosexualité au temps du sida*, Paris, ANRS, pp. 55–69.

Levine, A.S. (1982) 'The Epidemic of Acquired Immune Dysfunction in Homosexual Men and its Sequelae – Opportunistic Infections, Kaposi's Sarcoma, and Other Malignancies: An Update and Interpretation', *Cancer Treatment Reports*, vol. 66, no. 6, pp. 1391–6.

Levine, M. (1979) 'Gay Ghetto', *Journal of Homosexuality*, vol. 4, no. 4, pp. 363–77.

Levine, P. (2003) *Prostitution, Race and Politics: Policing Venereal Disease in the British Empire*, New York, Routledge.

Levy, V., Page-Shafer, K., Evans, J., Ruiz, J., Morrow, S., Reardon, J., Lynch, M., Raymond, H.F., Klausner, J.D., Facer, M., Molitor, F., Allen, B., Ajufo, B.G., Ferrero, D., Sanford, G.B. and McFarland, W. (2005) 'HIV-related Risk Behavior among Hispanic Immigrant Men in a Population-based Household Survey in Low-income Neighborhoods of Northern California', *Sexually Transmitted Diseases*, vol. 32, no. 8, pp. 487–90.

Lewis, N.M. (2009) 'Mental Health and Sexual Minorities: Recent Indicators, Trends, and their Relationships to Place in North America and Europe', *Health and Place*, vol. 15, no. 4, pp. 1029–45.

Lewis, N.M. (2012a) 'Gay in a "Government Town": The Settlement and Regulation of Gay-identified Men in Ottawa, Canada', *Gender, Place & Culture: A Journal of Feminist Geography*, vol. 19, no. 3, pp. 291–312.

Lewis, N.M. (2012b) 'Remapping Disclosure: Gay Men's Segmented Journeys of Moving Out and Coming Out', *Social & Cultural Geography*, vol. 13, no. 3, pp. 211–31.

Lewis, N.M. (2013a) 'Ottawa's Le/The Village: Creating a Gaybourhood Amidst the "Death of the Village"', *Geoforum*, vol. 49, pp. 233–42.

Lewis, N.M. (2013b) 'Beyond Binary Places: The Social and Spatial Dynamics of Coming Out in Canada', *ACME: An International E-Journal for Critical Geographies*, vol. 12, no. 2, pp. 305–30.

Lewis, N.M. (2014a) 'Moving "Out", Moving On: Gay Men's Migrations Through the Life Course', *Annals of the Association of American Geographers*, vol. 104, no. 2, pp. 225–33 [Online]. DOI: 10.1080/00045608.2013.873325 (accessed 20 April 2015).

Lewis, N.M. (2014b) 'Rupture, Resilience, and Risk: Relationships between Mental Health and Migration among Gay-Identified Men in North America', *Health & Place*, vol. 27, pp. 212–19.

Lewis, N.M. (2015) '"Placing" HIV beyond the Metropolis: Risks, Mobilities, and Health Promotion among Gay Men in the Halifax, Nova Scotia Region', *The Canadian Geographer* [Online]. DOI: 10.1111/cag.12173 (accessed 20 April 2015).

Leyshon, M., DiGiovanna, S. and Holcomb, B. (2013) 'Mobile Technologies and Youthful Exploration: Stimulus or Inhibitor?', *Urban Studies*, vol. 50, no. 3, pp. 587–605.

Liamputtong, P. (2007) *Researching the Vulnerable: A Guide to Sensitive Research Methods*, London, Sage.

Lieh-Mak, F., O'Hoy KM. and Luk, S.L. (1983) 'Lesbianism in the Chinese of Hong Kong'. *Archives of Sexual Behaviour*, vol. 12, no. 1, pp. 21–30.

Light, B. (2007) 'Introducing Masculinity Studies to Information Systems Research: The Case of Gaydar', *European Journal of Information Systems*, vol. 16, pp. 658–65.

Light, B., Fletcher, G. and Adam, A. (2008) 'Gay Men, Gaydar and the Commodification of Difference', *Information Technology and People*, vol. 21, no. 3, pp. 300–14.

Lim, J. and Fanghanel, A. (2013) '"Hijabs, Hoodies and Hotpants": Negotiating the "Slut" in SlutWalk', *Geoforum*, vol. 48, pp. 207–15.

Limoncelli, S. (2010) *The Politics of Trafficking: The First International Movement to Combat the Sexual Exploitation of Women*, Stanford, CA, Stanford University Press.

Listerborn, C. (2003) 'Prostitution as "Urban Radical Chic": The Silent Acceptance of Female Exploitation', *City*, vol. 7, no. 2, pp. 237–46.

Little, J. (2003) '"Riding the Rural Love Train": Heterosexuality and the Rural Community', *Sociologia Ruralis*, vol. 43, no. 4, pp. 401–17.

Little, J. (2007) 'Constructing Nature in the Performance of Rural Heterosexualities', *Environment and Planning D: Society and Space*, vol. 25, no. 5, pp. 851–66.

Livingstone, S. (2008) 'Taking Risky Opportunities in Youthful Content Creation: Teenagers' Use of Social Networking Sites for Intimacy, Privacy and Self-expression', *New Media and Society*, vol. 10, no. 3, pp. 392–411.

Lloyd, G. (1993) *The Man of Reason: 'Male' and 'Female' in Western Philosophy*, London, Routledge.

Lloyd, J. (2008) 'Selling New Domestic Spaces', in Hetherington, K. and Cronin, A. (eds) *Consuming the Entrepreneurial City: Image, Memory, Spectacle*, London, Routledge.

Lo, J. and Healy, T. (2000) 'Flagrantly Flaunting It? Contesting Perceptions of Locational Identity among Urban Vancouver Lesbians', in Valentine, G. (ed.) *From Everywhere to Nowhere: Lesbian Geographies*, London, Routledge, pp. 29–44.

Lobert, R. (2010) *A palavra mágica: a vida cotidiana do Dzi Croquettes*, Campinas, Unicamp.

LoBosco, S. and Badesha, M. (2014) *Pride across the Pattullo*, course work presentation, personal communication, 3 April.

Lockard, D. (1986) 'The Lesbian Community: An Anthropological Approach', *Journal of Homosexuality*, vol. 11, nos 3–4, pp. 83–95.

Loe, M. (2004) *The Rise of Viagra: How the Little Blue Pill Changed Sex in America*, London and New York, New York University Press.

Lombardi, E. and Wilchins, R.A. (2001) 'Gender Violence: Transgender Experience with Violence and Discrimination', *Journal of Homosexuality*, vol. 42, no. 1, pp. 89–101.

Long, S. (2009) 'Unbearable Witness: How Western Activists Misrecognize Sexuality in Iran', *Comparative Politics*, vol. 15, no. 1, pp. 119–36.

Longhurst, R. (1995) 'The Body and Geography', *Gender, Place and Culture*, vol. 2, no. 1, pp. 97–105.

Longhurst, R. (1997) '(Dis)embodied Geographies', *Progress in Human Geography*, vol. 21, no. 4, pp. 486–501.

Longhurst, R. (2001) *Bodies: Exploring Fluid Boundaries*, London, Routledge.

Longhurst, R. (2005) 'Situating Bodies', in Nelson, L. and Seager, J. (eds) *A Companion to Feminist Geography*, Malden, MA, Blackwell, pp. 337–49.

Loopmans, M. and Van den Broeck, P. (2011) 'Global Pressures, Local Measures: The Re-Regulation of Sex Work in the Antwerp Schipperskwartier', *Tijdschrift voor Economische en Sociale Geografie*, vol. 102, no. 5, pp. 548–61.

Loos, T. (2008) 'A Hstory of Sex and the State in Southeast Asia: Class, Intimacy and Invisibility', *Citizenship Studies*, vol. 12, pp. 27–43

Lopes, M. de A. and Simões, P.M. (2010) 'Os segredos da mulher brasileira', *Focus*, vol. 565, pp. 116–27.

Lorde, A. (1982) *Zami: A New Spelling of My Name – A Biomythography*, Berkeley, The Crossing Press.

Löw, M. and R. Ruhne (2009) 'Domesticating Prostitution: Study of an Interactional Web of Space and Gender', *Space and Culture*, vol. 12, pp. 232–49.

Lugones, M. (2007) 'Heterosexualism and the Colonial/Modern Gender System', *Hypatia*, vol. 22, no. 1, pp. 186–219.

Luibhéid, E. (2002) *Entry Denied: Controlling Sexuality at the Border*, Minneapolis, University of Minnesota Press.

Luibhéid, E. (2008a) 'Queer/Migration: An Unruly Body of Scholarship', *GLQ: A Journal of Lesbian and Gay Studies*, vol. 14, nos 2–3, pp. 170–90.

Luibhéid, E. (2008b) 'Sexuality, Migration, and the Shifting Line Between Legal and Illegal Status', *GLQ: A Journal of Lesbian and Gay Studies*, vol. 14, nos 2–3, pp. 290–315.

Luibhéid, E. and Cantú Jr, L. (eds) (2005) *Queer Migrations: Sexuality, US Citizenship, and Border Crossings*, Minneapolis, University of Minnesota Press.

Lumby, C. and Albury, K. (2010) 'Too Much? Too Young? The Sexualisation of Children Debate in Australia', *Media International Australia, Incorporating Culture & Policy*, vol. 135, pp. 141–52.

Luongo, M. (2007) *Gay Travels in the Muslim World*, Binghampton, Harrington Park Press.

Lupton, D. (1995) 'The Embodied Computer/User', in Featherstone, M. and Burrows, T. (eds) *Cyberspace, Cyberbodies, Cyberpunk: Cultures of Technological Embodiment*, London, Sage, pp. 97–112.

Lyod, B. and Rowntree, L. (1978) 'Radical Feminists and Gay Men in San Francisco: Social Space in Dispersed Communities', in Lanegran, D. and Palm, R. (eds) *An Invitation to Geography*, New York, McGraw-Hill, pp. 78–88.

Lyttleton, C. (2000) *Endangered Relations: Negotiating Sex and AIDS in Thailand*, New York, Harwood.

MacCallum-Stewart, E. (2008) 'Real Boys Carry Girly Epics: Normalising Gender Bending in Online Games', *Eludamos: Journal for Computer Game Culture*, vol. 2, no. 1, pp. 27–40.

MacDonnell, J.A. and Andrews, G.J. (2006) 'Placing Sexuality in Health Policies: Feminist Geographies and Public Health Nursing', *GeoJournal*, vol. 65, no. 4, pp. 349–64.

MacMillan, C. J. (2013) 'Repressed Identities: A Traveling Exploration of Sexuality, Gender and Place', in Pearce, W. and Hillabold, J. (eds) *Out Spoken: Perspectives on Queer Identities*, Regina, SK, University of Regina Press, pp. 145–58.

Maddison, S. (2007) *The Biopolitics of the Penis* [Online]. Available at http://cultural studiesresearch.org/wp–content/uploads/2012/10/MaddisonBiopoliticsPenis.pdf (accessed 20 March 2014).

Madison, D.S. (2012) *Critical Ethnography: Methods, Ethics, Performance*, Los Angeles, Sage.

Maginn, P.J. and Steinmetz, C. (eds) (2014) *(Sub)Urban Sexscapes: Geographies and Regulation of the Sex Industry*, London, Routledge.

Mahmood, S. (2005) *Politics of Piety: The Islamic Revival and the Feminist Subject*, Princeton, NJ, Princeton University Press.

Mai, N. (2009) 'Between Minor and Errant Mobility: The Relation between Psychological Dynamics and Migration Patterns of Young Men Selling Sex in the EU', *Mobilities*, vol. 4, no. 3, pp. 349–66.

Mai, N. and King, R. (2009) 'Love, Sexuality and Migration: Mapping the Issue(s)', *Mobilities*, vol. 4, no. 3, pp. 295–307.

Malbon, B. (1999) *Clubbing: Dancing, Ecstasy and Vitality*, London, Routledge.

Malek, A. (2006) 'Memoir as Iranian Exile Cultural Production: A Case Study of Marjane Satrapi's *Persepolis* Series', *Iranian Studies*, vol. 39, no. 3, pp. 353–80.

Malinowski, B. (1923) 'The Problem of Meaning in Primitive Languages', in Ogden, C.K. and Richards, I.A. (eds) *The Meaning of Meaning*, London, Routledge, pp.146–52.

Malpas, J. (1999) *Place and Experience: A Philosophical Topography*, Cambridge, Cambridge University Press.

Manalansan, M.F. (1995) 'In the Shadows of Stonewall: Examining Gay Transnational Politics and the Diasporic Dilemma', *GLQ: A Journal of Lesbian and Gay Studies*, vol. 2, pp. 425–38.

Manalansan, M. (2000) 'Diasporic Deviants/Divas: How Filipino Gay Transmigrants "Play with the World"', in Patton, C. and Sánchez-Eppler, B. (eds) *Queer Diasporas*, Durham, NC, Duke University Press, pp. 183–203.

Manalansan, M. (2003) *Global Divas: Filipino Gay Men in the Diaspora*, Durham, NC, Duke University Press.

Manalansan, M. (2006) 'Queer Intersections: Gender and Sexuality in Migration Studies', *International Migration Review*, vol. 40, no. 1, pp. 224–49.

Manderson, L. (1992) 'Public Sex Performances in Patpong and Explorations of the Edges of Imagination', *Journal of Sex Research*, vol. 29, no. 4, pp. 451–75.

Manderson, L. (1996) *Sickness and the State: Health and Illness in Colonial Malaya, 1870–1940*, New York, Cambridge University Press.

Manderson, L. (1997) 'Colonial Desires: Sexuality, Race, and Gender in British Malaya', *Journal of the History of Sexuality*, vol. 7, pp. 372–88.

Manifesto for Transfeminist Insurrection (2009) [Online]. Available at http://anarchalibrary. blogspot.co.uk/2010/10/manifesto-for-trans-feminist.html (accessed 2 September 2015).

Mann, J. and Tarantola, D. (1996) *AIDS in the World II: Global Dimensions, Social Roots, and Responses*, Vol. 2, Oxford, Oxford University Press.

Mao, L., Van de Ven, P. and McCormick, J. (2004) 'Individualism–Collectivism, Self-Efficacy, and Other Factors Associated With Risk Taking among Gay Asian and Caucasian Men', *AIDS Education and Prevention*, vol. 16, pp. 55–67.

Marçal, M.M. (1977) *Divisa/ Survivors*, bilingual edition (trans. S. D. Abrams), Barcelona, Institute of North American Studies (this edition 1993).

Marks, L. (2010) *Sexual Chemistry: A History of the Contraceptive Pill*, New Haven, CT, Yale University Press.

Markwell, K. (2002) 'Mardi Gras Tourism and the Construction of Sydney as an International Gay and Lesbian City', *GLQ: A Journal of Lesbian and Gay Studies*, vol. 8, nos 1–2, pp. 81–99.

Marmo, M. and Smith, E. B. (2012) 'Female Migrants: Sex, Value and Credibility in Immigration Control', in McCulloch, J. and Pickering, S. (eds) *Borders and Crime: Pre-Crime, Mobility and Serious Harm in an Age of Globalization*, London, Palgrave Macmillan, pp. 54–71.

Martey, R.M., Stromer-Galley, J., Banks, J., Wu, J. and Consalvo, M. (2014) 'The Strategic Female: Gender-switching and Player Behavior in Online Games', *Information, Communication & Society*, vol. 17, no. 3, pp. 286–300.

Martinez, J.M. (2003) 'On the Possibility of the Latino Postcolonial Intellectual', *Nepantla: Views from the South*, vol. 4, no. 2, pp. 253–6.

Martinez, O. and Dodge, B. (2010) 'El barrio de La Chueca en Madrid, Spain: An Emerging Epicenter of the Global LGBT Civil Rights Movement', *Journal of Homosexuality*, vol. 57, no. 2, pp. 226–48.

Martinsen, J. (2006) 'CPPCC: Exterminate the Super Girls', *Danwei* [Online]. Available at http://www.danwei.org/trends_and_buzz/cppcc_exterminate_the_super_girls.php (accessed 16 March 2012).

Marttila, A-M. (2008) 'Desiring the "Other": Prostitution Clients on a Transnational Red-light District in the Border area of Finland, Estonia and Russia', *Gender, Technology and Development*, vol. 12, no. 1, pp. 31–51.

Marwick, A. and boyd, d. (2011) 'The Drama! Teen Conflict, Gossip, and Bullying in Networked Publics', in *Proceedings* of the A Decade In Internet Time: Oxford Internet Institute Symposium on the Dynamics of the Internet and Society, Oxford, England, 21–24 September, University of Oxford.

Marx, K. (1845) 'Theses on Feuerbach', in McLellan, D. (ed.) *Karl Marx: Selected Writings*, Oxford, Oxford University Press, pp. 156–8, (this edition 1977).

Marx, K. (1846) *The German Ideology*, New York, International Publishers (this edition 1965).

Marx, K. (1857–61) *Grundrisse: Foundations of the Critique of Political Economy*, London, Penguin (this edition 1973).

Masanet, E. and Padilla, B. (2010) 'La inmigración brasileña en Portugal y España ¿Sistema migratório Ibérico?', *OBETS: Revista de Ciencias Sociales*, vol. 5, no. 1, pp. 49–86.

Mass, L.D. (1981) 'Disease Rumors Largely Unfounded', *New York Native*, 18 May.

Massachusetts SORB (2014) *Sex Offender Registry Board* [Online]. Available at: http://www.mass.gov/eopss/agencies/sorb/ (accessed 20 March 2014).

Massaro, V.A. and Williams, J. (2013) 'Feminist Geopolitics', *Geography Compass*, vol. 7, pp. 567–77.

Massey, D. (1994) *Space, Place and Gender*, Cambridge, Polity Press.

Massey, D. (2005) *For Space*, Cambridge, Polity Press.

Masur, H., Michelis, M.A., Greene, J. B., Onorato, I., Vande Stouwe, R.A., Holzman, R.S., Wormser, G., Brettman, L., Lange, M., Murray, H.W. and Cunningham-Rundles, S. (1981) 'An Outbreak of Community-acquired *Pneumocystis carinii* Pneumonia: Initial Manifestation of Cellular Immune Dysfunction', *New England Journal of Medicine*, vol. 305, no. 24, pp. 1431–8.

Masur, H., Michelis, M.A., Wormser, G.P., Lewin, S., Gold, J., Tapper, M.L., Giron, J., Lerner, C.W., Armstrong, D., Setia, U., Sender, J.A., Siebken, R.S., Nicholas, P., Arlen, Z., Maayan, S., Ernst, J.A., Siegal, F.P. and Cunningham-Rundles, S. (1982) 'Opportunistic Infection in Previously Healthy Women: Initial Manifestations of a Community-acquired Cellular Immune Dysfunction', *Annals of Internal Medicine*, vol. 97, no. 4, pp. 533–9.

Mathieu, L. (2011) 'Neighbors' Anxieties against Prostitutes' Fears: Ambivalence and Repression in the Policing of Street Prostitution in France', *Emotions, Space and Society*, vol. 4, no. 2, pp. 113–20.

Matrix (ed.) (1984) *Making Space: Women and the Man-made Environment*, London, Pluto Press.

Matter of Toboso-Alfonso [1990] 20 I.&N. Dec. 819.

Matthaei, J. (1997) 'The Sexual Division of Labor, Sexuality, and Lesbian/Gay Liberation: Toward a Marxist–Feminist Analysis of Sexuality in US Capitalism', in Gluckman, A. and Reed, B. (eds) *Homo Economics: Capitalism, Community, and Lesbian and Gay Life*, London, Routledge, pp. 135–64.

Mattilda (aka Matt Bernstein Sycamore) (2004) 'There's More to Life than Platinum: Challenging the Tyranny of Sweatshop-produced Rainbow Flags and Participatory Patriarchy', in Mattilda (ed.) *That's Revolting! Queer Strategies for Resisting Assimilation*, Berkeley, Soft Skull Press, pp. 1–7.

Maturana, H. R. (1985) 'Interview' [Online]. Available at http://www.oikos.org/maten.htm (accessed 6 April 2015).

Maurice, F. (2012) 'Villes friendly: le verdict des homos', *Têtu*, no. 189, pp. 80–91.

Mayer, K.H., Bekker, L-G., Stall, R., Grulich, A.E., Colfax, G. and Lama, J.R. (2012) 'Comprehensive Clinical Care for Men Who Have Sex with Men: An Integrated Approach', *The Lancet*, vol. 380, pp. 378–87.

McAdam, R. (2010) 'Queer in a Haystack: Queering Rural Space', *no more potlucks*, vol. 11, pp. 28–35.

McAllister, J. (2013) 'Tswanarising Global Gayness: The "UnAfrican" Argument, Western Gay Media Imagery, Local Responses and Gay Culture in Botswana', *Culture, Health and Sexuality*, vol. 15, pp. 88–101.

McCall, L. (2005) 'The Complexity of Intersectionality', *Signs: Journal of Women in Culture and Society*, vol. 30, pp. 1771–1800.

McClintock, A. (1995) *Imperial Leather: Race, Gender and Sexuality in the Colonial Contest*, New York, Routledge.

McCloskey, D. (1999) *Crossing: A Memoir*, Chicago, IL, University of Chicago Press.

McDermott, E. (2011) 'The World Some Have Won: Sexuality, Class and Inequality', *Sexualities*, vol. 14, pp. 63–78.

McDonald, S. and Hogue, A. (2007) *An Exploration of the Needs of Victims of Hate Crimes* [Online]. Available at http://www.justice.gc.ca/eng/rp-pr/cj-jp/victim/rr07_vic1/rr07_vic1.pdf (accessed 29 April 2013).

McDowell, L. (1999) *Gender, Identity and Place: Understanding Feminist Geographies*, Oxford, Polity Press.

McDowell, L. (2008) 'Thinking through Work: Complex Inequalities, Constructions of Difference and Trans-National Migrants', Progress in Human Geography, vol. 32, no. 4, pp. 491–507.

McFarlane, C. (2009) 'Translocal Assemblages: Space, Power and Social Movements', *Geoforum*, vol. 40, no. 4, pp. 561–67.

McGlotten, S. (2013) *Virtual Intimacies: Media, Affect, and Queer Sociality*, Albany, NY, SUNY Press.

McGonigal, J. (2011) *Reality is Broken*, London, Jonathan Cape.

McIlwaine, C. (2013) 'Urbanization and Gender-based Violence: Exploring the Paradoxes in the Global South', *Environment & Urbanisation*, vol. 25, no. 1, pp. 65–79.

McIntosh, W. and Harwood, P. (2002) 'The Internet and America's Changing Sense of Community', *The Good Society*, vol. 11, no. 3, pp. 25–28 [Online]. Available at http://muse.jhu.edu/journals/good_society/toc/gso11.3.html (accessed 4 March 2012).

McIntyre, M. (2013) 'Gay Owners to Close Restaurant, Sick of Insults', *Winnipeg Free Press*, 2 April [Online]. Available at http://www.winnipegfreepress.com/local/gay-owners-sick-of-insults-200996541.html (accessed 29 April 2013).

McKay, R.A. (2014) '"Patient Zero": The Absence of a Patient's View of the Early North American AIDS Epidemic', *Bulletin of the History of Medicine*, vol. 88, no. 1, pp. 161–94.

McKenna, K.Y.A. and Bargh, J.A. (1998) 'Coming Out in the Age of the Internet: Identity "Demarginalization" through Virtual Group Participation', *Journal of Personality and Social Psychology*, vol. 75, pp. 681–94.

McKewon, E. (2003), 'The Historical Geography of Prostitution in Perth, Western Australia', *Australian Geographer*, vol. 34, no. 3, pp. 297–310.

McKeown, A. (2008) *Melancholy Order: Asian Migration and the Globalization of Borders*, Columbia University Press, New York.

McLelland, M. (2002) 'Virtual Ethnography: Using the Internet to Study Gay Culture in Japan', *Sexualities*, vol. 5, no. 4, pp. 387–406.

McLelland, S.I. and Hunter, L.E. (2013) 'Bodies that are Always Out of Line: A Closer Look at "Age Appropriate Sexuality"', in Fahs, B., Dudy, M.L. and Stage, S. (eds) *Moral Panics about Sexuality*, London, Palgrave.

McLuhan, M. (1964) *Understanding Media: The Extensions of Man*, New York, McGraw-Hill.

McNeill, D. (2003) 'Rome, Global City? Church, State and the Jubilee 2000', *Political Geography*, vol. 22, no. 5, pp. 535–56.

McNeill, T. (2010) 'A Nation of Families: The Codification and (Be)longings of Heteropartriarchy', in Gray, H. and Gómez-Barris, M. (eds) *Toward a Sociology of the Trace*, Minneapolis, University of Minnesota Press, pp. 57–85.

McQueen, P. (2014) *Subjectivity, Gender and the Struggle for Recognition*, London and New York, Palgrave Macmillan.

Meadows, D.H., Meadows, D.L., Randers, J. and Behrens, W.W. (1972) 'The Limits to Growth', *The Top 50 Sustainability Books*, vol. 1, no. 116, pp. 31–7 (this edition 2009).

Meah, A. (2014) 'Reconceptualising Power and Gendered Subjectivities in Domestic Cooking Spaces', *Progress in Human Geography*, vol. 38, no. 5, pp. 671–90.

Mechant, M. (2013) 'Selling Sex in a Provincial Town: Prostitution in Bruges (1600–Present)', paper presented at Selling Sex in the City: Prostitution in World Cities, 1600 to the Present Conference, Amsterdam, 25–27 April.

Merry, S.E. (2001) 'Spatial Governmentality and the New Urban Social Order: Controlling Gender Violence through Law', *American Anthropologist*, NS 103, no. 1, pp. 16–29.

Merry, S.E. (2009) *Gender Violence: A Cultural Perspective*, Oxford, Wiley-Blackwell.

Meth, P. (2009) 'Marginalised Men's Emotions: Politics and Place', *Geoforum*, vol. 40, no. 5, pp. 853–63.

Meth, P. (2014) 'Violence and Men in Urban South Africa: The Significance of Home', in Gorman-Murray, A. and Hopkins, P. (eds) *Masculinities and Place*, Farnham, Ashgate, pp. 159–72.

Meyrowitz, J. (1985) *No Sense of Place: The Impact of Electronic Media on Social Behavior*, New York, Oxford University Press.

Meyerowitz, J. (2002) *How Sex Changed: A History of Transsexuality in the United States*, Cambridge, MA, Harvard University Press.

Mezzadra, S. and Neilson, B. (2013) *Border as Method, or The Multiplication of Labor*, Durham, NC, Duke University Press.

Michaelis (2014) *Moderno Dicionário da Língua Portuguesa* [Online]. Available at http://michaelis.uol.com.br/moderno/portugues/index.php?lingua=portugues-portugues&palavra=travesti (accessed 9 October 2014).

Mieli, M. (1977) *Elementi di critica omosessuale*, Milan, Feltrinelli (this edition 2002).

Mieli, M. (1980) *Homosexuality and Liberation: Elements of a Gay Critique*, London, Gay Men's Press.

Mies, M. and Shiva, V. (1993) *Ecofeminism*, London, Zed Books.

Migiro, K. (2014) 'Kenya: Anti-gay Groups in Kenya Rally to "Prevent Sodom" Promoted by the West', *AllAfrica*, 5 March [Online]. Available at http://allafrica.com/stories/201403061373. html (accessed 7 May 2014).

Mignolo, W.D. (1993) 'Colonial and Postcolonial Discourse: Cultural Critique or Academic Colonialism?', *Latin American Research Review*, vol. 28, no. 3, pp. 120–34.

Mignolo, W.D. (2000) *Local Histories/Global Designs: Coloniality, Subaltern Knowledges, and Border Thinking*, Princeton, NJ, Princeton University Press.

Mignolo, W.D. (2003a) 'Os Esplendores E as Misérias Da "Ciência": Colonialidade, Geopolítica Do Conhecimento E Pluri-Versalidade Epistémica', in de Sousa Santos, B. (ed.) *Conhecimento Prudente Para Uma Vida Decente: Um Discurso Sobre as Ciências' Revistado*, Porto, Edições Afrontamento, pp. 667–709.

Mignolo, W.D. (ed.) (2003b) 'Second Thoughts on the Darker Side of the Renaissance: Afterword to the Second Edition', in Mignolo, W.D., *The Darker Side of the Renaissance: Literacy, Territoriality, and Colonization*, Ann Arbor, University of Michigan Press, pp. 428–33.

Mignolo, W.D. (2009) 'Epistemic Disobedience, Independent Thought and Decolonial Freedom', *Theory, Culture & Society*, vol. 26, nos 7–8, pp. 159–81.

Mignolo, W.D. (2011) 'Epistemic Disobedience and the Decolonial Option: A Manifesto', *Transmodernity: Journal of Peripheral Cultural Production of the Luso-Hispanic World*, vol. 1, no. 2, pp. 44–66.

Miles, R. (1989) *Racism*, London, Routledge.

Miller, V. (2005) 'Intertextuality, the Referential Illusion, and the Production of a Gay Ghetto', *Social & Cultural Geography*, vol. 6, no. 1, pp. 61–79.

Mills, C.W. (1961) *The Sociological Imagination*, New York, Grove Press.

Millbank, J. (2002) 'Imagining Otherness: Refugee Claims on the Basis of Sexuality in Canada and Australia', *Melbourne University Law Review*, vol 26, no 1, pp. 144–77.

Millbank, J. (2003) 'Gender, Sex and Visibility in Refugee Claims on the Basis of Sexual Orientation', *Georgetown Immigration Law Journal*, vol. 18, no. 1, pp. 71–110.

Millbank, J. (2009) 'From Discretion to Disbelief: Recent Trends in Refugee Determinations on the Basis of Sexual Orientation in Australia and the United Kingdom', *International Journal of Human Rights*, vol. 13, no. 2, pp. 391–414.

Millward, L. (2012) 'Making a Scene: Struggles over Lesbian Place-making in Anglophone Canada, 1964–1984', *Women's History Review*, vol. 21, no. 4, pp. 553–69.

Minca, C. (2000) 'Venetian Geographical Praxis', *Environment and Planning D: Society and Space*, vol. 18, no. 3, pp. 285–9.

Minter, A. (2011) 'China's 'Super Girl' Goes Down, Raising Sparks', Bloomberg View, 22 September [Online]. Available at http://www.bloombergview.com/articles/2011–09–22/ china-s-super-girl-goes-down-raising-sparks-adam-minter (accessed 16 March 2012).

Mirzoeff, N. (2006) 'Invisible Empire: Visual Culture, Embodied Spectacle and Abu Ghraib', *Radical History Review*, vol. 95, pp. 21–44.

Mitchell, A., Patrick, K., Heywood, W., Blackman, P. and Pitts, M. (2014) *5th National Survey of Australian Secondary Students and Sexual Health 2013*, Melbourne, Australian Research Centre in Sex, Health and Society, La Trobe University.

Mitchell, D. (1995) 'There's No Such Thing as Culture: Towards a Reconceptualization of the Idea of Culture in Geography', *Transactions of the Institute of British Geographers*, vol. 20, pp. 102–16.

Mitchell, K. (2008) *Practicing Public Scholarship: Experiences and Possiblites beyond the Academy*, Oxford, Wiley-Blackwell.

Mittel, J. (2006) 'Narrative Complexity in Contemporary American Television', *The Velvet Light Trap*, vol. 58, pp. 29–40.

Mittel, J. (2009) 'Lost in a Great Story: Evaluation in Narrative Television (and Television Studies)', in Pearson, R. (ed.) *Reading Lost*, London, IB Tauris, pp. 119–38.

Mitter, R. (2005) *Bitter Revolution: China's Struggle with the Modern World*, Oxford, Oxford University Press.

Mohanty, C.T. (2008) 'Bajo los ojos de occidente. Academia Feminista y discurso colonial', in Suárez Navaz, L. and Hernández, A. (eds) *Descolonizando el Feminismo: Teorías y Prácticas desde los Márgenes*, Madrid, Ed. Cátedra, pp. 112–61.

Molloy, A. (2014) 'Kenya MP Likens Homosexuality to Terrorism', *The Independent*, 28 March.

Montagna, N. (2006) 'The De-commodification of Urban Space and the Occupied Social Centres in Italy', *City*, vol. 10, no. 3, pp. 295–304.

Moodie, T.D. (1988) 'Migrancy and Male Sexuality in the South African Gold Mines', *Journal of Southern African Studies*, vol. 14, no. 2, pp. 228–56.

Moores, S. (2004) 'The Doubling of Place: Electronic Media, Time–Space Arrangements and Social Relationships', in Couldry, N. and McCarthy, A. (eds) *MediaSpace: Place, Scale and Culture in a Media Age*, London, Routledge, pp. 21–36.

Moores, S. (2006) 'Media Uses and Everyday Environmental Experiences: A Positive Critique of Phenomenological Geography', *Particip@tions*, vol. 3, no. 2 [Online]. Available at http://www.participations.org/volume3/issuespecial/3_02_moores.htm (accessed 20 April 2014).

Morahan-Martin, J. (1999) 'The Relationship between Loneliness and Internet Use and Abuse', *Cyber Psychology and Behavior*, vol. 2, pp. 431–40.

Morato v Minister for Immigration, Local Government and Ethnic Affairs [1992] 39 FCR 401.

Moreira, P. (2012) *Backwater: Nova Scotia's Economic Decline*, Halifax, NS, Nimbus.

Morgan, K. (2004) 'The Exaggerated Death of Geography: Learning, Proximity and Territorial Innovation Systems', *Journal of Economic Geography*, vol. 4, no. 1, pp. 3–21.

Morgan, R. (1995) 'Television, Space, Education: Rethinking Relations between Schools and Media', *Discourse: Studies in the Cultural Politics of Education*, vol. 16, no. 1, pp. 39–57.

Morgensen, S. (2009) 'Arrival at Home: Radical Faerie Configurations of Sexuality and Place', *GLQ: A Journal of Lesbian and Gay Studies*, vol. 15, pp. 67–96.

Morris, J. (1986) *Conundrum: An Extraordinary Narrative of Transsexualism*, New York, Holt.

Morrison, C.A. (2012a) 'Heterosexuality and Home: Intimacies of Space and Spaces of Touch', *Emotion, Space and Society*, vol. 5, no. 1, pp. 10–18.

Morrison, C.A. (2012b) 'Solicited Diaries and the Everyday Geographies of Heterosexual Love and Home: Reflections on Methodological Process and Practice', *Area*, vol. 44, no. 1, pp. 68–75.

Mort, F. (1996) *Cultures of Consumption: Masculinities and Social Space in Late Twentieth-Century Britain*, London, Routledge.

Mortimer-Sandilands, C. (1993) 'On "Green" Consumerism: Environmental Privatization and "Family Values"', *Canadian Woman Studies*, vol. 13, no. 3, pp. 45–7.

Mortimer-Sandilands, C. (1999) 'Sex at the Limits', in Darier, E. (ed.) *Discourses of the Environment*, Oxford, Blackwell Publishers Ltd.

Mortimer-Sandilands, C. (2002) 'Lesbian Separatist Communities and the Experience of Nature: Toward a Queer Ecology', *Organisation and Environment*, vol. 15, pp. 131–63.

Mortimer-Sandilands, C. (2005) 'Unnatural Passions? Notes Toward a Queer Ecology', *Invisible Culture: An Electronic Journal for Visual Culture* [Online]. Available at www.rochester.edu/in_visible_culture/issue9/sandilands (accessed 10 February 2014).

Mortimer-Sandilands, C. (2010) 'Introduction: A Genealogy of Queer Ecologies', in Mortimer-Sandilands, C. and Erickson, B. (eds) *Queer Ecologies: Sex, Nature, Politics, Desire*, Bloomington, Indiana University Press.

Mortimer-Sandilands, C. and Erickson, B. (eds) (2010) *Queer Ecologies: Sex, Nature, Politics, Desire*, Bloomington, Indiana University Press.

Moss, A.R. (1996) 'AIDS Epidemiology: Investigating and Getting the Word Out', an oral history conducted in 1992–93 by Sally Smith Hughes, in *The AIDS epidemic in San Francisco: The medical response, 1981–1984, Volume II*, Berkeley, CA, Regional Oral History Office, The Bancroft Library, University of California, pp. 238–339.

Moss, P. (ed.) (2002) *Feminist Geography in Practice: Research and Methods*, Oxford, Blackwell.

Moss, P. and Dyck, I. (2002) *Women, Body, Illness: Space and Identity in the Everyday Lives of Women with Chronic Illness*, Lanham, MD, Rowman and Littlefield.

Motlagh, A. (2011) 'Autobiography and Authority in the Writings of the Iranian Diaspora', *Comparative Studies of South Asia, Africa and the Middle East*, vol. 31, no. 2, pp. 411–24.

Mottahedeh, N. (2004) 'Off the Grid: Reading Iranian Memoirs in our Time of Total War', *Middle East Research and Information* Project [Online]. Available at http://merip.org/mero/interventions/grid (accessed 1 July 2013).

Moussawi, G. (2013) 'Queering Beirut, the "Paris of the Middle East": Fractal Orientalism and Essentialized Masculinities in Contemporary Gay Travelogues', *Gender, Place & Culture*, vol. 20, no. 7, pp. 858–75.

Mowlabocus, S. (2008) 'Revisiting Old Haunts through New Technologies: Public (Homo) sexual Cultures in Cyberspace', *International Journal of Cultural Studies*, vol. 11, no. 4, pp. 419–39.

Mowlabocus, S. (2010a) *Gaydar Culture: Gay Men, Technology and Embodiment in the Digital Age*, Farnham, Ashgate.

Mowlabocus, S. (2010b) 'Look at Me! Images, Validation, and Cultural Currency on Gaydar', in Pullen, C. and Cooper, M. (eds) *LGBT Identity and Online New Media*, Abingdon, Routledge, pp. 201–14.

mrs kinpaisby (2008) 'Taking Stock of Participatory Geographies: Envisioning the Communiversity', *Transactions of the Institute of British Geographers*, vol. 33, pp. 292–9.

Mudu, P. (2004) 'Resisting and Challenging Neo-liberalism: The Development of Italian Social Centers', *Antipode*, vol. 36, no. 5, pp. 917–41.

Mugisha, F. (2014) 'Torment to Tyranny: Persecution in Uganda Now That the Anti-homosexuality Act is Law', *The Huffington Post*, 12 May [Online]. Available at http://www.huffingtonpost.com/frank-mugisha/torment-to-tyranny-persec_b_5311876.html (accessed 30 April 2014).

Muller, T.K. (2007) 'Liberty for All? Contested Spaces of Women's Basketball', *Gender, Place & Culture: A Journal of Feminist Geography*, vol. 14, no. 2, pp. 197–213 [Online]. DOI: 10.1080/09663690701213776 (accessed 20 April 2015).

Muller Myrdahl, T. (2013) 'Ordinary (Small) Cities and LGBQ Lives', *ACME: An International E-Journal for Critical Geographies*, vol. 12, no. 2, pp. 279–304.

Muller Myrdahl, T. (under contract) *Here is Queer: Sexual Difference and Urban Change in a Small Canadian City*, Vancouver, University of British Columbia Press.

Mummey, K. (2011) 'Prostitution: The Moral Economy of Medieval Prostitution', in Evans, R. (ed.) *A Cultural History of Sexuality in the Middle Ages*, Oxford and New York, Berg, pp. 165–80.

Muñoz, J. (1999) *Disidentifications: Queers of Color and the Performance of Politics*, Minneapolis, University of Minnesota Press.

Muñoz, J. (2009) *Cruising Utopia: The Then and There of Queer Futurity*, New York New York University Press.

Munoz-Laboy, M.A. (2004) 'Beyond "MSM": Sexual Desire among Bisexually-active Latino Men in New York City', *Sexualities*, vol. 7, no. 1, pp. 55–80.

Munt, S.R. (1995) 'The Lesbian Flâneur', in Bell, D. and Valentine, G. (eds) *Mapping Desire: Geographies of Sexualities*, London, Routledge, pp. 114–25.

Munt, S.R. (1998) *Heroic Desire: Lesbian Identity and Cultural Space*, New York, New York University Press.

Munt, S.R. (2000) '*The Lesbian Flaneur*', in Borden, I., Kerr, J., Pivaro, A. and Rendell, J. (eds) *The Unknown City: Contesting Architecture and Social Space*, Cambridge, MA, MIT Press, pp. 247–62.

Munt, S.R. and Medhurst, A. (1997) *The Lesbian and Gay Studies reader: A Critical Introduction*, London, Cassell.

Murdoch, J. (2006) *Post-structuralist Geography: A Guide to Relational Space*, London, Sage Publications.

Murphy, K.P., Pierce, J.L. and Knopp, L. (eds) (2010) *Queer Twin Cities: Twin Cities GLBT Oral History Project*, Minneapolis, University of Minnesota Press.

Murray, A. (1996) 'Minding Your Peers and Queers: Female Sex Workers in the AIDS Discourse in Australia and South-east Asia', *Gender, Place and Culture*, vol. 3, no. 1, pp. 43–60.

Murray, S.O. (2000) *Homosexualities*, Chicago, IL, University of Chicago Press.

Murray, S.O. and Roscoe, W. (1998) 'Southern Africa: Overview', in Murray, S.O. and Roscoe, W. (eds) *Boy-wives and Female Husbands: Studies of African Homosexualities*, Basingstoke, Macmillan.

Myers, J. (2010) 'Health, Sexuality and Place: The Different Geographies of HIV-positive Gay Men in Auckland, New Zealand', *New Zealand Geographer*, vol. 66, no. 3, pp. 218–27.

Myslik, W. (1996) 'Renegotiating the Social/Sexual Identity of Place', in Duncan, N. (ed.) *Body/Space: Geographies of Gender and Sexuality*, London, Routledge, pp. 156–69.

Naess, A. (1973) 'The Shallow and the Deep, Long-range Ecology Movement: A Summary', *Inquiry*, vol. 16, nos 1–4, pp. 95–100.

Nagar, R. (2006) *Playing with Fire: Feminist Thought and Activism through Seven Lives in India*, Minneapolis, University of Minnesota Press.

Nagar, R. (2014) *Muddying the Waters: Co-authoring Feminisms across Scholarship and Activism*, Urbana, Chicago and Springfield, University of Illinois Press.

Nagar, R. and Swarr, A. (2010) *Critical Transnational Feminist Praxis*, Albany, NY, SUNY Press.

Nakamura, L. (2002) 'Menu-driven Identities: Making Race Happen Online', in *Cybertypes: Race, Ethnicity, and Identity on the Internet*, New York, Routledge, pp. 101–36.

Nakamura, L. (2009) 'Don't Hate the Player, Hate the Game: The Racialization of Labor in World of Warcraft', *Critical Studies in Media Communication*, vol. 26, no. 2, pp. 128–44.

Nakamura, L. (2011) 'Race and Identity in Digital Media', in Curran, J. And Gurevitch, M. (eds) *Mass Media and Society*, London, Hodder Education, pp. 336–47.

Namaste, K. (1996) 'Gender Bashing: Sexuality, Gender, and the Regulation of Public Space', *Environment and Planning D: Society and Space*, vol 14, no. 2, pp. 221–40.

Namaste, V.K. (2000) *Invisible Lives: The Erasure of Transsexual and Transgendered People*, Chicago, IL, University of Chicago Press.

Nandy, A. (1983) *The Intimate Enemy: Loss and Recovery of Self Under Colonialism*, Delhi, Oxford University Press.

Nascimento, E.L. (2007) *The Sorcery of Color: Identity, Race, and Gender in Brazil*, Philadelphia, PA, Temple University Press.

Nash, C.J. (2001) 'Siting Lesbians: Sexuality, Space and Social Organization', in Goldie, T. (ed.) *In a Queer Country: Gay and Lesbian Studies in the Canadian Context*, Vancouver, Arsenal Pulp Press, pp. 235–56.

Nash, C.J. (2005) 'Contesting Identity: Politics of Gays and Lesbians in Toronto in the 1970s', *Gender, Place & Culture: A Journal of Feminist Geography*, vol. 12, no. 1, pp. 113–35 [Online]. DOI: 10.1080/09663690500083115 (accessed 20 April 2015).

Nash, C.J. (2006) 'Toronto's Gay Village (1969–1982): Plotting the Politics of Gay Identity', *Canadian Geographer/Le Géographe Canadien*, vol. 50, pp. 1–16.

Nash, C.J. (2010) 'Trans Geographies, Embodiment and Experience. Special Issue on Trans Geographies', *Gender, Place and Culture*, vol. 17, no. 5, pp. 579–95.

Nash, C.J. (2011) 'Trans Experiences in Lesbian and Queer Spaces', *The Canadian Geographer*, vol. 55, no. 2, pp. 192–207.

Nash, C.J. (2013a) 'The Age of the "Post-mo"? Toronto's Gay Village and a New Generation', *Geoforum*, vol. 49, pp. 243–52.

Nash, C.J. (2013b) 'Queering Neighbourhoods: Politics and Practice in Toronto', *ACME: An International E-Journal for Critical Geographies*, vol. 12, no. 2, pp. 243–52.

Nash, C.J. and Bain, A. (2007) '"Reclaiming Raunch"? Spatializing Queer Identities at Toronto Women's Bathhouse Events', *Social & Cultural Geography*, vol. 8, no. 1, pp. 47–62.

Nash, C.J. and Browne, K. (2015) 'Best for Society? Transnational Opposition to Sexual and Gender Equalities in Canada and Great Britain', *Gender, Place & Culture*, vol. 22, no. 4, pp. 561–77.

Nash, C.J. and Catungal, J.P. (2013) 'Introduction: Sexual Landscapes, Lives and Livelihoods in Canada', *ACME: An International E-Journal for Critical Geographies*, vol. 12, pp. 181–92.

Nash, C.J. and Gorman-Murray, A. (2014) 'LGBT Neighbourhoods and "New Mobilities": Towards Understanding Transformations in Sexual and Gendered Urban Landscapes', *International Journal of Urban and Regional Research*, vol. 38, no. 3, pp. 756–72.

Nash, C.J. and Gorman-Murray, A. (forthcoming) 'Recovering the Gay Village: A Comparative Historical Geography of Urban Change and Planning in Toronto and Sydney', *Journal of Historical Geography*, vol. 43.

Nast, H. (2002) 'Queer Patriarchies, Queer Racisms, International', *Antipode*, vol. 34, no. 5, pp. 874–909.

Naz Foundation v. Government of NCT of Delhi and Others [2009] [Online]. Available at http://www.lawyerscollective.org/vulnerable-communities/lgbt/section-377.html (accessed 31 March 2015).

Neilson, V. (2005) 'Uncharted Territory: Choosing an Effective Approach in Transgender-Based Asylum Claims', *Fordham Urban Law Journal*, vol. 32, no. 3, pp. 265–90.

Nel, J.A. and Judge, M. (2008) 'Exploring Homophobic Victiminsation in Gauteng, South Africa: Issues, Impacts and Responses', *Acta Criminologica*, vol. 21, no. 3, pp. 19–36.

Nelson, H. (1981a) 'Outbreaks of Pneumonia among Gay Males Studied', *Los Angeles Times*, 5 June, B3, B25 [Online]. Available at http://media.trb.com/media/acrobat/2011–06/62100915.pdf (accessed 28 May 2014).

Nelson, H. (1981b) 'Second Deadly Ailment Linked to Homosexuals', *Los Angeles Times*, 3 July, A3 [Online]. Available at http://media.trb.com/media/acrobat/2011–06/62101002.pdf (accessed 28 May 2014).

Nelson, H. (1982) 'Epidemic Affecting Gays Now Found in Heterosexuals', *Los Angeles Times*, 14 April, B22.

Nencel, L. (2001) *Ethnography and Prostitution in Peru*, London, Pluto Press.

Nestle, J. (1997) 'Restrictions and Reclamation: Lesbian Bars and Beaches on the 1950', in Ingram, G.B., Bouthillette, A.M. and Retter, Y. (eds) *Queers in Space: Communities, Public Places, Sites of Resistance*, Seattle, WA, Bay Press, pp. 61–8.

Neuts, B., Devos, T. and Dirckx, T. (2014) 'Turning off the Red Lights: Entrepreneurial Urban Strategies in "De Wallen", Amsterdam', *Applied Geography*, vol. 49, pp. 37–44.

Newman, B. (1997) 'The Use of Online Services to Encourage Exploration of Ego-dystonic Sexual Interests', *Journal of Sex Education & Therapy*, vol. 22, no. 1, pp. 45–8.

New South Wales (NSW) Government (2008) 'Safe Sexting: "No Such Thing" Information Sheet for Parents', NSW Government [Online]. Available at http//www.schools.nsw.edu.au (accessed 30 September 2009).

New York Post (1987) 'The Man Who Gave Us AIDS', 6 October, p. 1, p. 3.

Next Magazine (2008) 'Pride Map 2008', June.

Nguyen, V.K. (2005) 'Antiretroviral Globalism, Biopolitics and Therapeutic Citizenship', in Ong, A. and Collier, S. (eds) *Global Assemblages: Technology, Politics and Ethics as Anthropological Problems*, Oxford, Blackwell, pp. 124–45.

Nguyen, V.K. (2010) *The Republic of Therapy: Triage and Sovereignty in West Africa's Time of AIDS*, Durham, NC, Duke University Press.

Nicholls, W. (2007) 'The Geographies of Social Movements', *Geography Compass*, vol. 1, no. 3, pp. 607–22.

Nicholls, W. (2009) 'Place, Networks, Space: Theorising the Geographies of Social Movements', *Transactions of the Institute of British Geographers*, vol. 34, no. 1, pp. 78–93.

Noble, G. (2009) 'Countless Acts of Recognition: Young Men, Ethnicity and the Messiness of Identities in Everyday Life', *Social & Cultural Geography*, vol. 10, no. 8, pp. 875–91.

Noble, G. and Tabar, P. (2014) '"I am Lord, … I am Local": Migrant Masculinity, Sex and Making Yourself at Home', in Gorman-Murray, A. and Hopkins, P. (eds) *Masculinities and Place*, Farnham, Ashgate, pp. 77–91.

Nodin, N., Carballo-Diéguez, A., Ventuneac, A.M., Balan, I.C. and Remien, R. (2008) 'Knowledge and Acceptability of Alternative HIV Prevention Bio-medical Products among MSM who Bareback', *AIDS Care*, vol. 20, no. 1, pp. 106–15.

Nuñez, F. and Fuentes, P. (2013) 'Selling Sex in Mexico City', paper presented at Selling Sex in the City: Prostitution in World Cities, 1600 to the Present Conference, Amsterdam, 25–27 April.

Nussbaum, M.C. (2004) *Hiding from Humanity: Disgust, Shame and the Law*, Princeton, NJ, Princeton University Press.

Ochoa, T.T. (2012) 'Who Owns an Avatar? Copyright, Creativity, and Virtual Worlds', *Vanderbilt Journal of Entertainment & Technology Law*, vol. 14, pp. 959–93.

O'Dwyer, P. (2008) 'A Well–Founded Fear of Having My Sexual Orientation Heard in the Wrong Court', *New York School Law Review*, vol. 52, pp. 185–214.

Oleske, J., Minnefor, A., Cooper, R., Thomas, K., dela Cruz, A., Ahdieh, H., Guerrero, I., Joshi, V.V. and Desposito, F. (1983) 'Immune Deficiency Syndrome in Children', *Journal of the American Medical Association*, vol. 249, no. 17, pp. 2345–9.

Olivares, M., Masó, C., Duran, E., Gusí, T., Marçal, M.M. and Sentis, S. (1982) 'Dona i Nació: Feminisme i Nacionalisme', *Segones Jornades Catalanes de la Dona*, Barcelona, pp. 99–101.

Olsson, G. (1969) 'Inference Problems in Locational Analysis', in Cox, K.R. and Golledge, R.G. (eds) *Behavioral Models in Geography*, Evanston, IL, Northwestern University Press, pp. 14–34.

Olyslager, F. and Conway, L. (2007) 'On the Calculation of the Prevalence of Transsexualism', WPATH 20th International Symposium, Chicago, Illinois, 5–8 September [Online]. Available at http://ai.eecs.umich.edu/people/conway/TS/Prevalence/Reports/Prevalence%20of%20Transsexualism.pdf (accessed 27 April 2014).

O'Neill, B. and Kia, H. (2012) *Settlement Experiences of Lesbian, Gay and Bisexual Newcomers in BC (Metropolis British Columbia No. 12–15)*, Vancouver, Working Paper Series.

O'Neill, M., Campbell, R., Hubbard, P., Pitcher, J. and J. Scoular (2008) 'Living with the Other: Street Sex Work, Contingent Communities and Degrees of Tolerance', *Crime, Media, Culture*, vol. 4, no. 1, pp. 73–93.

Oommen, T.K. (1991) 'Internationalization of Sociology: A View from Developing Countries', *Current Sociology*, vol. 39, no. 1, pp. 67–84.

Ornelas-Chavez v Attorney General [2006] 458, F.3d, 1052.

O'Riordan, K. (2005) 'From Usenet to Gaydar: A Comment on Queer Online Community', *ACM SIGGROUP Bulletin (Special Issue on Virtual Communities)*, vol. 25, no. 2, pp. 28–32.

O'Riordan, K. and Phillips, D. J. (eds) (2007) *Queer Online: Media, Technology and Sexuality*, New York, Peter Lang.

Oswald, G.A., Theodossi, A., Gazzard, B.G., Byrom, N.A. and Fisher-Hoch, S.P. (1982) 'Attempted Immune Stimulation in the "Gay Compromise Syndrome"', *British Medical Journal*, vol. 285, no. 6348, p. 1082.

Oswin, N. (2004) 'Towards Radical Geographies of Complicit Queer Futures', *ACMe: An International E-Journal for Critical Geographies*, vol. 3, no. 2, pp. 79–86.

Oswin, N. (2005) 'Researching "Gay Cape Town" Finding Value-added Queerness', *Social & Cultural Geography*, vol. 6, no. 4, pp. 567–86.

Oswin, N. (2006) 'Decentering Queer Globalization: Diffusion and the "Global Gay"', *Environment and Planning D: Society and Space*, vol. 24, pp. 777–90.

Oswin, N. (2007a) 'The End of Queer (As We Knew It): Globalization and the Making of a Gay-friendly South Africa', *Gender, Place and Culture*, vol. 14, no. 1, pp. 93–110.

Oswin, N. (2007b) 'Producing Homonormativity in Neoliberal South Africa: Recognition, Redistribution, and the Equality Project', *Signs*, vol. 32, no. 3, pp. 649–69.

Oswin, N. (2008) 'Critical Geographies and the Uses of Sexuality: Deconstructing Queer Space', *Progress in Human Geography*, vol. 32, no. 1, pp. 89–103.

Oswin, N. (2010) 'The Modern Model Family at Home in Singapore: A Queer Geography', *Transactions of the Institute of British Geographers*, vol. 35, no. 2, pp. 256–68.

Oswin, N. (2012) 'The Queer Time of Creative Urbanism: Family, Futurity and Global City Singapore', *Environment and Planning A*, vol. 44, no. 7, pp. 1624–40.

Oswin, N. (2013) 'Geographies of Sexualities: The Cultural Turn and After', in Johnson, N.C., Schein, R.H. and Winders, J. (eds) *The Wiley Companion to Cultural Geography*, Chichester, John Wiley and Sons, pp. 105–16.

Oswin, N. (2015) 'World, City, Queer', *Antipode* [Online]. DOI: 10.1111/anti.12142 (accessed 20 April 2015).

O'Toole, L. (1999) *Pornocopia: Porn, Sex, Technology and Desire*, London, Serpents Tail.

Paasi, A. (2005) 'Globalisation, Academic Capitalism, and the Uneven Geographies of International Journal Publishing Spaces', *Environment and Planning A*, vol. 37, no. 5, pp. 769–89.

Packard, R.M. and Epstein, P. (1991) 'Epidemiologists, Social Scientists, and the Structure of Medical Research on AIDS in Africa', *Social Science and Medicine*, vol. 33, no. 2, pp. 771–94.

Paechter, C. (2004) '"Mens Sana in Corpore Sano": Cartesian Dualism and the Marginalisation of Sex Education', *Discourse: Studies in the Cultural Politics of Education*, vol. 25, no. 3, pp. 309–20.

Paglia, C. (1990) *Sexual Personae: Art and Decadence from Nefertiti to Emily Dickinson*, New Haven, CT, Yale University Press.

Paglia, C. (1994) 'No Law in the Arena: A Pagan Theory of Sexuality', in *Vamps and Tramps: New Essays*, New York, Random House, pp. 19–94.

Pain, R. (1991) 'Space, Sexual Violence and Social Control: Integrating Geographical and Feminist Analyses of Women's Fear of Crime', *Progress in Human Geography*, vol. 15, no. 4, pp. 415–31.

Pain, R. (1997) 'Social Geographies of Women's Fear of Crime', *Transactions of the Institute of British Geographers*, NS 22, pp. 231–44.

Pain, R. (2000) 'Place, Social Relations and the Fear of Crime: A Review', *Progress in Human Geography*, vol. 24, no. 3, pp. 365–87.

Pain, R. (2014a) 'Everyday Terrorism: Connecting Domestic Violence and Global Terrorism', *Progress in Human Geography*, vol. 38, no. 4, pp. 531–50.

Pain, R. (2014b) 'Seismologies of Emotion: Fear and Activism during Domestic Violence', *Social & Cultural Geography*, vol. 15, no. 2, pp. 127–50.

Pain, R., Grundy, S., Gill, S., Towner, E., Sparks, G. and Hughes, K. (2005) '"So Long as I Take My Mobile": Mobile Phones, Urban Life and Geographies of Young People's Safety', *International Journal of Urban and Regional Research*, vol. 29, no. 4, pp. 814–30.

Pain, R. and Smith, S. (eds) (2008) *Fear: Critical Geopolitics and Everyday Life*, Aldershot, Ashgate.

Palandri, M. and Green, L. (2000) 'Image Management in a Bondage, Discipline, Sadomasochist Subculture: A Cyber-ethnographic Study', *CyberPsychology & Behavior*, vol. 3, no. 4, pp. 631–41.

Papayanis, M. (2000) 'Sex and the Revanchist City: Zoning Out Pornography in New York', *Environment and Planning D: Society and Space*, vol. 18, no. 3, pp. 341–53.

Pardo, T. (2013) 'Disforias institucionales en las luchas transfeministas', in Solá, M. and Urko, E. *Transfeminismos: Epistemes fricciones y flujos*, Txalaparta, Tafalla, pp. 167–76.

Parker, E. (2011) 'Introduction: Queer, There and Everywhere', *Textual Practice*, vol. 25, no. 4, pp. 639–47.

Parker, R. (2009) 'Sexuality, Culture and Society: Shifting Paradigms in Sexuality Research', *Culture, Health and Sexuality*, vol. 11, no. 3, pp. 251–66.

Parker, R.G. (1999) *Beneath the Equator: Cultures of Desire, Male Homosexuality, and Emerging Gay Communities in Brazil*, New York, Routledge.

Parker, R.G., Barbosa, R.M. and Aggleton, P. (2000) 'Introduction', in Parker, R.G., Barbosa, R.M. and Aggleton, P. (eds) *Framing the Sexual Subject: The Politics of Gender, Sexuality and Power*, Berkeley, University of California Press, pp. 1–28.

Parr, H. (2002) 'Medical Geography: Diagnosing the Body in Medical and Health Geography, 1999–2000', *Progress in Human Geography*, vol. 26, no. 2, pp. 240–51.

Patal, P., Borkowf, C.B., Brooks, J.T., Lasry, A., Lansky, A. and Mermin, J. (2014) 'Estimating Per-act HIV Transmission Risk: A Systematic Review', *AIDS*, vol. 28 [Online]. DOI: 10.1097/QAD.0000000000000298 (accessed 20 April 2015).

Patton, C. (1990) *Inventing AIDS*, New York, Routledge.

Peace, R. (2001) 'Producing Lesbians: Canonical Proprieties', in Bell, D., Binnie, J., Holliday, R., Longhurst, R. and Peace, R. (eds) *Pleasure Zones: Bodies, Cities, Spaces*, Syracuse, NY, Syracuse University Press, pp. 29–54.

Peacock, B., Eyre, S.L., Quinn, S.C. and Kegeles, S. (2001) 'Delineating Differences: Sub-communities in the San Francisco Gay Community', *Culture, Health & Sexuality*, vol. 3, no. 2, pp. 183–201.

Peake, L. (1993) '"Race" and Sexuality: Challenging the Patriarchal Structuring of Urban Social Space', *Environment and Planning D: Society and Space*, vol. 11, no. 4, pp. 415–32.

Pearson, D. (2013) 'EA, Bioware Fire-fighting Reactions to SWtOR's "Gay Ghetto" Planet [Online]. Available at http://www.gamesindustry.biz/articles/2013–01–15-ea-bioware-fire-fighting-reactions-to-swtors-gay-ghetto-planet_(accessed 18 April 2013).

Peckham, M. (2006) *Sounds of Silence: Sanitizing Expression in Brave New Worlds* [Online]. Available at http://www.1up.com/features/sounds-of-silence_(accessed 12 March 2013).

Peixoto Caldas, J.M. (2010) 'Usos y apropriacion queer del espacio urbano: El Caso GayEixample en Barcelona y Chueca en Madrid', Comunicacion al XI Coloquio Internacional de Geocritica, Buenos Aires, 2–7 May [Online]. Available at http://rep ositorio-aberto.up.pt/bitstream/10216/55812/2/87067.pdf (accessed 1 April 2015).

Pelúcio, L. (2010) 'Erótica, Exótica e Travesti – nacionalidade e corporalidade no jogo das identidades no mercado transnacional do sexo', in Castro, A.L. (ed.) *Cultura Contemporânea, identidades e sociabilidades: olhares sobre corpo, mídia e novas tecnologias*, São Paulo, Cultura Acadêmica, pp. 197–214.

Pelúcio, L. (2011) 'Corpos indóceis – a gramática erótica do sexo transnacional e as travestis que desafiam fronteiras', in Souza, L.A.F., Sabatine, T.T. and Magalhães, B.R. (eds) *Michel Foucault: Sexualidade, corpo e direito*, São Paulo, Oficina Universitária/ Cultura Acadêmica, pp. 105–32.

Penteado, N. (2010) *Os segredo das mulheres brasileiras para manter os homens loucamente apaixonados*, Alfragide, Livros d'Hoje.

PEPFAR (2011) *Technical Guidance on Combination HIV Prevention* [Online]. Available at http://www.pepfar.gov/documents/organization/164010.pdf (accessed 30 April 2014).

Pérez, Kim y Mónica (1994) 'La transexualidad', in *Juntas y a por todas. Jornadas Feministas*, Madrid, Federación de Organizaciones Feministas del Estado Español.

Perlongher, N. (1987) *O negócio do michê: a prostituição viril*, São Paulo, Brasiliense.

Peršak, N. and Vermeulen, G. (2014) 'Faces and Spaces of Prostitution', in Peršak, N. and Vermeulen, G. (eds) *Reframing Prostitution. From Discourse to Description, from Moralisation to Normalisation?*, Antwerp, Maklu, pp. 13–24.

Petryna, A. (2009) *When Experiments Travel: Clinical Trials and the Global Search for Human Subjects*, Princeton, NJ, Princeton University Press.

Petzen, J. (2012) 'Queer Trouble: Centring Race in Queer and Feminist Politics', *Journal of Intercultural Studies*, vol. 33, no. 3, pp. 289–302.

Pew Research Center (2013a) *The Global Divide on Homosexuality: Greater Acceptance in More Secular and Affluent Countries* [Online]. Available at http://www.pewglobal.org/2013/06/04/the-global-divide-on-homosexuality/ (accessed 14 December 2014).

Pew Research Center (2013b) *A Survey of LGBT Americans: Attitudes, Experiences and Values in Changing Times* [Online]. Available at http://www.pewsocialtrends.org/2013/06/13/a-survey-of-lgbt-americans/2/ (accessed 25 April 2014).

Pheterson, G. (ed.) (1989) *A Vindication of the Rights of Whores*, Seattle, WA, Seal Press.

Phillips, R. (2002) 'Imperialism and the Regulation of Sexuality: Colonial Legislation on Contagious Diseases and Ages of Consent', *Journal of Historical Geography*, vol. 28, no. 3, pp. 339–62.

Phillips, R. (2006) *Sex, Politics and Empire: A Postcolonial Geography*, Manchester, Manchester University Press.

Phillips, R., Watt, D. and Shuttleton, D. (eds) (2000) *De-centring Sexualities: Politics and Representations beyond the Metropolis*, London, Routledge.

Philo, C. (2000) 'The Birth of the Clinic: An Unknown Work on Medical Geography', *Area*, vol. 32, pp. 11–19.

Philo, C. (2005) 'Sex, Life, Death, Geography: Fragmentary Remarks Onspired by "Foucault's Population Geographies"', *Population, Space and Place*, vol. 11, pp. 325–33.

Pickerill, J. (2007) '"Autonomy Online": Indymedia and Practices of Alter-globalisation', *Environment and Planning A*, vol. 39, pp. 2668–84.

Pickerill, J. and Chatterton, P. (2006) 'Notes towards Autonomous Geographies: Creation, Resistance and Self-management as Survival Tactics', *Progress in Human Geography*, vol. 30, no. 6, pp. 730–46.

Pile, S. (1994) 'Masculinism, the Use of Dualistic Epistemologies and Third Space', *Antipode*, vol. 26, pp. 255–77.

Pineda, E., Garaizábal, C. and Vázquez, N. (2001) 'Aquí. ¿Qué pasa con el lesbianismo?', in *Feminismo.es … y será. Jornadas Feministas de Córdoba*, Córdoba, Servicio de publicaciones Universidad de Córdoba.

Pini, B., Moletsane, R. and Mills, M. (2014) 'Education and the Global Rural: Feminist Perspectives', *Gender and Education*, vol. 26, no. 5, pp. 453–64.

Piscitelli, A. (2007) 'Brasileiras na indústria transnacional do sexo', *Nuevo Mundo–Mundos Nuevos*, vol. 7, p. 20 [Online]. Available at http://nuevomundo.revues.org/3744 (accessed 3 March 2014).

Piscitelli, A. (2009) 'Trânsitos: circulación de brasileñas en el ámbito de la transnacionalización de los mercados sexual y matrimonial', *Horizontes Antropológicos*, vol. 31, pp. 131–7.

Piscitelli, A., Assis, G. de O. and Olivar, J.M.N. (2011) *Gênero, sexo, afetos e dinheiro: mobilidades transnacionais envolvendo o Brasil*, Campinas, SP, UNICAMP / PAGU.

Pitcherskaia v INS [1997] 118 F.3d 641.

Plant. S. (2002) 'On the Mobile', *Vodafone Receiver Magazine*, vol. 6, pp. 1–9.

Platero, R,L. (2012) *Intersecciones: cuerpos y sexualidades en la Encrucijada*, Barcelona, Bellaterra.

Platero Mendez, R. (2009) 'La construcción del sujeto lésbico', *LES Online*, vol. 1, no. 1, pp. 36–44.

Plummer, K. (ed.) (1992) *Modern Homosexualities: Fragments of Lesbian and Gay Experience*, London, Routledge.

Pluskota, M. (2013) 'Selling Sex in Amsterdam, 1600s–2000s', paper presented at Selling Sex in the City: Prostitution in World Cities, 1600 to the Present Conference, Amsterdam, 25–27 April.

Podmore, J.A. (2001) 'Lesbians in the Crowd: Gender, Sexuality and Visibility along Montréal's Boul. St-Laurent', *Gender, Place and Culture*, vol. 8, no. 4, pp. 333–55 [Online]. DOI: 10.1080/09663690120111591 (accessed 20 April 2015).

Podmore, J.A. (2006) '"Gone Underground"? Lesbian Visibility and the Consolidation of Queer Space in Montréal', *Social & Cultural Geography*, vol. 7, no. 4, pp. 595–625 [Online]. DOI: 10.1080/14649360600825737 (accessed 20 April 2015).

Podmore, J.A. (2013a) 'Critical Commentary: Sexualities Landscapes beyond Homonormativity', *Geoforum*, vol. 49, pp. 263–7.

Podmore, J.A. (2013b) 'Lesbians as Village "Queers": The Transformation of Montréal's Lesbian Nightlife in the 1990s', *ACME: An International E-Journal for Critical Geographies*, vol. 12, no. 2, pp. 220–49.

Pollock, A. (2014) 'Places of Pharmaceutical Knowledge-making: Global Health, Postcolonial Science, and Hope in South African Drug Discovery', *Social Studies of Science*, vol. 44, no. 6, pp. 848–73.

Pommier, Y., Johnson, A.A. and Marchand, C. (2005) 'Integrase Inhibitors to Treat HIV/ AIDS', *Nature Reviews Drug Discovery*, vol. 4, no. 3, pp. 236–48.

Poniewozik, J. (2014) 'Why did Piers Morgan Get Cancelled? Pick a Reason', *Time Magazine*, 24 February [Online]. Available at http://time.com/9250/why-did-piers-morgan-get-cancelled-pick-a-reason/ (accessed 10 July 2014).

Pope, C. (2005) 'The Political Economy of Desire: Geographies of Female Sex Work in Havana, Cuba', *Journal of International Women's Studies*, vol. 6, no. 2, pp. 99–118.

Poppen, P.J., Reisen, C.A., Zea, M.C., Bianchi, F.T., Echeverry, J.J. (2004) 'Predictors of Unprotected Anal Intercourse among HIV-positive Latino Gay and Bisexual Men', *AIDS and Behavior*, vol. 8, no. 4, pp. 379–99.

Povinelli, E.A. and Chauncey, G. (1999) 'Thinking Sexuality Transnationally: An Introduction', *GLQ: A Journal of Lesbian and Gay Studies*, vol. 5, no. 4, pp. 439–49.

Pratt, M.L. (1991) 'Arts of the Contact Zone', *Profession*, vol. 91, pp. 33–40.

Preston, D.B., D'Augelli, A.R., Kassab, C.D., Cain, R.E., Schulze, F.W. and Starks, M.T. (2004) 'The Influence of Stigma on the Sexual Risk Behavior of Rural Men Who Have Sex with Men', *AIDS Education and Prevention*, vol. 16, no. 4, pp. 291–303.

Preston, M. (2013) '"Very Very Risky": Sexuality Education Teachers' Definition of Sexuality and Teaching and Learning Responsibilities', *American Journal of Sexuality Education*, vol. 8, pp. 18–35.

Prior, J. (2008) 'Planning for Sex in the City: Urban Governance, Planning and the Placement of Sex Industry Premises in Inner Sydney', *Australian Geographer*, vol. 39, no. 3, pp. 339–52.

Prior, J., Crofts, P. and Hubbard, P. (2013) 'Planning, Law, and Sexuality: Hiding Immorality in Plain View', *Geographical Research*, vol. 51, no. 4, pp. 354–63.

Pritchard, A. and Morgan, N. (2006) 'Hotel Babylon? Exploring Hotels as Liminal Sites of Transition and Transgression', *Tourism Management*, vol. 27, no. 5, pp. 762–72.

Pritchard, A., Morgan, N. and Sedgley, D. (2002) 'In Search of Lesbian Space? The Experience of Manchester's Gay Village', *Leisure Studies*, vol. 21, no. 2, pp. 105–23.

Probyn, E. (2004) 'Everyday Shame', *Cultural Studies*, vol. 18, pp. 328–49.

Prosser, J. (1998) *Second Skins: The Body Narratives of Transsexuality*, New York, Columbia University Press.

Provine, R.R., Spencer, R.J. and Mandell, D.L. (2007) 'Emotional Expression Online: Emoticons Punctuate Website Text Messages', *Journal of Language and Social Psychology*, vol. 26, no. 3, pp. 299–307.

Puar, J. (2006) 'Mapping US Homonormativities', *Gender, Place and Culture*, vol. 13, no. 1, pp. 67–88.

Puar, J.K. (2007) *Terrorist Assemblages: Homonationalism in Queer Times*, Durham, NC, Duke University Press.

Puar, J.K. (2013) 'Rethinking Homonationalism', *International Journal of Middle East Studies*, vol. 45, no. 2, pp. 336–9.

Puar, J.K., Rushbrook, D. and Schein, L. (2003) 'Sexuality and Space: Queering Geographies of Globalization', *Environment and Planning D: Society and Space*, vol. 21, no. 4, pp. 383–7.

Publishing for Non-Native Speakers of English, Session I (2014) YouTube video, added by Association of American Geographers [Online]. Available at https://www.youtube.com/watch?v=1dvtv1C0PX4 (accessed 30 May 2014).

Publishing for Non-Native Speakers of English, Session II (2014) YouTube video, added by Association of American Geographers [Online]. Available at https://www.youtube.com/watch?v=DbBSVFok8G8 (accessed 30 May 2014).

Pullen, C. (2010) 'Introduction', in Pullen, C. and Cooper, M. (eds) *LGBT Identity and Online New Media*, Abingdon, Routledge, pp. 1–13.

Pullen, C. and Cooper, M. (eds) (2010) *LGBT Identity and Online New Media*, Abingdon, Routledge.

Purcell, V. (1965) *The Memoirs of a Malayan Official*, London, Cassell and Co.

Pustianaz, M. (2010) 'Qualche domanda (sul) queer in Italia', *Italian Studies*, vol. 65, no. 2, pp. 263–77.

Quagliarello, V. (1982) 'The Acquired Immunodeficiency Syndrome: Current Status', *Yale Journal of Biology and Medicine*, vol. 55, pp. 443–52.

Quah, S. (1994) *Family in Singapore: Sociological Perspectives*, Singapore, Times Academic Press.

Queerblog (2010) *Napoli Pride 2010: manifesto politico e piattaforma rivendicativa* [Online]. Available at http://www.queerblog.it/post/8054/napoli-pride-2010-manifesto-politico-e-piattaforma-rivendicativa (accessed 21 March 2015)

Queer Days (2013) [Online]. Available at http://www.dailymotion.com/video/xy53hh_queer-days-rachele-borghi_shortfilms (accessed on 2 April 2015).

Quijano, A. (2000) 'Coloniality of Power, Eurocentrism, and Latin America', *Nepantla: Views from the South*, vol. 1, no. 3, pp. 533–80.

Quijano, A. (2007) 'Coloniality and Modernity/Rationality', *Cultural Studies*, vol. 21, no. 2, pp. 168–78.

Quilley, S. (1997) 'Manchester's "New Urban Village": Gay Space in the Entrepreneurial City', in Ingram, G.B., Bouthillette, A-M. and Retter, Y. (eds) *Queers in Space: Communities/ Public Places/Sites of Resistance*, Seattle, WA, Bay Press, pp. 275–92.

Rajan, K.S. (2007) 'Biocapital as an Emergent Form of Life: Speculations on the Figure of the Experimental Subject', in Gibbon, S. and Novas, C. (eds) *Biosocialities, Genetics and the Social Sciences: Making Biologies and Identities*, London, Routledge, pp. 157–86.

Rajan, K.S. (2012) 'Pharmaceutical Crises and Questions of Value: Terrains and Logics of Global Therapeutic Politics', *South Atlantic Quarterly*, vol. 111, no. 2, pp. 321–46.

Ramazanoğlu, C. and Holland, J. (2002) *Feminist Methodology: Challenges and Choices*, London, Sage.

Ramirez-Valles, J., Garcia, D., Campell, R.T.,Diaz, R.M. and Heckathorn, D.D. (2008) 'HIV Infection, Sexual Risk Behavior, and Substance Use among Latino Gay and Bisexual men and Transgender Persons', *American Journal of Public Health*, vol. 98, no. 6, pp. 1036–43.

Rao, D., Kekwaletswe, T.C., Hosek, S., Martinez, J. and Rodriguez, F. (2007) 'Stigma and Social Barriers to Medication Adherence with Urban Youth Living with HIV', *AIDS Care*, vol. 19, no. 1, pp. 28–33.

Rao, R. (2014) 'The Locations of Homophobia', *London Review of International Law*, vol. 2, no. 2, pp. 169–99.

Raunig, G. (2013) *Factories of Knowledge, Industries of Creativity*, Los Angeles, CA and Cambridge, MA., Semiotext(e), distributed by the MIT Press.

Ray, B. (2004) 'A Diversity Paradox: Montréal's Gay Village', in Andrew, C. (ed.) *Our Diverse Cities*, Ottawa, Federation of Municipalities, pp. 72–5.

Raymond, J. (1979) *The Transsexual Empire: The Making of the She-male*, Boston, MA, Beacon Press.

Reckless, W. (1933) 'The Distribution of Commercialized Vice in the City: A Sociological Analysis', *Publications of the American Sociological Society*, vol. 20, pp. 164–76.

Reddy, V. (2002) 'Perverts and Sodomites: Homophobia as Hate Speech in Africa', *Southern African Linguistics and Applied Language Studies*, vol. 20, no. 3, pp. 163–75.

Reed, B., Rhodes, S., Schofield, P. and Wylie, K. (2009) *Gender Variance in the UK: Prevalence, Incidence, Growth, and Geographic Distribution*, Ashtead, Gender Identity Research and Education Society, June.

Refugee Review Tribunal (RRT) (1995), V95/02999 [1995] RRTA 897, 26 April [Online]. Available at http://www.austlii.edu.au/cgi–bin/sinodisp/au/cases/cth/RRTA/1995/897.ht ml?stem=0&synonyms=0&query=RRTA%20897 (accessed 12 November 2012).

Refugee Review Tribunal (RRT) (1997), V97/06802 [1997] RRTA 3846, 30 September [Online]. Available at http://www.austlii.edu.au/cgi-bin/sinodisp/au/cases/cth/RRTA/1997/3846. html?stem=0&synonyms=0&query=%20RRTA%203846 (accessed 12 November 2012).

Refugee Review Tribunal (RRT) (1998a), V98/09160 [1998] RRTA 5331, 22 December [Online]. Available at http://www.austlii.edu.au/cgi-bin/sinodisp/au/cases/cth/RRTA/1998/5331. html?stem=0&synonyms=0&query=RRTA%205331 (accessed 12 November 2012).

Refugee Review Tribunal (RRT) (1998b), N97/16390 [1998] RRTA 4379, 23 September [Online]. Available at http://www.austlii.edu.au/cgi-bin/sinodisp/au/cases/cth/RRTA/1998/4379. html?stem=0&synonyms=0&query=RRTA%204379 (accessed 12 November 2012).

Refugee Review Tribunal (RRT) (1998c), N97/17155 [1998] RRTA 4386, 23 September [Online]. Available at http://www.austlii.edu.au/cgi-bin/sinodisp/au/cases/cth/RRTA/1998/4386. html?stem=0&synonyms=0&query=RRTA%204386 (accessed 12 November 2012).

Refugee Review Tribunal (RRT) (1999), N99/27818 [1999] RRTA 1607, 29 June [Online]. Available at http://www.austlii.edu.au/cgi-bin/sinodisp/au/cases/cth/RRTA/1999/1607. html?stem=0&synonyms=0&query=RRTA%201607 (Accessed 12 November 2012).

Refugee Review Tribunal (RRT) (2002), N02/42714 [2002] RRTA 808, 11 September [Online]. Available at http://www.austlii.edu.au/cgi-bin/sinodisp/au/cases/cth/RRTA/2002/808.ht ml?stem=0&synonyms=0&query=RRTA%20808 (accessed 10 November 2012).

Refugee Review Tribunal (RRT) (2003), N03/46498 [2003] RRTA 879, 22 September .

Refugee Review Tribunal (RRT) (2008), 0805932 [2008] RRTA 879, 28 November.

Refugee Review Tribunal (RRT) (2009), 0902671 [2009] RRTA 1035, 19 November.

Refugee Review Tribunal (RRT) (2010), 0903346 [2010] RRTA 41, 5 February.

Renkin, H.Z. (2014) 'Perverse Frictions: Pride, Dignity, and the Budapest LGBT March', *Ethnos: Journal of Anthropology* [Online]. DOI: 10.1080/00141844.2013.879197 (accessed 21 April 2015).

Report of the Chinese Marriage Committee (1926) Singapore, Government Printing Office.

Reyes-Reyes v Attorney General [2004] 384 F.3d 782.

Reynolds, R. (2009) 'Endangered Territory, Endangered Identity: Oxford Street and the Dissipation of Gay Life', *Journal of Australian Studies*, vol. 33, no. 1, pp. 79–92.

Rheingold, H. (1993) *The Virtual Community: Homesteading at the Electronic Frontier* (rev. edn), Reading, MA, Addison-Wesley.

Rhodes, T., Singer, M., Bourgois, P., Friedman, S.R. and Strathdee, S.A. (2005) 'The Social Structural Production of HIV Risk among Injecting Drug Users', *Social Science & Medicine*, vol. 61, no. 5, pp. 1026–44.

Ribeiro, M.A. and Oliveira, R.F (eds) (2011) *Território, Sexo e Prazer*, Rio de Janeiro, Gramma Editora.

Richards, R. and Ames, J. (1983) *Second Serve: The Renee Richards Story*, New York, Stein and Day.

Richardson, D. (1996a) *Theorising Heterosexuality: Telling it Straight*, Maidenhead, Open University Press.

Richardson, D. (1996b) 'Heterosexuality and Social Theory', in Richardson, D. (ed.) *Theorising Heterosexuality*, Buckingham, Open University Press, pp. 21–38.

Richardson, D. (2004) 'Locating Sexualities: From Here to Normality', *Sexualities*, vol. 7, no. 4, pp. 391–411.

Richardson, D. (2005) 'Desiring Sameness? The Rise of a Neoliberal Politics of Normalization', *Antipode*, vol. 37, pp. 515–35.

Richardson, I. (2005) 'FCJ-032 Mobile Technosoma: Some Phenomenological Reflections on Itinerant Media Devices', *The Fibreculture Journal*, issue 6 [Online]. Available at http://six. fibreculturejournal.org/fcj-032-mobile-technosoma-some-phenomenological-reflections-on-itinerant-media-devices/ (accessed 3 September 2015).

Richardson, I. (2007) 'Pocket Technospaces: The Bodily Incorporation of Mobile Media', *Continuum: Journal of Media and Cultural Studies*, vol. 21, no. 2, pp. 205–15.

Riff Raff Statue.Org (n.d.) [Online]. Available at www.riffraffstatue.org.com (accessed 5 March 2005).

Ringrose, J., Harvey, L., Gill, R. and Livingstone, S. (2013) 'Teen Girls, Sexual Double Standards and "Sexting": Gendered Value in Digital Image Exchange', *Feminist Theory*, vol. 14, no. 3, pp. 305–23.

Rispel, L. and Metcalf, C. (2009) 'Breaking the Silence: South African HIV Policies and the Needs of Men Who Have Sex with Men', *Reproductive Health Matters*, vol. 17, pp. 133–42.

Ristock, J., Zoccole, A. and Passante, L. (2010) *Aboriginal Two-Spirit and LGBTQ Migration*, Final Report, Winnipeg, Mobility and Health Research Project.

Ritchie, J. (2014) 'Pinkwashing, Homonationalism, and Israel–Palestine: The Conceits of Queer Theory and the Politics of the Ordinary', *Antipode* [Online]. DOI: 10.1111/anti12100 (accessed 21 April 2015).

Rivera, S. (2002) 'Queens in Exile: The Forgotten Ones', in Nestle, J., Howell, C. and Wilchins, R.A. (eds) *Genderqueer: Voices from Beyond the Gender Binary*, Los Angeles, CA, Alyson Books, pp. 67–85.

Robins, K. (2007) 'Against Virtual Community: For a Politics of Distance', in Bell, D. and Kennedy, B. (eds) *The Cybercultures Reader*, Abingdon, Routledge, pp. 227–35.

Robins, S. (2004) '"Long Live Zackie, Long Live!" AIDS Activism, Science and Citizenship after Apartheid', *Journal of Southern African Studies*, vol. 30, no. 3, pp. 651–72.

Robins, S. (2006) 'From "Rights" to "Ritual": AIDS Activism in South Africa', *American Anthropologist*, vol. 108, no. 2, pp. 312–23.

Robins, S. (2009) 'Foot Soldiers of Global Health: Teaching and Preaching AIDS Science and Modern Medicine on the Frontline', *Medical Anthropology*, vol. 28, no. 1, pp. 81–107.

Robinson, J. (2006) *Ordinary Cities: Between Modernity and Development*, London, Routledge.

Robinson, K.H., Bansel, P., Denson, N., Ovenden, G. and Davies, C. (2014) *Growing Up Queer: Issues Facing Young Australians Who Are Gender Variant and Sexuality Diverse*, Melbourne, Young and Well Cooperative Research Centre.

Rodó-de-Zárate, M. (2015) 'Young Lesbians Negotiating Public Space: An Intersectional Approach through Places', *Children's Geographies*, vol. 13, no. 4, pp. 413–34.

Rodríguez, E. and Pujol, J. (eds) (2008) *Dels drets a les llibertats. Una història política de l'alliberament gai a Catalunya (FAGC 1986–2006)*, Bilbao, Virus Editorial.

Rodríguez García, M. (2012) 'The League of Nations and the Moral Recruitment of Women', *International Review of Social History*, vol. 57, pp. 57–128.

Rodríguez García, M. (forthcoming) 'Ideas and Practices of Prostitution around the World', in Knepper, P. and Johansen, A. (eds) *The Oxford Handbook of the History of Crime*, New York, Oxford University Press.

Rodríguez-Pose, A. (2006) 'Is There an "Anglo-American" Domination in Human Geography? And, Is It Bad?', *Environment and Planning A*, vol. 38, no. 4, pp. 603–10.

Rofel, L. (2007) *Desiring China: Experiments in Neoliberalism, Sexuality and Public Culture*, Durham, NC, Duke University Press.

Romanillos, J.L. (2011) 'Geography, Death, and Finitude', *Environment and Planning A*, vol. 43, no. 11, pp. 2533–53.

Rooke, A. (2010) 'Trans Youth, Science and Art: Creating (Trans) Gendered Space', *Gender, Place and Culture*, vol. 17, no. 5, pp. 655–72.

Rose, G. (1993) *Feminism and Geography: The Limits of Geographical Knowledge*, Cambridge, Polity Press.

Rose, G. (2010) *Doing Family Photography: The Domestic, the Public and the Politics of Sentiment*, Farnham, Ashgate.

Rose, G. (2012) *Visual Methodologies: An Introduction to Researching with Visual Materials*, London, Sage.

Rosen, S. (2004) 'The State of Youth/Youth and the State in Early 21st-Century China', in Gries, P.H. and Rosen, S. (eds) *State and Society in 21st-Century China: Crisis, Contention, and Legitimation*, London, Routledge, pp. 159–79.

Rosenberg, M.W. (1998) 'Medical or Health Geography? Populations, Peoples, Places', *International Journal of Population Geography*, vol. 4, pp. 211–26.

Rosier, K. and Pearce, C. (2011) 'Doing Gender versus Playing Gender in Online Worlds: Masculinity and Femininity in *Second Life* and *Guild Wars*', *Journal of Gaming and Virtual Worlds*, vol. 3, no. 2, pp. 125–44.

Ross, B.L. (2010) 'Sex and (Evacuation from) the City: The Moral and Legal Regulation of Sex Workers in Vancouver's West End, 1975–1985', *Sexualities*, vol. 13, no. 2, pp. 197–218.

Ross, B.L. and Sullivan, R. (2012) 'Tracing Lines of Horizontal Hostility: How Sex Workers and Gay Activists Battled for Space, Voice, and Belonging in Vancouver, 1975–1985', *Sexualities*, vol. 15, nos 5–6, pp. 604–21.

Ross, C. (2008) 'Visions of Visibility: LGBT Communities in Turin', *Modern Italy*, vol. 13, no. 3, pp. 241–60.

Ross, C. (2009) 'Collective Association in the LGBT Movement', in Albertazzi, D., Brook, C., Ross, C. and Rothenberg, N. (eds) *Resisting the Tide: Cultures of Opposition Under Berlusconi (2001–2006)*, New York, Continuum.

Ross, C. (2013) 'Queering Spaces in Turin', in Storchi, S. (ed.) *Beyond the Piazza: Public and Private Spaces in Modern Italian Culture*, Brussels, Peter Lang, pp. 129–47.

Ross, M.B. (2005) 'Beyond the Closet as a Raceless Paradigm', in Johnson, E.P. and Henderson, M. G. (eds) *Black Queer Studies: A Critical Anthology*, Durham, NC, Duke University Press, pp. 161–89.

Rosser, S., West, W. and Weinmeyer, R. (2008) 'Are Gay Communities Dying or Just in Transition? Results from an International Consultation Examining Possible Structural Change in Gay Communities', *AIDS Care*, vol. 20, no. 5, pp. 588–95.

Rossi Barilli, G. (1999) *Il movimento gay in Italia*, Milan, Feltrinelli.

Rotello, G. (1997) *Sex Ecology: AIDS and the Destiny of Gay Men*, New York, Plume.

Roth, M. (2006) 'Marriage, Divorce, and the Prostitute in Ancient Mesopotamia', in Faraone, C.A. and McClure, L. (eds) *Prostitutes and Courtesans of the Ancient World*, Madison, University of Wisconsin Press, pp. 21–39.

Rothenberg, T. (1995) '"And She Told Two Friends … " Lesbians Creating Urban Social Space', in Bell, D. and Valentine, G. (eds) *Mapping Desire: Geographies of Sexualities*, London and New York, Routledge, pp. 165–81.

Rouhani, F. (2007) 'Religion, Identity and Activism: Queer Muslim Diasporic Identities', in Browne, K., Lim, J. and Brown, G. (eds) *Geographies of Sexualities: Theory, Practices and Politics*, Farnham, Ashgate, pp. 169–80.

Rouhani, F. (2012) 'Anarchism, Geography, and Queer Space-making: Building Bridges over Chasms We Create', *ACME: An International E-Journal for Critical Geographers*, vol. 11, no. 3, pp. 373–92.

Rouhani, F. (forthcoming) 'Queering the Iranian and the Diaspora of the Iranian Diaspora', in Ozyegin, G. (ed.) *Gender and Sexuality in Muslim Cultures*, Burlington, VT, Ashgate.

Routledge, P. (2003) 'Convergence Space: Process Geographies of Grassroots Globalization Networks', *Transactions of the Institute of British Geographers*, vol. 28, no. 3, pp. 333–49.

Rowan, L. (2009) *Using Internet-based Technologies to Assist LGBT Elders and Caregivers*, Knoxville, University of Tennessee Press.

Roy, S. (2011) 'It's Not Gay Rights; It's Human Rights: Clinton Breaks Down the Wall', *The Huffington Post*, 8 December [Online]. Available at http://www.huffingtonpost.com/sandip-roy/gay-rights-human-rights-clinton_b_1136340.html (accessed 30 March 2014).

Rubin, G.S. (1984) 'Thinking Sex: Notes for a Radical Theory of the Politics of Sexuality', in Rubin, G.S. (2012) *Deviations: A Gayle Rubin Reader*, Durham, NC, Duke University Press, pp. 137–181 (this edition 2012).

Rubin, H. (2003) *Self-Made Men: Identity and Embodiment Among Transsexual Men*, Nashville, TN, Vanderbilt University Press.

Rubinstein, T., Makov, S. and Sarel, A. (2013) 'Don't Bi-negative: Reduction of Negative Attitudes toward Bisexuals by Blurring the Gender Dichotomy', *Journal of Bisexuality*, vol. 13, no. 3, pp. 356–73.

Rucht, B. (2005) 'Un movimento di movimenti? Unità e diversità fra le organizzazioni per una giustizia globale', *Rassegna Italiana di Sociologia*, vol. 2, pp. 275–306.

Rudacille, D. (2005) *The Riddle of Gender: Science, Activism, and Transgender Rights*, New York, Pantheon Books.

Ruddick, S. (1996) 'Constructing Difference in Public Spaces: Race, Class, and Gender as Interlocking Systems', *Urban Geography*, vol. 17, no. 2, pp. 132–51.

Rushbrook, B. (2002) 'Cities, Queer Space, and the Cosmopolitan Tourist', *Gay and Lesbian Quarterly: A Journal of Lesbian and Gay Studies*, vol. 8, nos 1–2, pp. 183–206.

Russo, J. (2013) 'Fan Video and the Queerness of Media Convergence', paper presented to the New Media in Feminist Scholarship, Teaching, and Activism Colloquium, 2 February [Online]. Available at http://www.youtube.com/watch?v=eITak6WqLdo&feature=youtu be_gdata_player (accessed 13 August 2014).

Ruting, B. (2008) 'Economic Transformations of Gay Urban Spaces: Revisiting Collins' Evolution Gay District Model', *Australian Geographer*, vol. 39, no. 3, pp. 259–69.

Ryder, A. (2004) 'The Changing Nature of Adult Entertainment Districts: Between a Rock and a Hard Place or Going from Strength to Strength?', *Urban Studies*, vol. 41, no. 9, pp. 1659–86.

Ryder, A. (2006) 'The Changing Nature of Adult Entertainment Districts: Between a Rock and a Hard Place or Going from Strength to Strength?', in Collins, A. (ed.) *Cities of Pleasure: Sex and the Urban Socialscape*, London, Routledge, pp. 29–56.

Ryder, A. (2010) 'Red-light District', in Hutchinson, R. (ed.) *Encyclopedia of Urban Studies*, Vol. 2, Thousand Oaks, CA, Sage, pp. 638–42.

Said, E. W. (1978) *Orientalism*, Pantheon Books, New York.

Said, E.W. (2000) 'Invention, Memory, and Place', *Critical Inquiry*, vol. 26, no. 2, pp. 175–92 [Online]. Available at www.jstor.org/stable/1344120 (accessed 21 April 2015).

Salaff, J. (1988) *State and Family in Singapore: Restructuring a Developing Society*, Ithaca, NY, Cornell University Press.

Samar, V. J. (2000) 'Gay-rights as a Particular Instantiation of Human Rights', *Albany Law Review*, vol. 64, pp. 983–1030.

Samers, M. (2010) *Migration (Key Ideas in Geography)*, New York, Routledge.

SANAC (2011) *National Strategic Plan on HIV, STIs and TB 2012–2016* [Online]. Available at www.sanac.org.za/component/docman/doc_download/7-national-strategic-plan-on-hiv-stis-and-tb?Itemid= (accessed 14 March 2014).

Sanchez, L. (2004) 'The Global E-rotic Subject, the Ban, and the Prostitute-free Zone: Sex Work and the Theory of Differential Exclusion', *Environment and Planning D: Society and Space*, vol. 22, pp. 861–83.

Sánchez, R. (2006) 'On a Critical Realist Theory of Identity', in Mohanty, S.P., Alcoff, L.M., Hames-García, M. and Moya P.M.L. (eds) *Identity Politics Reconsidered*, New York, Palgrave, pp. 31–52.

Sanders, D. (1996) 'Getting Lesbian and Gay Issues on the International Human Rights Agenda', *Human Rights Quarterly*, vol. 18, no. 1, pp. 67–106.

Sanders, E.J., Graham, S.M., Okuku, H.S., van der Elst, E.M., Muhaari, A., Davies, A., Peshu, N., Price, M., McClelland, R.S. and Smith, A.D. (2007) 'HIV-1 Infection in High Risk Men Who Have Sex with Men in Mombasa, Kenya', *AIDS*, vol. 21, pp. 2513–20.

Sanders, T. (2004) 'The Risks of Street Prostitution: Punters, Police and Protesters', *Urban Studies*, vol. 41, no. 9, pp. 1703–17.

Sanders, T. (2008) *Paying for Pleasure: Men Who Buy Sex*, Cullompton, Willan Publishing.

Sanders, T. (2009) 'Controlling the "Anti Sexual" City: Sexual Citizenship and the Disciplining of Female Street Sex Workers', *Criminology and Criminal Justice*, vol. 9, no. 4, pp. 507–25.

Sandfort, J., Nel, J., Rich, E., Reddy, V. and Yi, H. (2008) 'HIV Testing and Self-reported HIV Status in South African Men Who Have Sex with Men: Results from a Community-based Survey', *Sexually Transmitted Infections*, vol. 84, no. 6, pp. 425–9.

Sani, S. (2002) 'Whose Place is this Space? Life in the Street Prostitution Area of Helsinki, Finland', *International Journal of Urban and Regional Research*, vol. 26, no. 2, pp. 343–59.

Sasajimi, J. (2012) 'From Red Light District to Art District', *Cities*, vol. 33, pp. 77–85.

Sassen, S. (2002) 'Women's Burden: Counter-Geographies of Globalization and the Feminization of Survival', *Nordic Journal of International Law*, vol. 71, no. 2, pp. 255–74.

Scannell, P. (1996) *Radio, Television and Modern Life: A Phenomenological Approach*, Oxford, Blackwell.

Schauer, E. and Wheaton, E.M. (2006) 'Sex Trafficking into the United States: A Literature Review', *Criminal Justice Review*, vol. 31, pp. 146–69.

Schettini, C. (2013) 'A Social History of Prostitution in Buenos Aires', paper presented at Selling Sex in the City: Prostitution in World Cities, 1600 to the Present Conference, Amsterdam, 25–27 April.

Schiltz, M-A. (1998) *Les homosexuels face au sida: enquête 1995: Regards sur une décennie d'enquêtes*, Paris, CERMES.

Schulman, S. (2012a) *Israel/Palestine and the Queer International*, Durham, NC, and London, Duke University Press.

Schulman, S. (2012b) *Gentrification of the Mind*, Berkeley, University of California Press.

Sears, A. (2005) 'Queer Anti-capitalism: What's Left of Lesbian and Gay Liberation?', *Science & Society*, vol. 69, no. 1, pp. 92–112.

Sedgwick, E.K. (1990) *Epistemology of the Closet*, Berkeley, University of California Press.

Seidman, S. (1993) 'Identity and Politics in a "Postmodern" Gay Culture: Some Historical and Conceptual Notes', in Warner, M. (ed.) *Fear of a Queer Planet: Queer Politics and Social Theory*, Minneapolis, University of Minnesota Press, pp. 105–42.

Seligmann, J., Gosnell, M., Coppola, V. and Hager, M. (1983) 'The AIDS Epidemic: The Search for a Cure', *Newsweek*, vol. 101, no. 16, pp. 74–9.

Sender, K. (2006) *Further Off the Straight and Narrow: New Gay Visibility on Television*, DVD documentary, Northampton, MA, Media Education Foundation.

Sengoba, N. (2014) 'Anti-gay Laws: Uganda has Won the Battle', *Daily Monitor*, 4 March.

Shakhsari, S. (2012) 'From Homoerotics of Exile to Homopolitics of Diaspora: Cyberspace, the War on Terror, and the Hypervisible Iranian Queer', *Journal of Middle East Women's Studies*, vol. 8, no. 3, pp. 14–40.

Sharing Space (2014) 'Call for Papers', Sharing Space Conference, Rennes, 9–11 April [Online]. Available at http://espacepartage.sciencesconf.org/ (accessed 2 April 2015).

Sharp, J. (2000) 'Remasculinising Geo(-)Politics? Comments on Gearóid Ó Tuathail's Critical Geopolitics', *Political Geography*, vol. 19, no. 3, pp. 361–4.

Sharp, J. (2001) 'A Feminist Geopolitics?', *Space and Polity*, vol. 5, no. 3, pp. 165–76.

Sharp, J. (2005) 'Geography and Gender: Feminist Methodologies in Collaboration and in the Field', *Progress in Human Geography*, vol. 29, pp. 304–9.

Sharp, J. (2007) 'Geography and Gender: Finding Feminist Political Geographies', *Progress in Human Geography*, vol. 31, no. 3, pp. 381–7.

Shaw, A. (2009) 'Putting the Gay in Games Cultural Production and GLBT Content in Video Games', *Games and Culture*, vol. 4, no. 3, pp. 228–53.

Sheller, M. (2004) 'Mobile Publics: Beyond the Network Perspective', *Environment and Planning D: Society and Space*, vol. 22, no. 1, pp. 39–52.

Sheller, M. (2008) 'Mobility, Freedom and Public Space', in Bergmann, S. and Sager, T. (eds) *The Ethics of Mobilities: Rethinking Place, Exclusion, Freedom and Environment*, Aldershot, Ashgate, pp. 25–38.

Sheller, M. and Urry, J. (2006) 'The New Mobilities Paradigm', *Environment and Planning A*, vol. 38, no. 2, pp. 207–26.

Shepard, B. (2010a) *Queer Political Performance and Protest*, New York, Routledge.

Shepard, B. (2010b) 'Bridging the Divide between Queer Theory and Anarchism', *Sexualities*, vol. 13, no. 5, pp. 511–27.

Shepard, B. and Hayduk, R. (eds) (2002) *From ACT UP to the WTO: Urban Protest and Community Building in the Era of Globalization*, London, Verso.

Sherry, M. (2004) 'Overlaps and Contradictions between Queer Theory and Disability Studies', *Disability and Society*, vol. 19, no. 7, pp. 769–83.

Shilts, R. (1987) *And the Band Played on: Politics, People and the AIDS Epidemic*, New York, St Martin's Press.

Short, J R., Boniche, A., Kim, Y. and Li, P.L. (2001) 'Cultural Globalization, Global English, and Geography Journals', *The Professional Geographer*, vol. 53, no. 1, pp. 1–11.

Shotwell, A. (2013) '"Women Don't get AIDS, They Just Die From It": Memory, Classification, and the Campaign to Change the Definition of AIDS', *Hypatia*, vol. 29, no. 2, pp. 509–25.

Shreve, A. (1990) *Women Together, Women Alone: The Legacy of the Consciousness-Raising Movement*, New York, Ballantine Books.

Shumsky, N. and Springer, L. (1981) 'San Francisco's Zone of Prostitution, 1880–1934', *Journal of Historical Geography*, vol. 7, no. 1, pp. 71–89.

Silva, J.M. (2011) 'Os desafios para expansao da geografia das sexualidades no Brasil e os limites do diálogo científico internacional', in Silva, J.M. and Pinheiro da Silva, A.C. (eds) *Espaço, gênero e poder: conectando fronteiras*, Ponta Grossa, Todapalavra Editora, pp. 187–99.

Silva, J.M., Ornat, M.J. and Chimin Jr, A.B. (eds) (2013) *Geografias malditas: corpos, sexualidades e espaços*, Ponta Grossa, Todapalavra.

Silva, J.M. and Vieira, P.J. (2014) 'Geographies of Sexualities in Brazil: Between National Invisibility and Subordinate Inclusion in Postcolonial Networks of Knowledge Production', *Geography Compass*, vol. 8, no. 10, pp. 767–77.

Silvey, R. (1998) '"Ecofeminism" in Geography', *Philosophy & Geography*, vol. 1, no. 2, pp. 243–9.

Silvey, R. (2004) 'Power, Difference and Mobility: Feminist Advances in Migration Studies', *Progress in Human Geography*, vol. 28, no. 4, pp. 490–506.

Silvey, R.M.(2010) 'Stigmatized Spaces: Gender and Mobility under Crisis in South Sulawesi, Indonesia', *Gender, Place and Culture*, vol. 7, no. 2, pp. 143–61.

Simbayi, L.C., Kalichmann, S., Strebel, A., Cloete, A., Henda, N. and Mqeketo, A. (2007) 'Internalised Stigma, Discrimination, and Depression among Men and Women Living with HIV/AIDS in Cape Town, South Africa', *Social Science & Medicine*, vol. 64, no. 9, pp. 1823–31.

Simmons, P. (2002) 'Subjects of the Visual Arts: Dildoes', *GLBTQ: An Encyclopedia of Gay, Lesbian, Bisexual, Transgender and Queer Culture* [Online]. Available at http://www.glbtq.com/arts/subjects_dildoes.html (accessed 20 March 2014).

Sinfield, A. (1996) 'Diaspora and Hybridity: Queer Identities and the Ethnicity Model', *Textual Practice*, vol. 10, no. 2, pp. 271–93.

Skeggs, B. (1997) *Formations of Class and Gender*, London, Sage.

Skeggs, B. (1999) 'Matter out of Place: Visibility and Sexualities in Leisure Spaces', *Leisure Studies*, vol.18, no. 3, pp. 213–32.

Skeggs, B. (2004) *Class, Self, Culture*, London, Routledge.

Skidmore, T.E. (1989) *Preto no branco: raça e nacionalidade no pensamento brasileiro*, Rio de Janeiro, Paz e Terra.

Small, C.B., Klein, R.S., Friedland, G.H., Moll, B., Emeson, E.E. and Spigland, I. (1983) 'Community-acquired Opportunistic Infections and Defective Cellular Immunity in Heterosexual Drug Abusers and Homosexual Men', *American Journal of Medicine*, vol. 74, no. 3, pp. 433–41.

Smallman-Raynor, M., Cliff, A. and Haggett, P. (1992) *London International Atlas of AIDS*, Oxford, Blackwell.

Smith, A.D., Tapsoba, P., Peshu, N., Sanders, E.J. and Jaffe, H.W. (2009) 'Men Who Have Sex with Men and HIV/AIDS in Sub-Saharan Africa', *The Lancet*, vol. 374, pp. 416–22.

Smith, A., Schlichthorst, M., Mitchell, A., Walsh, J., Lyons, A., Blackman, P. and Pitts, M. (2011) *Sexuality Education in Australian Secondary Schools 2010*, Monograph Series No. 80, Melbourne, Australian Research Centre in Sex, Health and Society, La Trobe University.

Smith, B. (1983) *Home Girls: A Black Feminist Anthology*, New Brunswick, NJ, Kitchen Table: Women of Color Press.

Smith, D. (2013) 'Zambian Gay Rights Activist Arrested', *The Guardian*, 9 April [Online]. Available at http://www.theguardian.com/world/2013/apr/09/zambian-gay-rights-activist-arrested (accessed 20 March 2014).

Smith, D.P. and Holt, L. (2005) 'Lesbian Migrants in the Gentrified Valley and "Other" Geographies of Rural Gentrification', *Journal of Rural Studies*, vol. 21, no. 3, pp. 313–22.

Smith, G. (2013) 'Sexuality, Space and Migration: South Asian Gay Men in Australia', *New Zealand Geographer*, vol. 68, no. 2, pp. 92–100.

Smith, G., Bartlett, A. and King, M. (2004) 'Treatments of Homosexuality in Britain since the 1950s – An Oral History: The Experience of Patients', *British Medical Journal* [Online]. DOI: 10.1136/bmj.37984.442419.EE (accessed 21 April 2015).

Smith, J.S. (2013) *Berlin Coquette: Prostitution and the New German Woman, 1890–1933*, Ithaca, NY, Cornell University Press.

Smith, N. (1996) *The New Urban Frontier: Gentrification and the Revanchist City*, London, Routledge.

Smith, N. (1998) 'Giuliani Time: The Revanchist 1990s', *Social Text*, vol. 57, pp. 1–20.

Smith, N.J. and Laing, M. (2012) 'Introduction: Working outside the (Hetero) Norm? Lesbian, Gay, Bisexual, Transgender and Queer (LGBTQ) Sex Work', *Sexualities*, vol. 15, nos 5–6, pp. 517–20.

Smith, S. (2011) 'She Says Herself, "I Have No Future": Love, Fate, and Territory in Leh District, India', *Gender, Place and Culture*, vol. 18, no. 4, pp. 455–76.

Soja, E. (1996) *Thirdspace*, Oxford, Blackwell.

Solá, M. (2011) 'Cartografia crítica de l'impacte de la teoria "queer" a les representacions del gènere i la identitat dels moviments socials trans-feministes', research study, Institut Català de les Dones.

Solá, M. (2013) 'Introducción', in Solá, M. and Urko, E. (eds) *Transfeminismos: Epistemes fricciones y flujos*, Tafalla, Txalaparta.

Solá, M. and Urko, E. (eds) (2013) *Transfeminismos: Epistemes fricciones y flujos*, Tafalla, Txalaparta.

Soley-Beltran, P. and Coll-Planas, G. (2011) '"Having Words for Everything". Institutionalizing Gender Migration in Spain (1998–2008)', *Sexualities*, vol. 14, pp. 334–53.

Sörensson, E. (2012) 'Providing Fun in the "World of Tourism": Servicing Backpackers in Indonesia', *Gender, Place and Culture*, vol. 19, no. 5, pp. 670–85.

Sos homophobie (2013) *Sos homophobie rapport annuel*, Paris, France [Online]. Available at http://www.sos-homophobie.org/rapport-annuel-2013/ (Accessed 31 March 2015).

Sothern, M. (2004) '(Un) Queer Patriarchies: Or, "What We Think When We Fuck"', *Antipode*, vol. 36, no. 2, pp. 183–90.

Sothern, M. (2006) 'On Not Living with AIDS: Or, AIDS-as-Post-Crisis', *ACME: An International E-Journal for Critical Geographers*, vol. 5, no. 2, pp. 144–62.

Sothern, M. (2007a) 'You Could Truly be Yourself if You Just Weren't You: Sexuality, Disabled Body Space, and the (Neo) Liberal Politics of Self-help', *Environment and Planning D: Society and Space*, vol. 25, no. 1, pp. 144–59.

Sothern, M. (2007b) 'HIV+ Bodyspace: AIDS and the Queer Politics of Future Negation in Aotearoa/New Zealand', in Browne, K., Lim, J. and Brown, G. (eds) *Geographies of Sexualities: Theory, Practice and Politics*, Farnham, Ashgate, pp. 181–94.

Sothern, M. and Dyck, I. (2010) '"… A Penis is Not Needed in Order to Pee": Sex and Gender in Health Geography' in Brown, T., McLafferty, S. and Moon, G. (eds) *The Companion to Health and Medical Geography*, Chichester, Wiley-Blackwell, pp. 224–241.

Spanger, M. (2010) 'Destabilising Sex Work and Intimacy? Gender Performances of Female Thai Migrants Selling Sex in Denmark', PhD thesis, Department of Society and Globalization, Roskilde University.

Spanger, M. (2011) 'Human Trafficking as Lever for Feminist Voices? Transformations of the Danish Policy Field of Prostitution', *Critical Social Policy*, vol. 31, no. 4, pp. 517–39.

Spanger, M. (2013a) 'Gender Performances as Spatial Acts: (Fe)male Thai Migrant Sex Workers in Denmark', *Gender, Place and Culture*, vol. 20, no. 1, pp. 37–52.

Spanger, M. (2013b) 'Doing Marriage and Love in the Borderland of Transnational Sex Work: Female Thai Migrants in Denmark', *NORA – Nordic Journal of Feminist and Gender Research*, vol. 21, no. 2, pp. 1–27.

Spencer, R. (2007) 'China Cracks Down on TV Talent Shows', *The Telegraph* [Online]. Available at http://www.telegraph.co.uk/news/worldnews/1563865/China-cracks-down-on-TV-ta lent-shows.html (accessed 16 March 2012).

Spivak, G.C. (1985) 'Can the Subaltern Speak?', in Ashcroft, B, Griffiths, G. and Tiffin, H. (eds) *The Post-Colonial Studies Reader*, London, Routledge, pp. 28–37 (this edition 1995).

Spivak, G. (1988) 'Can the Subaltern Speak?', in Nelson, C. and Grossberg, L. (eds) *Marxism and the Interpretation of Culture*, Basingstoke, Macmillan, pp. 271–313.

Spronk, S. and Webber, J.R. (2007) 'Struggles against Accumulation by Dispossession in Bolivia. The Political Economy of Natural Resource Contention', *Latin American Perspectives*, vol. 34, no. 2, pp. 31–47.

Staeheli, L. A. (1996) 'Publicity, Privacy, and Women's Political Action', *Environment and Planning D: Society and Space*, vol. 14, pp. 601–19.

Staeheli, L.A. and Kofman, E. (2005) 'Mapping Gender, Making Politics: Towards Feminist Political Geographies', in Staheli, L.A., Kofman, E. and Peake, L. (eds) *Mapping Women, Making Politics: Feminist Perspectives on Political Geography*, Abingdon, Routledge, pp. 1–14.

Stallabrass, J. (1996) *Garguantua: Manufactured Mass Culture*, London, Verso.

Stallybrass, P. and White, A. (1986) *The Politics and Poetics of Transgression*, London, Methuen.

Stanko, E.A. (1997) 'Safety Talk: Conceptualising Women's Risk Assessment as a "Technology of the Soul"', *Theoretical Criminology*, vol. 1, no. 4, pp. 479–99.

Stanko, E.A. (1990) *Everyday Violence: How Women and Men Experience Sexual and Physical Danger*, Pandora Press, London.

Stanko, E.A. (1995) 'Women, Crime, and Fear', *Annals of the American Academy of Political and Social Science*, vol. 539, pp. 46–58.

Staples, W.G. (1994) 'Small Acts of Cunning: Disciplinary Practices in Contemporary Life', *The Sociological Quarterly*, vol. 35, no. 4, pp. 645–64.

Statistics New Zealand (2013) 'Quick Stats about Hamilton City' [Online]. Available at http://www.stats.govt.nz/Census/2013-census-profile-and-summary-reports/quickstats-abo ut-a-place.aspx?request_value=13702&tabname=Culturaldiversity (accessed 10 October 2014).

Steier, F. (1991) 'Reflexivity and Methodology: An Ecological Constructionism', in Steier, F. (ed.) *Research and Reflexivity*, London, Sage, pp. 163–185.

Steinmetz, G. (ed.) (2013) *Sociology & Empire: The Imperial Entanglements of a Discipline*, Durham, NC, Duke University Press

Steinmetz, K. (2014) 'The Transgender Tipping Point', *Time Magazine*, 29 May, pp. 38–46.

Stine, G. (2013) *AIDS Update 2013*, New York, McGraw-Hill.

Stockwell, S. and Muir, A. (2003) 'The Military–Entertainment Complex: A New Facet of Information Warfare', *Fibreculture*, vol. 1, np.

Stoler, A.L. (1995) *Race and the Education of Desire: Foucault's History of Sexuality and the Colonial Order of Things*, Durham, NC, Duke University Press.

Stoler, A.L. (2002) *Carnal Knowledge and Imperial Power: Race and the Intimate in Colonial Rule*, Berkeley, University of California Press.

Stone, A.R. (1995) *The War of Desire and Technology at the Close of the Mechanical Age*, Cambridge, MA, MIT Press.

Straits Settlements (1915) *Proceedings of the Legislative Council of the Straits Settlements*, Singapore, Government Printing Office.

Straits Settlements (1927) *Proceedings of the Legislative Council of the Straits Settlements*, Singapore, Government Printing Office.

Straits Settlements (1933) *Proceedings of the Legislative Council of the Straits Settlements*, Singapore, Government Printing Office.

Straits Settlements (1936) *Annual Report*, Singapore, Government Printing Office.

Straits Settlements (1937) *Annual Report*, Singapore, Government Printing Office.

Straits Settlements (1938a) *Annual Report*, Singapore, Government Printing Office.

Straits Settlements (1938b) *Proceedings of the Legislative Council of the Straits Settlements*, Singapore, Government Printing Office.

Straughan, P. (1999) 'The Social Contradictions of the Normal Family: Challenges to the Ideology', *Department of Sociology. Working Papers Series*, vol. 135, Singapore, National University of Singapore.

Stryker, S. (1994) 'My Words to Victor Frankenstein above the Village of Chamounix: Performing Transgender Rage', *GLQ: A Journal of Lesbian and Gay Studies*, vol. 1, no. 3, pp. 237–54.

Stryker, S. (2000) 'Transsexuality: The Postmodern Body and/as Technology', in Bell, D. and Kennedy, B.M. (eds) *The Cybercultures Reader*, London, Routledge, pp. 588–97.

Stryker, S. (2006) '(De)subjugated Knowledges: An Introduction to Transgender Studies', in Stryker, S. and Whittle, S. (eds) *The Transgender Studies Reader*, London, Routledge, pp. 1–17.

Stychin, C.F. (2004) 'Same-sex Sexualities and the Globalisation of Human Rights Discourse', *McGill Law Review*, vol. 49, pp. 951–67.

Sullivan, B. (2000) 'Rethinking Prostitution and "Consent"', in Castles, F. and Uhr, J. (eds) *Proceedings of the 2000 Conference of the Australasian Political Studies Association*, Canberra, Australian National University, pp. 1–7.

Sullivan, R. (2009a) 'Exploring an Institutional Base: Locating a Queer Women's Community in Thunder Bay, Ontario, Canada', *Atlantis: A Women's Studies Journal/Revue d'estudes sur les femmes*, vol. 34, no. 1, pp. 78–88.

Sullivan, R. (2009b) 'The (Mis)translation of Masculine Femininity in Rural Space: (Re)reading "Queer" Women in Northern Ontario, Canada', *Thirdspace: A Journal of Feminist Theory & Culture*, vol. 8, no. 2 [Online]. Available at http://www.thirdspace.ca/journal/article/viewArticle/sullivan/247 (accessed 30 June 2011).

Sui, D. Z. (2007) 'Geographic Information Systems and Medical Geography: Towards a New Synergy', *Geography Compass*, vol. 1, no. 3, pp. 556–82.

Sun, W. (2007) 'Dancing with Chains: Significant Moments on China Central Television', *International Journal of Cultural Studies*, vol. 10, no. 2, pp. 187–204.

Sundén, J. (2009) 'Play as Transgression: An Ethnographic Approach to Queer Game Cultures', *Proceedings of DiGRA, Conference: Breaking New Ground: Innovation in Games, Play, Practice and Theory*, 1–4 September, London.

Suresh Kumar Koushal and Others v. Naz Foundation and Others [2013] [Online]. Available at http://indiankanoon.org/search/?formInput=naz%20foundation (accessed 31 March 2015).

Svänstrom, Y. (2004) 'Criminalising the John: A Swedish Gender Model?', in Outshoorn, J. (ed.) *The Politics of Prostitution: Women's Movements, Democratic States and the Globalisation of Sex Commerce*, Cambridge, Cambridge University Press, pp. 225–44.

Svänstrom, Y. (2013) 'Prostitution in Stockholm 1600 to the Present – Continuity and Change', paper presented at Selling Sex in the City: Prostitution in World Cities, 1600 to the Present Conference, Amsterdam, 25–27 April.

Swarr, A.L. (2012) *Sex in Transition: Remaking Gender and Race in South Africa*, Albany, NY, SUNY Press.

Swirski, B. (1993) 'Israeli Feminism New and Old', in Swirski, B. and Safir, M.P. (eds) *Calling the Equality Bluff: Women in Israel*, New York and London, Teachers College Press, Columbia University, pp. 285–302.

Sycamore, M.B. (aka Mattilda) (ed.) (2004) *That's Revolting! Queer Strategies for Resisting Assimilation*, New York, Soft Skull Press.

Symanski, R. (1974) 'Prostitution in Nevada', *Annals of the Association of American Geographers*, vol. 64, pp. 357–77.

Symanski, R. (1981) *The Immoral Landscape: Female Prostitution in Western Societies*, Toronto, Butterworth and Co.

S395/2002 v MIMIA [2003] 216 CLR 473.

Takahashi, L.M. (2009) 'Activism', in Kitchen, R. and Thrift, N. (eds) *International Encyclopedia of Human Geography*, Oxford, Elsevier, pp 1–6.

Take Back the Night (2014) *About Take Back the Night®* [Online]. Available at http://takebackthenight.org/about–tbtn/ (accessed 21 October 2014).

Tallon, K., Choi, A., Keeley, M., Elliott, J. and Maher, D. (2012) *New Voices / New Laws: School-age Young People in New South Wales Speak Out about the Criminal Laws that Apply to their Online Behaviour*, Sydney, National Children's and Youth Law Centre and Legal Aid NSW.

Tamale, S. (2009) 'A Human Rights Impact Assessment of the Ugandan Anti-homosexual Bill 2009', *The Equal Rights Review*, vol. 4, pp. 49–57. Available from: http://www.equalrightstrust.org/ertdocumentbank/Sylvia.pdf.

Tamale, S. (ed.) (2011) *African Sexualities: A Reader*, Oxford, Pambazuka.

Tan, K.P. (2007) 'Imagining the Gay Community in Singapore', *Critical Asian Studies*, vol. 39, pp. 179–204.

Tanaka, S. (2011) 'The Notion of Embodied Knowledge', in Stenner, P., Cromby, J., Motzkau, J., Yen, J. and Haosheng, Y. (eds) *Theoretical Psychology: Global Transformations and Challenges*, Concord, ON, Captus, pp. 149–57.

Tattelman, I. (1999) 'Speaking to the Gay Bathhouse: Communicating in Sexually Charged Spaces', in Leap, W.L. (ed.) *Public Sex/Gay Space*, New York, Columbia, pp. 71–94.

Taulke-Johnson, R. (2010) 'Queer Decisions? Gay Male Students' University Choices', *Studies in Higher Education*, vol. 35, no. 3, pp. 247–61.

Tauquir, T., Petzen, J., Haritaworn, J., Ekine, S., Bracke, S., Lamble, S., Jivraj, S. and Douglas, S. (2011) 'Queer Anti-Racist Activism and Strategies of Critique: A Roundtable Discussion', *Feminist Legal Studies*, vol. 19, pp. 169–91.

Taylor, T. (2003) 'Multiple Pleasures, Women and Online Gaming', *Convergence: The International Journal of Research into New Media Technologies*, vol. 9, no. 1, pp. 21–46.

Taylor, T. (2008) 'Does World of Warcraft Change Everything? How a PvP server, Multinational Playerbase, and Surveillance Mod Scene Caused Me Pause', in Corneliussen, H.G. and

Walker Rettberg, J. (eds) *Digital Culture, Play, and Identity*, Cambridge, MA, MITechnology Press, pp. 187–201.

Taylor, V. and Whittier, N.E. (1992) 'Collective Identity and Social Movement Communities: Lesbian Feminist Mobilization', in Morris, A.D. and Mueller, C.M. (eds) *Frontiers in Social Movement Theory*, New Haven, CT, Yale University Press, pp. 104–29.

Taylor, Y. (2007a) '"If Your Face Doesn't Fit ...": The Misrecognition of Working-class Lesbians in Scene Space', *Leisure Studies*, vol. 26, no. 2, pp. 161–78.

Taylor, Y. (2007b) *Working Class Lesbian Life: Classed Outsiders*, Basingstoke, Palgrave Macmillan.

Taylor, Y. (2008) '"That's Not Really My Scene": Working-class Lesbians in (and out of) Place', *Sexualities*, vol. 11, no. 5, pp. 523–46.

Taylor, Y. (2011) 'Sexualities and Class', *Sexualities*, vol. 14, pp. 3–11.

Taylor, Y., Hines, S. and Casey, M.E. (2011) *Theorizing Intersectionality and Sexuality*, Basingstoke, Palgrave Macmillan.

Tent, P. (2004) *Midnight at the Palace: My Life as a Fabulous Cockette*, Los Angeles, CA, Alyson Books.

Teo, Y.Y. (2007) 'Inequality for the Greater Good: Gendered State Rule in Singapore', *Critical Asian Studies*, vol. 39, pp. 423–45.

Têtu (2015) France, Paris [Online]. Available at http://www.tetu.com/ (accessed 31 March 2015).

The Autonomous Geographies Collective (2010) 'Beyond Scholar Activism: Making Strategic Interventions Inside and Outside the Neoliberal University', *ACME: An International E-Journal for Critical Geographies*, vol. 9, pp. 245–75.

The Colbert Report (2012) *The Beefstate Governors* [Online video]. Available at http://thecolbertreport.cc.com/videos/1bsxs9/the-beefstate-governors (accessed 9 August 2014).

The Colbert Report (2014) *Transgender Awareness – Janet Mock* [Online video]. Available at http://thecolbertreport.cc.com/videos/px4k4w/transgender-awareness-janet-mock (accessed 9 August 2014).

The Future We Want (2012) *UNCSD* [Online]. Available at http://www.uncsd2012.org/content/documents/727The%20Future%20We%20Want%2019%20June%201230pm.pdf (accessed 10 April 2014).

The Gay Centre Facebook Group (n.d.) *Facebook* [Online]. Available at http://www.facebook.com/groups/98485168653/members/ (accessed 30 March 2015).

The Whittington Family: Ryland's Story (2014) YouTube video, added by The Whittington Family [Online]. Available at https://www.youtube.com/watch?v=yAHCqnux2fk (accessed 9 August 2014).

Thomas, C.J. and Bromley, R.D.F. (2000) 'City-centre Revitalisation: Problems of Fragmentation and Fear in the Evening and Night-time City', *Urban Studies*, vol. 37, no. 8, pp. 1403–29.

Thomas, J. (1993) *Doing Critical Ethnography*, Newbury Park, CA, Sage.

Thomas, M.E. (2004) 'Pleasure and Propriety: Teen Girls and the Practice of Straight Space', *Environment and Planning D: Society and Space*, vol. 22, no. 5, pp. 773–90.

Thompson, L. and Cupples, J. (2008) 'Seen and Not Heard? Text Messaging and Digital Sociality', *Social & Cultural Geography*, vol. 9, no. 1, pp. 95–108.

Thrift, N. and Massey, D. (2003) 'The Passion of Place', in Johnston, R. and Williams, M. (eds) *A Century of British Geography*, British Academy Centenary Monographs, Oxford, Oxford University Press/British Academy, pp. 275–99.

Tiemeyer, P. (2013) *Plane Queer: Labor, Sexuality, and AIDS in the History of Male Flight Attendants*, Berkeley, University of California Press.

Tiresi@ (2010) *Appello ai Movimenti per la costruzione di uno spezzone LGBTIQ-Femminista-Antisessista-Antirazzista-Antifascista* [Online]. Available at http://tiresia.noblogs.org/post

/2010/06/09/appello-ai-movimenti-per-la-cotruzione-di-uno-spezzone-lgbtiq-femminis
ta-antisessista-antirazzista-antifascista (accessed 21 March 2015).

Tlostanova, M.V. and Mignolo, W. (2012) *Learning to Unlearn: Decolonial Reflections from Eurasia and the Americas*, Columbus, Ohio State University Press.

Todd, C. (2012) '"Troubling" Gender in Virtual Gaming Spaces', *New Zealand Geographer*, vol. 68, no. 2, pp. 101–10.

Tomsen, S. (2006) 'Homophobic Violence, Cultural Essentialism and Shifting Sexual Identities', *Social and Legal Studies*, vol. 15, no. 3, pp. 389–407.

Tongson, K. (2011) *Relocations: Queer Suburban Imaginaries*, New York, New York University Press.

Torrey, M. (1990) 'When Will We Be Believed? Rape Myths and the Idea of a Fair Trial in Rape Prosecutions', *UC Davis Law Review*, vol. 24, no. 4, pp. 1013–71.

Torrie, R. (2007) 'Making Space for Rural Lesbians: Homosexuality and Rurality in British Columbia, 1950–1970s', MA thesis, Simon Fraser University.

Trappolin, L. (2004) *Identità in azione. Mobilitazione omosessuale e sfera pubblica*, Rome, Carocci.

Trappolin, L. (2009) 'Lotte per il riconoscimento e ruolo dei mass–media. I significati del "Gay Pride"', *Partecipazione e conflitto*, vol. 1, pp. 123–45.

Trautner, M.N. (2005) 'Doing Gender, Doing Class: The Performance of Sexuality in Exotic Dance Clubs', *Gender and Society*, vol. 19, no. 6, pp. 771–88.

Treichler, P.A. (1987) 'AIDS, Homophobia, and Biomedical Discourse: An Epidemic of Signification', *October*, vol. 43, pp. 31–70.

Treichler, P. (1991) 'AIDS, Africa and Cultural Theory', *Transition*, vol. 51, pp. 86–103.

Treichler, P. (1999) *How to Have Theory in an Epidemic: Cultural Chronicles of AIDS*, Durham, NC, Duke University Press.

Trevisan, J.S. (1986) *Perverts in Paradise*, London, GMP.

Trujillo, G. (2008) *Deseo y resistencia. Treinta anos de movilización lesbiana en el Estado español*, Madrid, Egales.

Tsang, D. (2000) 'Notes on Queer 'n' Asian Virtual Sex', in Bell, D. and Kennedy, B.M. (eds) *The Cybercultures Reader*, London, Routledge, pp. 432–38.

Tucker, A. (2009a) *Queer Visibilities: Space, Identity and Interaction in Cape Town*, Oxford, Wiley-Blackwell.

Tucker, A. (2009b) 'Framing Exclusion in Cape Town's Gay Village: The Discursive and Material Perpetration of Inequitable Queer Subjects', *Area*, vol. 41, no. 2, pp. 186–97.

Tucker, A. (2010a) 'Shifting Boundaries of Sexual Identities: The Appropriation and Malleability of "Gay" in South African Township Spaces', *Urban Forum*, vol. 21, no. 2, pp. 107–22.

Tucker, A. (2010b) 'The "Rights" (and "Wrongs") of Articulating Race with Sexuality: The Conflicting Nature of Hegemonic Legitimisation in South African Queer Politics', *Social & Cultural Geography*, vol. 11, no. 5, pp. 433–49.

Tucker, A., de Swardt, G., Struthers, H. and McIntyre, J. (2013a) 'Understanding the Needs of Township Men Who Have Sex with Men (MSM) Health Outreach Workers: Exploring the Interplay between Volunteer Training, Social Capital and Critical Consciousness', *AIDS and Behavior*, vol. 17, no. 1, pp. 33–42.

Tucker, A., Liht, J., de Swardt, G., Jobson, G., Rebe, K., McIntyre, J. and Struthers, H. (2013b) 'An Exploration into the Role of Depression and Self-efficacy on Township Men Who Have Sex with Men's Ability to Engage in Safer Sexual Practices', *AIDS Care*, vol. 25, no. 10, pp. 1227–35.

Tucker, A., Liht, J., de Swardt, G., Jobson, G., Rebe, K., McIntyre, J. and Struthers, H. (2014) 'Homophobic Stigma, Depression, Self-efficacy and Unprotected Anal Intercourse for

Peri-urban Township Men Who Have Sex with Men in Cape Town, South Africa: A Cross-sectional Association Model', *AIDS Care*, vol. 26, no. 7, pp. 882–9.

Tudor, M. (2012) *Cyberqueer Techno-practices: Digital Space-making and Networking among Swedish Gay Men*, Stockholm, The Department of Journalism, Media and Communication (JMK).

Turkle, S. (1999) 'Cyberspace and Identity', *Contemporary Sociology*, vol. 28, pp. 643–48.

Turner, M. (2003) *Backward Glances: Cruising Queer Streets in London and New York*, London, Reaktion Books.

Tyler, T.R. (2002) 'Is the Internet Changing Social Life? It Seems the More Things Change the More They Stay the Same', *Journal of Social Issues*, vol. 58, no. 1, pp. 195–205. UNAIDS (2009) *UNAIDS Action Framework: Universal Access for Men Who Have Sex with Men and Transgender People*, Geneva, UNAIDS.

United Kingdom National Archives, CO 659/13, Letter from Government House, Singapore to Colonial Office.

United Nations High Commissioner for Refugees (UNHCR) (2012) *Guidelines on International Protection No. 9*, Geneva, UNHCR [Online]. Available at http://www.unhcr.org/509136ca9. pdf (accessed 1 October 2014).

United Nations Office of the High Commissioner for Human Rights Committee on the Elimination of Discrimination against Women (CEDAW) (1992) *Convention on the Elimination of All Forms of Discrimination Against Women, General Recommendation No. 19 (Eleventh Session)* [Online]. Available at http://www.un.org/womenwatch/daw/cedaw/ recommendations/recomm.htm (accessed 11 October 2014).

Usher, N. and Morrison, E. (2010) 'The Demise of the Gay Enclave, Communication Infrastructure Theory and the Transformation of Gay Space', in Pullen, C. and Cooper, M. (eds) *LGBT Identity and Online New Media*, New York and London, Routledge, pp. 271–87.

Vaid, U. (1995) *Virtual Equality: The Mainstreaming of Gay and Lesbian Liberation*, Doubleday, Anchor Books.

Vaiou, D. (2004) 'The Contested and Negotiated Dominance of Anglophone Geography in Greece', *Geoforum*, vol. 35, no. 5, pp. 529–31.

Valdivia Rude, M. (2014) *Laverne Cox on her Emmy Nomination, Music Video and Fighting for TWOC: The Autostraddle Interview* [Online]. Available at http://www.autostraddle. com/laverne-cox-on-her-emmy-nomination-music-video-and-fighting-for-twoc-the-autostraddle-interview-245773/ (accessed 13 August 2014).

Valenčius, C.B. (2001) 'Histories of Medical Geography', in Rupke, N.A. (ed.) *Medical Geography in Historical Perspective*, London, Wellcome Institute Trust for the History of Medicine.

Valentine, G. (1993a) 'Desperately Seeking Susan: A Geography of Lesbian Friendships', *Area*, vol. 25, no. 2, pp. 109–16.

Valentine, G. (1993b) 'Negotiating and Managing Multiple Identities: Lesbian Time–Space Strategies', *Transactions of the Institute of British Geographers*, vol. 18, no. 2, pp. 237–48.

Valentine, G. (1993c) '(Hetero)sexing Space: Lesbian Perceptions and Experiences of Everyday Spaces', *Environment and Planning D: Society and Space*, vol. 11, no. 4, pp. 395–413 [Online]. DOI: 10.1068/d110395 (accessed 21 April 2015).

Valentine, G. (1995) 'Out and About: Geographies of Lesbian Landscapes', *International Journal of Urban and Regional Research*, vol. 19, no. 1, pp. 96–111.

Valentine, G. (1996) '(Re)negotiating the Heterosexual Street: Lesbian Productions of Space', in Duncan, N. (ed.) *Bodyspace: Destabilising Geographies of Gender and Sexuality*, London, Routledge, pp. 145–55.

Valentine, G. (1997a) 'Making Space: Lesbian Separatist Communities in the United States', in Cloke, P. and Little, J. (eds) *Contested Countryside Cultures: Otherness, Marginalisation and Rurality*, London, Routledge, pp. 109–22.

Valentine, G. (1997b) 'Making Space: Separatism and Difference', in Jones III, J.P., Nast, H.J. and Roberts, S.M. (eds) *Thresholds in Feminist Geography: Difference, Methodology, Representation*, Lanham, MD, Rowman & Littlefield, pp. 65–76.

Valentine, G. (ed.) (2000) *From Nowhere to Everywhere: Lesbian Geographies*, London, Routledge.

Valentine, G. (2007) 'Theorizing and Researching Intersectionality: A Challenge for Feminist Geography', *The Professional Geographer*, vol. 59, no. 1, pp. 10–21 [Online]. DOI: 10.1111/j. 1467–9272.2007.00587.x (accessed 21 April 2015).

Valentine, G. and McKendrick, J. (1997) 'Children's Outdoor Play: Exploring Parental Concerns about Children's Safety and the Changing Nature of Childhood', *Geoforum*, vol. 28, no. 2, pp. 219–35.

Valentine, G. and Skelton, T. (2003) 'Finding Oneself, Losing Oneself: The Lesbian and Gay "Scene" as a Paradoxical Space', *International Journal of Urban and Regional Research*, vol. 27, no. 4, pp. 849–66.

Valentine, G. and Skelton, T. (2007) 'Re-defining "Norms": D/deaf Young People's Transitions to Independence', *Sociological Review*, vol. 55, no. 1, pp. 104–23.

Valentine, G. and Skelton, T. (2008) 'Changing Spaces: The Role of the Internet in Shaping Deaf Geographies', *Social & Cultural Geography*, vol. 9, no. 5, pp. 469–85.

Valentine, G., Skelton, T. and Butler, R. (2003) 'Coming Out and Outcomes: Negotiating Lesbian and Gay Identities with, and in, the Family', *Environment and Planning D: Society and Space*, vol. 21, no. 4, pp. 479–99.

Valentine, G., Vanderbeck, R., Sadgrove, J. and Andersson, J. (2013) 'Producing Moral Geographies: The Dynamics of Homophobia within a Transnational Religious Network', *The Geographical Journal*, vol. 179, no. 2, pp. 165–76.

Valiaho, P. (2014) 'Affectivity, Biopolitics and the Virtual Reality of War', *Theory, Culture and Society*, vol. 29, no. 2, pp. 63–83.

Valkyrie, Z.C. (2011) 'Cybersexuality in MMORPGs: Virtual Sexual Revolution Untapped', *Men and Masculinities*, vol. 14, no. 1, pp. 76–96.

Valocchi, S. (2010) *Social Movements and Activism in the USA*, New York, Routledge.

van Blerk, L. (2011) 'Negotiating Boundaries: The Sex Work Identities of "Bar Girls" in Nazareth, Ethiopia', *Gender, Place and Culture*, vol. 18, no. 2, pp. 217–33.

van den Berg, M. (2013) 'City Children and Genderfied Neighbourhoods: The New Generation as Urban Regeneration Strategy', *International Journal of Urban and Regional Research*, vol. 37, pp. 523–36.

Vanderbeck, R.M. (2007) 'Intergenerational Geographies: Age Relations, Segregation and re-engagements', *Geography Compass*, vol. 1, no. 2, pp. 200–21.

Vanderbeck, R.M. (2008) 'Reaching Critical Mass? Theory, Politics, and the Culture of Debate in Children's Geographies', *Area*, vol. 40, no. 3, pp. 393–400.

van der Elst, E.M., Smith, A.D., Gichuru, E., Wahome, E., Musyoki, H., Muraguri, N., Fegan, G., Duby, Z., Bekker, L., Bender, B., Graham, S.M., Operario, D. and Sanders, E.J. (2013) 'Men Who Have Sex with Men: Sensitivity Training Reduces Homoprejudice and Increases Knowledge among Kenyan Healthcare Providers in Coastal Kenya', *Journal of the International AIDS Society*, vol. 16, Supplement 3 [Online]. DOI: dx.doi.org/10.7448/IAS.16.4.18748 (accessed 21 April 2015).

van Doorn, N. (2011) 'Digital Spaces, Material Traces: How Matter Comes to Matter in Online Performances of Gender, Sexuality and Embodiment', *Media, Culture & Society*, vol. 33, no. 4, pp. 531–47.

Van Straaten, S. (2004) 'De Walletjes als Themapark voor Volwassenen', *Rooilijn*, vol. 33, pp. 438–43.

Veale, J. (2008) 'Prevalence of Transsexualism among New Zealand Passport Holders', *Australian & New Zealand Journal of Psychiatry*, vol. 42, no. 10, pp. 887–9.

Verouden, P. (2007) 'Soweto Gays Raise Safety Concerns at Soweto March', *The Star*, 1 October.

Vice (2014) [Online] Available at www.vice.com/en_uk/read/the–week–long–meth–fuelled –sex–parties–taking–over–londons–gay–scene (accessed 6 March 2015).

Visser, G. (2003a) 'Gay Men, Leisure Space and South African Cities: The Case of Cape Town', *Geoforum*, vol. 34, pp. 123–37.

Visser, G. (2003b) 'Gay Men, Tourism and Urban Space: Reflections on Africa's "Gay Capital"', *Tourism Geographies*, vol. 5, no. 2, pp. 168–89.

Visser, G. (2008a) 'The Homonormalisation of White Heterosexual Leisure Spaces in Bloemfontein, South Africa', *Geoforum*, vol. 39, no. 3, pp. 1347–61.

Visser, G. (2008b) 'Exploratory Notes on the Geography of Black Gay Leisure Spaces in Bloemfontein, South Africa', *Urban Forum*, vol. 19, no. 4, pp. 413–23.

Visser, G. (2010) 'Leisurely Lesbians in a Small City in South Africa', *Urban Forum*, vol. 21, no. 2, pp. 171–85.

Visser, G. (2013) 'Challenging the Gay Ghetto in South Africa: Time to Move On?', *Geoforum*, vol. 49, pp. 268–74 [Online]. DOI:10.1016/j.geoforum.2012.12.013 (accessed 21 April 2015).

Visweswaran, K. (1994) *Fictions of Feminist Ethnography, Minneapolis*, Minneapolis, University of Minnesota Press.

Vivienne, S. (2011) 'Trans Digital Storytelling: Everyday Activism, Mutable Identity and the Problem of Visibility', *Gay and Lesbian Issues and Psychology Review*, vol. 7, no. 1, pp. 43–54.

Vries, D.A. and Peter, J. (2013) 'Women on Display: The Effect of Portraying the Self Online on Women's Self-objectification', *Computers in Human Behaviour*, vol. 29, no. 4, pp. 1438–89.

VV.AA. (1998) *Vint anys de feminisme a Catalunya*, Barcelona, Associació per a la Celebració dels Vint Anys de les Primeres Jornades Catalanes de la Dona.

Wade, A.S., Kane, C.T., Diallo, P.A.N., Diop, A.K., Gueye, K., Mboup, S., Ndoye, I. and Lagarde, E. (2005) 'HIV Infection and Sexually Transmitted Infections among Men Who Have Sex with Men in Senegal', *AIDS*, vol. 19, no. 18, pp. 2133–40.

Waitt, G. and Gorman-Murray, A. (2011a) 'Journeys and Returns: Home, Life Narratives and Remapping Sexuality in a Regional City', *International Journal of Urban and Regional Research*, vol. 35, no. 6, pp. 1239–55.

Waitt, G. and Gorman-Murray, A. (2011b) '"It's About Time You Came Out": Sexualities, Mobility and Home', *Antipode*, vol. 43, no. 4, pp. 1380–403.

Waitt, G., Jessop, L. and Gorman-Murray, A. (2011) '"The Guys in there Just Expect to be Laid": Embodied and Gendered Socio-spatial Practices of a "Night Out" in Wollongong, Australia', *Gender, Place and Culture*, vol. 18, no. 2, pp. 255–75.

Waitt, G. and Johnston, L. (2013) '"It Doesn't Even Feel Like It's Being Processed By Your Head": Lesbian Affective Home Journeys to and within Townsville, Queensland, Australia', in Gorman-Murray, A., Pini, B. and Bryant, L. (eds) *Sexuality, Rurality, and Geography*, Lanham, MD, Lexington, pp. 143–58.

Waitt, G. and Markwell, K. (2006) *Gay Tourism: Culture and Context*, New York, Haworth Press.

Wakeford, N. (1999) 'Gender and the Landscapes of Computing in an Internet Café', in Crang, M., Crang, P. and May, J (eds) *Virtual Geographies: Bodies, Space and Relations*, London, Routledge, pp. 178–202.

Wakeford, N. (2000) 'Cyberqueer', in Bell, D. and Kennedy, B. (eds) *The Cybercultures Reader*, London, Routledge, pp. 403–15.

Wakeford, N. (2002) 'New Technologies and "Cyber-queer" Research', in Richardson, D. and Seidman, S. (eds) *Handbook of Lesbian and Gay Studies*, London, Sage, pp. 115–45.

Walker, K. (2000) 'Sexuality and Refugee Status in Australia', *International Journal of Refugee Law*, vol. 12, no. 2, pp. 175–211.

Walkowitz, J. (1982) 'Jack the Ripper and the Myth of Male Violence', *Feminist Studies*, vol. 8, no. 3, pp. 542–74.

Walkowitz, J. (2014) 'History and the Politics of Prostitution: Prostitution and the Politics of History', keynote address delivered at COST Action meeting, *Comparing European Prostitution Policies: Understanding Scales and Cultures of Governance*, Salamanca, 11 September.

Wallace, R., Wallance, D., Ullmann, J.E. and Andrews, H. (1999) 'Deindustrialisation, Inner-city Decay, and the Hierarchical Diffusion of AIDS in the USA: How Neoliberal and Cold War Policies Magnified the Ecological Niche for Emerging Infections and Created a National Security Crisis', *Environment and Planning A*, vol. 31, pp. 113–39.

Walmsley, D. (2000) 'Community, Place and Cyberspace', *Australian Geographer*, vol. 31, no. 1, pp. 5–19.

Walsh, C. (2007) '¿Son Posibles Unas Ciencias Sociales/ Culturales Otras? Reflexiones En Torno a Las Epistemologías Decoloniales', *Nómadas (Col)*, vol. 26, pp.102–13.

Walsh, C. (2012) 'Interculturalidad, Plurinacionalidad Y Razón Decolonial: Refundares Político–Epistémicos Em Marcha', in Grosfoguel, R. and Almanza Hernández, R. (eds) *Lugares Descoloniales: Espacios De Intervención En Las Américas*, Bogotá, DC, Pontificia Universidad Javeriana-Bogotá, pp. 95–118.

Walsh, K., Shen, H. and Willis, K. (2008) 'Introduction to Special Issue: Heterosexuality and Migration in Asia', *Gender, Place and Culture*, vol. 15, no. 6, pp. 575–9.

Wane, N., Kempf, A. and Simmons, M. (eds) (2011) *The Politics of Cultural Knowledge*, Rotterdam, Sense.

Ward, J. (2003) 'Producing "Pride" in West Hollywood: A Queer Cultural Capital for Queers with Cultural Capital', *Sexualities*, vol. 6, pp. 65–94.

Ward v Attorney–General (Canada) [1993] 2 SCR 689.

Warnke, G. (2007) *After Identity: Rethinking Race, Sex, and Gender*, Cambridge, Cambridge University Press.

Warren, J. (2003) *Ah Ku and Karayuki-san: Prostitution in Singapore 1880–1940*, Singapore, Singapore University Press.

Warrington, M. (2001) '"I Must Get Out": The Geographies of Domestic Violence', *Transactions of the Institute of British Geographers*, NS 26, pp. 365–82.

Washington, H. (2008) *Medical Apartheid: The Dark History of Medical Experimentation on Black Americans from Colonial Times to the Present*, New York, Random House.

Washington Post (2014) 'Nigeria's Anti-gay Law Demands a Response from the West', *Washington Post*, 11 February [Online]. Available at http://www.washingtonpost.com/opinions/nigerias-anti-gay-law-demands-a-response-from-the-west/2014/02/10/23b19570-9276-11e3-b227-12a45d109e03_story.html (accessed 30 April 2014).

Watkins, E.S. (2007) *On the Pill: A Social History of Oral Contraceptives, 1950–1970*, Baltimore, MD, Johns Hopkins University Press.

Watney, S. (1994) 'Missionary Positions: AIDS, "Africa" and Race', in *Practices of Freedom: Selected Writings on HIV/AIDS*, London, Rivers Oram Press, pp. 103–20.

Watts, S. (1983) 'Marriage Migration, a Neglected Form of Long-term Mobility: A Case Study from Ilorin, Nigeria', *International Migration Review*, vol. 17, no. 4, pp. 682–98.

'Wayne' (1989) 'Lying and Cheating to Get in a Protocol', *Newsline*, June, pp. 37–38.

Weatherburn, P., Hickson, F. and Reid, D. (2003) *Net Benefits: Gay Men's Use of the Internet and Other Settings where HIV Prevention Occurs*, London, Sigma Research.

Wee, C. J. W-L. (2007) *The Asian Modern: Culture, Capitalist Development, Singapore*, Singapore, NUS Press.

Weeks, J. (2007) *The World We Have Won*, London, Routledge.

Weightman, B. (1980a) 'Gay Bars as Private Places', *Landscape Research*, vol. 23, pp. 9–16.

Weightman, B. (1981) 'Commentary: Towards a Geography of the Gay Community', *Journal of Cultural Geography*, vol. 1, no. 2, pp. 106–12.

Weinberg, M. and Williams, C. (1975) 'Gay Baths and the Social Organisation of Impersonal Sex', *Social Problems*, vol. 23, pp. 124–34.

Weinberg, M.S., Shaver, F. and Williams, C. (1999) 'Gendered Sex Work in the San Francisco, Tenderloin', *Archives of Sexual Behavior*, vol. 28, pp. 503–20.

Weiss, M. (2008) 'Gay Shame and BDSM Pride: Neoliberalism, Privacy, and Sexual Politics', *Radical History Review*, vol. 100, pp. 87–101.

Weiss, M. (2011) *Techniques of Pleasure: BDSM and the Circuits of Sexuality*, Durham, NC, Duke University Press.

Weiss, M. (2005) 'Who Sets Social Policy in Metropolis? Economic Positioning and Social Reform in Singapore', *New Political Science*, vol. 27, no. 3, pp. 267–89.

Weitzer, R. (2014) 'The Social Ecology of Red-Light Districts: A Comparison of Antwerp and Brussels', *Urban Affairs Review*, vol. 50, no. 5, pp. 702–30 [Online]. DOI: 1078087413504081 (accessed 21 April 2015).

Wellman, B. (2001) 'Physical Place and Cyberculture: The Rise of Networked Individualism', in Keeble, L. and Loader, B. (eds) *Community Informatics: Shaping Computer-mediated Social Relations*, London, Routledge, pp. 17–42.

Wellman, B., Boase, J., Chen, W., Hampton, K., Quan-Haase, A. and de Isla, I.D. (2001) *Networking Community: The Internet in Everyday Life*, Toronto, University of Toronto Press.

Wellman, B. and Gulia, M. (1999) 'Net Surfers Don't Ride Alone: Virtual Communities as Communities', in Kollock, P. and Smith, M. (eds) *Communities and Cyberspace*, London, Routledge, pp. 167–94.

Wemos (2013) *The Clinical Trials Industry in South Africa: Ethics, Rules and Realities*, Amsterdam, Wemos.

Wesling, M. (2011) 'Neocolonialism, Queer Kinship, and Diaspora: Contesting the Romance of the Family in Shani Mootoo's *Cereus Blooms at Night* and Edwidge Danticat's *Breath, Eyes, Memory*', *Textual Practice*, vol. 25, no. 4, pp. 649–70.

Weston, K. (1995) 'Get Thee to a Big City: Sexual Imaginary and the Great Gay Migration', *GLQ: A Journal of Lesbian and Gay Studies*, vol. 2, no. 3, pp. 253–77 [Online]. DOI: 10.1215 /10642684-2-3-253 (accessed 21 April 2015).

White, L. (1990) *The Comforts of Home: Prostitution in Colonial Nairobi*, Chicago, University of Chicago Press.

White, R. (1988) *Ryan White's Testimony before the President's Commission on AIDS* [Online]. Available at http://en.wikisource.org/wiki/Ryan_White's_Testimony_before_the_Presid ent's_Commission_on_AIDS (accessed 1 May 2014).

Whitehand, J. W. R. (2005) 'The Problem of Anglophone Squint', *Area*, vol. 37, no. 2, pp. 228–30.

Whitesel, J. (2010) 'Gay Men's Use of Online Pictures in Fat-Affirming Groups', in Pullen, C. and Cooper, M. (eds) *LGBT Identity and Online New Media*, Abingdon, Routledge, pp. 215–29.

Whitlock, G. (2008) 'From Tehran to Tehrangeles: The Generic Fix of Iranian Exilic Memoirs', *Ariel*, vol. 39, nos 1–2, pp. 7–27.

Whittle, S. (2001) *The Transgender Debate: The Crisis Surrounding Gender Identity*, London, South Street.

Whitzman, C. (2007) 'Stuck at the Front Door: Gender, Fear of Crime and the Challenge of Creating Safer Space', *Environment and Planning A*, vol. 39, pp. 2715–32.

Whowell, M. (2009) 'Inappropriate Sexualities? The Practice, Performance and Regulation of Male Sex Work in Manchester', unpublished PhD dissertation, Loughborough University.

Whyte, S. (2009) 'Health, Identities and Subjectivities: The Ethnographic Challenge', *Medical Anthropology Quarterly*, vol. 23, no. 1, pp. 6–15.

Wickenhauser, J. (2012) 'Surprisingly Unexpected: Moose Jaw, Metronormativity and LGBTQ Activism', MA thesis, York University.

Wilchins, R. (2002) 'A Woman for her Time: In Memory of Stonewall Warrior Sylvia Rivera', *Village Voice*, 26 February [Online]. Available at http://www.villagevoice.com/2002-02-26/news/a-woman-for-her-time/ (accessed 13 August 2014).

Wilken, R. (2009) 'Mobilizing Place: Mobile Media, Peripatetics and the Renegotiation of Urban Places', *Journal of Urban Technology*, vol. 15, no. 2, pp. 39–55.

Wilkinson, E. (2009a) 'Perverting Visual Pleasure: Representing Sadomasochism', *Sexualities*, vol. 12, no. 2, pp. 181–98.

Wilkinson, E. (2009b) 'The Emotions Least Relevant to Politics? Queering Autonomous Activism', *Emotion, Space and Society*, vol. 2, pp. 36–43.

Wilkinson, E. (2011) '"Extreme Pornography" and the Contested Spaces of Virtual Citizenship', *Social & Cultural Geography*, vol. 12, no. 5, pp. 493–508.

Wilkinson, E. (2013) 'Learning to Love Again: "Broken Families", Citizenship and the State Promotion of Coupledom', *Geoforum*, vol. 49, pp. 206–13.

Willett, G. (2000) 'Australian Gay Activists: From Movement to Community', *Radical History Review*, vol. 76, pp. 169–87.

Williams, E.L. (2014) 'Sex Work and Exclusion in the Tourist Districts of Salvador, Brazil', *Gender, Place and Culture*, vol. 21, no. 4, pp. 453–70.

Willis, K. and Yeoh, B. (eds) (2000) *Gender and Migration*, Cheltenham, Edward Elgar.

Wills, K., Brickell, K. and Desai, V. (under review), '"You Still Can't Have Public Displays of Affection": Geographies of Love in Asian Cities', *Environment and Planning D: Society and Space*.

Willson, M. (2007) 'Community in the Abstract: A Political and Ethical Dilemma?' in Bell, D. and Kennedy, B. (eds) *The Cybercultures Reader*, Abingdon, Routledge, pp. 213–26.

Wilson, E. (1991) The Sphinx in the City: Urban Life, the Control of Disorder, and Women, Berkeley, University of California Press.

Wilson, M. (2002) '"I am the Prince of Pain, for I am a Princess in the Brain": Liminal Transgender Identities, Narratives and the Elimination of Ambiguities', *Sexualities*, vol. 5, no. 4, pp. 425–48.

Wilson, P.A. and Yoshikawa, H. (2004) 'Experiences of and Responses to Social Discrimination among Asian and Pacific Islander Gay Men: Their Relationship to HIV Risk', *AIDS Education and Prevention*, vol. 16, no. 1, pp. 68–83.

Wilton, R.D. (1996) 'Diminished Worlds? The Geography of Everyday Life with HIV/AIDS', *Health and Place*, vol. 2, no. 2, pp. 69–83.

Wimark, T. (2013) 'Is It Really Tolerance? Expanding the Knowledge About Diversity for the Creative Class', *Tijdschrift voor Economische en Sociale Geografie*, vol. 105, no. 1, pp. 46–63.

Wimark, T. (2014) 'Beyond Bright City Lights: The Migration Patterns of Gay Men and Lesbians', PhD thesis, Stockholm University.

Winett, L., Harvey, S.M., Branch, M., Torres, A. and Hudson, D. (2011) 'Immigrant Latino Men in Rural Communities in the Northwest: Social Environment and HIV/STI Risk', *Culture, Health & Sexuality*, vol. 13, no. 6, pp. 643–56.

Winner, L. (1986) *The Whale and the reactor: a search for limits in an age of high technology*, Chicago, University of Chicago Press.

Winnett, R., Furman, R. and Enterline, M. (2012) 'Men at Risk: Considering Masculinity during Hospital-based Social Work Intervention', *Social Work in Health Care*, vol. 51, no. 4, pp. 312–26.

Winter, S. and Conway, L. (2011) 'How Many Trans* People Are There? A 2011 Update Incorporating New Data' [Online]. Available at http://web.hku.hk/~sjwinter/Trans genderASIA/paper-how-many-trans-people-are-there.htm (accessed 25 April 2014).

Wirth, L. (1938) 'Urbanism as a Way of Life', *American Journal of Sociology*, vol. 44, no. 1, pp. 1–24.

Witt, E. (2015) 'Are You "Internet Sexual?"', *Medium* [Online]. Available at https://medium. com/matter/are-you-internet-sexual-1f855e113df (accessed 24 January 2015).

Wittman, C. (1970) *A Gay Manifesto*, New York, A Red Butterfly Publication.

Wolf, D.G. (1979) *The Lesbian Community*, Berkeley, University of California Press.

Wolfe, M. (1997) 'Invisible Women in Invisible Places: The Production of Social Space in Lesbian Bars', in Ingram, G.B., Bouthillette, A. and Retter, Y. (eds) *Queers in Space: Communities/Public Places/Sites of Resistance*, Seattle, WA, Bay Press, pp. 301–24.

Wolfe, M. and Sommella, L. (1997) 'This is about People Dying: The Tactics of Early ACT UP and Lesbian Avengers in New York City', in Ingram, G.B., Bouthillette, A. and Retter, Y. (eds) *Queers in Space: Communities/Public Places/Sites of Resistance*, Seattle, WA, Bay Press, pp. 407–38.

Wolmark, J. (1999) *Cybersexualities: A Reader on Feminist Theory, Cyborgs and Cyberspace*, Edinburgh, Edinburgh University Press.

Women and Geography Study Group of the Institute of British Geographers (1997) *Feminist Geographers: Explorations in Diversity and Difference*, London, Longman.

Wonders, N. and Michalowski, R. (2001) 'Bodies, Borders and Sex Tourism in a Globalized World: A Tale of Two Cities – Amsterdam and Havana', *Social Problems*, vol. 48, no. 4, pp. 545–71.

Wong, T., Yeoh, B.S.A., Graham, E.F. and Teo, P. (2004) 'Spaces of Silence: Single Parenthood and the "Normal Family" in Singapore', *Population, Space and Place*, vol. 10, pp. 43–58.

Wotherspoon, G. (1991) *City of the Plain: History of a Gay Sub-culture*, Sydney, Hale and Iremonger.

Wyers, M. (2013) 'Selling Sex in Istanbul: 1600 to the Present', paper presented at Selling Sex in the City: Prostitution in World Cities, 1600 to the Present Conference, Amsterdam, 25–27 April.

Wysocki, D. (1998) 'Let Your Fingers Do the Talking: Sex on an Adult Chat-line', *Sexualities*, vol. 1, no. 4, pp. 425–52.

Yang, L. and Bao, H. (2012) 'Queerly Intimate: Friends, Fans and Affective Communication in a Super Girl Fan Fiction Community', *Cultural Studies*, vol. 26, no. 6, pp. 842–71.

Yao, S. (1999) 'Social Virtues as Cultural Text: Colonial Desire and the Chinese in 19th Century Singapore', in Chew, P.G.L. and Kramer-Dahl, A. (eds) *Reading Culture: Textual Practices in Singapore*, Singapore, Times Academic Press, pp. 99–122.

Yea, S. (2012) '"Shades of Grey": Spaces in and beyond Trafficking for Thai Women Involved in Commercial Sexual Labour in Sydney and Singapore', *Gender, Place and Culture*, vol. 19, no. 1, pp. 42–60.

Yee, N. (2008) *Our Virtual Bodies, Ourselves?* [Online]. Available at http://www.nickyee.com/ daedalus/archives/print/001613.php (accessed 21 April 2015).

Yee, N. (2014) *The Proteus Paradox*, New Haven, CT, Yale University Press.

Yep, G.A., Lovaas, K. and Elia, J.P. (2004) *Queer Theory and Communication: From Disciplining Queers to Queering the Disciplines*, Binghampton, NY, Harrington Park Press.

Yoon, K. (2003) 'Retraditionalizing the Mobile: Young People's Sociality and Mobile Phone Use in Seoul, South Korea', *European Journal of Cultural Studies*, vol. 6, no. 3, pp. 327–43.

Yoshikawa, H., Wilson, P.A., Chae, H.W. and Cheng, J. (2004) 'Do Family and Friendship Networks Protect against the Effects of Discrimination on Mental Health and HIV Risk among Asian and Pacific Islander Gay Men?', *AIDS Education and Prevention*, vol. 16, pp. 84–100.

Young, I.M. (1990) *Justice and the Politics of Difference*, Princeton, NJ, Princeton University Press.

Yue, A. (2008) 'Same-sex Migration in Australia: From Interdependency to Intimacy', *GLQ: A Journal of Lesbian and Gay Studies*, vol. 14, nos 2–3, pp. 239–62.

Yue, A. (2012) 'Queer Asian Mobility and Homonational Modernity: Marriage Equality, Indian Students in Australia and Malaysian Transgender Refugees in the Media', *Global Media and Communication*, vol 8, no. 3, pp. 269–87.

Yue, A. and Hawkins, G. (2000) 'Going South', *New Formations*, vol. 40, pp 49–63.

Yuval-Davis, N. and Anthias, F. (eds) (1989) *Woman – Nation – State*, Basingstoke, Macmillan.

Zablotska, I., Holt, M. and Prestage, G. (2011) 'Changes in Gay Men's Participation in Gay Community Life: Implications for HIV Surveillance and Research', *AIDS Behavior*, vol. 16, pp. 666–75.

Zarra Bonheur (2015) *Zarra Bonheur* [Online]. Available at http://zarrabonheur.wix.com/zarrabonheur-en (accessed 2 April 2015).

Zea, M.C., Reisen, C.A., Poppen, P.J. and Bianchi, F.T. (2008) 'Unprotected Anal Intercourse among Immigrant Latino MSM: The Role of Characteristics of the Person and the Sexual Encounter', *AIDS and Behavior*, vol. 13, pp. 700–715.

Ziga, I. (2013) '¿El corto verano del transfeminismo?', in Solá, M. and Urko, E. (eds) *Transfeminismos: Epistemes fricciones y flujos*, Tafalla, Txalaparta, pp. 81–90.

Ziv, A. (2010) 'Performative Politics in Israeli Queer Anti-Occupation Activism', *GLQ: A Journal of Lesbian and Gay Studies*, vol. 16, no. 4, pp. 537–56.

Zook, M. and Graham, M. (2007) 'Mapping DigiPlace: Geocoded Internet Data and the Representation of Place', *Environment and Planning B: Planning and Design*, vol. 34, pp. 466–82.

Index

For Product Safety Concerns and Information please contact our EU
representative GPSR@taylorandfrancis.com Taylor & Francis Verlag GmbH,
Kaufingerstraße 24, 80331 München, Germany

Printed and bound by CPI Group (UK) Ltd, Croydon, CR0 4YY
17/12/2024
01807544-0021